NEWNES ALL COLOUR COOKBOOK

NEWNES ALL COLOUR COOKBOOK

NEWNES BOOKS

Editor: Mary Lambert

Published by
Newnes Books, a division of The Hamlyn Publishing Group Limited,
84–88 The Centre, Feltham, Middlesex TW13 4BH
and distributed for them by The Hamlyn Publishing Group Limited,
Rushden, Northants, England.

Original material © Marshall Cavendish Limited 1982
This arrangement © Marshall Cavendish Limited 1984
Produced by Marshall Cavendish Books Limited,
58 Old Compton Street, London W1V 5PA

ISBN 0 600 37317 7

Any editorial queries should be addressed to Marshall Cavendish Books Limited
Any trade queries should be addressed to Newnes Books

Printed and bound in Italy by New Interlitho SpA.

CONTENTS

SOUPS AND APPETIZERS

MAIN COURSES

DELIGHTFUL DESSERTS

QUICK 'N' EASY COOKING

VEGETABLE DISHES

PARTY COOKING

INTRODUCTION

Eating is one of life's great pleasures, but when it actually comes to preparing and cooking food for family and friends it can often be difficult to plan a varied and appetizing meal which does not take too long to cook or, more importantly, cost too much.

The Newnes All Colour Cookbook will help solve your problems. It is a book which covers all aspects of cookery in one volume. There are over 450 easy-to-follow recipes to suit all occasions – and they won't cost you a fortune! There are soups and appetizers, main courses and desserts plus extra sections on quick 'n' easy cooking for the person with very little time to spare; vegetable dishes for the vegetarian or vegetable lover and party cooking for those who do a lot of entertaining. Now you will easily be able to choose a simple supper snack, plan a mid-week meal or maybe a more elaborate dinner. Try the *Caribbean-Style Dinner* menu in 'Party Cooking'. It is a full three course meal and also has recipes for cocktail drinks to suit the mood of the evening. Suggestions on drinks or wine to suit the meals are also given in other menus in the 'Party Cooking' section. Make sangria for the Spanish Evening and have light, red French wine with the French dinner party.

All the recipes are illustrated in full colour so that you can see from the start how the dish will turn out. Every recipe also contains comprehensive 'Cook's Tips' which give you the timing of each dish, how many calories it contains and buying ideas. Suggestions are also made for alternative fillings to make the dish more economic or perhaps more exotic.

The Newnes All Colour Cookbook is an invaluable aid to everyday cooking and it is a title you will use time and time again.

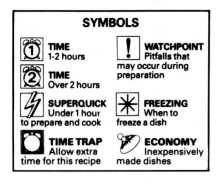

SYMBOLS

TIME
1-2 hours

TIME
Over 2 hours

SUPERQUICK
Under 1 hour
to prepare and cook

TIME TRAP
Allow extra
time for this recipe

WATCHPOINT
Pitfalls that
may occur during
preparation

FREEZING
When to
freeze a dish

ECONOMY
Inexpensively
made dishes

NOTE Both metric and imperial measurements are given. They are not exact equivalents, so please work from one set of measurements only. 1 tablespoon = 15 ml spoon; 1 teaspoon = 5 ml spoon. All spoon measures are level. Unless otherwise specified, eggs are medium (size 3/4) and sugar is granulated.

Dishes should be placed in centre of oven.

Calorie counts are given for generous servings and are approximate. Optional ingredients are not included in calorie counts.

Pressure cooking times are calculated using a cooker with 5 lb (L), 10 lb (M), 15 lb (H) weights.

SOUPS AND APPETIZERS

Planning a balanced menu for a dinner party or a pleasant family meal is never easy and often it can be very difficult to find that right first course. This section on soups and appetizers gives you a wide range of inexpensive and quick recipes to choose from.

You can make a warm filling soup, a tasty pâté or a more exotic seafood starter, often using some ingredients you already have in the store cupboard. There is also a good selection of meat and vegetable recipes to give you that extra variety.

SOUPS

Frankfurter and vegetable soup

SERVES 4

100 g/4 oz frankfurters, cut into 5 mm/¼ inch slices
2 tablespoons vegetable oil
175 g/6 oz carrots, cut into 1 cm/½ inch dice
1 celery stalk, thinly sliced
250 g/9 oz turnips, cut into 1 cm/½ inch dice
1 onion, chopped
1 clove garlic, crushed (optional)
700 ml/1¼ pints beef stock
400 g/14 oz can chopped tomatoes
salt and freshly ground black pepper
50 g/2 oz green cabbage leaves, shredded
25 g/1 oz pasta (see Buying guide)
50 g/2 oz Cheddar cheese, grated

1 Heat the oil in a heavy-based saucepan, add the carrots, celery, turnips, onion and garlic, if using, and cook over moderate heat for 7 minutes, stirring.

2 Remove from the heat and stir in the stock and tomatoes. Season to taste with salt and pepper.
3 Return the pan to the heat and bring to the boil. Lower the heat, cover the pan and simmer for 20 minutes.
4 Add the cabbage and pasta, then cover again and simmer for a further 10 minutes until the pasta is soft.
5 Stir in the frankfurters, taste and adjust seasoning, and cook for a further 3 minutes.
6 Ladle into warmed individual bowls or a soup tureen and serve at once. Hand the grated cheese in a separate bowl for sprinkling on top of the soup.

Cook's Notes

 TIME
Preparation takes 20 minutes, cooking 45 minutes.

BUYING GUIDE
Soup pasta, or pastina, as the Italians call it, comes in tiny star and circle shapes. If it is not available, use small pasta shapes or quick-cook pasta broken into 1 cm/½ inch lengths.

 VARIATION
Use potatoes or swedes in place of turnips.

 FREEZING
Transfer to a rigid container, cool quickly, then seal, label and freeze for up to 6 months. To serve: defrost at room temperature for 2-3 hours, then reheat thoroughly until bubbling.
Add a little more stock if necessary.

SERVING IDEAS
Serve this hearty soup with toast or wholemeal bread for a meal in itself.

●250 calories/1060 kj per portion

Quick meat and potato soup

SERVES 4

750 g/1½ lb potatoes, diced (see Buying guide)
1 tablespoon vegetable oil
1 large onion, finely chopped
600 ml/1 pint chicken stock
salt and freshly ground black pepper
200 g/7 oz can corned beef, diced
215 g/7½ oz can sweetcorn, drained
1 tablespoon chopped parsley

1 Heat the oil in a large saucepan, add the onion and cook gently for 2-3 minutes. Add the potatoes and cook for a further 1-2 minutes, stirring with a wooden spoon.

2 Stir the stock into the pan, season lightly with salt and pepper and bring to the boil. Lower the heat, cover and simmer for 10 minutes.

3 Add the corned beef and sweetcorn, bring back to the boil, then lower the heat again and simmer for a further 10 minutes.

4 Stir in parsley, taste and adjust seasoning, then pour into warmed soup bowls. Serve at once.

Salami and tomato soup

SERVES 4

50 g/2 oz sliced salami, skinned and roughly chopped

15 g/½ oz butter

100 g/4 oz potatoes, diced
100 g/4 oz carrots, diced
1 onion, roughly chopped
1 teaspoon sweet paprika
225 g/8 oz can chopped tomatoes
150 ml/¼ pint tomato juice
425 ml/¾ pint chicken stock
¼ teaspoon dried rosemary
salt and freshly ground white pepper
400 g/14 oz can cannellini beans, drained
1 tablespoon chopped fresh parsley

SESAME CROUTONS

25 g/1 oz butter, softened
1 tablespoon sesame seeds
1 teaspoon French mustard
4 thick slices white bread, crusts removed

1 Melt the butter in a saucepan, add the potatoes, carrots, onion and paprika and cook gently for 5 minutes until the onions are soft.

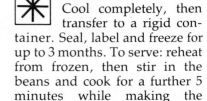

Cook's Notes

TIME
Preparation takes 20 minutes and cooking about 25 minutes.

VARIATIONS
Use ham or garlic sausage instead of the salami. Red kidney beans or butter beans could be used instead of cannellini beans.

ECONOMY
Use any left-over cooked meat such as pork or chicken for this recipe.

FOR CHILDREN
Use sliced frankfurters or cooked pork sausages instead of the salami.

FREEZING
Cool completely, then transfer to a rigid container. Seal, label and freeze for up to 3 months. To serve: reheat from frozen, then stir in the beans and cook for a further 5 minutes while making the sesame croûtons.

●330 calories/1375 kj per portion

2 Stir in the tomatoes and their liquid, the tomato juice and stock then bring to the boil. Lower the heat, stir in the rosemary and season with salt and pepper. Cover and simmer for 20 minutes until the vegetables are tender.

3 Remove from the heat and leave to cool slightly, then purée in a blender or work through a sieve.

4 Make the croûtons: put the butter in a bowl and beat in the sesame seeds and mustard. Spread on one side of each slice of bread. Cut the bread into 2 cm/¾ inch cubes and put them in a frying-pan. Cook gently for 5 minutes or until they are golden, turning frequently.

5 Return the soup to the rinsed-out pan and stir in the salami. ✳ Add the beans and heat through gently for 5 minutes, then taste and adjust the seasoning if necessary.

6 Ladle the soup into warmed individual bowls or a soup tureen, top with the sesame croûtons and then sprinkle over the chopped parsley. Serve the soup at once.

Spinach and liver pâté soup

SERVES 4

850 g/1 lb 12 oz can cream of chicken soup
225 g/8 oz chopped frozen spinach, defrosted, or canned spinach, drained
100 g/4 oz liver pâté (see Buying guide)
a little milk (optional)
2 teaspoons lemon juice
salt and freshly ground black pepper

TO GARNISH

25 g/1 oz margarine or butter
4 streaky bacon rashers, rinds removed and chopped
2 slices white bread, crusts removed and cut into small dice

1 Heat the oven to 110C/225F/Gas ¼. Make the garnish: melt the margarine in a frying-pan. Add the bacon and fry briskly for 2-3 minutes to release any fat. Add the diced bread and fry over moderate to high heat until both bacon and bread are lightly browned and crisp. Drain the bacon and croûtons well on absorbent paper and keep hot in the oven.
2 Pour the soup into a large saucepan, add the spinach and heat gently until simmering.
3 Using a balloon whisk, gradually whisk the liver pâté into the soup. If the soup seems too thick, add a little milk. Add the lemon juice and season carefully with salt and pepper.
4 Serve the soup piping hot in warmed individual soup bowls, sprinkled with the crispy bacon pieces and the croûtons.

Cook's Notes

TIME
Preparation takes about 20 minutes.

BUYING GUIDE
Canned liver pâté is an ideal choice for this soup. A can of pâté is handy for instant snacks. Or use it in savoury sauces.

SERVING IDEAS
With its interesting flavour and attractive green colour this soup is also perfect for a warming snack, served with crusty French bread. It is not, however, meant to be a complete meal in itself.

●370 calories/1550 kj per portion

Country soup

SERVES 4

1 potato, diced
1 large onion, sliced
1 small head celery, sliced
¼ head firm cabbage, shredded
225 g/8 oz can tomatoes
850 ml/1½ pints beef or ham
   stock
225 g/8 oz can kidney beans,
   drained
1 large or 2 medium frankfurter
   sausages
50 g/2 oz garlic sausage or salami,
   diced
50 g/2 oz smoked sausage, diced
salt and freshly ground black pepper
1 tablespoon finely chopped
   fresh parsley

1 Put the potato, onion, celery and cabbage in a large saucepan. Add the tomatoes with their juice, breaking them up against the sides of the pan with a wooden spoon.
2 Add the stock to the pan and bring quickly to the boil. Lower the heat to moderate, cover and simmer for 40 minutes.
3 Add the kidney beans, cover and cook for a further 20 minutes.
4 Meanwhile, bring a pan of water to the boil. Put the frankfurters into it and heat them through for 2 minutes. Remove with a slotted spoon and slice.
5 Add the garlic and smoked sausage and the frankfurters to the soup. Simmer over low heat for 15 minutes. Taste and adjust seasoning, [!] then pour into warmed individual soup bowls and sprinkle with chopped parsley. Serve at once.

Cook's Notes

TIME
Preparation takes about 20 minutes and cooking about 1¼ hours.

WATCHPOINT
The sausages can make the soup quite salty so do not add any extra salt until you have tasted it. If using ham stock, you will not need to use any salt at all.

VARIATIONS
Vary the vegetables in this soup according to what is in season and what is available. Leeks and carrots make tasty additions.

●265 calories/1125 kj per portion

Beefy soup

SERVES 4-6

425 g/15 oz can savoury minced beef
40 g/1½ oz lard
2 onions, finely chopped
1 large potato, cut into 1 cm/½ inch dice
1 large green pepper, deseeded and cut into chunks
2 teaspoons sweet paprika
2 tablespoons tomato purée
850 ml/1½ pints beef stock (see Cook's tip)
200 g/7 oz can sweetcorn, drained
salt and freshly ground black pepper
150 ml/¼ pint soured cream
1 tablespoon snipped chives, to garnish

1 Melt the lard in a large saucepan, add the onions and potato and fry gently for about 5 minutes. Add the green pepper and cook for a further 10 minutes, stirring the vegetables occasionally to prevent them from sticking.
2 Sprinkle the paprika into the pan and cook for 1-2 minutes. Add the tomato purée and minced beef, stirring with a wooden spoon to remove any lumps. Cook for 5 minutes, then pour in the beef stock and bring to the boil. Lower the heat and simmer for about 15 minutes, until the potatoes are tender.
3 Stir in the sweetcorn, heat through for 1-2 minutes, then taste and adjust seasoning if necessary.
4 Pour into warmed individual soup bowls. Top each serving with a swirl of soured cream, sprinkle with the chives and serve at once.

Cook's Notes

TIME
10 minutes preparation and 30 minutes cooking.

SERVING IDEAS
Serve warm rolls with this soup. Followed by cheese and biscuits, it can make a satisfying supper.

VARIATIONS
Add 50 g/2 oz mushrooms or a 225 g/8 oz can tomatoes.

COOK'S TIP
Use 2 beef stock cubes to make the stock.

●430 calories/1800 kj per portion

11

Mexican chilli soup

SERVES 4

175 g/6 oz lean minced beef
1 tablespoon corn oil
1 large onion, chopped
½ teaspoon ground cumin
15 g/½ oz plain flour
225 g/8 oz can tomatoes
½ teaspoon Tabasco (see Variations)
850 ml/1½ pints beef stock
salt and freshly ground black pepper
425 g/15 oz can red kidney beans, drained (see Variations)
fresh coriander or flat-leaved parsley, to garnish (optional)

1 Heat the oil in a saucepan and add the onion, minced beef and cumin. Cook over high heat until the meat is evenly browned, stirring with a wooden spoon to remove any lumps and mix thoroughly.
2 Sprinkle in the flour and stir well, then add the tomatoes with their juice, the Tabasco and the stock.
3 Bring to the boil, stirring. Season to taste with salt and pepper and simmer, uncovered, for 25 minutes.
4 Add the drained beans, stir them in and cook for a further 5 minutes or until heated through. Transfer to a warmed serving dish, sprinkle with coriander, if liked, then serve the soup at once (see Serving ideas).

Autumn soup

SERVES 4-6

1 large onion, chopped
2 carrots, cut into 1 cm/½ inch dice
1 small swede, cut into 1 cm/½ inch dice
½ green pepper, deseeded and thinly sliced
3 tablespoons vegetable oil
1 tablespoon tomato purée
1 L/1¾ pints beef stock
50 g/2 oz red lentils
salt and freshly ground black pepper
175 g/6 oz pork sausagemeat
25 g/1 oz fresh white breadcrumbs
½ teaspoon chopped fresh rosemary, or 1 teaspoon dried rosemary
1 cooking apple
1 large potato, cut into 1 cm/½ inch dice
snipped chives, to garnish

1 Heat the oil in a large flameproof casserole. Add the onion, carrots, swede and green pepper and fry gently for 3 minutes until the vegetables are soft but not coloured.
2 Stir in the tomato purée, stock and lentils, and season to taste with salt and pepper.
3 Bring to the boil, then lower the heat, cover and simmer for 20 minutes until the vegetables are just tender.
4 Meanwhile, put the sausagemeat, breadcrumbs and rosemary in a bowl. Mix thoroughly with your hands, then shape into 12 small balls.
5 Peel and core the apple, then cut into 1 cm/½ inch dice. Add to the soup with the potato and sausagemeat balls and simmer for a further 25 minutes until all the vegetables are tender.
6 Taste and adjust seasoning, then serve hot, sprinkled with chives.

Cook's Notes

 TIME
Preparation takes 20 minutes, cooking 50 minutes.

 SERVING IDEAS
An alternative serving idea is with crusty bread as a main-meal soup for lunch. Add grated cheese if liked.

VARIATIONS
In place of the sausage-meat balls, dice 75 g/3 oz skinned garlic sausage or salami and stir into the soup 10 minutes before the end of cooking. Pearl barley can be used instead of lentils, but you will need to allow at least another 30 minutes cooking time before adding the sausagemeat balls.

 COOK'S TIP
To give the sausage-meat balls a golden-brown colour fry them separately in a little oil, then add to the soup just before serving.

●380 calories/1575 kj per portion

13

Mussel soup

SERVES 4

2 kg/4½ lb fresh mussels (see
  Buying guide and Preparation)
2 tablespoons vegetable oil
25 g/1 oz butter
1 large onion, finely chopped
1 clove garlic, crushed (optional)
3 tablespoons finely chopped fresh
  coriander (see Variation)
700 ml/1¼ pints water
150 ml/¼ pint white wine
225 g/8 oz can tomatoes, drained
  and chopped
salt and freshly ground black pepper

1 Heat the oil and butter in a large
heavy-based saucepan, add the
onion, the garlic, if using, and the
coriander and fry gently for about
5 minutes until the onion is soft
and lightly coloured.
2 Pour in the water and wine and
add the tomatoes. Season to taste
with salt and pepper.

3 Add the mussels and bring to the
boil. Cover the pan, lower the heat
and simmer gently for about 10
minutes or until the mussel shells
have opened. Discard any mussels

that do not open during cooking.
4 Spoon the mussels and soup into
a warmed soup tureen or individual
soup bowls and serve at once (see
Serving ideas).

Cook's Notes

TIME
Preparing and cooking
the soup takes about 30
minutes. Allow extra time for
preparing the mussels.

PREPARATION
Check that the mussels
are fresh: tap any open
ones against a work surface and
discard if they do not shut. Pull
away any beards (pieces of
seaweed) gripped between the
shells of the mussels. Scrub the
mussels under cold running
water, then scrape away the
encrustations with a sharp
knife. Soak the mussels in fresh
cold water to cover for 2-3 hours,
changing the water several
times during this period.

BUYING GUIDE
Fresh mussels are
available from October-
March. Always buy them the
day you are going to eat them.
Look for closed mussels with
unbroken shells. Frozen shelled
mussels, which are available all
year round, can be used instead.

VARIATION
Use parsley or chervil
instead of coriander.

SERVING IDEAS
The mussels can be
eaten with the fingers
so provide napkins and a large
dish to put the empty shells in.

●255 calories/1050 kj per portion

Fish and vegetable soup

SERVES 4

225 g/8 oz cod steaks, defrosted if frozen, bones and skin removed and cut into 2 cm/¾ inch pieces
1 tablespoon vegetable oil
1 small onion, chopped
2 potatoes, cut into 1 cm/½ inch dice (see Buying guide)
2 carrots, cut into 1 cm/½ inch dice
25 g/1 oz plain flour
300 ml/½ pint warm milk
600 ml/1 pint warm chicken stock
1 bay leaf
salt and freshly ground black pepper
50 g/2 oz peeled prawns
½ bunch watercress, stalks removed, to garnish

1 Heat the oil in a large saucepan, add the onion, potatoes and carrots and cook over gentle heat, stirring, for 3 minutes. !
2 Sprinkle in the flour, stir for 1 minute, then remove from heat and gradually stir in the milk and stock.
3 Return the pan to the heat and bring to boil, stirring. Lower heat, add bay leaf and salt and pepper to taste. Simmer for 15 minutes.
4 Add the cod to the pan and simmer for a further 10 minutes.
5 Discard the bay leaf, stir the prawns into the soup and heat through for 5 minutes. ✳ Taste and adjust seasoning, then pour into warmed individual soup bowls and garnish with the watercress. Serve the soup at once.

Cook's Notes

TIME
Preparation takes 20 minutes and cooking about 35 minutes.

 FREEZING
Make the soup without adding the watercress. Cool quickly, then freeze in a polythene bag or rigid container for up to 3 months. Reheat from frozen, adding a little extra milk or stock if liked.

VARIATIONS
Any white fish may be used instead of cod. Use 2 tablespoons chopped parsley or snipped chives instead of the watercress.
Swirl 1 tablespoon top of the milk or cream on top of each bowl just before serving.

WATCHPOINT
Do not allow the vegetables to brown, or the soup will be light brown instead of pale and creamy.

 BUYING GUIDE
Choose floury potatoes such as King Edward. Waxy potatoes are not suitable for making soups, as they do not disintegrate so easily.

●250 calories/1050 kj per portion

Sweetcorn and tuna chowder

SERVES 4-6

350 g/12 oz can sweetcorn
200 g/7 oz can tuna
25 g/1 oz margarine or butter
1 large onion, finely chopped
2 tablespoons plain flour
2 teaspoons sweet paprika
pinch of cayenne pepper
850 ml/1½ pints milk
pinch of salt
grated zest of ½ lemon

TO FINISH
50 g/2 oz Cheddar cheese, finely
   grated
4 tablespoons chopped parsley

1 Drain the sweetcorn, reserving the juice. Drain off the oil from the tuna fish and discard. Place the fish on absorbent paper to remove excess oil. ! Flake the fish carefully into a bowl.

2 Melt the margarine in a saucepan, add the onion and cook gently until soft but not coloured.

3 Stir in the flour, paprika and cayenne pepper and cook for 1 minute, stirring constantly with a wooden spoon. Gradually stir in 300 ml/½ pint milk and the reserved sweetcorn juice and bring to the boil, stirring.

4 Stir in the remaining milk and bring the mixture to simmering point. Add the salt and the grated lemon zest.

5 Add the sweetcorn and simmer the soup, uncovered, for 5 minutes. Add the tuna fish and simmer for a further 5 minutes until heated through.

6 To finish: taste and adjust seasoning, then pour into warmed individual soup bowls. Sprinkle with the cheese ! and parsley and serve at once.

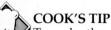

Cook's Notes

TIME
The soup takes 30 minutes to prepare and cook.

COOK'S TIP
To make the soup in advance, prepare it up to the end of stage 4, leave to cool, then refrigerate. To finish: re-heat until bubbling, stirring constantly, then continue from stage 5.

WATCHPOINT
It is important to re-move as much oil as possible from the tuna so that the chowder is not greasy.

Always add the cheese just before serving, when the soup is still hot enough for it to melt. Do not bring back to the boil after adding the cheese or the soup will be stringy.

●410 calories/1725 kj per portion

Provençal fish chowder

SERVES 4-6

750 g/1½ lb coley fillets, skinned
 and cut into 4 cm/1½ inch pieces
 (see Variation)
3 tablespoons vegetable oil
500 g/1 lb onions, grated
850 g/28 oz can tomatoes
bouquet garni
2 potatoes, cut into 1 cm/½ inch
 cubes
24 small black olives, halved and
 stoned
2 tablespoons capers, drained
300 ml/½ pint tomato juice
600 ml/1 pint vegetable stock (see
 Preparation)
salt and freshly ground black pepper
3 tablespoons finely chopped fresh
 parsley

1 Heat the oil in a large saucepan, add the onions and fry gently for 5 minutes until soft and lightly coloured. Add the tomatoes, with their juice, and the bouquet garni. Bring to the boil, then lower the heat and simmer for 5 minutes, stirring and breaking up the tomatoes with a wooden spoon.

2 Add all the remaining ingredients except the parsley and simmer uncovered, for 10-15 minutes, or until the potato is cooked (see Cook's tip).

3 Add the fish to the pan and simmer gently, uncovered, for about 5 minutes, or until the fish is tender but not breaking up. Remove the bouquet garni, stir in the parsley, then taste and adjust seasoning. Transfer to a warmed serving bowl and serve at once.

Cook's Notes

TIME
Total preparation and cooking time is about 50 minutes.

PREPARATION
For vegetable stock, save the liquid from cooked vegetables such as carrots and cabbage. Alternatively, use a vegetable stock cube, from health food shops.

SPECIAL OCCASION
This soup is a filling appetizer and can also make a lunch or supper party dish. Give it a real Mediterranean flavour by adding a crushed clove of garlic.

VARIATION
Use cod or haddock fillets as a substitute for the coley.

COOK'S TIP
You can prepare the chowder up to the end of stage 2 the day before, then add the fish and complete the cooking just before serving.

SERVING IDEAS
Serve with toasted French bread and butter.

● 395 calories/1650 kj per portion

Pea soup with cheese toast

SERVES 4

540 g/1 lb 3 oz can garden peas
1 tablespoon dried onion flakes
2 tablespoons boiling water
300 ml/½ pint chicken stock
½ teaspoon dried thyme
3 tablespoons instant potato powder (see Cook's tip)
1-2 teaspoons lemon juice
2-3 tablespoons evaporated milk or single cream
salt and freshly ground black pepper
1 tablespoon finely chopped fresh parsley

TOAST

4 small thick slices wholemeal bread
50 g/2 oz Cheddar cheese, grated
2 tablespoons evaporated milk or single cream
¼ teaspoon made English mustard

1 Put the dried onion flakes into a cup, pour over the boiling water and leave to stand for at least 15 minutes.
2 Put the peas with their liquid in the goblet of a liquidizer with the onion mixture and blend until smooth. Work through a sieve. Put into a saucepan with the stock and thyme and bring to the boil over moderate heat.
3 Lower the heat and sprinkle in the potato powder. Stir for 1-2 minutes then remove from heat and stir in the lemon juice and milk. Season to taste with salt and pepper. Return to the heat and simmer gently while you prepare the toast.
4 Heat the grill to high, and toast the bread on both sides. Remove from the grill.
5 Mix the cheese with the milk, mustard and salt and pepper.
6 Spread the cheese mixture on the toast, return to the grill and grill until the cheese mixture browns.
7 Ladle the soup into warmed individual bowls. Cut each slice of toast into 4 and serve at once.

Celery and peanut soup

SERVES 4

4 large celery stalks, chopped (see Economy)
6 tablespoons crunchy peanut butter
15 g/½ oz margarine or butter
1 tablespoon vegetable oil
1 onion, chopped
700 ml/1¼ pints light stock
salt and freshly ground black pepper
4 tablespoons single cream, to serve
chopped celery leaves, to garnish

1 Heat the margarine and oil in a saucepan, add the celery and onion and fry gently for 5 minutes until the onion is soft and lightly coloured.
2 Add the stock and bring to the boil. Lower the heat, cover and simmer gently for about 30 minutes until the celery is tender.
3 Cool the mixture a little, then work in a blender for a few seconds until smooth.
4 Return to the rinsed-out pan, place over low heat, then whisk in the peanut butter. Heat through until just boiling. ✳ Taste and then adjust seasoning.
5 Ladle the soup into 4 warmed individual bowls. Stir 1 tablespoon cream into each, then wait for a few seconds for the cream to rise to the surface. Sprinkle the chopped celery leaves in the centre of the bowls and serve at once.

Cook's Notes

TIME
Total preparation and cooking time is about 45 minutes.

FREEZING
Cool quickly, then pour into a rigid container, leaving 2 cm/¾ inch headspace. Seal, label and freeze for up to 2 months. To serve: defrost at room temperature for 2 hours, then reheat in a heavy-based pan, stirring frequently until bubbling. Taste and adjust seasoning, then proceed from the beginning of stage 5.

ECONOMY
This is a good way of using up outside celery stalks which may be a little tough, saving the more tender inner stalks for use in salads or serving with cheese.

SERVING IDEAS
Serve with freshly baked bread or rolls—crunchy brown granary rolls or those coated with a sprinkling of sesame or poppy seeds go particularly well with this soup.

● 265 calories/1100 kj per portion

Cheesy potato soup

SERVES 4

750 g/1½ lb potatoes, cut into
  even-sized pieces

salt

25 g/1 oz margarine or butter
1 large onion, finely chopped
2 large cloves garlic, finely chopped
  (optional)
3 celery stalks, finely chopped
1 large carrot, diced small
¼ small swede (weighing about
  50 g/2 oz), diced small
300 ml/½ pint chicken or vegetable
  stock (see Cook's tip)
150 ml/¼ pint milk
½ teaspoon dried thyme or
  marjoram
½ teaspoon celery salt
freshly ground black pepper
75 g/3 oz Cheddar cheese, grated
3 tablespoons chopped parsley

1 Cook the potatoes in boiling
salted water to cover for about 15
minutes or until tender.

2 When the potatoes are cooked,
leave them to cool slightly in the
water, then transfer both potatoes
and water to a blender and blend
until smooth. (If you do not have a
blender, pass them through a sieve.)
Return the purée to the rinsed-out
pan.

3 Melt the margarine in a large
frying-pan, add the onion and
garlic, if using, and fry over
moderate heat until beginning to
soften. Add the remaining
vegetables to the pan and cook,
stirring occasionally, for about 10
minutes, until just beginning to
colour.

4 Mix the vegetables with the
potato purée in the saucepan, then
stir in the stock, milk, thyme and
celery salt. Add pepper to taste.

5 Bring to the boil, lower the heat
and simmer gently for about 15
minutes or until the vegetables are
just soft. [!] Stir in the cheese,
reserving 2 tablespoons, and
simmer for a further 2-3 minutes.
Taste and adjust seasoning.

6 Pour into a warmed soup tureen.
Sprinkle with the chopped parsley
and the remaining cheese and serve
at once.

TIME
This very filling soup
takes just under 1 hour
to prepare and cook.

ECONOMY
Stretch the soup to 6
servings and give it a
slightly different flavour by
adding a small can of sweetcorn.

SERVING IDEAS
Serve the soup with hot
buttered toast.

WATCHPOINT
Thick soups sometimes
stick to the bottom of
the saucepan, so it is best to
stand the pan on an asbestos
mat or wire mesh if you are
using a gas cooker.

COOK'S TIP
If possible, use home-
made stock for a
fuller flavour.

● 335 calories/1400 kj per portion

Leek and barley soup

SERVES 4

 4 leeks, sliced
50 g/2 oz pearl barley
 1 tablespoon vegetable oil
1 small onion, chopped
2 carrots, sliced
400 g/14 oz can tomatoes
600 ml/1 pint vegetable stock or
    water (see Cook's tip)
½ teaspoon dried mixed herbs
1 bay leaf
salt and freshly ground black pepper
215 g/7½ oz can butter beans,
    drained

CHEESY BREAD
4 round slices French bread,
    2 cm/¾ inch thick
40 g/1½ oz butter, for frying
1 clove garlic, cut in half (optional)
100 g/4 oz Cheddar cheese, grated

1 Heat the oil in a large saucepan, add the onion, leeks and carrots and fry gently for 3-4 minutes.
2 Add the tomatoes with their juice, the stock and the barley, herbs and bay leaf. Season to taste with salt and pepper. Bring to the boil, stirring, then lower the heat, cover and simmer for 50 minutes. Stir occasionally during this time. ✳
3 Meanwhile, make the cheesy bread: melt the butter in a frying-pan and when it sizzles add the slices of French bread. Fry over fairly high heat, turning once, until the bread is crisp and golden brown on both sides. Remove from the pan, drain on absorbent paper and leave to cool.
4 Rub each side of fried bread with the cut sides of the garlic, if using. Press the grated cheese evenly on to the slices of bread, dividing it equally between them. Heat the grill to high.
5 Remove the bay leaf from the soup, stir in the drained beans and heat through. Adjust seasoning.

Cook's Notes

TIME
Preparation takes 15 minutes, cooking 1 hour.

COOK'S TIP
Vegetable stock cubes are difficult to obtain, but you may find them in a good continental delicatessen. To make your own vegetable stock, simply use the liquid in which you have cooked vegetables.

FREEZING
Cool the soup quickly after stage 2, discard the bay leaf, then freeze in a rigid container for up to 3 months. To defrost: place the soup in a large saucepan and cook over low heat, stirring from time to time. Make the cheesy bread and add the beans as from the beginning of stage 3.

●340 calories/1425 kj per portion

6 Toast the cheese-topped slices of bread until the cheese starts to bubble.
7 Ladle the soup into 4 warmed individual soup bowls and top each one with a slice of cheesy bread. Serve at once.

Chilled courgette and cheese soup

SERVES 6

500 g/1 lb courgettes, cut into 2.5 cm/1 inch lengths
850 ml/1½ pints chicken stock
1 mint sprig
25 g/1 oz margarine or butter
1 onion, chopped
1 clove garlic, crushed (optional)
175 g/6 oz full-fat soft cheese (see Economy)
150 ml/¼ pint milk
salt and freshly ground black pepper

TO SERVE

6 ice cubes
2 tablespoons double cream (see Economy)
extra mint sprigs, to garnish

1 Put the courgettes into a large pan with the stock and mint sprig. Bring to the boil, then lower the heat and simmer for 10 minutes.
2 Meanwhile, melt the margarine in a small pan, add the onion and garlic, if using, and fry gently for 5 minutes until the onion is soft and lightly coloured.
3 Remove the courgettes from the heat and stir in the onion and garlic. Allow to cool slightly, then pour the courgette mixture into a blender and work to a purée.
4 In a large bowl, blend the cheese with the milk a little at a time, then beat with a wooden spoon until smooth and creamy. Stir in the courgette purée.
5 Pour the soup into a clean large bowl or soup tureen, cover and refrigerate for about 4 hours or overnight.
6 To serve: season the soup to taste with salt and pepper (see Cook's tip). Add ice cubes, swirl over the cream and sprinkle with sprigs of mint. Serve at once.

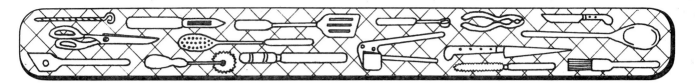

Chilled carrot and orange soup

SERVES 4
500 g/1 lb carrots, thinly sliced
1 tablespoon vegetable oil
1 onion, finely chopped
2 tablespoons medium-dry sherry
    (optional)
600 ml/1 pint chicken stock
salt and freshly ground black pepper
grated zest of 1 orange
juice of 3 large oranges
1 small carrot, grated, to garnish

1 Heat the oil in a saucepan, add the onion and fry gently for 5 minutes until soft and lightly coloured. Add the sherry, if using, and bring to the boil.
2 Add the sliced carrots and stock to the pan and season to taste.

Cook's Notes

TIME
15 minutes preparation, 45 minutes cooking, plus 2 hours chilling time.

VARIATION
4 tablespoons unsweetened concentrated orange juice may be substituted for the fresh orange juice.

SERVING IDEAS
If serving the soup at a summer dinner party,
give it a special garnish. Cut half an orange into 4 very thin slices. Remove the rind and pith. Float 1 orange slice on top of each bowl of chilled soup and arrange a little grated carrot on top of the slices.

The soup can also be served hot: prepare to stage 3 but do not cool, reduce to a purée at once and reheat gently with the orange zest and juice.

●130 calories/550 kj per portion

3 Bring to the boil, stirring, then lower the heat, cover and simmer gently for 45 minutes until the carrots are very tender. Leave to cool.
4 Pass the soup through a sieve or purée in a blender. Pour the soup into a bowl, cover and refrigerate for

at least 2 hours or overnight.
5 Just before serving, stir the orange zest and juice into the soup, then taste and adjust seasoning. Pour into 4 chilled individual soup bowls, sprinkle a little grated carrot on to each bowl and serve at once.

Mixed fish pâté

SERVES 4

175 g/6 oz can tuna fish in oil
125 g/4½ oz can mackerel fillets in oil
50 g/2 oz butter, melted and cooled
grated zest of 1 lemon
1 tablespoon lemon juice
1 clove garlic, crushed (optional)
salt and freshly ground black pepper
1 tablespoon single cream (optional)

TO GARNISH
few lemon slices
1-2 parsley sprigs

1 Place the tuna and mackerel, with their oil, in a blender or food processor. Pour over the melted butter and add the lemon zest and juice and the garlic, if using.
2 Blend to a smooth purée. Season well and stir in the cream, if using.
3 Spoon into individual dishes, cover and refrigerate for 2 hours.
4 Garnish with lemon slices and parsley. Serve chilled with toast.

Cook's Notes

TIME
10 minutes preparation, plus 2 hours chilling.

COOK'S TIPS
The beauty of this pâté is that it can be made in superquick time, from store-cupboard ingredients. This makes it ideal for an impromptu starter or snack.

VARIATION
Large supermarkets stock cans of tuna with vegetables in a curry sauce. If this is used instead of plain tuna in oil, it will make the pâté more exotic, with just a hint of curry.

●270 calories/1125 kj per portion

Quick pilchard pâté

SERVES 4

425 g/15 oz can pilchards in tomato
   sauce (see Cook's tip)
3 tablespoons double cream
½ teaspoon Worcestershire sauce
few drops of Tabasco
2 teaspoons lemon juice
25 g/1 oz gherkins, finely chopped
salt and freshly ground black pepper

TO GARNISH
1 tablespoon chopped fresh parsley
   or flat-leaved parsley sprigs
4 gherkin fans

1 Drain the pilchards and reserve 1
tablespoon of the tomato sauce. Cut
the pilchards in half and carefully
remove the bones.

Cook's Notes

TIME
Preparation takes about
5 minutes and chilling
takes 30 minutes.

SERVING IDEAS
Serve with slices of
warm pitta bread or oat-
cakes and butter. As a more
substantial starter, serve with a
seasonal salad.

● 180 calories/750 kj per portion

COOK'S TIP
If preferred, the can of
pilchards can be re-
frigerated unopened for 1 hour
before making the pâté — then
there is no need to chill the pâté
after it is made.

VARIATIONS
This pâté can also be
made with sardines in
tomato sauce or with canned
mackerel in tomato sauce.

2 Place the fish in a bowl with the
reserved tomato sauce, the cream,
Worcestershire sauce, Tabasco,
lemon juice and gherkins. Beat
together thoroughly with a fork and
season to taste with salt and
pepper.
3 Spoon the mixture into a serving
bowl or 4 individual bowls, cover
with cling film and then refrigerate
for 30 minutes.
4 To serve: garnish the pilchard
pâté with finely chopped parsley or
parsley sprigs and the prepared
gherkins fans and serve chilled (see
Serving ideas).

Egg pâté

SERVES 4

200 g/7 oz full-fat soft cheese
4 hard-boiled eggs, shelled and
 roughly chopped (see Cook's tip)
1 tablespoon finely snipped chives
salt and freshly ground black pepper
stuffed olives, sliced, to garnish

1 Put the cheese into a bowl and
beat until soft. Beat in the chopped
eggs and chives and season well
with salt and pepper.
2 Spoon into 4 individual dishes.
Smooth the top of each with a
palette knife, cover with cling film
and refrigerate for 30 minutes.
3 To serve: garnish with the olive
slices and serve at once.

Vegetable terrine

SERVES 4

12 cabbage leaves (see Buying guide), central midribs removed
salt
1 carrot (weight about 100 g/4 oz), cut into matchstick lengths
1 courgette (weight about 100 g/4 oz), cut into matchstick lengths
200 g/7 oz can sweetcorn and pimiento, drained
2 eggs, plus 1 egg yolk
150 ml/¼ pint milk
3 tablespoons double cream
¼ nutmeg, grated
freshly ground black pepper
vegetable oil, for brushing

TOMATO SAUCE
250 g/9 oz tomatoes, roughly chopped
3 tablespoons natural yoghurt
1 teaspoon French mustard
1 teaspoon Worcestershire sauce
1 teaspoon tomato ketchup
pinch of caster sugar

1 Heat the oven to 170C/325F/Gas 3.
2 Bring a saucepan of salted water to the boil and blanch the cabbage leaves for 2 minutes. Drain and dry on a clean tea-towel.
3 Bring a saucepan of salted water to the boil and put the carrot and courgette matchsticks in to simmer for 5 minutes. Drain and refresh under cold water, drain again.
4 Brush a 1 kg/2 lb loaf tin with vegetable oil. Line the loaf tin with 3 or 4 of the largest cabbage leaves and chop the remainder fairly finely.
5 Put half the carrot and courgette mixture into the lined loaf tin, add half the sweetcorn and pimiento, then half the chopped cabbage. Repeat the layering to make 6 layers in all.
6 Whisk the eggs lightly with the extra yolk, milk, cream and nutmeg. Season with salt and pepper. Carefully pour the egg mixture into the loaf tin, gently easing the vegetables apart in several places with a round-bladed knife, to make sure the egg mixture is evenly distributed through the tin and goes right to the bottom. Fold any protruding cabbage leaves over the filling. Cover the tin with foil.
7 Set the loaf tin in a roasting tin. Pour in hot water to come three-quarters up the sides of the loaf tin and cook for 1½-2 hours, until the custard is set and firm to the touch. Remove the loaf tin from the roasting tin and cool. Chill overnight in the refrigerator.
8 To make the sauce: put the tomatoes in a blender for a few seconds until liquidized, then sieve to remove the skins and seeds.
9 Mix the tomato purée with the remaining sauce ingredients, stirring to make sure they are well combined. Season to taste with salt and pepper. Cover with cling film and chill for at least 2 hours.
10 To serve: allow the terrine to stand at room temperature for about 10 minutes. Run a knife round the sides of the terrine, invert a serving plate on top and shake gently to unmould. Serve cut in slices (see Cook's tips) with the tomato sauce.

Three-tier pâté

SERVES 8

250 g/9 oz Continental liver sausage
65 g/2½ oz butter, softened
25 g/1 oz blanched almonds, finely chopped
a few black peppercorns, finely crushed
1 teaspoon medium sherry
salt
100 g/4 oz Cheddar cheese, grated
2 teaspoons snipped chives
2 teaspoons finely chopped fresh parsley
250 g/9 oz full-fat soft cheese
2 teaspoons tomato purée
good pinch of sweet paprika

1 Line the base of a freezerproof rigid container, approximately 10 cm/4 inches square and 7.5 cm/3 inches deep, with foil or grease-proof paper.

2 Using 15 g/½ oz of the butter, thoroughly grease the base and sides of the container, then coat with the chopped almonds.

3 Mix together the liver sausage, black peppercorns, sherry and salt to taste. Spoon this mixture into the prepared container and press down firmly. Smooth the surface with a wet palette knife.

4 In a bowl, beat together the remaining butter, the Cheddar cheese, chives, parsley and salt to taste. Spread this mixture over the liver sausage.

5 Beat the soft cheese in a separate bowl with the tomato purée, paprika and salt to taste. Spoon into the container and spread evenly on top of the Cheddar cheese mixture. ✳

6 Cover and refrigerate for 1-2 hours.

7 To serve: carefully run a knife around the sides of the container, then invert a serving plate on top. Invert the container on to the plate, remove the container and foil and slice the pâté. Serve chilled.

Meat terrine

SERVES 6

250 g/9 oz chicken livers
250 g/9 oz boneless belly pork, rind removed
1 small onion, cut into chunks
250 g/9 oz minced beef
1 tablespoon tomato purée
½ teaspoon dried oregano
1 clove garlic, crushed (optional)
3 tablespoons red wine (see Economy)
salt and freshly ground black pepper
100 g/4 oz stuffed olives
3 bay leaves
1 tablespoon chopped parsley, to garnish

1 Heat the oven to 180C/350F/Gas 4.
2 Wash and trim the livers, removing any discoloured parts with a sharp knife.
3 Mince the livers, pork and onion finely in a mincer or chop finely in a food processor (see Cook's tip). Place in a large bowl and stir in the minced beef, tomato purée, oregano, garlic, if using, and wine. Mix thoroughly and season generously with salt and pepper.
4 Reserve 3 of the olives for garnish, then halve the rest. Spoon half of the terrine mixture into a 700 ml/1¼ pint deep rectangular dish or tin. Arrange the halved olives in the dish (see Preparation).
5 Carefully spoon the remaining terrine mixture on top of the olives and arrange the bay leaves on top. Tap the base of dish a few times on a work surface so the mixture fills the gaps between the olives. Cover the dish loosely with foil.
6 Put the dish into a roasting tin, pour in boiling water to come halfway up the sides of the dish and cook in the oven for about 1½ hours. To test for doneness, tilt the dish and if the juices run clear the terrine is cooked. Remove the dish from the roasting tin and cover the surface of the terrine with foil. Put heavy weights on top, leave to cool, then refrigerate overnight.
7 To serve: turn the terrine out on to a platter. Slice the reserved olives and arrange them down the centre of the terrine. Sprinkle a row of chopped parsley either side.

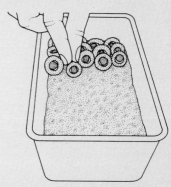

Pâté puffs

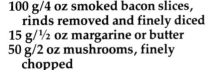

SERVES 4

100 g/4 oz smoked bacon slices, rinds removed and finely diced
15 g/½ oz margarine or butter
50 g/2 oz mushrooms, finely chopped
1 tablespoon chopped fresh parsley
celery or garlic salt (optional)
freshly ground black pepper
215 g/7½ oz frozen puff pastry, defrosted
100 g/4 oz liver pâté (see Buying guide)
1 egg, beaten
1-2 tablespoons sesame seeds

TO GARNISH (optional)
lettuce
tomato slices

1 Melt the margarine in a frying-pan over moderate heat, add the bacon and fry for 2-3 minutes. Add the mushrooms and cook for about 5 minutes. Stir in the parsley and season to taste with celery salt, if using, and pepper. [!] Set aside to cool slightly.

2 Heat the oven to 200C/400F/Gas 6.

3 Roll out the puff pastry on a floured surface to a square measuring about 30 cm/12 inches. Trim the edges to straighten them, then cut it into 16 squares 7.5 cm/3 inches each.

4 Mash the pâté with a fork to soften it then divide it between the 16 squares spreading it roughly in the centre of each one. Top with the bacon and mushroom mixture.

5 Brush the beaten egg round the edges of each pastry square. Carefully fold over the pastry to make a triangle, keeping the filling away from the edges. Press the edges of the pastry together firmly to seal them. [!] Brush with beaten egg.

6 Put the triangles on a large dampened baking sheet and sprinkle over the sesame seeds.

7 Bake for about 10-15 minutes until the pastry is puffy and golden. Lift the puffs off the baking sheet at once and cool slightly on a wire rack. Arrange the hot puffs on a plate garnished with lettuce and tomato, if using.

Chicken liver and walnut pâté

SERVES 12

500 g/1 lb chicken livers
100 g/4 oz walnut pieces, chopped
100 g/4 oz butter
1 small onion, finely chopped
1-2 cloves garlic, crushed (optional)
2 bay leaves
100 g/4 oz streaky bacon rashers,
   rinds removed and chopped
2 tablespoons dry or medium sherry
1 tablespoon brandy
2 large eggs, beaten
pinch of freshly grated nutmeg
salt and freshly ground black pepper

1 Melt the butter in a saucepan, add the chicken livers, onion, garlic, if using, bay leaves and bacon. Simmer gently for 10 minutes, stirring from time to time. Remove from the heat and leave to cool for about 30 minutes.

2 Heat the oven to 170C/325F/Gas 3.

3 Remove the bay leaves from the liver mixture and put the mixture through a mincer or chop finely. Stir in the remaining ingredients with salt and pepper to taste. Mix thoroughly.

4 Transfer the mixture to a 850 ml/1½ pint round, rectangular or oval terrine, ovenproof dish or tin.

5 Place the dish in a roasting tin and pour in enough water to come halfway up the dish. Bake in the oven for 1½ hours or until firm to the touch. ! Leave until cold then cover and refrigerate overnight.

6 Serve straight from the dish, or run a knife around the edge of the dish, then invert a serving plate on top of the dish. Hold the mould and plate firmly together and invert them giving a sharp shake halfway round. Serve cut into slices.

Quick tuna pâté

SERVES 4

200 g/7 oz can tuna, drained and
flaked
4 tablespoons thick bottled
mayonnaise
50 g/2 oz butter, melted
few drops of Tabasco
2 teaspoons lemon juice
2 teaspoons capers, drained and
chopped
salt and freshly ground black pepper
4 black olives, stoned and sliced
(optional)
4 tablespoons consommé (see
Cook's tip)

1 Mix the tuna, mayonnaise, butter,
Tabasco and the lemon juice in a
bowl until well blended. Stir in the
capers and season the mixture

with both salt and pepper to taste.
2 Spoon the mixture into 4 individual serving dishes. Smooth the
surfaces and arrange the olive slices
on top, if using.

3 Gently heat the consommé in a
saucepan and spoon 1 tablespoon
over each pâté. Refrigerate for
10 minutes, until the consommé
has set (see Serving ideas).

Quick pâté mousse

SERVES 4-6

2 × 200 g/7 oz cans pork or chicken pâté
175 g/6 oz full-fat soft cheese with chives
3 tablespoons snipped chives
2-3 tablespoons brandy
freshly ground black pepper
few stuffed olives and small gherkins, to garnish

1 Put all the ingredients, except the garnish, in a blender or food processor and work for several minutes until smooth (see Cook's tip).
2 Spoon the mixture into individual serving bowls, or 1 large bowl.
3 Cover and refrigerate for several hours or overnight.
4 Remove from the refrigerator 30 minutes before serving to allow to come to room temperature. Garnish with stuffed olives and gherkins.

Cook's Notes

TIME
The preparation only takes 10 minutes, but allow several hours chilling time.

COOK'S TIP
If you do not have a blender or food processor, mash the ingredients together with a fork. Add a little cream or top of the milk if the mixture is very stiff.

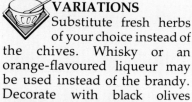

VARIATIONS
Substitute fresh herbs of your choice instead of the chives. Whisky or an orange-flavoured liqueur may be used instead of the brandy. Decorate with black olives instead of stuffed olives.

SERVING IDEAS
Serve with hot toast or crisp crackers as a starter or lunchtime or evening snack, or as part of a cold buffet.

●520 calories/2175 kj per portion

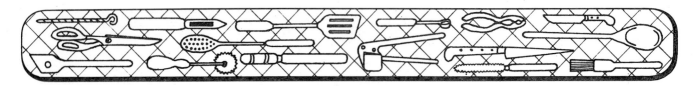

Salmon mousse

SERVES 4-6

200 g/7 oz can pink or red salmon,
  drained, with juice reserved
225-250 ml/8-9 fl oz milk
25 g/1 oz margarine or butter
25 g/1 oz plain flour
2 eggs, separated
1 rounded tablespoon (1 sachet)
  powdered gelatine
2 tablespoons lemon juice
2 tablespoons water
2 tablespoons tomato ketchup
150 ml/¼ pint single cream
salt and freshly ground black pepper
sprigs of dill
cucumber slices, to garnish

1 Strain the juice from the salmon
into a measuring jug and make up to
300 ml/½ pint with milk.
2 Melt the margarine in a small
saucepan, sprinkle in the flour and
stir over low heat for 1-2 minutes

until straw-coloured. Remove from
the heat and gradually stir in the
milk mixture. Return to the heat and
simmer, stirring, until thick and
smooth.
3 Remove from the heat and stir in
the egg yolks.
4 Mash the fish roughly with a fork,
discarding all skin and bones. Stir
into the sauce, then work the
mixture in a blender for a few
seconds until smooth. Pour into a
clean bowl and set aside to cool.
5 Sprinkle the gelatine over the
lemon juice and water in a small
heatproof bowl. Leave to soak for 5
minutes until spongy then stand the
bowl in a pan of gently simmering
water for 1-2 minutes, stirring
occasionally, until the gelatine has
dissolved.
6 Remove from the heat, leave to
cool slightly, then stir into the
salmon mixture with the tomato
ketchup and cream. Season to taste
with salt and pepper. Cover and
refrigerate for 2-3 hours, or until on
the point of setting.
7 In a clean, dry bowl, whisk the

Cook's Notes

TIME
Preparation time is
about 30 minutes, but
allow overnight refrigeration.

VARIATION
Omit dill sprigs and
set in a soufflé dish.
Do not turn out, but garnish the
top of the mousse decoratively
with thin cucumber and lemon
slices, if wished.

● 320 calories/1355 kj per portion

egg whites until standing in stiff
peaks, then fold into salmon
mixture with a large metal spoon.
8 Line base of an oiled 850 ml/1½
pint ring mould with dill sprigs.
Spoon salmon mixture carefully on
top. Refrigerate overnight.
9 Dip base of mould in hot water for
10 seconds, then turn mousse out on
to a serving plate. Serve chilled,
garnished with cucumber.

Egg and cucumber mousse

SERVES 6

4 hard-boiled eggs, chopped
250 g/9 oz cucumber, quartered
    lengthways
1 teaspoon salt
3 large spring onions
    (including green tops), finely
    chopped
4 tablespoons chopped fresh
    parsley
2 teaspoons powdered gelatine
3 tablespoons water
150 ml/¼ pint thick bottled
    mayonnaise
75 ml/3 fl oz natural yoghurt
freshly ground black pepper
1 egg white

1 Scrape out the cucumber seeds with a teaspoon and chop the cucumber finely. Spread it out on a plate and sprinkle with salt. Put another plate over the cucumber and place heavy weights on top. Leave for 30 minutes, then drain thoroughly.

2 Put the hard-boiled eggs, cucumber, onions and parsley into a bowl and mix well.

3 Sprinkle the gelatine over the water in a small heatproof bowl and leave to soak for 5 minutes, until spongy. Stand the bowl in a pan of gently simmering water and leave for 1-2 minutes, stirring occasionally, until gelatine has dissolved.

4 In a large bowl, blend the mayonnaise with the yoghurt. Allow the gelatine liquid to cool slightly, then stir it briskly into the mayonnaise mixture. Stir in the egg mixture and pepper to taste. Cover and refrigerate for 30-40 minutes, until beginning to set.

5 In a clean dry bowl, whisk the egg white until standing in stiff peaks, then fold it into the egg mixture with a large metal spoon. Turn the mousse into an 850 ml/1½ pint serving dish, cover and refrigerate for about 2 hours, until set. Serve chilled (see Serving ideas).

Cook's Notes

TIME
30 minutes draining for the cucumber, then 30 minutes preparation, plus about 2 hours setting time.

SERVING IDEAS
Garnish the mousse with slices of hard-boiled egg and drained canned anchovy fillets. (To reduce saltiness, soak the fillets in milk for 20 minutes, then drain and pat dry.) Serve as a starter or as a snack with Melba toast.

VARIATION
For an egg and sweet pepper mousse, omit the cucumber and parsley; deseed and dice 1 small red and 1 small yellow pepper and add to the chopped egg and onions. Garnish with strips of pepper.

●230 calories/975 kj per portion

Courgette and tomato mousse

SERVES 4-6

250 g/9 oz courgettes, sliced about
   1 cm/½ inch thick
25 g/1 oz margarine or butter
150 ml/¼ pint thick bottled
   mayonnaise
150 ml/¼ pint cold chicken stock
2 eggs, separated
3 tablespoons water
15 g/½ oz powdered gelatine
2 tablespoons snipped chives
few drops Tabasco (optional)
salt and freshly ground black pepper
250 g/9 oz tomatoes, skinned,
   deseeded and diced (see Cook's
   tip)

TO GARNISH
tomato slices
1 tablespoon snipped chives

1 Melt the margarine in a large frying-pan over low heat, add the courgettes and cook gently for about 15 minutes until soft, stirring so that the courgettes do not brown.

2 Place the courgettes with the mayonnaise, chicken stock and egg yolks in a blender or food processor and blend to a purée.

3 Put the water in a bowl, sprinkle over the gelatine and leave to soak until spongy. Then stand the bowl in a pan of hot water and stir until the gelatine is dissolved and the liquid is clear.

4 Turn the purée into a large bowl and stir in the chives and the Tabasco, if using. Taste and season. Then stir in the dissolved gelatine. Leave in the refrigerator for about 30 minutes until just setting.

5 Stir the purée until smooth then stir in the diced tomato. Whisk the egg whites until they stand in stiff peaks and then carefully fold into the purée.

6 Turn the mixture into a 1 L/2 pint soufflé dish and chill for about 1½ hours or until set.

7 Serve garnished with tomato slices and snipped chives.

Cook's Notes

TIME
The mousse takes about 30 minutes to prepare, allow 30 minutes for the mixture to come to setting point in the refrigerator, plus the chilling time.

COOK'S TIP
When deseeding the tomatoes, cut out the hard white piece of core under the stalk as it is rather dry and tough to eat and will spoil the texture of the mousse.

●355 calories/1500 kj per portion

FISH AND SEAFOOD

Fish gratin

SERVES 4

4 frozen cod steaks, total weight about 500 g/1 lb
150 ml/¼ pint water
1 small onion, sliced
1 bay leaf
salt and freshly ground black pepper
40 g/1½ oz margarine or butter
25 g/1 oz plain flour
150 ml/¼ pint milk
100 g/4 oz Cheddar cheese, grated
50 g/2 oz fresh white breadcrumbs
margarine, for greasing

1 Grease 4 scallop shells or individual ovenproof dishes.
2 Put the frozen fish steaks into a heavy-based frying-pan. Pour over the water, then add the onion and bay leaf and season to taste with salt and pepper. Bring to the boil, then lower the heat, cover and simmer for 15 minutes.
3 With a fish slice, lift the fish and onion from the liquid. Strain the liquid and reserve.
4 Leave the fish until cool enough to handle, then flake the flesh. Divide the fish between the prepared dishes and set aside.
5 Heat the grill to moderate.
6 Melt 25 g/1 oz of the margarine in a small saucepan, sprinkle in the flour and stir over low heat for 1-2 minutes until straw-coloured. Then remove from the heat and gradually stir in the reserved fish liquid and then the milk. Return to the heat and simmer, stirring, until thick and smooth. Remove from the heat and stir in half the grated cheese. Stir vigorously until the cheese has melted, then season to taste.
7 Spoon the cheese sauce over the fish in each shell, dividing it equally between them. Mix the breadcrumbs with the remaining cheese and sprinkle over the sauce in each shell. Dot with rest of margarine.
8 Grill until golden brown and heated through and serve at once.

Cook's Notes

TIME
Preparing and cooking take 40 minutes.

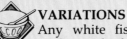

VARIATIONS
Any white fish fillets such as haddock or whiting may be used instead of the cod steaks. If using fresh fish, simmer 10 minutes.

●330 calories/1400 kj per portion

SPECIAL OCCASION
Pipe a border of mashed potatoes, to which some beaten egg has been added, around the edge of each shell before grilling.

Instead of cod, use monkfish, which tastes rather like lobster, and add 100 g/4 oz cooked prawns in stage 4.

Replace the water with white wine or dry cider.

Spicy fish

SERVES 4

350 g/12 oz rock salmon, bones removed, cut into 10 × 1 cm/ 4 × ½ inch strips (see Buying guide)
75 g/3 oz fresh white breadcrumbs
25 g/1 oz desiccated coconut
¼ teaspoon chilli powder
½ teaspoon ground coriander
½ teaspoon ground cumin
salt and freshly ground black pepper
25 g/1 oz plain flour
2 eggs, beaten
¼ cucumber, peeled and chopped
25 g/1 oz gherkins, chopped
6 tablespoons thick bottled mayonnaise
vegetable oil, for deep-frying
lemon and tomato, to garnish

1 Put the breadcrumbs in a bowl and stir in the coconut, chilli, coriander and cumin. Season with salt and black pepper to taste.

2 Spread the flour out on a large flat plate and season with salt and pepper. Beat the eggs in a shallow bowl. Dip the fish strips in the flour, turning to coat thoroughly, then in the egg, and then in the breadcrumb mixture until evenly coated.

3 Lay the strips on a baking sheet or tray and refrigerate for 10 minutes.

4 Meanwhile, mix the cucumber and gherkins into the mayonnaise and spoon into a small serving jug. Heat oven to 110C/225F/Gas ¼.

5 Pour enough oil into a deep-fat frier with a basket to come halfway up the sides. Heat the oil to 190C/ 375F, or until a stale bread cube turns golden in 50 seconds. Fry the fish strips a few at a time for 5-7 minutes until they are golden brown and crisp.

6 Drain on absorbent paper and keep warm in oven while frying remaining batches. Serve the fish strips at once garnished with thin wedges of lemon and tomato halves and with the cucumber and gherkin sauce handed separately.

Smoked mackerel salad

SERVES 4

500 g/1 lb smoked mackerel fillets, cut in half lengthways if large (see Buying guide)
4 tablespoons thick bottled mayonnaise
2 tablespoons natural yoghurt
¼ teaspoon French mustard
salt and freshly ground black pepper
3 celery stalks, chopped
175 g/6 oz green grapes, halved and seeds removed
100 g/4 oz radishes, thinly sliced
4 large lettuce leaves

GARNISH
1 punnet mustard and cress
1 lemon, cut into wedges

1 In a bowl, mix together the mayonnaise, yoghurt and mustard and season to taste with salt and pepper. Stir in the celery, grapes and radishes.

2 Put the lettuce leaves on a serving dish. Arrange the mackerel fillets over them, slightly overlapping.

3 Spoon the salad mixture in a line on top of the mackerel. Garnish with the mustard and cress and lemon wedges.

Cook's Notes

 TIME
Preparation takes about 20 minutes.

 BUYING GUIDE
Ready-cooked whole smoked mackerel can be bought from fishmongers and delicatessens and are easily filleted. Frozen vacuum-packed, or canned smoked mackerel fillets are available from supermarkets.

SERVING IDEAS
For an even more substantial salad, serve with plain cooked rice to which some chopped nuts have been added.

● 425 calories/1775 kj per portion

Baked stuffed kippers

SERVES 4

4 kippers, bones removed (see Preparation)
50 g/2 oz margarine or butter
3 eggs, hard-boiled and chopped while hot
2 tablespoons chopped parsley
grated zest and juice of ½ lemon
freshly ground black pepper
12 slices lemon and a few small parsley sprigs, to garnish

1 Heat the oven to 200C/400F/Gas 6.
2 Cream the margarine in a bowl with a wooden spoon and gradually work in the chopped eggs and parsley. Add the lemon zest and juice and season to taste with pepper. (Kippers can be salty so do not add salt.)
3 Cut 4 pieces of foil, each big enough to enclose a kipper.
4 Place a kipper on each piece of foil and spoon an equal amount of stuffing over one half of each kipper. Fold the kipper over the stuffing and wrap the foil into a loose parcel, turning in the ends of the foil to seal them tightly, so that the juices do not run out during cooking.
5 Place the parcels on a baking sheet and cook in oven for 15-20 minutes.
6 Fold back the foil around the kippers, then carefully remove the skin from the top side, leaving on the heads and tails. Lay 3 lemon slices along each kipper and place a sprig of parsley in the centre of each one.
7 Serve the kippers hot in the foil with their juices. If you prefer, use absorbent paper to drain away some of the juices first.

Cook's Notes

TIME
Preparation 20 minutes (including boning the kippers), cooking 15-20 minutes.

PREPARATION
Slide a sharp knife under the backbone and remove it with as many of the small bones as possible.

COOK'S TIP
If the kippers look dry, they can be made more succulent before cooking by placing them in a shallow dish and pouring over boiling water. Soak for 5 minutes, then dry thoroughly on absorbent paper.

SERVING IDEAS
Chunks of French or granary bread are perfect for mopping up the kipper juices.
A tomato and cucumber salad provides a refreshing contrast to the rich flavour of kippers.

VARIATIONS
Smoked mackerel can be substituted for the kippers. If kipper fillets are easier to obtain than whole kippers, use 2 per person and sandwich them together with the filling in between.

● 380 calories/1600 kj per portion

Creamy cod appetizer

SERVES 4

250 g/9 oz cod fillets, skinned
300 ml/½ pint milk
25 g/1 oz butter
25 g/1 oz plain flour
100 g/4 oz frozen peeled prawns, defrosted
2 tablespoons chopped fresh parsley

POTATO TOPPING
600 g/1¼ lb potatoes, cooked and mashed
25 g/1 oz butter
2 tablespoons milk
pinch of freshly grated nutmeg
salt and freshly ground black pepper

TO GARNISH
4 peeled prawns
parsley sprigs

1 Pour the milk into a saucepan and heat until simmering. Add the cod and cover the pan. Simmer for 15 minutes or until the fish is cooked. Using a fish slice, transfer the cod to a plate, then flake the flesh with a fork, discarding any bones. Strain the stock into a jug and set aside.
2 Make the potato topping: put the mashed potato in a bowl, then stir in the butter, milk ⚠ and nutmeg. Beat until smooth. Season to taste with salt and pepper, then spoon into a large piping bag fitted with a medium-sized nozzle. Set aside.
3 Melt the butter in a saucepan, sprinkle in the flour and stir over low heat for 1-2 minutes until straw-coloured. Remove from the heat and gradually stir in reserved stock. Return to the heat and simmer, stirring, until thick and smooth.
4 Stir in cod, prawns and parsley. Simmer gently for 5 minutes and season with salt and pepper.
5 Heat the grill to high.
6 Divide the fish mixture equally between 4 small shallow flameproof pots or dishes. Pipe a border of potato around the edge of each pot, then put under the grill for 3-4 minutes, until the potato border has browned a little.
7 Garnish each pot with a prawn and a sprig of parsley. Serve at once.

Fish rolls

SERVES 4

2 plaice, divided into 8 fillets
100 g/4 oz Cheddar cheese in 1 piece
2 large eggs, beaten
225 g/8 oz fresh white breadcrumbs
vegetable oil, for deep frying

1 Skin and wash the fillets, then dry them on absorbent paper.
2 Cut the cheese into 8 pieces, each long enough to fit just across the width of a fish fillet. Place a piece of cheese on each fillet and roll it up, starting from the tail end.
3 Pour the beaten eggs on to a shallow dish and put the bread-crumbs on a plate. Coat each fish roll all over in egg, then in bread-crumbs. Repeat, so that the rolls are coated twice, pressing the second coating of breadcrumbs on thoroughly. [!]
4 Pour enough oil into a deep-fat frier to cover the fish rolls and heat to 170C/325F (see Cook's tips).

Carefully lower the fish rolls into the hot oil and fry for about 7 minutes until they are golden brown and crisp (fry the rolls in 2 batches if necessary). Remove with a slotted spoon and drain on absorbent paper. Serve at once, with tartare sauce.

Cook's Notes

TIME
Preparation and cook-ing 30-45 minutes.

COOK'S TIPS
If you do not have a cooking thermometer or deep-fat frier with its own ther-mostat, test the heat of the oil by dropping in a 2.5 cm/1 inch cube of bread: this should brown in 75 seconds at a temperature of 170C/325F.

WATCHPOINT
It is very important to coat the rolls thoroughly in egg and breadcrumbs, or the cheese will melt and it will bubble out.

●510 calories/2150 kj per portion

Selsey soused herrings

SERVES 4

4 large herrings, each weighing
  about 250 g/9 oz, boned but left in
  1 piece (see Buying guide)
salt and freshly ground black pepper
1 small onion, sliced
150 ml/¼ pint white wine vinegar
125 ml/4 fl oz water
4 bay leaves
8 whole black peppercorns
1 stick cinnamon, 2.5 cm/1 inch long

TO SERVE

2 teaspoons creamed horseradish
  sauce
pinch of mustard powder
150 ml/¼ pint double cream
lemon and beetroot wedges, to
  garnish (optional)

1 Heat the oven to 170C/325F/Gas 3.
2 Season the herrings with salt and
pepper and roll them up, starting
from head end, with skin on outside and secure with cocktail sticks,
if necessary. Arrange them in a
single layer in a casserole just large
enough to hold them comfortably.
3 Add the onion, vinegar and
water. Push the bay leaves,
peppercorns and cinnamon
between the herring rolls. Cover
with a lid or foil and bake in the
oven for 1 hour. Leave to cool in the
cooking liquid for at least 8 hours.
4 Drain the herrings, reserving 4
tablespoons cooking liquid, and
place on a serving dish.
5 Put the reserved liquid into a
bowl with the horseradish sauce,
mustard powder and cream and
whisk until standing in soft peaks.
6 Spoon a little sauce over each
herring and garnish with lemon and
beetroot wedges, if liked. Serve
cold, with the remaining cream
sauce handed separately.

Cook's Notes

TIME
This recipe takes 10
minutes to prepare and
1 hour to cook, but allow a
further 8 hours for cooling.

BUYING GUIDE
Ask your fishmonger to
bone the fish and cut
off the head.

STORAGE
The flavour of soused
herrings is best after
they have been left for 24 hours,
but they can be left in the
refrigerator for up to 3-4 days.

SERVING IDEAS
Halve the herrings
lengthways before serv-
ing as a starter. Alternatively,
for a complete meal, serve with
potato salad and lettuce tossed
in an oil and vinegar dressing.

DID YOU KNOW
This dish gets its name
from Selsey in Sussex
and dates from a time when
herrings were plentiful in the
seas off England's south coast.

● 370 calories/1550 kj per portion

Salmon and macaroni layer

SERVES 4

215 g/7½ oz can salmon, drained with juice reserved, flaked (see Economy)
salt
175 g/6 oz short-cut macaroni
25 g/1 oz margarine or butter
25 g/1 oz plain flour
300 ml/½ pint milk
2 hard-boiled eggs, chopped
1 tablespoon chopped fresh parsley
pinch of ground mace
freshly ground black pepper
75 g/3 oz Cheddar cheese, grated
tomato wedges and
    watercress, to garnish

1 Bring a large pan of salted water to the boil, add the macaroni and cook for 10 minutes until tender but firm to the bite (*al dente*).

2 Meanwhile, melt the margarine in a saucepan, sprinkle in the flour and stir over low heat for 1-2 minutes until straw-coloured. Remove from the heat and gradually stir in the milk and reserved salmon juice. Return to the heat and simmer, stirring, until thick and smooth.

3 Remove the sauce from the heat and gently fold in the eggs and salmon with the parsley and mace. Season to taste with salt and pepper, then spoon into a flameproof dish (see Serving ideas).

4 Drain the macaroni thoroughly and turn into a bowl. Add half the cheese and toss to coat well. Spoon the macaroni over the salmon mixture. Sprinkle over the remaining cheese. Grill for 5 minutes until the cheese is golden and bubbling. Garnish with tomato and watercress. Serve at once, straight from dish.

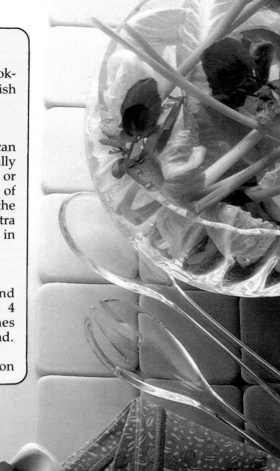

Herring salad

SERVES 4

250 g/9 oz salt herring fillets,
   drained (see Buying guide)

2 large waxy potatoes, cooked (see
   Watchpoint)
1 large beetroot, cooked (see Buying
   guide)
1 large pickled cucumber
1 large crisp dessert apple
2 tablespoons mayonnaise
6 tablespoons natural yoghurt or
   soured cream

1 Cut the herring fillets, potatoes,
beetroot and cucumber into small
dice and place in a large bowl (see
Preparation). Peel and core the
apple and cut it into small dice. Add
to the bowl (see Serving ideas).
2 Mix the mayonnaise and yoghurt
together until well blended and
smooth. Pour over the chopped
ingredients in the bowl and mix
thoroughly until everything is well
coated.

3 Cover the bowl with cling film
and refrigerate for several hours,
ideally overnight, before serving.

Cook's Notes

TIME
Preparation, including
boiling the potatoes and
beetroot, takes 1½ hours, plus
chilling time.

BUYING GUIDE
Any salt herring is
suitable for this salad.
Pickled rollmops in jars, or
herrings canned in wine are
available from delicatessens and
good supermarkets.
   Buy a ready-cooked beetroot
from the greengrocer, to cut
down on preparation time.

WATCHPOINT
Do not overcook the
potatoes—they should
be firm.

PREPARATION
Make sure the ingre-
dients are cut into small
dice for this salad—the flavours
will mingle more easily.

SERVING IDEAS
Serve as a main course,
with a green salad and
French bread.
   Salt herring fillets have a
strong, distinctive flavour, and
you may prefer not to mix them
into the salad. Combine the
other diced ingredients as in
stages 1 and 2, then roll the
drained fillets up tightly and
arrange around the dish, as in
the picture.

●365 calories/1525 kj per portion

Creamy pasta with tuna

 SERVES 4

 350 g/12 oz pasta shapes (see Buying guide)

salt

75 g/3 oz margarine or butter

1 small onion, chopped

1 clove garlic, crushed (optional)

2 tablespoons plain flour

300 ml/½ pint chicken stock

150 ml/¼ pint soured cream (see Variations)

freshly ground black pepper

100 g/4 oz button mushrooms, quartered

400 g/14 oz can tomatoes, drained and roughly chopped (see Economy)

100 g/4 oz Cheddar cheese, grated

200 g/7 oz can tuna, drained and flaked

SAVOURY BUTTER

75 g/3 oz butter

25 g/1 oz Parmesan cheese, grated

2 tablespoons finely chopped parsley

1 Heat the oven to 190C/375F/Gas 5. Set a large saucepan of salted water over high heat to boil.

2 Make the savoury butter: cream the butter with the Parmesan cheese and parsley. Put the savoury butter inside a piece of folded greaseproof paper and shape into a cylinder. Pat the ends to flatten and neaten, and twist the ends of the greaseproof paper. Chill in the refrigerator while you prepare the pasta.

3 Add the pasta to the pan of boiling water and cook for 10-12 minutes, or according to packet instructions, until tender yet firm to the bite. Drain well.

4 While the pasta is cooking, melt 50 g/2 oz of the margarine in a saucepan, add the onion and garlic, if using, and cook over gentle heat until soft but not coloured. Sprinkle in the flour and stir over low heat for 2 minutes until straw-coloured. Remove from the heat and gradually stir in the chicken stock.

5 Return the pan to the heat and simmer, stirring, until thick and smooth. Reduce the heat and stir in the soured cream. Remove from heat and season to taste with salt and pepper. Cover and set aside.

6 Melt the remaining margarine in a small saucepan, add the mushrooms and cook for 2-3 minutes.

7 Add the tomatoes to the sauce with the mushrooms and grated cheese. Stir in the cooked pasta. Put the tuna fish in the base of a large ovenproof dish. Spoon the pasta over the tuna.

8 Cut the chilled savoury butter into 8 slices and arrange them over the top of the pasta. Cook in the oven for about 15-20 minutes until the dish is piping hot.

Crab-stuffed tomatoes

8 large tomatoes
275-300 g/10-12 oz canned or frozen
    crabmeat (see Buying guide)
grated zest of 2 lemons
4 teaspoons lemon juice
2 tablespoons thick mayonnaise
4 tablespoons cottage cheese, sieved
2 punnets mustard and cress,
    snipped
salt and freshly ground black pepper
few drops of Tabasco

1 Slice off the top of each tomato and set aside. Using a grapefruit knife or teaspoon, gently scoop out the flesh and seeds, taking care not to pierce the tomato shells (see Economy). Turn them upside down on absorbent paper and leave them to drain while you prepare the crab filling.

2 In a bowl, mix together the crabmeat, lemon zest and juice, mayonnaise and sieved cottage cheese (see Cook's tip). Lightly stir in the mustard and cress and season to taste with salt, pepper and the Tabasco. Cover the bowl and chill the mixture in the refrigerator for 1-2 hours.

3 Spoon the crab mixture into the tomato shells, filling them as full as possible without letting the mixture run down the sides of the tomatoes. Carefully replace the tomato tops on the crab stuffing and serve the tomatoes at once.

Cook's Notes

TIME
Preparation takes 30 minutes. Allow 1-2 hours for chilling the stuffing.

SERVING IDEAS
These stuffed tomatoes are very versatile: they make an unusual starter for a dinner party, or may be served as a main meal with a mixed salad and French bread. For a tasty supper dish, serve the tomatoes on circles of fried or toasted bread, garnished with watercress.

BUYING GUIDE
Canned and frozen crabmeat is sold in varying weights according to individual brands. Exact weight of crabmeat is not critical for this recipe as the size of the tomatoes will vary as well.

ECONOMY
Discard the seeds and use the scooped-out tomato flesh for sandwiches.

COOK'S TIP
If you find the flavour of crab rather strong, use less crabmeat and add more cottage cheese when you are mixing the filling.

VARIATION
Tomatoes may be stuffed with all sorts of mixtures. Substitute drained, mashed tuna fish for the crabmeat in this recipe. Or try mixing equal quantities of cream cheese with sieved cottage cheese and adding some chopped prawns or chopped walnuts. You can also try lime juice instead of lemon juice.

●140 calories/600 kj per portion

Roes on toast

SERVES 4

500 g/1 lb soft cod roes, defrosted if frozen (see Buying guide)
75 g/3 oz margarine or butter
1 tablespoon lemon juice
1 tablespoon chopped parsley
salt and freshly ground white pepper (see Cook's tip)
4 large slices bread, crusts removed

TO GARNISH
lemon slices, halved
parsley sprigs

1 Drain the cod roes on absorbent paper.
2 Melt the margarine in a frying-pan, add the roes and fry fairly briskly for 3-4 minutes, turning the roes several times to brown. !
3 Add the lemon juice and parsley and season with salt and pepper.
4 While the roes are cooking, toast the bread and arrange the slices on a warmed serving dish. Spoon a portion of roes with the buttery juices on to each slice of toast (see Serving ideas).
5 Garnish the top of each serving with lemon slices and parsley sprigs. Serve at once.

Cook's Notes

TIME
This dish takes only 10 minutes to prepare.

COOK'S TIP
Use white pepper in pale-coloured dishes: black pepper spoils the colour of the finished dish.

WATCHPOINT
Soft roes break up easily and need careful cooking in a non-stick pan.

SERVING IDEAS
Grilled streaky bacon rolls may be served with the roes.

BUYING GUIDE
You can buy canned fish roes which are already cooked: simply turn them very briefly in some melted margarine or butter with the lemon juice added.

●285 calories/1200 kj per portion

Oriental seafood salad

SERVES 6

250 g/9 oz beansprouts
4 spring onions, chopped
1 celery stalk, finely sliced
1 red pepper, deseeded and cut into
   5 mm/¼ inch strips (optional)
100 g/4 oz peeled prawns, defrosted
   if frozen (see Economy)
175 g/6 oz can crabmeat, drained
   and flaked
6 Chinese leaves or lettuce leaves
spring onion tassels, to garnish

DRESSING

150 g/5 oz natural yoghurt
6 tablespoons thick bottled
   mayonnaise
finely grated zest of 1 lemon
1 tablespoon lemon juice
1 teaspoon ground ginger
salt and freshly ground black pepper

Cook's Notes

TIME
Preparation takes only 15 minutes plus 15-30 minutes chilling time.

SERVING IDEAS
Serve as a starter to a Chinese-style meal — it makes 6 servings. Follow salad with a main course of stir-fried vegetables with beef or pork strips and a bowl of rice. Shred some of the leftover Chinese leaves and add to the vegetables.

Alternatively, serve this refreshing salad with fried prawn crackers available from many large supermarkets.

ECONOMY
Omit the prawns and use 200 g/7 oz can drained sweetcorn instead. Or you can substitute a 200 g/7 oz can tuna, drained and flaked, for the canned crabmeat.

●250 calories/1050 kj per portion

1 Combine the beansprouts, spring onions and celery in a bowl with the red pepper, if using.
2 Make the dressing: put the yoghurt in a bowl with the mayonnaise, lemon zest and juice and ginger. Mix together and season with salt and pepper to taste.
3 Add the dressing to the bean- sprouts mixture and toss to coat well, then fold the prawns and crabmeat into the salad. Cover with cling film and refrigerate the salad for about 15-30 minutes.
4 Arrange the Chinese leaves on a serving plate and spoon the salad on top. Garnish with spring onion tassels and serve at once.

Mussel omelettes

MAKES 4

2 × 150 g/5 oz jars mussels in their own juice, drained, with juice reserved (see Variations)
100 g/4 oz butter
1 onion, finely chopped
2 celery stalks, finely chopped
40 g/1½ oz plain flour
3 tablespoons dry or medium white wine
8 eggs
salt and freshly ground black pepper
2-3 tablespoons double cream
1 tablespoon finely chopped fresh parsley

1 Melt 50 g/2 oz butter in a saucepan. Add the onion and celery and cook very gently, stirring with a wooden spoon, for about 10 minutes until soft.
2 Sprinkle in the flour and stir for 1-2 minutes. Gradually stir in 125 ml/4 fl oz reserved mussel juice and the wine and simmer, stirring, until thick and smooth, then stir in the mussels and enough cream to make a thick sauce (see Cook's tip). Season to taste with salt and pepper, being cautious with the salt, and stir in the chopped parsley. Leave the sauce on very low heat, stirring occasionally, while you make the omelettes.
3 Lightly beat 2 eggs and season sparingly with salt and pepper. Melt 15 g/½ oz butter in a frying-pan. When it sizzles, pour in the eggs, and cook for 2-3 minutes, drawing the edges towards the centre with a fork as they cook. The omelette is ready when the centre is still slightly runny.
4 Spoon one-quarter of the mussel sauce on to one-half of the omelette in the pan and fold the omelette over. Carefully slide it out on to a warmed individual serving plate and serve at once. Make the other 3 omelettes in the same way serving each as soon as it is made.

Cook's Notes

TIME
These omelettes take only 30 minutes to prepare and cook.

COOK'S TIP
The mussel mixture is very thick. Add the cream gradually until you have the sauce consistency to suit your taste.

VARIATIONS
Use 250 g/9 oz shelled frozen mussels, defrosted, and substitute milk for the mussel juice. Mussels or clams in brine can be used. They should be drained and milk used in place of the brine to prevent the sauce from becoming salty.

●453 calories/1905 kj per portion

Devilled prawns and eggs

SERVES 4

175 g/6 oz frozen prawns
4 eggs
400 g/14 oz can tomatoes
1 tablespoon tomato purée
2 tablespoons brown sugar
2 tablespoons wine vinegar
1 tablespoon Worcestershire sauce
salt and freshly ground black pepper

1 Put the tomatoes in a saucepan with half the juice from the can, the tomato purée, sugar, vinegar, and Worcestershire sauce. Reserve the remaining tomato juice for future use in a casserole.
2 Bring to the boil, stirring well to break up the tomatoes.
3 Reduce the heat a little and simmer, uncovered, for 10 minutes.
4 Meanwhile, cook the eggs in gently simmering water for 7-8 minutes until hard-boiled.
5 Stir the prawns into the tomato sauce and cook for a further 5 minutes. Season to taste with salt and pepper.
6 Peel and halve the eggs and place in a warmed serving dish. Spoon the tomato and prawn mixture over them. Serve at once.

Cook's Notes

TIME
20 minutes to prepare and cook.

COOK'S TIPS
Adjust the consistency of the sauce before adding the prawns. If it is too thick, add some of the reserved juice from the tomatoes. If it is too runny, boil it rapidly for about 5 minutes to evaporate some of the liquid.
Always use wine vinegar for a delicate flavour. Malt vinegar is much too harsh in flavour for most dishes.

SERVING IDEAS
For a starter, serve in individual dishes, without the rice accompaniment. For a main meal, surround with boiled rice.

VARIATION
Use canned crabmeat in place of prawns.

●175 calories/725 kj per portion

Crab and cheese florentines

SERVES 4

175 g/6 oz can crabmeat, drained and flaked, or the same weight of frozen crabmeat, defrosted
3 tablespoons vegetable oil
1 tablespoon white wine vinegar
juice of 1 lemon
salt and freshly ground black pepper
100 g/4 oz raw spinach, shredded
150 g/5 oz natural yoghurt
finely grated zest of ½ lemon
1 tablespoon snipped chives
225 g/8 oz cottage cheese

TO GARNISH (OPTIONAL)
cayenne pepper
radish waterlilies (see Preparation)

1 Put the oil, vinegar and half the lemon juice into a large bowl and season well with salt and pepper. Whisk together with a fork, then add the spinach and toss it with 2 forks until thoroughly coated. Use it to line 4 individual dishes.
2 Put the yoghurt, lemon zest and the chives into a bowl with the remaining lemon juice and salt and pepper to taste. Mix thoroughly.
3 In a separate bowl, fork together the cottage cheese and crabmeat. Fold in the yoghurt and spoon on to the spinach.
4 Sprinkle with cayenne pepper, if liked, then garnish with radish waterlilies. Serve at once.

Cook's Notes

 TIME
Preparation time is about 25 minutes, but remember to allow time for radishes to soak if using them.

 VARIATIONS
Use prawns or other shellfish in place of the crab. For a milder garnish, use sweet paprika, not cayenne.

? **DID YOU KNOW**
Spinach is a rich source of iron and vitamins and is even more nutritious when eaten raw as suggested here.

PREPARATION
To make radish waterlilies:

1 *Slice off the stalk and root ends, then with the stalk end downwards, cut 5 shallow petal shapes, cutting almost to the base.*

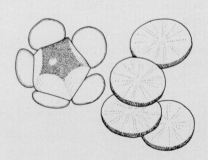

2 *Place in ice-cold water for at least 30 minutes for the petals to open. Then arrange the radish on a circle of very thin radish slices.*

●225 calories/950 kj per portion

Slimmers' crab dip with crudités

SERVES 4
175 g/6 oz can crabmeat
150 g/5 oz natural yoghurt
1 tablespoon snipped chives
salt
few drops of Tabasco

CRUDITES
1 red pepper
1 cucumber
3 celery stalks
2 carrots
75 g/3 oz button mushrooms

1 Drain the crabmeat and flake it into a bowl. Beat in the yoghurt and chives and season to taste with salt and Tabasco. Refrigerate the dip while preparing the vegetables.
2 Deseed the pepper and cut into strips about 5 cm/2 inches long and 1 cm/½ inch thick.

3 Peel the cucumber and cut into sticks the same size as the pepper. Cut the celery and carrots into the same size sticks. Halve the button mushrooms lengthways.

4 Beat the dip again and spoon into a serving bowl. Put the bowl on a large platter and surround with the prepared vegetables. Serve at once (see Cook's tip and Serving ideas).

Cook's Notes

TIME
Preparation takes about 15 minutes, including the chilling time.

COOK'S TIP
The dip will separate if it is left to stand – if this happens, whisk it vigorously until evenly blended again. If a smoother dip is preferred, work the dip in an electric blender before serving.

VARIATION
Canned tuna fish or pink salmon can be used instead of the crab but they are more fattening. A 175 g/6 oz can crabmeat, drained, is 145 calories/600 kj; the same weight of tuna in brine, drained, is 185 calories/ 775 kj; tuna in oil, drained, 370 calories/1550 kj; and pink salmon 270 calories/1125 kj.

SERVING IDEAS
For an attractive display, spoon the dip into a crab shell and arrange the crudités in separate bowls.
Use savoury biscuits and crisps instead of the vegetables, but remember that the calorie count will be higher.

●85 calories/350 kj per portion

CHEESE AND EGG DISHES

Fruit and cheese kebabs

SERVES 4

50 g/2 oz curd cheese
25 g/1 oz seedless raisins, chopped
2 tablespoons walnuts or unsalted
 peanuts, finely chopped
50 g/2 oz Danish blue cheese
50 g/2 oz smoked cheese
50 g/2 oz Leicester or Red Cheshire
 cheese
1 large red-skinned dessert apple
juice of 1 lemon
300 g/11 oz can mandarin orange
 segments, well drained, or 2 fresh
 mandarin oranges, peeled and
 divided into segments
225 g/8 oz can pineapple chunks,
 well drained
100 g/4 oz black or green grapes,
 washed and dried
6 lettuce leaves, shredded, to serve

1 Put the curd cheese into a bowl
with the raisins and mix well. Roll
into 8 small even-sized balls.

2 Spread the chopped nuts out on a
flat plate and roll the balls in them.
Transfer to a plate and refrigerate
while you prepare the other
ingredients.
3 Cut the Danish blue cheese into 8
even-sized cubes. Repeat with both
the smoked cheese and the Leicester
cheese.
4 Quarter and core the apple, but do
not peel it. Cut in even sized slices

and immediately squeeze the lemon
juice over them to prevent
discoloration.
5 On 8 individual skewers, spear 1
curd cheese ball and 1 cube each of
Danish blue, smoked and Leicester
cheeses, interspersed with apple
slices, mandarin orange segments,
pineapple chunks and grapes. Serve
2 skewers per person on a bed of
shredded lettuce.

Cook's Notes

TIME
Total preparation time
is about 20 minutes.

SERVING IDEAS
These kebabs make an
interesting and refresh-
ing snack or an unusual, fresh-
tasting dinner party starter.
Slices of brown bread and butter
go well with them, or they can
be served inside wholemeal
pitta bread.

● 355 calories/1450 kj per kebab

VARIATIONS
You can vary the
ingredients according
to the cheese, nuts and fruit you
prefer and have available; you
can also add salad ingredients
such as red or green pepper,
chunks of cucumber, radishes
or tiny tomatoes.

ECONOMY
If you have any fruit left
over, tip it into a bowl
and add a can of guavas for a
quick fruit salad.

Cottage cheese pancakes

MAKES 12

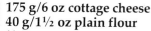

175 g/6 oz cottage cheese
40 g/1½ oz plain flour
½ teaspoon salt
25 g/1 oz butter, melted
3 eggs, separated
vegetable oil, for greasing

1 Heat the oven to 110C/225F/Gas ¼.
2 Sift the flour and salt into a bowl, then add the cottage cheese, butter and egg yolks and mix well.
3 In a clean, dry bowl, whisk the egg whites until they form soft peaks. With a metal spoon, fold 3 tablespoons of the egg white into the cottage cheese mixture and then carefully fold in the remainder. !
4 Heat a little oil in a heavy-based frying-pan. Drop about 6 tablespoons of the mixture into the pan, spacing them well apart, and fry over moderate heat for 2-3 minutes on each side until they are golden brown.
5 Remove the pancakes with a fish slice and keep hot in the oven while frying the second batch. Serve at once (see Serving ideas).

Cook's Notes

TIME
The pancakes take less than 1 hour to make.

 WATCHPOINT
The air trapped in the whisked egg whites makes the mixture light, so fold them into the cottage cheese mixture very gently to avoid losing the air and making the pancakes heavy.

SERVING IDEAS
Spread the pancakes with smoked cod's roe pâté (taramosalata), available in tubs from supermarkets and delicatessens, or with curd cheese mixed to a spread with tomato purée, snipped chives and salt and pepper to taste.

●65 calories/275 kj per pancake

Cottage cheese and ham cocottes

SERVES 4

225 g/8 oz cottage cheese
1 tablespoon vegetable oil
1 small onion, finely chopped
100 g/4 oz mushrooms, chopped
2 eggs, lightly beaten
50 g/2 oz ham, diced
pinch of freshly grated nutmeg
salt and freshly ground black pepper
25 g/1 oz butter, melted
parsley sprigs, to garnish

1 Heat the oven to 200C/400F/Gas 6.
2 Heat the oil in a small sauce-pan, add the onion and fry gently until it is soft.
3 Add the mushrooms and fry for 1-2 minutes only, stirring constantly. Remove the saucepan from the heat and cool.
4 Sieve the cottage cheese into a bowl and beat in the beaten eggs, a little at a time.
5 Add the diced ham to the cheese mixture with the onion and mush-rooms. Add the nutmeg, then season to taste with salt and pepper.
6 Brush 4 ramekins or cocottes with the melted butter and divide the mixture between them.
7 Place on a baking sheet and bake for about 20-25 minutes or until well risen, and brown and bubbly on top. Serve immediately, garnished with sprigs of parsley.

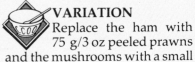

Cook's Notes

TIME
Preparation 10 minutes, baking 25 minutes.

VARIATION
Replace the ham with 75 g/3 oz peeled prawns and the mushrooms with a small amount of canned or frozen sweetcorn.

● 210 calories/875 kj per portion

Crunchy Camembert

SERVES 4
4 Camembert triangle portions
15 g/½ oz plain flour
salt and freshly ground black pepper
1 large egg
15 g/½ oz fresh white breadcrumbs
25 g/1 oz blanched almonds, finely chopped

FRUITY SALAD
2 oranges
1 grapefruit
2 teaspoons caster sugar
4 tomatoes, each cut into 6 wedges
1 tablespoon olive oil
1 teaspoon chopped fresh parsley
vegetable oil, for deep frying

1 Chill the cheese portions in the freezer or freezing compartment of the refrigerator for 30 minutes (see Cook's tips).
2 Put the flour in a large polythene bag; season with salt and pepper.
3 Lightly beat the egg in a shallow dish. Mix together the breadcrumbs and almonds and spread out on a flat plate.
4 Add the cheeses to the flour and shake until well coated. Dip them into the egg and then into the breadcrumbs. Coat the portions in the egg and breadcrumbs again until evenly coated. Put on a plate and refrigerate for 30 minutes.
5 Meanwhile, make the salad: divide the fruit into segments making sure that all white pith and any pips are removed then put the segments into a bowl and mix together with the sugar. Add the tomato wedges and mix well.
6 Drain off any liquid then divide the salad mixture between 4 serving plates. Spoon over the olive oil and sprinkle with parsley.
7 Pour enough oil into a deep-fat frier to cover the cheeses. Heat to 180C/350F, or until a stale bread cube browns in 60 seconds.
8 Using a slotted spoon, lower the cheeses into the hot oil and deep-fry for 30-60 seconds until the coating begins to turn golden. Drain on absorbent paper and serve at once, with the salad (see Cook's tips).

Parsley cheese bites

SERVES 4

75 g/3 oz full-fat soft cheese
100 g/4 oz Cheddar cheese, grated
50 g/2 oz Danish Blue cheese, at
   room temperature
freshly ground black pepper
4-5 tablespoons finely chopped
   fresh parsley
2-3 tablespoons plain flour

1 Work the cheeses together with a fork to form a smooth paste. Add pepper to taste.
2 Put the chopped parsley and flour on separate flat plates. Dip your hands in the flour, shaking off any excess, then shape the cheese mixture into 20 small balls, reflouring your hands as necessary. Roll each ball in chopped parsley.
3 Transfer to a serving plate and refrigerate for 30 minutes before serving. Serve chilled.

Cook's Notes

TIME
Total preparation time is only 10-15 minutes but allow a further 30 minutes for chilling.

VARIATIONS
Any mixture of cheese can be used and it is fun to experiment with different flavours, but the base must always be made from full-fat soft cheese to make the bites cling together. Try soft cheese flavoured with chives and, instead of Cheddar, use grated Wensleydale, Cheshire, Caerphilly or Lancashire cheese. A Blue Stilton or Italian Dolcelatte or Gorgonzola can be used in place of Danish Blue.

SERVING IDEAS
Serve on cocktail sticks, with sticks of celery and Melba toast as a snack or starter or alternatively, add them to a cheeseboard to end a meal.

●250 calories/1025 kj per ball

Dutch fondue

SERVES 4

250 g/9 oz flat mushrooms with
  their stalks, finely chopped
600 ml/1 pint chicken stock
4 tablespoons cornflour
150 ml/¼ pint milk
250 g/9 oz Gouda cheese, finely
  grated (see Variations)
1 tablespoon finely chopped fresh
  parsley
1 teaspoon Worcestershire sauce
salt and freshly ground black pepper
mushroom slices, to garnish

TO SERVE

1 small French loaf, cut into 2.5 cm/
  1 inch cubes
500 g/1 lb pork sausages, fried and
  thickly sliced

1 Put the chopped mushrooms in a
saucepan with the stock and bring
to the boil. Lower the heat, cover

Cook's Notes

TIME
Preparation and cooking
take 40 minutes.

VARIATIONS
Add 50 g/2 oz finely
grated mature Cheddar
cheese with the Gouda, and stir
1 tablespoon dry sherry into the
fondue just before serving.

Lightly steamed still crunchy
broccoli spears or cauliflower
florets may be used for dipping.

WATCHPOINTS
It is vital not to allow the
mixture to simmer (no
sign of a bubble should appear
on the surface) or the fondue
will become stringy and
separate and will not look as nice.

Make sure that the serving
bowl or bowls are well heated,
or the fondue will cool and
thicken around the edges.

●665 calories/2800 kj per portion

and simmer gently for 10 minutes.
2 In a small bowl, blend the
cornflour to a smooth paste with a
little of the milk. Stir into the
mushroom stock, then add the
remaining milk. Bring to the boil,
lower the heat and simmer for 2
minutes, stirring all the time.
3 Turn the heat under the pan to the
lowest setting. Add the grated
cheese to the pan, 2 tablespoons at a
time, stirring well until all the

cheese has melted. Do not allow the
mixture to simmer. [!]
4 Remove the pan from the heat and
stir in the fresh parsley and
Worcestershire sauce, with salt and
pepper to taste. Pour the fondue
into a warmed serving bowl, [!] or 4
individual bowls, garnish with
mushroom slices and serve at once.
Hand the bread cubes and sliced
fried sausages separately (see Variations). Provide forks for dipping.

Tomato, cheese and basil flan

SERVES 6-8

150-175 g/6 oz shortcrust pastry,
  defrosted if frozen
4 large tomatoes (about 250 g/9 oz),
  sliced
300 ml/½ pint milk
3 large eggs
1½ teaspoons dried basil (see Did
  you know)
75 g/3 oz mature Cheddar cheese,
  grated
salt and freshly ground black pepper
a few tomato slices, to garnish
  (optional)

1 Heat the oven to 190C/375F/Gas 5.
2 Roll out the shortcrust pastry on a floured surface and use to line a 20 cm/8 inch plain flan ring set on a baking sheet.
3 Arrange the 250 g/9 oz tomato slices overlapping in the flan case. In a bowl, whisk together the milk, eggs, basil, 50 g/2 oz of the cheese and salt and pepper to taste.
4 Pour the mixture into the flan case and sprinkle over the remaining cheese. Bake in the oven for 40-45 minutes until the filling is set and golden brown on top.
5 Allow the flan to cool for 5 minutes, then carefully remove the flan ring. Transfer the flan to a serving dish, then garnish with tomato slices, if liked.

Cook's Notes

TIME
Preparation takes about 20 minutes, baking 40-45 minutes.

DID YOU KNOW
The flavour of sweet basil perfectly complements tomato, and this is a classic combination in many dishes, particularly those of Italian origin.
  Fresh herbs are always preferable in cooking, but fresh basil is not readily available, though it can sometimes be found in specialist greengrocers during the summer months.

Remember, if you want to grow basil, that it is an annual and so you will need to buy a new plant each year. It likes a sunny, sheltered spot.
  There are two main kinds, with which you can experiment. Sweet basil has largish, shiny dark green leaves and white flowers. Bush basil has many small pale green leaves and tiny white flowers. Bush and sweet basil have an equally good flavour.
  The strong, aromatic flavour of basil is delicious in egg, mushroom and pasta dishes, as well as with tomatoes.

SERVING IDEAS
The flan is equally good served warm or cold. It serves 6-8 as an appetizing starter for either a lunch or supper party. Try accompanying it with a spicy tomato relish. This tasty flan also makes perfect picnic food.

●385 calories/1600 kj per portion

Stilton quiche

SERVES 6-8

150-175 g/6 oz shortcrust pastry, defrosted if frozen
100 g/4 oz Stilton cheese, grated
150 ml/¼ pint milk
150 ml/¼ pint double cream
3 large eggs
2 tablespoons chopped parsley
25 g/1 oz Stilton cheese, crumbled, to garnish (optional)

1 Heat the oven to 200C/400F/Gas 6.
2 Roll out the pastry on a floured surface and use to line a 20 cm/8 inch flan ring placed on a baking sheet. Refrigerate for 30 minutes.
3 Put 100 g/4 oz grated Stilton, the milk, cream, eggs and parsley in a bowl and whisk together, using a fork, until well blended. Pour the mixture into the prepared flan ring and bake in the oven for 40-45 minutes, until the filling has set.
4 Carefully remove the flan ring and transfer the quiche to a serving dish. Serve hot or cold, garnished with crumbled cheese if liked.

Cook's Notes

 TIME
If using ready-made pastry, the quiche takes 15 minutes to prepare. Allow 30 minutes for chilling the unbaked pastry case. Baking takes 40-45 minutes.

SERVING IDEAS
Serve the quiche with a crisp green salad.

● 550 calories/2300 kj per portion

Eggs Florentine

SERVES 4

500 g/1 lb fresh spinach
4 large eggs, hard-boiled and sliced
salt
40 g/1½ oz margarine or butter
1 small onion, grated
25 g/1 oz plain flour
300 ml/½ pint milk
65 g/2½ oz Cheddar cheese, grated
½ teaspoon French mustard
freshly ground black pepper
40 g/1½ oz Red Leicester cheese,
    grated (see Buying guide)

1 Wash the spinach in several changes of water to remove all the grit. Remove the stalks and mid-ribs and discard. Put the spinach in a large saucepan with just the water that adheres to the leaves after washing. Sprinkle with salt.

2 Cook the spinach over moderate heat for about 15 minutes, stirring occasionally with a wooden spoon. Turn the cooked spinach into a colander and drain thoroughly, pressing with a large spoon or a saucer to extract as much moisture as possible. Keep hot.

3 Meanwhile melt the margarine in a pan, add the onion and fry gently for about 5 minutes until soft and lightly coloured. Sprinkle in the flour and stir over low heat for 1-2 minutes. Remove from the heat and gradually stir in the milk. Return to the heat and simmer, stirring, until thick and smooth. Mix in Cheddar cheese and the mustard, season to taste with salt and pepper and remove from the heat.

4 Heat the grill to high.

5 Divide the spinach between 4 individual gratin dishes. Arrange a row of egg slices on top of the spinach. Pour sauce over, covering the surface as much as possible. Sprinkle the Red Leicester cheese

on top of the rows of egg slices.

6 Place under the grill for about 5 minutes or until the cheese has melted. Serve hot. (see Serving ideas.)

Egg and spinach nests

SERVES 4

250 g/9 oz spinach, stalks and large midribs removed, shredded
25 g/1 oz margarine or butter
salt and freshly ground black pepper
4 eggs
4 tablespoons double cream
cayenne, to garnish
margarine, for greasing

1 Heat the oven to 190C/375F/Gas 5. Grease 4 individual ovenproof dishes or ramekins.
2 Melt the margarine in a saucepan, add the spinach and cook gently for 8 minutes, or until soft. Season to taste with salt and pepper.
3 Divide the spinach between the prepared dishes. Break 1 egg into each dish on top of the cooked spinach mixture.
4 Place the dishes on a baking sheet and bake in oven for 10 minutes, until the egg whites begin to set. Remove from the oven and spoon 1 tablespoon cream over each egg. Return to the oven and cook for a further 5 minutes. Sprinkle a little cayenne over each egg and serve at once (see Serving ideas).

Cook's Notes

TIME
Preparation 20 minutes, cooking 15 minutes.

SERVING IDEAS
Ideal as a first course for a dinner party or serve with wholemeal toast for a light lunch or supper.

DID YOU KNOW
In France the nests are served in cocotte dishes – small dishes with a handle. Cocotte dishes hold one egg.

VARIATIONS
Place 4 tablespoons chopped cooked mushrooms or asparagus in the dish in place of the spinach.

● 195 calories/825 kj per portion

Chinese egg rolls

SERVES 4

- 175 g/6 oz cooked chicken, cut into 2.5 cm/1 inch strips
- ½ teaspoon cornflour
- 3-4 tablespoons vegetable oil
- 2 tablespoons soy sauce
- 1 teaspoon sherry
- 3 celery stalks, sliced
- 8-10 spring onions, sliced
- 75 g/3 oz beansprouts, well drained if canned
- 6 eggs, beaten
- 1 tablespoon water
- salt and freshly ground black pepper

1 Heat the oven to 130C/250F/Gas ½. Put the chicken on a plate and sprinkle with the cornflour.

2 Pour 2 tablespoons of the oil into a heavy frying-pan or wok. Stir in the soy sauce and sherry and heat over high heat until very hot.

3 Add the celery and spring onions and toss for 2 minutes, either by lifting and shaking the pan, or using a large flat spoon.

4 Add the chicken to the pan with the beansprouts. Toss over high heat for about 1 minute, [!] then transfer to a plate and keep warm.

5 Put the eggs and water into a bowl with salt and pepper to taste and beat until thoroughly mixed.

6 Clean the frying-pan with several sheets of absorbent paper. Add 1 tablespoon vegetable oil and heat over moderate heat. Pour in a quarter of the egg mixture, tilting the pan so that it spreads over the surface to make a thin pancake.

7 Place a quarter of the chicken and beansprout mixture in the middle of the pancake, spreading it out a little. Fold in the sides and then roll up into a parcel (see Preparation). Transfer to a warmed serving dish and keep warm in the oven.

8 Repeat with the remaining egg and chicken mixture to make 3 more egg rolls, adding more oil to the pan if necessary. Serve at once.

Cook's Notes

TIME
This nutritious starter takes less than 20 minutes to prepare and cook.

ECONOMY
Instead of sherry, use a little more soy sauce. Any kind of left-over cooked meat can be cut into strips and used in this recipe.

WATCHPOINT
Do not cook the beansprouts for too long or they will go limp and lose their vitamin C content.

PREPARATION
To make the egg roll parcels:

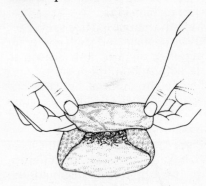

● 295 calories/1235 kj per roll

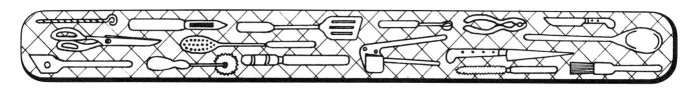

Small corn quiches

MAKES 12

200 g/7 oz can sweetcorn, drained
150-175 g/6 oz shortcrust pastry,
 defrosted if frozen
100 g/4 oz streaky bacon, rinds
 removed and cut into 1 cm/½ inch
 strips
1 large egg
75 ml/3 fl oz milk
salt and freshly ground black pepper
1 tablespoon chopped fresh parsley

1 Heat the oven to 190C/375F/Gas 5.
2 Roll out the pastry on a lightly
floured surface to a circle 5 mm/¼
inch thick. Cut into rounds with a
7.5 cm/3 inch cutter. Roll out the
trimmings to make 12 rounds
altogether. Press the rounds lightly
into 12 patty tins, then refrigerate
while making the filling.

3 Put the bacon into a non-stick
frying-pan (see Cook's tip) and fry
over moderate heat for 3-5 minutes.
Drain on absorbent paper.
4 Mix the bacon with the drained
sweetcorn and spoon into the prepared pastry cases.

5 Beat the egg with the milk. Season
with salt and pepper to taste, then
stir in the parsley. Spoon carefully
over the sweetcorn mixture. !
6 Bake in the oven for 20-25 minutes
until the pastry is golden and the
filling firm. Serve hot or cold.

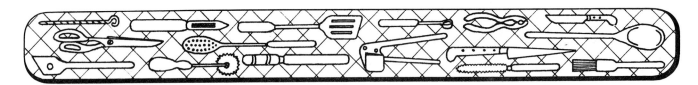

Egg mousse

SERVES 4

3 hard-boiled eggs, yolks and
   whites separated
15 g/½ oz powdered gelatine
150 ml/¼ pint chicken stock
300 ml/½ pint thick bottled
   mayonnaise
1-2 teaspoons curry paste (see Did
   you know)
few drops of Worcestershire sauce
salt and freshly ground black pepper
1 egg white
parsley sprigs, to garnish

1 Sprinkle the gelatine over the
stock in a small pan and leave for 1-2
minutes to soften and become
spongy. Set the pan over very gentle
heat without allowing it to boil,
until the gelatine is completely
dissolved ! (the liquid should be
absolutely clear).
2 Leave the gelatine to cool, then
whisk it slowly into the mayonnaise
in a bowl until smooth.

3 Sieve the egg yolks and stir into
the mayonnaise mixture with the
curry paste and Worcestershire
sauce. Chop the egg whites and fold
two-thirds of them into the mixture.
Season carefully with salt and
pepper.
4 Whip the egg white stiffly and

fold it into the mixture with a large
metal spoon until evenly incorporated. Pour into an 850 ml/1½
pint soufflé dish (see Serving ideas).
5 Refrigerate for about 3 hours or
until set. Just before serving,
garnish with the remaining chopped
egg white and the parsley sprigs.

Cook's Notes

TIME
Preparation takes about
30 minutes including
hard-boiling the eggs; allow 3
hours for the mousse to set.

DID YOU KNOW
Curry paste is a blend of
curry powder, oil and
vinegar. It is very handy for
adding to sauces and liquid
mixtures, as it dissolves more
readily than curry powder.

WATCHPOINT
If soaked gelatine is
allowed to boil, it will
lose its setting power. As an
extra precaution, you can dis-

solve gelatine in a bowl set over
a pan of simmering water, but
this is not absolutely necessary.

SERVING IDEAS
An attractive way to
serve this mousse, and
one that is ideal for a dinner
party starter, is to set the
mixture in 4 ramekins and
accompany with toast.
   To serve the mousse turned
out, rinse inside of dish with
cold water before putting in
mixture: when set, run knife
round edge before unmoulding
on to inverted plate.

● 555 calories/2325 kj per portion

Cauliflower and salami soufflés

SERVES 4

1 small cauliflower, broken into very small florets
50 g/2 oz salami, skinned and chopped (see Buying guide)
40 g/1½ oz margarine or butter
salt
25 g/1 oz plain flour
300 ml/½ pint milk
pinch of freshly grated nutmeg
freshly ground white pepper
2 large eggs, separated

1 Heat the oven to 200C/400F/Gas 6. Use 15 g/½ oz of the margarine to grease four 300 ml/½ pint soufflé or ovenproof dishes.
2 Bring a pan of salted water to the boil and add the cauliflower. Simmer for 4-5 minutes, or until the cauliflower is just cooked.
3 Meanwhile, melt the remaining margarine in a small saucepan, sprinkle in the flour and stir over low heat for 1-2 minutes until straw-coloured. Remove from the heat and gradually stir in the milk. Return to the heat and simmer, stirring, until thick and smooth. Add the nutmeg and salt and pepper to taste, remove from the heat and leave to cool for a few minutes, then stir in the egg yolks.
4 Drain cauliflower and set aside.

Cook's Notes

TIME
20 minutes to prepare plus 30 minutes cooking time in all.

WATCHPOINT
Serve the soufflés immediately they come from the oven as they tend to sink after a few minutes.

VARIATIONS
Diced potatoes or parsnips can replace the cauliflower.
Use cooked bacon or left-over cooked meat like chicken instead of the salami.

BUYING GUIDE
There is a huge range of salami available from supermarkets and delicatessens. Both with and without garlic and including different spices, they come from many countries including Italy, Poland, Hungary and France. Any type of salami is suitable for this tasty recipe.

●260 calories/1075 kj per portion

5 In a clean, dry bowl, whisk the egg whites until standing in stiff peaks. Using a metal spoon, fold into the sauce with the salami.
7 Arrange the cauliflower in the prepared dishes and spoon the soufflé mixture on top. Bake in the oven for 30 minutes until well risen and golden. Remove from the oven and serve at once.

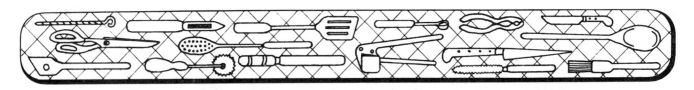

Cheese and chive soufflé

SERVES 4

150 g/5 oz Cheddar cheese, finely grated
50 g/2 oz margarine or butter
1 small onion, finely chopped
40 g/1½ oz plain flour
pinch of mustard powder
pinch of cayenne pepper
300 ml/½ pint milk
4 large eggs, separated
1 tablespoon snipped chives
salt and freshly ground black pepper
melted margarine, for greasing

1 Brush the inside of a 1 L/2 pint soufflé dish with melted margarine. Heat the oven to 180C/350F/Gas 4.
2 Melt the margarine in a saucepan, add the onion and cook gently for about 5 minutes until soft and lightly coloured but not browned.
3 Sprinkle the flour, mustard and cayenne into the pan and stir over low heat for 2 minutes.
4 Remove from the heat and gradually stir in the milk. Return to the heat and simmer, stirring, until thick and smooth.
5 Remove the pan from heat, stir in the cheese, then leave the sauce to cool slightly. Beat the egg yolks, then stir them into the cheese sauce with the chives. Season well with pepper, and salt if necessary.
6 Whisk the egg whites until stiff but not dry. Fold them into the cheese mixture with a large metal spoon, in a figure-of-eight motion, using the edges of the spoon to cut through the mixture.
7 Pour the mixture into the prepared soufflé dish. Run a round-bladed knife through the mixture, to make an attractive 'crown' effect (see Preparation).
8 Bake in the oven for 50 minutes or until the soufflé is well-risen and golden. When lightly shaken, it should only wobble slightly. Serve at once straight from the dish.

Eggs in potato nests

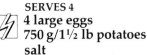

SERVES 4
4 large eggs
750 g/1½ lb potatoes
salt
1 large egg yolk
25 g/1 oz margarine or butter
about 100 ml/3½ fl oz creamy milk
1 tablespoon vegetable oil
100 g/4 oz mushrooms, finely
chopped
1 small onion, finely chopped
75 g/3 oz cooked ham, diced
1 teaspoon tomato purée
freshly ground black pepper
1 small egg, beaten, to glaze
1 tablespoon chopped parsley
margarine, for greasing

1 Cook the potatoes in boiling salted water until tender. Drain well and press them through a sieve.

Beat in the egg yolk, half the margarine and just enough of the creamy milk to make a firm mixture.
2 Put the creamed potato into a piping bag fitted with a large star nozzle and pipe 4 'nests' on to a greased baking sheet. To form the nests: using a spiral motion, make a round of potato about 12.5 cm/5 inches in diameter, then pipe a wall about 5 cm/2 inches high around the outer edge. Or shape the mixture with a teaspoon.
3 Heat the oven to 180C/350F/Gas 4. Heat the oil in a frying-pan. Add the mushrooms and onion and cook gently until soft. Stir in the ham and the tomato purée with salt and pepper to taste, then mix well. Remove from the heat.
4 Brush the potato nests with beaten egg to glaze and spoon in the mushroom and ham mixture, dividing it equally between the nests.
5 Break 1 egg at a time into a cup and slide the eggs into the potato nests.
6 Spoon a little creamy milk on top of each egg to cover the yolk and dot

with the remaining margarine to protect the yolk during cooking.
7 Bake nests in the oven for 10-15 minutes until the whites of the eggs have just set and the yolks are still soft. With a fish slice, carefully remove the nests from the baking sheet without breaking the egg yolks, then place them on warmed serving plates or individual dishes. Sprinkle with chopped parsley and serve at once.

VEGETABLE APPETIZERS

Cheese-stuffed courgettes

SERVES 4

4 large courgettes
salt
1 tablespoon vegetable oil
1 onion, chopped
225 g/8 oz cottage cheese, sieved
50 g/2 oz Parmesan cheese, grated
1 egg, beaten
1 tablespoon finely chopped parsley
freshly ground black pepper
4 tablespoons day-old soft white breadcrumbs
50 g/2 oz Cheddar cheese, grated
50 g/2 oz margarine or butter, melted
margarine, for greasing

1 Heat the oven to 200C/400F/Gas 6.
2 Bring a large saucepan of salted water to the boil, add the courgettes, bring back to the boil, reduce the heat and simmer for about 10 minutes until barely tender. [!] Drain and refresh under cold running water for 1 minute. Drain again.

3 Cut the courgettes into half lengthways and with a teaspoon or grapefruit knife carefully scrape out the core and seeds from the centre, leaving a good shell. Reserve the scooped-out flesh and seeds (see Cook's tip). Sprinkle the insides of the courgettes with salt, place upside down on absorbent paper and leave to drain for 5-10 minutes.
4 Meanwhile, chop the reserved courgette flesh. Heat the oil in a frying-pan, add the onion and courgette flesh and fry over moderate heat for about 10 minutes until the onion is just beginning to brown. Transfer to a bowl and leave to cool.
5 Mix the cottage cheese with the onion and courgette mixture. Stir in the Parmesan cheese, egg and parsley and season to taste with salt and pepper. The mixture should hold its shape: if it is too soft, add a few of the breadcrumbs.
6 Grease a large shallow ovenproof dish and stand the courgette halves in it in a single layer, skin side down. Using a teaspoon, fill the courgettes with the stuffing, heaping it in a mound on each half.
7 Mix together the breadcrumbs and grated Cheddar cheese and

sprinkle evenly over the courgettes. Drizzle the melted margarine over the top and bake in the oven for 25-30 minutes until golden and bubbling. Serve hot.

70

Egg and avocado bake

SERVES 6

6 eggs, separated
1 large avocado
6 tablespoons browned
   breadcrumbs (see Preparation)
3 tablespoons vegetable oil
1 onion, finely chopped
1 clove garlic, crushed (optional)
4 tablespoons finely chopped fresh
   parsley
salt and freshly ground black pepper
75 g/3 oz Cheddar cheese, grated
melted margarine or butter, for
   greasing

1 Heat the oven to 200C/400F/Gas 6. Brush 6 individual ovenproof dishes with melted margarine, then coat them evenly with 4 tablespoons of the breadcrumbs. Set aside.

2 Heat the oil in a frying-pan, add the onion and garlic, if using, and fry gently for 3-4 minutes until the onion is soft but not coloured. Set aside to cool for about 5 minutes.

3 Cut the avocado in half. Remove the stone, scoop out the flesh into a bowl, then mash with a fork to a purée. Beat in the egg yolks and parsley, then the cooled onion and salt and pepper to taste.

4 Beat the egg whites until standing in stiff peaks, then fold them into the avocado mixture. Pile into the dishes, scatter remaining crumbs on top and bake in the oven for 20 minutes.

5 Sprinkle the top of the rising mixture with the cheese, then return dishes to the oven for a further 15 minutes until they are well risen and golden. Serve at once.

Cook's Notes

TIME
Preparation takes about 30 minutes, plus 30 minutes for making breadcrumbs, cooking 35 minutes.

PREPARATION
To make the quantity of browned breadcrumbs needed for this recipe: toast 3-4 slices of day-old white bread in a 180C/350F/Gas 4 oven for 20 minutes until golden. Cool, then put in a polythene bag and crush with a rolling pin.

SERVING IDEAS
Serve with French bread and a salad.

● 330 calories/1385 kj per portion

Salad kebabs

SERVES 4

½ small cauliflower, divided into
  florets (see Watchpoint)
350 g/12 oz can luncheon meat, cut
  into 2.5 cm/1 inch cubes (see
  Cook's tips)
175 g/6 oz Edam cheese, rind
  removed and cut into
  2 cm/¾ inch cubes
1 tablespoon olive oil
1 teaspoon wine vinegar
1 teaspoon chopped fresh parsley
1 red dessert apple
2 teaspoons lemon juice
½ teaspoon caster sugar

SAUCE
4 tablespoons thick bottled
  mayonnaise
2 tablespoons soured cream
1 teaspoon tomato purée
½ teaspoon French mustard

Cook's Notes

TIME
Preparation takes about
30 minutes.

WATCHPOINT
Make sure the cauli-
flower florets are large
enough to thread easily on to
the skewers without breaking.

SERVING IDEAS
These kebabs are ideal
for starters or perhaps
for a picnic: wrap them in cling
film or foil or pack in a rigid
container. Put the sauce in a
separate container with a tight-
fitting lid.

COOK'S TIPS
If you chill the can of
luncheon meat for 30
minutes before dicing, it makes
it easier to cut.
   The prepared kebabs can be
covered and stored in the refrigerator for up to 1 hour.

● 560 calories/2325 kj per portion

1 Whisk the olive oil, vinegar and parsley together in a bowl. Add the cauliflower, mix well and leave to stand for 5-10 minutes.
2 Meanwhile, leaving the skin on, cut the apple into 8 wedges and remove the core. Mix the lemon juice and sugar together and toss the apple in this mixture.
3 Thread the cauliflower, apple, luncheon meat and cheese alternately on to 4 long kebab skewers. Transfer to a serving plate and, if liked, use remaining pieces of apple or cauliflower to garnish.
4 Make the sauce: whisk the sauce ingredients together, then transfer to a small bowl. Serve the kebabs (see Cook's tips) with the sauce handed separately.

Spinach and Brie puffs

SERVES 4

225 g/8 oz frozen spinach, defrosted and well drained (see Cook's tip)
50 g/2 oz Brie, thinly sliced (see Buying guide)
1 egg, beaten
¼ teaspoon freshly grated nutmeg
salt and freshly ground black pepper
215 g/7½ oz frozen puff pastry, defrosted
15 g/½ oz grated Parmesan cheese

1 Heat the oven to 220C/425F/Gas 7.
2 Put the spinach in a bowl, stir in half the beaten egg and the nutmeg. Season to taste with salt and pepper.
3 Roll out the pastry on a lightly floured surface. Trim to a 30 cm/12 inch square, then cut into four 15 cm/6 inch squares.
4 Divide the spinach equally between the squares, spreading it diagonally over one-half of each and leaving a 1 cm/½ inch border. Top the squares with Brie slices, dividing them equally between the 4 squares.
5 Brush the edges of the pastry with beaten egg, then fold the pastry over to form a triangle and enclose the filling. Press the edges firmly together to seal them, then knock up with a knife and flute. Brush the tops with beaten egg, then use a sharp knife to make 2 small slits to allow the steam to escape. Sprinkle over the Parmesan cheese.
6 Dampen a baking sheet and carefully transfer the triangles to it.
7 Bake in the oven for about 10 minutes, until the pastry is golden. Serve the puffs hot or cold.

Cook's Notes

TIME
The puffs take about 20 minutes to prepare and 10 minutes to cook.

SERVING IDEAS
Make the puffs smaller (cut 7.5 cm/3 inch squares) for an unusual starter or snack to serve with drinks.

COOK'S TIP
Put the spinach into a colander or sieve and drain thoroughly, pressing the spinach with a large spoon or a saucer to extract as much moisture as possible.

BUYING GUIDE
Look for Brie that is not too ripe. If it is quite soft, put it in the freezer or freezing compartment of the refrigerator for about 30 minutes before making the puffs.

● 320 calories/1350 kj per puff

Gingered aubergine dip

SERVES 4

1 kg/2 lb firm aubergines, stems
   removed
175 ml/6 fl oz natural yoghurt
1 clove garlic, crushed (optional)
1 tablespoon light soft brown sugar
1 teaspoon grated fresh root
   ginger
½ teaspoon cumin powder
salt and freshly ground black pepper
fresh coriander or parsley sprigs, to
   garnish (optional)

1 Heat the oven to 200C/400F/Gas 6. Prick the aubergines all over with a fork, then put them into a roasting tin and bake in the oven for 45-60 minutes, until they feel really soft when they are pressed with the back of a spoon.

2 Remove the aubergines from the oven and leave until cool enough to handle. Cut them in half lengthways, and squeeze gently in your hand to drain off the bitter juices (see Preparation). Scoop out flesh and leave until cold.

3 Put aubergine flesh in a blender with the yoghurt, the garlic, if using, sugar, ginger, cumin and salt and pepper to taste. Blend until smooth. Transfer to 1 large or 4 small serving dishes. Refrigerate for 2-3 hours to allow dip to firm up.

4 Just before serving, garnish with coriander or parsley sprigs, if liked.

Avocado and apple grill

SERVES 4

2 ripe avocados
4 crisp dessert apples
25 g/1 oz margarine
25 g/1 oz plain flour
300 ml/½ pint milk
75 g/3 oz Cheddar cheese, grated
2 teaspoons Dijon mustard
salt and freshly ground black pepper
juice of ½ lemon
25 g/1 oz fresh brown breadcrumbs

1 Heat the grill to high.
2 Make the sauce: melt the margarine in a small saucepan, sprinkle in the flour and stir over a low heat for 1-2 minutes until it is straw-coloured. Remove from the heat and gradually stir in the milk. Return to the heat and simmer, stirring, until thick and smooth. Stir in 50 g/2 oz of the cheese and the mustard and season to taste with salt and pepper. Stir until the cheese has melted, then remove the pan from the heat.
3 Peel the avocados, cut in half and remove the stones. [!] Cut lengthways into thin slices. Peel, quarter and core the apples. Cut into thin slices. Arrange the slices of avocado and apple in layers in 1 large or 4 individual shallow gratin dishes (see Serving ideas). Squeeze the lemon juice over them immediately to prevent discoloration.
4 Pour the sauce over the avocado and apple. Mix together the remaining cheese and the breadcrumbs and sprinkle evenly over the top.
5 Place under the grill for about 5 minutes until golden brown and bubbling. Serve at once.

Cook's Notes

TIME
Preparation and cooking take about 20 minutes.

WATCHPOINT
Prepare the avocados just before they are needed as their flesh quickly turns black if exposed to the air when left to stand.

SERVING IDEAS
Served in individual gratin dishes, this makes a most delicious first course for a dinner party. The number of servings can be easily adjusted up or down by allowing ½ an avocado and 1 apple per person – the quantity of cheese sauce remains the same for up to 8 servings.

Gruyère or Emmental cheese and a combination of half milk and half dry white wine would make a richer sauce for special occasions.

● 455 calories/1900 kj per portion

Stuffed cucumber salad

SERVES 4

1 large cucumber, cut into 24 even slices (see Buying guide)
1 round lettuce, leaves separated (see Buying guide)
350 g/12 oz carrots, finely grated
3 tablespoons sultanas
small parsley sprigs and a few chopped walnuts, to garnish

FILLING

250 g/9 oz curd cheese
75 g/3 oz shelled walnuts, chopped
2 teaspoons finely chopped fresh parsley
2 teaspoons snipped fresh chives or finely chopped spring onion
½ teaspoon sweet paprika
salt and freshly ground black pepper

DRESSING

5 tablespoons vegetable oil
2 tablespoons white wine or cider vinegar
large pinch of mustard powder
pinch of caster sugar

1 Make the filling: put all the filling ingredients in a bowl, season with salt and pepper and mix well with a fork.

2 Remove the seeds from each slice of cucumber with an apple corer or a small sharp knife. Season on both sides with salt and pepper and set out on a flat plate.

3 Divide the filling between the cucumber slices, pressing it into the central hole and piling it up on top.

4 Make the dressing: put all the dressing ingredients in a small screw-top jar, season with salt and pepper then shake the jar well to mix together.

5 Arrange the lettuce leaves on 4 individual plates and drizzle a teaspoonful of the dressing over each serving. Carefully transfer 6 cucumber slices to each plate, arranging them in a ring.

6 Mix the grated carrots with the sultanas in a bowl and add the remaining dressing. Toss to coat thoroughly, then pile into the centre of the rings of stuffed cucumber slices. Garnish 3 cucumber slices on each plate with a parsley sprig and 3 slices with a few chopped walnuts. Serve at once.

Cook's Notes

 TIME
Preparation time is about 45 minutes.

 BUYING GUIDE
Choose a straight cucumber so that it will be easy to slice evenly.
A curly, soft-leaved lettuce is best for this recipe because it gives an added attraction, but any soft-leaved lettuce will do.

 SERVING IDEAS
Serve the stuffed cucumber slices, with the lettuce as a garnish, as a tasty starter or with drinks. As an alternative suggestion, the salad could be accompanied by cold, sliced meat to make a much more filling supper or lunch.

 VARIATION
Use chopped muscatel raisins instead of sultanas.

● 410 calories/1730 kj per portion

Aubergines on waffles

SERVES 4

2 large aubergines, cut into cubes
salt
2 tablespoons vegetable oil
300 ml/½ pint beef stock
4 teaspoons tomato purée
2 cloves garlic, crushed (optional)
½ teaspoon dark soft brown sugar
freshly ground black pepper
4 potato waffles
75 g/3 oz Cheddar cheese, grated
coriander sprigs or parsley, to
  garnish

1 Layer the aubergine cubes in a colander, sprinkling each layer with salt. Put a plate on top and weight down. Leave to drain for about 30 minutes to remove the bitter juices. Rinse under cold running water, pat dry with absorbent paper or a clean tea-towel and set aside.

2 Heat the oil in a large frying-pan, add the aubergines, stock, tomato purée, garlic, if using, and sugar. Season with salt and pepper.

3 Bring to the boil, then lower the heat, cover the pan and simmer for 8-10 minutes, stirring frequently, until the liquid is absorbed and the aubergines are tender.

4 Meanwhile, heat the grill to high and toast the waffles for 4 minutes on each side or fry as directed on the packet.

5 Place the waffles in a flameproof dish, pile the aubergine mixture on top and sprinkle over the grated cheese. Grill for 1-2 minutes (see Cook's tip).

6 Garnish waffles with coriander sprigs or parsley and serve at once.

MEAT DISHES

Bacon and onion crispies

SERVES 4
**4 rashers back bacon, rinds
  removed and diced**
1 small onion, chopped
40 g/1½ oz margarine or butter
25 g/1 oz plain flour
150 ml/¼ pint milk
1 teaspoon dried mixed herbs
1 egg, lightly beaten
50 g/2 oz fresh white breadcrumbs
vegetable oil, for deep-frying

1 Melt the margarine in a small
saucepan, add the bacon and onion
and fry over moderate heat for 3-4
minutes.
2 Sprinkle in the flour and stir over
low heat for 1-2 minutes until straw-
coloured. Remove from the heat and
gradually stir in the milk.
3 Return the pan to the heat and
cook for 2-3 minutes, stirring all the
time until very thick and creamy.
Remove from the heat and leave to
cool.
4 Stir the herbs into the mixture,
divide into 8 equal portions, then
form each portion into a ball (see
Preparation). Put the egg and
breadcrumbs in separate shallow
dishes.
5 Roll each ball in the egg, then coat
with the breadcrumbs.
6 Heat enough oil to cover the balls
in a deep-fat frier to 180C/350F or
until a stale bread cube browns in 60
seconds. Add the balls to the oil a
few at a time and deep-fry for 2-3
minutes until golden brown on all
sides.
7 Drain the crispies on absorbent
paper and serve at once.

Saucy ham and prawn rolls

SERVES 4

8 slices cooked ham, total weight
   250 g/9 oz
100 g/4 oz packet parsley and thyme
   stuffing mix
50 g/2 oz peeled prawns, defrosted
   if frozen, chopped
parsley sprigs, to garnish

CHEESE SAUCE

75 g/3 oz Cheddar cheese, grated
25 g/1 oz margarine or butter
25 g/1 oz plain flour
300 ml/½ pint milk
pinch of freshly grated nutmeg
½ teaspoon made English mustard
salt and freshly ground black pepper

1 Heat the oven to 200C/400F/Gas 6.
2 Make the stuffing according to packet instructions. Allow to cool slightly and mix in the prawns.

3 Divide the stuffing between the ham slices, spooning it in a strip about 1 cm/1½ inch from one edge. Starting at the edge nearest the stuffing, carefully roll up each slice of ham. Place the prawn-filled ham rolls, with the join side down, in a shallow ovenproof dish large enough to hold them in a single layer.
4 Make the sauce: melt margarine in a saucepan, sprinkle in the flour and stir over low heat for 1-2 minutes until straw-coloured. Remove from heat and gradually stir in the milk. Add the nutmeg and mustard and season to taste with salt and pepper. Return to the heat and simmer, stirring, until thick and smooth. Remove the pan from the heat and stir in half the grated Cheddar cheese.
5 Pour the sauce over the ham rolls and sprinkle with the remaining cheese. Bake in the oven for 20 minutes until the sauce is golden and bubbling. Garnish with parsley and serve at once straight from the dish (see Serving ideas).

Bacon kebabs with peanut dip

SERVES 4
350 g/12 oz collar bacon, trimmed
  and cut into 1-2 cm/¾-1 inch
  cubes
3 tablespoons crunchy peanut
  butter
25 g/1 oz desiccated coconut
150 ml/¼ pint water
salt and freshly ground black pepper
coriander leaves, to garnish

MARINADE
2 tablespoons vegetable oil
2 teaspoons curry paste
2 teaspoons lemon juice
½ teaspoon ground coriander
¼ teaspoon ground turmeric

1 Make the marinade: blend the marinade ingredients in a bowl.
2 Add the bacon cubes and coat thoroughly in the marinade. Cover and leave to stand for 30 minutes.
3 Heat the grill to moderate.

4 Remove the bacon cubes from the marinade with a slotted spoon. Reserve marinade. Thread the bacon pieces on to each of 12 wooden cocktail sticks (see Cook's tip).
5 Grill the kebabs for 10 minutes, turning occasionally, until cooked.
6 Meanwhile, pour the reserved marinade into a saucepan and add peanut butter, coconut and water. Season to taste with salt and pepper and heat through gently, stirring constantly until well mixed.
7 Arrange the bacon kebabs on a warmed serving plate and garnish with coriander. Serve at once with the dip handed separately in a warmed bowl (see Serving ideas).

Cook's Notes

 TIME
Preparation and cooking take 25 minutes plus 30 minutes marinating.

 COOK'S TIP
Soak the cocktail sticks in cold water for 30 minutes to prevent them from becoming too brown when grilling the bacon. Or, if wished, small metal skewers may be used instead.

 VARIATIONS
Use either gammon steaks or picnic rashers in place of the collar bacon.
To make a tomato dip for the bacon, heat the marinade with a 300 g/10 oz can condensed tomato soup with 65 ml/2½ fl oz water added to it.

 SERVING IDEAS
For an unusual party platter, arrange the bacon kebabs on a serving plate in alternating rows with peeled cucumber strips. Garnish with coriander, put dip in a coconut shell and place on the plate.

●280 calories/1175 kj per portion

Chicken fritters

SERVES 4

100 g/4 oz boneless cooked chicken, skinned and finely chopped
25 g/1 oz margarine
40 g/1½ oz plain flour
150 ml/¼ pint milk
1 egg yolk
50 g/2 oz cooked ham, finely chopped
4 button mushrooms, finely chopped
½ teaspoon dried oregano
salt and freshly ground black pepper
125 g/4 oz packet batter mix
6 rashers streaky bacon, rinds removed
vegetable oil, for deep frying

1 Make the sauce: melt margarine in a saucepan, sprinkle in 25 g/1 oz flour and stir over low heat for 1-2 minutes until straw-coloured. Remove from heat and gradually stir in the milk and the egg yolk. Return to heat and simmer, stirring, until thick and smooth.

2 Stir in the chicken, ham, mushrooms and oregano and season to taste with salt and pepper. Pour the mixture on to a large plate, spread it out with a knife and leave to cool for 15-20 minutes.

3 Meanwhile, heat the oven to 110C/225F/Gas ¼ and make up the batter according to the packet instructions. ⚠️

4 Stretch each of the bacon rashers with the back of a knife and then cut them in half.

5 Divide the chicken mixture into 12, then roll each piece into a ball, and shape it into a roll. Wrap each roll with bacon.

6 Spread out the remaining 15 g/½ oz flour on a flat plate and season with salt and pepper. Dip each roll in the flour until evenly coated.

7 Heat the oil in a deep-fat fryer to 190C/375F or until a day-old bread cube browns in 50 seconds.

8 Dip the rolls one at a time into the batter, then drop into the hot oil and deep fry 6 at a time for about 6 minutes until golden and crispy.

9 Drain on absorbent paper and keep warm in oven while cooking the second batch. Serve at once.

Cook's Notes

TIME
Preparation, including cooling, takes about 40-45 minutes. Cooking takes 12 minutes.

SERVING IDEAS
Serve the fritters with a crisp green salad, or for a more substantial dish, serve with a tasty rice salad.

WATCHPOINT
Follow the packet instructions for making batter for frying as opposed to batter for pancakes. No egg is required for the batter.

●505 calories/2125 kj per portion

Curried chicken salad

SERVES 4

500 g/1 lb boneless cooked chicken, skinned and cut into 10 cm/4 inch strips

150 ml/¼ pint thick bottled mayonnaise

150 g/5 oz natural yoghurt

1 teaspoon curry paste (see Cook's tip)

juice of ½-1 lemon

2 dessert apples

4 celery stalks, chopped

4 spring onions or 1 small onion, finely chopped

100 g/4 oz green grapes, halved and deseeded

75 g/3 oz shelled walnuts, coarsely chopped

salt and freshly ground black pepper

1 small lettuce, shredded

Cook's Notes

TIME
Preparing the salad takes about 20-25 minutes.

COOK'S TIP
This quantity of curry paste will give a mild-flavoured dressing for this salad. Increase the quantity a little at a time, tasting as you add the curry paste, if you prefer a hotter flavour.

SPECIAL OCCASION
Decorate the salad with a little whipped cream and top with a few walnut halves. Alternatively, garnish with watercress.

VARIATION
Use a 225 g/8 oz can of pineapple pieces, drained, instead of grapes.

● 590 calories/2475 kj per portion

1 In a bowl, mix together the mayonnaise and yoghurt. Mix the curry paste with the juice of half a lemon and fold into the mayonnaise mixture.

2 Core and slice but do not peel the apples and mix them into the mayonnaise mixture with the celery, onions, grapes and walnuts.

3 Add the chicken strips to the mixture turning them to coat evenly with the mayonnaise. Taste and season with salt and pepper if necessary, and add more lemon juice if liked.

4 Arrange the lettuce in individual dishes. Pile the salad on top and serve at once.

Peanut drumsticks

SERVES 4

8 chicken drumsticks, skinned (see Preparation)

75 g/3 oz smooth peanut butter
1 egg, beaten
75 ml/3 fl oz milk
salt and freshly ground black pepper
200 g/7 oz plain potato crisps
50 g/2 oz plain flour
vegetable oil, for greasing

1 Heat the oven to 190C/375F/Gas 5. Brush a baking sheet with oil.
2 Put the peanut butter into a bowl and beat in the egg with a wooden spoon. Gradually beat in the milk, then season to taste with salt and pepper. Pour the mixture into a shallow bowl.

3 Put the potato crisps into a polythene bag and crush with a rolling pin. Spread out on a flat plate.
4 Spread the flour out on a separate plate.
5 Coat each chicken drumstick in flour, then in the peanut mixture

followed by the crushed crisps. Make sure that each layer is evenly covered.
6 Place the coated drumsticks on the prepared baking sheet and bake in the oven for 45-50 minutes, or until crisp and lightly browned. Serve hot or cold.

Cook's Notes

 TIME
Total preparation and cooking time is about 1 hour.

VARIATIONS
Crunchy peanut butter can be used instead of smooth. Dried breadcrumbs or crushed cornflakes can replace the crushed potato crisps.

● 590 calories/2450 kj per portion

PREPARATION
To skin the drumsticks, cut through the skin lengthways with a sharp knife or scissors, then pull the skin away with a sharp tug.

 SERVING IDEAS
Serve hot with buttered noodles or jacket potatoes, or cold with a chicory and cress salad or as part of a finger buffet with a relish.

Savoury bacon fritters

SERVES 4

275 g/10 oz lean bacon, rinds
 removed (see Buying guide)
100 g/4 oz plain flour
2 teaspoons mustard powder
large pinch of celery salt
large pinch of sweet paprika
freshly ground black pepper
2 eggs, separated
125-150 ml/4-5 fl oz beer
1 tablespoon vegetable oil
1 onion, finely chopped
½ green pepper, deseeded and
 chopped
vegetable oil, for deep-frying
tomato wedges, to serve

1 Sift the flour into a bowl with the mustard powder, celery salt, paprika and pepper to taste. Make a well in the centre, add the egg yolks and beat to mix thoroughly, gradually working the dry ingredients into the centre. Beat in enough beer to make a batter with a thick coating consistency.

2 Cover the bowl with cling film, then set aside in a cool place for 2 hours (see Time).

3 Grill the bacon until cooked but not crisp. Drain on absorbent paper, then cut into 2.5 cm/1 inch lengths.

4 Heat a little oil in a frying-pan. Add the onion and pepper and fry gently for 5 minutes until the onion is soft and lightly coloured. Remove with a slotted spoon and add to the bacon.

5 Pour enough oil into a deep-fat frier to come halfway up the sides. Heat the oil gently to 190C/375F, or until a stale bread cube turns golden in 50 seconds.

6 Meanwhile, in a clean dry bowl, whisk the egg whites until they are standing in stiff peaks. Using a large metal spoon, carefully fold the egg whites into the batter with the bacon, onion and green pepper.

7 Drop a few tablespoonfuls of batter into the hot oil and deep-fry for 3-4 minutes, until puffed and golden brown. Drain well on absorbent paper and keep hot while frying the remainder, but remember to reheat the oil between each batch.

8 Serve with tomato wedges.

 Cook's Notes

 TIME
Preparation, 20 minutes, cooking 15 minutes, and 2 hours for batter to rest. To save time, use milk instead of beer and rest it 30 minutes.

BUYING GUIDE
Collar rashers are lean and less expensive than back bacon; they are ideal for this recipe.

 SERVING IDEAS
Serve with a selection of relishes, and with a colourful white and red cabbage coleslaw.

●595 calories/2500 kj per portion

MAIN COURSES

The highlight of any meal is the main course, but it is often hard to achieve the variety of dishes that you would like without spending too much money. This section contains a balanced selection of Pork, Beef and Veal, Lamb, Poultry, Fish and Seafood and Offal dishes to suit all palates – and they don't take ages to make. There is a good choice of casseroles, dishes with joints of meat or spicy dishes like *Stir-fried beef with cashews* or *Chicken paprikash*. If you prefer more traditional fare try making *Pot-roasted leg of lamb* or perhaps the tasty *Family fish pie*.

PORK

Pork escalopes with plums

SERVES 4

8 pork escalopes, each weighing
    50 g/2 oz
540 g/1 lb 3 oz can red plums,
    drained (see Buying guide)
2 tablespoons vegetable oil
25 g/1 oz margarine or butter
1 onion, finely chopped
150 ml/¼ pint cider or dry white
    wine
1 teaspoon ground cinnamon
½ teaspoon ground coriander
salt and freshly ground black pepper

1 Carefully remove the stones from the plums, keeping them as whole as possible if using canned ones.

2 Make the sauce: heat half the oil and half the margarine in a pan, add the onion, fry gently for 10 minutes until softened. Pour in the cider and bring to the boil. Add the spices and salt and pepper to taste. Stir well, then lower the heat, cover and cook the sauce gently for 5 minutes.

3 Add the plums to the sauce, cover and simmer very gently for a further 5 minutes, taking care not to break up the plums. Taste and adjust seasoning.

4 Meanwhile, divide the remaining oil and margarine between 2 large frying-pans and heat gently. Add the pork escalopes and cook over high heat for 3 minutes on each side, until browned.

5 To serve, arrange the escalopes on a warmed serving dish and spoon over the sauce. Serve at once.

Cook's Notes

TIME
This dish takes 35 minutes to prepare and cook.

WATCHPOINT
Do not overcook or keep the escalopes warm as they will toughen. They should be cooked while the sauce and plums are cooking.

BUYING GUIDE
If you use fresh plums you will need 250 g/9 oz, stoned and sliced. Add them to the sauce with the cider and cook for 10-15 minutes.

●455 calories/1900 kj per portion

Marinated pork chops

SERVES 4

8 thin pork breakfast chops, or 4 rib chops

MARINADE

4 tablespoons soy sauce
2 tablespoons orange juice
2 tablespoons olive oil or corn oil
2 tablespoons tomato ketchup
2 tablespoons light soft brown sugar
1 teaspoon ground ginger
grated zest of 1 orange
salt and freshly ground black pepper
small bunch spring onions, thinly sliced

1 Make the marinade: mix all the ingredients together, including the spring onions, making sure the sugar dissolves.

2 Put 4 of the chops in a dish so they do not overlap one another. Spoon over half the marinade, putting a few pieces of spring onion on each chop.

3 Put the remaining chops on top and spoon the rest of the marinade over them. Cover with cling film and refrigerate for at least 6 hours, basting occasionally.

4 Remove chops from the marinade and grill under high heat for about 4 minutes on each side. (Rib chops will need about 7-8 minutes each side.) Spoon the marinade with the onions on to the chops when you turn them, so that the onions become brown and crispy. Serve at once on a warmed serving plate.

Cook's Notes

TIME
Preparation 10 minutes but allow at least 6 hours to marinate the chops. Cooking takes 8-15 minutes.

VARIATIONS
Marinades are infinitely variable. Try substituting lemon juice for the orange juice, or add a splash of wine.

SERVING IDEAS
Serve with new potatoes or boiled potatoes mashed with soured cream and chives plus a simple green salad. Garnish with orange slices.

●550 calories/2325 kj per portion

Mediterranean pork casserole

SERVES 4

750-850 g/1½-1¾ lb pork spare-rib chops, trimmed of bone and fat and cut into small cubes
15 g/½ oz lard
1 onion, sliced
1 clove garlic, crushed (optional)
1-2 teaspoons sweet paprika
¼ teaspoon dried thyme
salt and freshly ground black pepper
1 large green pepper, deseeded and cut into strips
400 g/14 oz can tomatoes
100 g/4 oz button mushrooms, quartered
2 teaspoons cornflour

1 Melt the lard in a large flameproof casserole and fry the pork cubes over brisk heat for about 5 minutes, stirring continuously. Lower the heat, add the onion and garlic, if using, and cook for about 5 minutes until the onion is soft and translucent.

2 Sprinkle over the sweet paprika and thyme and season to taste. Stir in the green pepper, tomatoes and mushrooms and bring to the boil. Lower the heat, cover the pan and simmer gently for 1 hour or until the pork is tender, stirring occasionally.

3 Mix the cornflour to a smooth paste with a little cold water, stir in a spoonful of the hot liquid from the pork, then stir this mixture back into the pork. Bring to the boil, stirring, then simmer for 1-2 minutes until thickened. Taste and adjust seasoning. Serve at once, straight from the casserole.

Cook's Notes

TIME
Preparation takes about 30 minutes and cooking just over 1 hour.

COOK'S TIP
This casserole improves in flavour if made a day in advance. It can be kept, covered, in the refrigerator overnight.

BUYING GUIDE
Use lean spare-rib chops for this dish, not the spare ribs used in Chinese cooking.

VARIATION
If you prefer a slightly spicier flavour, simply add more paprika according to taste.

SERVING IDEAS
Boiled noodles or potatoes plus a bright-coloured vegetable such as carrots or broccoli, are good accompaniments to this casserole.

FREEZING
Allow the cooked casserole to cool and then remove the excess fat from the surface. Freeze in a rigid container for up to 3 months. Defrost overnight in the refrigerator, then heat through until bubbling.

●525 calories/2200 kj per portion

Pork ragoût

SERVES 4

850 g/1¾ lb belly pork, trimmed of excess fat, cut into strips 2.5 cm/1 inch long and 2 cm/¾ inch wide
2 tablespoons vegetable oil
1 large onion, chopped
40 g/1½ oz plain flour
600 ml/1 pint chicken stock
4 large carrots, cut into thin slices
thinly pared zest of 1 lemon, cut into strips
100 g/4 oz black-eyed beans, soaked overnight in cold water, drained
½ teaspoon ground coriander
½ teaspoon ground turmeric
¼ teaspoon ground ginger
freshly ground black pepper
salt
strips of lemon zest and chopped parsley, to garnish

1 Heat the oven to 170C/325F/Gas 3.
2 Heat three-quarters of the oil in a flameproof casserole, add the pork and fry for 3-4 minutes until lightly browned and sealed on both sides. Remove with a slotted spoon and drain on absorbent paper.
3 Heat the remaining oil in the casserole, add the onion and fry gently for 5 minutes until soft and lightly coloured. Sprinkle in the flour and stir over low heat for 1-2 minutes. Gradually stir in stock. Bring to the boil and then simmer, stirring, until thick.
4 Add the carrots, lemon strips, beans and spices, and season to taste with ground black pepper. Bring back to the boil and then boil for 10 minutes. Return the meat to the casserole, cover and cook in the oven for about 2 hours.
5 Before serving, add salt and black pepper to taste, and garnish with the strips of lemon zest and the chopped parsley. Serve at once.

Cook's Notes

TIME
30 minutes to prepare and 2 hours to cook.

FREEZING
Cool quickly, then pour into a rigid container. Seal, label and freeze for up to 2 months. To serve: defrost overnight in the refrigerator, then reheat in a 180C/350F/Gas 4 oven for 30 minutes, until the ragoût is bubbling.

? DID YOU KNOW
In Classic French cookery, a *ragoût* is a stew made with meat or fish cut into even-sized pieces. These are browned all over first and then casseroled.

●810 calories/3400 kj per portion

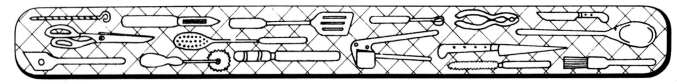

Stir-fried pork and cucumber

SERVES 4-6

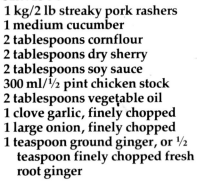

1 kg/2 lb streaky pork rashers
1 medium cucumber
2 tablespoons cornflour
2 tablespoons dry sherry
2 tablespoons soy sauce
300 ml/½ pint chicken stock
2 tablespoons vegetable oil
1 clove garlic, finely chopped
1 large onion, finely chopped
1 teaspoon ground ginger, or ½
    teaspoon finely chopped fresh
    root ginger

Cook's Notes

TIME
40 minutes to prepare and cook.

SERVING IDEAS
Serve with a mixture of boiled Chinese noodles and lightly fried beansprouts topped with finely chopped spring onions.

BUYING GUIDE
Streaky pork rashers are cut from the belly of the pig and are often simply described as 'belly pork'. You can buy streaky pork in the piece as a joint for roasting, but for this dish the meat needs to be cut into rashers. Most butchers sell ready-prepared rashers, but if not, ask your butcher to cut them for you and bone them at the same time. Remember too, that the thick end of belly pork (from the middle of the pig) has far more meat on it than the thin end, so it is worth asking for it.

●935 calories/3900 kj per portion

1 Trim the rinds, bones and any excess fat from the pork rashers. Cut the rashers into thin strips about 5 cm/2 inches long.
2 Wipe but do not peel the cucumber, then cut into quarters lengthways, trimming off the ends. Scoop out the seeds with a teaspoon. Cut the quarters lengthways again and cut the pieces into 2.5 cm/ 1 inch lengths.
3 Mix the cornflour to a paste in a bowl with a little of the sherry or soy sauce, then stir in the remainder with the stock.
4 Put the oil and garlic into a frying-pan and set over high heat until the garlic sizzles.
5 Add the pork and fry over high heat for about 15 minutes until all the pieces are crisp and well browned, stirring briskly all the time.
6 Pour all but about 1 tablespoon of the fat from the frying-pan and then set the pan back over low heat.
7 Stir in the cucumber, onion and ginger and cook, stirring, for about 5 minutes until the onion is translucent.
8 Give the cornflour mixture a stir and pour it into the pan. Increase the heat and bring the mixture to the boil. Cook over high heat for 3 minutes until a thick, translucent sauce is formed.
9 Transfer to a warmed serving dish and serve at once.

Baked honey ribs

SERVES 4

1.5 kg/3 lb pork spare ribs, Chinese style (see Buying guide)
4 tablespoons clear honey
3 tablespoons soft brown sugar
1 tablespoon Worcestershire sauce
2 tablespoons tomato ketchup
1 tablespoon mild French mustard
2 tablespoons red wine vinegar
salt and freshly ground black pepper

1 Heat the oven to 200C/400F/Gas 6.
2 If necessary, cut through the ribs to separate them. Put them in a single layer in 1 large or 2 small roasting tins.
3 Combine the remaining ingredients in a small saucepan and season well with salt and pepper.

Heat gently over low heat until just simmering.
4 Brush the ribs with the sauce on both sides, using a pastry or similar kitchen brush, then pour over any remaining syrup, making sure the ribs are well coated.

5 Bake in the oven uncovered, for 1 hour, basting and turning the ribs frequently, then turn the oven down to lowest for 30 minutes more, or until the flesh is well cooked and the ribs thoroughly coated in syrupy sauce. Serve at once.

Cook's Notes

 TIME
Preparation 15 minutes. Cooking 1½ hours.

 BUYING GUIDE
Most butchers will supply sheets of Chinese-style spare ribs, but some need a few days notice. Ordinary spare rib chops will not make a satisfactory substitute.

●310 calories/1300 kj per portion

 COOK'S TIP
Marinate the ribs in the sauce ingredients for a few hours, before barbecuing them, basting with the sauce.

SERVING IDEAS
Eat the ribs with your fingers (making sure you have plenty of napkins to hand). Excellent accompaniments for these honey ribs are hot Greek pitta bread and fresh green salad.

Pork fillet in puff pastry

SERVES 4-6

2 pieces pork fillet (tenderloin),
   each weighing about 350 g/12 oz
1 tablespoon vegetable oil
215 g/7½ oz frozen puff pastry,
   defrosted
50 g/2 oz button mushrooms, sliced
1 dessert apple

STUFFING
50 g/2 oz fresh white breadcrumbs
1 tablespoon shredded suet
1 small onion, grated
1 teaspoon dried sage
salt and freshly ground black pepper
1 egg, beaten

1 Heat the oven to 200C/400F/Gas 6.
2 Slit the pork fillets ready for stuffing (see Preparation).
3 Heat the oil in a large frying-pan and cook the fillets over moderate heat until they are lightly browned. Remove from the frying-pan and drain on absorbent paper.
4 To make the stuffing: put the breadcrumbs in a bowl with the suet, onion and sage, and season with salt and pepper. Add enough egg to bind the mixture, reserving the remaining egg for sealing and glazing the pastry.
5 Roll out the pastry thinly on a floured surface to make a rectangle measuring about 40 × 30 cm/16 × 12 inches. Trim edges of the pastry and reserve for decorating. Place the pastry on a dampened baking sheet.
6 Place 1 pork fillet in centre of the pastry and sprinkle the mushrooms over it. Peel, core and grate the apple and sprinkle over the mushrooms. Place the second pork fillet on top of mushroom and apple layer and spread the stuffing mixture over this.
7 Fold over the ends of the pastry, then the sides, so that the meat is enclosed in a pastry parcel with the join on the top. Seal the edges with some of the reserved egg.
8 Decorate along the seam of the parcel with pastry leaves made from the trimmings. Brush with the remaining beaten egg and bake in the oven for 40 minutes until the pastry has risen and is golden. Transfer to a warmed serving dish and serve at once.

Cook's Notes

 TIME
Total preparation and cooking time is 50 minutes.

 SERVING IDEAS
Serve with broccoli, or Brussels sprouts sprinkled with ground mace and mushroom sauce.

 PREPARATION
To cut the pork fillet so that it is ready for the stuffing:

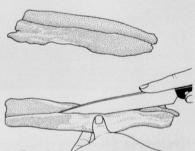

1 Carefully slit each piece of pork fillet (tenderloin) without cutting right through. Open out each piece flat so that there are 2 rectangular pieces of meat, each about 20 cm/8 inches long and 13 cm/5 inches wide.

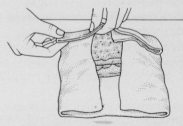

2 Make a pastry parcel around the meat and stuffing to enclose it completely.

●805 calories/3375 kj per portion

Roast pork with peaches

SERVES 4

1.25 kg/2½ lb boned pork joint (see
   Buying guide)
salt
1 tablespoon vegetable oil

STUFFED PEACHES
4 ripe fresh peaches, skinned (see
   Preparation)
2 tablespoons lemon juice
25 g/1 oz margarine or butter
50 g/2 oz fresh white breadcrumbs
1 onion, finely chopped
2 celery stalks, finely chopped
1 teaspoon dried sage
½ teaspoon grated lemon zest
freshly ground black pepper
1 teaspoon grated Parmesan cheese

1 Heat the oven to 190C/375F/Gas 5.
2 Using a sharp knife, score the skin
of the pork at 5 mm/¼ inch intervals, cutting into the fat below the
skin but not into the meat.
3 Wipe the pork dry with absorbent
paper. Sprinkle the scored skin

Cook's Notes

TIME
Preparation of joint, 5
minutes, then 30 min-
utes to prepare the stuffed
peaches once the pork is in the
oven. Cooking 1½ hours.

BUYING GUIDE
Joints suitable for this
recipe are: chump end
of loin, thick end of belly,
quarter cut of leg and rolled
sparerib. Ask your butcher to
bone the joint for you and to tie
it into a neat shape.

PREPARATION
To skin the peaches,
immerse in very hot
water for 1 minute. Drain, then
nick the skin near the stalk and
peel away the skin.

●740 calories/3100 kj per portion

liberally with salt and rub it in with
the oil.
4 Place the joint in a small roasting
tin and roast in the oven for 1 hour.
5 Meanwhile, prepare the stuffed
peaches. Halve the peaches, remove
the stones and sprinkle the cut sides
of the fruit with a little lemon juice.
6 Melt the margarine in a small
saucepan, add the breadcrumbs,
onion and celery and fry gently for
4-5 minutes, stirring constantly to
prevent sticking. Remove from the
heat and add the sage, lemon zest
and 1 tablespoon lemon juice. Mix
the ingredients together and season

well with salt and pepper.
7 Place 1 tablespoonful of the
stuffing in the hollow of each peach
and smooth over with a knife.
Sprinkle lightly with the Parmesan
cheese.
8 When the joint has cooked for 1
hour, remove the roasting tin from
the oven, and place the stuffed
peaches around the joint. Return to
the oven for a further 30 minutes or
until the pork is tender, basting
once with the dripping in the tin.
Transfer the joint to a warmed
serving platter and surround with
the stuffed peaches. Serve at once.

Hawaiian pork parcels

SERVES 4

4 thick pork chops, each weighing about 175 g/6 oz
425 g/15 oz can pineapple rings in natural juice, drained, with juice reserved (see Economy)
15 g/½ oz margarine or butter
1 small onion, chopped
100 g/4 oz fresh wholemeal breadcrumbs
1 teaspoon malt or cider vinegar
1 tablespoon finely chopped fresh parsley
dash of Tabasco
salt and freshly ground black pepper
parsley sprigs, to garnish

SAUCE

1 tablespoon cornflour
150 ml/¼ pint chicken stock
1 teaspoon Worcestershire sauce
1 teaspoon malt or cider vinegar

1 Cut 4 squares of foil each large enough to contain a chop easily.

2 Using a sharp knife, slit each pork chop horizontally, from the fatty outside edge to the bone, without cutting all the way through, to make a small pocket.

3 Make the stuffing (see Cook's tips): chop 1 pineapple ring finely. Melt the margarine in a frying-pan, add the onion and fry gently for 5 minutes until soft and lightly coloured. In a bowl combine the onion mixture with the chopped pineapple, breadcrumbs, vinegar, 1 tablespoon pineapple juice, the parsley and Tabasco. Season with salt and pepper.

4 Heat the grill to moderate. Heat the oven to 190C/375F/Gas 5.

5 Divide the stuffing mixture into 4 portions. Using a teaspoon, spoon a portion of stuffing into the pocket of each chop. Grill the chops for about 5 minutes on each side, until lightly browned (see Cook's tips).

6 Place a chop on each piece of foil and top each with a pineapple ring. Fold over the edges of the foil to make a loose parcel, then seal the edges tightly.

7 Arrange the parcels in a large, shallow roasting tin and bake in the oven for about 50 minutes, or until the juices run clear when the meat is pierced with a fine skewer.

8 About 5 minutes before the end of cooking time, make the sauce: measure out 150 ml/¼ pint of the reserved pineapple juice into a saucepan. In a cup, blend the cornflour with a little of the measured pineapple juice to a smooth paste. Stir the mixture into the pineapple juice with the stock, Worcestershire sauce and vinegar, and season to taste with salt and pepper. Bring slowly to the boil, stirring, until the sauce is thickened and smooth.

9 Remove the Hawaiian pork chops from their foil parcels and place them on a warmed serving plate. Garnish each pork chop with a sprig of parsley placed in the centre of the pineapple ring. Hand the sauce separately in a warmed jug.

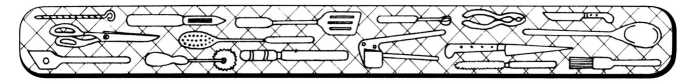

Pork and pears

SERVES 4

4 pork chops, trimmed of fat and
  rind
25 g/1 oz margarine or butter
salt and freshly ground black pepper
425 g/15 oz can pear halves
1 tablespoon chopped fresh
  marjoram, or 1½ teaspoons dried
  marjoram
1 tablespoon lemon juice

1 Heat the oven to 190C/375F/Gas 5.
2 Melt the margarine in a large
frying-pan. Add the chops and fry
for 3-4 minutes on each side until
golden brown.
3 Remove with a slotted spoon and
place in a single layer in an ovenproof dish. Sprinkle with salt and
pepper to taste. Drain the pears,

reserving the juice, and fry in the
hot fat for about 10 minutes until
brown. Place on top of the chops in
the dish.
4 Pour the reserved pear juice into
the pan and stir with a wooden
spoon to dislodge any sediment at
the bottom. Add the marjoram and
lemon juice, and raise the heat.

Bring to the boil and boil rapidly,
stirring frequently, for about 5
minutes until reduced by about
half. ☐ Pour over the chops and
pears, then cover the dish.
5 Bake in the oven for 25 minutes or
until the chops are tender. Transfer
to a warmed serving dish and serve
at once.

Cook's Notes

TIME
25 minutes preparation,
25 minutes to cook.

VARIATION
Try canned apricot
halves, or pineapple
rings instead of pears.

WATCHPOINT
When reducing the pear
juice, do not boil for
longer than 5 minutes or it will

become too thick and syrupy at
this stage and not coat the chops
and pears. It will reduce further
during baking in the oven.

SERVING IDEAS
Good accompaniments
are cauliflower or leeks,
lightly boiled then drained and
tossed with butter and 25 g/1 oz
chopped flaked almonds.

●490 calories/2050 kj per portion

Quick Portuguese pork

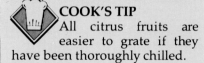

SERVES 4
- 750 g/1½ lb pork fillets (tenderloin), sliced into thin strips
- 1 large grapefruit (see Cook's tip)
- 2 teaspoons ground coriander
- salt and freshly ground black pepper
- 3 tablespoons olive oil
- 4 tablespoons dry white wine
- 175 g/6 oz can pimientos, drained and cut into strips (see Buying guide)

1 Grate the zest from the grapefruit and reserve. Remove all the remaining rind and pith, then divide the flesh into segments, cutting away all membranes.

2 Put the strips of pork in a bowl, sprinkle with the ground coriander, the reserved grated zest of the grapefruit and salt and pepper to taste and turn the meat over until thoroughly coated.

3 Heat the oil in a frying-pan until very hot. Add the pork and fry briskly turning from time to time until evenly browned on all sides. Lower the heat.

4 Pass the juice from a quarter of the grapefruit segments through a sieve. Add to the frying-pan and stir in the wine and pimientos. Fry for 3-4 minutes until the pork is tender, stirring all the time.

5 Transfer the pork and pimientos to a warmed serving dish with a slotted spoon. Keep hot in the lowest possible oven.

6 Bring the liquid in the pan to the boil and boil rapidly until reduced slightly. Lower the heat, add the remaining grapefruit segments and heat through.

7 Remove the grapefruit segments from the pan with a slotted spoon and reserve. Pour the pan juices over the pork and pimientos, then garnish with the reserved grapefruit segments. Serve at once.

Cook's Notes

TIME
10 minutes preparation, 15 minutes to cook.

BUYING GUIDE
Canned red pimientos are available from most supermarkets. They are small, sweet peppers, and the fact that they are ready-skinned and sliced makes them a handy store-cupboard item. If you prefer to use a fresh red pepper for this dish, cut it into strips, discarding the white membrane and seeds. Plunge into boiling water for 2-3 minutes then refresh under cold running water.

COOK'S TIP
All citrus fruits are easier to grate if they have been thoroughly chilled.

●400 calories/1675 kj per portion

Dynasty pork

SERVES 4

750 g/1½ lb lean stewing pork, trimmed and cut into 2.5 cm/1 inch cubes
25 g/1 oz plain flour
salt and freshly ground black pepper
2 tablespoons vegetable oil
25 g/1 oz margarine or butter
1 onion, chopped
1 green pepper, deseeded and sliced
1 clove garlic, crushed (optional)
300 ml/½ pint chicken stock
300 g/11 oz can mandarin orange segments, drained, with syrup reserved
1 tablespoon wine vinegar
1 tablespoon soy sauce
2 tomatoes, skinned and chopped

1 Put the flour in a polythene bag and season with salt and pepper. Place the pork in the bag and shake until the meat is well coated with flour. Reserve any flour remaining in the bag.

2 Heat the oil and margarine in a flameproof casserole, add the onion, green pepper and garlic, if using, and fry over gentle heat for 5 minutes until the onion is soft and lightly coloured. Remove with a slotted spoon and set aside.

3 Add the pork to the pan together with any flour remaining in the bag. Fry over brisk heat for 4-5 minutes, turning constantly until browned on all sides.

4 Gradually blend in the chicken stock, mandarin orange syrup, vinegar and soy sauce. Return the cooked vegetables to the pan, bring to the boil and simmer for 2-3 minutes, stirring constantly. Add salt and pepper to taste.

5 Lower the heat cover the pan and simmer very gently for about 1½ hours or until the pork is tender. Add the orange segments and chopped tomatoes and cook for a further 5 minutes. Taste and adjust seasoning, then transfer to a warmed serving dish. Serve hot.

Cook's Notes

 TIME
Preparation 25 minutes, cooking 1½-1¾ hours.

 FREEZING
Transfer the cooked dish to a foil container, cool quickly, then remove any excess solidified fat. Seal, label and freeze for up to 6 months. To serve: reheat from frozen in a 190C/375F/Gas 5 oven for 1 hour or until bubbling.

 PRESSURE COOKING
Do not add flour until end of cooking time. Bring to high (H) pressure and cook for 15 minutes. Release pressure quickly. Blend flour with a little fruit syrup, and stir in with tomatoes and orange segments. Bring to the boil and simmer for 2 minutes.

●710 calories/2975 kj per portion

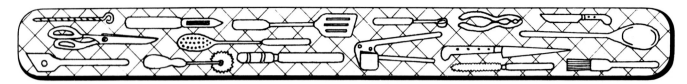

Fruity stuffed pork chops

SERVES 4

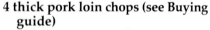

4 thick pork loin chops (see Buying guide)
2 tablespoons vegetable oil

STUFFING
15 g/½ oz margarine or butter
1 small onion, chopped
50 g/2 oz prunes, soaked overnight, stones removed and finely chopped
1 small dessert apple, peeled, cored and grated
25 g/1 oz walnuts, roughly chopped
50 g/2 oz soft day-old white breadcrumbs
salt and freshly ground black pepper
1 small egg, beaten

1 Heat the oven to 190C/375F/Gas 5.
2 Make the stuffing: melt the margarine in a frying-pan, add the onion and fry gently for 5 minutes until soft and lightly coloured. Put the prunes in a bowl with the apple, walnuts and breadcrumbs and stir in the onion. Season with salt and pepper and stir in the egg to bind.
3 Using a sharp knife, slit each pork chop horizontally, from the fatty outside edge to the bone, without cutting right the way through. Fill the chops with the stuffing mixture and secure the slit edges with wooden cocktail sticks.
4 Brush a baking or roasting tin with half the oil. Put in the chops and brush with the remaining oil.
5 Cook the chops in the oven for about 20 minutes, then cover the dish with foil and return to oven for 30-40 minutes until cooked through. Remove cocktail sticks to serve.

Cook's Notes

TIME
Preparing the stuffing and the chops takes about 25 minutes. Allow overnight soaking for the prunes. Cooking in the oven takes 50-60 minutes.

BUYING GUIDE
Choose chops without kidney and with as little bone as possible.

COOK'S TIP
If there is any stuffing left over, put it in a small ovenproof dish, cover with foil and bake in the oven below the chops for 20 minutes.

●465 calories/1925 kj per portion

Pork and peas

SERVES 4

1 kg/2 lb boneless shoulder of pork, trimmed and cut into 1 cm/½ inch cubes
275 g/10 oz shelled fresh peas
salt
15 g/½ oz lard
1 large onion, finely chopped
1 clove garlic, finely chopped (optional)
2 teaspoons sweet paprika
¼ teaspoon cayenne pepper
125 ml/4 fl oz hot chicken stock
75 ml/3 fl oz dry white wine
2 tablespoons chopped fresh parsley

1 Cook the peas in boiling salted water for 10 minutes.
2 Meanwhile, melt the lard in a large frying-pan, add the pork and fry over brisk heat for 5 minutes until browned on all sides. Remove from the pan with a slotted spoon and set aside.

3 Lower the heat and stir in the onion, garlic, if using, paprika and cayenne pepper. Raise the heat to moderate and cook for 5 minutes until the onion is soft.
4 Drain the peas, then add to pan with the pork. Stir well, pour in stock and wine. Bring to the boil.

5 Lower the heat, add the parsley, then cover the pan and simmer for 40 minutes or until the pork is tender.
6 Taste and adjust seasoning, then transfer the pork and peas to a warmed serving dish and serve at once, while piping hot.

Cook's Notes

TIME
Total preparation and cooking time 1¼ hours.

FREEZING

Transfer the pork and peas to a rigid container, cool quickly, then seal, label and freeze for up to 2 months. To serve: reheat from frozen until heated through and bubbling. Stir frequently and add a little stock or water if the mixture sticks.

COOK'S TIP
To use frozen peas, do not defrost, simply stir into pan in last 10 minutes.

PRESSURE COOKING
Heat the lard in the base of cooker, fry the onion, then remove and drain. Fry pork and, if very fatty, drain off excess fat. Return onion and pork to pressure cooker, add liquid (200 ml/7 fl oz chicken stock and 75 ml/3 fl oz white wine) and bring to the boil. Skim liquid if necessary, then bring to high (H) pressure and cook for 12 minutes. Reduce pressure quickly, add peas. Bring back to high (H) pressure and cook a further 3 minutes. Reduce pressure quickly.

●700 calories/2925 kj per portion

Stilton steak

SERVES 4

 4 rump steaks, each weighing 175 g/6 oz (see Buying guide)
1 tablespoon finely chopped onion
1 tablespoon Worcestershire sauce
75 ml/3 fl oz vegetable oil
50 ml/2 fl oz port or sweet sherry
freshly ground black pepper
1 bay leaf, crumbled
75 g/3 oz Blue Stilton cheese, grated
watercress sprigs and tomato slices, to garnish

1 Put the steaks in a large shallow dish. Combine the onion, Worcestershire sauce, oil, port, pepper and bay leaf and pour over the steaks. Cover and leave to marinate for at least 3 hours at room temperature, turning the steaks several times.
2 Line grill rack with foil, and heat the grill to moderate.
3 Using a fish slice, lift the steaks from the marinade and arrange them on the grill rack. Grill for 5-8 minutes, depending on whether you like your steak medium or well done, basting from time to time with the marinade. Turn the steaks and grill for 2-5 minutes.
4 Sprinkle the Stilton over each steak, dividing it equally between them and pressing down with the back of the spoon. Grill for a further 3 minutes until the Stilton topping is melted and bubbling.
5 Transfer the steaks to a warmed serving dish, garnish with watercress and tomato and serve at once.

Cook's Notes

TIME
Allow at least 3 hours marinating time. Cooking takes about 15 minutes.

BUYING GUIDE
Rump steak is cut from the lower part of the sirloin. Choose rump steaks that have a slightly purplish tinge which shows that they have been well-hung and will be tender. Some supermarkets sell smallish pieces of rump steak in special economy packs: these would be ideal.
Frying steak, which is much cheaper than rump steak, may be used instead; it will need to be cooked for slightly longer.

COOK'S TIP
If steaks are marinated there is no need to beat the meat to tenderize it. The alcohol in the marinade will break down fibres of the meat.

SERVING IDEAS
Serve the steaks with baked or new potatoes and a green salad.

●380 calories/1600 kj per portion

Steak and parsnip pie

SERVES 4

750 g/1½ lb chuck steak, cut into
  bite-sized pieces
2 tablespoons vegetable oil
1 large onion, sliced
25 g/1 oz plain flour
400 g/14 oz can tomatoes
1 chicken stock cube
bouquet garni
salt and freshly ground black pepper
250 g/9 oz parsnips, cut into chunky
  pieces
215 g/7½ oz packet frozen puff
  pastry, defrosted
a little beaten egg, to glaze

1 Heat the oven to 180C/350F/Gas 4.
2 Heat the oil in a flameproof casserole, add the meat and onion and fry until the onion is soft and the meat is browned on all sides. Sprinkle in the flour, then cook for 1-2 minutes, stirring constantly.
3 Stir in the tomatoes and their juice, crumble in the stock cube and stir well to mix. Add the bouquet garni and season to taste with salt and pepper. Bring to the boil, stirring, then cover and transfer to the oven. Cook for 1½ hours or until the meat is just tender.
4 Stir in the parsnips and cook for a further 45 minutes.
5 Meanwhile, roll out the pastry on a floured surface to a shape slightly larger than the circumference of a 1 L/2 pint pie dish. Cut off a long narrow strip of pastry all around the edge. Reserve this and other trimmings.
6 Transfer the meat and parsnip mixture to the pie dish, then discard the bouquet garni and taste and adjust seasoning. Increase the oven

Cook's Notes

TIME
Preparation time is 15 minutes. Cooking time is 2¾ hours but remember to allow time for the pastry to defrost.

● 675 calories/2825 kj per portion

VARIATIONS
You could use blade or stewing steak, in which case the meat will need longer to cook. Turnips, carrots or swedes can be used instead of the parsnips or try using a mixture of root vegetables.

temperature to 220C/425F/Gas 7. Brush the rim of the pie dish with water, then press the narrow strip of pastry all around the rim. Brush the strip with a little more water, then place the large piece of pastry on top. Trim the edge of the pastry, then knock up and flute.
7 Make leaves or other shapes with the pastry trimmings, then place on top of the pie, brushing the underneath with water so that they do not come off during baking. Make a small hole in the centre of the pie for the steam to escape, then brush all over the pastry with beaten egg.
8 Bake the pie in the oven for 25-30 minutes until the pastry is well risen and golden brown. Serve hot.

minutes or until just tender. Drain well and mix with the potatoes in a bowl. While the vegetables are still warm, pour over 2 tablespoons of the marinade from the beef and gently turn them with a fork, without breaking them up, to coat thoroughly with the marinade. Cover and chill in the refrigerator for 1 hour.

6 When ready to serve, mix the grated carrots and the tomatoes with the potatoes and beans. Remove the meat slices from the marinade, draining off any excess marinade from the slices. Remove the onions from the marinade with a slotted spoon and mix them into the mixed vegetables.

7 Pile the vegetable salad into the centre of a serving platter and arrange the marinated beef slices around it. Garnish the platter with black olives and chopped parsley. Serve at once.

Cook's Notes

TIME
Cooking the beef takes about 1 hour. Allow 5-6 hours or overnight for marinating the beef. Preparing the vegetable salad, including cooking the potatoes and beans, takes about 30 minutes. Allow 1 hour for chilling the salad.

BUYING GUIDE
Most supermarkets have a selection of beef roasting joints. Choose one that is lean and without gristle. Rolled topside would be a good choice for this dish, or boned rolled fore rib, which is slightly less expensive.

COOK'S TIPS
How long you cook the beef depends on whether you like it rare or well done, but this dish is most attractive if the meat is still pink. A joint of this weight will be just turning from pink after 1 hour's cooking. Cook for only 50 minutes if you like your beef rare, and for 1¼ hours if you like a joint to be well done.

●440 calories/1825 kj per portion

Marinated summer beef

SERVES 4

750 g-1 kg/1½-2 lb beef roasting joint (see Buying guide)
100 ml/3½ fl oz vegetable oil
150 ml/¼ pint dry white wine
1 teaspoon mild French mustard
1 teaspoon dried thyme
1 tablespoon lemon juice
1 clove garlic, crushed (optional)
salt and freshly ground black pepper
1 small onion, finely sliced

SALAD

2 potatoes
100 g/4 oz French beans, fresh or frozen
2 carrots, grated
2 tomatoes, quartered

GARNISH

8-10 black olives
1 tablespoon chopped fresh parsley

1 Heat the oven to 180C/350F/Gas 4.
2 Wrap the beef in foil and place in a roasting tin. Roast in the oven for about 1 hour (see Cook's tips). Remove from the oven and leave the beef, still wrapped in foil, to cool for about 45 minutes.

3 Make the marinade: put the oil, wine, mustard, thyme, lemon juice and garlic, if using, in a bowl or in the goblet of a blender. Season with salt and pepper and beat well with a fork, or process in the blender for 30 seconds.

4 Slice the cooled beef into even, neat slices and arrange them in a shallow dish. Arrange the onion slices on top of the beef and pour over the marinade. Cover the dish of beef with cling film and refrigerate for at least 5-6 hours or overnight if possible.

5 Make the salad: cook the potatoes in boiling salted water for 15-20 minutes or until just tender. Drain, cool slightly and cut into bite-sized chunks. Meanwhile, cook the beans in boiling salted water for 5-10

Tasty hamburgers

SERVES 4

750 g/1½ lb lean minced beef
1 small onion, finely grated
1 tablespoon tomato ketchup
salt and freshly ground black pepper
75 g/3 oz Danish Blue cheese,
   mashed
2 tablespoons vegetable oil

1 In a large bowl, mix together the minced beef, onion and tomato ketchup and season well with salt and pepper. ✳ Cover the mixture and refrigerate for 1 hour.
2 Divide the mashed cheese into 4 portions. Shape each portion into a ball and flatten slightly. Divide the chilled beef mixture into 4 portions and mould 1 portion around each ball of cheese. Shape into a fairly thick hamburger, making sure that

the cheese is completely enclosed by the meat mixture.
3 Heat the oil in a large frying-pan, add the hamburgers and fry for about 5-8 minutes on each side,

until they are done to your liking.
4 Remove the hamburgers from the pan with a fish slice, drain quickly on absorbent paper and serve at once (see Serving ideas).

Cook's Notes

TIME
Preparation takes 10 minutes but allow 1 hour chilling time. Cooking then takes 10-15 minutes.

FREEZING
Shape beef mixture round the cheese as in stage 2. Open freeze hamburgers until solid, then wrap individually in foil and pack together in a polythene bag. Seal, label and return to the freezer for up to 3 months. To serve: defrost at room temperature, then proceed from the beginning of stage 3.

VARIATIONS
Grated mature Cheddar cheese or finely shredded Mozzarella may be substituted for the Danish Blue.
   Add a few drops of Tabasco to the minced beef mixture, for a more piquant taste.

SERVING IDEAS
Serve in the traditional sesame bun with lettuce, sliced tomato and various relishes or mustard. Alternatively, serve with French fried potatoes, without the bun.

●415 calories/1750 kj per portion

Pot roast brisket

SERVES 4

1 kg/2 lb fresh brisket of beef,
   rolled and tied (see Buying guide)
25 g/1 oz margarine or butter
1 onion, quartered
2 large carrots, sliced
2 celery stalks, sliced
425 ml/¾ pint beef stock
½ teaspoon dried thyme
½ teaspoon dried marjoram
1 tablespoon soy sauce
freshly ground black pepper
4 teaspoons cornflour
salt

1 Melt the margarine in a large flameproof casserole and fry the brisket over high heat until browned on all sides. Transfer to a plate.
2 Add the onion, carrots and celery to the pan, lower the heat and fry gently for 5 minutes, stirring. Return the meat to the pan and add the stock, thyme, marjoram, soy sauce and freshly ground black pepper to taste.
3 Bring to the boil, then lower the heat, cover and simmer gently for

2½ hours, turning the meat over every 30 minutes. !
4 When tender, remove the meat from the pan and keep warm.
5 Blend the cornflour to a paste with a little cold water, stir into the pan and bring to the boil. Lower the heat and simmer for 2-3 minutes, stirring constantly, then mash the onions,

carrots and celery into the gravy in the pan with a potato masher. Taste and adjust seasoning.
6 Place the meat on a warmed serving platter, cutting a few thin slices from one end, if wished. Pour over a little of the gravy, then serve at once, with the remaining gravy handed separately in a sauceboat.

Cook's Notes

TIME
20 minutes preparation; 2½ hours cooking, turning the meat every 30 minutes. Allow an extra 5-10 minutes to finish the gravy and slice the meat.

BUYING GUIDE
Make sure you buy a fresh brisket, not a salted one. Look for a good, lean joint.

PRESSURE COOKING
Calculate the cooking time at 20 minutes per 500 g/1 lb meat. Remove the trivet from the pressure cooker pan. Brown the meat and vegetables in the pan as described, then add the stock and flavour-

ings. Cover with the lid, bring up to pressure according to manufacturer's instructions, then cook at high (H) pressure for the calculated cooking time (about 50 minutes). Reduce pressure with cold water, lift out the meat and thicken the gravy as described.

WATCHPOINT
To turn the brisket over without splashing or burning yourself, use 2 large kitchen forks, or a fork and a wooden spoon. Make sure you have a firm grip on the joint before you lift it; if it slips back into the pan the hot stock will splash dangerously.

●505 calories/2125 kj per portion

Flemish beef casserole

SERVES 4

750 g/1½ lb chuck steak, trimmed
    and cut into 2.5 cm/1 inch cubes
3 tablespoons vegetable oil
3 medium onions, sliced
100 g/4 oz smoked streaky bacon,
    rinds removed, chopped
1 clove garlic, crushed (optional)
2 tablespoons plain flour
200 ml/7 fl oz brown ale
75 ml/3 fl oz beef stock
1 tablespoon red wine vinegar
1 tablespoon soft brown sugar
bouquet garni (parsley, thyme, bay
    leaf)
salt and freshly ground black pepper
1 tablespoon finely chopped
    parsley, to garnish

MUSTARD CROUTONS
2 large slices white bread, crusts
    removed, each cut into 4 triangles
    or squares
2 teaspoons made English mustard
vegetable oil, for frying

1 In a large saucepan or flameproof casserole, heat the oil over fairly high heat, and fry the meat, a few pieces at a time, until evenly brown all over. Remove with a slotted spoon to a plate and keep warm.
2 Reduce the heat and fry the onions and bacon, stirring occasionally, for 5-7 minutes until softened and beginning to colour. Add the garlic, if using, and fry for 1 minute.
3 Add the flour and stir, scraping the crusty bits off the bottom of the pan. Cook until it begins to brown. Stir in the ale and stock and bring to the boil, stirring. Return the meat to the pan, then add the remaining ingredients, except the parsley. Stir well, reduce the heat, cover and simmer gently over low heat for 1¾-2 hours until the meat is tender.
4 Spread both sides of the bread triangles or squares with mustard.
5 Heat the oil in a frying-pan and fry the croûtons for a few seconds until they are evenly browned on all sides.
6 Drain on absorbent paper.
7 When the meat is tender, check and adjust seasoning. Serve hot, garnished with parsley and the mustard croûtons.

Cook's Notes

 TIME
Preparation 25 minutes, cooking 2 hours.

BUYING GUIDE
Ready-made bouquets garnis are available from most good supermarkets and delicatessens. Remember to remove before serving.

 FREEZING
Cool quickly, remove any excess solidified fat and pack in a rigid container or heavy-duty polythene bag. Seal, label and freeze for up to 3 months. To use, defrost gently over low heat, bring to boiling point and cook for about 20 minutes until thoroughly heated.

COOK'S TIPS
This casserole can be cooked in the oven at 180C/350F/Gas 4 for the same length of time.
    Like most casseroles, the flavour is improved if it is made one day, cooled, then reheated thoroughly the next day.

ECONOMY
If you use a cheaper cut of stewing steak, such as shin beef, the dish will be less expensive, but remember to trim away all the fat and gristle. Shin beef is tougher than chuck and will need to cook for at least an hour longer.

●620 calories/2600 kj per portion

Mexican beef

SERVES 4

500 g/1 lb minced beef (see Buying
    guide)
1-2 tablespoons vegetable oil
1 small onion, finely chopped
3-4 teaspoons chilli seasoning
2 tablespoons quick-cooking
    porridge oats
300 ml/½ pint beef stock
1 tablespoon tomato purée
pinch of freshly grated nutmeg
salt and freshly ground black pepper
350 g/12 oz can sweetcorn with
    sweet peppers, drained
1 large or 2 medium avocados
1 tablespoon lemon juice
100 g/4 oz Cheddar cheese, cut into
    2.5 cm/1 inch cubes

1 Heat 1 tablespoon oil in a heavy-
based saucepan. Add the beef and
fry over moderate heat for 3
minutes, stirring constantly until all
the beef has browned, breaking up
any lumps with a wooden spoon.
Remove the beef with a slotted
spoon. Add the onion to the pan and
fry for 5 minutes until soft and
lightly coloured, adding a further
tablespoon oil if necessary, to
prevent overbrowning.
2 Return the beef to the pan, stir in 3
teaspoons chilli seasoning, then the
oats, stock, tomato purée, nutmeg,
salt to taste and add a light sprinkling of pepper.
3 Bring to the boil, stirring, then
reduce the heat, cover and simmer
gently for 40-45 minutes or until the
oats are soft and the meat cooked.
4 Stir the drained sweetcorn and
peppers into the beef mixture and
continue to cook, uncovered, for 5
minutes until most of the excess
liquid has evaporated. Taste and
adjust seasoning, adding more chilli
if a slightly hotter flavour is liked.
5 Just before serving, cut the
avocado in half lengthways and
discard the stone. Cut into quarters
lengthways and peel away the skin,
then cut the flesh into neat thin
slices lengthways. Brush with the
lemon juice to prevent discoloration.
6 Stir the cheese into the beef until
just beginning to melt, then spoon
the mixture into a warmed serving
dish and arrange the avocado slices
around the edge. Serve at once.

Cook's Notes

TIME
Preparation 30 minutes,
cooking 45 minutes.

BUYING GUIDE
Various grades of
minced beef are avail-
able, but for this dish choose a
good-quality, lean mince and
use it on the day of purchase.
  Cheaper grades of mince will
require longer cooking and any
excess fat should be skimmed
from the top before serving.

VARIATION
If you do not have any
chilli seasoning (avail-
able in jars from most supermarkets), use the same quantity
of mild curry powder; this will
season the beef, but will not be
sufficient to give a strong curry
flavour. Chilli powder can be
used, but as it is hotter than
chilli seasoning, add a little at a
time to the required strength.

PRESSURE COOKING
Pre-brown the beef and
onion in the base of the
pressure cooker, then add all the
other ingredients, except for the
sweetcorn, avocado, lemon
juice and cheese. Bring to high
(H) pressure and cook for 7
minutes. Reduce the pressure
quickly, then add the sweetcorn. Bring to the boil,
uncovered, remove from the
heat and stir in the cheese.
Garnish with the avocado slices.

●555 calories/2325 kj per portion

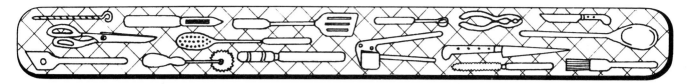

Beef curry

SERVES 4

750 g/1½ lb stewing steak, trimmed of excess fat and cut into 1 cm/ ½ inch cubes
1 teaspoon ground coriander
1 teaspoon ground turmeric
1 teaspoon chilli powder
½ teaspoon ground ginger
2 tablespoons vegetable oil
1 onion, sliced
1 clove garlic, crushed (optional)
350 ml/12 fl oz beef stock
1 tablespoon desiccated coconut
1 tablespoon lemon juice
salt

1 Put the coriander, turmeric, chilli and ginger in a bowl and gradually add a little water, stirring all the time until a smooth paste is formed. Set aside.

2 Heat the oil in a large flameproof casserole, add the onion and garlic, if using, and fry for 5 minutes until the onion is soft and lightly coloured.

3 Stir in the spicy paste and fry for a further 3-4 minutes, stirring all the time.

4 Add the meat and fry for a further 3-4 minutes, stirring to cook on all sides in the spices. Stir in the stock and bring to the boil, then lower the heat and stir in the coconut, lemon juice and salt to taste. Cover and simmer gently for 2 hours ✳ until the meat is tender.

5 Taste and adjust seasoning (see Cook's tips) then serve hot, straight from the casserole.

Cook's Notes

TIME
15 minutes initial preparation, then 2 hours cooking time.

COOK'S TIPS
All curries have an infinitely better flavour if left to go cold overnight and are reheated the following day.
For extra 'bite', add more lemon juice before serving.

●405 calories/1700 kj per portion

Stir-fried beef with cashews

SERVES 4

500 g/1 lb rump steak or flash-fry
   steak, cut 1 cm/½ inch thick and
   all fat removed (see Cook's tip)
3 tablespoons vegetable oil
1 clove garlic, crushed (optional)
4 spring onions, cut into 2.5 cm/
   1 inch pieces
1 large onion, chopped
50 g/2 oz unsalted cashew nuts
1 small green or red pepper,
   deseeded and cut into thin strips
1 teaspoon ground ginger
1 tablespoon cornflour
150 ml/¼ pint chicken stock
2 teaspoons medium sherry
2 teaspoons soy sauce
salt and freshly ground black pepper

1 Dry the beef on absorbent paper.
Place it between 2 sheets of greaseproof paper and beat to flatten, with
a wooden rolling pin. Using kitchen
scissors, snip the beef into thin
strips about 5 cm/2 inches long.

2 Heat 1 tablespoon of oil in a large
frying-pan or wok, add half the beef
strips, stir for about 1 minute until
browned on all sides, [!] remove
from the pan with a slotted spoon
and reserve. Heat 1 further tablespoon of oil in the pan, add the
remaining beef strips, stir-fry in the
same way and reserve.

3 Heat the remaining oil in the pan,
add the garlic, if using, spring
onions, onion, cashew nuts and
pepper strips and fry gently for 3-4
minutes, stirring, until the
vegetables are tender and the nuts
lightly browned. Remove the pan
from the heat and stir in the ginger.

4 Blend the cornflour with the
chicken stock, sherry and soy sauce
to make a smooth paste, and stir into
the pan.

5 Return to the heat, bring to the
boil, lower heat and simmer gently
for 1 minute, stirring constantly.
Season to taste with salt and pepper.

6 Return the reserved cooked beef
strips to the pan and stir over gentle
heat until heated through. Serve at
once in individual bowls.

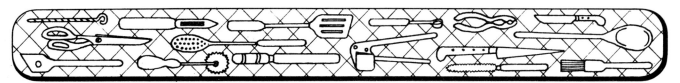

Beef goulash

SERVES 4

500 g/1 lb chuck steak, cubed
250 g/9 oz stewing veal, cubed
25 g/1 oz margarine or butter
2 tablespoons vegetable oil
2 large onions, finely chopped
2 teaspoons sweet paprika
400 g/14 oz can tomatoes, drained
100-175 g/4-6 oz button
    mushrooms
300 ml/½ pint beef stock or water
1 tablespoon tomato purée
salt and freshly ground black
    pepper
150 ml/¼ pint soured cream
1 tablespoon chopped parsley

1 Heat the oven to 170C/325F/Gas 3.
2 Heat the margarine and half the oil in a frying-pan, add the onions and cook without browning over low heat. Drain and remove to a casserole.
3 Add the remaining oil to the pan and fry the meat over high heat until evenly browned. Sprinkle the paprika over, fry for 1-2 minutes and remove to the casserole.
4 Chop the tomatoes, lay them on top of the meat, and add the whole mushrooms, stock and tomato purée. Season with salt and pepper. Cover and cook until the meat is tender in the oven for about 2-2½ hours. Taste and adjust seasoning.
✳ Before serving, stir in half the soured cream and pour the rest over the top. Sprinkle with chopped parsley. Serve at once.

Cook's Notes

TIME
Preparation will take 25-30 minutes. Cook the goulash for 2-2½ hours, until the meat is tender when tested with a fork.

• 530 calories/2225 kj per portion

SERVING IDEAS
Small new boiled potatoes are nicest with goulash, but you can also serve mashed potatoes, macaroni or noodles with a crisp green vegetable such as broccoli or French beans.

FREEZING
Freeze in casserole. Tip out, wrap in foil, and replace in freezer. When ready to use, turn back into the casserole which was used for cooking. Cover and reheat until the goulash is bubbling.

Serbian beef

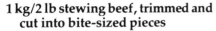

SERVES 4-5

1 kg/2 lb stewing beef, trimmed and
  cut into bite-sized pieces
25 g/1 oz dripping
2 large onions, sliced
1 tablespoon sweet paprika
1 celery stalk, chopped
2 cloves garlic, crushed (optional)
1 bay leaf
1 tablespoon chopped parsley
salt and freshly ground black pepper
150 ml/¼ pint red wine vinegar (see
  Cook's tip)
4 potatoes, thinly sliced
vegetable oil, for brushing

1 Heat the oven to 150C/300F/Gas 2
and lightly brush a large ovenproof
dish with oil.

2 Melt half the dripping in a heavy
flameproof casserole over high heat
and fry the meat in batches, if

necessary, until crisp and golden on
all sides. Transfer the meat with a
slotted spoon to a plate.

3 Add the remaining dripping to
the pan and fry the onions gently for
about 5 minutes until soft and
translucent.

4 Return the meat and any juices to
the pan. Add the paprika and stir
over low heat for 2 minutes.

5 Add the celery, garlic, if using,
bay leaf, parsley, salt and pepper to
taste and the wine vinegar. Bring to
the boil, remove from the heat and
allow to cool for a few minutes.

6 Put half the potatoes in a layer on
the bottom of the oiled ovenproof
dish, cover with the meat mixture
and then add the remaining
potatoes in a neat layer on top.
Cover tightly with a lid or foil and
cook in the oven for about 2½ hours
until the meat is tender.

7 Brush the potatoes with oil and
place the casserole under a high grill
for 5 minutes until the potatoes are
browned. Serve hot straight from
the dish.

Apple-stuffed veal chops

SERVES 4

4 veal chops, each weighing about 175-250 g/6-9 oz, trimmed of excess fat (see Buying guide)
2 large cooking apples
juice of ½ lemon
2 tablespoons sultanas
1½ teaspoons ground cloves
salt and freshly ground black pepper
1 tablespoon vegetable oil
25 g/1 oz margarine or butter
2 tablespoons sultanas, soaked in 1 tablespoon sherry, to garnish

1 Using a very sharp knife, make a pocket in each chop: slit horizontally, from the outside edge to the bone, cutting through to within 1 cm/½ inch of the edge.

2 Quarter, peel and core 1 apple. Cut into 5 mm/¼ inch slices and put into a bowl with the lemon juice. Toss the apple slices in the lemon juice, then add the sultanas and 1 teaspoon of ground cloves. Mix together well.

3 Spoon the apple mixture into the pocket of each chop, dividing it equally between them. Secure the slit edges with wooden cocktail sticks. Sprinkle the chops with the remaining ground cloves and season well with salt and freshly ground black pepper.

4 Heat the oven to 110C/225F/Gas ¼.

5 Heat the oil and margarine in a large frying-pan, add the veal chops and fry them over high heat for 2-3 minutes on each side, to brown and seal. Lower the heat and cook for 10-15 minutes on each side, until cooked through and the juices run clear when the meat is pierced with a sharp knife.

6 Peel and core the remaining apple. Slice into rings. Using a fish slice, transfer chops to a warmed serving platter and keep warm in the oven. Add the apple rings to the frying-pan and fry gently, turning carefully so that the rings do not break up, until golden brown.

7 Arrange the fried apple rings on top of the chops, spoon the sultanas into the centre of the apple rings and serve the apple-stuffed veal chops at once (see Serving ideas).

Cook's Notes

 TIME
Preparing and cooking the veal chops take only 30 minutes.

 BUYING GUIDE
Veal chops are cut from the loin. As the loin is usually sold in one piece for roasting, veal chops may have to be ordered in advance from the butcher.

 ECONOMY
Use 4 pork chump chops, in place of the veal chops used here.

SERVING IDEAS
Serve the veal chops with a cider sauce, if liked. Pour off excess fat from the frying-pan after cooking the apples. Pour in 150 ml/¼ pint cider, then bring slowly to the boil, stirring and scraping the sediment from the bottom of the pan with a wooden spoon. Remove from the heat and stir in 3 tablespoons double cream. Season to taste with salt and pepper. Spoon the sauce over the apples and veal to serve.

●305 calories/1275 kj per portion

Italian veal rolls

500 g/1 lb veal topside or rump, cut across the grain of the meat into 8 equal-sized pieces
4 thin square slices cooked ham, halved
1 tablespoon French mustard (optional)
150 g/5 oz Edam or Gouda cheese, cut into 8 sticks 5 × 1 cm/2 × ½ inch (see Watchpoint)
25 g/1 oz butter
2 tablespoons vegetable oil
1 onion, chopped
1 clove garlic, crushed (optional)
100 g/4 oz mushrooms, sliced
400 g/14 oz can tomatoes, drained and chopped
75 ml/3 fl oz chicken stock
½ teaspoon dried oregano
1 bay leaf
salt and freshly ground black pepper
snipped chives, to garnish

1 Place the veal pieces between 2 sheets of greaseproof paper and pound with a wooden rolling pin or mallet, to flatten to the same size as the halved ham slices. Spread the ham slices with the mustard, if using.

2 Place a slice of ham on each piece of veal, mustard side down if used. Place a cheese stick at one end, then roll the veal and ham up around the cheese. Tie the rolls at both ends with fine string (see Preparation).

3 Heat the butter with the oil in a large frying-pan. When sizzling, add the veal rolls and fry over moderate heat for about 6 minutes to brown on all sides. Remove the rolls from the pan with a slotted spoon or kitchen tongs and leave to drain on absorbent paper.

4 Add the onion and garlic, if using, to the pan and fry for 5 minutes over gentle heat until soft and lightly coloured. Add the mushrooms to the pan and fry for a further 3 minutes.

5 Stir the tomatoes, stock and oregano into the pan, add the bay leaf and season to taste with salt and pepper. Bring to the boil. Return the veal rolls to the pan and turn in the sauce.

6 Lower the heat, cover the pan and cook gently for 10 minutes. Uncover and cook for a further 10 minutes or until the veal is tender and the sauce has reduced by about one-half.

7 Remove the rolls from the pan and carefully remove the string. Place the rolls in a warmed serving dish and keep hot. Discard the bay leaf from the sauce and taste and adjust seasoning.

8 Spoon the sauce over the veal rolls and sprinkle with chives. Serve.

Cook's Notes

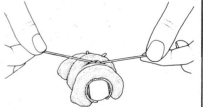

TIME
Preparation takes about 45 minutes, cooking 35-40 minutes.

PREPARATION
Make the veal rolls in the following way:

1 *Place the cheese stick at one end of the ham and roll up.*

2 *Tie the rolls at either end with fine string as shown.*

WATCHPOINT
The cheese sticks must not protrude from the ends of the rolls, or the cheese will ooze out during cooking.

SPECIAL OCCASION
Use Gruyère cheese, Parma ham, and dry white wine or vermouth instead of chicken stock.

● 415 calories/1750 kj per portion

Ratatouille veal

SERVES 4-6

1.5 kg/3-3½ lb boned breast of veal
  (boned weight)
1 teaspoon chopped fresh basil or
  ½ teaspoon dried basil
50 g/2 oz dripping or lard

RATATOUILLE STUFFING
3 tablespoons olive oil
1 onion, finely chopped
1 aubergine, weighing about 250 g/
  9 oz, peeled and cut into 1 cm/
  ½ inch cubes, salted, drained,
  rinsed and dried
1 small green pepper, deseeded and
  finely chopped
2 large tomatoes, skinned and
  chopped
1 teaspoon chopped fresh basil or
  ½ teaspoon dried basil
salt and freshly ground black pepper

1 Make the stuffing: heat the oil in a saucepan, add the onion and fry gently for 5 minutes until soft and lightly coloured. Add the remaining stuffing ingredients with salt and pepper to taste and cook gently for 15 minutes, stirring from time to time. Remove the stuffing from the heat and leave to cool.

Cook's Notes

 TIME
Preparation takes about 30 minutes, cooking about 1½ hours.

PREPARATION
To stuff the veal with ratatouille:

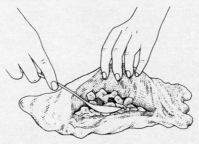

Spoon the ratatouille into the pocket, packing it in well.

Sew up the opening in the veal with trussing thread.

SERVING IDEAS
This tasty and unusual dish may be accompanied with croquette potatoes and, if liked, a green salad.

●760 calories/3200 kj per portion

---

2 Heat the oven to 190C/375F/Gas 5.
3 Pat the veal dry with absorbent paper. With a very sharp knife make a pocket in the veal by slitting horizontally through one long edge to within 2.5 cm/1inch of other 3 edges. Spoon the cooled ratatouille into the pocket (see Preparation). Using a trussing needle and fine string, sew up the opening (see Preparation).
4 Place the ratatouille-stuffed veal in a roasting tin. Sprinkle with the basil, season with salt and pepper and dot with the dripping. Cover the veal with foil and then roast in the oven for ¾ hour, basting often. Remove foil and roast for a further ¾ hour, basting often, until the veal is tender (the juices run clear when the meat is pierced with a fine skewer).
5 Remove from oven and cut away trussing string. Transfer veal to a warmed serving dish and serve at once, cut into slices.

Veal with Stilton and walnuts

SERVES 4-6

1.5 kg/3-3½ lb boned shoulder of veal
1 tablespoon vegetable oil
15 g/½ oz butter
425 ml/¾ pint chicken stock
bouquet garni
175 g/6 oz mushrooms, sliced
2 teaspoons cornflour
2 teaspoons water
walnut halves, to garnish

STUFFING

100 g/4 oz Stilton cheese
50 g/2 oz shelled walnuts, chopped
3 tablespoons parsley and thyme packet stuffing mix
salt and freshly ground black pepper
1 egg
2 tablespoons water

1 Heat the oven to 180C/350F/Gas 4.
2 Make the stuffing: put the Stilton into a bowl and mash it with a fork. Stir in the walnuts and the stuffing mix. Season with salt and pepper. Beat the egg with the water and stir into the mixture.
3 Lay the veal skin side down on a board or work surface. Spread the stuffing mixture over it. Roll the veal up from one short end, then tie securely with string in several places to neaten joint.
4 Heat the oil and butter in a large flameproof casserole. Add the veal and fry over brisk heat, turning, to brown and seal the meat. Drain any excess fat from the casserole and pour the stock round the veal. Add the bouquet garni. Cover with foil, then with the lid and cook in the oven for 1 hour (see Cook's tip).
5 Add the mushrooms to the casserole, cover again with the foil and lid and cook for a further 30 minutes, or until the veal is cooked through and the juices run clear when the meat is pierced with a skewer.
6 Place the veal on a warmed serving dish and remove the string. Keep the veal warm in the oven turned to its lowest setting while making the sauce.
7 Transfer the casserole to the top of the cooker and bring the cooking liquid to the boil. Blend the cornflour to a smooth paste with the water in a small bowl, stir in a little of the hot cooking liquid, then stir this mixture back into the casserole. Cook, stirring, for 1-2 minutes until the sauce thickens, then taste and adjust seasoning.
8 Carve veal into neat slices, then garnish with walnuts. Pour over a little sauce and hand the rest separately in a warmed sauceboat.

LAMB

Pot-roasted leg of lamb

SERVES 4-6

1.5 kg/3 lb leg of lamb
  (see Buying guide)
150 ml/¼ pint red wine
150 ml/¼ pint water
1 tablespoon white wine vinegar
1 medium onion, finely chopped
1 teaspoon dried oregano
2 tablespoons vegetable oil
2 tablespoons tomato purée
pinch of sugar
salt and freshly ground black pepper
chopped parsley, to garnish

1 Put the lamb into a large bowl. Mix together the wine, water, vinegar, onion and oregano and pour over the lamb. Cover and leave to marinate in the refrigerator for several hours, preferably overnight. Turn the lamb in the marinade from time to time.
2 Remove the lamb and reserve the marinade. Pat the lamb all over with

absorbent paper until dry.
3 Heat the oil in a large flameproof casserole, add the lamb and fry over moderate heat until browned on all sides. Pour over the reserved marinade and cover the casserole with a tight-fitting lid. Cook over low heat for 1½-2 hours or until the meat is cooked to your liking.
4 Remove the lamb and keep hot. Skim off any fat from the cooking

liquid with a slotted spoon, then stir in the tomato purée and sugar. Bring to the boil, add salt and pepper to taste, then lower the heat and return the lamb to the casserole. Simmer gently for a further 5 minutes.
5 To serve: transfer the lamb to a warmed serving dish, pour over the sauce and sprinkle with parsley. Serve at once.

Cook's Notes

TIME
Preparation takes only a few minutes, but the lamb needs several hours to marinate. Cooking time is 1½-2 hours.

SERVING IDEAS
A pot roast makes a welcome, often more succulent, change to the traditional roast joint on a Sunday, but it can still be served with all the traditional accompaniments to a roast meal.

BUYING GUIDE
Ask for the chump end of a large leg of lamb. Not only is it the meatiest part of the leg, it is also neater in shape and therefore easier to fit into a casserole dish.

ECONOMY
For a more economical dish, use 300 ml/½ pint well-flavoured stock instead of the wine and water.

●655 calories/2750 kj per portion

Breast of lamb and apple rounds

SERVES 4

2 breasts of lamb, each weighing
   600 g/1¼ lb
1 small onion, halved
1 small carrot, roughly chopped
1 celery stalk, roughly chopped
1 tablespoon chopped celery leaves
   (optional)
1 teaspoon whole cloves
7.5 cm/3 inch cinnamon stick
2 bay leaves
1 sprig each fresh rosemary and
   thyme, or pinch each dried
   rosemary and thyme
2 tablespoons cider vinegar or white
   wine vinegar
1 teaspoon black peppercorns
1 teaspoon salt

APPLE FILLING

2 large cooking apples, peeled,
   cored and chopped
6 tablespoons cider vinegar
4 whole cloves

1 Put the vegetables, spices, herbs and vinegar in a large saucepan with the peppercorns and salt. Pour in enough water to cover the lamb—but do not add the lamb at

this stage. Bring to the boil, then lower the heat and simmer for 10 minutes.

2 Add the lamb, cover the pan and bring back to the boil. Lower the heat and simmer for 1½ hours or until the meat is tender.

3 Let the lamb cool in the liquid in the pan.

4 Meanwhile, make the apple filling: put the apples into a saucepan with the vinegar and cloves. Cover and cook over low heat for 15 minutes or until the apple is very soft. Remove the cloves and, using a wooden spoon, mash the apples to a purée.

5 When the lamb is cool enough to handle, lift out of the liquid and remove the bones and as much of the skin and the fat as possible (see Preparation).

6 Spread the lamb breasts with the apple purée, then roll them up and tie with fine cotton string. Leave in a cool place for at least 4 hours to set into shape.

7 Heat the grill to high.

8 Bring the breasts of lamb to room temperature, then cut each roll into 4 thick slices, leaving the string in place.

9 Grill the rounds of lamb until they are brown and crisp on both sides (10-15 minutes in all). Remove the string and serve at once.

Cook's Notes

TIME
Preparation and cooking time 3¾ hours, but allow 4 hours for the lamb to cool before slicing.

PREPARATION
A way to bone and skin the breast of lamb is shown below:

1 *Once the lamb has been boiled, the bones pull out easily.*

2 *To remove the thick piece of skin between the layers, gently ease the meat apart and pull away the skin.*

●545 calories/2275 kj per portion

116

Lamb chops and peppers

SERVES 4

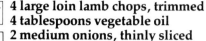

4 large loin lamb chops, trimmed
4 tablespoons vegetable oil
2 medium onions, thinly sliced
1 clove garlic, chopped (optional)
500 g/1 lb tomatoes, skinned,
    deseeded and chopped
2 green peppers, deseeded and cut
    into strips
1 red pepper, deseeded and cut into
    strips
1 teaspoon crushed coriander seeds
    (optional)
salt and freshly ground black pepper
150 ml/¼ pint dry white wine
1 tablespoon tomato purée

1 Heat the oil in a large frying-pan over high heat. Brown the chops on both sides, frying in 2 batches if necessary.

2 With all the chops in the pan, lower the heat, put in onions and garlic, if using, and cover pan. Cook for about 10 minutes until the onions and garlic are soft and beginning to colour.

3 Add the tomatoes, peppers, coriander and salt and pepper to taste. Re-cover the pan and cook for a further 15 minutes or until the chops are tender.

4 Remove chops from pan and keep hot. Raise the heat and stir the wine into the pan. Cook rapidly, uncovered, until the liquid in the pan is reduced by half, stirring constantly.

5 Stir in the tomato purée and simmer, uncovered, for 5 minutes. Taste and adjust seasoning. ✳

6 Place the chops on a warmed serving platter, then spoon the sauce over them. Serve at once.

Roast lamb with courgette sauce

SERVES 4

½ shoulder lamb, weighing about
   1 kg/2 lb
1 clove garlic (optional), cut into
   thin slices
grated zest of ½ lemon
1½ teaspoons clear honey

SAUCE

25 g/1 oz margarine or butter
1 small onion, finely chopped
250 g/9 oz courgettes, grated
juice of ½ lemon
300 ml/½ pint chicken stock
1 teaspoon caster sugar
salt and freshly ground black pepper

1 Heat the oven to 200C/400F/Gas 6.
2 Place the lamb in a roasting tin, skin side up. Score the surface with a sharp knife to make a trellis pattern. Make a series of small slits within the trellis squares; press a garlic sliver, if using, into each.
3 Sprinkle the surface of the lamb with the lemon zest, then spread thinly with the honey.

4 Roast the lamb for about 1¼ hours (see Cook's tip), until the juices run clear when the thickest part of the meat is pierced with a sharp knife or skewer.
5 Meanwhile, make the sauce: melt the margarine in a frying-pan, add the onion and fry gently for about 5 minutes until soft and lightly coloured. Stir in the grated courgettes, and fry, stirring, for a further 2-3 minutes, then stir in the lemon juice and stock. Bring to the boil,

add the sugar and season to taste with salt and pepper. Remove from the heat and leave to cool slightly, then pour into a blender and work to a smooth purée. Reheat gently, if necessary, to serve.
6 Remove the lamb from the oven and transfer to a warmed serving platter. Carve a few slices and pour over a little of the sauce. Serve at once, with the remaining sauce handed separately in a warmed sauceboat.

Cook's Notes

TIME
Preparing the lamb and making the sauce takes 30 minutes. Roasting in the oven takes about 1¼ hours.

COOK'S TIP
The total cooking time for shoulder of lamb is calculated at 25 minutes per 500 g/1 lb, plus 25 minutes.

BUYING GUIDE
Choose the blade joint half of the shoulder: it is meatier than the knuckle.

PRESSURE COOKING
Make sure the joint fits comfortably in the cooker and that there is enough headroom. Pre-brown the lamb in hot fat, then drain. Put the trivet into the base of the cooker, place the lamb on it and pour in 300 ml/½ pint stock. Cook at high (H) pressure for 24 minutes. Release pressure quickly. Crisp the lamb in a 200C/400F/Gas 6 oven for 10-12 minutes, while making the sauce.

● 470 calories/1975 kj per portion

Egg and almond lamb

SERVES 4

500 g/1 lb boneless lean lamb,
   minced (see Economy)
50 g/2 oz crustless bread
300 ml/½ pint milk
15 g/½ oz lard or dripping
1 large onion, finely chopped
2 teaspoons curry powder
2 teaspoons sugar
2 teaspoons lemon juice
50 g/2 oz sultanas
½ teaspoon salt
2 eggs, beaten
25 g/1 oz flaked almonds

1 Heat the oven to 190C/375F/Gas 5.
2 Put the bread into a bowl and pour over the milk. Leave to soak.
3 Meanwhile, melt the lard in a large frying-pan, add the onion and fry gently until soft. Stir in the curry powder, sugar and lemon juice and cook for 1-2 minutes, stirring.
4 Squeeze the milk from the bread, reserving the milk. Beat the bread with a fork to break it up.
5 Add the meat and bread to the onion mixture and cook until the meat is well browned. Stir in the sultanas and salt; remove from heat.
6 Add a quarter of the beaten eggs to meat mixture and pour into a greased ovenproof dish. Level the surface, then bake for 30 minutes.
7 Meanwhile, beat the reserved milk into the remaining eggs.
8 Lower the oven heat to 180C/350F/Gas 4. Drain away fat from the lamb, then pour over the egg mixture. Scatter the almonds on top and cook for 30 minutes.

Cook's Notes

TIME
Preparation 30 minutes, cooking 1 hour.

ECONOMY
Shoulder of lamb is probably the most economical cut to use for this recipe, but you will have to trim it well before cooking or the finished dish may be too fatty. This recipe is also an excellent way to use up left-over lamb from the weekend joint. Mince or chop it finely, then follow the method above, omitting the initial 30 minutes baking.

 DID YOU KNOW
Almonds are one of the world's most popular nuts. They are often mentioned in the Old Testament and were known by the Romans as 'the Greek nut'. They were also eaten before meals in medieval times, in the belief this would prevent drunkenness.

SERVING IDEAS
As this is a substantial dish on its own, it needs nothing more than a seasonal vegetable or salad.

●620 calories/2600 kj per portion

Indian skewered lamb

SERVES 4

750 g/1½ lb lean lamb (preferably cut from the fillet or top end of the leg) cut into 2.5 cm/1 inch cubes, trimmed of excess fat

300 g/10 oz natural yoghurt

1 onion, finely grated

1 teaspoon ground ginger

2 tablespoons garam masala (see Buying guide)

½ teaspoon chilli powder

salt

1 large green pepper, deseeded and cut into 2.5 cm/1 inch squares

1 large red pepper, deseeded and cut into 2.5 cm/1 inch squares

24 button mushrooms, trimmed

vegetable oil, for greasing

1 In a large bowl, mix together the yoghurt, onion, ginger, garam masala, chilli powder and salt to taste. Add the cubes of lamb to the mixture, turning them over so that each piece is well-coated. Cover with cling film and leave to marinate in a cool place (not in the refrigerator) overnight.

2 Heat the oven to 190C/375F/Gas 5.

3 Remove the lamb from the marinade but do not wipe off the yoghurt coating. Thread the meat, the red and green peppers and mushrooms in turn on to 8 oiled kebab skewers.

4 Brush the inside of a large roasting tin with oil and place the skewers in it side-by-side (see Cook's tips). Brush the meat with a little oil, then cook in the oven for about 1 hour, until the meat is tender, turning the skewers and brushing them with more oil every 15 minutes. Transfer the skewers to a bed of plain boiled rice and serve at once, with the tasty juices from the roasting tin spooned carefully over the kebabs.

Lamb and asparagus casserole

SERVES 4

1.25 kg/2½ lb half shoulder of lamb, boned, excess fat removed, cut into 2.5 cm/1 inch cubes (see Buying guide)
1 tablespoon plain flour
1 tablespoon chopped fresh thyme, or 1 teaspoon dried thyme
salt and freshly ground black pepper
1 tablespoon vegetable oil
2 shallots, chopped
1 clove garlic, crushed (optional)
300 ml/½ pint water
75 ml/3 fl oz medium white wine
500 g/1 lb fresh or frozen asparagus (see Preparation)
100 g/4 oz mushrooms, sliced
2 tablespoons double cream and asparagus spears, to finish

1 Heat the oven to 170C/325F/Gas 3.
2 Put the flour in a large polythene bag, add half the thyme and salt and pepper to taste. Add lamb cubes and shake to coat well. Reserve any excess seasoned flour.
3 Heat the oil in a large flameproof casserole, add the lamb cubes and fry quickly over brisk heat to brown and seal on all sides. Remove from the pan with a slotted spoon and leave to drain thoroughly on absorbent paper.
4 Add the shallots to the casserole with the garlic, if using, and fry gently for 5 minutes until soft and lightly coloured. Sprinkle in any excess seasoned flour, stir in the water and wine and season to taste with salt and pepper. Bring to the boil, then return the lamb cubes to the casserole and stir in the remaining thyme.
5 Cover and cook in the oven for about 1½ hours.
6 Add the blanched asparagus and the mushrooms to the casserole and cook for a further 30 minutes, until the lamb is cooked through and tender when pierced with a sharp knife. Swirl over the cream, garnish with asparagus spears. Serve at once, straight from the casserole.

Cook's Notes

TIME
Preparation 30 minutes, cooking 2 hours.

PREPARATION
Fresh asparagus needs to be blanched: trim off woody bases of stems and cut stems into 5-7 cm/2-3 inch lengths. Simmer 5 minutes in salted water, drain. Add frozen asparagus straight to casserole.

FREEZING
Cook the casserole in a foil container, cool quickly, then seal, label and freeze for up to 3 months. To serve: defrost overnight in the refrigerator, then reheat in a 180C/350F/Gas 4 oven for 30-40 minutes until bubbling.

BUYING GUIDE
Half shoulder of lamb is an economical cut, very suitable for casseroles.
The asparagus season is short, so it is worth making the most of it while home-grown asparagus is least expensive. Choose thick-stemmed asparagus, usually sold in bundles, for this recipe: the less expensive, thin-stemmed sprue asparagus is unsuitable.

●590 calories/2450 kj per portion

Lamb ratatouille

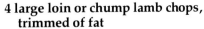

SERVES 4

4 large loin or chump lamb chops, trimmed of fat

3 tablespoons olive or corn oil

1 onion, roughly chopped

350 g/12 oz tomatoes, skinned and roughly chopped

1 aubergine, unskinned, cut into 2.5 cm/1 inch cubes

2 courgettes, cut into 2.5 cm/1 inch slices

1 green pepper, deseeded and chopped

1-2 garlic cloves, crushed with ½ teaspoon salt

1 teaspoon dried basil

salt and freshly ground black pepper

1 Heat the oil in a heavy-based deep saucepan, add the onion and fry gently for about 5 minutes until soft and lightly coloured.

2 Stir in the tomatoes, then the aubergine, the courgettes, green pepper, garlic and basil. Bring the mixture to the boil, then lower the heat, cover and simmer for about 30 minutes until the aubergine cubes are soft when pressed with a spoon. Stir the mixture frequently during this time.

3 Heat the grill to high.

4 Uncover the pan of ratatouille, increase the heat and boil rapidly until most of the liquid has evaporated. Taste and season with salt and pepper, then cover the pan again and keep the ratatouille warm on the lowest possible flame, stirring occasionally.

5 Lay the chops on the hot grill rack and grill for about 7 minutes on each side until browned and cooked through.

6 Spoon half the ratatouille into a warmed serving dish, arrange the chops in a single layer on top, then top each with a spoonful of the remaining ratatouille. Serve at once.

Cook's Notes

TIME
1 hour to prepare and cook the dish.

DID YOU KNOW
Ratatouille is best described as a French vegetable stew. Native to Provence in the south of France, it is made there with the best of the summer vegetables—aubergines, courgettes, peppers, tomatoes, onions and garlic.

SERVING IDEAS
Serve with spaghetti, pasta shells or spirals, or boiled or steamed rice.

FREEZING
Ratatouille freezes very successfully, and is a useful vegetable dish to keep in the freezer to serve with any roast or grilled meats. Transfer to a rigid container, cool quickly, then seal, label and store in the freezer for up to 3 months. To serve: reheat from frozen in a heavy-based saucepan, stirring frequently until bubbling. Take care not to overcook the vegetables or they will be mushy. Taste and adjust seasoning before serving.

●750 calories/3125 kj per portion

Lamb with plums

SERVES 4

1.25 kg/2½ lb best end neck of lamb in one piece, boned (see Buying guide)
500 g/1 lb dark cooking plums
15 g/½ oz margarine or butter
1 small onion, finely chopped
1 tablespoon chopped fresh parsley
2 teaspoons dried mixed herbs
75 g/3 oz wholemeal breadcrumbs
2 tablespoons hot chicken stock
salt and freshly ground black pepper

SAUCE

15 g/½ oz margarine or butter
1 small onion, finely chopped
2 teaspoons plain flour
300 ml/½ pint hot chicken stock
bouquet garni
4 tablespoons dry white wine
few drops of red food colouring (optional)

1 Heat the oven to 180C/350F/Gas 4.
2 Make a slit across the width of the thick end of the lamb, to make a pocket for the stuffing. Make the slit about 4 cm/1½ inches deep, but do not cut right through.
3 Reserve 2 whole plums for the garnish. Stone and chop the rest.
4 To make the stuffing: melt the margarine in a small frying-pan, add the onion and fry gently for 5 minutes until soft and lightly coloured.
5 Remove the pan from the heat and stir in the parsley, herbs, breadcrumbs and one-third of the chopped plums. Gradually add the stock and stir well. Season with salt and pepper to taste.
6 Place the lamb skin side down on a flat surface and spread the stuffing over it, and also push it into the slit. Roll the lamb and tie it with trussing thread or fine string in several places. Place the lamb in a roasting tin and roast in the oven for 45 minutes.
7 Turn the lamb over and roast for a further 45 minutes or until cooked to your liking. Meanwhile, make the sauce: melt the margarine in a small saucepan, add the onion and fry gently for 5 minutes until soft and lightly coloured. Sprinkle in the flour and stir over low heat for 1-2 minutes. Gradually stir in the stock, bring to the boil, then add the remaining chopped plums, the bouquet garni and salt and pepper to taste. Lower the heat, cover and simmer for 30 minutes, stirring occasionally.
8 Remove the bouquet garni from the sauce, then strain the sauce through a sieve, pressing hard with a wooden spoon to extract as much liquid as possible. Set the sauce aside. Halve, stone and slice the 2 remaining plums.
9 When the lamb is cooked, lift it out of the roasting tin and keep hot with any loose stuffing from the tin.
10 Pour off all the fat from the roasting tin and place the tin on top of the cooker. Pour in the wine and bring to the boil, scraping up all the sediment from the sides and bottom of the pan with a wooden spoon.
11 Stir in the sauce, lower the heat and simmer for 1 minute, then strain to remove any black specks if necessary. If liked, stir in food colouring to make the sauce pink. Taste and adjust seasoning. Keep hot.
12 Carve the lamb into 8 thick slices and arrange on a warmed serving platter. Spoon a little sauce over each slice. Garnish with the sliced plums. Serve at once with the remaining sauce handed separately.

Cook's Notes

 TIME
Preparation 35 minutes, cooking takes 1¾ hours.

BUYING GUIDE
Ask your butcher to bone the lamb for you.

● 560 calories/2350 kj per portion

Summer lamb

SERVES 4

½ leg of lamb, weighing about
   1 kg/2 lb (see Buying guide)
2 sprigs fresh rosemary
2 bay leaves
salt and freshly ground black pepper
25 g/1 oz dripping

TUNA MAYONNAISE

200 g/7 oz can tuna, drained and
   flaked
3 tablespoons thick bottled
   mayonnaise
150 g/5 oz natural yoghurt
2 teaspoons anchovy essence
grated zest of 1 lemon
1 tablespoon lemon juice

TO GARNISH

1 small red pepper, deseeded and
   cut into strips
12 black olives

1 Heat the oven to 190C/375F/Gas 5.
2 Place the lamb on a large sheet of foil, and tuck the sprigs of rosemary and the bay leaves into the meat. Sprinkle with salt and pepper and dot with the dripping. Wrap the foil around the meat and place in a roasting tin. Roast in the oven for 1¼ hours or until the meat is tender (the juices run clear when the meat is pierced with a skewer).
3 Remove from the oven and leave the meat to cool overnight in its wrappings (see Cook's tips).
4 Make the tuna mayonnaise: put the tuna in a blender with the mayonnaise, yoghurt, anchovy essence, lemon zest and juice. Blend until the mixture is smooth. Alternatively, if you do not have a blender, mash the ingredients with a fork until well combined.
5 Pour into a bowl, then taste and add salt and pepper if necessary.

Cover with cling film and refrigerate until ready to serve.
6 Plunge the strips of pepper into boiling water for 1 minute to blanch them, then drain and refresh under cold running water. Drain thoroughly.
7 Carve the cold lamb into thin slices. Lay the slices in a single layer on a serving dish and cover with the tuna mayonnaise (see Cook's tips). Arrange the strips of pepper in a lattice pattern over the mayonnaise and place the olives in the squares. Serve cold.

Cook's Notes

TIME
Cooking time for the lamb is 1¼ hours, but remember to allow it to cool overnight in a cold place.

Preparation of the tuna mayonnaise takes 10-15 minutes, and allow 10 minutes to finish.

COOK'S TIPS
You can use left-over lamb for this dish, but meat cooked and left to cool in the piece has a better flavour and is also moister.

If the slices of lamb will not fit in the dish in a single layer, make 2 layers and separate them with a layer of half the mayonnaise mixture.

If you have any tuna mayonnaise left over it will make a delicious snack or starter served the following day spooned over halved hard-boiled eggs or a bed of shredded lettuce.

BUYING GUIDE
The frozen lamb joints sold in supermarkets are ideal for this recipe. If you are using frozen lamb make sure the joint is thoroughly defrosted before cooking.

●565 calories/2350 kj per portion

Lamb bake

SERVES 4

500 g/1 lb cooked lamb, cut into
   small cubes
50 g/2 oz margarine or butter
1 tablespoon plain flour
½ teaspoon mustard powder
300 ml/½ pint canned beef
   consommé, undiluted
150 ml/¼ pint single cream
1 teaspoon Worcestershire sauce
2 hard-boiled eggs, quartered
100 g/4 oz mushrooms, sliced
salt and freshly ground black pepper
50 g/2 oz fresh wholemeal
   breadcrumbs
1 tablespoon chopped parsley

1 Heat the oven to 180C/350F/Gas 4.
2 Over low heat, gently melt half the margarine in a flameproof casserole. Stir in the flour and mustard, mix well, raise the heat and cook for about 1 minute, stirring constantly. Add the consommé and bring to the boil, stirring briskly. Continue to boil 2-3 minutes until sauce is cooked.
3 Lower the heat and add the cream, Worcestershire sauce, hard-boiled eggs, sliced mushrooms and the cooked lamb. Fold gently to mix, taking care not to break the eggs. Taste and adjust seasoning.
4 Melt the remaining margarine in a separate pan and mix with the breadcrumbs and parsley. Sprinkle on top of the casserole.
5 Bake uncovered in the heated oven for about 30 minutes until the casserole is golden on top, and the meat heated through. Serve at once.

Cook's Notes

TIME
15 minutes preparation, 30 minutes cooking.

ECONOMY
This is an excellent way of using up leftover roast lamb.

SERVING IDEAS
Serve with golden brown sauté potatoes (potatoes boiled until nearly cooked, then sliced and fried in hot oil), and a green vegetable.

VARIATIONS
Use 2-4 tablespoons red wine in place of some of the consommé for a richer flavour.
  For a sharper taste, use natural yoghurt in place of some or all of the single cream.

COOK'S TIP
To hard-boil eggs: put eggs in a pan, cover with cold water and bring to the boil. Simmer for 7-8 minutes only, then drain and immediately plunge into cold water. Remove shells and keep in cold water to prevent a black ring forming around yolks.

● 655 calories/2600 kj per portion

7 Cut a piece of foil nearly large enough to enclose the lamb. Line a roasting tin with the foil, then put the lamb, skin side up, in the tin. Season with salt and pepper and dust with flour. Pour the oil evenly over the surface of the lamb.

8 Bring the foil up closely around the sides of the lamb but do not cover the surface.

9 Roast the lamb in the oven for 2 hours, basting occasionally with the juices in the foil.

10 Increase oven heat to 200C/400F/ Gas 6, open out foil and cook for a further 30 minutes until the skin is crisp and browned and the meat is cooked through (the juices run clear when the lamb is pierced with a fine meat skewer).

11 Remove skewer and transfer lamb to a warmed carving dish. Return to oven turned to lowest setting for 10-15 minutes for meat to 'settle' so that it is easier to carve, then slice and serve.

Spinach-stuffed lamb

SERVES 8

1.5 kg/3-3½ lb shoulder of lamb, blade bone removed (see Buying guide)
plain flour, for dusting
3 tablespoons vegetable oil

SPINACH STUFFING
50 g/2 oz margarine or butter
1 onion, finely chopped
2 celery stalks, finely chopped
225 g/8 oz frozen chopped spinach
250 g/9 oz pork sausagemeat
1 egg, beaten
1 tablespoon finely chopped fresh mint, or 1 teaspoon dried mint
good pinch of freshly grated nutmeg
salt and freshly ground black pepper

1 Make the stuffing: melt the margarine in a saucepan, add the onion and celery and cook gently for about 5 minutes until the vegetables are soft and lightly coloured but not browned.

2 Meanwhile, cook the spinach in a separate pan for about 4 minutes, stirring occasionally. Drain through a fine sieve, pressing with the back of a spoon to remove as much liquid from it as possible.

3 Mix the spinach into the fried onion mixture and cook gently for 1 minute, stirring constantly.

4 Mash the sausagemeat in a bowl. Add spinach mixture and stir well. Stir in the egg, mint and nutmeg. Season well with salt and pepper and mix thoroughly. Cover and refrigerate for 30 minutes.

5 Meanwhile, heat the oven to 170C/325F/Gas 3.

6 With a sharp knife, carefully enlarge pocket left in the lamb by removal of the bone. Pack in prepared stuffing, pressing it down well. Draw edges of pocket together and secure with a meat skewer (see Cook's tip).

Cook's Notes

TIME
Preparing the stuffing takes about 20 minutes, but allow 30 minutes chilling. Preparing the lamb for roasting takes about 15 minutes; cooking 2½ hours; 10-15 minutes for the meat to settle before carving.

BUYING GUIDE
Order the lamb in advance and ask your butcher to remove the blade bone. When stuffed in this way, the shoulder should retain its shape.

COOK'S TIP
If the meat is firmly secured the stuffing should stay in place, but if a little does escape, use it as a garnish for the sliced lamb on the serving dish.

SERVING IDEAS
Serve with roast potatoes and buttered carrots to make an attractive colour contrast with that of the spinach stuffing.

● 395 calories/1650 kj per portion

POULTRY

Chicken in lychee sauce

SERVES 4

3 chicken breasts, each weighing 175 g/6 oz, skinned
3 tablespoons cornflour
3 tablespoons vegetable oil
1 onion, thinly sliced
1 chicken stock cube
2 tablespoons boiling water
2 tablespoons tomato ketchup
2 teaspoons soy sauce
312 g/11 oz can lychees, drained and quartered, with syrup reserved
2 large tomatoes, skinned and roughly chopped
2 tablespoons snipped chives or chopped spring onions
1-2 tablespoons lemon juice
freshly ground black pepper

1 Cut away any bones from the chicken with a sharp knife. Discard any fat. Cut the chicken into 1 cm/½ inch cubes.
2 Put the cornflour into a polythene bag then add the chicken cubes and shake until well coated.
3 Heat the oil in a large frying-pan, add the onion and fry gently for 5 minutes until soft and lightly coloured.
4 Raise the heat, add the chicken and fry for about 5 minutes, turning frequently until lightly browned all over. Remove the pan from the heat.
5 In a bowl, dissolve the stock cube in the boiling water. Stir in the tomato ketchup and soy sauce, then stir this mixture into the chicken together with the quartered lychees and reserved syrup, the tomatoes and half the chives. Mix well.
6 Return to the heat, bring to the boil, then simmer for 1 minute, stirring constantly. Cover with a lid or foil and simmer gently for a further 5 minutes, or until the chicken is tender and cooked through. Stir in lemon juice and pepper to taste, then transfer to a warmed serving dish. Sprinkle with remaining chives. Serve at once.

Cook's Notes

TIME
40 minutes to prepare and cook.

SERVING IDEAS
Serve with fresh peas and fried, fresh beansprouts or boiled Chinese noodles.

DID YOU KNOW
Lychees are a small fruit with a stone, of Chinese origin. When bought fresh, they have a hard, parchment-like skin which is reddish-brown in colour. The flesh is firm and slippery, with a slightly perfumed taste.

VARIATION
Use a diced pepper instead of tomatoes.

PRESSURE COOKING
Without coating in cornflour, pre-brown the chicken in the cooker, then add the rest of the ingredients, except for the lychees. Bring the pressure to high (H) and cook for 5 minutes. Reduce the pressure quickly, add the cornflour mixed with a little water, and simmer uncovered for 2 minutes. Add lychees, heat through, stir in lemon juice.

●325 calories/1350 kj per portion

Spanish stuffed chicken

SERVES 4-6

1.5 kg/3-3½ lb roasting chicken
vegetable oil, for brushing

STUFFING
25 g/1 oz margarine or butter
1 small onion, chopped
50 g/2 oz soft white breadcrumbs
25 g/1 oz blanched almonds, chopped
1 canned red pimiento, chopped
8 green olives, stoned and quartered
1 large tomato, skinned and chopped
½ teaspoon salt
freshly ground black pepper

1 Heat the oven to 180C/350F/Gas 4.
2 Make the stuffing: melt the margarine in a frying-pan, add the onion and fry gently for 5 minutes until soft and lightly coloured. Remove the pan from the heat.
3 Add the remaining stuffing ingredients to the pan and mix well.
4 Wash the chicken and pat dry with absorbent paper. Using a small sharp knife, remove the wishbone

from the neck end of the chicken by cutting away the flesh around it (see Cook's tip). Break off the bone at the joints and lift it out.
5 Fill the neck cavity with the stuffing, fold the neck skin back into position, then fold the wing tips over it. Secure with a metal skewer. Carefully truss the drumsticks with string, if necessary.

6 Lightly oil a roasting tin. Place the chicken in the tin, brush with oil and season with salt and pepper.
7 Roast the chicken in the oven for 1½ hours until cooked (the juices run clear when the thigh is pierced with a skewer). Remove skewer and any string and, if serving hot, transfer to a warmed serving dish (see Serving ideas).

Cook's Notes

TIME
Preparation, including making the stuffing, takes about 30 minutes. Cooking takes about 1½ hours.

SERVING IDEAS
Make a gravy to serve with the hot chicken: pour off most of the fat in the tin, leaving about 2 tablespoons of sediment. Stir in 2 teaspoons plain flour and cook over gentle heat for 1-2 minutes, stirring constantly. Gradually blend in 300 ml/½ pint hot chicken stock. Bring to the boil and cook for 2-3 minutes. Taste and adjust seasoning if necessary. Strain into a warmed sauceboat.

COOK'S TIP
Removing the wishbone makes carving easier: the chicken can be sliced right down through the stuffing.

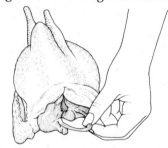

Cut away the flesh around the wishbone with a small sharp knife, then break at joints and remove.

●525 calories/2200 kj per portion

Chicken curry

SERVES 4

4 chicken joints, each weighing about 350 g/12 oz
25 g/1 oz margarine or butter
2 onions, chopped
1 clove garlic, crushed (optional)
1 tablespoon plain flour
1 tablespoon curry powder
3 tomatoes, skinned and roughly chopped
2 celery stalks, chopped
2 bananas, thickly sliced
1 dessert apple, roughly chopped
125 ml/4 fl oz chicken stock
salt and freshly ground black pepper
150 g/5 oz yoghurt or soured cream
1½ tablespoons toasted flaked almonds, to garnish

1 Melt the margarine in a large frying-pan and fry the chicken joints over moderate heat until browned on both sides. Remove from the pan with a slotted spoon and set aside.
2 Add the onions to the pan with the garlic, if using, and fry for 5 minutes until the onion is trans-lucent. Stir in the flour and curry powder and cook for 2-3 minutes, then stir in all the remaining ingredients except the salt, pepper and yoghurt.
3 Bring to the boil, stirring constantly, then return the chicken joints to the pan and season to taste with salt and pepper. Lower the heat, cover and cook gently for about 45 minutes or until the chicken is tender when pierced with a skewer (see Cook's tips).
4 Remove the chicken from the pan and keep hot on a serving plate. Boil the sauce until thick, then remove the pan from the heat and stir in the yoghurt.
5 Taste and adjust seasoning (see Cook's tips), pour over the chicken and sprinkle with the flaked almonds. Serve at once.

Cook's Notes

TIME
The curry takes 20 minutes preparation plus 45 minutes cooking.

SERVING IDEAS
Serve with rice, chapati, or poppadoms and pre-pare separate bowls of mango chutney and sliced onion or cucumber.

COOK'S TIPS
The flavour of the dish will improve if it is left overnight. If you intend to do this, reduce the cooking time by 10 minutes and ensure the meat is thoroughly heated before serving the next day. If, at the end of the cooking the flavour is too hot for your taste, add a little more yoghurt or cream.

FREEZING
Transfer to a rigid container, cool quickly, then seal, label and freeze for up to 3 months. To serve: defrost in refrigerator overnight, then reheat until the chicken is heated through and the sauce bubbling. Stir in a little chicken stock or water if the sauce is too thick. Continue from the beginning of stage 4.

●460 calories/1925 kj per portion

Rosé chicken

SERVES 4

 1.5 kg/3-3½ lb oven-ready chicken
salt and freshly ground black pepper
 25 g/1 oz margarine or butter
2 sprigs fresh tarragon, chopped, or
  1 teaspoon dried tarragon
 1 small onion, halved
150 ml/¼ pint rosé vermouth
2 good pinches sweet paprika
2 teaspoons tomato purée
1 tablespoon cornflour
4 tablespoons milk
150 ml/¼ pint chicken stock
1-2 teaspoons lemon juice,
  according to taste

1 Heat the oven to 190C/375F/Gas 5.
2 Pat the chicken dry with absorbent paper, then sprinkle inside and out with salt and pepper.
3 Place half the margarine inside the chicken with half the tarragon and the onion halves. Truss with thread or fine string.
4 Place the chicken in an ovenproof dish and spread with the remaining margarine. Sprinkle over the remaining tarragon, then pour the vermouth around the chicken.
5 Roast in the oven for 1¼ hours or until the chicken is tender and the juices run clear when the thickest part of the thigh is pierced with a skewer. Baste occasionally during the cooking time.
6 Remove the chicken from the dish and discard the trussing thread. Place the chicken on a warmed serving platter and keep hot in the lowest possible oven.
7 To make the sauce: pour the juices from the chicken into a saucepan. Stir in a pinch of paprika and the tomato purée. In a bowl, blend the cornflour to a paste with the milk, gradually stir in the chicken stock and add to the pan. Stir well to combine, bring to the boil, then simmer for 2 minutes, stirring constantly. Taste and adjust seasoning, then add lemon juice to taste, for a sharper flavour.
8 Pour a little of the sauce over the chicken and sprinkle with the remaining paprika. Serve at once, with the remaining sauce handed separately.

Cook's Notes

TIME
Preparation 10 minutes and cooking time 1¼ hours. Last-minute finishing touches, 10 minutes.

WATCHPOINT
Choose an ovenproof dish just large enough to take the chicken. The vermouth will evaporate too quickly if a large space is left around the bird.

FREEZING
Cut the chicken into portions, arrange in a freezer container and cover completely with the sauce. Cool quickly, then seal, label and freeze for up to 6 months. To serve: reheat from frozen in a 200C/400F/Gas 6 oven for about 1 hour, or until defrosted.

PRESSURE COOKING
Weigh the chicken and calculate exact cooking time at 7 minutes per 500 g/1 lb. Pre-brown the chicken, drain, then stand on the trivet, rim-side down. Pour vermouth and 300 ml/½ pint stock into base of cooker. Bring to high (H) pressure, then cook for calculated time. Release pressure quickly. Make the sauce using liquid in base of cooker.

●395 calories/1650 kj per portion

Crunchy chicken salad

SERVES 4

275 g/10 oz boneless cooked
   chicken
225 g/8 oz brown rice
600 ml/1 pint chicken stock
1 large red pepper, deseeded and
   finely chopped
1 bunch spring onions, chopped
100 g/4 oz frozen peas, cooked and
   cooled
50 g/2 oz carrot, grated
75 g/3 oz walnuts, roughly
   chopped
200 g/7 oz commercial mayonnaise
1 tablespoon tomato purée
generous pinch of sugar
1 tablespoon chopped parsley
   (optional)

DRESSING

2 tablespoons olive or salad oil
1 tablespoon lemon juice
2 teaspoons wine vinegar or dry
   white wine
pinch of mustard powder
salt and freshly ground black pepper

1 Cook the brown rice in the chicken stock for about 45 minutes or until tender. If necessary, top up the pan with boiling water during the latter part of the cooking time.

2 Meanwhile, make the dressing: combine all the ingredients in a screw-top jar and shake well to mix.

3 Drain any excess liquid from the rice, then mix in the red pepper, spring onions, peas and carrot.

4 While the rice is still warm, fork the dressing through the mixture. Cover the bowl with cling film and chill in the refrigerator for at least 1 hour.

5 When ready to serve, add the walnuts to the rice and mix thoroughly. Spoon into a serving dish and arrange the cooked chicken on top of the rice.

6 Mix the mayonnaise with the tomato purée and sugar. It should be the consistency of a coating sauce; if it is too thick, stir in a little hot water.

7 Carefully spoon the mayonnaise on top of the cooked chicken, then sprinkle the top with chopped parsley, if liked.

Cook's Notes

 TIME
The rice will take 45 minutes to cook and 1 hour to chill, during which time the other preparations can be completed.

 COOK'S TIP
Brown rice takes longer to cook than long-grain white rice, but has a lovely, nutty flavour. It will absorb the dressing better if you fork it through while the rice is still warm.

 ECONOMY
Cut down the cooking time for the rice by soaking it for 2 hours in cold water before cooking.

 VARIATIONS
Add finely chopped celery, green peppers, drained canned sweetcorn, chopped French beans or any other crisp vegetable to the salad.

● 865 calories/3600 kj per portion

Chicken paprikash

SERVES 4

 4 chicken pieces, skinned
15 g/½ oz margarine or butter
 500 g/1 lb onions, finely chopped
1 clove garlic, crushed (optional)
 1 tablespoon sweet paprika
salt and freshly ground black pepper
about 150 ml/¼ pint hot chicken
   stock
150 ml/¼ pint soured cream
snipped chives, to garnish

1 Heat the oven to 180C/350F/Gas 4.
2 Melt the margarine in a large, shallow flameproof casserole big enough to take the chicken pieces in a single layer (see Cook's tip). Add onions and garlic, if using, cover and fry gently for about 45 minutes until a soft, golden brown purée is formed.
3 Raise the heat slightly, then sprinkle in the paprika and salt and pepper to taste. Add the chicken and spoon over the onion mixture.
4 Cover the casserole and bake in the oven for 45 minutes or until the juices run clear when the thickest part of the chicken flesh is pierced with a skewer. Check the casserole contents regularly and add a little stock from time to time if the chicken appears to be becoming a little too dry.
5 Heat the soured cream in a pan; do not boil, or it will curdle. Pour over the chicken; sprinkle with chives and serve at once.

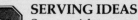

Chicken lasagne

SERVES 4

6 strips lasagne (see Buying guide)
salt

1 teaspoon vegetable oil
freshly ground black pepper
100 g/4 oz Cheddar cheese, grated
margarine, for greasing

CHICKEN SAUCE
3 tablespoons vegetable oil
1 large onion, sliced
100 g/4 oz streaky bacon, rinds
  removed and chopped
25 g/1 oz plain flour
300 ml/½ pint chicken stock
225 g/8 oz can tomatoes
250 g/9 oz boneless cooked chicken,
  chopped (see Buying guide)
1 tablespoon tomato purée

WHITE SAUCE
25 g/1 oz margarine or butter
25 g/1 oz plain flour
pinch of freshly grated nutmeg
300 ml/½ pint milk

1 Heat the oven to 180C/350F/Gas 4 and grease a shallow ovenproof dish. ✳

2 Make the chicken sauce: heat the oil in a frying-pan, add the onion and fry gently until soft and lightly coloured. Add the bacon and cook for 1 minute.

3 Sprinkle in the flour and cook for 1 minute, stirring, until straw-coloured. Remove from the heat and gradually stir in stock, tomatoes, chicken and tomato purée.

4 Return to the heat and bring to the boil, stirring constantly, then lower the heat and simmer for 3 minutes. Remove from the heat and set aside.

5 Bring a large pan of salted water to the boil and cook the lasagne with the oil for 10 minutes.

6 Meanwhile, make the white sauce: melt the margarine in a saucepan, sprinkle in the flour and nutmeg and stir over low heat for 2 minutes until straw-coloured. Remove from the heat and gradually stir in the milk, return to the heat again and simmer, stirring, until thick and smooth. Set aside.

7 Drain the lasagne and pat dry with absorbent paper.

8 Spread half the chicken sauce in the bottom of the greased ovenproof dish and sprinkle with salt and pepper. Place 3 strips of lasagne on top.

9 Spread the remaining chicken sauce over the lasagne, sprinkle with more salt and pepper and cover with a second layer of lasagne. Pour the white sauce over the lasagne and sprinkle with salt and pepper.

10 Sprinkle the grated cheese over the top of the white sauce, then bake in the oven for 1 hour until bubbling and golden. If the topping is not golden at the end of the cooking time, heat the grill to high and transfer the lasagne to the grill for 2-3 minutes to brown the cheese. Serve hot, straight from the dish.

Cook's Notes

TIME
Preparation 35 minutes, cooking 1 hour.

BUYING GUIDE
Lasagne varies in width, from one manufacturer to another—'strips' of lasagne are narrow; 'sheets' are wider.
For 250 g/9 oz boneless chicken, buy 2 large chicken breasts and cook, skin and bone them before using, or buy half a roasted chicken and simply remove the meat.

FREEZING
Do not pre-cook the lasagne strips. Arrange them over the chicken sauce in layers as in stage 8. Cook the lasagne in a foil freezer container, cool quickly, then seal, label and freeze. Store for up to 1 month. To serve: reheat from frozen, uncovered, in the foil container in a 200C/400F/Gas 6 oven for 1¼ hours until bubbling.

● 655 calories/2750 kj per portion

Chicken polka pie

SERVES 4

350 g/12 oz boneless cooked chicken, cut into bite-sized pieces (see Buying guide)

1 kg/2 lb potatoes

salt

100 g/4 oz frozen mixed vegetables with sweetcorn

300 ml/½ pint packet parsley sauce mix

300 ml/½ pint milk

1 teaspoon Worcestershire sauce

pinch of freshly grated nutmeg

freshly ground black pepper

3 hard-boiled eggs, chopped (see Freezing)

40 g/1½ oz margarine or butter

75 g/3 oz Cheddar cheese, grated

25 g/1 oz flaked almonds (optional)

1 Cook the potatoes in boiling salted water for about 15 minutes until tender but still firm. At the same time, cook the frozen vegetables according to packet directions.

2 While the potatoes and vegetables are cooking, make up the parsley sauce with the milk according to packet directions. Stir in the Worcestershire sauce, nutmeg and salt and pepper to taste.

3 Drain the frozen vegetables and fold into the sauce with the chicken and hard-boiled eggs. Simmer over very gentle heat until the chicken is thoroughly heated through, stirring occasionally.

4 Meanwhile, drain the potatoes and, when cool enough to handle, slice thickly. Grease a shallow flameproof dish ✳ with 15 g/½ oz margarine. Heat the grill to high.

5 Pour the chicken mixture into the dish and level the surface. Place the potato slices on top, overlapping them so that they cover the chicken mixture completely. Dot with the remaining margarine and sprinkle with the cheese.

6 Place under the heated grill for 7-10 minutes until crisp and golden brown. Sprinkle the flaked almonds over the top, if using, and replace under the grill until the almonds are lightly toasted. ⚠ Serve at once, straight from the dish.

Cook's Notes

TIME
Preparation and cooking about 1 hour; grilling, 7-10 minutes.

FREEZING
If freezing this dish, leave out the hard-boiled eggs because they become rubbery in the freezer. Make the pie up to the end of stage 6 in a freezerproof casserole dish instead of the flameproof dish. Leave until cold, then seal, label and freeze for up to 6 months. To serve: cook from frozen, uncovered, in a 200C/400F/Gas 6 oven for about 1 hour or until heated through and golden brown.

SERVING IDEAS
As the dish already contains potatoes and vegetables, serve with a contrasting, crisp salad of lettuce and watercress. Sliced tomatoes can be used as a garnish in place of the almonds.

VARIATION
Use cheese or onion sauce mix instead of parsley.

COOK'S TIP
For an even quicker dish to prepare use canned new potatoes for the topping. Drain them well.

WATCHPOINT
Keep a strict eye on the dish at this stage, the almonds can easily burn and spoil the flavour.

BUYING GUIDE
Left-over cooked chicken can be used for this dish, but if you are buying ready-cooked chicken pieces, you will need 3 with a total weight of about 600 g/1¼ lb in order to have 350 g/12 oz meat when all the skin and bones have been removed.

●620 calories/2600 kj per portion

Turkey parcels

SERVES 4

8 turkey escalopes (see Buying guide)
175 g/6 oz dried apricots, soaked overnight and drained
50 g/2 oz ground almonds
50 g/2 oz margarine or butter
8 tablespoons dry white wine
salt and freshly ground black pepper
watercress, to garnish
margarine, for greasing

1 Heat the oven to 190C/375F/Gas 5. Cut 8 pieces of foil, large enough to enclose the turkey escalopes, and then lightly grease them with margarine.
2 Roughly chop two-thirds of the apricots and mix in a bowl with the ground almonds. Spread equal portions of this mixture on one half of each escalope and then fold the other half over to make a sandwich.
3 Place each stuffed escalope on a piece of greased foil. Fold up the sides of the foil without sealing, put a knob of margarine on each escalope and then pour 1 tablespoon wine over each. Season well with salt and pepper and loosely fold the foil to enclose the stuffed escalope.

Seal and place the parcels on a baking sheet and cook in the oven for about 30 minutes.
4 To serve the escalopes: remove the foil and transfer the meat to a warmed serving platter, pour over the juices, then garnish with the remaining apricot halves and top with the watercress.

Cook's Notes

TIME
Allow 30 minutes for preparation and 30 minutes for cooking.

VARIATIONS
Use pork escalopes or chicken breasts instead of the turkey. Replace the dried apricots with 8 tablespoons of thick apple purée flavoured with grated nutmeg, or use 1½ tablespoons of natural yoghurt in each parcel instead of the margarine and wine.

SERVING IDEAS
Serve with croquette potatoes, French beans or a crisp fennel and courgette salad.

BUYING GUIDE
Turkey escalopes, thin slices of meat cut from the breasts, are available in packets at large supermarkets. You will need 2 escalope parcels per person.

●420 calories/1775 kj per portion

Creamy almond turkey

SERVES 4

500 g/1 lb turkey fillets
25 g/1 oz butter
2 teaspoons plain flour
300 ml/½ pint chicken stock
2 teaspoons tomato purée
25 g/1 oz ground almonds
salt and freshly ground black pepper
25 g/1 oz flaked almonds
100 ml/3½ fl oz single cream

1 Heat the oven to 180C/350F/Gas 4.
2 Melt the butter in a shallow flameproof casserole. Add the turkey fillets and fry over moderate heat for 2-3 minutes on each side until lightly coloured. Remove from the casserole with a slotted spoon and reserve.
3 Sprinkle the flour into the hot butter in the casserole and stir over low heat for 1-2 minutes until straw-coloured. Gradually stir in the chicken stock, then simmer, stirring, until thick and smooth.
4 Stir in the tomato purée and ground almonds and mix well. Season to taste with salt and pepper. Return the turkey fillets to the casserole. Cover and bake in the oven for 30 minutes.
5 Meanwhile, brown the flaked almonds: put them into a heated, ungreased, frying-pan and shake the pan over the heat until the almonds are light brown all over.
6 Add the cream to the cooked turkey and stir it into the sauce. Sprinkle over the browned almonds and serve at once.

Cook's Notes

 TIME
Preparation takes 20 minutes. Cooking in the oven takes about 30 minutes.

 VARIATION
Chicken breast may be used instead of turkey.

 WATCHPOINT
Watch the almonds carefully as they can burn.

 SERVING IDEAS
For a pretty colour contrast with the pink sauce, serve with green pasta and spinach or broccoli.

●285 calories/1195 kj per portion

136

Macaroni turkey

SERVES 4

750 g/1½ lb boneless turkey meat, cut into 2.5 cm/1 inch cubes (see Buying guide)
1 tablespoon vegetable oil
50 g/2 oz margarine or butter
1 large onion, chopped
2 celery stalks, chopped
2 teaspoons plain flour
300 g/10 oz can condensed cream of chicken soup
300 ml/½ pint chicken stock
salt and freshly ground black pepper
2 teaspoons French mustard
175 g/6 oz wholewheat macaroni
250 g/9 oz mushrooms, sliced
2 tablespoons chopped parsley
50 g/2 oz fresh white breadcrumbs
tomato slices, to garnish

1 Heat oil and half the margarine in a large frying-pan. Add the onion and celery and fry gently for 1-2 minutes. Add the turkey and fry briskly for a further 3-4 minutes, stirring often, to brown on all sides.
2 Sprinkle the flour into the frying-pan and stir over low heat for 1-2 minutes. Remove from the heat and stir in the soup and the chicken stock. Return to heat and bring to the boil, stirring. Season to taste. Lower the heat, add the mustard and simmer for 20 minutes.
3 Heat the oven to 200C/400F/Gas 6.
4 Meanwhile, bring a large pan of salted water to the boil and cook the macaroni for 10 minutes. Drain well. Melt the remaining margarine in the rinsed-out pan, add the macaroni and stir it well to coat thoroughly.
5 Spoon the macaroni over the base of a large ovenproof dish.
6 Stir the sliced mushrooms into

the turkey mixture and spoon over macaroni. Sprinkle with the parsley and breadcrumbs and bake for 20 minutes. Serve hot, straight from the dish, garnished with tomato slices.

Turkey in breadcrumbs

SERVES 4

4 turkey fillets, each weighing about 100 g/4 oz, thoroughly defrosted if frozen
15 g/½ oz plain flour
salt and freshly ground black pepper
75 g/3 oz fresh white breadcrumbs
2 eggs
vegetable oil, for frying
tomato wedges and parsley sprigs, to garnish

SAUCE
15 g/½ oz butter
2 tomatoes, skinned and chopped
225 g/8 oz frozen sweetcorn (see Cook's tip)
2 tablespoons double cream

1 Place the turkey fillets between 2 large sheets of greaseproof paper and beat with a rolling pin or mallet until they are very thin and twice their original size.

2 Heat the oven to 110C/225F/Gas ¼.
3 Spread the flour out on a flat plate and season with salt and pepper. Spread the breadcrumbs out on a separate flat plate. Beat the eggs in a shallow dish.
4 Dip the turkey escalopes in flour, then in beaten egg, and then in breadcrumbs, to coat evenly.
5 Pour oil into a large frying-pan to a depth of about 5 mm/¼ inch. Heat the oil, add 2 turkey escalopes and fry over brisk heat for about 3 minutes on each side, until golden brown and crisp.
6 Drain the escalopes on both sides on absorbent paper. Transfer to a warmed serving dish and keep warm in the oven while frying the remaining escalopes in same way.
7 While the last 2 escalopes are cooking, make the sauce: melt the butter in a small saucepan, add the tomatoes and cook for 1-2 minutes until very soft. Stir in the sweetcorn and cook for 3 minutes, then stir in the cream and heat through gently. Season with salt and pepper.
8 Drain the last 2 turkey escalopes on both sides on absorbent paper

and transfer to the serving dish. Garnish with tomato wedges and parsley sprigs and serve at once, with the sauce handed separately in a warmed sauceboat.

Cook's Notes

TIME
Preparation takes about 25 minutes. Cooking, including making the sauce, takes 15 minutes.

SERVING IDEAS
Serve with sauté potatoes and peas cooked in the French way with tiny onions, shredded lettuce and diced bacon.

COOK'S TIP
The sweetcorn does not need to be defrosted: just stir into the pan and heat thoroughly without overcooking, as this will toughen it.

●435 calories/1825 kj per portion

Farmhouse turkey and ham pie

SERVES 4

400 g/13 oz frozen puff pastry,
    defrosted
350 g/12 oz cooked turkey, chopped
250 g/9 oz cooked ham, chopped
2 hard-boiled eggs, quartered
a little beaten egg, to glaze

SAUCE
25 g/1 oz margarine or butter
25 g/1 oz plain flour
300 ml/½ pint milk
finely grated zest and juice of
    ½ lemon
1 tablespoon chopped fresh parsley
salt and freshly ground black pepper

1 Heat the oven to 220C/425F/Gas 7.
2 Roll out the pastry on a lightly floured surface to a shape slightly larger than the circumference of an 850 ml/1½ pint pie dish. Cut off a long narrow strip all round edge. Reserve with other trimmings.
3 Mix the turkey and ham together in the pie dish and arrange the quartered eggs on top.
4 Make the sauce: melt the margarine in a small saucepan, sprinkle in the flour and stir over low heat for 1-2 minutes until straw-coloured. Remove from the heat and gradually stir in the milk. Return to the heat and simmer, stirring, until it is thick and smooth.
5 Remove from the heat and stir in the lemon zest and juice, and the parsley. Season to taste with salt and pepper and allow to cool. Pour evenly over the turkey and ham in the pie dish.
6 Brush the rim of the pie dish with water, and then press the narrow strip of pastry all around the rim. Brush the strip with a little more water, then place the large piece of pastry on top. Trim the edge of the pastry, then knock up and flute.
7 Make leaves with the pastry trimmings, brush the undersides with water and place on top of the pie. Brush with beaten egg and make a small hole in the centre of the pastry lid.
8 Bake in the oven for 25-30 minutes until the pastry is well risen and golden brown. Serve hot or cold.

Cook's Notes

TIME
Preparation takes about 20 minutes, baking in the oven 25-30 minutes.

SPECIAL OCCASION
Add 1 tablespoon dry white wine instead of the lemon juice to the sauce.

FREEZING
Omit the hard-boiled eggs in stage 3, then prepare the pie to stage 7, but do not brush with beaten egg. Open freeze until solid, then wrap in a polythene bag. Seal, label and return to the freezer for up to 2 months. To serve: remove from bag, defrost overnight in the refrigerator, then brush with beaten egg and make a hole in the lid. Bake in a 220C/425F/Gas 7 oven for 30 minutes.

SERVING IDEAS
A green salad is the best accompaniment to the turkey and ham pie.

● 825 calories/3450 kj per portion

Stuffed turkey drumsticks

SERVES 4

4 turkey drumsticks, unskinned
100 g/4 oz streaky bacon rashers, rinds removed, chopped
1 onion, finely chopped
1 red pepper, deseeded and finely chopped
50 g/2 oz button mushrooms, finely chopped
50 g/2 oz fresh white breadcrumbs
3 tablespoons finely chopped fresh parsley
1 egg, beaten
salt and freshly ground black pepper
vegetable oil, for brushing

1 Heat the oven to 180C/350F/Gas 4.
2 Bone the drumsticks: with a sharp knife cut through the tendons at each end of the bone, then starting at the thigh end work the flesh down towards the knuckle and ease the flesh over the narrow end, to expose the bone.
3 Place the blade of the knife across the bone at the knuckle. Bang the knife sharply with a rolling pin to cut through the bone, so that only a small piece is left inside the flesh.!
4 Put the bacon in a frying-pan and fry over gentle heat until the fat runs (see Cook's tips). Add the onion and red pepper and fry gently for 5 minutes until softened. Stir in the mushrooms and cook for 2 minutes.
5 Put the fried bacon and vegetables in a bowl and combine with the breadcrumbs, parsley and egg, stirring well to mix. Season with salt and pepper.
6 Allow the stuffing mixture to cool, then pack it into the drumsticks. Secure the ends with wooden cocktail sticks and place drumsticks in a small roasting tin. Brush with oil and sprinkle with salt (see Cook's tips).
7 Bake in the oven for 45-50 minutes, until golden. Remove the cocktail sticks and serve hot or cold.

Cook's Notes

 TIME
Preparation, including boning the drumsticks, making the stuffing and stuffing the drumsticks takes about 1 hour. Cooking in the oven takes about 50 minutes.

 FREEZING
Cool quickly, open freeze until solid, then pack in a polythene bag. Seal, label and return to the freezer for up to 6 months. To serve: defrost at room temperature for 3-4 hours, then serve cold (the drumsticks tend to go dry if reheated after freezing).

WATCHPOINT
During the boning process be careful not to split the skin.

COOK'S TIPS
The bacon cooks in its own fat: no extra fat or oil for frying is needed.
Sprinkling with salt makes the skin deliciously crisp.

●275 calories/1155 kj per portion

Roast duck with grapes

SERVES 4

1 duck, weighing 2-2.25 kg/4½-5 lb, giblets reserved
salt
1 small onion, quartered
bouquet garni
freshly ground black pepper
425 ml/¾ pint water
grapes and watercress, to garnish

SAUCE
1 onion, very finely chopped
25 g/1 oz plain flour
300 ml/½ pint duck giblet stock
150 ml/¼ pint dry white wine
50-75 g/2-3 oz each green and black grapes, quartered and deseeded
2 tablespoons double cream

1 Heat the oven to 180C/350F/Gas 4.
2 Pat the duck dry inside and out with absorbent paper. Prick the skin all over and sprinkle with salt.
3 Weigh the duck and calculate the roasting time at 30 minutes per 500 g/1 lb. Place the duck breast side up, on a grill rack or trivet in a roasting tin. Roast, without basting, in the oven for the calculated cooking time, until the skin is brown and crisp, and the juices run clear when thigh is pierced with a fine skewer.

4 Meanwhile, rinse the giblets in cold water and place in a saucepan together with the quartered onion and bouquet garni. Season with salt and pepper and cover with the water. Bring to the boil, then lower heat and simmer gently for 1 hour. Strain and set aside.
5 Drain the cooked duck well, saving 2 tablespoons dripping (see Economy). Place the duck on a warmed serving dish and keep hot in the oven turned down to 110C/225F/Gas ¼, while making sauce.
6 Pour the 2 tablespoons of hot duck dripping into a small saucepan. Add the chopped onion, cover the pan and cook gently for 10 minutes, shaking the pan from time to time until the onion is soft and golden brown. Sprinkle in the flour and stir over low heat for 1-2 minutes, then gradually stir in 300 ml/½ pint of the strained giblet stock and the wine. Bring to the boil, and simmer for 2 minutes, stirring, until thickened.
7 Add the grapes and heat through gently for a further 2 minutes. Remove from the heat and stir in the cream. Pour into a warmed bowl or sauceboat and hand separately with the roast duck (see Cook's tip), garnished with grapes and watercress.

Cook's Notes

 TIME
Preparation takes about 25 minutes, cooking 2¼-2½ hours, including roasting the duck, preparing the stock and making the sauce.

 SERVING IDEAS
This makes a perfect Christmas dinner for 4 people and a more suitable alternative to turkey, which is best for serving larger numbers.

 COOK'S TIP
For easier serving, cut the duck in half lengthways, using sharp kitchen scissors to cut down the breastbone and along backbone. Then cut each half into 2 even portions.
Arrange the 4 portions on a warmed serving dish.

 ECONOMY
Strain the remaining dripping from the duck into a bowl. Cover and keep in the refrigerator for roasting potatoes. Duck dripping can also be used for roasting parsnips.

●490 calories/2060 kj per portion

Honey duck salad

SERVES 4

2 kg/4½ lb duck, defrosted if
   frozen
salt
2 tablespoons clear honey
1 tablespoon hot water

SALAD GARNISH
2 heads chicory leaves, separated
1 bunch watercress, divided into
   small sprigs
2 oranges, divided into segments

DRESSING
4 tablespoons vegetable oil
1 tablespoon tarragon vinegar
1 tablespoon fresh orange juice
pinch of sugar
½ teaspoon French mustard
salt and freshly ground black pepper

1 Heat the oven to 180C/350F/Gas 4.
2 Pat the duck dry inside and out
with absorbent paper. Prick the skin
all over with a fork and sprinkle
evenly with salt.
3 Place the duck breast side up, on
a rack in a roasting tin. Roast in the
oven for 1 hour, then drain off the
fat from the tin. Blend the honey
with the hot water and brush the
duck all over with the mixture.
4 Return the honey duck to the
oven and roast for a further 1¼
hours, basting 2-3 times to glaze
and brown. Drain the duck over the
tin, transfer to a plate and leave
until completely cold (3-4 hours).
5 Divide the duck into 4 (see Preparation). Arrange on a serving dish.
Garnish with chicory leaves, watercress sprigs and orange segments.
6 Place ingredients for dressing
in a screw-top jar, with salt and
pepper to taste, and shake well
together. Sprinkle over the salad
just before serving.

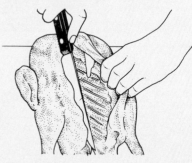

Duck 'n' beans

SERVES 4

4 duck pieces, each weighing about 400 g/14 oz, defrosted if frozen (see Buying guide)
salt and freshly ground black pepper
1 onion, chopped
1 clove garlic, crushed (optional)
425 ml/¾ pint chicken stock
1 tablespoon medium sherry
425 g/15 oz can baked beans in tomato sauce
1 tablespoon tomato ketchup
175 g/6 oz spicy garlic sausage, chopped
1 teaspoon dried thyme
1 bay leaf

TOPPING

4 tablespoons chopped fresh parsley
100 g/4 oz fresh white breadcrumbs

1 Heat the oven to 190C/375F/Gas 5.
2 Prick the duck pieces all over with a fork, season with salt and pepper and place on a rack in a roasting tin. Roast for 1¼ hours, until the duck pieces are cooked through (the juices run clear when the meat is pierced with a fine skewer). Remove the duck pieces from the tin, drain on absorbent paper and place in a large casserole. Turn the oven down to 180C/350F/Gas 4.
3 Drain off all but 1 tablespoon fat from the tin and transfer the tin to the top of the cooker. Add the onion and garlic, if using, and fry gently for 2 minutes.
4 Gradually stir in the stock and sherry and bring to the boil, stirring constantly. Stir in the baked beans in their sauce, the tomato ketchup, garlic sausage, thyme and bay leaf. Season to taste with salt and freshly ground black pepper.
5 Pour the mixture over the duck pieces in the casserole. Cover and cook the casserole in the oven for about 30 minutes.

Cook's Notes

TIME
Preparation takes about 20 minutes, cooking about 2¼ hours.

BUYING GUIDE
Duck pieces, consisting of the breast and wing, are available from high-quality butchers, large supermarkets and freezer centres.

SERVING IDEAS
Serve with jacket-baked potatoes and a salad.

●840 calories/3525 kj per portion

6 Increase the oven heat to 220C/425F/Gas 7. Mix the parsley and breadcrumbs together and sprinkle evenly over the surface of the casserole. Return to the oven and cook for a further 15 minutes, uncovered, to brown the topping. Serve hot.

FISH AND SEAFOOD

Spiced fried herrings

SERVES 4

8 herrings, each weighing about
    100 g/4 oz, heads removed,
    cleaned, boned and roes reserved
    (optional)
1 egg yolk
1 tablespoon milk
3 tablespoons plain flour
½ teaspoon sweet paprika
salt and freshly ground black pepper
vegetable oil, for frying
lemon and lime wedges and
    coriander or parsley sprigs, to
    garnish

SPICE MIXTURE
3 tablespoons finely chopped fresh
    coriander or parsley
2 tablespoons olive or sunflower
    oil
1 tablespoon ground cumin
1 teaspoon sweet paprika
½ teaspoon cayenne
½ teaspoon ground cinnamon
¼ teaspoon salt

1 Heat the oven to 110C/225F/Gas ¼.
2 Combine all ingredients for the
spice mixture in a small bowl and
mix well together. Open out the
herrings and lay them flat, skin side
down, on a board or work surface.
Spread with spice mixture, then
close the herrings up, cover and set
aside in a cool place for 3 hours.
3 Beat the egg yolk with the milk in
a small bowl. Spread the flour out
on a large flat plate and season with
the paprika and salt and pepper to
taste. Brush the herrings with the
egg yolk mixture, then turn in the
flour to coat evenly. Shake off the
excess flour and reserve for the
herring roes, if using.
4 Heat enough oil in a large frying-
pan just to cover the base. Add 4 of
the herrings and fry over moderate
heat for 4-5 minutes on each side
until cooked through (the flesh
should be opaque). Using a fish
slice, transfer the cooked herrings

to a warmed serving dish and keep
warm in the oven. Heat a little more
oil in the pan, add the remaining
herrings and fry in the same way.
5 Turn the reserved roes, if using,
in the remaining flour to coat
evenly. Add to pan and fry for 2-3
minutes, turning once, until just
cooked Remove and drain on
absorbent paper.
6 Arrange the herrings with roes, if
using, on serving dish. Garnish
with lemon and lime wedges and
coriander or parsley sprigs.

Cook's Notes

TIME
Preparation takes about
30 minutes. Allow
3 hours standing. Cooking then
takes about 20-25 minutes.

SERVING IDEAS
Serve with salad and
rolls and butter.

●410 calories/1725 kj per portion

144

Breton steaks

SERVES 4

4 × 225 g/8 oz cod or hake steaks
salt and freshly ground black pepper
50 ml/2 fl oz sweet vermouth

SAUCE
75 g/3 oz butter
2 celery stalks, thinly sliced
2 small leeks, thinly sliced
1 small onion, thinly sliced
100 g/4 oz mushrooms,
   thinly sliced
40 g/1½ oz plain flour
150 ml/¼ pint milk

1 Heat the oven to 180C/350F/Gas 4.
2 Season the fish steaks well with salt and pepper. Arrange in the base of a casserole and pour over the vermouth. Cover and bake in the oven for 30 minutes until the fish is tender and the flesh flakes easily when pierced with a knife.
3 Meanwhile, make the sauce: melt

Cook's Notes

TIME
This dish takes 1 hour to prepare and cook.

SERVING IDEAS
Serve with boiled new potatoes and broccoli or mange-tout peas, and chilled white wine. Traditionally these fish steaks are garnished with small crescents of flaky pastry known as *fleurons*. To make *fleurons*: cut out crescent shapes of puff pastry, using a metal cutter, and put them on a baking sheet. At stage 4 remove fish steaks from the oven and keep warm. Increase heat to 200C/400F/Gas 6 and bake the *fleurons* for 10 minutes.

DID YOU KNOW
In French cookery the term *à la bretonne*, when applied to fish, indicates that the dish is served with a sauce made with leeks, onions, celery and mushrooms.

●405 calories/1700 kj per portion

half the butter in a large frying-pan, add the celery, leeks, onion and mushrooms and fry gently for 5-6 minutes until soft. Set aside.
4 Using a fish slice, transfer the fish steaks to a warmed serving dish and keep warm in the oven turned to its lowest setting. Reserve the fish cooking juices.
5 In a small pan, melt remaining butter, sprinkle in the flour and stir over low heat for 1-2 minutes until it is light straw-coloured. Remove from the heat and gradually stir in the milk and the fish juices. Return to the heat and simmer, stirring, until thick and smooth.
6 Stir in the vegetables and heat through gently for about 5 minutes. Pour the sauce over the fish steaks and serve the dish at once, while still piping hot (see Serving ideas).

Peanut plaice

 SERVES 4

8 plaice fillets, each weighing about 75 g/3 oz, skinned
1 large egg
2 tablespoons single cream or top of the milk
2 teaspoons lemon juice
salt and freshly ground black pepper
40 g/1½ oz toasted breadcrumbs. (see Preparation)
100 g/4 oz peanuts, finely chopped (see Cook's tip)
1 tablespoon vegetable oil
25 g/1 oz margarine or butter
lemon wedges, to serve

1 Put the egg, cream and lemon juice in a shallow bowl with salt and pepper to taste. Beat well to mix.
2 Mix the breadcrumbs and peanuts together on a plate.

3 Dip the fillets one by one into the egg mixture, lift by the tail to drain off the surplus egg, then coat in the breadcrumb and peanut mixture. Press the crumbs into the fish and make sure each fillet is well coated on both sides.
4 Heat the oil and margarine together in a large frying-pan until the mixture is foaming. Fry the fish, in 2 batches if necessary, for 4-5 minutes on each side until light golden in colour. Keep hot on absorbent paper until all are cooked, then serve at once with wedges of lemon.

Cook's Notes

TIME
Preparation takes 20-25 minutes, cooking 10 minutes.

COOK'S TIP
Use ordinary raw peanuts, not the roasted or salted varieties, for this recipe. You can leave the skins on or remove them, before chopping, by rubbing them between your fingers. The peanuts can be chopped in a coffee grinder, blender or food processor, but do not chop too finely or the coating will not be crunchy.

 PREPARATION
To make 40 g/1½ oz toasted breadcrumbs, toast 4 thin slices of bread until golden on each side. Cut off the crusts, then work for a few seconds in a blender or food processor until reduced to crumbs.

●430 calories/1800 kj per portion

Halibut special

SERVES 4

4 × 175 g/6 oz halibut steaks,
  skinned (see Buying guide)
150 ml/¼ pint dry cider
1 tablespoon cornflour
1 tablespoon cold water
fresh thyme, to garnish

TOPPING
25 g/1 oz butter
1 onion, chopped
2 celery stalks, chopped
3 tomatoes, skinned and chopped
100 g/4 oz mushrooms, chopped
1 teaspoon chopped fresh thyme or
  ½ teaspoon dried thyme
salt and freshly ground black pepper

1 Heat the oven to 170C/325F/Gas 3.
2 Make the topping: melt the butter in a saucepan. Add the onion and fry gently for 5 minutes until soft and lightly coloured. Add celery, tomatoes and mushrooms and cook for 1 further minute, stirring once or twice. Add the thyme, season well with salt and pepper and set aside.
3 Arrange the halibut steaks in a single layer in a large shallow oven-proof dish. Spoon the vegetable mixture evenly over the halibut and pour around the cider. Cover the dish with foil and bake in the oven for about 40 minutes, until the halibut is cooked through and flakes easily when pierced with a sharp knife. Transfer the halibut steaks to a warmed serving dish.
4 Pour the cooking liquid into a small saucepan. Blend the cornflour with the water to make a smooth paste and stir into the liquid. Bring to the boil, stirring constantly. Taste and adjust the seasoning if necessary, then pour over the halibut. Garnish with thyme and serve the halibut at once (see Serving ideas).

Cook's Notes

TIME
Preparation takes about 15 minutes, cooking in the oven about 40 minutes.

SERVING IDEAS
Serve simply with minted garden peas and potatoes gratin dauphinois (sliced and baked with cheese).

BUYING GUIDE
Halibut has a delicious delicate flavour, but is a more expensive white fish than cod or haddock, which can be used instead. Some freezer centres sell economy packs of halibut (1.5 kg/3½-4½ lb).

●230 calories/975 kj per portion

Celery-stuffed trout

SERVES 4

 4 rainbow trout, each weighing 300-350 g/10-12 oz, cleaned with heads and tails left on
margarine, for greasing
celery leaves, to garnish

CELERY STUFFING
25 g/1 oz margarine or butter
1 tablespoon vegetable oil
1 small onion, finely chopped
2 large celery stalks, finely chopped
75 g/3 oz fresh wholemeal breadcrumbs
finely grated zest of 1 orange
finely grated zest of ½ lemon
1 teaspoon dried basil
1 teaspoon mustard powder
1 egg, beaten
2-3 tablespoons fresh orange juice
salt and freshly ground black pepper

1 Heat the oven to 190C/375F/Gas 5. Cut out and grease 4 foil squares each large enough to contain a whole rainbow trout.

2 Make celery stuffing: heat the margarine and oil in a saucepan, add the onion and fry gently for 5 minutes until soft and lightly coloured. Add celery and cook for a further 2-3 minutes, stirring the mixture once or twice.

3 Remove from the heat and stir in the breadcrumbs, orange and lemon zests, the basil and mustard. Stir in the egg and enough orange juice just to bind. Season to taste with salt and pepper.

4 Spoon the stuffing into the trout cavities, dividing it equally between them. Place each trout on a piece of greased foil and seal tightly to make neat parcels (see Cook's tips).

5 Place the parcels on a baking tray and cook in the oven for 25-30 minutes (see Cook's tips) until the fish is cooked through and the flesh flakes very easily when pierced with a sharp knife.

6 Open up the foil parcels and carefully transfer the trout to a warmed serving plate. Garnish with celery leaves and serve at once.

Cook's Notes

TIME
Preparation, including making the stuffing, takes 35 minutes. Cooking the trout in the oven takes about 25-30 minutes.

SERVING IDEAS
Top the fish with pats of herb butter if liked or garnish with thin orange and lemon slices or a sprinkling of herbs. Serve with potatoes boiled in their skins and oven-baked tomatoes.

COOK'S TIPS
The trout may be prepared in advance up to the end of stage 4, then refrigerated for up to 4 hours until ready to cook.
  To brown the fish: turn back the foil for last 10 minutes.

 VARIATION
Use fennel instead of celery and use the feathery leaves as a garnish.

● 505 calories/2125 kj per portion

148

Family fish pie

SERVES 4

500 g/1 lb cod fillets
425 ml/¾ pint milk

1 small onion, quartered
2 bay leaves
4 cloves
6 whole black peppercorns
1 kg/2 lb potatoes
salt
225 g/8 oz packet frozen mixed
  vegetables
65 g/2½ oz margarine or butter
75 ml/3 fl oz creamy milk
4 tablespoons snipped chives, or
  finely chopped spring onion tops
2 hard-boiled eggs, chopped
2 tablespoons chopped parsley
freshly ground black pepper
40 g/1½ oz plain flour
1 tablespoon tomato purée
3 tomatoes, sliced, to finish

1 Heat the oven to 180C/350F/Gas 4.
2 Put the fish in an ovenproof dish and cover with the milk. Add the onion quarters, bay leaves, cloves and peppercorns. Cover with grease-proof paper and bake in the oven for about 20 minutes until the fish flakes easily.
3 Meanwhile, cook the potatoes in boiling salted water for 20 minutes until tender. Cook the frozen vegetables as directed on the packet, then drain.
4 When the fish is cooked, remove it from the dish and strain the cooking liquid into a jug. Increase the oven heat to 190C/375F/Gas 5.
5 Drain the potatoes and mash with 25 g/1 oz margarine and the creamy milk. Beat in the chives.
6 Flake the fish into a bowl, removing any skin and bones. Stir in the mixed vegetables, the hard-boiled eggs and the parsley. Season well with salt and pepper. Put the mixture in a large saucepan.
7 Melt the remaining 40 g/1½ oz margarine gently in a separate saucepan and sprinkle in the flour. Stir over low heat for 2 minutes until straw-coloured, then remove from the heat and gradually stir in the reserved cooking liquid from the fish. Return to the heat, stir in the tomato purée and simmer, stirring

constantly until the sauce is thick and smooth.
8 Pour the sauce into the fish mixture and fold gently to mix over low heat until heated through. Taste and adjust seasoning.
9 Turn the fish mixture into a buttered ovenproof dish. Spoon the mashed potato evenly over the top,

level the surface and mark with a fork in a criss-cross pattern. ✳
10 Put the fish in the oven for 20-30 minutes until heated through. Arrange the sliced tomatoes on the top, then place the pie under a heated grill for 5 minutes, to brown the topping. Serve very hot, straight from the dish.

Cook's Notes

TIME
Preparing and cooking the fish and potatoes takes about 1 hour. Heating through the finished pie takes 20-30 minutes.

COOK'S TIP
This pie is a meal in itself, and is well worth the time it takes to prepare because you do not need to serve an accompanying vegetable with it.

ECONOMY
Any economical white fish, such as coley, may be used instead of cod.

SPECIAL OCCASION
Substitute a few frozen or canned prawns, or canned mussels, for the mixed vegetables and mash the potatoes with single cream.

FREEZING
Make the pie without hard-boiled eggs and freeze after stage 9. Freeze for up to 2 months. To serve: defrost overnight in the refrigerator, top with the tomatoes and give the pie slightly longer in the oven to heat through.

● 635 calories/2650 kj per portion

Salmon parcels

SERVES 4

4 x 175-225 g/6-8 oz salmon
  steaks, skinned and bones
  removed, defrosted if
  frozen (see Buying guide)
40 g/1½ oz butter, softened
1 tablespoon finely chopped fresh
  parsley
½ teaspoon chopped fresh thyme,
  or ¼ teaspoon dried thyme
pinch of sweet paprika
salt and freshly ground black pepper
400 g/13 oz frozen puff pastry,
  defrosted
4 teaspoons lemon juice
little beaten egg, to glaze
4 lemon slices sprinkled with
  paprika, to garnish

1 Heat the oven to 200C/400F/Gas 6.
2 Put the butter in a small bowl with parsley, thyme and paprika. Season well with salt and pepper and beat with a wooden spoon until the herbs and spices are thoroughly blended with the butter.
3 Divide the pastry into 4 equal pieces. Roll each piece out on a lightly floured board into a circle about 18 cm/7 inches in diameter, or large enough to enclose a salmon steak.
4 Spread each salmon steak with a quarter of prepared butter and place, buttered side up, on one-half of a pastry circle. Sprinkle the salmon steak with a little lemon juice and season lightly with salt and freshly ground black pepper.
5 Moisten edges of each pastry circle with water, then fold over to cover salmon and seal firmly to make neat parcels. Make diagonal cuts on top and decorate with pastry trimming, if wished.
6 Dampen a baking sheet and place the pastry parcels on it. Brush the parcels with beaten egg to glaze.
7 Bake just above centre of the oven for 20 minutes, then lower the heat to 180C/350F/Gas 4 and cook for a further 15 minutes or until the pastry is well risen and golden brown. Serve the salmon parcels hot or cold, garnished with lemon slices dusted with paprika (see Serving ideas).

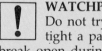

Cook's Notes

 TIME
Preparation and cooking take about 1 hour.

 BUYING GUIDE
Fresh salmon is at its best from May to July and many large supermarkets now sell trimmed steaks in their chilling cabinets. Frozen salmon steaks are available most of the year from large supermarkets and freezer centres.

! WATCHPOINT
Do not try to make too tight a parcel or it may break open during baking. But be sure to seal parcels firmly.

 SERVING IDEAS
Serve hot with new potatoes, garden peas and soured cream dressing.
  Serve cold with potato salad, sliced cucumber and lettuce salad and mayonnaise. Or, for picnics, wrap each parcel carefully in foil, then pack in a rigid container.

 VARIATION
Omit the seasoned butter and spread each salmon steak with 1 teaspoon of soured cream with chives before wrapping in pastry.

●865 calories/3625 kj per portion

Haddock thermidor

SERVES 6
750 g/1½ lb haddock steaks
½ bay leaf
1 small carrot, sliced
½ small onion, sliced
4 black peppercorns (optional)
salt
100 g/4 oz margarine or butter
50 g/2 oz plain flour
600 ml/1 pint milk
½ teaspoon mustard powder
pinch of cayenne pepper
250 g/9 oz mushrooms, sliced
2 tablespoons dry sherry (optional)
50 g/2 oz Parmesan cheese, grated
margarine or butter, for greasing
lemon slices, to garnish

1 Heat the oven to 220C/425F/Gas 7. Lightly grease an ovenproof baking dish.

2 Put the fish steaks in a wide shallow frying-pan in 1 layer, and scatter over the bay leaf, carrot, onion, peppercorns and salt. Add water to cover and bring to the boil. Lower the heat and cook gently until the fish flakes easily when tested with a fork, about 10 minutes. With a slotted spoon, remove the fish carefully and keep warm.

3 Meanwhile, make the sauce: melt 50 g/2 oz margarine in a small sauce-pan, sprinkle in the flour and stir over low heat for 1-2 minutes until straw-coloured. Remove from the heat and gradually stir in the milk. Return to the heat and simmer, stirring, until thick and smooth. Add the mustard powder, cayenne pepper and salt to taste. Remove from the heat.

4 Melt the remaining margarine in a frying-pan and fry the mushrooms for about 3 minutes, stirring. Mix into the sauce with the sherry, if using.

5 Cut the fish into bite-sized pieces and carefully combine with the sauce. ✳

6 Pour the fish and sauce into the greased baking dish, sprinkle the Parmesan over the top and bake in the oven for about 15 minutes until the top is golden brown and bubbling. Serve hot, straight from the dish, garnished with lemon.

Cook's Notes

TIME
Cooking the fish, preparing the sauce and cooking the mushrooms takes 20 minutes. Allow 15 minutes cooking time in the oven.

COOK'S TIP
This dish with its rich sauce may be prepared as much as 8 hours in advance, up to the end of stage 5. Allow to cool, cover with cling film and refrigerate. Bring back to room temperature before baking.

VARIATIONS
Instead of Parmesan cheese, use grated Gruyère or Emmental for a different flavour. Cod steaks may be substituted for haddock.

SERVING IDEAS
Serve in vol-au-vent shells or with mashed potatoes. Broccoli or spinach are colourful accompaniments.

FREEZING
Cool the fish and mush-room sauce mixture quickly, pack into a foil container, seal, label and freeze for up to 3 months. To serve: defrost at room temperature and reheat in a 180C/350F/Gas 4 oven for 30 minutes. Sprinkle over the cheese and bake as in stage 6. If you are serving the dish in frozen vol-au-vent shells, bake according to packet instructions.

●335 calories/1400 kj per portion

Herby fish kebabs

SERVES 4

 750 g/1½ lb boneless cod steaks, skinned
 2 tablespoons lemon juice
1 tablespoon vegetable oil
 1 teaspoon Worcestershire sauce
1 tablespoon chopped mixed fresh herbs, or 1 teaspoon dried basil
good pinch of fresh chopped dill or dried chopped dillweed
salt and freshly ground black pepper
1 large green pepper, deseeded
4 small tomatoes, halved
vegetable oil, for greasing

1 Cut the fish into 32 cubes and place on a large plate. In a bowl mix together the lemon juice, oil, Worcestershire sauce and herbs. Season well with salt and pepper and pour over the fish. Leave to stand for 5 minutes, turning the cubes of fish in the marinade from time to time.

2 Put the green pepper in a bowl and cover with boiling water. Leave to stand for 5 minutes. Drain well, then cut into chunky pieces big enough to thread on to skewers.

3 Heat the grill to moderate. Slide alternate pieces of fish and green pepper on to 8 oiled skewers, 25 cm/ 10 inches long. Complete each skewer with a halved tomato.

4 Place the skewers in a grill pan and cook under the grill for 15-20 minutes, turning as necessary and basting with the juices from the pan ⚠ until the fish is cooked through and lightly browned. Serve at once.

Cook's Notes

TIME
Preparation 15 minutes, cooking 15-20 minutes.

WATCHPOINT
The basting is necessary to avoid the fish becoming dry during cooking.

SERVING IDEAS
Prepare 4 portions of creamed potato and spread evenly over a shallow heatproof serving dish. Sprinkle with a little grated cheese and place under the hot grill until golden brown. Keep hot below the grill pan while cooking the fish. Arrange the fish kebabs on top of the browned potato and garnish with lemon slices and watercress. Serve with mayonnaise or tartare sauce.

In summer, cook the fish on skewers over the barbecue, and serve on a bed of shredded and chopped fresh salad ingredients.

 VARIATIONS
Use raw cucumber instead of blanched green pepper. Add 1 tablespoon dry vermouth to the marinade.

●180 calories/750 kj per portion

Smoked cod and spinach roll

SERVES 4

500 g/1 lb smoked cod fillets
300 ml/½ pint milk

2 bay leaves
1 lemon
225 g/8 oz frozen spinach
4 eggs, separated
3 hard-boiled eggs, finely chopped
¼ nutmeg, freshly grated
salt and freshly ground black pepper
40 g/1½ oz margarine or butter
2 tablespoons plain flour
vegetable oil, for greasing

TO GARNISH
few tomato slices (optional)
parsley sprigs (optional)

1 Heat the oven to 180C/350F/Gas 4.
2 Put the fish in an ovenproof dish and add the milk and bay leaves. Grate the zest from the lemon and reserve. Cut 2 slices from the lemon and put them on top of the fish. Cover the surface of the dish with greaseproof paper and bake in the oven for 15-20 minutes, until the flesh flakes easily.
3 Cook the spinach according to packet instructions, then drain thoroughly in a sieve pressing out all excess moisture with the back of a spoon.
4 Grease a 34 cm × 24 cm/13½ × 9½ inch Swiss roll tin and line it with greaseproof paper. Grease the paper well (see Cook's tip).
5 Lift the fish from the pan with a slotted spoon and reserve the cooking liquid. Flake the flesh into a bowl, discarding all skin and bones. Mash the flesh well with a fork, then stir in the lemon zest.
6 Increase the oven temperature to 200C/400F/Gas 6.
7 Beat the egg yolks and stir them into the fish. Whisk the egg whites until stiff and standing in peaks, then fold into the fish. Turn the mixture out of the bowl into the Swiss roll tin and spread it evenly over the base with a knife. Place in the oven and cook for 10-12 minutes until the mixture is firm to the touch and beginning to brown.
8 Place the drained spinach in a saucepan with 15 g/½ oz margarine.

Stir in the chopped egg, nutmeg and a little salt ⚠ and pepper to taste. Reserve, keeping warm.
9 Meanwhile, melt the remaining margarine in a small saucepan, sprinkle in the flour and stir over low heat for 2 minutes until straw-coloured. Remove from the heat and gradually strain in the reserved cooking liquid. Return to the heat and simmer, stirring, until thick and smooth. Keep warm.
10 Remove the fish from the oven and turn it out of the Swiss roll tin

on to a clean sheet of greaseproof paper. Gently ease the fish away from the lining paper. ⚠
11 Spread the warm spinach mixture over the surface of the fish, then roll it up like a Swiss roll, using the greaseproof paper to help you roll the fish. Slide the roll on to a warmed serving dish, join side down, and garnish the top with tomato slices and parsley sprigs, if liked. Cut a few slices off the roll and serve at once with the sauce handed separately.

Cook's Notes

TIME
This dish takes 1¼ hours to prepare and cook.

COOK'S TIP
To help avoid the fish mixture sticking to the greaseproof paper during baking, brush the paper liberally with oil, or use a silicone paper or non-stick baking parchment, available from large chemists, supermarkets and hardware stores.

WATCHPOINTS
Add salt sparingly because the smoked cod has a salty flavour.
If the greaseproof paper needs a little coaxing to come away from the fish mixture—run a knife carefully between them.

●405 calories/1700 kj per portion

Squid salad

SERVES 4

750 g/1½ lb squid (see Buying guide)
7 tablespoons olive oil
1 clove garlic, crushed (optional)
2 spring onions, finely chopped
3 tomatoes, skinned, deseeded and chopped
1 small green and 1 small red pepper, deseeded and roughly chopped
100 g/4 oz peeled prawns, defrosted and drained if frozen
juice of ½ lemon
salt and freshly ground black pepper

1 Clean the squid (see Kitchen Basics, back cover) and slice the flesh thinly into rings.

2 Heat 3 tablespoons of the oil in a frying-pan, add squid and garlic, if using, and cook, stirring often, for about 10 minutes or until the squid is tender. Drain on absorbent paper and then set aside until the squid is completely cold.

3 Put the squid, spring onions, tomatoes, peppers and prawns into a serving dish. Blend the remaining oil with the lemon juice and season with salt and pepper. Pour the dressing over the squid salad, then, using two forks, gently toss until coated in dressing. Cover the salad and refrigerate for 1 hour.

Cook's Notes

 TIME
Total preparation takes about 45 minutes, including cleaning the squid. Allow 1 hour chilling time.

 SERVING IDEAS
Serve with potato salad and a salad of lettuce and cucumber. Accompany with chunks of French bread and butter, and a glass of dry white wine.

BUYING GUIDE
Many fishmongers now sell squid and it is becoming increasingly popular, as it represents good value for money. Small squid (no more than 10 cm/4 inches long) are the most tender.
Ready-prepared, skinned and cleaned squid is sometimes sold, but it is more expensive.

●375 calories/1575kj per portion

Seafood macaroni bake

SERVES 4

350 g/12 oz fresh or frozen haddock
  fillets, skinned (see Cook's tips)
600 ml/1 pint milk
1 lemon (see Preparation)
1 bay leaf
3 whole black peppercorns
salt
50 g/2 oz margarine or butter
250 g/9 oz mushrooms, thinly sliced
250 g/9 oz short-cut macaroni,
  boiled, drained and rinsed (see
  Watchpoint)
150 g/5 oz jar mussels, drained
40 g/1½ oz plain flour
250 g/9 oz peeled prawns (see
  Cook's tips)
pinch of freshly grated nutmeg
freshly ground black pepper
margarine, for greasing
extra lemon slices and unpeeled
  fresh prawns, to garnish
  (optional)

1 Put the haddock in a large frying-pan with a lid and pour in enough of the milk to just cover. Add 2 slices of lemon, the bay leaf, peppercorns and a good pinch of salt. Bring gradually to the boil, then cover and turn off the heat under the pan. Leave to stand for 5 minutes, then remove the haddock with a fish slice. Flake the flesh into 4 cm/1½ inch pieces, discarding any bones. Strain all the cooking liquid and reserve.

2 Melt 15 g/½ oz margarine in the rinsed-out frying-pan, add the sliced mushrooms and fry for 2-3 minutes. Stir in the lemon juice and remove from heat.

3 Heat the oven to 180C/350F/Gas 4.

4 Put the macaroni into a greased large ovenproof dish with the haddock, mushrooms and mussels. Stir carefully to mix, without breaking up the fish.

5 Melt the remaining margarine in a saucepan, sprinkle in the flour and stir over low heat for 1-2 minutes until straw-coloured. Remove from the heat and gradually stir in rest of milk and reserved cooking liquid. Return to the heat and simmer, stirring, until thick and smooth. Remove from heat, stir in the prawns, nutmeg and salt and pepper to taste, then pour evenly over macaroni and fish mixture. Cook in the oven for 20 minutes.

6 Garnish with lemon slices and unpeeled prawns, if liked, and serve hot, straight from the dish.

Cook's Notes

 TIME
Preparation, 30 minutes; cooking in the oven, 20 minutes.

 COOK'S TIPS
If using frozen haddock, there is no need to defrost before using: after bringing to the boil in stage 1, simmer for a few minutes until thoroughly defrosted before turning off heat under pan.

If using frozen prawns, there is no need to defrost them before adding to the sauce.

 PREPARATION
Squeeze the juice from one-half of the lemon and slice the other half.

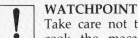 **WATCHPOINT**
Take care not to overcook the macaroni at this stage, as it will continue cooking in the oven. Rinsing it under cold running water after it has been boiled prevents it from sticking together.

●610 calories/2550 kj per portion

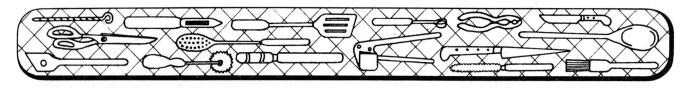

Mussel and prawn pie

 SERVES 4
215 g/7½ oz frozen puff pastry, defrosted
lightly beaten egg white, for glazing
lemon wedges, to garnish

FILLING
425 g/15 oz jar mussels in brine, drained
50 g/2 oz frozen prawns, defrosted
40 g/1½ oz margarine or butter
1 small onion, chopped
25 g/1 oz plain flour
200 ml/7 fl oz milk
75 ml/3 fl oz dry white wine
salt and freshly ground black pepper
1 tablespoon chopped fresh parsley

1 On a lightly floured surface, roll out the pastry to 4 cm/1½ inches larger all round than the top of an 850 ml/1½ pint ovenproof pie dish.

Invert the pie dish on the rolled out pastry and cut round the edge with a sharp knife to make a lid. Then cut a strip the same width as the rim of the pie dish, from the outer edge.

2 Use the trimmings for decorations and refrigerate with the pastry.

3 Make the filling: melt margarine in a heavy-based saucepan, add the onion and fry gently for about 5 minutes until it is soft and lightly coloured. Sprinkle in the flour and stir over low heat for 1-2 minutes. Remove from heat and gradually stir in milk. Return to heat and simmer, stirring, until thick.

4 Stir in the wine, mussels and prawns and season to taste with salt and pepper. Simmer for 2 minutes, then stir in the parsley. Pour the mixture into the pie dish and leave until cold (see Cook's tip).

5 Heat the oven to 220C/425F/Gas 7.

6 Dampen the rim of the dish with water. Place the pastry strip on the rim and press down lightly. Brush the strip with egg white, place pastry lid on top of dish and press round the edge to seal. Trim any surplus pastry, then flute the edge.

Brush pastry decorations with egg white and stick on to pastry lid. Brush lid with egg white.

7 Bake in the oven for 20 minutes, then lower oven temperature to 190C/375F/Gas 5 and bake for a further 15 minutes until the pastry is puffed up and golden. Serve the pie hot (see Serving ideas).

Cook's Notes

 TIME
Preparation takes about 30 minutes and cooking 35 minutes. Allow extra time for cooling and chilling.

SERVING IDEAS
Serve pie with spinach and grilled tomatoes or with peas and sweetcorn.

 COOK'S TIP
The pie filling must be cold before covering or the pastry will be soggy.

●430 calories/1800 kj per portion

Kedgeree special

SERVES 4-6

500 g/1 lb smoked cod fillets, defrosted if frozen (see Did you know)

250 g/9 oz white or brown rice

25 g/1 oz margarine or butter

1 onion, chopped

225 g/8 oz frozen mixed vegetables, defrosted

150 g/5 oz natural yoghurt

juice of ½ lemon

100 g/4 oz can smoked mussels, drained

100 g/4 oz peeled prawns, defrosted if frozen

2 hard-boiled eggs, roughly chopped

2 tablespoons finely chopped fresh parsley

salt and freshly ground black pepper

thick lemon wedges, to garnish (optional)

1 Put the smoked cod in a large saucepan, cover with cold water and bring to the boil. Lower the heat, cover the pan, and simmer gently for 10 minutes, until the fish flakes easily when pierced with a sharp knife.

2 Remove the fish with a slotted spoon, reserving the poaching liquid in the pan. Leave the fish until cool enough to handle, then flake the flesh into small pieces, discarding the skin and any remaining bones.

3 Make the fish poaching liquid up to 1 L/1¾ pints with water. Bring to the boil, add the rice, cover and simmer for 15 or 40 minutes until tender. Turn into a sieve and leave to drain.

4 Meanwhile, melt the margarine in a separate large saucepan, add the onion and fry gently for 5 minutes until soft and lightly coloured. Stir in the mixed vegetables and cover the pan. Continue cooking over low heat for 5 minutes, shaking the pan from time to time.

5 Add the flaked fish and drained rice to the vegetables, with the yoghurt, lemon juice, mussels, prawns, hard-boiled eggs and parsley. Season to taste with salt and pepper. Taking care not to break up the ingredients, fork through lightly over gentle heat until well mixed and heated through.

6 Pile the kedgeree into a warmed serving dish, garnish the ends of the dish with lemon wedges, if liked, and serve at once.

Seafood and orange kebabs

SERVES 4
500 g/1 lb haddock fillet, skinned and cut into 2.5 cm/1 inch cubes
250 g/9 oz unpeeled prawns
4 large oranges
watercress sprigs, to garnish

MARINADE
4 tablespoons vegetable oil
4 tablespoons lemon juice
½ teaspoon dried marjoram
1 large clove garlic, crushed (optional)
salt and freshly ground black pepper

1 Combine all the marinade ingredients in a large shallow dish. Add the haddock cubes and prawns and turn to coat (see Cook's tip). Leave to marinate for 30 minutes at room temperature.
2 Meanwhile, peel and segment the

Cook's Notes

TIME
Preparation takes 20-25 minutes. Allow 30 minutes for marinating. Cooking the kebabs takes about 10 minutes.

PREPARATION
When threading the prawns on to the kebab skewers, push the skewer through the thickest part of the body so that they do not fall off during cooking.

COOK'S TIP
If you prefer not to peel the cooked prawns at the table, grill peeled jumbo prawns on the kebabs instead.

WATCHPOINT
Take care not to overcook the prawns, or they will become hard and tough. Lower the heat if they begin to brown too quickly.

●270 calories/1125 kj per portion

oranges over the marinade, so that any juice drips into it. Set the orange segments aside on a plate.
3 Line the grill rack with a piece of foil. Heat the grill to moderate.
4 Remove the haddock cubes and prawns from the marinade and thread them and the orange segments on to 4 oiled long kebab skewers (see Preparation).

5 Place the kebabs on the grill rack and brush well with some of the marinade. Grill for about 5 minutes, then turn the kebabs and grill for a further 5 minutes, brushing once or twice with more marinade.
6 Arrange the cooked kebabs on a warmed large serving plate. Brush with marinade, garnish with watercress sprigs and serve at once.

OFFAL

Kidney and orange simmer

SERVES 4

500 g/1 lb lamb kidneys, skinned and chopped, with cores removed (see Buying guide)
1 tablespoon vegetable oil
1 onion, chopped
1 clove garlic, crushed (optional)
300 ml/½ pint chicken stock
1 tablespoon white wine vinegar
pinch of mustard powder
pinch of cayenne pepper
2 teaspoons chopped fresh tarragon
finely grated zest of 1 orange
1 tablespoon orange juice
100 g/4 oz mushrooms, sliced
salt and freshly ground black pepper

TO GARNISH
1 tablespoon chopped fresh parsley
orange slices

1 Heat the oil in a large frying-pan with a lid, add the onion and garlic, if using, and fry over moderate heat for 1-2 minutes. Add the kidneys to the pan and fry for a further 2-3 minutes, stirring all the time.
2 Stir the stock, vinegar, mustard, cayenne pepper and tarragon into the pan, with the grated orange zest and juice. Add the mushrooms, stir well and season to taste with salt and pepper.
3 Bring to the boil, then lower the heat, cover the pan and simmer for 15 minutes until the kidneys are tender.
4 Transfer to a warmed serving dish, sprinkle with parsley and garnish with orange slices. Serve at once, piping hot.

Cook's Notes

TIME
Preparation takes 10 minutes, cooking about 20 minutes.

SPECIAL OCCASION
Stir in 2 tablespoons single cream just before serving.

BUYING GUIDE
Kidneys go 'off' very quickly and must be eaten the day they are bought. Frozen kidneys may be used, but must be defrosted completely before using.

SERVING IDEAS
Serve with plain boiled white rice. This is a rich dish, which is best served with a simple green salad.

● 150 calories/625 kj per portion

Kidney and pork medley

SERVES 4

4 lamb kidneys, halved and cores removed
250 g/9 oz lean pork fillet, cut into 2.5 cm/1 inch cubes
2 tablespoons vegetable oil
1 onion, chopped
350 g/12 oz tomatoes, skinned and quartered
3 tablespoons sweet red vermouth
½ teaspoon dried oregano
salt and freshly ground black pepper
150 ml/¼ pint natural yoghurt

1 Heat the oil in a large saucepan, then add the onion and fry very gently for 5 minutes until soft and lightly coloured.
2 Add the pork to the pan and fry, turning from time to time, for 10 minutes until lightly browned.
3 Cut each kidney half into 4 pieces. Add to the pan and fry, stirring frequently, for 5 minutes.
4 Stir in the tomatoes, vermouth and oregano, and season to taste with salt and pepper. Cover and cook for 10 minutes, then remove the lid and cook for a further 5 minutes until the pork is tender when pierced with a sharp knife.
5 Remove from the heat, taste and adjust seasoning, then swirl in the yoghurt. Turn into a warmed serving dish and serve at once.

Cook's Notes

 TIME
Preparation and cooking take 40 minutes.

 SERVING IDEAS
Serve with boiled noodles or rice and a fresh green vegetable such as broccoli. Or, use as a topping for jacket-baked potatoes (it will serve 8 this way). Alternatively, try using as a tasty stuffing for a baked marrow.

 ECONOMY
Chicken stock may be used as a substitute for the red vermouth.

 VARIATIONS
Add 100 g/4 oz button mushrooms, quartered and fried in butter, just before serving. Substitute dried sage for the oregano.

●250 calories/1050 kj per portion

Liver loaf

SERVES 6

500 g/1 lb lamb liver, trimmed and sliced
15 g/½ oz lard or dripping
250 g/9 oz pork sausagemeat
75 g/3 oz fresh white breadcrumbs
1 large onion, grated
1 tablespoon Worcestershire sauce
2 small eggs, beaten
1 teaspoon dried thyme
salt and freshly ground black pepper

TOMATO SAUCE
1 tablespoon vegetable oil
1 small onion, finely chopped
1 clove garlic, crushed (optional)
400 g/14 oz can tomatoes
150 ml/¼ pint water
1 teaspoon tomato purée
½ teaspoon sugar
½ teaspoon dried sweet basil

TO GARNISH
1-2 tomatoes, sliced
parsley sprigs

1 Heat the oven to 180C/350F/Gas 4.
2 Grease a 1 kg/2 lb loaf tin. Melt the lard in a frying-pan, add the liver and fry over brisk heat until browned on all sides. Remove with a slotted spoon, drain and cool on absorbent paper, then mince.
3 Mix the minced liver with all the remaining ingredients, adding salt and pepper to taste. Make sure that all the ingredients are combined.
4 Spoon the mixture into the prepared tin, pressing it down firmly. Cover with foil, then place the tin in a roasting pan half filled with hot water.
5 Bake in the oven for about 1 hour or until the juices run clear when the loaf is pierced in the centre with a knife.
6 Meanwhile, make the tomato sauce: heat the oil in a saucepan, add the onion and garlic (if using) and fry gently until soft. Add the remaining sauce ingredients with salt and pepper to taste, then bring to the boil, stirring constantly to break up the tomatoes.
7 Lower the heat, half cover with a lid and simmer gently for about 20 minutes, stirring from time to time.

Remove from the heat, leave to cool for a few minutes, then purée in a blender or work through a sieve. Return to the pan, taste and adjust seasoning, then simmer gently on top of the cooker until cooked.
8 Remove the cooked liver loaf from the roasting pan, leave to stand for 5 minutes, ⚠ then pour off any fat and juices from the tin.
9 Turn the loaf out on to a warmed serving platter then pour a little of the hot tomato sauce over the top (see Variation). Serve at once, with the remaining sauce handed separately in a sauceboat.

Cook's Notes

TIME
25 minutes preparation, plus about 1 hour baking. Allow an extra 5-10 minutes for turning out.

FREEZING
Leave until cold, then unmould, wrap in cling film and overwrap in a polythene bag. Seal, label and freeze for up to 3 months. Defrost in wrappings overnight in the refrigerator.

● 385 calories/1625 kj per portion

VARIATION
Use about 50 g/2 oz instant mashed potato mix, made according to packet instructions, to cover the loaf. Pipe it over, or use a fork to mark it decoratively. Garnish with tomatoes and parsley.

WATCHPOINT
The loaf must be left to stand in the tin for at least 5 minutes after cooking to allow the mixture to settle. If the loaf is turned out immediately it will be difficult to slice neatly.

Liver and bacon hotpot

SERVES 4

500g/1 lb lamb or pig liver, cut
    into 16 small slices
1 tablespoon vegetable oil
25 g/1 oz margarine or butter
2 medium onions, sliced into thin
    rings
4 bacon rashers, rinds removed
1 cooking apple, peeled, cored and
    sliced
salt and freshly ground black
    pepper
few drops of Worcestershire sauce
300 ml/½ pint hot beef stock
1 teaspoon cornflour

1 Heat the oven to 180C/350F/Gas 4.
2 Heat oil and margarine in a large frying-pan and fry the liver slices over moderate heat until brown on both sides. Remove with a slotted spoon and transfer to a plate.
3 Lower the heat and fry the onion rings for 5 to 10 minutes. Spread the onions evenly over the base of an ovenproof serving dish.
4 Sandwich ½ rasher of bacon between 2 apple slices and 2 liver slices. Turn the liver sandwiches on their sides and arrange in rows on top of the onions. Sprinkle with salt and pepper.
5 Add a few drops of Worcestershire sauce to the stock. Blend the cornflour to a paste in a small saucepan with a little cold water, then gradually stir in the stock. Bring to the boil stirring constantly, then lower the heat and simmer gently until thickened. Pour over the liver.
6 Cover and bake in the oven for about 30 minutes. ! Serve hot, straight from the serving dish.

Cook's Notes

TIME
An easy dish taking less than an hour.

COOK'S TIP
If using pig liver, soak it in a little milk for about an hour to remove the strong flavour. Drain and dry it before cooking.

WATCHPOINT
Always use liver on the day it is bought, or within 24 hours if kept well wrapped in a refrigerator. Do not be tempted to leave the liver in the oven for longer than 30 minutes — overcooked liver is tough and leathery, and the apple slices will disintegrate.

SERVING IDEAS
Serve with creamy mashed potatoes — made extra special with a large knob of butter, a few tablespoons of cream and a beaten egg. Beat them well until soft and fluffy.

● 365 calories/1525 kj per portion

Liver cobbler

SERVES 4

350 g/12 oz lamb liver, cut into
    bite-sized pieces
300 ml/½ pint milk
1 tablespoon plain flour
salt and freshly ground black pepper
50 g/2 oz margarine or butter
6 streaky bacon rashers, rinds
    removed, cut into thin strips
2 large onions, sliced
225 g/8 oz can tomatoes
½ teaspoon dried mixed herbs

TOPPING
225 g/8 oz self-raising flour
pinch of salt
50 g/2 oz margarine or butter, diced
½ teaspoon dried mixed herbs
150 ml/¼ pint milk
a little milk, to glaze

1 Put the liver pieces in a shallow dish, pour over the milk and leave to marinate at room temperature for 1 hour (see Cook's tip).

2 Remove the liver from the milk and dry on absorbent paper. Spread out the flour on a flat plate and season with salt and pepper. Dip the liver strips in the seasoned flour, turning them to coat thoroughly.

3 Melt the margarine in a frying-pan, add the bacon and onions and fry gently for 5 minutes until soft. Remove with a slotted spoon and put in a round 23 cm/9 inch diameter 1.25 L/2 pint casserole.

4 Add the liver to the frying-pan and fry for 1-2 minutes, turning the pieces to seal.

5 Gradually stir the milk into the pan and bring to the boil, stirring. Cook for 2-3 minutes.

6 Using a slotted spoon, transfer the liver to the casserole with the onions and bacon. Pour in the milk and stir in the tomatoes with their juice and herbs. Season to taste with salt and pepper.

7 Heat the oven to 220C/425F/Gas 7.

8 Make the cobbler topping: sift the flour and salt into a bowl. Add the margarine and rub it into the flour with the fingertips until the mixture resembles fine breadcrumbs. Add the herbs and gradually mix in the milk to form a soft dough.

9 Turn the dough on to a lightly floured surface and knead gently until smooth. Roll out to about 1 cm/½ inch thickness. Cut into rounds, using a 6 cm/2½ inch cutter.

10 Arrange the rounds of dough overlapping in a circle on top of the liver mixture in the casserole. Brush the dough topping with a little milk to glaze.

11 Bake the cobbler in the oven for 20-25 minutes until the topping is well risen and golden brown. Serve at once, straight from the casserole.

Cook's Notes

TIME
Preparation, including pre-cooking, takes about 30 minutes. Cooking in the oven takes 20-25 minutes, but allow 1 hour for the liver to marinate in the milk.

COOK'S TIP
Marinating the liver in milk makes it beautifully tender, and the milk also gives a deliciously creamy sauce.

VARIATION
Add a 215 g/7½ oz can mushrooms, drained, to the liver mixture.

SERVING IDEAS
Serve the cobbler with carrots and green beans. The topping is starchy, so there is no need for a potato accompaniment.

●770 calories/3225 kj per portion

Chinese-style liver

SERVES 4-5

750 g/1½ lb lamb liver, trimmed and thinly sliced (see Preparation)
4 tablespoons vegetable oil
12 large spring onions, cut into 1 cm/½ inch lengths (see Preparation)
100 g/4 oz button mushrooms, sliced
2 tablespoons dry or medium sherry
1-2 tablespoons soy sauce
1 tablespoon wine vinegar
1 teaspoon sugar
½ teaspoon ground ginger
2 tablespoons cornflour
425 ml/¾ pint water
thin carrot strips, to garnish

MARINADE
1 teaspoon salt
½ teaspoon freshly ground black pepper
4 teaspoons cornflour
4 teaspoons dry sherry
4 teaspoons vegetable oil

1 To make the marinade: mix the marinade ingredients together in a large bowl. Add the sliced liver, stir well and leave for 10 minutes.
2 Heat 3 tablespoons oil in a large saucepan over moderate heat. Drain the liver and add to the pan. Stir-fry (see Did you know) over high heat for 2-3 minutes only, until the liver is browned all over. Remove from the pan with a slotted spoon, and reserve.
3 Heat the remaining tablespoon oil in the pan, add the spring onions and mushrooms and stir-fry over high heat for 1 minute.
4 Remove the pan from the heat and stir in the sherry, soy sauce, wine vinegar, sugar and ginger.
5 In a large bowl, mix the cornflour to a paste with a little of the water. Gradually stir in remaining water.
6 Return the pan to the heat and bring to the boil, scraping up all the sediment from the sides and bottom of the pan with a wooden spoon.
7 Stir in the cornflour mixture, add the liver and bring to the boil, stirring. Simmer gently for 2 minutes. Transfer the mixture to a warmed serving dish (see Serving ideas). Garnish with carrot strips and serve at once.

Cook's Notes

TIME
Preparation and cooking take 30 minutes.

PREPARATION
Slice the liver no more than 5 mm/¼ inch thick, or it will not cook in the specified time.
To trim the spring onions: remove the outside layer of each one, cut off most of the green part and slice off the root.

DID YOU KNOW
Stir-frying is a term frequently used in Chinese cooking. It means literally stirring and frying at the same time. The ingredients are kept on the move over high heat so that they cook quickly and evenly.

SERVING IDEAS
Serve with boiled rice or noodles, and a stir-fried vegetable accompaniment.

● 495 calories/2075 kj per portion

164

DELIGHTFUL DESSERTS

A delicious dessert can be the ideal and fitting end to an enjoyable meal. This section contains a tantalising choice of different types of hot and cold desserts – some fruity, others light and creamy and the always popular ice creams and the more filling cakes, pies and flans. The recipes are as ideal for the busy cook as they are easy to follow and quick to make. There is also a selection of extremely quick desserts for those occasions when time is really at a premium. The family's favourites are also included – dishes like apple crumble and chocolate pudding that you are asked to make time and time again.

FRUITY DESSERTS

Pineapple bread pudding

SERVES 4

4 medium eggs
3 tablespoons caster sugar
375 g/13 oz can crushed pineapple
1 teaspoon ground mixed spice
75 g/3 oz butter, melted
4 thick slices bread, crusts removed,
    cut into 1 cm/½ inch cubes

TO DECORATE
4 rings canned pineapple
4 glacé cherries

1 Put the eggs and sugar into a 1L/2 pint ovenproof dish and whisk lightly with a fork until the sugar has dissolved.
2 Stir in the crushed pineapple with its syrup, the spice and butter. Fold in the bread cubes.
3 Press down the bread cubes lightly to level the surface, then cover the dish. Leave to soak in the refrigerator overnight.
4 The next day, when ready to cook, heat the oven to 170C/325F/Gas 3.
5 Uncover the dish and bake the pudding for 40-45 minutes or until the top is golden brown. Decorate with pineapple rings and glacé cherries, if liked.

166

Chilled cherry compote

SERVES 4

2 × 450 g/1 lb cans stoned cherries, drained, with syrup reserved (see Buying guide)
5 cm/2 inch stick cinnamon, or large pinch of ground cinnamon
5 cm/2 inch strip lemon zest (see Cook's tips)
1 teaspoon lemon juice
about 2 tablespoons redcurrant jelly, or to taste
2 teaspoons arrowroot
2 tablespoons water

TO SERVE

4 tablespoons thick natural yoghurt
8 ratafias (see Did you know)

1 Put the cherries into a large bowl and set aside.
2 Pour the reserved cherry syrup into a medium heavy-based saucepan. Add the cinnamon, lemon zest and juice and 2 tablespoons redcurrant jelly. Stir over low heat to dissolve the jelly, then bring to the boil and simmer for 1 minute. Remove from the heat.
3 Blend the arrowroot with the water, then stir into the syrup. Return to the heat and bring to the boil, stirring. Simmer for 1-2 minutes, stirring constantly, until the syrup thickens slightly and is clear. Taste and stir in more redcurrant jelly to sweeten, if necessary.
4 Strain the syrup through a nylon sieve over the cherries. Mix well, then leave to cool. Cover and refrigerate the compote for 1-2 hours (see Cook's tips).
5 To serve: spoon the cherries and syrup into 4 individual glass dishes. Top each with 1 tablespoon yoghurt and 2 ratafias. (Stand the ratafias upright and at a slight angle, like butterfly wings.)

Spiced banana dumplings

MAKES 12

375 g/13 oz frozen puff pastry, defrosted

3 large firm bananas
1 tablespoon lemon juice

[!] 75 g/3 oz caster sugar
1 teaspoon ground mixed spice
1 egg, beaten

1 Heat the oven to 220C/425F/Gas 7. Brush a baking sheet with water.
2 On a floured board, roll out the pastry into a rectangle about 50 × 37.5 cm/20×15 inches. [!] Trim the edges with a knife to straighten them. Let the pastry rest for 5-10 minutes, then cut into 12 squares about 12.5 cm/5 inches each.
3 Cut each banana into quarters crossways and toss in lemon juice to prevent discoloration. Place 1 banana quarter diagonally in the centre of each pastry square. Mix the sugar and spice, then sprinkle 1 teaspoon over each banana piece.
4 Brush the edges of 1 dough square with some of the beaten egg, then wrap the banana (see Preparation). Repeat for each dumpling.
5 Brush the dumplings with the remaining beaten egg and sprinkle over the remaining spiced sugar. Arrange the dumplings on the baking sheet, then bake in the oven for 15-20 minutes or until the pastry is puffed up and golden brown.
6 Carefully lift the dumplings with a fish slice. Serve warm.

Cook's Notes

TIME
Preparation time 30 minutes, cooking time 15-20 minutes.

PREPARATION
Roll up the spiced banana dumplings as shown below:

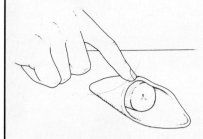

1 *Bring the 2 opposite corners of the pastry together across the length of the banana. Overlap the ends of the dough over the top of the banana and press firmly to seal.*

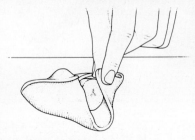

2 *Bring the other 2 corners to the centre and overlap them on top of the first 2 corners. Press firmly to seal.*

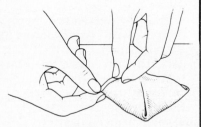

3 *Fold over the open edges slightly and press to seal.*

[!] **WATCHPOINT**
Do not stretch pastry or it will shrink during baking. To prevent this, let the dough rest for 5-10 minutes after rolling out.

●170 calories/700 kj each

Oranges in Cointreau

SERVES 4

8 small oranges
100 g/4 oz caster sugar
4 tablespoons water
4 tablespoons Cointreau (see
Buying guide)

1 Using a small sharp knife, pare the zest from oranges, then cut the zest into shreds (see Cook's tip).
2 Put the sugar and water in a large heavy-based saucepan. Stir over very low heat until the sugar has dissolved, then bring to the boil.
3 Add the orange shreds and boil for 1 minute, then remove with a slotted spoon and pat them dry on absorbent paper. Transfer to a saucer, cover and refrigerate until required. Leave syrup to cool.
4 Peel the oranges with a sharp knife, removing every scrap of

Cook's Notes

TIME
About 30-40 minutes to prepare; 1 hour to chill.

COOK'S TIP
To pare the zest as thinly as possible, use a potato peeler. There should be no pith attached to the zest.

BUYING GUIDE
The Cointreau may be replaced by another orange liqueur such as Grand Marnier or a Curaçao, but the flavour will be subtly different.

PREPARATION
Reshape each orange as follows:

Slice the orange and lay the slices flat, one on top of each other.

●230 calories/950 kj per portion

white pith and taking care not to damage the orange flesh.
5 Cut the oranges across into thin slices, then stack the slices (see Preparation), to reshape each orange. Spear together with cocktail sticks and carefully transfer to a serving dish.

6 Add the Cointreau to the cooled syrup, then pour over the oranges. Refrigerate for at least 1 hour, spooning the juice over the oranges from time to time.
7 To serve: sprinkle the oranges with the chilled shreds and serve at once.

Mango spoon sweet

SERVES 4-6

2 ripe mangoes, total weight about 750 g/1½ lb (see Preparation)
225 g/8 oz can pineapple rings in natural juice, drained with 100 ml/3½ fl oz juice reserved
100 g/4 oz green grapes, halved and seeded
100 g/4 oz black grapes, halved and seeded

1 Put the mangoes in a blender with their juice and the measured pineapple juice. Work to a purée, then pour into a large bowl.

2 Cut each pineapple ring into 6 pieces and add to the mango purée together with the grapes. Cover and refrigerate for 30 minutes.

3 Spoon the mixture into 4-6 small dishes. Serve chilled.

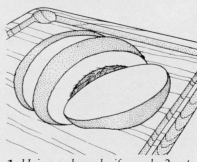
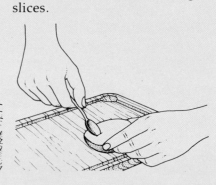

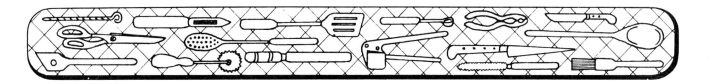

Plum and banana compote

SERVES 4

500 g/1 lb plums (see Buying guide)
300 ml/½ pint water
75 g/3 oz sugar
4 tablespoons red wine or orange
    juice
2 small bananas
15 g/½ oz flaked almonds

1 Wash and wipe the plums, then halve them and remove the stones (see Preparation).
2 Put the water and sugar into a heavy-based saucepan and heat very gently until the sugar has dissolved, stirring occasionally. Bring the syrup slowly to the boil, without stirring, then boil for 2-3 minutes.
3 Carefully add the plums to the hot syrup; allow it to bubble up over them, then reduce the heat and cook the plums gently until they are just tender when pierced with a fine skewer. ⚠️
4 Using a slotted spoon, transfer the plums to a serving bowl.
5 Add the wine to the syrup and boil rapidly until thickened and reduced by about half. Remove from the heat and allow to cool for a few minutes, then pour over the plums. Leave until completely cold.

6 Just before serving, peel the bananas and cut diagonally into slices. Fold gently into the plums, then sprinkle the flaked almonds over the top. Serve at once or the bananas will discolour.

Cook's Notes

TIME
About 30 minutes preparation, plus a few hours cooling time.

BUYING GUIDE
Plums vary in size, colour, juiciness, and flavour according to variety. Dark, purple-skinned plums are best for this dish, but you can use another variety if preferred. If the fruit is very large, cut it into quarters rather than halves.

When fresh plums are scarce or out of season, substitute frozen plums and defrost them before cooking. Alternatively, use drained, canned plums and do not cook them; use the syrup and boil it with the red wine.

PREPARATION
To stone plums, cut round them along the indentation from the stalk end, then twist the halves in opposite directions to separate them.

Ease out the stone with your fingers or the tip of a knife.

WATCHPOINT
Cooking time depends on the variety of plum used. It is important that the plums retain their shape for this dish, so take care not to overcook them or they will become mushy and the appearance of the dessert will be spoilt.

● 175 calories/725 kj per portion

Harvest pudding

SERVES 4-6

225 g/8 oz cooking plums, halved and stoned

500 g/1 lb cooking apples, peeled, cored and sliced

275 g/10 oz sugar

225 g/8 oz fresh or frozen blackberries

8 trifle sponge cakes, cut in half horizontally

softly whipped cream, to serve (optional)

1 Put the plums, apples and 200 g/ 7 oz sugar into a heavy-based saucepan. Cover and cook gently for 10 minutes, stirring occasionally. Add the blackberries and remaining sugar, replace the lid and cook for a further 10 minutes, until all the fruit is very soft.

2 Turn the fruit into a nylon sieve set over a bowl to drain off the excess juice.

3 Arrange a few slices of sponge cake in the base of a 1.5 L/2½ pint pudding basin. Cover the cake with a layer of fruit and sprinkle over about 1 tablespoon of the drained juice. Continue making layers in this way [!] until all the cake and fruit are used, finishing with a layer of cake (see Economy).

4 Stand the basin on a plate, then cover the pudding with cling film. Put a small plate or lid which fits just inside the rim of the basin on top of the pudding. Weight the plate down, then leave the pudding in the refrigerator overnight.

5 To serve: run a palette knife around the sides of the pudding to loosen it, then invert a serving plate on top. Hold the plate and basin firmly and invert, giving a sharp shake halfway round. Carefully lift off the basin. Serve the pudding chilled, with cream, if liked.

Cook's Notes

TIME
40 minutes preparation, plus at least 8 hours chilling.

WATCHPOINT
Take care not to add too much juice: if the pudding is very soggy it will collapse when turned out on the serving plate.

ECONOMY
Do not throw the remaining juice away. It can be poured over the pudding after it has been turned out, or it can be kept in the refrigerator for 3-4 days and diluted with lemonade, cream soda or tonic water to make a delicious cold drink.

●510 calories/2140 kj per portion

Gooseberry and apple amber

SERVES 4

225 g/8 oz gooseberries, topped and tailed if fresh, defrosted if frozen
225 g/8 oz cooking apples, peeled, quartered, cored and sliced
1 tablespoon water
25 g/1 oz margarine or butter
25-50 g/1-2 oz sugar
15 g/½ oz fresh cake- or breadcrumbs (see Cook's tip)
2 eggs, separated
¼ teaspoon ground cloves or mixed spice
100 g/4 oz caster sugar

1 Heat the oven to 180C/350F/Gas 4.
2 Put the gooseberries, apples, water and margarine into a heavy-based pan. Cover and cook over moderate heat for about 10 minutes, until tender. Remove from the heat and beat in the sugar to taste, the crumbs, egg yolks and cloves.
3 Turn the mixture into four 150 ml/¼ pint ramekins and level the surface. Stand the dishes on a baking sheet and bake in the oven for about 15 minutes, until just set.
4 Meanwhile, in a clean, dry bowl whisk the egg whites until standing in stiff peaks. Whisk in the caster sugar, 1 tablespoon at a time, whisking the mixture thoroughly after each addition and continue whisking until the meringue is stiff and glossy. Swirl or pipe the meringue over the gooseberry mixture in the ramekins.
5 Lower the heat to 140C/275F/Gas 1, then return the dish to the oven for about 30 minutes, until the meringue is crisp on the outside and lightly browned. Serve hot or cold.

Cook's Notes

TIME
Preparation and cooking take about 1¼ hours.

VARIATIONS
For apple amber, omit the gooseberries and increase the apples to 500 g/1 lb. Add the grated zest of 1 lemon with the cloves.
Use ground cinnamon or grated nutmeg instead of cloves.

COOK'S TIP
The crumbs absorb the fruit juices and prevent the pudding separating when the egg yolks are added.

WATCHPOINT
Take meringue right to the rim of each dish, otherwise it may 'weep'.

●270 calories/1125 kj per portion

Fruit flambé

SERVES 6

1 can (about 1 lb) peach slices
1 can (about 1 lb) red cherries
1 can (about 14 oz) pear slices
1 can (about 8 oz) pineapple rings
¼ cup brandy or rum
¼ cup sweet butter (see Cook's tips)
¼ cup superfine sugar
1 teaspoon ground allspice
6 portions vanilla ice cream, to
   serve

1 Drain the fruits thoroughly, then blot dry on paper towels. Pit the cherries (see Preparation), and quarter the pineapple rings.
2 Pour the brandy into a cup and stand in a pan or bowl of hot water to warm through gently.
3 Melt the butter in a large, heavy-bottomed saucepan. Add the superfine sugar and allspice and cook over low heat, stirring occasionally, until the sugar has dissolved. ⚠

Cook's Notes

⏰ TIME
Preparation and cooking take about 20 minutes.

👨‍🍳 COOK'S TIPS
It is worth using sweet butter for this dish, otherwise the flavor will not be so good.

Use a spatula and palette knife to turn the fruits gently so that they remain whole and do not break.

📖 PREPARATION
A cherry pitter is useful when you have a lot of fruit to prepare. If you do not have one, slit the cherries down one side, then flick out the pits with the point of a knife.

⚠ WATCHPOINTS
Keep the heat low, so that the butter does not burn.

Make sure that the excess liquid from the fruit has evaporated before you add the brandy — if the spirit is diluted too much it will not ignite.

Hold the match just above the side of the pan and stand well back since the flames will shoot high for a few seconds and could be dangerous.

● 290 calories per portion

4 Add the fruit and turn carefully until evenly coated, (see Cook's tips), then cook gently to heat through.
5 Meanwhile, put the ice cream into 6 dessert bowls.
6 When the fruit is heated and all excess liquid has evaporated ⚠ turn off the heat. Pour the warmed brandy over the fruit and immediately set light to it. ⚠ Let the flames die completely, then spoon the fruit over the ice cream. Serve at once.

Gingered fruit cocktails

fruit mixture and sweeten with brown sugar, if necessary, then leave to cool.

2 Divide fruit mixture between 4 dessert glasses. Cover each glass

with cling film and refrigerate for 20-30 minutes.

3 To serve: spoon the soured cream over the fruit and sprinkle the crushed biscuits on top.

SERVES 4

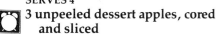

- 3 unpeeled dessert apples, cored and sliced
- 2 large oranges, peeled and chopped, with pips removed (see Preparation)
- ½ small melon, peeled, seeded and cubed (see Buying guide)
- 2 tablespoons light soft brown sugar (optional)
- 150 ml/¼ pint soured cream
- 8-10 gingernut biscuits, coarsely crushed

1 Place the prepared fruit in a heavy-based saucepan. Cover and cook gently until the apples and melon are tender but not mushy. Remove from the heat. Taste the

Cook's Notes

 TIME
25 minutes preparation, plus cooling and chilling time.

 PREPARATION
Use a sharp knife to peel the oranges and take care to remove every scrap of bitter white pith.

BUYING GUIDE
Choose a cantaloupe or charentais melon for this dessert as they have very sweet orange-coloured flesh,

which is highly scented. If either variety is unobtainable, use ½ small honeydew instead.

WATCHPOINTS
When you check for sweetness, remember that chilling will tone down the flavour and natural sweetness of the fruit mixture.

Serve the fruit cocktails as soon as they are assembled; if left to stand the biscuits will become soggy.

● 255 calories/1075 kj per portion

175

Fruit kebabs

SERVES 4

75 g/3 oz butter
¼ teaspoon ground cinnamon
4 tablespoons white wine, or 3
   tablespoons water mixed with
   1 tablespoon lemon juice
2 tablespoons thick honey
2 dessert apples
1 large or 2 small ripe dessert pears
2 small bananas
8 whole dates, stoned
8 maraschino cherries
4 slices bread, crusts removed

1 Beat 50 g/2 oz butter with the cinnamon and set aside.
2 Put the remaining butter into a small saucepan. Add the wine and honey and stir over low heat until melted and blended. Bring slowly to the boil and cook for 1-2 minutes until the sauce is slightly syrupy. Remove from the heat and set aside.

3 Peel and core the apples and pear, then cut into chunky pieces. Peel the bananas and cut each across into 8 pieces. Thread the apples, pears, bananas, dates and the maraschino cherries alternately on to eight 15 cm/6 inch long skewers (see Preparation).
4 Lay a sheet of foil over the grill rack and heat the grill to moderate.
5 Place the skewers on the foil, brush liberally with some of the sauce, then place as far as possible away from the heat and grill for 10 minutes, turning them over frequently and basting with more sauce.
6 Remove the kebabs and foil from the grill pan and keep warm.
7 Increase the heat of the grill to high, then toast the bread on 1 side only. Spread the untoasted side with the cinnamon butter, then grill until crisp at the edges.
8 Meanwhile, reheat any remaining sauce until bubbling. Place the toast on individual serving plates and place 2 kebabs on each. Pour over the hot sauce and serve at once.

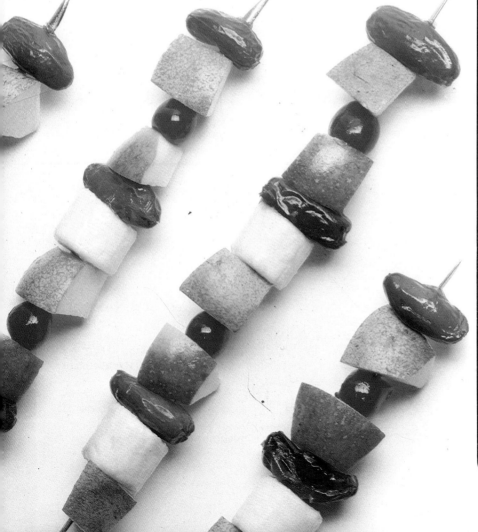

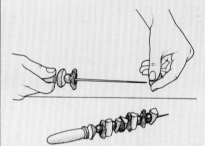

Coupe Jacques

SERVES 6

350 g/12 oz mixed fresh fruits, cut into small pieces (see Cook's tips)
3 tablespoons kirsch or orange-flavoured liqueur (see Economy)
caster sugar, to taste
475 ml/17 fl oz lemon sorbet
475 ml/17 fl oz strawberry sorbet

1 Place 6 shallow bowls in the refrigerator to chill.
2 Put the fruits into a bowl and sprinkle with 2 tablespoons of the liqueur and caster sugar to taste. Mix gently but thoroughly, then cover and refrigerate for at least 1 hour.
3 To serve: put 1 scoop or large spoonful each of lemon and strawberry sorbet side by side in each of the chilled bowls. Carefully drain off any excess juice from the mixed chilled fruits, then divide the fruits equally between the bowls, spooning them in between and on top of the 2 sorbets. Sprinkle over the remaining liqueur and serve at once.

Cook's Notes

TIME
20-30 minutes preparation (depending on the fruits used), plus chilling time.

COOK'S TIP
You can use any combination of fruits. If using those which discolour when peeled (such as bananas or apples), turn the pieces in lemon juice before adding to the bowl.

ECONOMY
Use orange juice in place of the orange-flavoured liqueur.

DID YOU KNOW
This is a classic French fruit salad which is always served with kirsch and lemon and strawberry sorbets. What is not known about the dish is who the original Jacques was!

VARIATIONS
Other flavoured sorbets, or water ices, can be used. If you find the sorbets difficult to obtain, use vanilla and strawberry ice cream instead.

● 220 calories/925 kj per portion

Grilled pineapple

SERVES 4

1 large pineapple
4 tablespoons dark soft brown sugar
25 g/1 oz butter
4 tablespoons rum

1 Heat the grill to high.
2 Cut the pineapple lengthways into quarters, slicing through the green crown. Cut out the core and loosen the flesh (see Preparation). Wrap foil around each crown.
3 Arrange the pineapple quarters in the grill pan. Sprinkle each quarter with 1 tablespoon sugar and dot with butter. Grill for 4-5 minutes until the pineapple is heated through. Transfer to warmed dishes and remove the foil.
4 Put the rum into a small saucepan, heat it through gently, then remove from the heat and immediately set light to it. As soon as the flames subside, pour the rum over the pineapple together with any juice from the grill pan. Serve at once.

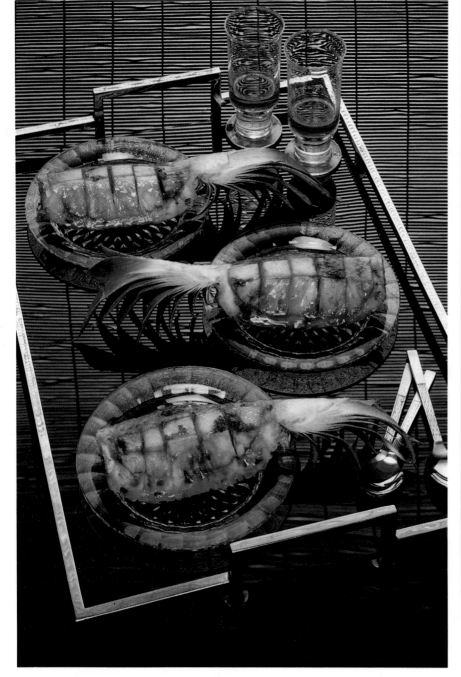

Cook's Notes

TIME
Preparation and cooking take 15 minutes.

PREPARATION
To prepare the pineapple 'boats':

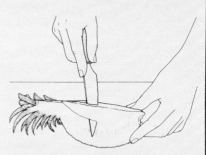

1 Put the pineapple quarters on to a plate or chopping board. Using a sharp, serrated knife, carefully cut out the core.

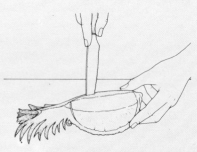

2 Cut all round the edge between flesh and skin, about 1 cm/½ inch from the skin.

3 Slide the knife underneath the flesh to separate it from the skin completely but do not remove it from the 'boat'. Cut the flesh lengthways and then across into bite-size cubes ready for serving.

FOR CHILDREN
Omit the rum and decorate the pineapple with halved glacé cherries.

●235 calories/975 kj per portion

Date rice

SERVES 4

50 g/2 oz pudding rice
600 ml/1 pint milk
15 g/½ oz margarine or butter
50 g/2 oz pressed dates, chopped
   (see Buying guide)
grated zest of 1 orange
melted margarine, for greasing

1 Heat the oven to 150C/300F/Gas 2. Brush the inside of an 850 ml/1½ pint ovenproof pie dish with melted margarine.
2 Put the rice, milk and margarine into a saucepan. Bring just to boiling point, then remove from the heat. Stir in the dates and orange zest. Pour into the prepared oven-proof pie dish and place the dish on a baking sheet.
3 Bake in the oven for about 2 hours, or until the rice is tender and most of the milk has been absorbed. Serve hot (see Serving ideas).

Cook's Notes

TIME
Preparation 20 minutes, cooking time 2 hours.

ECONOMY
If you are using the oven heated to 170C/325F/ Gas 3 for a main dish, the pudding may be baked on the bottom shelf.

VARIATIONS
Use other dried fruits, such as raisins or sultanas in place of some or all of the dates. For added flavour, grate a little nutmeg over the top.

BUYING GUIDE
Buy dates that are already stoned—available from most supermarkets.

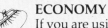
SERVING IDEAS
Serve hot, topped with chilled fresh orange segments, or drained canned mandarins.

COOK'S TIP
Heating the milk and rice first helps to keep baking time to a minimum.

●220 calories/925 kj per portion

CAKES, PIES AND FLANS

Ginger cream refrigerator cake

MAKES 8 SLICES

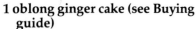
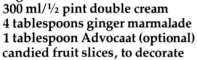 1 oblong ginger cake (see Buying guide)
300 ml/½ pint double cream
4 tablespoons ginger marmalade
1 tablespoon Advocaat (optional)
candied fruit slices, to decorate

1 Remove the cake from its paper wrapper. Scrape off the remnants of cake sticking to the wrapper with a round-bladed knife, then crumble them between your fingers and reserve for decoration, if liked.
2 Cut the cake vertically into 4 equal slices, as shown in photograph.
3 Whip the cream until thick, then fold in the marmalade and Advocaat, if using. Sandwich the cake back together with about half of the cream mixture, then place on a narrow serving dish.

4 Spread the remaining cream mixture all over the cake to cover it completely.
5 Decorate the top with candied fruit slices and sprinkle with the reserved cake crumbs, if using. Refrigerate the cake for 1-2 hours before serving.

Cook's Notes

 TIME
20 minutes preparation, plus 1-2 hours chilling.

BUYING GUIDE
Choose a moist, oblong cake (sometimes sold as 'Jamaica' cake).

 FREEZING
Make the cake up to the end of stage 4, assembling it on a freezer tray. Open freeze until solid, then place carefully in a rigid container. Seal, label and store in the freezer for up to 3 months. To serve: remove from container and place on a serving dish; defrost at room temperature for 3 hours, then decorate.

 VARIATIONS
Use an orange- or lemon-flavoured cake and add orange or lemon jelly marmalade to the whipped cream. Drained mandarin segments or fresh orange slices can be used to decorate the top of the cake, if liked.

DID YOU KNOW
Advocaat is a thick and creamy, yellow Dutch liqueur; it is based on brandy and thickened with egg yolks and sugar.

●335 calories/1400 kj per slice

180

Chocolate éclairs

MAKES 8

100 g/4 oz packet choux pastry mix
   (see Buying guide)
225 ml/8 fl oz tepid water
vegetable oil and flour, for baking
   sheet

FILLING AND ICING

150 ml/¼ pint whipping cream
2 drops vanilla flavouring
15 g/½ oz caster sugar
50 g/2 oz plain chocolate, broken
   into pieces
knob of butter
2-3 tablespoons water
175 g/6 oz icing sugar

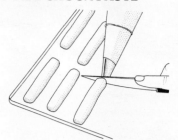
1 Heat the oven to 200C/400F/Gas 6. Prepare a large baking sheet (see Preparation).
2 Put the pastry mix into a small bowl, add the water and beat with a rotary or hand-held electric whisk for 4 minutes. Put paste in piping bag fitted with a 2 cm/¾ inch plain nozzle, and pipe on to prepared baking sheet (see Preparation).
3 Bake in the oven for 40 minutes, until puffed and golden. With a palette knife, ease the éclairs off the baking sheet and transfer to a wire rack. Split each one lengthways in half with a sharp knife, then scrape out and discard any uncooked pastry from the inside with a teaspoon. Leave to cool completely.
4 Make the filling: whip the cream until beginning to thicken, then add vanilla flavouring and caster sugar and continue whisking until thick but not stiff. Pipe or spoon the cream into the bottom half of each éclair, then replace the tops.
5 Put the chocolate, butter and 1 tablespoon water in a heatproof bowl set over a pan of hot water. Leave, stirring occasionally, until the chocolate has melted. Remove the bowl from the pan and beat in the sifted icing sugar, a little at a time. If necessary, beat in 1-2 more tablespoons water to thin the icing.
6 Spoon or spread the icing over the tops of the éclairs, then leave in a cool place to set. Serve as soon as possible.

Cherry cream slices

MAKES 6 SLICES

400 g/13 oz frozen puff pastry, defrosted

FILLING

425 g/15 oz can stoned black cherries in syrup
2 tablespoons cornflour
2 tablespoons water
300 ml/½ pint double cream
3 drops vanilla essence
25 g/1 oz sugar

ICING

225 g/8 oz icing sugar, sifted
2-3 tablespoons warm water
25 g/1 oz dessert chocolate, melted

1 Heat the oven to 230C/450F/Gas 8. Dampen a large baking sheet with water. Cut the pastry in half and roll out each piece to a rectangle, about 30 × 15 cm/12 × 6 inches. ! Place on the prepared baking sheet and prick well with a fork. Bake in the oven for 15 minutes, turning the pieces round halfway through the cooking time so that they become evenly browned. Transfer to a wire rack and leave to cool completely.

2 Meanwhile, make the filling: place the cherries, with their syrup, in a small saucepan and bring slowly to simmering point. Blend the cornflour to a smooth paste with the water. Remove the pan from the heat and stir in the cornflour mixture. Return to low heat and bring back to the boil, stirring constantly, then set aside to cool completely. !

3 Make the icing: blend the icing sugar with enough warm water to give a thick coating consistency.

4 Turn one layer of pastry over and spread the icing over the surface (see Cook's tips).

5 Whip the cream until it begins to thicken; add the vanilla essence and sugar. Continue whipping until the cream stands in stiff peaks.

6 Assemble the dessert: spread the cold cherry mixture over the other layer of pastry, then cover with the whipped cream.

7 Put the iced layer of pastry on top of the cream, iced side up, then lift on to a wooden board and place in the refrigerator for 30 minutes, or the freezer for 20 minutes (see Cook's tips).

8 With a sharp serrated knife, and a sawing motion, carefully cut the pastry into 6 slices. Using a tea-spoon, drizzle melted chocolate over the top of each slice in a zig-zag pattern. Return to the refrigerator for 10 minutes to set before serving.

Cook's Notes

TIME
About 4 hours total pre-paration and cooking time, including cooling the cherry mixture which can take as long as 2 hours.

WATCHPOINTS
When rolling the pastry, keep a good rectangular shape with neat edges.

Before filling, ensure that the cherry mixture and the pastry are well cooled or the cream will melt. To speed up cooling of any mixture, place in a cool container and stand on a wire rack so the air can circulate freely.

COOK'S TIPS
Icing the flat underside of the layer, before turning it over, gives a better finished appearance.

Placing the dessert in the refrigerator or freezer for a short time makes it easier to slice.

STORAGE
Keep covered in a large plastic container in the refrigerator for up to 2 days.

●735 calories/3075 kj per slice

Frozen macaroon mould

SERVES 6-8

150 ml/¼ pint double cream
1 L/1¾ pints soft-scoop vanilla ice cream (see Buying guide)
4 tablespoons orange juice
100 g/4 oz macaroons, crushed
25 g/1 oz whole almonds, split and lightly toasted

SAUCE
350 g/12 oz raspberries, defrosted if frozen
4 tablespoons redcurrant jelly
1 teaspoon cornflour
2 tablespoons water

1 Whip the cream until thick. Add the ice cream and orange juice and whisk gently together until evenly combined. Quickly fold in the macaroons. Turn the mixture immediately into a 1.5 L/2½ pint freezerproof mould and level the surface. Cover tightly and freeze for at least 8 hours or overnight, until firm (see Cook's tip).

2 When the mixture is firm, make the sauce: reserve some of the whole raspberries for decoration; sieve the remainder, then pour the purée into a saucepan and add the redcurrant jelly. Blend the cornflour to a smooth paste with the water and stir into the pan. Bring slowly to the boil, stirring, and simmer for 2-3 minutes. Pour the sauce into a jug and cool. Cover and refrigerate. ✳

3 Turn the frozen mixture out of the mould on to a chilled, deep serving plate. [!] Pour the sauce over the dessert and spike with the almonds.

Cook's Notes

 TIME
20 minutes preparation (including turning out and decorating), plus at least 8 hours freezing.

 WATCHPOINT
When the dessert is turned out of the mould the mixture melts slightly, so have absorbent paper ready to mop up liquid from the base.

BUYING GUIDE
Use soft-scoop ice cream for this dessert, not the block variety which is too hard to blend in easily.

COOK'S TIP
You can make this dessert in the freezer compartment of the refrigerator. Turn the refrigerator to its coldest setting at least 1 hour beforehand, and pour the ice cream and macaroon mixture into a well-chilled metal mould.

FREEZING
The ice cream and macaroon mixture can be stored in the freezer for up to 3 months. Freeze the sauce separately; defrost before use.

● 400 calories/1675 kj per portion

Mocha meringue

SERVES 8

3 large egg whites
175 g/6 oz light soft brown sugar, sifted
1 teaspoon instant coffee powder
vegetable oil, for greasing

FILLING

100 g/4 oz plain dessert chocolate, broken into squares
4 tablespoons water
300 ml/½ pint whipping cream
2 teaspoons instant coffee powder
grated chocolate, to finish

1 Heat the oven to 150C/300F/Gas 2. Line 3 baking sheets with non-stick parchment paper or greaseproof paper (see Cook's tips). Mark each piece with a 15 cm/7 inch circle. If using greaseproof paper, lightly brush each circle with oil.
2 Put the egg whites into a dry, grease-free large bowl. Whisk until stiff and white and standing in firm peaks.
3 Add the sugar, 1 tablespoon at a time, whisking well after each addition so that the meringue is firm and glossy. Whisk in the instant coffee powder.

4 Spread the meringue mixture evenly over the marked circles on the baking sheet linings. Bake in the oven for 1½ hours or until crisp and dry in the centre. Swap the top and bottom sheets after 45 minutes to ensure even cooking. Set aside to cool, then peel off lining paper.
5 Prepare the filling: put the chocolate and water into a small bowl over a pan of simmering water and heat until the chocolate has melted. Stir, then set aside to cool for about 10 minutes or until the chocolate begins to thicken.
6 Whisk the cream until stiff, then put half of it into another bowl. Stir the chocolate mixture into one half and the instant coffee powder into the other half.

7 To finish: put 1 meringue round on to a serving plate and spread it with half the coffee cream. ⚠ Cover with another meringue round and spread with half the chocolate cream. Cover with the third meringue round. Spread the remaining coffee cream over the top and mark decoratively with a fork.
8 Lightly whip the remaining chocolate cream until stiff. Put the cream into a piping bag fitted with a small star nozzle. Pipe 8 rosettes around the edge of the cake. Sprinkle the rosettes with a little grated chocolate. Serve as soon as possible, or within 2 hours if kept in the refrigerator, otherwise the mocha meringue will lose its fresh, crisp appearance.

Cook's Notes

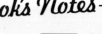

TIME
Preparation time 20 minutes, cooking time 1½ hours. Allow another 15 minutes for decoration.

COOK'S TIPS
If you do not have 3 baking sheets, use large flan tins, or put 2 meringue rounds on 1 large sheet.
If possible, use an electric beater to whisk the meringue.

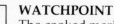

WATCHPOINT
The cooked meringue is very brittle, so it must be handled with a great deal of care at this stage otherwise it may crack badly or break.

VARIATION
Stir 100 g/4 oz thick fruit purée into the cream in place of the chocolate.

● 295 calories/1250 kj per portion

Chocolate cheesecake

SERVES 6-8

275 g/10 oz packet bourbon biscuits (12 biscuits), finely crushed
150 g/5 oz butter, melted

FILLING

225 g/8 oz cottage cheese
225 g/8 oz full-fat soft cheese
50 g/2 oz caster sugar
juice of ½ lemon
¼ teaspoon vanilla essence
300 ml/½ pint single cream
1 tablespoon powdered gelatine
3 tablespoons warm water
75 g/3 oz plain dessert chocolate, broken into pieces

1 Mix the crushed biscuits with the butter. Press on to the base and sides of an oiled 20 cm/8 inch loose-bottomed cake tin. Cover and chill for 30 minutes, until firm.

2 To make the filling: press the cottage cheese through a nylon sieve into a mixing bowl. Add the soft cheese and beat with a wooden spoon until well combined.

3 Add the sugar, lemon juice, vanilla and cream and mix well.

4 Sprinkle the gelatine over the water in a heatproof bowl. Leave to soak for 2-3 minutes until spongy. Place the bowl over a saucepan of simmering water and stir until the gelatine has dissolved.

5 Remove from the heat, leave to cool slightly, then stir gradually into the cheese mixture.

6 Put the chocolate pieces in a heatproof bowl and place over a pan of gently simmering water. Heat until the chocolate has melted.

7 Pour the cheese mixture on top of the biscuit crust, then drizzle the melted chocolate over and swirl in with the point of a skewer. ⓘ

8 Cover and chill for about 3 hours. ✳

9 To serve: run a knife round the edge of the cake, carefully remove the sides of the tin and slide the cheesecake on to a serving plate. Serve chilled.

Spicy apple crunch

SERVES 4

750 g/1½ lb cooking apples (see Buying guide)

1 tablespoon light soft brown sugar
1 teaspoon ground cinnamon
2 tablespoons cold water
margarine, for greasing

TOPPING
75 g/3 oz porridge oats
50 g/2 oz light soft brown sugar
25 g/1 oz wholemeal flour
¼ teaspoon salt
40 g/1½ oz margarine or butter, melted

1 Heat the oven to 190C/375F/Gas 5.
2 Grease a shallow 1.5 L/2½ pint ovenproof dish thoroughly with margarine (see Cook's tips). Peel, quarter and core the apples, then slice them thinly. Mix the sugar with the cinnamon. Layer the apple slices in the dish, sprinkling the

spiced sugar mixture in between. Sprinkle over the water.
3 Make the topping: mix the oats, sugar, flour and salt in a bowl. Stir in the melted margarine with a knife until thoroughly mixed.

4 Sprinkle the topping evenly over the apples. Bake in the oven for 50-60 minutes, until the apples are very tender and the topping is crisp and browned. Serve hot or warm, straight from the dish.

Cook's Notes

 TIME
Preparation takes 20 minutes and baking 50-60 minutes.

 SERVING IDEAS
This pudding is delicious served hot or warm with vanilla ice cream, chilled soured cream or natural yoghurt. It is also good cold.

VARIATIONS
You can use plain white flour instead of wholemeal flour, if preferred. Gooseberries (topped and tailed) or halved and stoned plums can replace the apples, but they will need an extra tablespoon of sugar; alternatively, you could use a mixture of apples and blackberries.

 BUYING GUIDE
The best type of cooking apples to use are Bramleys, which reduce to a soft pulp when cooked.

COOK'S TIPS
This pudding is served straight from the dish, so choose an attractive one to bake it in. You can make the pudding ahead and reheat it, if liked, in the oven at 170C/325F/Gas 3 for about 30 minutes.

●335 calories/1400 kj per portion

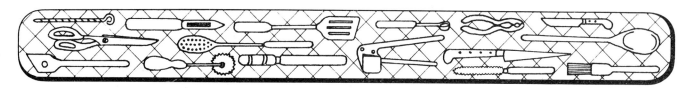

Redcurrant jelly tart

MAKES 10 SLICES
500 g/1 lb redcurrant jelly
150 g/5 oz butter, softened
150 g/5 oz caster sugar
few drops of vanilla flavouring
1 egg, lightly beaten
100 g/4 oz ground almonds
175 g/6 oz plain flour, sifted
icing sugar, for dredging (optional)
lightly whipped cream, to serve
extra softened butter, for greasing

1 Heat the oven to 180C/350F/Gas 4. Butter a 20 cm/8 inch springform cake tin (see Cook's tips).
2 Beat the butter and caster sugar together until very pale and fluffy, then beat in the vanilla. Add the egg, a little at a time, beating thoroughly after each addition. Using a wooden spoon, gradually work in the almonds and flour.

3 Draw the mixture into a ball with your fingers, turn out on to a lightly floured surface and knead briefly until smooth (see Cook's tips).
4 Reserve one-quarter of the dough in a cool place. With your hand, gently press the remaining dough over the base and 4 cm/1½ inches of the way up the sides of the prepared tin. Neaten the edges.
5 Spread the jelly evenly in the pastry case.
6 On a lightly floured surface, roll out the reserved dough to a 22× 5 cm/8½×2 inch strip. Trim edges with a sharp knife, then cut lengthways into 6 narrow strips.
7 Dampen the ends of the pastry strips, then arrange over the jelly in a lattice pattern. Press the ends against the pastry edge to seal, then flute the rim of the pastry. Bake in the oven for 45 minutes, or until the pastry is cooked and browned.
8 Sift icing sugar over the top of the hot tart, if liked. Leave to cool completely, then remove from the tin and transfer to a serving plate.

American chocolate pie

MAKES 6-8 SLICES

175 g/6 oz gingernut biscuits, finely
crushed

50 g/2 oz margarine or butter,
melted

margarine or butter, for greasing

FILLING AND TOPPING
300 ml/½ pint milk
100 g/4 oz plain dessert chocolate,
broken into pieces
100 g/4 oz caster sugar
3 tablespoons plain flour
50 g/2 oz margarine or butter
2 large egg yolks, lightly beaten
150 ml/¼ pint double cream
1 piece drained stem ginger, finely
chopped, to decorate (optional)

1 Grease an 18-20 cm/7-8 inch loose-based flan tin. Mix the finely crushed biscuits with the melted margarine until evenly coated.

2 Spoon the crumbs into the greased tin and press evenly over the base and up the sides with the back of a metal spoon (see Cook's tip). Cover and refrigerate for 30 minutes.

3 Meanwhile, make the chocolate filling: put the milk and broken chocolate into a saucepan and heat gently, stirring frequently, until the chocolate has melted. [!] Remove from the heat.

4 Combine the sugar, flour, margarine and beaten egg yolks in a bowl and mix together thoroughly with a fork. Stir in the hot chocolate milk, mixing well.

5 Return the mixture to the pan and bring slowly to the boil, stirring constantly. Reduce the heat and cook, still stirring, for about 5 minutes until the mixture is very thick and smooth.

6 Remove the pan from the heat and let the mixture cool for 5 minutes before pouring it into the biscuit-lined tin. Leave for about 30 minutes until the chocolate filling is cold and set.

7 Carefully remove the pie from the tin and place on a serving plate. Whip the cream until thick, then spread over the chocolate filling. Decorate with the stem ginger, if liked. Refrigerate until required.

Cook's Notes

TIME
Preparation takes about 1 hour and setting about 30 minutes.

COOK'S TIP
For a really smooth finish, work an empty jam jar over the base and sides of the biscuit case.

WATCHPOINT
Be sure to use a heavy-based saucepan to avoid scorching the mixture.

VARIATIONS
For a richer chocolate flavour, use chocolate digestive biscuits instead of gingernuts, and sprinkle the top with grated chocolate or orange zest rather than ginger. If preferred, a baked shortcrust pastry case can be used instead of biscuit crust—use 150-175 g/6 oz pastry.

●570 calories/2375 kj per slice

Nectarine tart

MAKES 6 SLICES

100 g/4 oz fresh cream cheese (see
    Cook's tip)
100 g/4 oz plain flour, sifted
1 tablespoon caster sugar

FILLING

4 nectarines
300 ml/½ pint water
50 g/2 oz sugar
1 tablespoon lemon juice
4 tablespoons redcurrant jelly or
    sieved apricot jam, for glazing

1 Make the pastry: beat the cream
cheese with a wooden spoon until
soft and smooth. Add the flour and
sugar and continue beating until the
mixture is evenly crumbly. Using
your fingers, draw the mixture
together to make a soft dough.

2 Turn the dough out on to a lightly
floured surface and knead briefly;
wrap in cling film and refrigerate for
1 hour (and up to 24 hours).

3 Heat the oven to 200C/400F/Gas 6.

4 On a lightly floured surface, roll
out the pastry and use to line a
loose-based, 20 cm/8 inch fluted flan
tin. Prick the base with a fork, then
line with a large circle of greaseproof paper or foil and weight
down with baking beans.

5 Bake in the oven for 10 minutes.
Remove paper or foil and baking
beans and return to the oven for a
further 10-15 minutes until pastry is
set and lightly coloured. Remove
the sides of the tin, slide the pastry
case on to a wire rack and leave to
cool completely.

6 Meanwhile, prepare the filling:
put the water into a heavy-based
saucepan with the sugar and lemon
juice. Stir over low heat until the
sugar has dissolved, then bring to
the boil, without stirring, and
simmer for 1-2 minutes.

7 Halve and stone the nectarines
and lower into the syrup with a
slotted spoon. Cover and poach
gently for above 5 minutes until just
tender. Remove the pan from the
heat. Lift nectarines out of the
syrup with the slotted spoon and
leave to cool completely. Reserve
1 tablespoon of syrup in the pan.

8 Assemble the tart: place the
pastry case on a serving plate. Skin
nectarines, if liked, then cut into
thick slices or leave the halves intact
and arrange them carefully in the
pastry case.

9 Add jelly or jam to reserved
syrup and stir well over low heat
until melted. Allow the glaze to cool
until beginning to thicken, then
brush over the nectarines. Leave to
set before serving.

Cook's Notes

TIME
10-15 minutes, plus
chilling the pastry, then
1¼ hours, plus setting.

WATCHPOINT
Do not overcook the
nectarines: they must
keep their shape or the whole
look of the tart will be spoilt.

VARIATION
Firm peaches can be
used instead. Do not
use canned fruit for this recipe.

COOK'S TIP
Pastry made with cream
cheese is richer and
more crumbly than shortcrust.
There are also fewer calories.
It has a delicious flavour which
goes beautifully with fresh nectarines, but plain shortcrust can
be used instead, if you prefer.
When using ordinary shortcrust
pastry, you will need 150-175 g/
6 oz dough for a 20 cm/8 inch
fluted flan tin.

●245 calories/1025 kj per slice

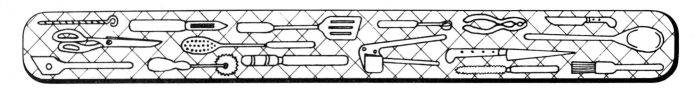

Raised plum pie

SERVES 6

1 350 g/12 oz shortcrust pastry,
    defrosted if frozen
milk and caster sugar, for glazing

FILLING
1 tablespoon cornflour
1 teaspoon ground cinnamon
175 g/6 oz caster sugar
750 g/1½ lb ripe plums (see Buying
    guide), halved and stoned
pouring cream or custard, to serve

1 Heat the oven to 190C/375F/Gas 5.
2 On a lightly floured surface, roll
out just under half of the pastry and
use to line a 20 cm/8 inch pie dish.
3 Place the cornflour, cinnamon

and sugar in a strong, large polythene bag, then add the plums and
shake well until the fruit is coated
with the sugar mixture.
4 Turn the plum and sugar mixture
into the pastry-lined plate, mounding it slightly in the centre. Brush
the pastry edges with water.
5 On a lightly floured surface, roll

out the remaining pastry to a 24 cm/
9½ inch circle and use to cover the
pie. Brush the pastry lid with milk,
then sprinkle with caster sugar.
Pierce the top with a skewer or fork
to make a steam vent.
6 Bake in the oven for about 45
minutes, until the pastry is golden
brown. Serve hot or warm.

Cook's Notes

TIME
Preparation takes 20-25
minutes; baking time is
about 45 minutes.

VARIATION
Cherry plum pie: use
only 350 g/12 oz plums
and 75 g/3 oz caster sugar; omit
cinnamon and cornflour and
mix the sweetened plums with a

400 g/14 oz can commercial
cherry pie filling.

BUYING GUIDE
Victoria plums are ideal
for this recipe. Other
ripe plums can be used, but they
must be firm—soft plums do not
make a good filling.

●410 calories/1725 kj per portion

Raisin pie

MAKES 4-6 SLICES
175 g/6 oz plain flour
pinch of salt
25 g/1 oz caster sugar
75 g/3 oz margarine or butter, diced
1 egg, beaten
a little milk, for brushing
caster sugar, for sifting

FILLING
350 g/12 oz seedless raisins
grated zest and juice of 1 lemon
½ teaspoon ground cinnamon
50 g/2 oz sugar
150 ml/¼ pint water
2 teaspoons cornflour
2 teaspoons water

1 Sift the flour with the salt and sugar into a bowl. Add the diced margarine and rub it into the flour until the mixture resembles fine breadcrumbs. Add the beaten egg and mix to a stiff dough. Wrap in cling film or foil and refrigerate.
2 Heat the oven to 220C/425F/Gas 7.
3 Prepare the filling: put the raisins, lemon zest and juice, cinnamon, sugar and water into a saucepan and cook gently for 5 minutes. Mix the cornflour to a smooth paste with the water, then stir into the raisin mixture. Bring to the boil, stirring all the time. Remove from the heat and leave to cool completely.
4 Cut off one-third of the pastry and set it aside. Roll out the remaining pastry and use to line a 20 cm/8 inch loose-bottomed fluted flan tin or a flan ring set on a baking sheet.
5 Spoon the cold raisin filling into the pastry-lined tin. ! Roll out the reserved piece of pastry to a round large enough to cover the pie. Dampen the pastry rim with water, then place the pastry lid on top and press the edges together to seal. Brush the top of the pie with milk, then prick it with a fork. ✳
6 Bake the pie in the oven for 25-30 minutes. Remove the sides of the tin or the flan ring and return the pie to the oven for a further 5 minutes to brown the sides. Remove the pie from the oven and immediately sift over caster sugar (see Serving ideas).

TIME
40 minutes preparation, plus 30-35 minutes baking.

WATCHPOINT
Make sure that the raisin filling is quite cold before it is put into the pastry-lined tin. If hot filling is put into raw pastry it will make the fat in the pastry melt and thus cause the pastry base to become soggy.

FREEZING
Prepare the pie up to the end of stage 5. Open freeze, then remove from the tin, or ring, and wrap in foil. Return to the freezer and store for up to 3 months. To serve: unwrap and replace in the flan tin or ring; bake from frozen, allowing an extra 10 minutes.

SERVING IDEAS
This pie can be served hot, warm or cold, with vanilla ice cream, custard, whipped cream or natural yoghurt.

STORAGE
The pastry and filling can be prepared and stored separately in the refrigerator for 2-3 days.

●630 calories/2625 kj per slice

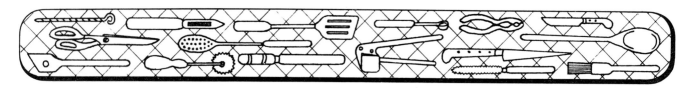

Frangipani tart

MAKES 6 SLICES

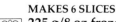 225 g/8 oz frozen puff pastry,
    defrosted
 6 canned apricot halves, drained
    and finely chopped
½ teaspoon finely grated orange
    zest
100 g/4 oz soft tub margarine
100 g/4 oz caster sugar
2 eggs, lightly beaten
100 g/4 oz ground almonds
melted margarine, for greasing

ICING

50 g/2 oz icing sugar, sifted
2 tablespoons orange juice, warmed

1 Heat the oven to 190C/375F/Gas 5.
Lightly grease a 20 cm/8 inch flan or
sandwich tin with a loose base.
2 Roll out the pastry on a lightly
floured surface and use to line the
tin. Mix the apricots and orange zest

together and sprinkle over the base
of the pastry case.
3 Beat the margarine with the sugar
until pale and fluffy. Beat in the
eggs, a little at a time, then stir in the
ground almonds. Spoon the mixture
into the pastry case and level the
surface.
4 Bake in the oven for about 40

minutes, until the filling is set and
browned. Leave to cool in the tin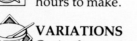
for 10-15 minutes, then remove from
the tin and place on a serving dish.
5 Make the icing: blend the icing
sugar and orange juice until
smooth. Using a pastry brush,
brush the icing over the top of the
flan. Serve warm or cold.

Cook's Notes

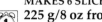 **TIME**
The flan takes 1¼-1½
hours to make.

VARIATIONS
Omit the apricots and
orange zest and spread
3 tablespoons apricot jam over
the base of the pastry case. Add
2 tablespoons chopped blanched
almonds to the filling.

 FREEZING
Cool completely, then
remove from the tin. Do
not ice. Wrap in a polythene

bag, seal, label and freeze for up
to 1 month.
    To serve: defrost in wrap-
pings at room temperature for
4-5 hours. Warm through in a
170C/325F/Gas 3 oven for 15
minutes, then ice.

DID YOU KNOW
This aromatic tart is
named after the frangi-
pani, a tropical plant noted for
its fragrancy; its oils are used to
make perfume.

●505 calories/2125 kj per slice

Pineapple meringue pie

MAKES 6 SLICES

175 g/6 oz digestive biscuits, finely crushed

75 g/3 oz butter, melted

FILLING
2 tablespoons custard powder
2 tablespoons sugar
375 g/13 oz can crushed pineapple, well drained, with syrup reserved
2 large eggs, separated (see Watchpoints)
100 g/4 oz caster sugar

1 Mix the biscuit crumbs with the melted butter. Spoon into a loose-based 20 cm/8 inch sandwich or flan tin and press evenly and firmly over the base and up the sides. Cover and refrigerate for at least 30 minutes.
2 Heat the oven to 200C/400F/Gas 6.

3 Make the filling: in a small, heavy-based saucepan, mix together the custard powder and sugar. Stir in a little of the reserved pineapple syrup to make a smooth paste, then blend in the remainder. Bring gently to the boil, stirring constantly, then remove from the heat.
4 Allow the mixture to cool slightly, then beat in the egg yolks. Stir in the crushed pineapple. Spoon the pineapple mixture into the biscuit case and level the surface.
5 In a spotlessly clean, dry bowl, whisk the egg whites until they stand in stiff peaks. Whisk in the caster sugar, 1 tablespoon at a time, and continue whisking until the meringue is stiff and glossy.
6 Pipe swirls of meringue over pie or spread with a palette knife, then draw up into peaks. Bake in the oven for 10-15 minutes, until the meringue is golden brown. Leave to cool completely, [!] then remove from the tin and place on a serving plate. Serve at room temperature.

Cook's Notes

TIME
30 minutes preparation, 10-15 minutes baking, plus at least 4 hours cooling.

WATCHPOINTS
Use eggs at room temperature.
Resist the temptation to remove the pie from the tin before it is completely cold as the biscuit case may crumble.

STORAGE
The biscuit case will keep for up to 2 days in the refrigerator. Wrap it well in foil or place in a polythene bag and seal tightly. The baked pie will keep fresh overnight if left loosely covered in a cool place, but not the refrigerator.

●400 calories/1675 kj per slice

Citrus apple flan

SERVES 4

RICH SHORTCRUST PASTRY
175 g/6 oz plain flour
pinch of salt
100 g/4 oz margarine or butter
2 tablespoons water, chilled

FILLING
75 g/3 oz margarine or butter
75 g/3 oz caster sugar
100 g/4 oz fresh white breadcrumbs
grated zest of 1 orange
½ teaspoon ground mixed spice
4 tablespoons thick-cut marmalade
2 cooking apples
icing sugar, to dust

1 To make the pastry: sift the flour and salt into a large bowl. Cut the margarine into 1 cm/½ inch cubes, add to the flour and rub in until the mixture resembles coarse crumbs. Sprinkle over the water, then draw the mixture together to a firm dough. Wrap in cling film and refrigerate for at least 30 minutes before using.

2 Heat the oven to 200C/400F/Gas 6.

3 Roll out the pastry on a floured surface and use to line a 20 cm/8 inch loose-based sandwich tin or a plain or fluted flan ring placed on a baking sheet. Prick lightly in several places with a fork.

4 In a saucepan, melt the margarine over low heat. Remove from the heat and stir in the sugar, breadcrumbs, orange zest and mixed spice.

5 Spread the marmalade over the base of the flan. Peel, core and slice the apples and arrange over the marmalade. Spoon the breadcrumb mixture evenly over the top and press down lightly.

6 Bake in the oven for 25 minutes, then reduce the heat to 180C/350F/Gas 4 and bake for a further 10-15 minutes until golden.

7 Remove from the tin (see Cook's tip), sift icing sugar lightly and evenly over the top to dust and serve the flan hot.

Tropical flan

SERVES 6

25 cm/10 inch sponge flan case
3 oranges
425 g/15 oz can pineapple rings in natural juice, drained with juice reserved
1 mango
1-2 tablespoons caster sugar
2 teaspoons arrowroot (see Buying guide)
150 ml/¼ pint whipping or double cream, to serve

1 Put the flan case on a flat serving dish.

2 Peel and slice the oranges over a bowl to reserve any juice. Remove any pips and the central pith and arrange around the edge of the sponge flan.

3 Cut the pineapple rings in half and arrange, overlapping, in a ring inside the ring of orange slices.

4 Again working over a bowl, score the skin of the mango lengthways into several sections and remove the skin with a small sharp knife. Chop the mango flesh neatly and pile into the centre of the flan. Squeeze the mango stone, which will have some flesh clinging to it, over the bowl to extract all the juice.

5 Strain the reserved orange, pineapple and mango juice into a measuring jug and make up to 175 ml/6 fl oz with water. Stir in 1-2 tablespoons caster sugar, to taste, and mix until dissolved.

6 Spoon 50 ml/2 fl oz of this juice over the sponge around the rim of the flan to moisten it.

7 Put the arrowroot into a bowl. Stir in a little of the fruit juice to make a smooth paste, then gradually stir in the remainder. Transfer to a small saucepan and bring to the boil over moderate heat, stirring constantly, until thick, smooth and clear.

8 Spoon the hot glaze over the fruit, allowing a little to run down the sides of the flan.

9 Leave in a cool place for 30 minutes, or up to 8 hours, then serve accompanied by the cream. (If liked the cream can be whipped until standing in soft peaks and piped around the edge instead).

Latticed gooseberry tart

SERVES 4

275 g/10 oz shortcrust pastry, defrosted if frozen
little beaten egg, for glazing
caster sugar, for dredging
custard or cream, to serve

FILLING

225 g/8 oz gooseberries, topped and tailed if fresh, defrosted and well drained if frozen
2 tablespoons fresh white breadcrumbs (see Cook's tips)
25 g/1 oz sugar
½ teaspoon finely chopped fresh mint (optional)

1 Heat the oven to 200C/400F/Gas 6.
2 Cut off one-third of the pastry and reserve. On a lightly floured surface, roll out the remaining pastry and use to line a 23 cm/9 inch pie plate.
3 Mix the gooseberries with the breadcrumbs, sugar and mint, if using. Spoon into the pastry-lined pie plate and spread evenly. Brush the edges of the pastry with water.

4 Use the reserved pastry to make a lattice decoration over the tart (see Preparation). Brush the pastry lattice with beaten egg.
5 Bake the tart in the oven, just above the centre, for 20 minutes; then lower the heat to 190C/375F/Gas 5 and bake for about 15 minutes

more, until the gooseberries are tender (see Cook's tips). Cover the top with greaseproof paper if the pastry is browning too quickly.
6 Remove the tart from the oven and sift caster sugar thickly over the top. Serve hot, warm or cold, with custard or cream.

Cook's Notes

 TIME
30 minutes preparation, plus about 35 minutes baking.

COOK'S TIPS
Breadcrumbs absorb the juices produced by the filling during baking and help prevent the pastry becoming soggy.

Use a fine skewer to test that the gooseberries are tender.

 VARIATIONS
Fresh mint gives a pleasant flavour to gooseberries, but you could use a little grated orange or lemon zest, or ¼ teaspoon ground mixed spice instead.

PREPARATION
A lattice is a very decorative way of topping a tart. If using a very soft or moist filling, make the lattice on greaseproof paper, then gently shake it on to the tart.

For a scalloped effect, the strips can be cut with a pastry lattice. A plain lattice is made as follows: roll out the pastry to a rectangle, 1 cm/½ inch larger than diameter of the pie plate. Cut in 1 cm/½ inch wide strips. Place half the strips over the tart in parallel lines. Lay the remaining strips in parallel lines across the first set. Trim the edges and press to seal.

●345 calories/1450 kj per portion

Mediterranean rice dessert

SERVES 4

450 g/15½ oz can creamed rice milk
    pudding
1 tablespoon cornflour
150 ml/¼ pint milk
2 tablespoons sugar
1 large egg yolk
grated zest of 1 small lemon
grated chocolate, to decorate

1 Turn the creamed rice into a saucepan and set over low heat.
2 Blend the cornflour with 2-3 tablespoons of milk, then stir in half the remaining milk. Add the cornflour mixture to the rice together with the sugar. Bring slowly to the boil, stirring, and simmer for 2 minutes.
3 Beat the egg yolk with the remaining milk, then stir into the rice pudding. Add the lemon zest and simmer, stirring, for 2 minutes more.
4 Remove the pan from the heat and pour the pudding into 4 individual dessert bowls. Sprinkle a little grated chocolate over each pudding. Serve hot or chilled.

Cook's Notes

TIME
Preparation and cooking take about 10 minutes. Remember to allow chilling time if serving cold.

ECONOMY
This is a quick and easy way to stretch a can of rice pudding to serve 4.

DID YOU KNOW
This type of pudding is popular in the Mediterranean, where it is often sprinkled with cinnamon.

● 185 calories/775 kj per portion

Coffee mousse

SERVES 6

4 teaspoons instant coffee
50 g/2 oz caster sugar
3 tablespoons boiling water
1 rounded tablespoon (1 sachet)
   powdered gelatine
3 tablespoons cold water
300 ml/½ pint double cream
2 egg whites
small chocolate curls, to decorate
   (see Preparation)

1 Dissolve the coffee and caster sugar in the boiling water.
2 Sprinkle the gelatine over the cold water in a small heatproof bowl and leave to soak for 5 minutes, then stand the bowl in a pan of gently simmering water for 1-2 minutes until the gelatine has completely dissolved, stirring occasionally.
3 Pour the coffee into the gelatine liquid, stirring well to mix. Remove the bowl from the pan and leave the coffee mixture until tepid. ⚠
4 Meanwhile, whip the cream until standing in soft peaks. Just before the coffee mixture is ready, whisk the egg whites until stiff in a clean, dry bowl and using clean beaters.

5 Using a large metal spoon, quickly blend the coffee mixture into the cream, then fold in the egg whites. Divide the mixture equally between 6 small dishes. Cover and refrigerate for 2-3 hours, until set.
6 Just before serving, decorate each mousse with chocolate curls.

Cook's Notes

⏰ TIME
15 minutes preparation plus 2-3 hours chilling.

⚠ WATCHPOINT
You need to keep a close watch on the coffee mixture as it cools very quickly. Test the mixture frequently with a clean finger; it should feel just warm. Do not let it become too cool or it will set in threads as soon as it comes into contact with the whipped cream.

● 280 calories/1175 kj per **mousse**

PREPARATION
For a 2-tone effect, make curls from bars of white and dairy milk chocolate.

Draw a swivel potato peeler towards you, along the side of bar, to shave off small curls.

Rhubarb and orange cream

SERVES 4

540 g/1 lb 3 oz can rhubarb
finely grated zest and juice of
1 orange
1 tablespoon caster sugar, or to
taste
3 eggs
150 ml/¼ pint whipping or double
cream
sweet biscuits, to serve

1 Put the rhubarb and 2 tablespoons juice from the can into a blender with the orange zest and juice and sugar. Blend at high speed until a smooth purée.
2 Whisk the eggs together thoroughly in a heatproof bowl, then whisk in the rhubarb purée.
3 Place the bowl over a saucepan of simmering water and cook for 10-15 minutes, whisking constantly with a balloon whisk until the mixture is thick and creamy. !
4 Remove the bowl from the heat, leave to cool, then chill in the refrigerator until absolutely cold. !
5 Whip the cream until it stands in soft peaks, then fold into the cooled rhubarb mixture. Cover and chill in the refrigerator for at least 6 hours (preferably overnight) before serving.
6 Serve chilled in individual dishes or glasses, with sweet biscuits.

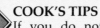 *Cook's Notes*

 TIME
1 hour 25 minutes, plus at least 6 hours chilling.

VARIATIONS
Use fresh rhubarb when in season. Weigh 500 g/ 1 lb, trim and slice, then cook with sugar to taste until tender. Drain, reserving 2 tablespoons juice.

Try using canned plums instead of rhubarb, but sieve them after puréeing to remove the skins. Add a pinch of ground cinnamon to give a deliciously different flavour.

COOK'S TIPS
If you do not have a blender, simply mash the rhubarb thoroughly until it is a smooth, creamy pulp.

Use the finest part of the grater to grate the orange rind. Do not grate for too long in one place, but simple take off the zest, or the orange-coloured part of the skin, because the pith underneath is rather bitter.

WATCHPOINT
It is important the bowl containing the eggs and rhubarb purée should not come in contact with the water simmering in the pan. It should rest just above the surface of the water so the mixture does not boil and curdle or separate.

The cooked mixture must be quite cold before you add the cream, or the cream will flop.

 SERVING IDEAS
This dessert has a soft, creamy consistency which is complemented by crisp biscuits such as *langues de chat* or sponge fingers.

●250 calories/1050 kj per portion

Fruit mallow

SERVES 6

175 g/6 oz pink and white
  marshmallows (see Buying
  guide)
400 g/14 oz can fruit cocktail, well
  drained
300 ml/½ pint whipping cream
2 tablespoons milk
extra marshmallows and fan
  wafers, to decorate (optional)

1 Snip the marshmallows into
pieces (see Preparation) and put
into a large bowl. Using a wooden
spoon, gently stir in the fruit cocktail and mix until evenly blended.
2 In a separate bowl, whip the
cream with the milk until standing
in stiff peaks. Using a large metal
spoon, fold the cream into the fruit
and marshmallow mixture.

3 Spoon the mixture into 6 tall
glasses. Cover each with cling film
and refrigerate for at least 8 hours,
or overnight, to allow the flavours
to blend and the texture to firm.

4 Remove the desserts from the
fridge 15 minutes before serving
to take chill off. Just before serving,
decorate with marshmallows and
wafers if liked.

Cook's Notes

TIME
Preparation takes only
15 minutes, but allow at
least 8 hours chilling time. Decorating the desserts takes a few
extra minutes.

BUYING GUIDE
Some supermarkets sell
their own brand of
marshmallow in a 175 g/6 oz
packets. They are also available
in 130 g/4½ oz packets; in which
case, buy 2 packs and use the
extra to decorate the desserts
just before you serve them.

● 290 calories/1200 kj per portion

PREPARATION
Cut the marshmallows
as follows:

*Using kitchen scissors, cut each
marshmallow in half across, then
cut each half into 3 pieces. Dip the
scissors into hot water at frequent
intervals – this will prevent the
blades becoming too sticky.*

Apple flummery

SERVES 4

2 large eggs, separated
50 g/2 oz sugar
600 ml/1 pint milk
25 g/1 oz semolina
pinch of salt
1 large cooking apple, weighing
  about 300 g/11 oz, peeled, cored
  and puréed
juice of ½ small lemon

TO SERVE
1 red-skinned dessert apple
few drops of lemon juice

1 Put the egg yolks and sugar in a bowl and beat together until creamy.
2 Put the milk into a large saucepan and warm it over moderate heat. Sprinkle in the semolina and bring to the boil, stirring. Add the salt and lower the heat, then simmer for 10 minutes, stirring constantly.
3 Gradually stir in the egg yolk and sugar mixture until well mixed, then continue cooking very gently for a further 2 minutes, stirring all the time. Do not allow the mixture to boil or it will stick to the bottom of the pan and may burn.
4 Remove the pan from the heat, then stir in the apple purée and lemon juice until well blended.
5 Whisk the egg whites until stiff and fold into the mixture in the pan, using a metal spoon.
6 Carefully spoon the mixture into individual glasses and leave to cool for about 30 minutes.
7 To serve: thinly slice the apple, discarding the core, but leaving the skin on. Sprinkle immediately with lemon juice to prevent discoloration. Place a few slices on each serving and serve at once.

Cook's Notes

TIME
About 50 minutes, including 15 minutes to prepare and purée the apple.

COOK'S TIP
The flummery is a particularly light and re-freshing dessert—it separates slightly into a shallow layer of liquid at the bottom, topped with a fluffy mixture.

DID YOU KNOW
According to the dictionary, flummery is an old Welsh word of unknown derivation, but it refers to a traditional sweet dish (popular in the British Isles) which is milk and egg-based and always eaten cold.

●250 calories/1050 kj per portion

Honeyed apricot whips

SERVES 4

100 g/4 oz dried apricots
300 ml/½ pint hot water
2 tablespoons clear honey
300 g/10 oz natural yoghurt
2 egg whites
boudoir biscuits or chocolate
fingers, to serve

1 Put the apricots in a small bowl with the hot water and leave to soak for at least 4 hours or, if possible, overnight.
2 Turn the apricots and water into a heavy-based saucepan. Add the honey, cover and simmer very gently for about 20 minutes, until the apricots are tender. Remove from the heat and leave to cool completely.
3 Purée the apricots with the cooking syrup and yoghurt in a blender. Alternatively, press the apricots through a nylon sieve, then stir in the cooking syrup and fold in the yoghurt.
4 Whisk the egg whites until they stand in soft peaks. Using a metal spoon, lightly stir 1 tablespoon of the whisked egg whites into the apricot purée mixture, then fold in the remainder.
5 Spoon the whip into stemmed glasses. Serve at once, or refrigerate until serving time. Serve with the biscuits.

Cook's Notes

TIME
1¼ hours (including cooling time), but remember that the apricots need to be soaked for a minimum of 4 hours before they are ready to be cooked.

DID YOU KNOW
Yoghurt is a high-protein, low-calorie food, and dried apricots are a good source of iron. This dessert is suitable for anyone on a low-fat diet.

●135 calories/575 kj per portion

Mango yoghurt foam

SERVES 4

 1 orange
 **2 large, ripe mangoes, sliced (see
    Preparation)**
1 teaspoon powdered gelatine
3 tablespoons cold water
300 ml/½ pint thick natural yoghurt
2-3 tablespoons caster sugar
1 egg white

1 Using a potato peeler, pare several strips of zest from the orange. ⚠ With a small, sharp knife, shred the zest into matchstick-sized strips.
2 Bring a small pan of water to the boil and blanch the strips for 2-3 minutes; drain and refresh under cold running water. Drain again, then pat dry on absorbent paper and set aside.

3 Squeeze the juice from the orange, then purée the prepared mangoes and orange juice in a blender, or work the mangoes through a nylon sieve and stir in the orange juice.
4 Sprinkle the gelatine over the water in a small, heavy-based pan. Leave to soak for 5 minutes, then set over very low heat for 1-2 minutes, until the gelatine is dissolved.
5 Stirring constantly with a wooden spoon, pour the dissolved gelatine in a thin stream on to the mango purée (see Cook's tip). Gradually beat in the yoghurt, then sweeten to taste with caster sugar.
6 In a spotlessly clean, dry bowl, whisk the egg white until standing in stiff peaks. Using a large metal spoon, fold the egg white into the mango mixture. Taste and fold in more caster sugar, if necessary.
7 Spoon the foam into 4 dessert dishes or stemmed glasses and decorate with the strips of orange zest. Serve within 2 hours.

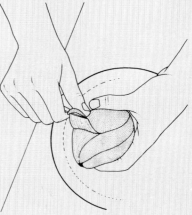

TIME
30 minutes preparation, plus cooling and setting.

WATCHPOINT
Be sure to use a nylon sieve; metal may taint or discolour the melon flesh.

SERVING IDEAS
Decorate with slices of kiwi fruit, or drained and chopped stem ginger; serve with crisp biscuits.

COOK'S TIP
The mixture itself needs to be quite strongly coloured, as the cream and egg whites will make it paler.

PREPARATION
Use a large metal spoon and a 'figure of eight' action to fold the egg whites into the melon mixture.

● 145 calories/600 kj per portion

Melon mousse

SERVES 6

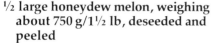

½ large honeydew melon, weighing about 750 g/1½ lb, deseeded and peeled
1 rounded tablespoon (1 sachet) powdered gelatine
1 tablespoon lemon juice
1 tablespoon water
50 g/2 oz caster sugar
few drops of green food colouring
2 pinches ground ginger (optional)
2 egg whites
150 ml/¼ pint whipping cream

1 Sprinkle the gelatine over the lemon juice and water in a heatproof bowl and leave to soak for 5 minutes until spongy.
2 Meanwhile, cut the melon flesh into chunks and work through a nylon sieve, !|or purée in a blender then sieve to remove fibres.
3 Pour the purée into a saucepan. Add the sugar and heat gently, stirring constantly, until the sugar is dissolved. Remove from the heat.
4 Stand the bowl containing the gelatine in a pan of gently simmering water and heat gently for 1-2 minutes until the gelatine has dissolved, stirring occasionally.
5 Stir the dissolved gelatine into the melon mixture, then add enough colouring to tint it a fairly strong green. Stir in ginger, if using. For a streaky effect, lightly stir in a little extra colouring.
6 Pour the mixture into a bowl; cool, then cover and refrigerate until beginning to set.
7 In a clean, dry bowl, whisk the egg whites until standing in stiff peaks. Whip the cream in a separate bowl until it will just hold its shape. Fold the cream and then the egg whites into the melon mixture (see Preparation).
8 Divide the mixture between 6 individual glasses or glass bowls, cover and refrigerate for 8 hours, or overnight, until set. Serve chilled (see Serving ideas).

Tangerine jelly

SERVES 6

8 tangerines
2 tablespoons caster sugar
2 tablespoons lemon juice
2 tablespoons water
1 rounded tablespoon powdered
   gelatine
125 ml/4 fl oz double cream
1 tablespoon orange liqueur
   (optional)

1 Rinse out an 850 ml/1½ pint metal jelly or ring mould with cold water and place it in the refrigerator to chill.

2 Squeeze the juice from 4 of the tangerines and strain into a measuring jug. Stir in the sugar, adding a little more to taste if liked.

3 Mix the lemon juice and water in a small bowl; sprinkle gelatine on top and leave to soak for about 5 minutes, until opaque and spongy. Then stand the bowl in a pan of hot water and stir until the gelatine is dissolved and the liquid is clear.

4 Remove the bowl from the pan and cool slightly. Pour the gelatine solution in a thin stream on to the strained fruit juice, stirring constantly. Make up to 600 ml/1 pint with water and refrigerate for about 1 hour, until just beginning to set.

5 Using a sharp serrated knife, peel the remaining tangerines, taking care to remove every bit of bitter white pith. Divide the fruit into segments and remove any pips.

6 Fold the segments through the almost set jelly ! and pour into the chilled mould. Refrigerate at least 4 hours, or overnight, until set.

7 Unmould the tangerine jelly carefully and allow to stand at room temperature for about 30 minutes to take the chill off the flavour. Lightly whip the cream and flavour with liqueur if liked. Use the cream to decorate the jelly or serve it in a separate bowl.

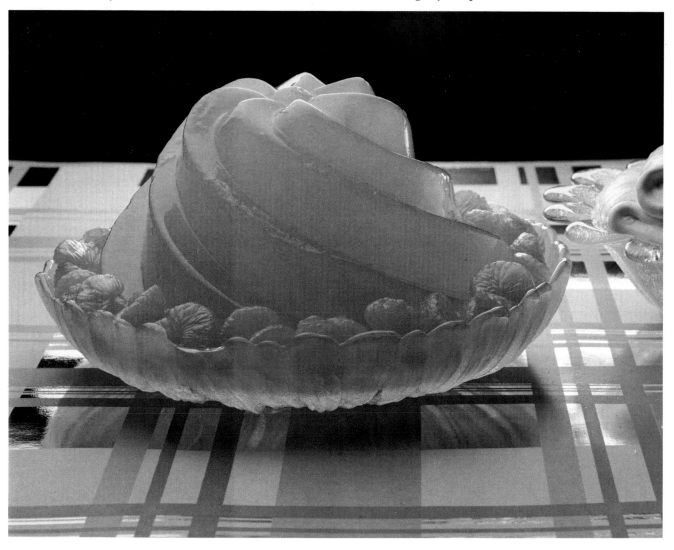

205

Chocolate
mousse special

SERVES 4

 100 g/4 oz plain chocolate, broken
    into pieces
1 tablespoon water
few drops of vanilla flavouring
3 eggs, separated
20-24 sponge finger biscuits (see
    Cook's tip)
chocolate curls and orange slices, to
    decorate (optional)

1 Put the chocolate, water and
vanilla flavouring into a heatproof
bowl. Set the bowl over a pan half
full of simmering water and leave,
stirring occasionally, until the
chocolate is melted. Set aside to cool
slightly.
2 In a large bowl, whisk the egg

yolks until pale. Add the melted
chocolate and continue whisking
until the mixture is thick.
3 In a clean, dry bowl and using
clean beaters, whisk the egg whites
until standing in stiff peaks. Fold
the egg whites into the chocolate
mixture with a large metal spoon.
4 Use half the biscuits to line the
base of an oblong 850 ml/1½ pint

serving dish. (Trim the biscuits, if
necessary, so they fit neatly.)
5 Pour the chocolate mixture over
the biscuits, then cover with cling
film; refrigerate at least 2 hours.
6 To serve: arrange the remaining
biscuits, cut in half, on top of the
mousse. Decorate with chocolate
flakes and orange slices, if liked,
and serve chilled.

Cook's Notes

 TIME
This easy-to-make des-
sert takes only 30
minutes to prepare, but needs at
least 2 hours chilling.

 COOK'S TIP
The number of sponge
fingers you need de-
pends on the shape of your
serving dish.

 STORAGE
The mousse can be pre-
pared up to the end of
stage 5 and kept, covered, in the
refrigerator for up to 48 hours.

SERVING IDEAS
Serve with a dish of
sliced oranges.

●275 calories/1150 kj per portion

Rich caramel mould

SERVES 6-8

75 g/3 oz sugar
3 tablespoons cold water
300 ml/½ pint milk
8 trifle sponge cakes, cut in half horizontally
4 tablespoons apricot jam
300 ml/½ pint single cream
4 large eggs, lightly beaten
vegetable oil, for greasing

TO FINISH

300 ml/½ pint double cream
grated chocolate

1 Put the sugar and water into a small, heavy-based saucepan and heat very gently, without stirring, until the sugar has dissolved. ! Bring to the boil and boil rapidly until the syrup turns a rich caramel colour. !
2 Immediately remove from heat and plunge base of pan into a bowl of cold water until the sizzling stops. Pour the milk on to the caramel, ! then return to low heat and leave, stirring occasionally, until caramel has dissolved. Set aside.
3 Heat the oven to 180C/350F/Gas 4. Lightly oil a 1 L/2 pint charlotte mould or soufflé dish, line the base with greaseproof paper, then oil the paper.
4 Spread the cut side of each cake with jam. Arrange, jam-side-up, in the prepared mould. Lightly whisk the cream, and then the caramel milk into the eggs; strain into the mould and leave for 15 minutes.
5 Lay a piece of oiled greaseproof paper over the top of the pudding. Stand the mould in a small roasting tin and pour in enough cold water to come halfway up the sides of the mould. Carefully transfer to the oven and bake for about 2 hours, until the custard is set.
6 Lift the mould out of the tin. Cool for 30 minutes, then remove grease-proof covering and run a palette knife around the side of the pudding. Invert a serving plate on top of the mould. Hold mould and plate firmly and invert them. Do not remove mould. Refrigerate for at least 3 hours, or overnight.
7 To serve: carefully lift off mould, then mop up any liquid on the plate with absorbent paper. Whip the double cream until standing in soft peaks, then pipe over pudding. Decorate with grated chocolate.

Cook's Notes

TIME
1 hour preparation (including decoration), 2 hours baking, plus chilling.

WATCHPOINTS
Make sure every granule of sugar has dissolved or the syrup will crystallize.
Watch the caramel constantly as it can easily scorch.
Stand well back as the milk will splutter for 1-2 seconds.

● 620 calories/2600 kj per portion

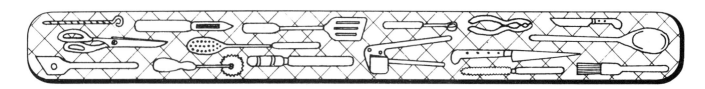

Ginger syllabub

SERVES 4

 5 tablespoons Advocaat
3 tablespoons ginger marmalade
   (see Cook's tip)
300 ml/½ pint double cream
crystallized ginger or drained stem
   ginger, cut into small pieces, to
   decorate
crisp biscuits, to serve

1 Mix the Advocaat and marmalade together in a small bowl.
2 Whip the cream until standing in soft peaks. [!] Using a large metal spoon, fold the marmalade mixture into the cream.
3 Spoon the mixture into 4 stemmed

Cook's Notes

TIME
10 minutes preparation, plus a minimum 30 minutes chilling time and a maximum of 2 hours.

COOK'S TIP
A jar of ginger marmalade is a useful store-cupboard item, as it can be used to enliven both sweet and savoury dishes. It makes a delicious filling for sponge cakes and 1 tablespoon is enough to pep up a beef casserole. Alternatively, try 1 tablespoon with cooked rhubarb or in a rhubarb fool.

WATCHPOINTS
Do not whip the cream until standing in stiff peaks, or the syllabubs will be too solid.
Syllabubs are always chilled before serving so that the flavours can mingle, but do not leave any longer than the specified time or the mixture will separate.

●425 calories/1775 kj per portion

dishes, cover with cling film and refrigerate for at least 30 minutes, or up to 2 hours. [!]

4 Just before serving, decorate each syllabub with pieces of ginger. Serve chilled, with crisp biscuits.

Cranberry brûlés

SERVES 4

250 g/9 oz cranberries (see Cook's tips)
5 tablespoons water
150 g/5 oz light soft brown sugar, or to taste
1½ teaspoons arrowroot

TOPPING

150 ml/¼ pint soured cream (see Cook's tips)
25 g/1 oz light soft brown sugar
large pinch of ground mixed spice

1 Put the cranberries and 4 tablespoons water into a heavy-based saucepan. Cover and simmer gently for 5 minutes, then stir in 150 g/5 oz sugar and cook for a further 3-4 minutes.
2 Blend the arrowroot with the remaining water and stir into the cranberry mixture. Bring to the boil and simmer for 1-2 minutes until thickened and no longer cloudy, stirring constantly.
3 Cool the cranberry mixture for 30 minutes, then taste and stir in more sugar if liked. Divide the mixture equally between 4 ramekins or other small flameproof dishes.
4 Heat the grill to hot.

5 Spread the soured cream over the cranberry mixture, almost to the edges. Mix the sugar and spice and sprinkle evenly on top of the cream.
6 Place under the grill for a few seconds, until the sugar is melted and bubbling. Remove immediately from the heat, leave to settle for 1-2 minutes, then serve hot. Alternatively, serve chilled (see Variation).

Cook's Notes

 TIME
Preparation (including cooling and grilling time) is 45-50 minutes.

COOK'S TIPS
Frozen cranberries can be used if fresh are not available; there is no need to defrost first, simply simmer for 3-4 minutes longer.
If the cream is very thick and stiff, stir well before using so it is easy to spoon.

 VARIATION
This dessert can also be served chilled: leave to cool after grilling, then cover with cling film and refrigerate for at least 2 hours.

DID YOU KNOW
Brûlés is from the French verb brûler to burn or scald and refers here to the delicious toffee-like topping.

●225 calories/1075 kj per portion

Marbled lime soufflé

SERVES 6

4 limes
1 rounded tablespoon (1 sachet)
   powdered gelatine
6 tablespoons water
4 large eggs, separated
225 g/8 oz caster sugar
300 ml/½ pint double cream
few drops of green food colouring
unsalted pistachio nuts, blanched
   and chopped, to decorate (see
   Economy)

1 Prepare a 16-19 cm/6½-7½ inch
(1.5 L/2½ pint) soufflé dish: cut a
58 × 25 cm/23 × 10 inch strip of foil
or greaseproof paper. Fold in half
lengthways. Wrap the strip around
the dish so it stands above the rim
and secure with adhesive tape.
Lightly oil inside of collar, above
rim of dish.
2 Finely grate the zest from 3 limes;

squeeze the juice from all the limes
and measure 100 ml/3½ fl oz for the
soufflé.
3 Sprinkle the gelatine over the
water in a heatproof bowl. Leave to
soak for 5 minutes until spongy,
then set the bowl over a pan of
simmering water and heat gently
for 1-2 minutes until gelatine has
dissolved, stirring occasionally.
Remove gelatine liquid from heat
and leave to cool slightly.
4 Meanwhile, put the egg yolks
into a bowl with 200 g/7 oz caster
sugar, the lime zest and reserved
juice. Using an electric whisk, beat
until very pale, thick and creamy.
5 Whisk in the gelatine. Leave the
mixture for 5-10 minutes, whisking
occasionally, until it is beginning to
thicken.
6 Meanwhile, whip the cream until
standing in soft peaks.
7 In a clean, dry bowl, whisk the
egg whites until standing in stiff
peaks. Whisk in the remaining
sugar, 1 tablespoon at a time, and
continue whisking until meringue is
firm and glossy.

8 Fold the whipped cream into the
lime mixture, then gently fold in the
meringue. Put half the mixture into
another bowl and tint pale green
with food colouring.
9 Put alternate spoonfuls of the
2 mixtures into prepared dish. Level
the surface carefully, then chill for 4
hours, until set.
10 Remove tape from collar, then
carefully peel away from soufflé
with the aid of a round-bladed
knife. Press chopped nuts around
the sides of the soufflé. Serve as
soon as possible.

Pancake Alaska

SERVES 4

100 g/4 oz plain flour
1½ teaspoons baking powder
¼ teaspoon salt
2 egg yolks
1 tablespoon caster sugar
1 tablespoon vegetable oil
175 ml/6 fl oz milk
extra vegetable oil, for frying

FILLING
225 g/8 oz apricot jam
1 tablespoon brandy or orange-
   flavoured liqueur (see Economy)
425 g/15 oz can pineapple pieces,
   drained

MERINGUE
2 egg whites
100 g/4 oz caster sugar
1 tablespoon flaked almonds

1 Heat the oven to 220C/425F/Gas 7.
2 Sift the flour, baking powder and salt into a bowl. Add the egg yolks, sugar, oil and milk and whisk until just smoothly blended.
3 Brush a 15 cm/6 inch heavy-based frying-pan lightly with oil; place over moderately high heat. Remove from the heat and pour in about 2 tablespoons batter. Using the back of the spoon, spread the batter to the sides of the pan.
4 Return to the heat and cook until the bubbles burst on top. Loosen with a palette knife, then turn the pancake over and cook on the other side for a further 20-30 seconds, until browned. Lift on to grease-proof paper and keep warm.
5 Continue making pancakes, interleaving them with greaseproof paper, until you have about 7. Stir the batter frequently and grease the pan with more oil as necessary.
6 Warm the jam with the brandy in a small pan. Reserve 1 pancake; spread the rest with warmed jam.
7 Place 1 pancake, jam side up, on an ovenproof serving plate and top with a few pineapple pieces. Cover with another pancake, jam side up. Continue layering in this way, ending with the reserved plain pancake on top.
8 Make the meringue: in a clean, dry bowl, whisk the egg whites until stiff, then whisk in the sugar, 1 tablespoon at a time.
9 Swirl the meringue over the top and sides of pancake stack, taking it right down on to the plate. Sprinkle with the almonds. Bake immediately in the oven for 10 minutes, or until the meringue is tinged with brown and the nuts are golden. Serve at once, cut into wedges.

Cook's Notes

TIME
This spectacular dessert takes about 50 minutes to prepare (including 10 minutes baking time).

ECONOMY
Use syrup from the can of pineapple instead of the brandy or liqueur.

●575 calories/2400 kj per portion

Raspberry soufflés

SERVES 4

200 ml/7 fl oz raspberry purée (see
   Cook's tip)
1 tablespoon powdered gelatine
3 tablespoons cold water
4 large eggs, separated
100 g/4 oz caster sugar
300 ml/½ pint whipping cream
vegetable oil, for greasing
crushed ratafias, extra caster sugar
   and fresh hulled raspberries,
   to finish

1 Secure paper collars around 4
straight-sided, 175 ml/6 fl oz
ramekins (see Preparation). Reserve
4 tablespoons of the purée.
2 Sprinkle the gelatine over the
water in a cup; leave until spongy,
then stand the cup in a bowl of very
hot water until the gelatine is
completely dissolved.
3 Meanwhile, whisk the egg yolks
and sugar together in a heatproof
bowl over barely simmering water
until thick and pale.
4 Remove from the heat. Whisk in
the dissolved gelatine and the
remaining raspberry purée. Turn
into a clean large bowl, cover and
chill, stirring occasionally, until on
the point of setting.
5 Whip 225 ml/8 fl oz of the cream
until it forms soft peaks. Using clean
beaters, whisk the egg whites until
standing in soft peaks. Fold the
cream and egg whites into the
raspberry mixture. Divide between
the prepared dishes, cover lightly
and chill for about 2 hours, until set.
6 Remove the adhesive tape from
paper collars; then gently peel away
from the soufflés with the aid of a
round-bladed knife. Press crushed
ratafias around the sides.
7 Sweeten the reserved purée with
caster sugar, to taste. Spread 1
tablespoon purée over the top of
each soufflé.
8 Whip the remaining cream with 2
teaspoons caster sugar until
standing in soft peaks. Decorate the
top of each soufflé with raspberries
and piped cream.

Cook's Notes

TIME
50 minutes, plus chilling
and setting.

COOK'S TIP
Work 500-600 g/1-1¼ lb
fresh or defrosted frozen
raspberries through a sieve
or purée in a blender, then
sieve.

PREPARATION
The collars enable you
to overfill the dish so
that, when they are removed,
the soufflés appear 'risen'.
   Measure the depth and circumference of the dishes with
string. Cut 4 strips of double
thickness greaseproof paper, 2.5
cm/1 inch longer and 2.5 cm/1
inch deeper. Wrap 1 strip tightly
around each dish and secure
with adhesive tape. Lightly oil
inside of paper, above rim.

●505 calories/2125 kj per portion

Hot coffee soufflés

SERVES 4

25 g/1 oz margarine or butter
25 g/1 oz plain flour
150 ml/¼ pint milk
3 eggs, separated
25 g/1 oz caster sugar
2 teaspoons coffee essence
melted margarine, for greasing

SAUCE
175 ml/6 fl oz hot strong black coffee
1½-2 tablespoons sugar
1½ teaspoons arrowroot
1 tablespoon water
1-2 tablespoons Tia Maria

1 Heat the oven to 180C/350F/Gas 4. Brush the insides of four 150 ml/¼ pint soufflé dishes with butter, then stand them on a baking sheet.
2 Melt the margarine in a fairly large saucepan, sprinkle in the flour and stir over low heat for 1-2 minutes until straw-coloured. Remove from the heat and gradually stir in the milk. Return to the heat and simmer, stirring, until very thick and smooth. [!]
3 Remove from the heat, allow to cool for a few minutes, then beat in the egg yolks one at a time. Stir in the caster sugar and coffee essence.
4 In a clean, dry bowl, whisk the egg whites until they stand in stiff peaks. Using a large metal spoon, lightly but thoroughly fold egg whites into the coffee mixture. [!]
5 Spoon into dishes. Mark a circle with a knife in the top of each soufflé. Bake in the oven, above centre, for 25-30 minutes until risen well above the rims of the dishes and browned on top.
6 Meanwhile, make the sauce: pour the hot coffee into a small pan and then stir in 1½ tablespoons sugar. Blend the arrowroot with the water, add to the sweetened coffee and simmer gently, stirring, until thickened and no longer cloudy. Remove from the heat and flavour with Tia Maria and more sugar, if liked. Keep hot. Serve the soufflés *immediately* they are cooked, with a little of the sauce poured over them and the rest handed around separately in a jug.

Cook's Notes

TIME
These light soufflés take about 1 hour to prepare and bake.

WATCHPOINTS
The small amount of mixture thickens quickly on the base of the pan, so stir briskly to keep it smooth.
Use as light an action as you can when folding the egg whites into the mixture so that as little as possible of the air trapped in the whisked whites is crushed out. Stop folding as soon as the egg white and coffee mixture are evenly blended.

COOK'S TIP
Individual soufflés cook more quickly and are easier to serve than baking 1 large one. But if you do want to make 1 large soufflé, use a 850 ml/1½ pint soufflé dish and bake for 40 minutes.

VARIATIONS
Vary the flavour by stirring a few drops of vanilla or almond essence, or 40 g/1½ oz grated chocolate into the mixture before folding in the egg whites.

●215 calories/900 kj per portion

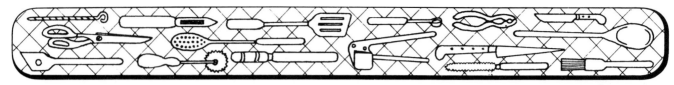

Baked mincemeat soufflé

SERVES 4-6

 175 g/6 oz mincemeat
6 tablespoons dry cider
 2 tablespoons brandy (optional)
25 g/1 oz blanched almonds, chopped
4 large eggs, separated
pinch of salt
¼ teaspoon grated lemon or orange zest
2 tablespoons plain flour
75 g/3 oz caster sugar
icing sugar, to dredge

1 Heat the oven to 180C/350F/Gas 4.
2 Put the mincemeat, cider, brandy (if using) and the blanched almonds into a saucepan and heat the mixture through gently.
3 Meanwhile, put the egg yolks, salt and lemon zest in a bowl and whisk together lightly. Add the flour and continue whisking until the mixture is pale and thick.
4 Whisk the egg whites in a separate bowl until frothy. ! Gradually whisk in the caster sugar and whisk until the mixture forms soft peaks. Fold thoroughly into the egg yolk mixture with a metal spoon.
5 Pour the heated mincemeat mixture into a shallow ovenproof dish. Carefully spread the soufflé mixture on top.
6 Bake in the oven for about 15 minutes or until the topping is puffed up and golden brown.
7 Sift icing sugar thickly over the top and serve at once.

ICE CREAMS AND SORBETS

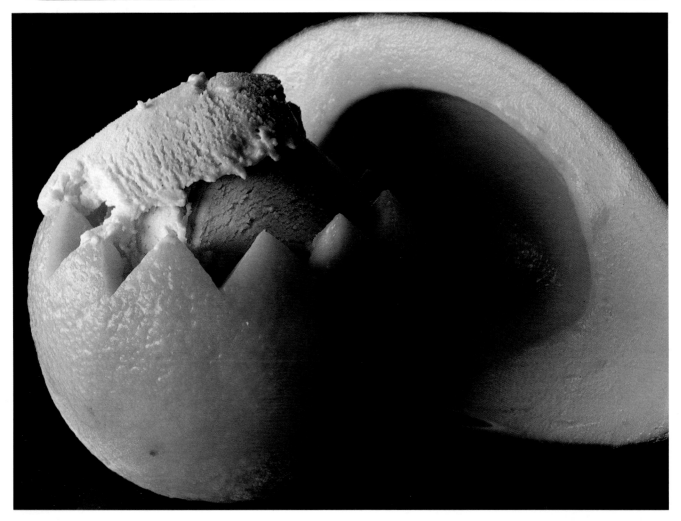

Avocado ice cream

SERVES 6-8
2 ripe avocados
2 eggs
75 g/3 oz caster sugar
300 ml/½ pint single cream
finely grated zest and juice of 1
    large orange
300 ml/½ pint double cream

1 Put the eggs and sugar into a bowl and beat together with a wooden spoon until thick and creamy.
2 Pour the single cream into a small saucepan and heat gently until almost boiling then immediately remove from the heat and pour on to the egg mixture, stirring vigorously. Leave the custard to cool.
3 Halve, stone and peel the avocados, then roughly chop the flesh. Purée with the orange zest and juice in a blender.
4 In a large bowl, whip the double cream until it forms soft peaks. Using a large metal spoon, fold in the avocado purée and the custard.
5 Turn into a large freezerproof container, cover and freeze until the mixture is frozen 2.5 cm/1 inch around the edges. Scrape the mixture into a bowl and whisk until smooth, then return to the container, cover and freeze until firm.
6 Transfer to the main part of the refrigerator about 30 minutes before serving to soften.

Mixed fruit ice

SERVES 4-6

 175 g/6 oz can evaporated milk, chilled (see Watchpoint)

 50 g/2 oz icing sugar, sifted

2 bananas

 juice of 2 lemons

375 g/13 oz can crushed pineapple

175 g/6 oz jar maraschino cherries, drained and halved with 2 tablespoons syrup reserved

1 Pour the milk into a large bowl and whisk until thick and frothy, then whisk in the icing sugar.

2 Peel and mash the bananas with the lemon juice, then stir into the milk mixture together with the pineapple and its syrup.

3 Set aside a few cherries for decoration; stir the rest into the fruit and milk mixture together with the reserved syrup.

4 Pour the mixture into a rigid plastic container and freeze uncovered (see Cook's tip), for about 2 hours, until frozen around the edges. Loosen the frozen mixture with a fork and stir through the whole mixture. Cover and return to the freezer for a further 8 hours, or overnight, until firm.

5 To serve: transfer the container to the main part of the refrigerator for about 30 minutes until softened, then scoop into dishes and decorate with reserved cherries.

Cook's Notes

 TIME
15 minutes preparation, 10 hours freezing and 30 minutes softening time.

COOK'S TIP
If using the freezing compartment of the refrigerator, turn it to its lowest setting 1 hour beforehand. Remember to return it to the original setting afterwards.

SPECIAL OCCASION
Use half a pineapple as a 'plate' for the fruit ice. Or, put a drained canned pineapple ring on 4-6 individual plates and top with scoops of the ice mixture.

 WATCHPOINT
The milk must be chilled for at least 3 hours, or it will not whisk to a thick consistency.

 FREEZING
Prepare up to the end of stage 4, then cover, label and freeze for up to 6 weeks. To serve: follow stage 5.

●280 calories/1175 kj per portion

216

Iced passion fruit dessert

SERVES 4

100 ml/3½ fl oz passion fruit pulp (see Preparation)
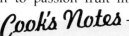
150 g/5 oz strawberry yoghurt (see Variations)
1 teaspoon powdered gelatine
100 ml/3½ fl oz water
3 tablespoons caster sugar
2 egg whites

1 Put the passion fruit pulp into a large bowl with the yoghurt and stir well until evenly blended.

2 Sprinkle the gelatine over the water in a heatproof bowl and leave to soak for 5 minutes, then stand bowl in a pan of gently simmering water for 1-2 minutes until the gelatine has completely dissolved, stirring occasionally.

3 Cool the gelatine slightly, then pour on to passion fruit mixture, stirring vigorously all the time to blend. Add the sugar and stir until dissolved.

4 Pour the mixture into an 850 ml/1½ pint metal or other freezerproof container. Leave, uncovered, in the freezer or freezing compartment of the refrigerator for 45-60 minutes until the mixture is frozen around the edges.

5 In a clean, dry bowl, whisk egg whites until standing in stiff peaks. Turn passion fruit mixture into a large bowl and whisk until smooth and creamy, then fold in egg whites with a large metal spoon.

6 Return mixture to the container, cover tightly and freeze for a further 4 hours or until firm. ✳

7 About 45 minutes before serving, transfer the mixture to the main part of the refrigerator to soften slightly. To serve: carefully scoop into individual glasses.

Cook's Notes

TIME
15 minutes preparation, plus about 5 hours freezing and 45 minutes softening.

PREPARATION
You will need about 8 passion fruit. Cut in half, then scoop out the pulp.

SERVING IDEAS
This dessert is delicious served with slices of pineapple and sweet biscuits.

VARIATIONS
Use passion fruit and melon or mandarin yoghurt instead of strawberry. (In this case, the dessert will be pale yellow, rather than a pale apricot.)

FREEZING
Seal the container, label and return to freezer for up to 6 weeks. To serve the passion fruit dessert: see stage 7.

●95 calories/400 kj per portion

Brown bread ice cream

SERVES 4
50 g/2 oz fresh wholemeal
    breadcrumbs
25 g/1 oz sugar
2 large eggs, separated
50 g/2 oz light soft brown sugar
    (see Cook's tips)
150 ml/¼ pint double cream,
    whipped until in soft peaks
1 tablespoon coffee and chicory
    essence, or dark rum

1 Heat the grill to high. Mix the breadcrumbs and sugar together; spread over the base of a small baking tray and toast under the grill for about 5 minutes, turning occasionally, until golden and crunchy.
2 Turn the crunchy crumbs on to a plate and leave to cool completely, then crush coarsely with the back of a wooden spoon.
3 Beat the egg yolks with a fork until well blended, then set aside.
4 In a spotlessly clean and dry large bowl, whisk egg whites until stiff. Whisk in brown sugar, 1 tablespoon at a time. Using a large metal spoon, fold in the egg yolks, whipped cream, crushed breadcrumbs and coffee and chicory.
5 Turn the mixture into a 1 L/2 pint metal container and cover securely with foil. Freeze (see Cook's tips) for 2 hours, stirring lightly every 30 minutes, [!] then leave for a further 2 hours, or until firm. ✳
6 Let the ice cream stand at room temperature for about 5 minutes, to soften slightly, before serving.

Cook's Notes

 TIME
5 minutes toasting plus cooling time for the breadcrumbs, then 30-40 minutes preparation and about 4 hours freezing time.

COOK'S TIPS
Soft brown sugar gives a lovely pale coffee colour, but caster sugar can be used for a whiter ice cream. Sift soft brown sugar if it is lumpy.

To make the ice cream in the freezing compartment of the refrigerator: turn the temperature to the lowest setting and chill the container 1 hour beforehand.

 SERVING IDEAS
Scoop into dessert bowls or stemmed glasses and top with fan wafers, or serve as an accompaniment to poached or canned fruit.

 FREEZING
Overwrap, then return to the freezer and store for up to 3 months.

WATCHPOINT
The ice cream mixture should be lightly stirred and turned over at regular times during the first 2 hours or the crumbs will sink.

●320 calories/1350 kj per portion

Lime ice box pudding

SERVES 10

grated zest of 2 limes
juice of 3 limes
3 eggs, separated
100 g/4 oz caster sugar
425 ml/¾ pint double cream
8 plain sweet biscuits, crushed
fresh lime slices, to decorate

1 Line the base of a 1.7 L/3 pint loaf tin with greaseproof paper.
2 Put the egg yolks in a large heatproof bowl over a pan half full of gently simmering water. Using a rotary or hand-held electric mixer, slowly whisk in the sugar until pale and thick. ! Remove from heat and stir in lime zest and juice.
3 Whip the cream until standing in soft peaks and fold into the lime mixture.
4 In a clean, dry bowl and using clean beaters, whisk the egg whites until standing in soft peaks. Using a large metal spoon, fold the egg whites into the lime mixture.
5 Sprinkle a thin layer of biscuit crumbs over the base of the tin. Carefully pour in the lime mixture and top with a layer of the remaining biscuit crumbs.
6 Cover with foil, then place in the freezer compartment of the refrigerator or in the freezer and freeze for about 8 hours, or overnight, until firm. ✳
7 To serve (see Cook's tip): uncover the tin, then run a palette knife around the edges of the pudding to loosen it. Turn out on to a flat serving plate and remove the greaseproof paper. Decorate the pudding with slices of lime and serve at once.

Cook's Notes

 **TIME**
Preparation takes 40 minutes, plus about 8 hours freezing time.

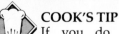 **COOK'S TIP**
If you do not want to serve all the pudding at once, cut off as many slices as you need, then wrap the (undecorated) surplus in foil and return it to the freezer for up to 1 month.

WATCHPOINT
Make sure that the egg yolks and sugar are really thick before removing from the heat.

 **FREEZING**
Freeze at the end of stage 6. Overwrap and return to the freezer for up to 1 month.

●365 calories/1525 kj per portion

Cherries jubilee

SERVES 4

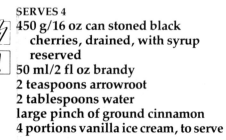

450 g/16 oz can stoned black
   cherries, drained, with syrup
   reserved
50 ml/2 fl oz brandy
2 teaspoons arrowroot
2 tablespoons water
large pinch of ground cinnamon
4 portions vanilla ice cream, to serve

1 Pour the brandy into a cup and
stand in a pan or bowl of hot water
to warm through gently.
2 In a small bowl, blend the arrowroot to a smooth paste with the
water.
3 Pour the reserved cherry syrup
into a saucepan. Add the cinnamon,
then bring to the boil and boil
briskly for 4 minutes, until reduced
by one-quarter.
4 Remove pan from the heat and
stir in the arrowroot mixture.
Return to the heat, bring back to the
boil and cook, stirring, until the
mixture thickens and clears.
5 Add the cherries to the pan and
simmer gently for 1-2 minutes.
6 Meanwhile, put the ice cream into
4 dessert bowls.
7 Turn off the heat under the pan.
Pour the warmed brandy over the
cherries and immediately set light to
it. Let the flames die down
completely, then spoon the cherries
over the ice cream. Serve at once.

Cook's Notes

TIME
Preparation and cooking
take 15-20 minutes.

WATCHPOINTS
Remove the pan from
the heat immediately, or
the cherry sauce will burn.

  Hold the match just above the
sides of the pan and stand well
back since the flames will shoot
high for a few seconds.

●210 calories/875 kj per portion

Tutti frutti ice cream

SERVES 4

150 ml/¼ pint double cream
425 g/15 oz can custard (see Cook's tips)
50 g/2 oz glacé cherries, chopped
15 g/½ oz cut mixed peel
25 g/1 oz seedless raisins or sultanas
25 g/1 oz chocolate dots
25 g/1 oz chopped mixed nuts (optional)
fan-shaped wafers, to serve

1 Whip the cream until just thickened, then stir in the custard and mix until evenly combined. Turn the mixture into a shallow 850 ml/1½ pint freezerproof container. Freeze uncovered (see Cook's tips) for about 1 hour, or until frozen around the edges and slushy in the centre.

2 Scrape the mixture into a bowl and beat well with a wooden spoon or hand-held electric whisk. Stir in the cherries, peel, raisins, chocolate and nuts, if using, making sure they are evenly distributed (see Economy). Return the mixture to the container, cover and freeze for a further 2 hours, or until solid. ✳

3 Transfer the ice cream to the main part of the refrigerator for about 2 hours to soften slightly (see Cook's tips). Scoop into individual glass dishes and serve at once, with fan (or other shaped) wafers to give a texture contrast.

Cook's Notes

 TIME
15 minutes preparation and about 3 hours freezing, plus softening time.

 COOK'S TIPS
To shorten freezing time, refrigerate the custard 2 hours in advance.

If using the freezing compartment of the refrigerator, turn it to its coldest setting 1 hour before making the ice cream. Return it to the original setting afterwards.

If you are in a hurry, soften the ice cream for 30 minutes at room temperature.

 FREEZING
The ice cream can be stored in the freezer for up to 2 months.

FOR CHILDREN
Scoop the ice cream into cones and press half a chocolate flake into the top.

ECONOMY
Whisk 1 egg white until standing in soft peaks and fold into the mixture after adding the fruit and chocolate. This gives a greater volume.

●405 calories/1700 kj per portion

Watermelon frappé

SERVES 4

1.4 kg/3 lb watermelon, seeded, peeled and cut into cubes (see Cook's tips)
100 g/4 oz caster sugar
finely grated zest and juice of 1 large orange
finely grated zest of ½ lemon
1 tablespoon lemon juice

1 Purée watermelon, in batches, in a blender, or crush to a pulp with a potato masher, then work the pulp through a nylon sieve.
2 Put the sugar into a large bowl with the orange and lemon zest. Slowly stir in the orange and lemon juice. Add the watermelon purée, a little at a time, stirring constantly to dissolve the sugar.
3 Pour the mixture into a 1 L/2 pint rigid polythene container and freeze, uncovered, for about 3 hours, or until the mixture is slushy (see Cook's tips).
4 Turn the mixture into a large bowl and whisk to break up large ice crystals. Return to the container, cover and freeze for a further 2-3 hours, until firm.
5 Transfer to the main part of the refrigerator and leave for 1-1½ hours, until softened. Mash the ice briefly with a fork to break up large lumps, then spoon into dishes and serve at once before it begins to melt (see Serving ideas).

Cook's Notes

TIME
20 minutes preparation, plus freezing and softening time.

DID YOU KNOW
Frappé means iced in French, and aptly describes this cooling dessert with its granular, icy texture.

FREEZING
Overwrap the container, then return to the freezer for up to 2 months. To serve see stage 5.

● 160 calories/650 kj per portion

COOK'S TIPS
The easiest way to remove the seeds is to scrape them out with a fork.
If making the ice in the freezing compartment of the refrigerator, turn it to the lowest setting for 1 hour beforehand. Return to the original setting afterwards.

SERVING IDEAS
This refreshing ice is an ideal dessert after a rich main course. Spoon it into stemmed glass dishes and provide long-handled spoons for easy eating.

Sicilian orange cassata

SERVES 6-8

150 ml/¼ pint orange juice
10 trifle sponge cakes
400 g/14 oz Ricotta cheese (see Buying guide)
100 g/4 oz caster sugar
50 g/2 oz cut mixed peel
50 g/2 oz plain dessert chocolate, broken up into small pieces
finely grated zest of 1 orange
3 teaspoons medium sherry
vegetable oil, for greasing

TO DECORATE
150 ml/¼ pint double cream
3 orange slices, halved

1 Brush a 1.25 L / 2 pint bombe mould or pudding basin very lightly with oil. Pour the orange juice into a shallow bowl.

2 Using three-quarters of the trifle sponge cakes, dip one side of each into the orange juice and use to line completely the sides and base of the mould with the darker sugar-coated sides facing inwards (see Preparation).

3 Place all the Ricotta cheese in a large bowl and stir in the remaining ingredients, mixing well. Spoon into the prepared mould and level the surface. If necessary, trim the ends of the sponge cakes level with the top of the filling.

4 Dip the remaining sponge cakes in the orange juice and use to cover the top of the cassata. Cover and refrigerate overnight.

5 Uncover, then carefully run a palette knife down the sides of the sponge lining to loosen. Invert a serving plate on top of the mould. Hold the plate and mould firmly and invert, giving a sharp shake halfway round. Carefully remove the mould from the cassata.

6 To decorate: whip the cream until standing in stiff peaks, then spoon into a piping bag fitted with a star nozzle. Pipe cream decoratively around base of the cassata, then pipe a ring on top. Arrange the halved orange slices overlapping on top of the ring of cream and serve at once or refrigerate for up to 1 hour before serving.

Cook's Notes

TIME
30-40 minutes to make cassata, plus chilling overnight and 10 minutes for decorating.

PREPARATION
To line the mould with trifle sponge cakes:

Press a soaked sponge cake into centre of base, then press the rest against the sides.

DID YOU KNOW
This is a version of the famous Sicilian sponge cake that is traditionally served at weddings to celebrate the start of a new life.

BUYING GUIDE
Ricotta is made from the whey of cow's milk and is a smooth, mild cheese. It is always sold fresh and is available from Italian delicatessens or the delicatessen counters of some large supermarkets. If it is unavailable, use curd or cottage cheese instead but pass through a sieve before using.

●520 calories/2175 kj per portion

Grapefruit ice

SERVES 4

 grated zest and juice of 2 grapefruit
100 g/4 oz caster sugar
300 ml/½ pint water
2 grapefuit slices, quartered, to decorate

1 Place the sugar and water in a saucepan and heat gently until the sugar has dissolved, then bring to the boil and boil for about 5 minutes, without stirring, until a thick syrup is formed.
2 Remove the syrup from the heat and leave until completely cold.
3 Add the grapefruit zest and juice to the cold syrup and pour into a 1.25 L/2 pint shallow freezerpoof tin or ice cube tray without the divisions. Freeze in the freezer

compartment of a refrigerator or in the freezer for about 30 minutes (see Cook's tip) until slushy.
4 Remove from the freezer and stir well with a metal spoon until evenly blended.
5 Return to the freezer for 30 minutes, then stir again. Repeat this process once more, then cover and freeze for at least 8 hours.
6 To serve: stir the mixture well, to break up any large pieces of ice, then spoon into glasses or small dishes. Decorate each portion with quartered grapefruit slices. Serve at once (see Serving ideas).

Pear wine sorbet

SERVES 4

 4 firm dessert pears, peeled, cored and sliced (see Buying guide)

 150 ml/¼ pint white wine (see Buying guide)

 75 g/3 oz caster sugar

strip of lemon rind

maraschino cherries, to decorate

1 Put wine, sugar and rind in a saucepan and stir over low heat until the sugar has dissolved. Bring to the boil, add the pears, then cover the pan and poach the pears gently for about 5 minutes, or until opaque. Remove the pan from the heat and set aside to cool.

2 Discard the lemon rind, reserve a few pear slices for decoration, then purée the cold mixture in a blender or press it through a sieve.

3 Pour into a freezer container, cover and freeze for several hours until firm (see Cook's tips).

4 Remove from the freezer and turn into a large bowl. ⚠ Break the sorbet up with a fork, then whisk it well until slushy.

5 Spoon the mixture back into its freezer container, cover and return to the freezer for a further 3-4 hours until firm.

6 Remove the sorbet from the freezer and allow it to soften at room temperature for about 15 minutes. Then spoon it into individual glasses and serve decorated with pear slices and maraschino cherries.

Cook's Notes

TIME
Preparation takes only about 20 minutes, but remember to allow several hours for freezing time.

 FREEZING
The sorbet can be stored in the freezer for up to 2 months.

BUYING GUIDE
Choose firm pears such as Conference or Comice for this sorbet. Avoid Williams which will be too soft.

It is worth choosing a good wine, or the flavour of the finished sorbet will be disappointing. Choose sweet or dry according to your taste.

 WATCHPOINT
If the sorbet is too firm to mash, let it soften slightly at room temperature.

COOK'S TIPS
To make the sorbet in the freezing compart-ment of an ordinary refrigerator, use a pre-chilled shallow metal tray for freezing the sorbet and turn the refrigerator down to its coldest setting at least 1 hour before you start making the sorbet. This will help speed up the freezing process.

VARIATION
Decorate the sorbet with a few sprigs of fresh mint in season.

● 140 calories/575 kj per portion

Mint sorbet

SERVES 4

 25 g/1 oz fresh mint leaves (see Buying guide)

 425 ml/¾ pint water

100 g/4 oz caster sugar

 thinly pared zest and juice of 2 lemons

few drops of green food colouring

1 egg white

sprigs of mint, to decorate

1 Pour the water into a heavy-based saucepan. Add the sugar and lemon zest and stir over low heat until the sugar has dissolved, then bring to the boil and simmer, without stirring, for 5 minutes.

2 Remove the syrup from the heat, stir in the lemon juice and mint leaves and leave to cool completely.

3 Strain the syrup into an 850 ml/ 1½ pint freezerproof container. Stir in the colouring, then cover and freeze (see Cook's tips) for about 3 hours, or until the mixture is frozen about 1 cm/½ inch around the edges and slushy in the centre.

4 Turn the mint mixture into a large bowl and mash well with a fork (see Cook's tips). In a clean, dry bowl, whisk the egg white until standing in stiff peaks. Whisk the mint mixture to break up large lumps, then whisk in the egg white about a third at a time and continue whisking until evenly incorporated.

5 Return the mixture to the container, cover and freeze for a further 3 hours, or until firm.

6 To serve: allow the sorbet to soften for 5 minutes at room temperature, then scoop into stemmed glasses. Decorate with a sprig of mint and serve at once.

Cook's Notes

TIME
20 minutes preparation (excluding cooling the syrup), plus 6 hours freezing.

FREEZING
Overwrap container, seal, label and return to freezer for up to 3 months.

COOK'S TIPS
If using freezing compartment of refrigerator, turn to coldest setting at least 1 hour before making the sorbet. Remember to return it to original setting afterwards.
    If the mint mixture is solid, allow it to soften slightly before mashing it with the fork.

BUYING GUIDE
Any variety of mint — spearmint, peppermint or applemint — is excellent for this sorbet. As they all grow profusely it is worth asking friends with gardens if they have any mint to spare. Do not use dried mint for this recipe; it will not give a good flavour.

● 105 calories/450 kj per portion

Tea sorbet

SERVES 8

10½ teaspoons China tea (see Buying guide)

150 g/5 oz sugar

600 ml/1 pint boiling water

juice of 2 lemons

4 egg whites

1 Put the tea into a large heatproof bowl with the sugar. Pour over the boiling water and stir until the sugar has dissolved, then cover and leave to stand for 1 hour.

2 Strain the tea through a very fine sieve into a jug. Stir in the lemon juice, then pour into a 1 L/2 pint metal loaf tin or other freezerproof container. Cover tightly with foil and freeze in the freezer (or freezing compartment of refrigerator turned to its coldest setting) for 2½ hours, or until half-frozen and slushy.

3 Remove from the freezer, turn into a bowl and mash with a fork to break up the ice crystals, then whisk briefly until smooth. Return to container, cover and freeze for a further 2 hours, or until firm.

4 In a clean, dry bowl, whisk egg whites until standing in soft peaks.

5 Remove the tea ice from freezer, turn into a large bowl and break up with a fork as before, mashing well. Whisk the ice until smooth, then slowly whisk in the egg whites. Return the mixture to the container, cover and freeze for a further 4 hours, until firm.

6 To serve: remove from the freezer and soften at room temperature for 20-30 minutes. Scoop or spoon into small serving dishes. Serve at once (see Serving ideas).

Cook's Notes

TIME
10-15 minutes preparation, plus 1 hour standing and about 8½ hours freezing, plus softening time.

BUYING GUIDE
Choose black China tea: either Lapsang Suchong or Keemam, both of which are available from good supermarkets and specialist food shops. Do not use Indian or other teas: they are too strong.

FREEZING
Seal the container, label and return to the freezer for up to 3 months. Soften and serve as in stage 6.

SERVING IDEAS
The subtle, slightly bitter, flavour of this sorbet is best complemented with a sweet fruit such as strawberries or raspberries. Frosted fruit and rose petals can make a pretty decoration.

●80 calories/350 kj per portion

Lemon layer sponge

SERVES 4

3 large eggs, separated
3 tablespoons plain flour
3 tablespoons caster sugar
175 ml/6 fl oz milk
25 g/1 oz butter, melted
grated zest and juice of 1 lemon
icing sugar, to dredge
pouring cream, to serve

1 Heat the oven to 170C/325F/Gas 3.
2 Place the egg yolks, flour, caster sugar, milk, butter and lemon zest in a large bowl and whisk until smoothly blended.
3 In a clean dry bowl, and using clean beaters, whisk the egg whites until stiff. Gently but thoroughly fold them into the lemon mixture, using a large metal spoon.
4 Spoon the mixture into a buttered 1 L/2 pint baking dish standing in a roasting tin. Pour enough hot water into the tin to come about 2.5 cm/1 inch up the side of the dish (see Preparation).
5 Bake the pudding in the oven for about 1 hour until risen, golden, and just firm to the touch. Remove the dish from the tin. Sift icing sugar thickly over the top of the pudding. Serve while still warm, with cream.

Cook's Notes

TIME
About 15 minutes to prepare and 1 hour to bake.

PREPARATION
Standing the dish in a tin of hot water for baking helps keep the pudding deliciously soft and moist.
During baking, the mixture separates into layers: a light sponge on top and a rich custard sauce underneath.

●210 calories/875 kj per portion

Creamy blackcurrant cheesecake

MAKES 8-10 SLICES
90 g/3½ oz butter
50 g/2 oz caster sugar
200 g/7 oz shortbread biscuits, finely crushed
butter, for greasing

FILLING AND TOPPING
500 g/1 lb full-fat soft cheese (see Buying guide)
175 g/6 oz caster sugar
3 eggs, separated
finely grated zest of ½ lemon
few drops of vanilla flavouring
150 ml/¼ pint whipping cream
5 teaspoons powdered gelatine
5 tablespoons water
400 g/14 oz can blackcurrant pie filling
lemon twists (optional)

1 Grease a deep, 23 cm/9 inch round cake tin with a loose base.

2 Put the butter and sugar into a small, heavy-based saucepan and stir over low heat until melted. Remove from the heat and stir in the biscuit crumbs, then press the mixture evenly over the base of the prepared tin. Refrigerate.

3 Put the cheese into a large bowl and beat until softened. Beat in 75 g/3 oz sugar, the egg yolks, lemon zest, vanilla and cream.

4 Sprinkle the gelatine over the water in a heatproof bowl. Leave to soak for 5 minutes until spongy, then stand the bowl in a pan of barely simmering water for 1-2 minutes, stirring occasionally, until the gelatine has dissolved.

5 Allow the gelatine to cool slightly, then beat it into the cheese mixture. Leave in a cool place for about 15 minutes, until on point of setting.

6 In a clean, dry bowl, whisk the egg whites until standing in stiff peaks, then gradually whisk in the remaining sugar. Fold the meringue into the cheese mixture.

7 Turn filling into prepared tin and level the surface. Cover and chill for at least 3 hours, until set.

8 To serve: loosen cake with a palette knife, then remove sides of tin. Spread pie filling over the top. Add lemon twists, if liked.

229

Date and walnut baked apples

SERVES 4

4 large cooking apples (see Buying guide)
6 tablespoons natural unsweetened apple juice
whipped double cream, to serve

FILLING
50 g/2 oz dates, stoned and coarsely chopped
15 g/½ oz shelled walnuts, chopped
25 g/1 oz Demerara sugar
½ teaspoon ground cinnamon

1 Heat the oven to 180C/350F/Gas 4.
2 Using an apple corer or a small sharp knife, remove the core from each apple. Score the skin around the middle of each apple with a sharp knife (see Cook's tip).
3 Make the filling: mix together the dates, walnuts, sugar and ground cinnamon in a bowl. Use to fill cavities, pressing down firmly with the back of a teaspoon.
4 Place in an ovenproof dish, then pour apple juice around apples.
5 Bake in oven for 50-60 minutes, basting occasionally with the apple juice, until the apples are soft when pierced through the centre with a sharp knife.
6 Serve at once, accompanied by whipped double cream.

Cook's Notes

 TIME
15 minutes preparation; 50-60 minutes cooking.

 VARIATION
Replace the dates with chopped figs.

 COOK'S TIP
Scoring the apples will prevent the skins from exploding during baking.

 BUYING GUIDE
Choose Bramley apples, each weighing about 200 g/7 oz.

●175 calories/725 kj per portion

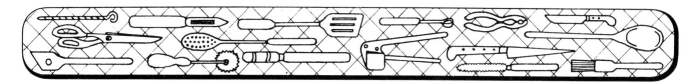

Magic chocolate pudding

SERVES 4

75 g/3 oz self-raising flour
2 tablespoons cocoa powder
pinch of salt
100 g/4 oz margarine or butter,
  softened
100 g/4 oz caster sugar
½ teaspoon vanilla flavouring
2 eggs, lightly beaten
1-2 tablespoons milk
margarine, for greasing

SAUCE
100 g/4 oz light soft brown sugar
2 tablespoons cocoa powder
300 ml/½ pint boiling water

1 Heat the oven to 190C/375F/Gas 5. Lightly grease a 1.5 L/2½ pint fairly deep ovenproof pie dish.
2 Sift flour into a bowl with cocoa powder and salt, then set aside.
3 Beat the margarine and caster sugar together until pale and fluffy, then beat in the vanilla. Beat in the eggs, a little at a time, adding 1 tablespoon of the flour mixture with the last few additions of egg. Gradually stir in the remaining flour mixture and mix well, then add enough milk to give a smooth dropping consistency.
4 Spoon the mixture into the prepared dish, spread it evenly and level the surface.
5 Make the sauce: mix together the brown sugar and cocoa powder,
then gradually blend in the water, stirring vigorously to avoid lumps. Pour the sauce over the mixture in the pie dish (see Cook's tip).
6 Bake just above the centre of the
oven for 40 minutes, or until the pudding is well risen and browned and the chocolate sauce beneath is syrupy. Serve the pudding while it is hot (see Serving ideas).

Cook's Notes

TIME
15 minutes preparation and 40 minutes baking.

COOK'S TIP
This quick and easy pudding, which is very popular with children, has the added bonus of an 'instant' chocolate sauce that cooks with
the mixture in the oven. Do not worry if the mixture looks unpromising when you pour over the sauce: during baking it rises above the sauce.

SERVING IDEAS
The pudding is rich enough to eat as it is, but if you are feeling really
indulgent, serve it with ice cream or whipped cream.

SPECIAL OCCASION
Use dark rum instead of milk. Stir in 25 g/1 oz chopped walnuts or blanched almonds at the end of stage 3.

● 520 calories/2175 kj per portion

231

Queen of puddings

SERVES 4

50 g/2 oz fresh white breadcrumbs
25 g/1 oz sugar
grated zest of ½ lemon

425 ml/¾ pint milk
15 g/½ oz margarine or butter
2 egg yolks
5 tablespoons lemon curd
margarine or butter, for greasing

MERINGUE
2 egg whites
75 g/3 oz caster sugar

1 Mix the breadcrumbs, sugar and lemon zest together in a bowl. In a small saucepan, bring the milk and margarine almost to the boil, then remove from the heat and pour over the crumb mixture. Stir well, then leave to soak for 10-15 minutes.

2 Meanwhile, heat the oven to 180C/350F/Gas 4. Grease an 850 ml/1½ pint pie dish.
3 Beat the egg yolks into the milky crumbs, then spoon the mixture into the dish and spread it evenly. Bake in the oven for 35-40 minutes, until just set in the centre. ⚠️
4 Remove the dish from the oven and spread the lemon curd over the pudding. In a spotlessly clean and dry bowl, whisk the egg whites until standing in stiff peaks. Reserve 2-3 teaspoons of the caster sugar; whisk the remaining sugar into the egg whites, 1 tablespoon at a time, and continue whisking until the meringue is stiff and glossy. Spread it over the pudding, then form into peaks (see Preparation) and sprinkle over the reserved sugar.
5 Return the dish to the oven and bake for 10-15 minutes, until the surface of the meringue is crisp and lightly browned.
6 Serve the pudding at once, straight from the dish.

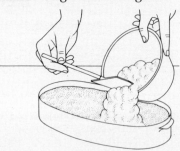
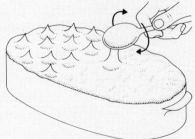

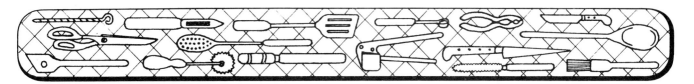

Tropical crumble

SERVES 4-6

4 oranges, peeled and chopped
4 fresh apricots, stoned and
  chopped or 8 canned apricot
  halves, chopped
2 large bananas, peeled and sliced
100 g/4 oz fresh pineapple,
  chopped, or canned pineapple
  chunks
single cream or ice cream, to serve

TOPPING
50 g/2 oz plain flour
½ teaspoon ground ginger
25 g/1 oz rolled or porridge oats
25 g/1 oz desiccated coconut
150 g/5 oz dark soft brown sugar
65 g/2½ oz butter, melted

1 Heat the oven to 180C/350F/Gas 4.
2 First make the topping: sift the flour and ginger into a mixing bowl. Add the oats, coconut and sugar and mix together. Stir in the melted butter.
3 Put all the fruit into a deep ovenproof dish, turning the banana slices in the juice from the oranges to prevent them from discolouring.
4 Sprinkle the topping evenly over the fruit and press down gently to level the surface.
5 Bake for about 40 minutes or until the fruit mixture is bubbling up around the edge of the topping. Serve hot with single cream or, if you prefer ice cream.

Cook's Notes

TIME
The preparation of the fruit and the crumble topping will take about 20 minutes. The cooking time is about 40 minutes.

COOK'S TIP
If using canned pineapple, try to find a can that has unsweetened syrup, because the topping mixture for the crumble is itself very sweet.

VARIATIONS
Use other fruits such as apple or rhubarb with the same crumble topping. If you use dried fruit allow an extra 3 hours soaking time.

● 510 calories/2150 kj per portion

Bread and butter pudding

SERVES 4

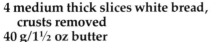

- 4 medium thick slices white bread, crusts removed
- 40 g/1½ oz butter
- 50 g/2 oz sultanas
- 25 g/1 oz caster sugar
- 2 large eggs
- 300 ml/½ pint milk
- ¼ teaspoon freshly grated nutmeg

1 Butter the bread well on one side. Cut each slice into 4.

2 Layer bread, buttered side up, in a well-greased 1 L/2 pint ovenproof dish, sprinkling sultanas and sugar between each layer and on top of the last layer.

3 Whisk the eggs and milk together and strain over the bread. Leave to stand in a cool place for 30 minutes.

4 Heat the oven to 180C/350F/Gas 4.

5 Sprinkle the nutmeg over the pudding and bake in the oven for 25-30 minutes until set and golden brown. Serve hot.

Cook's Notes

 TIME
Preparation 10 minutes, cooking time 30 minutes, but allow another 30 minutes soaking time.

 ECONOMY
This is an excellent way of using up stale white or brown bread.

●665 calories/2775 kj per portion

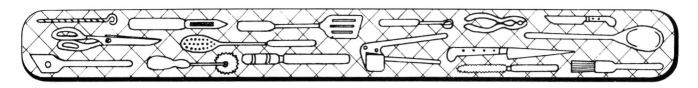

Sherry trifle

SERVES 4-6

8 trifle sponges, cut in half horizontally
100 g/4 oz raspberry jam
4 tablespoons medium sherry
385 g/13½ oz can raspberries, drained with syrup reserved
3 large eggs
2 tablespoons caster sugar
600 ml/1 pint milk
1 teaspoon vanilla flavouring
300 ml/½ pint whipping or double cream
red glacé cherries, halved
a little angelica, to finish

1 Spread the trifle sponges with the jam, then sandwich together again. Cut each across in half and arrange in the base of a glass serving bowl.
2 Stir the sherry into the reserved raspberry syrup, then pour over the sponges. Scatter the raspberries over the top.

3 Whisk the eggs and sugar lightly together in a large bowl (see Cook's tip). Heat the milk until almost boiling in a small saucepan, then pour on to the egg and sugar mixture, whisking constantly.
4 Strain the mixture into a heavy-based pan. Cook over low heat for 10-15 minutes, stirring constantly with a wooden spoon, until the custard is thick enough to coat the back of the spoon. Remove from the heat, stir in the vanilla and leave to cool for 10 minutes.
5 Pour the custard over the raspberries and sponges and leave to cool completely. Cover and refrigerate for 3-4 hours, or overnight.
6 Whip the cream until it forms soft peaks. Spread one-third of the cream over the custard and mark the surface with a fork or small palette knife, if liked. Put the remaining cream into a piping bag fitted with a large star nozzle. Pipe a border of cream and a lattice on the trifle, then decorate with cherries and angelica. Serve at once, or cover and refrigerate for 2-3 hours.

Nutty apple crumble

SERVES 4

 3 large dessert apples (about 500 g/ 1 lb) preferably Cox's

 50 g/2 oz sultanas
50 g/2 oz light soft brown sugar
2 tablespoons water

CRUMBLE TOPPING
100 g/4 oz wholewheat flour
1 teaspoon ground mixed spice
100 g/4 oz chilled margarine or butter, cubed [!]
50 g/2 oz walnuts, roughly chopped
50-75 g/2-3 oz light soft brown sugar, according to taste

1 Heat the oven to 190C/375F/Gas 5.
2 Make the crumble topping: put the flour in a mixing bowl with the spice. Stir well to mix. Add the margarine and cut it in with a round-bladed knife, then rub in the pieces until the mixture resembles coarse bread-crumbs. Stir in the walnuts and sugar to taste, then set aside.
3 Peel, core and slice the apples (see Cook's tip) and layer them with the sultanas and the sugar in a well-buttered 1.5 L/2½ pint ovenproof dish. Sprinkle over the water.
4 Sprinkle the crumble mixture over the apples and press down lightly to level the surface.
5 Bake in the oven for 40-50 minutes or until the crumble topping is crisp and golden and the apples are tender. Serve hot or warm.

Cook's Notes

 TIME
Preparation 15 minutes, cooking time 50 minutes.

 SERVING IDEAS
This sweet pudding is best served with a sharp-tasting natural yoghurt, rather than custard or cream.

[!] **WATCHPOINT**
Make sure the margarine is well chilled or it will be impossible to rub in. Do not overwork the mixture or it will become sticky and doughy and impossible to work with.

 COOK'S TIP
Slice the apples thinly so they will be cooked at the same time as the topping.

VARIATION
Use cooking apples and the full amount of sugar for the topping.

●560 calories/2350 kj per portion

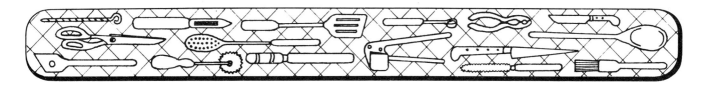

Jam soufflé omelettes

MAKES 2, TO SERVE 4

6 eggs
2 tablespoons caster sugar
few drops of vanilla flavouring
40 g/1½ oz butter
6-8 tablespoons jam, warmed
4 tablespoons icing sugar, to dredge

1 Make the first omelette: separate 3 of the eggs, placing the whites in a clean, dry bowl. Whisk the egg whites until standing in soft peaks. In a separate bowl, whisk the egg yolks with half the sugar and 1-2 drops vanilla.
2 Heat the grill to high.
3 Melt half the butter in an omelette or frying-pan with a base diameter of 20 cm/8 inches. ⚠ Meanwhile, quickly fold the beaten egg yolks into the egg whites with a large metal spoon.
4 As soon as the butter is foaming, pour in the egg mixture and turn down the heat to low. Cook the omelette, without stirring, ⚠ for

Cook's Notes

TIME
Each omelette takes about 10 minutes to prepare and cook.

WATCHPOINTS
The size of the pan is important: if it is too small the omelette will be too thick to fold; if it is too large the omelette will be disappointingly thin.

If stirred, the omelette will lose its light, fluffy texture.

COOK'S TIP
If you only need to serve 2 people, make just 1 omelette, but if serving 4, do not try to keep the first omelette hot

while cooking the second one. Pick an occasion when it does not matter if everyone is served at one time. To cut down the time between servings whisk the second batch of egg whites while the first omelette is cooking.

DID YOU KNOW
This type of sweet omelette is traditionally decorated with a criss-cross pattern, made by placing heated metal skewers on top of the folded omelette until the icing sugar is caramelized, as shown in the photograph.

● 340 calories/1425 kj per portion

2-3 minutes, until the underside is set and golden. Then place the pan under the grill for 2-3 minutes, until the top of the omelette is golden brown.
5 Spread half the warmed jam over one-half of the omelette. Using a large palette knife or fish slice, fold

the omelette in half to enclose jam.
6 Slide the omelette on to a warmed dish and sift half the icing sugar over the top. Cut across in half and serve at once.
7 Use the remaining ingredients to make the second omelette in the same way (see Cook's tip).

Orange jelly castles

SERVES 4

135 g/4¾ oz packet tangerine or
   orange jelly, cubed
125 ml/4 fl oz boiling water
425 g/15 oz can semolina pudding
   (see Cook's tips)

TO DECORATE

about 4 tablespoons desiccated
   coconut
300 g/11 oz can mandarin orange
   segments, drained
'leaves' of angelica

1 Rinse out four 150 ml/¼ pint
moulds (see Cook's tips) with cold
water.
2 Place the jelly in a small pan with
the boiling water and stir over very
low heat until the jelly is dissolved.
Remove from the heat and cool for
about 5 minutes.

3 Using a fork or balloon whisk,
beat the semolina pudding into the
jelly until evenly blended. Divide
the mixture between the prepared
moulds, cover with cling film and
refrigerate for 1-2 hours, until set.
4 Unmould the jellies, one at a time:
run a round-bladed knife around
the sides of the jelly to loosen it. Dip
the base of the mould in a bowl of
hot water for 2-3 seconds, then
invert a dampened dessert plate on
top. Hold the mould and plate
firmly and invert them, giving a
sharp shake halfway round (see
Cook's tips). Lift off the mould.
5 Sprinkle the coconut over the
jellies, covering the tops and as
much of the sides as possible. Using
the tip of a round-bladed knife, lift
the loose coconut from the plates
and gently press it on to the sides of
the jellies.
6 Arrange mandarin orange
segments on the top and around the
base of each jelly, then decorate
with 'leaves' of angelica. Serve at
once, or refrigerate for up to 2 hours.

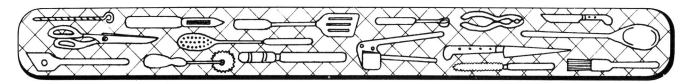

Iced chocolate boxes

MAKES 6

475 ml/17 fl oz block chocolate
ice cream (see Watchpoint)
24 peppermint chocolates (see
Buying guide)
150 ml/¼ pint double cream
300 g/11 oz mandarin orange
segments, drained
6 small sprigs fresh mint, to
decorate (optional)

1 Cut the ice cream into 6 equal
cubes and place on a freezerproof
plate. Press 1 chocolate on to 4 sides
of each cube leaving the top and
bottom plain. Return to the freezer,
or freezing compartment of the
refrigerator ✳ while you prepare
the cream.

2 Whip the cream until thick, but
not stiff, then put into a piping bag
fitted with a large star nozzle (see
Cook's tip).
3 Remove the chocolate boxes from
the freezer and pipe the cream on

the top of each box. Top with
mandarin orange segments and a
sprig of mint, if liked. Place on
chilled, individual serving plates
and serve immediately, before the
ice cream melts.

Raisin semolina

SERVES 4-6

600 ml/1 pint milk
40 g/1½ oz semolina

40 g/1½ oz seedless raisins
1 egg, beaten
50 g/2 oz Demerara sugar
½ teaspoon ground cinnamon
15 g/½ oz margarine or butter,
   shaved into flakes
melted margarine or butter,
   for greasing

1 Brush the inside of a 600 ml/1 pint flameproof dish with margarine.
2 Pour the milk into a heavy-based saucepan and heat gently until just below boiling point. Sprinkle in the semolina and stir until the mixture comes to the boil. Add the raisins, then reduce the heat and cook gently for 15 minutes, stirring frequently.
3 Heat the grill to high.
4 Remove the pan from the heat. Allow the semolina mixture to cool slightly, then beat in the egg, a little at a time. ⚠ Return the pan to low heat and cook, stirring, for 1 minute.
5 Turn the semolina mixture into the prepared dish and level the surface. Mix the sugar with the cinnamon and sprinkle over the surface of the pudding, then dot with the margarine.
6 Place under the grill for 2-3 minutes, until the sugar is melted and bubbling. ⚠ Serve hot or cold, straight from the dish.

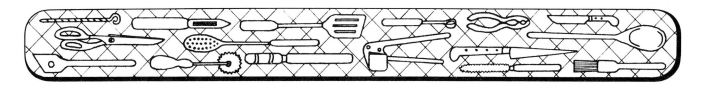

Treacle tart

SERVES 4-6

225 g/8-9 oz shortcrust pastry,
   defrosted if frozen
225 g/8 oz golden syrup (see Cook's
   tips)
75 g/3 oz white breadcrumbs, made
   from stale bread
grated zest and juice of ½ lemon
double cream or custard, to serve
   (optional)

1 Heat the oven to 200C/400F/Gas 6.
2 Roll out the pastry thinly on a
lightly floured surface and use to
line a 20 cm/8 inch loose-bottomed
flan tin. Trim the edges and reserve
the trimmings. Prick the pastry base
with a fork and refrigerate.
3 To make the filling: put the syrup,
breadcrumbs, lemon zest and juice
into a small saucepan and heat
gently, stirring, until the ingre-

dients are thoroughly combined.
[!] Leave to cool before spooning
into the prepared pastry case.
4 Roll out the reserved pastry
trimmings and cut into long, 5 mm/
¼ inch-wide strips. Use to decorate
the top of the tart in a lattice pattern,
moistening the ends of the lattice

strips and pressing them firmly
against the edge of the pastry case so
they do not come loose during
baking.
5 Bake in the oven for about 25
minutes or until the pastry is golden
and the filling is just set. Serve warm
or cold with cream or custard.

Cook's Notes

TIME
Preparation 20 minutes,
cooking time 25 minutes.

COOK'S TIPS
To weigh the golden
syrup, first warm the
golden syrup container in a
bowl of hot water so the syrup
flows freely. Next place a small
saucepan on the scales and reset
to zero. Pour the golden syrup
directly into the saucepan until
it weighs 225 g/8 oz.

●460 calories/1925 kj per portion

WATCHPOINT
Do not allow the mix-
ture to boil or it will resemble toffee.

VARIATION
Make tart on a 23 cm/
9 inch pie plate and
decorate with a sunflower edge
as shown in the photograph: cut
the pastry edge into 2.5 cm/1
inch strips, fold the strips
diagonally in half and press
down firmly. Glaze the edge by
brushing with egg yolk beaten
with a little milk.

Banana fan flambé

SERVES 4

 4 large bananas, cut into fans (see
    Preparation)

 4 tablespoons rum
juice of 1½ oranges
¼ teaspoon ground cinnamon
large pinch of freshly grated
    nutmeg
75 g/3 oz butter
little lightly beaten egg white
4 tablespoons light soft brown
    sugar
vanilla ice cream or whipped cream,
    to serve

1 Pour the rum into a cup and stand
in a pan or bowl of hot water to
warm through gently. In a separate
cup, mix the orange juice with the
cinnamon and nutmeg.
2 Melt the butter in a large, heavy-

Cook's Notes

TIME
Preparation and cooking
take about 20 minutes.

 WATCHPOINTS
Use a fish slice and turn
the fans very gently so
that they do not break or lose
their attractive shape.
   Hold the match just above the
side of the pan and stand well
back since the flames will shoot
high for a few seconds and could
be dangerous.

● 330 calories/1375 kj per portion

PREPARATION
Make banana fans as
follows:

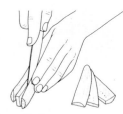

*Cut each banana across in half.
With a sharp knife, make 3-4
parallel cuts lengthways in each
half towards tapered end. Do not
cut right through. Fan out slices.*

based frying-pan over low heat.
Lightly brush fans with egg white,
then add them to the pan and fry
gently for about 5 minutes, turning
once, until golden brown on both
sides. [!] Sprinkle over the sugar.
3 Pour in the spiced orange juice

and heat through gently. Turn off
the heat. Pour the warmed rum over
the bananas and immediately set
light to it. [!] Let the flames die
completely, then divide the fans and
sauce between 4 warmed individual
dishes and serve with ice cream.

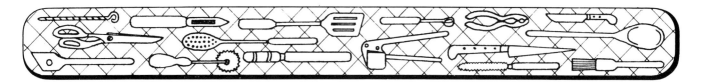

Gooseberry fool

SERVES 4

500 g/1 lb gooseberries, topped and
   tailed if fresh (see Preparation),
   defrosted and well drained if
   frozen (see Watchpoints)
2 tablespoons water
50 g/2 oz caster sugar
425 g/15 oz can custard
few drops of green food colouring
150 g/5 oz natural yoghurt
4 teaspoons coloured sugar crystals
   (optional)

1 Put the gooseberries into a heavy-
based saucepan with the water.
Cover and cook over moderate heat
for about 8 minutes, until soft.
2 Press the gooseberries through a
nylon sieve, or cool slightly, then
purée in a blender and sieve the
purée to remove seeds. Sweeten to
taste with caster sugar, then leave to
cool completely.
3 Stir the purée into the custard
until evenly blended, then add
enough colouring to tint the fool
pale green. Cover and refrigerate for
1-2 hours, if liked.
4 Divide the fool between 4 dessert
glasses or bowls. Spoon a little
yoghurt carefully on to each portion.
5 Just before serving, scatter the
yoghurt with sugar crystals if liked.
⚠ Serve at room temperature or,
if preferred, chilled.

Cook's Notes

TIME
25 minutes preparation,
plus cooling and chill-
ing time.

WATCHPOINTS
If using defrosted goose-
berries, drain them on
absorbent paper before cooking
otherwise the purée will be too
watery.
   Sugar crystals will dissolve if

added more than 5 minutes
before serving.

SERVING IDEAS
This smooth, light des-
sert needs to be served
with crisp biscuits for texture
contrast.

STORAGE
Prepare up to the end of
stage 3; cover with cling

film and refrigerate for up to 24
hours.

PREPARATION
Use a small, sharp stain-
less steel knife to trim
off the small fibrous stalks and
'tails' from fresh gooseberries.
This is called 'topping and
tailing'.

●200 calories/825 kj per portion

243

Flaky rice sundae

SERVES 4

600 ml/1 pint milk
50 g/2 oz flaked rice (see Buying guide)
25 g/1 oz sugar
few drops of vanilla flavouring

TOPPING
15 g/½ oz margarine or butter
1 tablespoon golden syrup
25 g/1 oz corn flakes or rice crispies

1 Pour the milk into a medium heavy-based saucepan. Bring slowly to simmering point over low heat, then sprinkle in the flaked rice. Simmer gently, stirring frequently, for 15-20 minutes, until the rice is tender and thickened. ⚠
2 Remove from the heat and stir in the sugar and vanilla, to taste. Cool slightly, then spoon into 4 dessert dishes. Leave to cool completely.
3 Make the topping: melt the margarine with the syrup in a saucepan over low heat. Remove from the heat, add the corn flakes and stir gently with a large metal spoon until evenly coated.
4 Spoon the topping over the puddings. ⚠ Leave to set about 30 minutes before serving.

Cook's Notes

TIME
35 minutes preparation, plus cooling time.

BUYING GUIDE
You can buy white and brown rice flakes. The brown variety, which are sold in health food stores, have a pleasant 'nutty' flavour and more food value.

WATCHPOINTS
The milk should only simmer gently, otherwise it will evaporate and the pudding will be too thick.
The topping sticks together and hardens as it cools, so it must be divided between the dishes while still warm.

SERVING IDEAS
This easy-to-make milk pudding with its tempting crisp, sweet topping can also be served hot. Spoon the pudding into the dishes, but do not cool; make and add the topping, then serve at once.

VARIATIONS
Try this topping over other milk puddings (canned, if liked), such as sago or semolina.

● 240 calories/1000 kj per portion

QUICK 'N' EASY COOKING

This is the section for the cook who never has enough time. All the dishes can be prepared and cooked in under an hour, giving you an infinite variety of meals for snacks, brunch, lunch and supper. There are salads and vegetables, soups and snacks, rice 'n' pasta and egg 'n' cheese dishes. There is also a selection of recipes for those main meals when you just haven't much time or guests arrive unexpectedly. Try making the delicious *Country goulash* or *Baconburgers* which children will love. Appetizing and filling sandwiches are also included for those quick lunches or late-night impromptu snacks.

SALADS AND VEGETABLES

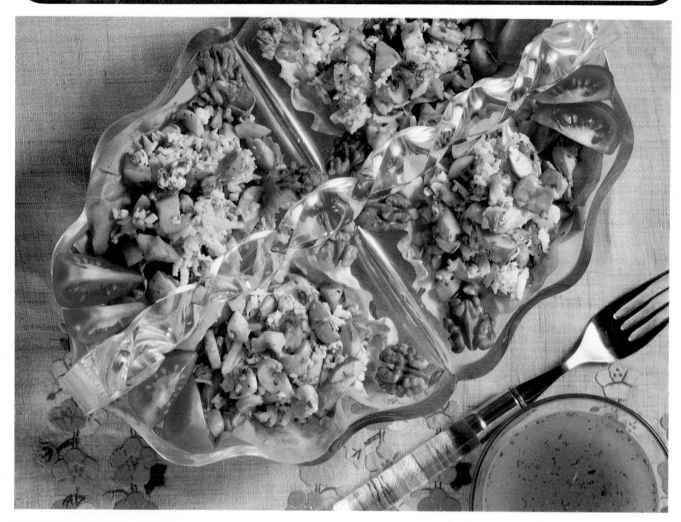

Mushroom and Stilton salad

SERVES 4
100 g/4 oz button mushrooms, chopped
100 g/4 oz Stilton cheese, grated
75 g/3 oz shelled walnut halves
4 large lettuce leaves
2 tomatoes, quartered

VINAIGRETTE DRESSING
1 tablespoon white wine vinegar
2 teaspoons lemon juice
3 tablespoons vegetable oil
1 teaspoon dried mixed herbs (optional)
about ½ teaspoon sugar
salt and freshly ground black pepper

1 Mix the mushrooms and Stilton cheese together in a bowl, forking them through gently until thoroughly combined. Cover and refrigerate for at least 1 hour.
2 Meanwhile, make the vinaigrette dressing: in a bowl mix together the vinegar, lemon juice and oil. Add the dried herbs, if using, and sugar to taste. Season with salt and freshly ground black pepper.
3 Reserve 8 walnut halves to garnish and chop the remainder roughly. Mix with the mushrooms and Stilton cheese.
4 Spoon a little of the dressing into the mixture and fork through gently until well combined.
5 Arrange the lettuce leaves on 4 individual serving plates. Carefully spoon a quarter of the mushroom and Stilton cheese mixture on to the top of each of the lettuce leaves.
6 Garnish each serving with 2 walnut halves and 2 tomato quarters. Hand the remaining vinaigrette dressing separately.

Cook's Notes

TIME
The salad takes about 15 minutes to prepare but allow time for chilling the mushrooms and the Stilton.

SERVING IDEAS
This salad is very rich, but very tasty. Serve it with warm granary toast or rolls for a supper or lunch dish.

●315 calories/1325 kj per portion

246

Tropical salad

SERVES 4-6

75 g/3 oz pasta shapes
2 grapefruits, peeled and segmented
2 oranges, peeled and segmented
2 large dessert apples, diced
3 celery stalks, finely chopped
100 g/4 oz salami, skinned and
    roughly chopped
1 tablespoon snipped chives
25 g/1 oz salted cashew nuts

DRESSING

4 tablespoons thick bottled
    mayonnaise
2 tablespoons fresh orange juice
finely grated zest and juice of 1
    lemon
2 tablespoons rosehip syrup
salt and freshly ground black pepper

TO GARNISH

slices of unpeeled orange
watercress

1 Bring a pan of salted water to the boil and cook the pasta for about 10 minutes or until just tender. Rinse in cold water and drain well.

2 Turn the pasta into a large bowl and stir in the prepared fruit, celery and salami. Mix thoroughly.

3 To make the dressing: mix together the mayonnaise, orange juice, lemon zest and juice and the rosehip syrup. Whisk with a fork until thoroughly combined. Season with salt and pepper.

4 Toss the salad and dressing well together, then turn into a salad bowl and sprinkle over the chives and cashews.

5 Serve garnished with slices of unpeeled orange and watercress.

Cook's Notes

TIME
Preparation of this salad takes 20 minutes plus 10 minutes to cook the pasta.

SERVING IDEAS
This makes a refreshing summer lunch.

● 430 calories/1800 kj per portion

Tuna salad

SERVES 4

 200 g/7 oz can tuna, drained and flaked

1 crisp lettuce (see Buying guide)
75 g/3 oz can pimientos, drained
425 g/15 oz can red kidney beans, drained
175 g/6 oz black olives, stoned
1 onion, sliced into rings

DRESSING
3 tablespoons olive oil
1 tablespoon wine vinegar
½ teaspoon mustard powder
pinch of sugar
1 clove garlic, crushed (optional)
salt and freshly ground black pepper

1 Make the dressing: put all the dressing ingredients into a screw-top jar with salt and pepper to taste. Shake thoroughly to mix, then chill in the refrigerator until ready to use.

2 Line the sides of a large salad bowl with the outside leaves of the lettuce, discarding any damaged leaves.

3 Cut the pimientos into strips.

4 Shred the remaining lettuce (see Preparation) and combine it with the flaked tuna, kidney beans, pimientos and olives. Place in the centre of the salad bowl.

5 Place the sliced onion decoratively on top of the prepared tuna salad to garnish.

6 Pour the dressing over the salad, but do not toss it or you will spoil its appearance, then serve at once. !

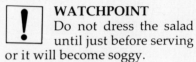

Cook's Notes

 TIME
Preparation takes 10 minutes.

 BUYING GUIDE
A small Webb's or an iceberg lettuce is the best kind for this recipe.

WATCHPOINT
Do not dress the salad until just before serving or it will become soggy.

 VARIATIONS
Use canned butter or white haricot beans instead of the kidney beans. Add sliced hard-boiled egg for extra nourishment and colour.

 SERVING IDEAS
Serve with hot French bread and/or potato salad.

 PREPARATION
To shred lettuce:

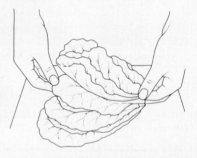

1 *Pile several lettuce leaves on top of each other with the stem ends at right angles to you.*

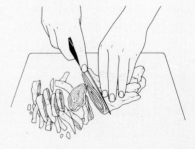

2 *Roll up the leaves, rolling away from you, then slice the roll into thin strips.*

● 305 calories/1275 kj per portion

JOHN WOODCOCK

Harvest ham salad

SERVES 4

250 g/9 oz cooked ham, diced
600 ml/1 pint water
salt
150 g/5 oz fresh peas (shelled weight)
250 g/9 oz courgettes, sliced diagonally into 1 cm/½ inch lengths
2 tablespoons thick bottled mayonnaise
4 tablespoons natural yoghurt
½ teaspoon mustard powder
freshly ground black pepper
250 g/9 oz white cabbage, finely shredded
snipped chives, to garnish

1 Bring the water to the boil in a saucepan, add salt to taste, then the peas. Bring back to the boil, then lower the heat, cover and simmer for 3 minutes.

2 Add the sliced courgettes to the pan, cover again and simmer for a further 4-5 minutes until the vegetables are just tender. Drain, rinse under cold running water, then spread out on absorbent paper to cool and drain thoroughly.

3 In a large bowl, mix the mayonnaise, yoghurt and mustard with salt and pepper to taste. Fold in the cabbage, ham, peas and courgettes.

4 Turn the mixture into a serving dish and garnish with snipped chives. Serve at once or place ungarnished in a covered container and refrigerate overnight, then garnish just before serving.

Chef's layered salad

SERVES 4

8 lettuce leaves, shredded
4 hard-boiled eggs, sliced

4 tomatoes, sliced
275 g/10 oz boneless cooked
   chicken, diced (see Economy)
¼ small cucumber (about 5 cm/2
   inch), unpeeled and thinly sliced
1 large carrot, grated
100 g/4 oz Cheddar or Edam cheese,
   grated

DRESSING
4 tablespoons olive oil
1 tablespoon cider vinegar
salt and freshly ground black pepper

1 Arrange the shredded lettuce in the base of a large glass bowl (see Serving ideas).
2 Arrange the sliced eggs on the lettuce and then sliced tomatoes in a third layer over the eggs.
3 Place the diced chicken on top, then add layers of cucumber, carrot and finally grated cheese. When you arrange the cheese, leave a 2 cm/1 inch border of carrot showing around the edge.
4 Make the dressing: mix the oil and vinegar together and season to taste with salt and pepper. Pour evenly over the salad and serve at once.

Cook's Notes

TIME
Preparation, including hard-boiling and cooling the eggs, takes 45 minutes.

COOK'S TIP
The salad can be prepared in advance and covered with cling film, and the dressing mixed and stored in a screw-top jar, to be added at the last minute.

ECONOMY
Buy chicken thighs and roast them in foil. This will be far less expensive than buying a whole chicken. Five thighs will yield about 275 g/10 oz chicken meat.

SERVING IDEAS
Be sure to make the salad in a glass bowl, to display the layers to best effect. Vary the arrangement of the layers as you wish.
  This substantial main-course salad makes a complete meal served either with potato salad or with thinly sliced brown bread and butter.

●430 calories/1800 kj per portion

Aubergine and pasta bake

SERVES 4

2 × 420 g/14¾ oz cans aubergines in sunflower seed oil (see Buying guide)
2 tablespoons vegetable oil
1 large onion, chopped
1 red pepper, deseeded and chopped
1 teaspoon dried mixed herbs
large pinch of ground cinnamon (see Cook's tips)
salt and freshly ground black pepper
175 g/6 oz wholewheat short-cut macaroni (see Variation)

TOPPING

2 eggs
300 ml/½ pint natural yoghurt
50 g/2 oz mature Cheddar cheese, grated
sweet paprika, for sprinkling

1 Heat the oven to 200C/400F/Gas 6.
2 Heat the oil in a heavy-based saucepan. Add the onion and red pepper and cook gently, stirring frequently, for about 10 minutes until the vegetables are softened. Stir in the aubergines and their oil, herbs, cinnamon and salt and pepper to taste. Cover and keep warm.
3 While the vegetables are cooking, bring a large pan of salted water to the boil. Add the macaroni and stir once. Bring the water back to the boil and cook for 9-11 minutes, until the macaroni is just tender.
4 Drain the macaroni thoroughly, then stir into the aubergine mixture. Check the seasoning, then turn into a 1.5-1.75 L/2½-3 pint baking or gratin dish and level the surface.
5 Make the topping: whisk the eggs into the yoghurt, then stir in the cheese and salt and pepper to taste. Pour over the aubergine mixture and sprinkle with paprika according to taste.
6 Bake in the oven for about 40 minutes, until the topping is set and browned (see Cook's tips). Serve hot, straight from the casserole.

Paprika potatoes

SERVES 4
750 g/1½ lb potatoes
salt
2 tablespoons vegetable oil
1 medium onion, sliced
1 teaspoon sweet paprika
300 ml/½ pint chicken stock
**½ teaspoon caraway seeds
    (optional)**
**1 large tomato, skinned and
    chopped**
freshly ground black pepper
3 tablespoons soured cream
extra sweet paprika, to garnish

1 Boil the potatoes in salted water until they are beginning to soften—about 7 minutes. Drain and cut into 5 mm/¼ inch slices.
2 Heat the oil in a large saucepan and fry the onion over moderate heat for about 4 minutes, or until it is just beginning to turn light brown. Add the paprika, chicken stock, caraway seeds, if using, tomato and pepper. Stir well and add the potatoes, stirring carefully.
3 Bring slowly to the boil, cover the pan and simmer for 20-25 minutes. The potatoes should have absorbed most of the liquid.
4 Pour over the soured cream and allow just to heat through. Turn on to a warmed serving dish. Sprinkle with a little extra paprika to garnish.

Cook's Notes

TIME
This dish takes 45 minutes to make.

DID YOU KNOW
Caraway seeds have an aniseed taste which imparts a very definite flavour to food.

●265 calories/1100 kj per portion

Sunshine supper

SERVES 4

1 large aubergine
salt
4 tablespoons olive oil
1 clove garlic, crushed (optional)
1 onion, chopped
1 green pepper, deseeded and finely
    chopped
400 g/14 oz can tomatoes, chopped
    (see Economy)
75 ml/3 fl oz red wine
2 teaspoons tomato purée
½ teaspoon sugar
1 teaspoon dried basil
freshly ground black pepper
100 g/4 oz ribbon noodles (see
    Buying guide)
6 slices processed cheese
25 g/1 oz Parmesan cheese, grated
melted butter, for greasing

1 Wipe the aubergine with a damp cloth and trim off the stalk. Slice the aubergine into 5 mm/¼ inch thick slices and put them in a colander in layers, sprinkling salt between each layer. Cover with a plate and place a heavy weight on top. Leave for about 1 hour to draw out the bitter juices then rinse the slices and pat dry on absorbent paper.

2 Heat the oven to 180C/350F/Gas 4.

3 Heat 1 tablespoon of the oil in a saucepan, add the garlic, if using, the onion and green pepper and fry gently for about 5 minutes until the onion is soft and lightly coloured. Stir in tomatoes with juices, wine and tomato purée. Bring to boil, stir in the sugar and basil and season with salt and pepper to taste. Let the sauce boil gently to reduce and thicken.

4 Meanwhile, bring a pan of salted water to the boil and add 1 teaspoon of oil. Cook the noodles for 10-12 minutes until just tender then drain thoroughly.

5 Heat the remaining oil in a frying-pan, add the aubergine slices and fry gently until they are lightly coloured on both sides. Remove with a slotted spoon and drain on absorbent paper.

6 Grease an ovenproof dish with melted butter and spread a third of the tomato sauce over the bottom.

Put half the noodles on top, followed by half the aubergine slices and half the processed cheese. Cover with another third of the tomato sauce and then the remaining noodles, aubergine slices and processed cheese. Spread the remaining tomato sauce over the cheese slices and sprinkle the Parmesan cheese on top.

7 Cook in the oven for about 20 minutes, until heated through. Serve immediately straight from the dish.

Cook's Notes

 TIME
Draining the aubergines takes 1 hour; allow another 20-25 minutes for the rest of the preparation. Cooking takes 20 minutes.

 BUYING GUIDE
Look for green noodles available in most supermarkets; they are particularly suitable for this dish.

●355 calories/1500 kj per portion

 SERVING IDEAS
This delicious supper dish needs only a salad accompaniment to make it a complete meal.

 ECONOMY
Use fresh tomatoes for the sauce when they are plentiful and low in price—you will need 350 g/12 oz. Skin and chop them and add to the onion and green pepper with a little extra wine.

Creamed leek pastry

750 g/1½ lb leeks, finely sliced
100 g/4 oz butter
350 g/12 oz frozen puff pastry,
  defrosted
1 small egg
salt
freshly grated nutmeg
3 tablespoons single cream
freshly ground black pepper

1 Heat the oven to 200C/400F/Gas 6.
2 Melt the butter in a large saucepan and add the leeks, stir and cover. Cook over very gentle heat for about 15 minutes, stirring occasionally until leeks are soft.
3 Meanwhile, roll out the pastry on a lightly floured surface to a 33 × 23 cm/12 × 9 inch rectangle. Fold the pastry in half lengthways so that it measures 33 × 11½ cm/12 × 4½ inches. Lightly roll over the pastry to expel any air bubbles.

4 Press the edges of the pastry together well. Prick with a fork all over. Place the pastry strip on a dampened baking sheet and bake in the oven for 10 minutes.
5 Beat the egg lightly with a pinch of salt. Remove the pastry from the oven and brush with the egg, pressing the pastry down gently as you brush. Return to the oven for a

further 10 minutes until golden.
6 Add a little nutmeg to the cooked leeks, stir in the cream and season to taste with salt and pepper. Keep the leeks warm, but do not boil.
7 Carefully lift the pastry from the baking sheet and place on a serving plate (see Cook's tip). Spoon the leek mixture on top of the pastry and serve at once.

 Cook's Notes

 TIME
Preparation is about 10 minutes, cooking time 15 minutes for the leeks and 20 minutes for the pastry.

COOK'S TIP
If the pastry has risen unevenly, gently prick it to let the air escape and it will sink and become flat.

WATCHPOINT
Be careful not to let the leeks burn—cook them on the lowest possible heat.

SERVING IDEAS
Serve as a starter or a snack, with a tomato and cucumber salad.
Make individual portions by cutting the long strip of pastry into four pieces before cooking.

VARIATIONS
Instead of leeks use grated or finely chopped carrots with ginger, or cabbage finely chopped with cinnamon added.

●630 calories/2625 kj per portion

Lentil layer pie

SERVES 4

100 g/4 oz split red lentils (see
    Buying guide)
1 large onion, chopped
¼ teaspoon dried basil
¼ teaspoon dried thyme
225 g/8 oz can tomatoes
425 ml/¾ pint beef stock
salt and freshly ground black pepper
25 g/1 oz margarine or butter
50 g/2 oz fresh white breadcrumbs
4 large hard-boiled eggs, sliced
margarine, for greasing

1 Heat the oven to 190C/375F/Gas 5
and grease a 1 L/2 pint baking dish.
2 Put the lentils, onion, herbs,
tomatoes and stock into a pan.
Season with salt and pepper and
bring to the boil. Lower the heat and
cook gently for 15-20 minutes,
stirring occasionally until the lentils
are just tender. The liquid will not
be completely absorbed.
3 Meanwhile, melt the margarine in
a separate pan, remove from the
heat and stir in the breadcrumbs.
Season with salt and pepper.
4 Cover the base of the prepared
dish with a layer of the lentil
mixture then top with a layer of
sliced eggs. Continue these layers
until all the ingredients are used,
finishing with a layer of lentils.
5 Sprinkle the breadcrumbs over
the top and bake near the top of the
oven for 25-30 minutes until the
crumbs are browned. Serve at once,
straight from the dish.

Cook's Notes

TIME
This layered pie takes
only about 1 hour to
prepare and cook.

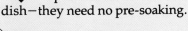
BUYING GUIDE
Be sure to buy the small
split red lentils for this
dish—they need no pre-soaking.

SERVING IDEAS
For a satisfying supper
dish, serve the pie with
a green salad and 'quickie' garlic
bread: spread slices of French
bread with softened butter
mixed with garlic salt and finely
chopped parsley, then wrap in
foil and heat in a 190C/375F/
Gas 5 oven for 7 minutes.

VARIATION
Layer the lentils with
chopped or minced
meat instead of, or as well as,
the hard-boiled eggs.

● 260 calories/1100 kj per portion

Herby beans with eggs

SERVES 4

225 g/8 oz fresh or frozen sliced French or runner beans (see Cook's tip)
225 g/8 oz fresh or frozen broad beans
225 g/8 oz fresh or frozen peas
salt
4 large eggs, hard-boiled and quartered

SAUCE

25 g/1 oz margarine or butter
25 g/1 oz plain flour
425 ml/¾ pint milk
2 tablespoons chopped fresh parsley
2 tablespoons chopped fresh tarragon or 1½ teaspoons dried tarragon
2 teaspoons lemon juice
freshly ground black pepper

1 Heat the oven to 110C/225F/Gas ¼. Bring a large saucepan of salted water to the boil. Add the fresh or frozen vegetables and cook for 10-15 minutes until just tender.

2 Meanwhile, make the sauce: melt the margarine in a small saucepan, sprinkle in the flour and stir over low heat for 1-2 minutes until straw-coloured. Remove from the heat and gradually stir in the milk. Add the parsley and tarragon, return to the heat and simmer, stirring, until thickened and smooth. Stir in the lemon juice, and season to taste with salt and pepper.

3 Drain the vegetables. Reserve one-third of the sauce and mix the rest into the vegetables. Heat through, very gently, transfer to a warmed serving dish and keep warm in the oven.

4 Heat the remaining sauce in the same pan. When it is very hot but not boiling, arrange the eggs on the vegetables and drizzle the hot sauce over them. Serve at once straight from the dish.

Cauliflower polonaise

SERVES 4

1 cauliflower

DRESSING
3 tablespoons vegetable oil
1 tablespoon wine vinegar
½ teaspoon mustard powder
salt and freshly ground black pepper

TO GARNISH
2 large eggs, hard-boiled
50 g/2 oz margarine or butter
2 tablespoons dried white
    breadcrumbs
chopped parsley

1 To make the dressing: combine all the ingredients in a screw-top jar with salt and pepper to taste.

2 Heat the oven to 130C/250F/Gas ½. Put the cauliflower in boiling salted water and cook for 10-20 minutes, until the stalk is just tender when pierced. Drain thoroughly and keep warm in the oven.

3 Make the garnish: separate the yolks from the whites of the eggs. Chop whites finely, sieve yolks.

4 Melt the margarine in a frying-pan, add the breadcrumbs and fry over brisk heat, stirring, until golden brown and crisp. !

5 Transfer cauliflower to a serving dish. Shake the dressing well to mix and pour it over. Carefully turn the cauliflower in the dressing, so it is evenly coated. Spoon the fried breadcrumbs evenly over the cauliflower, then arrange the chopped egg white and sieved yolk decoratively on top. Sprinkle with parsley and serve at once.

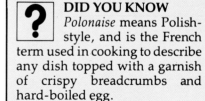

Brussels sprouts and Stilton

SERVES 4

250 g/9 oz Brussels sprouts, shredded
200 g/7 oz can pimientos, drained and sliced
250 g/9 oz Stilton cheese, diced
4 celery stalks, sliced
2 green dessert apples, cored and chopped

DRESSING
6 tablespoons vegetable oil
2 tablespoons cider vinegar or white wine vinegar
1 teaspoon mustard powder
1 tablespoon snipped chives or spring onion tops
salt and freshly ground black pepper

1 Make the dressing: combine the oil, vinegar, mustard and 2 teaspoons of the chives in a screw-top jar. Season with salt and pepper, then shake well to mix.
2 Put the Brussels sprouts in a large bowl. Pour in half the dressing and toss to coat thoroughly. Set aside for 5 minutes.
3 Put the pimientos cheese, celery and apple into the bowl and toss in the remaining dressing until all the ingredients are thoroughly coated.
4 Serve at once, garnished with the remaining chives.

Cook's Notes

 TIME
Preparation time for this unusual salad is about 30 minutes.

 SERVING IDEAS
Serve as a light lunch or supper dish with slices of crusty French bread.

 **VARIATIONS**
Shredded raw spinach or any well-flavoured cabbage can be used instead of the sprouts.
Use other firm blue cheeses such as Danish Blue.

● 530 calories/2225 kj per portion

Vegetable soup

SERVES 4

225 g/8 oz packet frozen mixed
   vegetables
425 ml/¾ pint boiling chicken stock
40 g/1½ oz margarine or butter
1 medium onion, chopped
40 g/1½ oz plain flour
425 ml/¾ pint warm milk
1 tablespoon tomato purée
salt and freshly ground black pepper

CROUTONS

4 tablespoons vegetable oil
4 slices day-old bread, crusts
   removed, cut into small cubes

1 Pour the stock into a saucepan.
Add the frozen vegetables and cook
gently for 8 minutes.
2 Melt the margarine in a heavy-
based saucepan over moderate heat.
When the foam subsides, add the
onion and fry until golden.

3 Sprinkle in the flour and stir over
low heat for 2 minutes until straw-
coloured. Remove from the heat and
gradually stir in the milk, then
return to the heat and simmer,
stirring with a wooden spoon until
the mixture is thick and smooth. Stir
in the tomato purée.
4 Add the mixture to the stock and
vegetables, and season with salt and
pepper to taste. Stir well and cook
gently for 15 minutes, stirring
occasionally.
5 To prepare the croûtons: heat the
oil in a frying-pan over moderate
heat until very hot. Fry the bread
cubes until golden brown. [!]
Remove from the pan and drain on
absorbent paper.
6 Reserve 2 tablespoons vegetables,
then blend the remaining ingredients in a blender or rub them
through a sieve. Return to the pan,
taste and adjust seasoning and heat
through until boiling.
7 Pour the soup into heated
individual bowls, then stir in the
reserved vegetables. Hand the
croûtons around separately.

Cook's Notes

TIME
This soup takes 30
minutes to make.

VARIATIONS
Use just one vegetable,
such as peas or carrots.
For a change leave the soup
unblended or blend for only 2
seconds so that the vegetables
are only partially chopped.

SERVING IDEAS
To make the soup more
substantial, hand round
a bowl of grated Parmesan or
Cheddar cheese for sprinkling
on the soup while it is still
piping hot.

[!] **WATCHPOINT**
Watch the croûtons
carefully while they are
frying so that they do not burn.

●420 calories/1750 kj per portion

Corned beef soup

SERVES 6

200 g/7 oz can corned beef, diced
2 tablespoons vegetable oil
2 large onions, chopped
250 g/9 oz carrots, cut into 5 mm/¼ inch dice
750 g/1½ lb potatoes, cut into 1 cm/½ inch dice
850 ml/1½ pints hot beef stock
salt and freshly ground black pepper
chopped fresh parsley, to garnish

1 Heat the oil in a pan and fry the onions gently for 5 minutes until soft and lightly coloured. Add the carrots and potatoes and fry gently, stirring, for a further 3 minutes.

2 Pour on the stock and bring to the boil. Cover and simmer for 10 minutes until the carrots and potatoes are just tender.

3 Add the corned beef and season to taste with salt and pepper. Simmer gently, uncovered, for a further 5 minutes (see Cook's tip). Serve at once, sprinkled with a little parsley.

Cook's Notes

TIME
This quick and easy dish takes 45 minutes to prepare and cook.

COOK'S TIP
For a thicker, smoother soup, sieve or purée in a blender with a little cream or milk. Reheat before serving.

VARIATIONS
A dash of Tabasco makes the soup slightly spicy. Try sprinkling with grated cheese before adding the parsley. Swedes are a good alternative to carrots, and they make an equally filling dish.

●235 calories/985 kj per portion

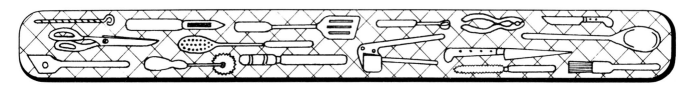

Carrot and parsley soup

SERVES 4

500 g/1 lb carrots, sliced
2 tablespoons freshly chopped
parsley
25 g/1 oz butter
1 onion, finely chopped
600 ml/1 pint chicken stock (see
Cook's tip)
300 ml/½ pint milk
salt and freshly ground black pepper

1 Melt the butter in a large sauce-pan. Add the carrots and onion and cook gently covered, for 15 minutes, stirring occasionally until softened but not browned.
2 Pour in the chicken stock and bring to the boil, then lower the heat and simmer gently, covered, for a further 20 minutes.

3 Allow to cool slightly, then press the soup through a sieve or work in a blender until smooth.
4 Return the puréed soup to the rinsed-out pan and stir in the milk and parsley. Season to taste with salt and freshly ground black pepper. Heat the soup through gently for about 5 minutes.
5 Pour the soup into 4 warmed individual soup bowls and serve at once (see Serving ideas).

Cook's Notes

 TIME
Total preparation time is 20 minutes. Cooking takes about 40 minutes.

 COOK'S TIP
This soup is best made with a subtle, delicately flavoured homemade stock.

 SERVING IDEAS
Garnish each serving with cheese and mustard toast: cut half a small French loaf into 8 slices. Toast one side of each slice under the grill, then spread untoasted sides with butter and a little made English mustard. Top each slice with grated Cheddar cheese and toast until cheese is bubbling. Place a slice on top of each bowl of soup and hand remaining bread separately.

 **VARIATION**
For a really creamy soup, stir 2-3 tablespoons single cream into the soup just before serving.

●135 calories/575 kj per portion

Mushroom soup with dumplings

SERVES 4

250 g/9 oz flat mushrooms, finely
   chopped
295 g/10½ oz can condensed
   consommé
700 ml/1¼ pints cold water
1 onion, finely chopped
bouquet garni
salt and freshly ground black pepper
chopped fresh parsley, to garnish
   (optional)

DUMPLINGS
75 g/3 oz self-raising flour
40 g/1½ oz shredded suet
½ teaspoon salt
1-2 tablespoons finely chopped
   fresh parsley
2-3 tablespoons cold water

1 Put the consommé into a saucepan and stir in the water. Add the chopped mushrooms, onion, and bouquet garni and season to taste with salt and pepper. [!] Bring to the boil, then lower the heat, cover and simmer for 10 minutes, stirring occasionally.

2 Meanwhile, stir all the dry dumpling ingredients together in a bowl. Mix to form a soft but not sticky dough with the cold water. Shape into 12-16 small balls with your hands.

3 Drop the dumplings into the soup, bring back to the boil, then lower the heat again and simmer for a further 15 minutes until the dumplings are cooked through.

4 To serve: remove the bouquet garni and pour the soup into warmed individual soup bowls. Add a few dumplings to each bowl, then sprinkle with a little chopped parsley, if wished.

Cook's Notes

TIME
The soup takes about 35 minutes to make.

WATCHPOINT
Add salt sparingly because canned consommé tends to have a salty flavour.

SERVING IDEAS
Serve this soup as a filling starter before a light lunch or dinner.

VARIATION
Substitute the parsley in the dumplings with ½ teaspoon dried mixed herbs or caraway seeds.

●170 calories/725 kj per portion

Tomato rice soup

SERVES 4

500 g/1 lb fresh tomatoes, chopped
400 g/14 oz can tomatoes
1 tablespoon tomato purée
150 ml/¼ pint water
salt and freshly ground black pepper
50 g/2 oz long-grain rice
2 tablespoons medium sherry
   (optional, see Variation)
1 tablespoon finely chopped
   parsley, to garnish

1 Put all the ingredients except the rice, sherry, if using, and parsley into a large saucepan. Bring to the boil, stirring, then lower the heat, cover and simmer for 30 minutes.
2 Pass the contents of the saucepan through a sieve, or leave to cool slightly, then purée in a blender and sieve (see Cook's tip).
3 Pour the sieved tomato purée back into the rinsed-out pan and bring back to the boil. Stir in the rice, lower the heat, cover and simmer for about 15 minutes or until the rice is tender.
4 Stir in the sherry, if using, taste and adjust seasoning, then pour into warmed individual soup bowls. Sprinkle with parsley and serve at once.

Cook's Notes

TIME
Preparation and cooking take about 1 hour.

VARIATION
Use 2 tablespoons single cream instead of the sherry, and swirl a little into each bowl just before sprinkling with parsley.

SERVING IDEAS
Serve with hot whole-meal rolls.

COOK'S TIP
It is essential to sieve the tomato mixture, to remove the pips and skins.

●80 calories/325 kj per portion

Tasty meat triangles

SERVES 4

350 g/12 oz lean minced beef (see Buying guide)
good pinch of cayenne pepper
salt
8 × 15 g/½ oz triangular portions cheese spread (see Buying guide)
2 eggs
175 g/6 oz day-old breadcrumbs
vegetable oil, for deep frying

1 Put the beef in a bowl and mix in the cayenne pepper and salt to taste.
2 Divide into 8 portions and put on a clean board. Then, using a small palette knife or your fingers, flatten each one into a triangular shape about 10 cm/4 inches on each side.
3 Press a cheese portion into the centre of each beef triangle. Mould and seal the beef evenly and completely around the cheese, being very careful to cover the corners.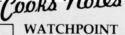
4 Beat the egg in a shallow bowl and spread out the breadcrumbs on a large flat plate. Dip each triangle into the egg and then into the breadcrumbs, pressing firmly to coat evenly. Repeat a second time with each triangle.
5 Pour enough oil into a deep-fat frier to come halfway up the sides of the triangles and heat to 180C/350F, or until a day-old bread cube will brown in 60 seconds.
6 Using a slotted spoon, lower half the triangles into the hot oil and deep-fry for about 7 minutes until well browned.
7 Drain on absorbent paper and keep warm while cooking the second batch. Serve as soon as they are all cooked.

Cook's Notes

TIME
Total preparation and cooking time 30-40 minutes from start to finish.

BUYING GUIDE
Buy very lean minced beef so that it does not shrink during cooking.
Processed cheese triangles are available in different flavours, individually wrapped in flat round boxes.

WATCHPOINT
It is important to seal the cheese well inside the beef to prevent it leaking out as it melts during cooking.

VARIATION
Instead of processed cheese portions, use small cubes of cheese and shape the beef into balls. Any soft melting cheese, such as Mozzarella, would be suitable.

SERVING IDEAS
Serve with lettuce, grilled whole tomatoes and fried onion or with boiled rice, sweetcorn or peas and tomato sauce. For parties, make bite-size triangles or balls and serve them hot with a chutney-flavoured dip. You can double or treble the quantities when catering for large numbers.

●385 calories/1600 kj per portion

Ham fritters with fried bananas

SERVES 4

175 g/6 oz cooked ham, minced
3 eggs, beaten
50 g/2 oz fresh breadcrumbs
150 ml/¼ pint milk
freshly ground black pepper
75 g/3 oz butter
4 bananas
parsley sprigs, to garnish

1 Heat the oven to 110C/225F/Gas ¼.
2 In a bowl, beat together the ham, eggs and breadcrumbs.
3 Put the milk in a small saucepan and bring to the boil. Stir the milk into the ham mixture. Season to taste with pepper and mix everything together thoroughly.
4 Melt 15 g/½ oz butter in a large frying-pan over moderate heat. When the butter is hot and foaming, spoon tablespoonsfuls of half the mixture into the pan. Cook for 1-2 minutes until well browned, then turn them over using a fish slice and cook for a further 1-2 minutes. Drain on absorbent paper and keep warm in the oven while you prepare the next batch.
5 Melt another 15 g/½ oz butter and cook the other half of the mixture in the same way. Drain on absorbent paper and keep warm.
6 Lower the heat and melt the remaining butter in the same pan. Peel the bananas and cut each in half lengthways. Fry gently in the butter for 3-4 minutes, shaking the pan so that the butter coats all the bananas thoroughly.
7 Arrange the fritters on a warmed serving dish and put the bananas around them. Garnish with sprigs of parsley.

Cook's Notes

TIME
The fritters take about 5 minutes to make and 8 minutes or so to cook.

SERVING IDEAS
As the fritters and bananas make a rather rich, filling meal, serve with something sharp-flavoured as a contrast. A mixed green salad tossed in an oil and vinegar dressing would be ideal.

VARIATIONS
Use any cold left-over meat in these fritters. Add a few fried mushrooms, a finely chopped small onion or ½ a green or red pepper.

●280 calories/1175 kj per fritter

Sausage twists

SERVES 4

8 large pork sausages
100 g/4 oz frozen puff pastry,
    defrosted
1 tablespoon tomato ketchup

1 In a large non-stick frying-pan, gently fry the sausages for about 5 minutes, without adding any extra fat to the pan, or heat the grill to low and grill them. Do not allow the sausages to become too brown (see Cook's tip). Remove from the heat and leave to cool.

2 Heat the oven to 200C/400F/Gas 6.
3 On a floured surface, roll out the pastry very thinly to a rectangle 24 × 20 cm/9½ × 8 inches. Trim the edges straight and cut into 8 equal-sized rectangles.
4 Spread a little tomato ketchup over the rectangles and then place a sausage, on the ketchup, diagonally across the pastry.To make the 'twist': lift the bottom right-hand corner of the pastry and wrap in a band over the sausage. Press it on to the pastry underneath the sausage to seal it (see Preparation). Make the rest and place on a dampened baking sheet join-side down.
5 Bake in the oven for 40 minutes until browned. Lift from the sheet with a fish slice. Serve hot.

Cook's Notes

TIME
Preparation, including pre-cooking the sausages, takes about 20 minutes. Cooking in the oven takes 40 minutes.

COOK'S TIP
The sausages must be pre-cooked to remove some of the fat before they are baked in the oven.

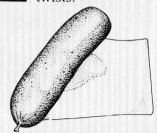
PREPARATION
To make the sausage twists:

1 *Place the sausage, on the ket-chup, diagonally across the pastry rectangle as shown.*

2 *Lift bottom right-hand corner of pastry and fold over sausage to seal.*

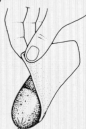
VARIATIONS
Use mustard or Worcestershire sauce in place of tomato ketchup. Or use a herby pastry by rolling the pastry out, sprinkling it with 1 teaspoon herbs, folding and rolling the pastry out again. These variations are less suitable for children.

CHILDREN
Children will enjoy the sausage twists by themselves, or served with canned spaghetti in tomato sauce or baked beans.

●520 calories/2175 kj per portion

Beefburger parcels

MAKES 4

4 fresh or frozen beefburgers
400 g/13 oz frozen puff pastry,
   defrosted
100 g/4 oz smooth pâté (see Buying
   guide)
1 egg, lightly beaten

1 Heat the oven to 220C/425F/Gas 7.
2 Fry or grill the beefburgers according to packet instructions. Drain well on absorbent paper, then set aside to cool for 5-10 minutes. [!]
3 Roll out the pastry on a floured surface to a 35 cm/14 inch square then, using a saucer, cut it into 4 rounds so that each is about 4 cm/ 1½ inches larger all round than the cooked beefburger. Reserve the pastry trimmings.
4 Spread a quarter of the pâté on top

Cook's Notes

 TIME
Preparation time, including cooking and cooling the beefburgers is 20 minutes; baking in the oven is 15-20 minutes.

[!] **WATCHPOINTS**
It is important to drain and cool the beefburgers before placing on the pastry or the pastry will melt.
   If the edges are not completely sealed, the pâté may leak out.

 VARIATIONS
Replace the pâté with horseradish sauce and sliced tomatoes. Alternatively, top each beefburger with a ring of pineapple or green pepper.

BUYING GUIDE
Use a can of liver pâté for this recipe, or choose a smooth pâté from a delicatessen counter.

●608 calories/2555 kj per portion

of each beefburger and place pâté side down on the pastry rounds. Brush the pastry edges with water and draw them together over the meat to form a neat parcel. Seal the edges carefully. [!]
5 Dampen a baking sheet and place the parcels on it with their seams underneath.

6 Make leaves from the pastry trimmings, brush them underneath with water and place them on top of the parcels. Brush the pastry all over with beaten egg, make 2 slits in the top of each for the steam to escape and bake in the oven for 15-20 minutes until golden and well risen. Serve hot.

Cheese and chicken pockets

SERVES 4

 200 g/7 oz Gruyère cheese, cut into thin strips

 250 g/9 oz cooked chicken, thinly sliced (see Buying guide)

4 pitta breads

1 small green pepper, deseeded and sliced into thin rings

2 large firm tomatoes, thinly sliced

salt and freshly ground black pepper

3 tablespoons mango chutney

1 Heat the oven to 200C/400F/Gas 6. Cut out 8 squares of foil each large enough to enclose half a pitta.

2 Cut each pitta bread in half crossways and ease the pockets open with a knife, taking care not to pierce the sides of the bread.

3 Divide the ingredients for the filling into 8, then hold each pitta pocket open with one hand and,

with the other, layer the ingredients into the pockets in the following order: green pepper, cheese, tomato and chicken. [!] Sprinkle each layer with a little salt and pepper, then spread the chicken with chutney.

4 Place each filled pocket, chicken layer uppermost, on a square of foil, and wrap securely in a parcel. Put the parcels on 1 or 2 baking sheets, and heat through in the oven for about 20 minutes. Serve at once.

Cook's Notes

 TIME
Preparation takes about 30 minutes. Heating through takes 20 minutes.

SERVING IDEAS
These tasty chicken pockets can be heated on a barbecue instead of in the oven. They are best eaten with fingers so provide each person with just a plate and a napkin.

VARIATIONS
Try using cooked lamb, beef, ham or turkey instead of chicken. Another good melting cheese, such as

Mozzarella, can be used instead of the Gruyère.

 WATCHPOINT
The order in which the pittas are filled is important. If tomato is put next to the bread, the bread will become soggy.

 BUYING GUIDE
Sliced, pressed rolled chicken, available from supermarkets and delicatessens, is ideal for this recipe and saves preparation time.

● 570 calories/2400 kj per portion

Grilled corned beef baps

SERVES 4

350 g/12 oz can corned beef
2 tablespoons sweet pickle
1 tablespoon mild mustard
6 tablespoons mayonnaise
freshly ground black pepper
4 soft baps, cut in half
175 g/6 oz Double Gloucester or
 mature Cheddar cheese, grated
8 tomato slices, to garnish

1 Heat the grill to moderate.
2 Mash the corned beef with the pickle, mustard and mayonnaise until smooth. Taste and season with a little pepper.
3 Spread the cut surfaces of the baps evenly all over with the corned beef mixture.
4 Grill gently for 4-5 minutes or until the corned beef mixture begins to brown.
5 Sprinkle the cheese over the top. Return to the heat and grill for a further 3-4 minutes or until the cheese has melted and is browned. Serve hot, garnished with tomato.

Cook's Notes

TIME
Preparation takes 10 minutes. Cooking time is 8-10 minutes.

COOK'S TIP
The corned beef mixture may be kept, covered, in the refrigerator for 3-4 days, and is ideal for snacks or impromptu meals.

●645 calories/2700 kj per portion

Eggs Benedict

SERVES 4

4 eggs
4 rashers streaky bacon, rinds
    removed
2 muffins (see Buying guide)
25 g/1 oz butter, for spreading

SAUCE
2 teaspoons lemon juice
2 teaspoons wine vinegar
100 g/4 oz butter
2 egg yolks
few drops of Tabasco
salt and freshly ground black pepper
sweet paprika, to finish

1 Heat the oven to 110C/225F/Gas ¼. Heat the grill to moderate.
2 Grill the bacon rashers for about 8 minutes, turning once, until cooked through. Cut the rashers in half and keep them warm in the oven.
3 Slit the muffins in half horizontally, turn grill to high and toast the muffins lightly on both sides. Spread the cut side of each muffin thinly with butter, top each one with 2 bacon rasher halves and return to the oven.
4 Heat a large frying-pan of water just to simmering point (see Cook's tips).
5 Make the sauce: put the lemon juice and vinegar in a small sauce-pan and bring to the boil. [!] Melt the butter in a separate pan until it is sizzling, but do not let it start to brown. [!]
6 Warm the goblet of the blender (see Cook's tips) by filling it with very hot water. Tip the water out and put the lemon juice and vinegar into the goblet together with the egg yolks and the Tabasco. Season well with salt and pepper. Blend for a few seconds.
7 With the motor switched on, gradually pour the melted butter in a very thin stream through the hole in lid of blender. The sauce will thicken as the butter is added.
8 Pour the sauce into a heatproof bowl standing over a pan of gently simmering water. Keep hot while poaching the eggs, stirring from time to time.

9 Cook the eggs by breaking them one by one into a cup and slipping them into the frying-pan of just simmering water for 3-4 minutes, until set. Remove them with a slotted spoon if using a frying-pan or by running round the outside of each egg with a round-bladed knife if using a poacher. Slip a poached egg on to each half muffin.
10 Transfer the egg-topped muffins to warmed plates. Spoon a little sauce over each, sprinkle with sweet paprika and serve at once.

Cook's Notes

TIME
Preparation and cooking take about 30 minutes.

COOK'S TIPS
If you have one, you can use an egg poacher for this recipe; you do not need to prepare it until end of stage 8.
 You really do need a blender to make this a quick and easy recipe. Made in the traditional way in a double boiler it takes much longer.

WATCHPOINTS
The vinegar and lemon juice mixture evaporates quickly, so watch it carefully.
 Butter browns very quickly, so also needs careful watching.

DID YOU KNOW
The sauce in this recipe is a simplified version of hollandaise, one of the most famous of all French sauces.

BUYING GUIDE
Muffins should be available from bakers and supermarkets. If you cannot obtain them, use 4 crumpets instead for this recipe.

●465 calories/1925 kj per portion

Tuna strudel

SERVES 4

200 g/7 oz can tuna, drained
6 stuffed olives, chopped
1 hard-boiled egg, chopped
2 tablespoons single cream
2 tablespoons finely chopped fresh
   parsley
salt and freshly ground black pepper
215 g/7½ oz frozen puff pastry,
   defrosted
beaten egg yolk, for brushing
lightly beaten egg white, to glaze

1 Heat the oven to 200C/400F/Gas 6.
2 Put the tuna into a bowl with the olives, hard-boiled egg, cream and parsley. Season to taste with salt and pepper and mix thoroughly with a fork.
3 Roll out the pastry on a floured surface into a thin rectangle about 38 × 28 cm/15 × 11 inches; trim edges.

Cook's Notes

TIME
Preparation takes 15 minutes, cooking 20 minutes.

VARIATIONS
Use capers instead of olives and add chopped anchovies to the tuna mixture. For a more substantial dish, add about 75 g/3 oz cooked rice to the tuna mixture.

WATCHPOINTS
Make sure the ends of the pastry roll are firmly sealed or the filling will leak out during cooking.
   Take care when transferring the pastry to the baking sheet. The pastry is thin and the roll is long—so use 2 fish slices and place diagonally on the baking sheet, if necessary.

SPECIAL OCCASION
For a dinner-party starter, serve each slice topped with soured cream and snipped chives.

● 395 calories/1650 kj per portion

4 Spread the tuna mixture over the pastry leaving a pastry border all round of about 1 cm/½ inch. Starting at a long edge roll up the pastry. Brush the opposite long edge with beaten egg yolk and press down firmly so that it sticks. Gently press the roll to flatten its shape slightly. Tuck the ends in, brushing with egg yolk so that they stick. [!]
5 Dampen a large baking sheet and carefully transfer the pastry roll to it, join side down. [!] Brush all over with beaten egg white.
6 Bake in the oven for 20 minutes. Serve hot or cold, cut into slices.

Sherried cod

SERVES 4

500 g/1 lb cod fillets, skinned and
    cut into 2.5 cm/1 inch cubes
2 tablespoons plain flour
½ teaspoon dried thyme
salt and freshly ground black pepper
50 g/2 oz margarine or butter
2 tablespoons vegetable oil
½ red pepper and ½ green pepper,
    deseeded and cut into narrow
    strips 4 cm/1½ inches long
1 onion, finely chopped
100 g/4 oz button mushrooms,
    sliced
2-3 tablespoons dry sherry
150 ml/¼ pint soured cream

1 Mix the flour and thyme on a large
plate and season with salt and
pepper. Dip the fish pieces in the
seasoned flour, turning until well
coated, then set aside.

2 Melt half the margarine and oil in
a saucepan, add the peppers and
onion and cook over moderate heat
for 5 minutes, stirring. Add the
mushrooms and cook, stirring, for a
further 2 minutes. Keep warm.

3 Melt the remaining margarine
and oil in a large frying-pan, add the
fish pieces and fry over moderate
heat for about 4 minutes until just
cooked, turning once.

4 Pour over the sherry, allow to
bubble, then stir in the soured
cream, turning the fish very gently.
Arrange on a serving plate, spoon
over the pepper mixture and serve at
once (see Serving ideas).

Cook's Notes

TIME
Preparation and cook-
ing only take about 45
minutes from start to finish.

SERVING IDEAS
Serve with 250 g/9 oz
green or white taglia-
telle which has been well tossed
in 25 g/1 oz margarine or butter
and 1½ teaspoons poppy seeds.

VARIATION
Use other firm white
fish such as haddock,
hake or coley instead of the cod
fillets used here.

●335 calories/1400 kj per portion

Fruity chicken pie

SERVES 4-6

350 g/12 oz boneless cooked
   chicken, cut into bite-sized
   pieces
50 g/2 oz margarine or butter
1 onion, chopped
1 cooking apple, peeled, quartered
   and sliced
2 teaspoons curry powder
25 g/1 oz plain flour
300 ml/½ pint chicken stock
100 g/ 4 oz mushrooms, sliced
salt and freshly ground black pepper
3 tomatoes, skinned and roughly
   chopped
215 g/7½ oz frozen puff pastry,
   defrosted
beaten egg, to glaze

1 Heat the oven to 220C/425F/Gas 7.
2 Melt the margarine in a large
frying-pan, add the onion and fry
for 5 minutes until soft and lightly
coloured. Add the apple and curry
powder and cook gently for another
5 minutes. Sprinkle in the flour and
stir until blended. Gradually stir in
the stock and simmer, stirring, until
thick and smooth.
3 Stir in the chicken pieces and
mushrooms and season with salt
and pepper to taste. Cook for a
further 5 minutes, then stir in the
chopped tomatoes. Pour the mixture into an 850 ml/1½ pint pie dish.
4 Roll out the pastry on a floured
surface to a shape slightly larger
than the top of the pie dish. Cut off
a strip of pastry all around edge.
5 Brush the rim of the dish with
water and press the strip of pastry
on the rim. Brush the strip with a
little more water, then place the
large piece of pastry on top. Press to
seal, then knock up and flute.
6 Make decorations with the pastry
trimmings, brush the undersides
with water and arrange on top of
the pie. Brush the pastry all over
with the beaten egg and make a
small hole in the centre of the pie.
Bake in the oven for 30 minutes
until golden. Serve at once.

Cook's Notes

TIME
Preparation 40 minutes,
cooking 30 minutes.

VARIATIONS
Turkey makes a deli-
cious alternative to
chicken. A chopped green pepper may be used instead of the
sliced mushrooms.

SERVING IDEAS
Serve with a creamy
potato purée and a
fresh green vegetable such as
broccoli, or with French bread
and a green salad. For special
occasions, pop the pie dish into
a paper frill to serve.

●535 calories/2250 kj per portion

Chicken and yogurt curry

SERVES 4

2 large chicken breasts, each weighing 250 g/9 oz, skinned and cut into 1 cm/½ inch pieces
25 g/1 oz margarine or butter
1 tablespoon vegetable or olive oil
1 large onion, chopped
1 clove garlic, crushed (optional)
1½ teaspoons ground ginger
2 teaspoons garam masala (see Variations)
150 ml/¼ pint chicken stock
150 g/5 oz natural yoghurt
½ cucumber, cut into 1 cm/½ inch pieces
40 g/1½ oz roasted salted peanuts (see Watchpoint)
coriander or parsley sprigs, to garnish

1 Heat the margarine and oil in a large frying-pan, add the onion and garlic, if using, and fry gently for 5 minutes until soft and lightly coloured. Stir in the spices and cook for a further 2 minutes.
2 Add the chicken and fry over moderate heat until sealed on all sides. Mix in the stock, bring to the boil, then lower the heat and simmer, uncovered, for 20 minutes or until the chicken is cooked.
3 Turn the heat to very low, then stir the yoghurt into the pan. Heat gently until warmed through, stirring constantly. Remove from the heat and mix in the cucumber.
4 Divide the mixture equally between 4 small bowls and sprinkle a few peanuts on top of each. Garnish with coriander or parsley sprigs and serve at once.

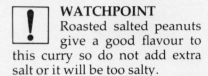

Apricot barbecue chicken

SERVES 4

12 chicken drumsticks, each
  weighing 100 g/4 oz, skinned
toasted almonds, to garnish
  (optional)

BARBECUE SAUCE
400 g/14 oz can apricots
2 tablespoons malt vinegar
2 tablespoons light soy sauce
1 clove garlic, crushed (optional)
2.5 cm/1 inch piece fresh root
  ginger, peeled and crushed
pinch of dried tarragon (optional)
salt and freshly ground black pepper

1 Heat the oven to 200C/400F/Gas 6.
2 Make the sauce: put the apricots
and their syrup into the goblet of a
blender, add the remaining sauce
ingredients with salt and pepper to
taste and work for a few seconds to
a rough purée.
3 Turn the apricot mixture into a
saucepan and bring to the boil. Boil,
stirring, for 2-3 minutes until it
thickens to a coating consistency.
4 Fill a roasting tin to a depth of
1 cm/½ inch with cold water and set
a rack over the tin (see Cook's tip).
Arrange the drumsticks on the rack
and brush thickly with half the
sauce. Cook in the oven, on the
shelf above centre, for 40-45 minutes until the juices run clear when
the thickest part of the drumsticks is
pierced with a fine skewer. Turn the
drumsticks over once or twice
during cooking time and brush with
the remaining sauce.
5 Transfer drumsticks to a serving
platter and spoon over any sauce
and juices which have collected in
the tin. Garnish with the toasted
almonds, if using, and serve.

Cook's Notes

TIME
Preparing and cooking
take about 1 hour.

VARIATIONS
Use 350 g/12 oz fresh
ripe apricots instead of
canned. Simmer the peeled,
halved and stoned apricots with
300 ml/½ pint water and 75 g/
3 oz sugar for 10-15 minutes
then follow the recipe.

Use sauce to baste chicken
wings and grill them on an
outdoor barbecue they make
tasty finger food.

COOK'S TIP
Water in the roasting
tin helps to keep any
sauce that drips through the
rack from spitting and burning
and spoiling the dish.

●300 calories/1250 kj per portion

275

Turkey toss

SERVES 4

300 g/10 oz boned, cooked turkey, diced (see Economy)
250 g/9 oz Basmati rice (see Buying guide)
25 g/1 oz margarine or butter
300 ml/½ pint boiling water
2 tablespoons turkey dripping or vegetable oil (see Economy)
1 onion, finely chopped
2 celery stalks, sliced
1 clove garlic, crushed (optional)
100 g/4 oz frozen peas, cooked
1 green pepper, deseeded and diced
2 tablespoons currants
190 g/6½ oz can sweet pimientos, drained and sliced
1-2 tablespoons soy sauce
salt and freshly ground black pepper
a few bay leaves, to garnish

1 Rinse the rice thoroughly in several changes of cold water. Place in a pan with the margarine and boiling water and bring rapidly to the boil. Lower the heat, cover with a tight-fitting lid and simmer very gently for 10 minutes, or until all the liquid has evaporated and the rice is just tender.
2 Meanwhile, heat the dripping in a large frying-pan or wok. Add the onion, celery and garlic, if using, and fry gently for 5 minutes until the onion is soft and lightly coloured.
3 Add the rice, cooked peas, turkey, green pepper, currants and half the pimiento. Cook over moderate heat, stirring frequently, until heated all through.
4 Stir in the soy sauce and season with salt and pepper to taste.
5 Transfer to a warmed serving dish, garnish with the remaining pimiento slices and a few bay leaves, and serve at once while still piping hot.

Pork turnovers

SERVES 4

8 cured pork loin steaks, trimmed of all visible fat (see Buying guide)
freshly ground black pepper
400 g/13 oz frozen puff pastry, defrosted
1 egg yolk
1 tablespoon cold water

STUFFING
40 g/1½ oz dry white breadcrumbs
3 tablespoons finely chopped fresh parsley
1 tablespoon grated or very finely chopped onion
finely grated zest of 1 lemon
2 teaspoons lemon juice
½ teaspoon ground ginger
1½ teaspoons mild curry powder
pinch of cayenne
3-4 tablespoons melted butter
celery salt or salt

1 Put the pork steaks between 2 sheets of greaseproof paper and beat with a rolling pin until 5 mm/¼ inch thick. Season the steaks on both sides with black pepper.
2 Mix together all the stuffing ingredients, except the melted butter and salt. Add enough melted butter to bind the mixture and season to taste with celery salt and pepper.
3 Heat the oven to 220C/425F/Gas 7.
4 Spread the stuffing mixture on 4 of the steaks, to within 1 cm/½ inch of the edges. Cover with the remaining steaks, to make sandwiches with stuffing filling.
5 Cut the pastry into 4 equal pieces and roll out each piece on a floured surface to a 20-23 cm/8-9 inch square. Trim the edges of each square. Mix the egg yolk with the cold water and brush the pastry squares with a little of this mixture, making sure you brush right to the edges of the squares.
6 Place a pork 'sandwich' on one-half of each square, fold the pastry over and press the edges together to seal. Trim the edges to a semi-circular shape, leaving a 2 cm/ ¾ inch pastry border around the pork. Seal edges, knock up and flute.

Cut 3 small slits in the top of each turnover with a sharp knife.
7 With a fish slice, transfer the turnovers to a dampened baking sheet and brush them all over with the remaining egg yolk mixture. Bake in oven for 20-25 minutes, until deep golden brown. Serve hot.

Cook's Notes

 TIME
Preparation takes 30-40 minutes, cooking in the oven 20-25 minutes.

BUYING GUIDE
Danish cured pork loin steaks are available from large supermarkets. They are an excellent buy as they are tender and lean, with very little waste. Or buy a 750 g/1½ lb boneless pork loin joint and cut it into 8 pieces.

 SERVING IDEAS
Serve these tasty stuffed pork turnovers with a mixed green salad tossed in an oil and vinegar dressing.

● 685 calories/2875 kj per portion

Pork chops in cider sauce

SERVES 4

4 medium pork chops, each
    weighing 175-225 g/6-8 oz
3 tablespoons plain flour
salt and freshly ground black
    pepper
pinch of ground mace (optional)
50 g/2 oz butter

SAUCE

8 spring onions, trimmed and thinly
    sliced
150 ml/¼ pint dry cider
1 teaspoon tomato purée
4 thin slices lemon, or 2 teaspoons
    concentrated lime juice
1 tablespoon top of the milk
    (optional)

1 Trim the meat, discarding any
rind or fat.

2 Put the flour into a greaseproof or
polythene bag and season with salt
and pepper and a pinch of ground
mace, if using. Toss the chops in the
seasoned flour one at a time until
they are thoroughly coated and dry.
Put on one side.

3 Melt the butter in a large frying-
pan over moderate heat. When it
stops foaming, add the chops and
fry them gently for 8 minutes. Turn
each one over very carefully, taking
care not to pierce the meat, and fry
for a further 5 minutes or until they
are cooked through and well
browned.

4 Using a slotted spoon remove the
meat from the pan and transfer it to a
warmed serving dish. Cover the
dish with the foil and keep it warm
in a low oven until the cider sauce is
prepared.

5 Add the chopped onions to the fat
remaining in the pan. Stir well and
cook, stirring occasionally, for 3
minutes. Pour on the cider, stir in the
tomato purée and bring rapidly to
the boil, stirring all the time. Add
the lemon slices or lime juice and
boil for 1 minute. Taste the sauce
and season with salt and pepper. If
the sauce is a little too sharp, stir in
the milk.

6 Pour the sauce over the pork and
heat the dish through for a further 5
minutes. Serve at once.

Cook's Notes

TIME
The whole dish takes
about 30 minutes.

SERVING IDEAS
Serve with buttered
pasta shells, boiled rice
or new potatoes plus a crisp
green vegetable such as sprouts.

COOK'S TIP
When adding the cider
to the juices and fat in
the pan, use a flat-edged
wooden spoon so that you can
scrape all the delicious brown
pieces from the pan. Their
flavour will make all the
difference to the sauce.

SPECIAL OCCASION
Replace the cider with
dry white wine, or with
half dry sherry and half water.
    For a real celebration, substi-
tute sliced pork tenderloin.

 FREEZING
Place in one or more
aluminium or similar
containers, seal, label and
freeze. Store for up to 6 months.
To serve, reheat thoroughly,
either from frozen or after
defrosting. Add a tablespoon of
stock, cider or water if the sauce
is too thick.

● 530 calories/2175 kj per portion

Bacon burgers

SERVES 4

250 g/9 oz cooked bacon
salt
350 g/12 oz potatoes
1 small onion
1 tablespoon tomato purée
freshly ground black pepper
1 egg, beaten
4 tablespoons vegetable oil
4 baps or rolls, halved horizontally
4 canned pineapple rings, well
   drained

1 Bring a pan of salted water to the boil and cook the potatoes for about 20 minutes or until tender.
2 Meanwhile, mince the cooked bacon and onion.
3 Drain the cooked potatoes very thoroughly [!] and mash them.
4 Mix the potato, bacon, onion and tomato purée together in a bowl. Season with pepper and add enough beaten egg to bind the mixture together. [!]

5 Divide the mixture into 4 and shape each portion into a flat round 7.5 cm/3 inches in diameter. ✳
6 Heat the grill to high.
7 Heat the oil in a frying-pan, add the burgers and fry for 5-7 minutes on each side until golden.
8 Meanwhile, lightly toast the cut sides of each of the bap halves.
9 Remove the burgers from the pan, place on the bottom halves of the baps and keep warm. Fry the pineapple rings for 1 minute on each side and place on top of the burgers. Replace the bap lids and serve the burgers at once.

Cook's Notes

 TIME
Preparation and cooking take 45-50 minutes.

VARIATIONS
These burgers can be made with cooked minced chicken or corned beef instead of the bacon.

 WATCHPOINTS
Make sure that the potatoes are very well drained before mashing or they will make the mixture too moist.

Add just enough egg to bind the mixture. If too much is added the burgers will become soft and difficult to handle.

FOR CHILDREN
Children may prefer this served as a main meal without the pineapple ring and bap. Serve the burgers instead with spaghetti in tomato sauce.

FREEZING
Open freeze the burgers on a tray and then pack in polythene bags and seal, label and return to freezer. Store for up to 3 months. To serve: defrost at room temperature for 1-2 hours and then continue from step 6 of the recipe.

●430 calories/1800 kj per portion

Streaky pork with mandarin sauce

SERVES 4

500 g/1 lb lean belly of pork
   rashers, rind, bones and excess
   fat removed, and cut in half
   across (see Buying guide)
1 tablespoon vegetable oil
1 large onion, sliced
300 g/11 oz can mandarin orange
   segments, drained with juice
   reserved
about 150 ml/¼ pint chicken stock
¼ teaspoon ground ginger
1 tablespoon lemon juice or vinegar
1 green pepper, deseeded and
   chopped
salt and freshly ground black pepper
1 tablespoon cornflour
2 tablespoons water

1 Heat the oil in a large frying-pan. Add the pork and fry over moderate heat for 5 minutes turning, until brown on both sides.

2 Add the onion to the pan and fry for a further 5 minutes until the onion is soft. Pour off excess fat from the pan.

3 Make up the reserved fruit juice to 300 ml/½ pint with the chicken stock and pour into the pan. Add the ginger, lemon juice and green pepper and season to taste with salt and pepper. Bring to the boil, then lower the heat, cover, and simmer for 30-40 minutes until the pork is cooked (the juices run clear when the meat is pierced with a skewer).

4 Remove from the heat (see Cook's tip). Blend the cornflour with the water, then stir in a little of the liquid from the pan. Pour back into the pan and bring to the boil, stirring constantly, then simmer for 3 minutes until the liquid is thick and has a smooth consistency. ❗ Add the mandarin orange segments and stir carefully to coat in sauce.

5 Turn into a warmed serving dish and serve at once.

Cook's Notes

TIME
Preparation takes 20 minutes; cooking takes about 40 minutes.

BUYING GUIDE
Belly of pork is sold in supermarkets cut into rashers and is often labelled 'streaky pork rashers'. If buying from the butcher, ask him to cut the belly of pork into rashers.

WATCHPOINT
The sauce should be of a coating consistency. If it gets too thick, however, add some remaining chicken stock.

COOK'S TIP
Belly of pork is a fatty meat. If liked, blot the surface of the sauce with some absorbent paper to remove the excess fat at this stage.

VARIATION
Use a 225 g/8 oz can pineapple pieces instead of the mandarins.

SERVING IDEAS
For a delicious supper dish, serve with plain boiled rice and a mixed salad.

● 380 calories/1500 kj per portion

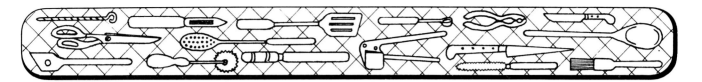

Beef and bean crumble

SERVES 4

500 g/1 lb lean minced beef
25 g/1 oz margarine or butter
1 onion, chopped
2 carrots, coarsely grated
2 celery stalks, finely chopped
150 ml/¼ pint beef stock
150 g/5 oz can tomato purée
½ teaspoon dried oregano
salt and freshly ground black pepper
425 g/15 oz can baked beans in tomato sauce

CRUMBLE TOPPING

75 g/3 oz porridge oats
25 g/1 oz plain flour
½ teaspoon dried oregano
50 g/2 oz Cheddar cheese, finely grated
40 g/1½ oz margarine, melted

1 Heat the oven to 200C/400F/Gas 6. Melt the margarine in a large saucepan, add the onion, carrot and celery and fry gently for 5 minutes until the onion is soft and lightly coloured. Add the minced beef and fry over moderate heat for 3-4 minutes until browned.

2 Add the stock to the pan with the tomato purée, oregano and salt and pepper to taste, and simmer, uncovered, for 10 minutes, stirring.

3 Meanwhile, make the crumble topping: mix the oats in a small bowl with the flour, oregano and grated cheese. Add ¼ teaspoon salt, then season well with black pepper. Stir in the melted margarine.

4 Stir the baked beans into beef mixture and heat through, then transfer the mixture to a 1.75 L/3 pint ovenproof dish. Sprinkle the crumble mixture over the top.

5 Bake in the oven for 30 minutes, until the topping is golden brown. Serve hot, straight from the dish.

Spaghetti with meat balls

SERVES 4

350 g/12 oz spaghetti
3 tablespoons vegetable oil
1 onion, chopped
1 clove garlic, crushed (optional)
400 g/14 oz can tomatoes
75 ml/3 fl oz hot chicken stock
1 tablespoon tomato purée
¼ teaspoon dried thyme
1 teaspoon dried oregano
salt and freshly ground black pepper
500 g/1 lb minced beef
2 tablespoons chopped fresh
   parsley
a knob of butter, for tossing
grated Parmesan cheese (optional)

1 Heat 1 tablespoon oil in a large saucepan, add the onion and garlic, if using, and fry gently for 5 minutes until soft and lightly coloured. Add the tomatoes with their liquid, the stock, tomato purée, thyme and half the oregano. Season to taste with salt and pepper. Bring to the boil, cover and simmer for 30-40 minutes.
2 Meanwhile, in a bowl mix the beef with the remaining oregano and the parsley and season well with salt and pepper. Shape into 32 small balls.
3 Heat the rest of the oil in a frying-pan over moderate heat and fry the meat balls on all sides for 6-8 minutes until golden brown. Drain on absorbent paper and keep warm.
4 Bring a pan of salted water to the boil and cook the spaghetti for about 10 minutes until *al dente* (tender, yet firm to the bite).
5 Meanwhile, sieve the tomato sauce, or purée in a blender. Return to the pan to reheat, adding a little water if the sauce is too thick. Stir in the meat balls and then transfer to a warmed serving dish.
6 Drain the pasta thoroughly and toss in butter. Transfer to warmed individual serving bowls. Spoon 8 meat balls and a quarter of the sauce over each spaghetti serving. Serve at once, with cheese, if liked.

Country goulash

SERVES 4

2 onions, sliced
2 tablespoons vegetable oil
2 carrots, sliced
2 celery stalks, sliced
2 courgettes, sliced
1 green pepper, deseeded and diced
50 g/2 oz mushrooms, sliced
500 g/1 lb hard white cabbage, finely shredded
400 g/14 oz can tomatoes
1 tablespoon tomato purée
1 teaspoon lemon juice
300 ml/½ pint water
4½ teaspoons sweet paprika
1 tablespoon caraway seeds
salt and freshly ground black pepper
150 ml/¼ pint soured cream

Cook's Notes

TIME
Preparation and cooking the goulash take about 55 minutes.

SERVING IDEAS
Serve as a vegetarian meal with hot granary rolls. Or serve as an accompaniment to hot salt beef.

COOK'S TIP
Paprika loses colour when exposed to strong light. Store it in a cool, dark place to preserve the bright red colour which adds greatly to the distinctive appearance and taste of this dish.

●235 calories/975 kj per portion

1 Heat the oil in a large saucepan, add the onions, carrots and celery and fry for about 5 minutes until soft and lightly coloured.

2 Add courgettes, green pepper, mushrooms and white cabbage and cook over moderate heat for 10 minutes, stirring occasionally to prevent the vegetables sticking to the saucepan.

3 Stir in the tomatoes with their juices, the tomato purée, lemon juice and water. Sprinkle in the paprika and caraway seeds and season well with salt and pepper.

4 Cover the pan and simmer for 20 minutes or until the vegetables are just tender. Taste and add more seasoning if necessary.

5 Transfer the goulash to a hot serving dish and spoon over the soured cream. Serve at once.

Lamb and apricot salad

SERVES 4

350 g/12 oz cooked lamb, diced
400 g/14 oz can apricot halves, drained and chopped
150 ml/¼ pint thick bottled mayonnaise
4 tablespoons natural yoghurt
1 tablespoon clear honey
2 teaspoons finely grated lemon zest
½ teaspoon ground cinnamon
salt and freshly ground black pepper
350 g/12 oz potatoes, boiled and roughly chopped
1 small lettuce
25 g/1 oz toasted flaked almonds

1 Put the mayonnaise in a large bowl and stir in the yoghurt, honey, lemon zest and cinnamon. Season to taste with salt and pepper, then cover and refrigerate for 30 minutes (see Cook's tip).

2 Mix together the lamb, potatoes and apricots and gently fold into the mayonnaise mixture.

3 Arrange the lettuce leaves in a bowl or shallow dish. Spoon the salad into the centre and sprinkle the almonds over the top. Serve the salad at once.

Cook's Notes

TIME
Preparation is about 10 minutes, but allow 30 minutes for chilling.

VARIATIONS
Use canned mandarins or pineapple instead of the apricots, and chicken, ham or tongue instead of the lamb. Substitute 250 g/9 oz cooked rice for the boiled potatoes. If cooking the rice especially for this dish, you will need 75 g/3 oz of raw rice.

COOK'S TIP
Chilling the mayonnaise mixture improves the flavour but is not essential.

● 575 calories/2400 kj per portion

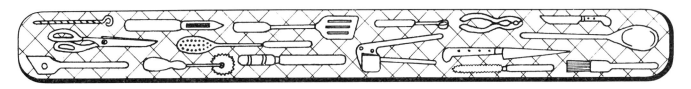

Lamb and pasta medley

SERVES 4

500 g/1 lb minced raw lamb
2 tablespoons olive oil
1 onion, chopped
1 green pepper, deseeded and chopped
2 courgettes, finely chopped
400 g/14 oz can tomatoes
300 ml/½ pint water
250 g/9 oz pasta shapes
½ teaspoon dried basil
½ teaspoon dried thyme
salt and freshly ground black pepper
100 g/4 oz mushrooms, sliced

1 Heat the oil in a saucepan and fry the onion, green pepper and courgettes gently for 2-3 minutes until they are beginning to soften.
2 Add the lamb, turn the heat to high and fry until the meat is evenly browned, stirring with a wooden spoon to remove any lumps. Pour off any excess fat.
3 Stir in the tomatoes with their juice and the water, breaking up the tomatoes with the spoon. Bring to the boil, stirring frequently.

4 Add the pasta, herbs and salt and pepper to taste and mix well. Cover the pan and simmer the lamb and pasta for 15 minutes.
5 Stir in mushrooms and simmer, uncovered, for 10 minutes. Serve the lamb and pasta medley at once (see Serving ideas and Variations).

Cook's Notes

TIME
About 45 minutes to prepare and cook.

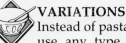

VARIATIONS
Instead of pasta shapes, use any type of pasta from the store cupboard. Break up spaghetti into small pieces.
Minced beef can be used as an alternative to the lamb.
Dried mixed herbs may be used instead of the dried basil and thyme.

SERVING IDEAS
This dish needs no accompaniment as it is a meal in itself, but grated hard cheese such as Parmesan or mature Cheddar may be served separately for sprinkling.

ECONOMY
Use left-over cooked lamb, chopped finely, and omit all of stage 2.

●570 calories/2375 kj per portion

Maytime flan

SERVES 4

215 g/7½ oz frozen shortcrust pastry, defrosted

FILLING
225 g/8 oz cottage cheese with chives
3 eggs
25 g/1 oz butter
100 g/4 oz button mushrooms, sliced
½ teaspoon dried thyme
salt and freshly ground black pepper
1 tomato, thinly sliced

1 Heat the oven to 200C/400F/Gas 6.
2 Roll out the pastry on a lightly floured surface and use to line an 18 cm/7 inch loose-bottomed flan tin or flan ring standing on a baking sheet. Prick the pastry with a fork, line with greaseproof paper and fill with baking beans. Bake blind in the oven for 10 minutes.
3 Meanwhile, make the filling: put the cottage cheese into a bowl with the eggs and beat together with a fork until well mixed.
4 Melt the butter in a small saucepan, add the mushrooms and fry gently for 2 minutes, stirring. Drain well, then add the mushrooms to the cottage cheese mixture. Stir in the thyme and season to taste with salt and pepper.
5 Remove the greaseproof paper and beans from the pastry case, pour in the cottage cheese mixture and arrange the tomato slices around the edge. Return to the oven and bake for 35 minutes until the filling is golden brown and set.
6 Leave to stand for 5-10 minutes. Remove sides of tin and place the flan on a serving plate. Serve while still warm or leave until cold.

Cook's Notes

TIME
Preparation and cooking take 50-55 minutes.

SERVING IDEAS
Serve the flan with white wine and salad.

VARIATION
This flan can be made with homemade wholemeal pastry. Use half wholemeal flour and half plain flour, if wished.

●385 calories/1625 kj per portion

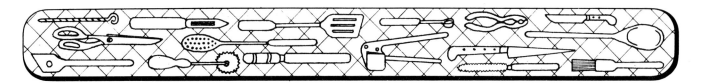

Pan pizza

SERVES 2-4

225 g/8 oz can tomatoes, drained
  and chopped
1 teaspoon dried marjoram
freshly ground black pepper
1 tablespoon vegetable oil
75 g/3 oz Mozzarella cheese, sliced
  (see Buying guide)
45 g/1¾ oz can anchovy fillets in
  oil, drained and soaked in milk
  for 20 minutes

DOUGH BASE
100 g/4 oz self-raising flour
pinch of salt
25 g/1 oz margarine
3 tablespoons water

1 Mix the tomatoes and marjoram
together and season with pepper.

2 Make the dough: sift the flour and
salt in a bowl and rub in the
margarine. Bind with the water.
3 Heat the oil in a 20 cm/8 inch
frying-pan. Roll the dough out
lightly to fit the frying-pan base and
put it into the pan. Cook the pizza
over moderate heat for 4 minutes,

then turn it over and cook the
other side for about 3-4 minutes.
4 Spread the tomato and herb mixture over the cooked dough. Cover
with cheese; top with anchovies.
5 Heat the grill to high.
6 Place the frying-pan under the
grill to brown the pizza. Serve hot.

Cook's Notes

TIME
Preparation 15 minutes,
cooking 12 minutes.

BUYING GUIDE
If Mozzarella cheese is
unobtainable, Edam can
be substituted. Also, canned
sardines may be used instead of
anchovies.

SERVING IDEAS
The pizza will serve 4 as
a snack, or 2 as a more

substantial dish for supper or
lunch.
   A green salad makes a cool,
crisp accompaniment to this
dish.

VARIATION
Garnish the pizza with
juicy black olives or thin
mushroom slices brushed with
vegetable oil before being put
under the grill.

●510 calories/2125 kj per portion

Salmon in puff pastry

SERVES 4

215 g/7½ oz can red salmon (see
   Buying guide), drained and
   flaked, skin and bones discarded
50 g/2 oz long-grain rice
salt
2 hard-boiled eggs, chopped
2 tablespoons chopped parsley or
   snipped chives
50 g/2 oz margarine or butter,
   melted
2 tablespoons tomato ketchup
freshly ground black pepper
375 g/13 oz frozen puff pastry,
   defrosted
1 small egg, beaten

1 Heat the oven to 220C/425F/Gas 7.
2 Rinse the rice thoroughly under
cold running water, then cook in a
saucepan of boiling salted water for
12 minutes. Drain and rinse again
under cold running water to
separate the grains.
3 Put the salmon in a large bowl
with the rice, hard-boiled eggs,
parsley, melted margarine, tomato
ketchup and salt and pepper to
taste. Fold gently to mix, taking care
not to break up the pieces of salmon
and egg.
4 Roll out the pastry on a floured
surface to a rectangle about 35 × 25
cm/14 × 10 inches. Transfer to a
dampened baking sheet.
5 Place the salmon and rice mixture
in the centre of the pastry,
spreading it out evenly. Dampen
the edges of the pastry and press
them together over the top of the
filling. Crimp the edges and make
3-4 cuts each side.
6 Brush the pastry all over with
beaten egg, then bake in the oven
for about 40 minutes until golden
brown. ! Serve hot or cold.

Cook's Notes

TIME
Preparation about 20
minutes, including
cooking the rice and hard-
boiling the eggs. Cooking takes
about 40 minutes.

BUYING GUIDE
Red, rather than pink
salmon is recom-
mended for this pie because of
its finer flavour and colour.

WATCHPOINT
If the pastry browns too
quickly, cover with foil.

DID YOU KNOW
This is an easy version
of a delicious Russian
fish pie, called *kulibyaka*.

●630 calories/2625 kj per portion

288

Seafood quickie

SERVES 4

4 tomatoes, skinned and sliced
500 g/1 lb cod or other white fish fillets, skinned and defrosted if frozen (see Buying guide)
100 g/4 oz peeled prawns, defrosted if frozen
300 g/10 oz can condensed cream of asparagus soup
15 g/½ oz butter
4 tablespoons vegetable oil
3 slices white bread, crusts removed and cut into triangles or fish shapes
extra tomato slices or small can asparagus tips, to garnish (optional)

1 Heat the oven to 190C/375F/Gas 5.
2 Place the sliced tomatoes in the bottom of a 1.5 L/2½ pint shallow ovenproof dish and arrange the fish on top (see Preparation). Sprinkle the prawns evenly over the surface of the fish and pour the can of condensed asparagus soup over the top.

3 Cover the dish with a lid or foil and bake in the oven for 35 minutes. Remove the lid or foil, then continue to cook in the oven, uncovered, for a further 10-15 minutes, until the fish pieces are cooked through (see Cook's tip).

4 Meanwhile, melt the butter with the oil in a frying-pan. When sizzling, add the bread shapes and fry over high heat for 2-3 minutes, turning once until golden brown on each side. Drain on absorbent paper.

5 Arrange the fried bread shapes around the edge of the fish in the dish, then garnish with tomato slices, if liked. Serve at once, straight from the dish.

Mackerel pilaff

SERVES 4

2 mackerel, each weighing about
500 g/1 lb (see Variations)
25 g/1 oz margarine or butter
1 onion, chopped
1 red pepper, deseeded and cut into
5 mm/¼ inch strips
250 g/9 oz long-grain brown rice
1 L/1¾ pints boiling chicken stock
salt and freshly ground black pepper
25 g/1 oz whole blanched almonds
or salted peanuts
150 g/5 oz courgettes, cut into 5 mm/
¼ inch slices
parsley sprigs and lemon slices, to
garnish (optional)

1 Melt the margarine in a heavy-based saucepan. Add the onion and red pepper and fry gently for 5 minutes until the onion is soft and lightly coloured.

2 Stir in the rice and cook for 1 minute. Remove from the heat and stir in the stock. Season with salt and pepper, return to the boil then simmer, covered, for 30 minutes until the rice is tender and nearly all the liquid has been absorbed. Check the pan during cooking and add more boiling stock or water if necessary.

3 Heat the grill to high. Cover the grill rack with foil.

4 Spread the almonds out on the foil and toast under the grill until golden on all sides turning them constantly. Remove from grill and leave to cool.

5 Grill the mackerel for 10-12 minutes on each side, or until the flesh flakes easily.

6 Meanwhile, bring a pan of salted water to the boil and cook the courgettes for 3-4 minutes until just tender. ⚠ Drain well.

7 Flake the mackerel flesh into large pieces with a fork, removing all the skin and bones.

8 Drain any liquid from the rice and carefully fork in the courgettes and fish. Heat through for a few seconds then taste and adjust seasoning.

9 Spoon on to a large serving platter, and sprinkle over the toasted almonds. Garnish with parsley sprigs and lemon slices, if liked, and serve hot or cold.

Spicy sausage macaroni

SERVES 6

500 g/1 lb chorizo sausages (see Buying guide)

salt

350 g/12 oz short-cut macaroni

15 g/½ oz lard

1 small onion, finely chopped

2 × 250 g/9 oz cans tomato or mushroom spaghetti sauce

1 teaspoon dried oregano (optional)

freshly ground black pepper

175 g/6 oz mild Cheddar cheese, grated

margarine, for greasing

1 Bring a large saucepan of salted water to the boil. Meanwhile, skin the sausages.

2 Heat the oven to 180C/350F/Gas 4. Drop the macaroni into the boiling water and cook according to packet instructions until just tender.[!] Drain thoroughly.

3 While the macaroni is cooking, melt the lard in a large frying-pan, add the sausages and fry, turning, until brown on all sides. Remove the sausages from the pan, drain on absorbent paper and set aside.

4 Add the onion to the pan and fry gently, stirring often, until it is soft and golden. Remove from the pan with a slotted spoon and pour away the fat left in the pan.

5 Cut the sausages into 1 cm/½ inch pieces. Return to the pan with the onion, spaghetti sauce and oregano, if using. Season carefully with salt and pepper. Bring the contents of the pan to simmering point.

6 Lightly grease a 1.75 L/3 pint casserole. Form separate layers of macaroni, sausage and sauce, and one-third of the cheese. Repeat these layers once, then finish with a layer of macaroni. Sprinkle the top with the remaining one-third of the grated cheese, making sure all the macaroni is covered.[!]

7 Bake in the oven for about 30 minutes, until the topping is golden and the macaroni heated through.

Cook's Notes

TIME
Preparation, including boiling the pasta, takes about 20 minutes. Cooking in the oven takes about 30 minutes.

BUYING GUIDE
Chorizos are sold cooked and uncooked in delicatessens: make sure you buy the uncooked variety for this dish.

WATCHPOINTS
The macaroni should be only just tender after boiling, so it does not become mushy when heated through in the oven.
It should be completely covered with cheese, so that the top layer does not become hard or brittle.

●850 calories/3575 kj per portion

Pasta and ham supper

SERVES 4

225 g/8 oz pasta shells
salt
2 teaspoons vegetable oil
2 × 300 g/10 oz cans condensed
 chicken soup
175 g/6 oz Parma ham (see
 Economy), fat removed and cut
 into thin strips
225 g/8 oz frozen peas, defrosted
2 egg yolks (see Economy)
2 tablespoons snipped chives or
 chopped fresh parsley
freshly ground black pepper

1 Heat the oven to 110C/225F/Gas ¼.
Bring a saucepan of salted water to
the boil, add the vegetable oil and
cook the pasta for about 12 minutes,
or until it is just soft. Drain well and
turn into a warmed serving dish.
Cover and keep warm in the oven.

2 While the pasta is cooking, heat
the chicken soup in a saucepan. Add
the ham strips and the peas. Heat
until the soup is just bubbling.
3 Beat the egg yolks into the
contents of the pan and warm

through very gently without
boiling. Stir in half the chives and
season to taste with black pepper.
Spoon the sauce over the pasta and
sprinkle with the remaining chives.
Serve at once.

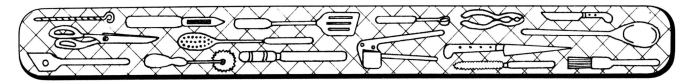

Cannelloni with tuna

SERVES 4-6

12 cannelloni tubes (see Buying guide)
50 g/2 oz margarine or butter
50 g/2 oz plain flour
500 ml/18 fl oz milk
200 g/7 oz can tuna, drained and flaked
100 g/4 oz frozen petits pois (see Buying guide)
salt and freshly ground black pepper
1 tablespoon tomato purée
generous pinch of sweet paprika
50 g/2 oz mature Cheddar cheese, finely grated
2 tablespoons grated Parmesan cheese
margarine or butter, for greasing

1 Heat the oven to 200C/400F/Gas 6. Grease a shallow ovenproof dish.
2 Make the filling: melt the margarine in a saucepan, sprinkle in the flour and stir over low heat for 1-2 minutes until straw-coloured. Remove from the heat and gradually stir in 300 ml/½ pint of the milk. Return to the heat and simmer, stirring, until thick and smooth. Remove from the heat.
3 Spoon half the sauce into a bowl, then fold in the tuna and peas with salt and pepper to taste.
4 With a small teaspoon, or a forcing bag fitted with a large plain nozzle, fill the cannelloni with the filling mixture, pushing it well into the tubes with your little finger.
5 Over low heat, gradually stir the remaining milk into the reserved sauce in the pan. Whisk vigorously until smooth, then add the tomato purée, sweet paprika and salt and pepper to taste, then simmer for a few minutes until thickened.
6 Cover the bottom of the prepared dish with a little of the hot sauce, then arrange the cannelloni on top, separating each one with a little sauce. Cover with the remaining sauce. Mix the cheeses together,

then sprinkle over the top.
7 Bake in the oven for 30-35 minutes until the sauce is bubbling at the edges and the cannelloni are cooked through. Serve hot, straight from the dish.

Cook's Notes

 TIME
Preparation takes 40 minutes, baking 30-35 minutes.

 VARIATION
Use 100 g/4 oz cooked ham or Italian salami, finely chopped, instead of the tuna.

 BUYING GUIDE
Be sure to buy cannelloni that do not need pre-cooking. Instructions are printed on the packet.
Petits pois are the smallest variety of frozen peas available, and are, therefore, the most suitable for filling cannelloni tubes. If difficult to obtain, use ordinary frozen peas.

 DID YOU KNOW
Cannelloni is a favourite dish in Italy; the filling often includes veal, ham, curd cheese or spinach.

 SERVING IDEAS
Serve the cannelloni with a mixed salad.

●530 calories/2225 kj per portion

Spaghetti with olives

SERVES 4

400 g/14 oz spaghetti
150 ml/¼ pint olive oil (see Cook's tip)
1 onion, finely chopped
1 green pepper, deseeded and thinly sliced
4 tomatoes, skinned and chopped
salt and freshly ground black pepper
100 g/4 oz black olives, stoned and halved (see Buying guide)
50 g/2 oz Parmesan cheese, grated, to finish

1 Heat the oil in a large frying-pan with a lid. Add the onion, green pepper and tomatoes, with salt and pepper to taste, then cover the pan and cook over moderate heat for 20 minutes, stirring from time to time.
2 Add the olives to the tomato and pepper mixture in the frying-pan and cook gently for 5 minutes.

3 Meanwhile, bring a large saucepan of salted water to the boil and cook the spaghetti for about 10 minutes, until *al dente* (tender yet firm to the bite). Drain well.

4 Add the drained spaghetti to the frying-pan and turn gently to coat evenly with the sauce. Transfer to a warmed serving dish and serve, sprinkled with Parmesan cheese.

Cook's Notes

TIME
Preparation takes about 15 minutes. Cooking takes 25 minutes.

COOK'S TIP
It is essential to use olive oil for this dish, to ensure the sauce has the right flavour and a consistency just to coat the spaghetti.

BUYING GUIDE
There are many different varieties of olive, some very large, some very small. They are available pickled in brine in jars, or loose from delicatessens. Choose medium-sized olives for this recipe.

VARIATION
2 large celery stalks, thinly sliced, could replace the pepper: the flavour of celery combines very well with olives too.

DID YOU KNOW
Olives grow profusely in Mediterranean countries, especially in France, Italy, Spain and Greece. Black olives, which are fully ripe when picked, are often used in the cooking of these countries. Green olives, which are picked unripe, are most often used for garnishing rather than cooking.

● 810 calories/3375 kj per portion

Creamy rigatoni

SERVES 4

500 g/1 lb rigatoni (see Buying
  guide)
salt
1 tablespoon vegetable oil
150 g/5 oz butter
100 g/4 oz button mushrooms,
  sliced
150 ml/¼ pint single cream
2 egg yolks
75 g/3 oz Parmesan cheese, grated
pinch of freshly grated nutmeg
freshly ground black pepper
100 g/4 oz frozen peas, cooked

1 Bring a large saucepan of salted
water to the boil. Add the rigatoni
and oil, lower the heat and simmer
for about 12 minutes until just
tender.
2 Meanwhile, melt 25 g/1 oz butter
in a frying-pan. Add the mushrooms and fry over moderate heat
until just tender. Set aside.
3 Make the sauce: melt the
remaining butter in a large saucepan. Remove from the heat and set
aside. In a bowl, quickly mix the
cream, egg yolks and Parmesan with
the nutmeg. Season with salt and
plenty of pepper. Add this mixture
to the melted butter in the pan and
stir well.
4 When the rigatoni is nearly
cooked, set the saucepan with the
sauce mixture over very low heat to
warm it through slightly.
5 Drain the cooked rigatoni, add to
the cream sauce with the peas and
the mushrooms and stir continuously for a few seconds, then pile
into warmed individual serving
dishes and serve at once.

Cook's Notes

TIME
Preparation time is
about 10 minutes, total
cooking time 15 minutes.

WATCHPOINT
When heating the cream
mixture, watch it very
carefully so that the eggs do not
begin to scramble.

SERVING IDEAS
Serve with a tossed
green salad, and offer
extra Parmesan for sprinkling
over the pasta just before eating.

VARIATION
Use 100 g/4 oz chopped
cooked ham in place of,
or in addition to the peas.

BUYING GUIDE
Rigatoni, a pasta that
looks like large, ribbed
macaroni, is available from
delicatessens and some supermarkets. If it is difficult to
obtain, use ordinary short-cut
macaroni instead.

●870 calories/3650 kj per portion

Creamy mushroom noodles

SERVES 4

350 g/12 oz noodles (see
   Variation)

salt
1 tablespoon vegetable oil
250 g/9 oz streaky bacon rashers,
   rinds removed
250 g/9 oz button mushrooms, very
   thinly sliced
150 ml/¼ pint milk
3 eggs
150 ml/¼ pint double cream
75 g/3 oz Cheddar cheese, grated
2 tablespoons chopped parsley
100 g/4 oz cooked ham, diced
freshly ground black pepper
40 g/1½ oz butter
2 tablespoons freshly grated
   Parmesan cheese (optional)

1 Bring a large saucepan of salted water to the boil. Add the oil and drop in the noodles. Bring back to the boil and cook according to packet instructions, until just tender, (see Cook's tip). Drain and rinse with boiling water to remove the excess starch.

2 Meanwhile, heat the grill to high. Grill the bacon until really crisp. Drain on absorbent paper, then cut into small strips and keep warm.

3 Put the mushrooms and milk in a saucepan and simmer for 3 minutes. Drain the mushrooms and keep warm. Reserve half the milk.

4 Beat the eggs, cream and the reserved milk together. Stir in the grated Cheddar cheese, half the parsley, the ham and salt and pepper to taste.

5 Melt the butter in a large saucepan, add the drained noodles, and toss over very gentle heat, to heat through.

6 Stir the cream and egg mixture into the noodles, and toss quickly until they are well coated and the ingredients well mixed. Stir in the mushrooms.

7 Turn the noodles into a warmed serving dish. Scatter the bacon, the remaining parsley and Parmesan, if using, on top. Serve at once.

Cook's Notes

TIME
This takes about 40 minutes to prepare and cook.

COOK'S TIP
Freshly made pasta, if available, takes less time to cook than commercially prepared pasta.
   You will find that the smooth surface of a wooden spoon and fork makes it specially easy to mix the sauce evenly into the noodles.

VARIATION
For an attractive colour contrast, use half white and half green noodles.

WATCHPOINT
The noodles must be tossed very quickly in the cream and egg mixture, so that the eggs do not scramble.

●1085 calories/4550 kj per portion

Englishman's paella

SERVES 4

150 g/5 oz jar mussels in vinegar, drained
125 g/4 oz can brislings, drained
2 tablespoons vegetable oil
2 onions, chopped
250 g/9 oz long-grain rice
400 g/14 oz can tomatoes
600 ml/1 pint chicken stock
2 cloves garlic, crushed (optional)
1 bay leaf
½ teaspoon ground turmeric
¼ teaspoon ground cinnamon
100 g/4 oz runner or French beans, cut into 5 mm/¼ inch lengths
salt and freshly ground black pepper

Cook's Notes

 TIME
Preparation and cooking take a total of about 50 minutes.

 VARIATION
Substitute canned sardines or pilchards for the brisling.

 SERVING IDEAS
Serve on its own garnished with bay leaves, coriander and lemon. For a more substantial meal, serve with crusty bread and a salad.

●410 calories/1700 kj per portion

1 Heat the oil in a large frying-pan, add the onions and fry gently for about 10 minutes until browned. Stir in the rice and cook until the oil is absorbed, about 2 minutes.

2 Add the tomatoes and their juices, the stock, garlic, if using, bay leaf, turmeric, cinnamon, and the beans. Season to taste with salt and pepper and bring to boil, stirring. Lower the heat, cover pan and simmer for 20-25 minutes until the rice is tender and most of the liquid has been absorbed.

3 Gently stir in the mussels and brisling and allow to heat through for 3-4 minutes. Serve straight from the pan, while piping hot.

Chicken biriani

SERVES 4-6

350 g/12 oz cooked chicken, cut
   into cubes
50 g/2 oz butter
225 g/8 oz long-grain rice
2 tablespoons Madras curry
   powder
50 g/2 oz seedless raisins
16 black peppercorns
¼ teaspoon salt
1 chicken stock cube
850 ml/1½ pints hot water
1 large onion, quartered
25 g/1 oz flaked almonds
1 hard-boiled egg, quartered
   lengthways, to garnish

1 Melt 25 g/1 oz butter in a heavy-based saucepan and fry the rice over moderate heat for about 1 minute, until the rice is only just beginning to brown on all sides.

Cook's Notes

TIME
This tasty dish takes only about 25 minutes to prepare and cook.

SERVING IDEAS
Serve accompanied by mango chutney and a side dish of natural yoghurt mixed with chopped fresh mint.

DID YOU KNOW
Birianis are normally finished by drizzling saffron water or food colouring over them so that some of the grains of rice turn a golden yellow to contrast vividly with those that remain white.

● 520 calories/2175 kj per portion

2 Lower the heat, add half the curry powder and stir well. Reserve a few raisins and add the rest to the pan with the peppercorns and salt.

3 Crumble the stock cube into the water, stir to dissolve and add to the rice mixture. Cover the pan and cook gently for about 10 minutes until the rice is almost cooked but there is still some liquid left in the bottom of the pan.

5 Meanwhile, melt the remaining butter in a frying-pan and add the chicken and onion. Fry gently for about 2 minutes, turning the chicken and onion frequently.

6 Add the remaining curry powder and fry quickly, stirring well, until the chicken is brown and well coated in spices while the onion stays crisp.

7 Add the chicken mixture to the rice. Reserve a few almonds and stir into the pan. Cook gently until all the remaining liquid is absorbed. Serve at once, garnished with the reserved raisins and almonds and the hard-boiled egg quarters.

Farmhouse chicken and rice

SERVES 4-6

350 g/12 oz boneless cooked chicken meat, skin removed and cut into bite-sized pieces
25 g/1 oz margarine or butter
1 large onion, chopped
2 celery stalks, chopped
2 carrots, sliced
100 g/4 oz Chinese leaves or summer cabbage, shredded
400 g/14 oz can tomatoes, drained and chopped (see Cook's tips)
350 g/12 oz cooked long-grain rice (see Cook's tips)
200 g/7 oz can sweetcorn kernels, drained
salt and freshly ground black pepper
1 tablespoon chopped parsley
50 g/2 oz mature Cheddar cheese, grated

1 Melt the margarine in a large saucepan, add the onion, celery, carrots and Chinese leaves and fry for about 10 minutes or until the vegetables are just tender, stirring occasionally.
2 Stir in the chicken, tomatoes, rice and sweetcorn and season to taste with salt and pepper. Cover and cook gently for a further 10 minutes or until piping hot.
3 Add the parsley and cheese and stir until the cheese has melted. Transfer to a warmed serving dish and serve at once.

Cook's Notes

TIME
Preparation and cooking in total, take about 35 minutes.

COOK'S TIPS
The liquid from the tomatoes can be added to the dish if a moister mixture is preferred.
  This is a good way of using up left-over rice. If using raw rice you will need 100 g/4 oz to make the amount required for this dish.

●405 calories/1700 kj per portion

Kabanos risotto

SERVES 4

2 tablespoons vegetable oil
1 onion, finely chopped
1 small green pepper, deseeded and finely chopped
400 g/14 oz can tomatoes
1 teaspoon sweet paprika
½ teaspoon sugar
salt and freshly ground black pepper
175 g/6 oz kabanos sausages, cut into 1 cm/½ inch slices (see Buying guide)
350 g/12 oz cooked long-grain rice (see Cook's tip)
2 tablespoons chopped parsley, to garnish

1 Heat the oil in a saucepan and fry the onion and the pepper over moderate heat for 3 minutes until soft and lightly browned.

2 Add the tomatoes and their juice, paprika, sugar, and salt and pepper to taste. Bring to the boil, breaking up the tomatoes with a wooden spoon and simmer, uncovered, for about 10 minutes, stirring the tomato sauce from time to time.

3 Add the kabanos and rice to the sauce, stir well and simmer for a further 5 minutes or until piping hot all the way through.

4 Serve immediately in a warmed serving dish, garnished with the chopped parsley.

Cook's Notes

TIME
Preparing and cooking take 30 minutes.

VARIATION
Add 100 g/4 oz frozen peas with the tomatoes.

BUYING GUIDE
Kabanos, a Polish pork sausage, is available in delicatessens – 2 sausages should provide the amount needed. If unavailable, use some pepperoni or chorizos.

COOK'S TIP
This is a good way of using up left-over rice. If using raw rice, you will need 100 g/4 oz at stage 1.

●375 calories/1575 kj per portion

Chicken and courgette salad

SERVES 4

350 g/12 oz boneless cooked
   chicken meat, cut into
   bite-sized pieces
250 g/9 oz long-grain rice
2 tablespoons vegetable oil
350 g/12 oz courgettes, thickly
   sliced
2 teaspoons curry powder
1½ tablespoons lemon juice
salt and freshly ground black pepper
2 tablespoons thick bottled
   mayonnaise
2 bananas

1 Bring a pan of salted water to the boil and cook the rice for 12-15 minutes until just tender. Rinse well under cold running water to separate the grains. Drain well and set aside for 30 minutes until cold.
2 Meanwhile, heat half the oil in a frying-pan and fry courgettes and curry powder briskly for about 4-5 minutes, turning, until golden and cooked through. Remove from pan with a slotted spoon and drain.
3 Put 1 tablespoon of the lemon juice and the remaining oil in a large serving bowl, season to taste with salt and pepper and mix well. Stir in the cold rice and courgettes.
4 Put mayonnaise into a separate bowl. Add the cooked chicken pieces and stir them into the mayonnaise until well coated.
5 Fold the chicken into the rice mixture until evenly distributed. Peel and slice the bananas and arrange on top, then sprinkle with the remaining lemon juice. Serve at once (see Serving ideas).

Cook's Notes

 TIME
Total preparation and cooking time for the dish is 1 hour.

 WATCHPOINT
The courgettes should be only just tender; if they are overcooked and too soft they will break up and spoil the appearance of the salad.

SERVING IDEAS
Sprinkle the finished dish with a little lightly toasted shredded coconut and garnish with a border of lemon slices.

VARIATIONS
Use chunks of cooked ham instead of chicken and, if liked, add chopped, well-drained canned pineapple segments.

●515 calories/2150 kj per portion

Quick beef curry

SERVES 4

500 g/1 lb lean minced beef
1 large onion, chopped
1 clove garlic, crushed (optional)
1 tablespoon curry powder (see
 Did you know)
¼ teaspoon ground ginger
¼ teaspoon ground cumin
1 dessert apple, peeled and grated
2 tablespoons sultanas or seedless
 raisins
300 g/10 oz can condensed beef
 consommé
salt and freshly ground black pepper
100 g/4 oz mushrooms, quartered

TIME
A quick and easy dish taking about 40 minutes to prepare and cook.

DID YOU KNOW
Curry powder is made from many different spices, including allspice, cardamom, chilli, cumin, saffron and turmeric. It is available in various strengths, from mild to very hot, so be sure to check the label carefully.

SERVING IDEAS
Serve with boiled rice and sliced onions.

●400 calories/1675 kj per portion

1 Place the beef, onion and garlic in a saucepan and fry over moderate heat until the beef is well browned, stirring constantly to break up lumps.
2 Stir in the spices and cook for 2 minutes, then stir in the apple, sultanas and the beef consommé. Season to taste with salt and pepper.
3 Bring to the boil, then simmer gently for 5 minutes.
4 Stir in the mushrooms and simmer a further 10 minutes. Taste and adjust seasoning. Serve at once.

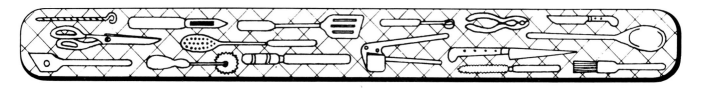

Savoury rice mountain

SERVES 4

250 g/9 oz cooked long-grain rice
(see Cook's tip)
350 g/12 oz can luncheon meat,
diced
2 hard-boiled eggs, chopped
200 g/7 oz can sweetcorn, drained
75 g/3 oz frozen peas, cooked
3 tablespoons thick bottled
mayonnaise
salt and freshly ground black pepper
vegetable oil, for greasing

TO SERVE
2 tablespoons snipped chives
grated carrot
extra mayonnaise

1 Brush the inside of a 1.2L/2 pint jelly mould or pudding basin with vegetable oil. Set aside.
2 In a large bowl, toss the rice,

luncheon meat, eggs, sweetcorn and peas. Mix in the mayonnaise and season with salt and pepper.
3 Spoon the rice into the prepared mould and then press down firmly. Cover with a plate and weight down. Refrigerate at least 1 hour.
4 Remove the weight and place

from the mould and invert a serving plate on top. Holding mould and plate firmly together, turn them over, then carefully lift off the mould to release the rice. Arrange chives on top and grated carrot around the rice mountain and hand a bowl of mayonnaise separately.

Cook's Notes

TIME
This dish, ideal for using up leftovers, takes less than 10 minutes to prepare plus 1 hour chilling in mould.

COOK'S TIP
Rice trebles in weight when it is cooked so use 75 g/3 oz raw rice to give the required amount of cooked rice.

VARIATION
Left-over cooked vegetables such as carrots and beans can be chopped and

added to the rice mixture to give colour and added flavour.
Use 250 g/9 oz smoked mackerel or a 200 g/7 oz can tuna instead of the luncheon meat.

 WATCHPOINT
Make sure the rice mixture is firmly packed down in the mould or basin and that it is well chilled so that it will not fall apart when it is turned out.

● 660 calories/2750 kj per portion

EGG 'N' CHEESE DISHES

Celery soufflé

SERVES 4
300 g/10 oz condensed celery soup
3 celery stalks, chopped
3 egg yolks
pinch of freshly grated nutmeg
salt and freshly ground black pepper
4 egg whites
1 tablespoon grated Parmesan
  cheese
margarine, for greasing

1 Heat the oven to 180C/350F/Gas 4. Grease a 2 L/3½ pint soufflé or ovenproof dish.
2 Pour the celery soup into a saucepan and warm through gently. Stir in the celery.
3 Remove the soup from the heat and stir in the egg yolks and nutmeg. Season to taste with salt and freshly ground black pepper.
4 In a clean, dry bowl whisk the egg whites until they are standing in stiff peaks.
5 Using a metal spoon, fold a spoonful of the egg whites into celery mixture and then fold in the remainder of the egg whites.
6 Pour the mixture into the prepared dish and bake in the oven for 40 minutes.
7 Carefully slide the oven shelf out a little way, sprinkle the grated Parmesan over the soufflé and return it to the oven for a further 5 minutes. Serve at once.

Cook's Notes

 TIME
This soufflé takes 10 minutes to prepare and 45 minutes to cook.

 VARIATIONS
Use can of condensed mushroom soup and some sliced fresh mushrooms instead of the celery soup and celery. Cheddar cheese can be used instead of Parmesan, or the cheese can be omitted altogether, if you prefer.

 COOK'S TIP
Reserve the spare egg yolk and add it to a sauce for a savoury dish to give it extra richness.

• 150 calories/625 kj per portion

Ham and egg cobbler

SERVES 4-6

SCONE TOPPING
115 g/4½ oz self-raising flour
115 g/4½ oz wholemeal flour
1½ teaspoons baking powder
½ teaspoon mustard powder
½ teaspoon salt
1 tablespoon chopped parsley
pinch of dried sage
40 g/1½ oz lard
1 egg, beaten
125 ml/4 fl oz milk

FILLING
40 g/1½ oz margarine or butter
1 large onion, finely chopped
3 tablespoons plain flour
½ teaspoon mustard powder
450 ml/16 fl oz milk
350 g/12 oz lean cooked ham, diced
4 eggs, hard-boiled and coarsely chopped
350 g/12 oz potatoes, boiled and cut into 2 cm/¾ inch cubes
2 tablespoons chopped parsley
salt and freshly ground black pepper

1 Heat the oven to 200C/400F/Gas 6. Melt the margarine in a saucepan, add the onion, cover and cook very gently for about 10 minutes, until soft but not coloured.
2 Meanwhile, make the scone topping: sift the flours, baking powder, mustard powder and salt into a large bowl. Stir in the herbs. Using your fingertips, rub the lard into the dry ingredients until the mixture resembles breadcrumbs. Make a well in the centre, pour in the egg and milk and stir with a fork until all the dry ingredients are drawn into the liquid to form a soft dough.
3 Knead the dough lightly on a floured surface, then roll out to a thickness of 1 cm/½ inch. Cut into rounds with a floured 5 cm/2 inch scone cutter. Set the dough rounds aside while you prepare the filling.
4 Sprinkle the flour and mustard powder for the filling into the onion mixture over the heat. Stir over low heat for 1-2 minutes, then remove from the heat and gradually stir in the milk. Return to the heat and simmer, stirring, until thick and smooth.
5 Remove the sauce from the heat

and lightly stir in the ham, eggs, potatoes and parsley. Add salt and pepper to taste. Transfer the mixture to a 1.5-1.75 L/2½-3 pint pie dish and arrange the rounds of dough on top. Bake the cobbler in the oven for 25 minutes or until the topping is risen and golden brown, and the filling is heated through. Serve hot, straight from the dish.

Leek and bacon flan

SERVES 4

215 g/7½ oz shortcrust pastry, defrosted if frozen

40 g/1½ oz margarine or butter
500 g/1 lb leeks, sliced
3 large rashers lean bacon, rinds removed and cut into 1 cm/ ½ inch strips
1½ teaspoons plain flour
1½ teaspoons sweet paprika
1 teaspoon lemon juice
100 ml/3½ fl oz milk
salt and freshly ground black pepper
2 eggs, beaten

1 Heat the oven to 200C/400F/Gas 6.
2 Roll out the pastry on a floured surface and use to line a 20 cm/8 inch flan tin.✳ Prick the base with a fork. Place a large circle of greaseproof paper or foil in the case, weight it down with baking beans and bake blind in the oven for 10 minutes. Remove the baking beans and greaseproof paper then return to the oven for 10-15 minutes until crisp and lightly coloured.
3 Meanwhile, prepare the filling: melt the margarine in a saucepan, add the leeks, cover and cook gently for about 10 minutes until soft.
4 Place the bacon in a frying-pan and fry it gently in its own fat for about 10 minutes until coloured. Set aside.
5 When the leeks have softened, sprinkle in the flour and sweet paprika and cook for 1-2 minutes stirring. Gradually blend in the lemon juice and milk and bring to the boil, stirring. Add salt and pepper to taste (remembering that the bacon will be salty), then remove from the heat and stir in the eggs.
6 When the flan case is cooked, lower the oven temperature to 180C/350F/Gas 4. Spread the bacon pieces over the base of the prepared case, then pour the leek mixture over the top. Return to the oven and bake for 20-25 minutes. Serve warm.

Scrambled eggs and onions

SERVES 4

6 eggs
3 tablespoons milk
salt and freshly ground black pepper
50 g/2 oz margarine or butter
1 tablespoon vegetable oil
4 onions, thinly sliced
2 tablespoons snipped chives
8 slices of French bread,
    toasted, to serve

1 Beat the eggs in a bowl with the milk; season with salt and pepper.
2 Heat the margarine and oil in a frying-pan, add the onions and fry gently for about 20 minutes or until golden (see Cook's tips).
3 Add the egg mixture and cook over low heat, stirring constantly until the eggs are just set but not dry (see Cook's tips). Taste and adjust seasoning.
4 Pile on slices of French bread, sprinkle over chives and serve.

Spanish vegetable omelette

SERVES 4

500 g/1 lb potatoes, cut into 1 cm/½
    inch dice (see Cook's tip)
salt
175 g/6 oz fresh French beans or
    100 g/4 oz frozen French beans
2 tablespoons vegetable oil
1 onion, chopped
1 red pepper, deseeded and diced
7 eggs, beaten
2 tablespoons finely chopped fresh
    parsley
½ teaspoon sweet paprika
freshly ground black pepper
a little extra finely chopped fresh
    parsley, to garnish

1 Bring a pan of salted water to the boil and cook the potatoes for about 5 minutes, until just tender but not mushy. Drain, refresh in cold water and drain again. Put the potatoes in a large bowl.
2 If using fresh beans, bring a pan of salted water to the boil and cook them for about 8 minutes until tender but still crisp. If using frozen beans, cook for about 5 minutes. Drain, refresh in cold water and drain again. Cut the beans into 2.5-4 cm/1-1½ inch lengths and add to the potatoes in the bowl.

3 Heat the oil in a large non-stick frying-pan, add the onion and red pepper and cook gently for about 5 minutes, stirring occasionally, until softened but not coloured. Remove the onion and pepper from the pan with a slotted spoon, draining all the oil back into the pan, and add to the potatoes and beans.
4 Add the beaten eggs, parsley and sweet paprika to the vegetables in the bowl and stir lightly together. Season to taste with salt and pepper.
5 Reheat the oil in the pan over low heat and pour in the omelette

mixture. Level out the vegetables and leave to cook very gently for 15-20 minutes, until the bottom is set but the top is still creamy. Meanwhile, heat the grill to high.
6 Set the frying-pan under the grill at the lowest position from the heat for 2-3 minutes, until the top of the omelette is set and light golden. Loosen the omelette from the pan with a palette knife, then with a fish slice slide it carefully on to a large plate. Sprinkle lightly with chopped parsley and leave to cool slightly. Serve the omelette cut into wedges.

Cook's Notes

TIME
Preparation and cooking take about 1 hour.

SERVING IDEAS
Serve the omelette warm or cold, on its own for a snack, or with French bread and salad for a lunch or supper dish. Alternatively, try slipping wedges of the hot omelette into lightly toasted pitta bread pockets, adding slices of cucumber or tomato.

VARIATIONS
Use peas or broad beans instead of French beans, or replace half the potato with

diced carrot. Use 8 spring onions, trimmed and cut into 5 mm/¼ inch slices, in place of ordinary onion, and finely chopped fresh mint makes a refreshing alternative to parsley. Add 50 g/2 oz left-over cooked chicken, ham or sausage, finely chopped, to the recipe for extra flavour and nourishment.

COOK'S TIP
If you want to use up left-over potatoes in this recipe, you will need about 350 g/12 oz cooked potatoes.

●315 calories/1325 kj per portion

Creole eggs

SERVES 4

8 eggs
1 tablespoon vegetable oil
2 onions, sliced
1 small green pepper, deseeded and
    sliced
2 tablespoons cornflour
425 ml/¾ pint milk
4 tomatoes, skinned and quartered
salt and freshly ground black pepper
pinch of cayenne pepper (optional)
2 tablespoons chopped fresh
    parsley
onion and green pepper rings, to
    garnish

1 Heat the oil in a large saucepan, add the onions and green pepper and fry gently for 5 minutes until the onions are soft and lightly coloured.
2 Put the cornflour into a bowl and mix with a little of the milk to form a smooth paste. Mix in the remaining milk and stir into the vegetables. Bring slowly to the boil, stirring, then when the mixture thickens, add the tomatoes with salt, pepper and cayenne, if using, to taste.
3 Lower the heat, cover the pan and simmer for about 10 minutes, stirring from time to time.
4 Meanwhile, hard-boil the eggs, remove their shells and halve the eggs lengthways. Arrange the halves in a single layer on the base of a warmed serving dish.
5 Pour the sauce over the eggs, sprinkle with chopped parsley and garnish with rings of onion and green pepper. Serve at once.

Cook's Notes

TIME
This easy dish takes about 25 minutes to prepare and cook.

DID YOU KNOW
Dishes using a combination of tomatoes and peppers are a popular feature of Creole cookery in the southern United States.

●275 calories/1150 kj per portion

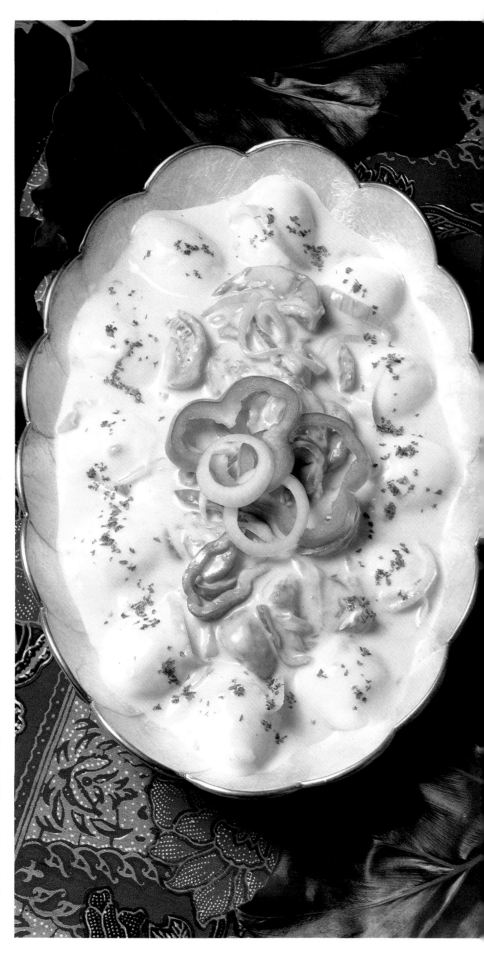

Eggs in a nest

SERVES 4

 8 eggs
25 g/1 oz margarine or butter
 100 g/4 oz bacon rashers, rinds
    removed, cut into strips
25 g/1 oz plain flour
300 ml/½ pint milk
285 g/10 oz can sweetcorn, drained
1 teaspoon Worcestershire sauce
salt and freshly ground black pepper
1 small packet potato crisps,
    crushed
1 tablespoon chopped fresh parsley

1 Put the eggs into a saucepan,
cover with cold water and bring to
the boil. Simmer for 5 minutes.
2 Meanwhile, heat the grill to high.
3 Run cold water over the eggs

and remove shells. Put the eggs into
a bowl, cover with warm water and
set aside until needed.
4 Melt the margarine in a small
frying-pan, add the bacon and fry
for 4-5 minutes until lightly
browned. Sprinkle in the flour and
stir over low heat for 1-2 minutes.
Remove from the heat and gradually
stir in the milk. Return to the heat
and simmer, stirring, until the
mixture is thick and smooth.
5 Stir the sweetcorn and the
Worcestershire sauce into the bacon
sauce. Taste and season with salt, if
necessary, and pepper.
6 Spread the sweetcorn mixture in a
flameproof serving dish, dry the
eggs on absorbent paper and
arrange them in the corn. Sprinkle
over the crushed crisps. Put the dish
under the grill for a few minutes to
warm the crisps. Sprinkle parsley
over the top and serve at once,
straight from the dish.

Cheese puff

SERVES 4

100 g/4 oz Gruyère or Gouda cheese, coarsely grated

400 g/14 oz frozen puff pastry, defrosted

50 g/2 oz plain flour

150 ml/¼ pint milk

25 g/1 oz margarine or butter, cut into small pieces

2 large eggs, beaten

3 tablespoons double cream

cayenne pepper

freshly grated nutmeg

salt and freshly ground black pepper

beaten egg, to seal and glaze

TIME
Preparation 30 minutes, baking 40 minutes.

COOK'S TIP
If the sauce is too thick, thin with a little more cream. If too runny, chill in the refrigerator until thickened.

FREEZING
Prepare up to the end of stage 8, open freeze raw on a baking sheet, then wrap in foil and freeze for 3 months. Bake from frozen, uncovered, allowing an extra 10 minutes.

VARIATIONS
For a meaty version, add 50 g/2 oz diced ham or grilled bacon to the cheese sauce; for a cheesier flavour, add 50 g/2 oz diced blue cheese (such as Stilton, Danish Blue, Gorgonzola).

SERVING IDEAS
Eat hot for supper cut into thick slices with either hot vegetables or a salad. Or serve cut into small squares for a snack to eat with drinks.

● 680 calories/2850 kj per portion

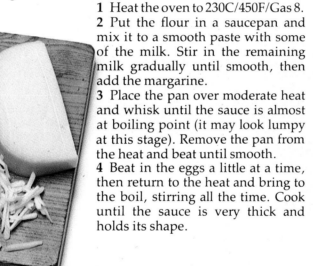

1 Heat the oven to 230C/450F/Gas 8.

2 Put the flour in a saucepan and mix it to a smooth paste with some of the milk. Stir in the remaining milk gradually until smooth, then add the margarine.

3 Place the pan over moderate heat and whisk until the sauce is almost at boiling point (it may look lumpy at this stage). Remove the pan from the heat and beat until smooth.

4 Beat in the eggs a little at a time, then return to the heat and bring to the boil, stirring all the time. Cook until the sauce is very thick and holds its shape.

5 Remove from the heat and leave to cool slightly, then stir in the cheese and cream with a pinch of cayenne and nutmeg, and salt and pepper to taste. To prevent a skin forming on top, press a piece of cling film or damp greaseproof paper on to the surface of the sauce, then leave to cool.

6 Roll out half the pastry on a floured board to about a 30 × 18 cm/12 × 7 inch rectangle, 2 mm/⅛ inch thick. Trim the edges square, then place on a dampened baking sheet.

7 Spread the cheese sauce over the pastry, leaving a 3.5 cm/1½ inch margin around the edge. Turn in this pastry border to partially cover the cheese filling. Roll out the remaining pastry to a rectangle the same size as the first and trim the edges square. Brush all round the edge with water or beaten egg, then place on top of the first rectangle, pressing the edges together firmly to seal. Knock up the edges with the back of a knife, then flute.

8 Brush the top with more beaten egg, then slash across at 2.5 cm/1 inch intervals with a sharp knife. ✳

9 Bake in the oven for 20 minutes, then cover the pastry with foil or greaseproof paper to prevent it becoming too brown. Lower the heat to 200C/400F/Gas 6 and continue baking for a further 20 minutes.

10 Slide on to a wire rack, sprinkle lightly with cayenne pepper, if liked, then leave to cool for 5 minutes before serving.

Cheese fondue

SERVES 4

225 g/8 oz Gouda or Gruyère
   cheese, finely grated

225 g/8 oz mature Cheddar cheese,
   finely grated

1 clove garlic (optional)
300 ml/½ pint dry white wine
1 tablespoon plain flour
1 teaspoon kirsch (optional)
pinch of freshly grated nutmeg
salt and freshly ground black pepper

TO SERVE
selection of raw crisp vegetables
   (celery stalks, cauliflower florets,
   carrot sticks)
French bread, cut into cubes

1 Halve garlic, if using and rub cut surfaces on inside of a heavy-based fondue pan or saucepan.

2 Pour the wine into the pan and heat until it starts to boil.

3 Put the flour in a polythene bag, add the cheeses, and shake.

4 Turn the heat to low and slowly add the cheese to the wine, stirring.

5 Add the kirsch, if using, and nutmeg, salt and pepper to taste, then cook for 10-15 minutes on the lowest possible heat to allow the fondue flavours to develop.

6 To serve: place fondue pan over spirit burner, or pour fondue into warmed individual soup bowls. Serve at once, using forks to dip crisp vegetables and cubes of bread into the fondue.

Cook's Notes

TIME
30-40 minutes, including preparation.

WATCHPOINT
Do not let the mixture become too hot during cooking or the cheese will become stringy.

ECONOMY
This is an inexpensive version of the traditional Swiss cheese fondue which uses equal quantities of Gruyère and Emmental. Mature Cheddar is more economical.

● 275 calories/1150 kj per portion

Cheese and apple pie

SERVES 4-6

 375 g/13 oz frozen shortcrust pastry,
    defrosted
 500 g/1 lb tart dessert apples
    juice of ½ lemon
    50 g/2 oz Demerara sugar
    ½ teaspoon ground cinnamon
 25 g/1 oz sultanas
    75 g/3 oz Cheddar or Red Leicester
    cheese, grated
    milk and Demerara sugar, for
    glazing

1 Heat the oven to 200C/400F/Gas 6.
2 Roll out half the pastry on a floured surface and use to line a 20 cm/8 inch pie plate.
3 Core, peel and thinly slice apples. Arrange half the slices on the pastry; sprinkle at once with half the lemon juice and half each of the sugar, cinnamon and sultanas. Top with the remaining apple slices, followed by the remaining lemon juice, sugar, cinnamon and sultanas.
4 Sprinkle the grated cheese evenly over the top of the apples. Brush around the edges of the pastry with milk, then roll out the remainder of

the pastry and cover the apples and cheese. Trim round the edge of the plate with a sharp knife.
5 Press the edges of the pastry together firmly, then knock up with back of a knife and scallop or flute to make an attractive finish.
6 Roll out the pastry trimmings and cut out leaves or diamonds to decorate the top of the pie. Brush with a little milk and fix on top.

7 Brush the top of the pie with milk and sprinkle with a little Demerara sugar. Bake the pie in the oven for about 20 minutes, turning the pie once so that it browns evenly.
8 Reduce the oven temperature to 180C/350F/Gas 4 and cook for a further 20 minutes or so, [!] until the apples feel tender when pricked with a fine skewer. Serve warm or cold.

Cook's Notes

TIME
Preparation takes about 20 minutes, cooking 40 minutes.

SERVING IDEAS
This pie makes a perfect cut-and-come-again sweet snack, by itself or with a wedge of cheese. It can be eaten warm or cold.

You could also serve the pie for a family tea, or with cream as a dessert.

WATCHPOINT
If the pastry becomes too brown before the pie filling is cooked, cover the top with foil.

FREEZING
The cooked pie can be successfully frozen. Let it cool completely, then open freeze on the pie plate. When solid, carefully remove from the plate and pack in a rigid container (cooked frozen pastry is very fragile and tends to crumble easily). Seal, label and return to the freezer for up to 6 months. To serve: place the frozen pie, uncovered, into a heated 220C/425F/Gas 7 oven. Bake for 20 minutes, reduce the oven temperature to 180C/350F/Gas 4 and bake for a further 20 minutes until warm through.

●615 calories/2575 kj per portion

Cheese and ham rolls

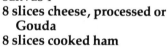

SERVES 4

8 slices cheese, processed or
  Gouda
8 slices cooked ham
225 g/8 oz cottage cheese
freshly ground black pepper
1 tablespoon chopped parsley or
  snipped chives

TOMATO SAUCE
15 g/½ oz butter
1 tablespoon vegetable oil
1 small onion, finely chopped
1 clove garlic, crushed
400 g/14 oz can tomatoes
1 teaspoon sugar
1 bay leaf
1 teaspoon chopped parsley
  or basil
salt and freshly ground black
  pepper

1 Heat the oven to 200C/400F/Gas 6.
2 To make the sauce: melt the butter with the oil in a saucepan and lightly cook the onion and crushed garlic until soft. Add all the remaining ingredients, breaking up the tomatoes if necessary. Bring to the boil, then lower the heat, cover the pan and simmer for 30 minutes. Adjust seasoning if necessary. ✳
3 Meanwhile, place a slice of cheese on each piece of ham. Season the cottage cheese with pepper, stir in the parsley or chives and divide evenly between the ham and cheese slices. Roll up and place in a single layer in an ovenproof dish, with the joins underneath. Pour the tomato sauce over the ham slices and place in the oven for 10 minutes until bubbly on top. For a crisper topping, scatter a little grated cheese mixed with a few breadcrumbs over the top before baking.

Cheesy vegetable curry

SERVES 4

150 g/5 oz mature Cheddar cheese, cut into 1 cm/½ inch cubes
40 g/1½ oz margarine or butter
1 large onion, chopped
1 small green pepper, deseeded and cut into strips
2 small carrots, halved lengthways and thinly sliced
4 small or 2 large courgettes, halved lengthways and cut into 1 cm/ ½ inch slices
1 large cooking apple, peeled, cored and cut into 2 cm/¾ inch dice
2 teaspoons curry powder
40 g/1½ oz plain flour
600 ml/1 pint chicken stock
25 g/1 oz sultanas
salt
2 tablespoons mango chutney, chopped

1 Melt the margarine in a saucepan, add the onion, green pepper and carrots and fry gently for 3-4 minutes, stirring, until the onions are soft but not coloured. Add the courgettes, apple and curry powder and cook for 2 minutes, stirring.
2 Sprinkle in the flour, cook for 1-2 minutes, stirring, then gradually blend in the stock. Bring to the boil, stirring, then add the sultanas and salt to taste. Lower the heat, cover the pan and simmer for 5 minutes.
3 Add the mango chutney, then stir in the cubed cheese. ☐ Serve at once in an attractive bowl.

Cheese and tomato loaf

SERVES 4

350 g/12 oz mature Cheddar cheese,
    grated (see Buying guide)
500 g/1 lb firm tomatoes, very finely
    chopped
8 large gherkins, finely chopped
6 spring onions, finely chopped
2 teaspoons natural yoghurt
1 teaspoon French mustard
1 tablespoon chopped fresh parsley
salt and freshly ground black pepper
melted margarine or butter, for
    greasing

TO GARNISH
1 tomato, sliced
2 large or 4 cocktail gherkins, sliced
sprigs of parsley

1 Brush a 500 g/1 lb loaf tin with the
melted margarine or butter.

2 Put all the loaf ingredients in a
large bowl with salt and pepper to
taste and mix together until
thoroughly combined.
3 Spoon the mixture into the
prepared loaf tin, press down and
cover with greaseproof paper and
weight down. Chill overnight.
4 Drain off liquid, then turn out loaf
on to a serving dish and garnish
with tomato and gherkin slices and
sprigs of parsley.

Cook's Notes

 TIME
This loaf only takes
about 10 minutes to
prepare, but remember to allow
for chilling overnight.

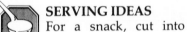 **VARIATIONS**
Ordinary Cheddar can
be used for a less
expensive, milder-tasting loaf.
Try one of the flavoured
Cheddars with mixed herbs or
pickled onions for a different
flavour.
    Instead of yoghurt, use
mayonnaise, soured cream or
double cream.

 **SERVING IDEAS**
For a snack, cut into
slices with fresh bread
and butter and a mixed salad or
a salad of sliced beetroot and
chicory. If you are short of time,
do not chill, simply spoon the
mixture on to a bed of shredded
lettuce. For a starter to serve 6
people, serve with crisp toast.

 BUYING GUIDE
Mature or Farmhouse
Cheddar gives a good
cheese flavour to the dish.

●400 calories/1675 kj per portion

SANDWICHES

Spicy club sandwich

MAKES 4

100 g/4 oz cooked chicken, chopped
    into bite-sized pieces
4 rashers back bacon, rinds
    removed
2 teaspoons mild curry powder
4 tablespoons mayonnaise
8 slices brown bread
4 slices white bread
50 g/2 oz butter, softened
4 small lettuce leaves
16 thin slices cucumber
2 tomatoes, sliced

1 Heat the grill to moderate. In a bowl, stir the curry powder into the mayonnaise and mix in the chicken. Lightly grill the bacon, drain well on absorbent paper and keep warm.

2 With a very sharp knife, remove the crusts from the bread and trim the slices to exactly the same size. Butter both sides of the white, and one side of the brown bread slices. Spread the chicken mixture equally over 4 slices of the brown bread. Top with the white bread slices.

3 Put a lettuce leaf and 4 slices of cucumber on each sandwich. Top with remaining brown bread slices.

4 Finally top each sandwich with the tomato slices and a grilled bacon rasher.

Chicken and banana double deckers

SERVES 4

175 g/6 oz boneless cooked chicken
1 tablespoon vegetable oil
1 small onion, chopped
1-2 teaspoons curry powder
2 tablespoons thick bottled
   mayonnaise
juice of 1 lemon
1 tablespoon sultanas
butter, for spreading
8 slices brown bread, crusts
   removed
4 slices white bread, crusts removed
8 teaspoons mango chutney
2 bananas
4 teaspoons desiccated coconut

1 Heat the oil in a small pan, add the onion and fry gently for 5 minutes until soft and lightly coloured. Sprinkle over curry powder (see Cook's tips) and cook for 2 minutes.

2 Put the chicken and the onion mixture into a blender. Add the mayonnaise and 2 teaspoons lemon juice and blend for 1-2 minutes (see Cook's tips). Transfer to a bowl.

3 Stir the sultanas into the chicken mixture until well blended.

4 Spread butter on one side of all the slices of bread. Lay 4 brown slices, buttered side up, on a board. Divide the chicken mixture between them, spreading it evenly. Top with slices

of white bread, buttered side down.

5 Spread the mango chutney over the top of the white bread slices. Slice the bananas evenly. Put the banana slices on top of the chutney and brush with the remaining lemon juice. Sprinkle over the desiccated coconut and top with the remaining brown bread slices, buttered side down.

6 Cut sandwiches in quarters and arrange on a serving plate.

Cook's Notes

TIME
20-30 minutes for pre-paration.

COOK'S TIPS
The amount of curry powder you use will depend on how strong a curry flavour you like.

If you do not have a blender, chop the chicken finely, then put the onion mixture into a

bowl and mix in the mayonnaise, lemon juice and chicken stirring well to combine all the ingredients.

 SERVING IDEAS
These sandwiches make a tasty snack on their own, or serve a tomato and onion salad with them.

● 620 calories/2575 kj per portion

Fried sardine sandwiches

SERVES 4
100 g/4 oz sardines in oil, drained
2 large eggs, hard-boiled and
  chopped
2 tablespoons snipped chives or
  finely chopped spring onion tops
freshly ground black pepper
75 g/3 oz margarine or butter,
  softened
grated zest of 1 lemon
1 tablespoon lemon juice
generous pinch of sweet paprika
8 thin slices bread, crusts removed

1 Mash the sardines until smooth, then mix in the chopped eggs, chives and plenty of pepper.
2 Using a wooden spoon, beat the margarine in a separate bowl until light and creamy, then beat in the lemon zest, lemon juice and paprika.
3 Spread the bread slices on 1 side with the lemon-flavoured margarine. [!] Turn 4 of the slices over, and spread evenly with the sardine mixture. Top with the remaining 4 slices of bread, margarine side facing upwards.
4 Set a large frying-pan over fairly high heat and leave it for about 30 seconds to heat through (see Cook's tip). Put the sardine sandwiches into the pan and press them down gently with a fish slice.
5 Fry the sandwiches for about 3 minutes until golden brown, then carefully turn them over, using a fish slice, and cook for a further 3 minutes until golden brown. Serve at once.

Cook's Notes

 TIME
Preparation takes about 20 minutes, including hard-boiling the eggs. Frying the sandwiches takes about 6 minutes.

 VARIATION
Mix the mashed sardines with skinned, chopped tomatoes or peeled, diced cucumber instead of the egg.

[!] **WATCHPOINT**
Make sure you spread the margarine right to the edges of the slices of bread. This ensures an even, golden-brown finish.

 COOK'S TIP
No fat for frying is needed, as the sandwiches are spread on the outside with the margarine.

SERVING IDEAS
These sandwiches are best eaten with a knife and fork.
  Or cut each sandwich into 4 triangles with a sharp knife, and serve the triangles skewered with cocktail sticks and a garnish of tiny lemon wedges or lemon twists.

●350 calories/1475 kj per portion

Baked ham and tomato sandwiches

SERVES 4
8 slices smoked ham
3-4 large tomatoes, sliced
6 tablespoons mayonnaise
1 tablespoon French mustard
½ teaspoon Worcestershire sauce
½ teaspoon soy sauce
3 spring onions, finely chopped
225 g/8 oz mature Cheddar cheese, grated
salt and freshly ground black pepper
225 g/8 oz loaf French bread

1 Heat the oven to 200C/400F/Gas 6.
2 In a bowl mix together the mayonnaise, mustard, Worcestershire sauce, soy sauce, spring onions (reserving a little to garnish), cheese and salt and pepper to taste.
3 Cut the French loaf in half across, then cut each half open horizontally. Cut off the rounded ends so that you have 4 rectangular pieces of bread.
4 Spread the cheese mixture over the cut surfaces of the bread. Lay 2 ham slices on each piece of bread, then top with tomato slices. Season with salt and pepper.
5 Wrap each open sandwich in a piece of foil and arrange them side by side on a baking sheet.
6 Bake for 30 minutes or until the cheese mixture is melted and bubbling. Serve hot, garnished with the reserved spring onion.

Cook's Notes

 TIME
Preparation and cooking take 45 minutes.

 VARIATION
Substitute any other strong-flavoured cheese, such as Lancashire, for Cheddar, or use a mixture of cheeses.

 COOK'S TIP
If liked, these sandwiches may be prepared ahead of time and kept, wrapped in their foil, in the refrigerator. In this case, increase the cooking time by 10-15 minutes.

●670 calories/2800 kj per portion

Melted Mozzarella sandwiches

SERVES 4
8 large slices white bread
50 g/2 oz butter, softened
freshly ground black pepper
Worcestershire sauce
100 g/4 oz Mozzarella cheese (see
   Buying guide)
3 eggs, beaten
vegetable oil, for frying
parsley sprigs, to garnish

1 Spread the bread with the butter and cut off the crusts (see Cook's tip) with a sharp knife. ⚠Season 4 of the bread slices with pepper and a few drops of Worcestershire sauce.
2 Cut the Mozzarella into thin slices and arrange them in a single layer on the seasoned bread, leaving a 5 mm/¼ inch margin all round the edge of the bread.
3 Top with the remaining 4 bread slices. Press the edges firmly together.
4 Put beaten eggs on a plate and dip in each sandwich to coat thoroughly all over. Make sure that the edges are well covered with egg so that they are sealed.
5 Heat the oven to 110C/225F/Gas ¼. Pour enough oil into a large frying-pan to come to a depth of 5 mm/¼ inch. Heat gently until a bread crust sizzles and turns golden brown when dropped into the oil.
6 Fry the sandwiches 2 at a time for 3-4 minutes on each side until golden brown.
7 Drain very thoroughly on absorbent paper. Keep warm in the oven while frying the remaining sandwiches. Serve at once, garnished with parsley sprigs.

Cook's Notes

TIME
The sandwiches take about 15 minutes to prepare and cook.

DID YOU KNOW
In Italy these sandwiches are called Mozzarella in *carrozza* (a small covered carriage).

COOK'S TIP
Use a little of the removed bread crust to test the temperature of the oil.

WATCHPOINT
It is important that the bread slices are exactly the same size so that they can be sealed neatly.

BUYING GUIDE
Mozzarella cheese has outstanding melting qualities. If you can, buy an individually packed Mozzarella cheese from an Italian delicatessen; a single cheese will weigh about 100 g/4 oz.

●365 calories/1525 kj per portion

Sandwiches in batter

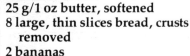

MAKES 4 SANDWICHES
8 small rashers back bacon, rinds
   removed
25 g/1 oz butter, softened
8 large, thin slices bread, crusts
   removed
2 bananas

BATTER
50 g/2 oz plain flour
pinch of salt
2 large eggs, separated
4 tablespoons water
vegetable oil, for frying

1 Heat the grill to high. Grill the
bacon on both sides until crisp, then
drain on absorbent paper.
2 While the bacon is grilling, butter
the bread and then just before
ready to use, mash the bananas
well with a fork.
3 Spread the mashed banana over 4
slices of bread, dividing it equally
between them. Cut the grilled bacon

rashers in half and arrange 4 halves
on each banana-topped slice of
bread. Top with the remaining
bread slices and press down well.
4 Make the batter: sift the flour into
a large bowl with the salt. Make a
well in the centre. Beat the egg yolks
with the water and pour into the
well, gradually drawing the flour
into the liquid with a wooden
spoon. When all the liquid is
incorporated, beat well to make a
smooth batter.
5 Beat the egg whites until stiff but

not dry, then fold into the batter.
6 Dip the sandwiches into the
batter, ensuring that they are
thoroughly and evenly coated on all
sides.
7 Pour enough oil into a large
frying-pan to cover the base and
heat over moderate to high heat,
until sizzling. Add the batter-coated
sandwiches and fry until crisp and
golden brown on both sides,
turning once with a fish slice.
8 Drain the fried sandwiches on
absorbent paper and serve at once.

Cook's Notes

TIME
Preparation and cooking
take about 25 minutes.

VARIATIONS
Instead of the bananas,
substitute 8 stoned,
sliced prunes.

FOR CHILDREN
Children will enjoy the
sandwiches spread with
yeast extract or peanut butter.

 WATCHPOINTS
Bananas discolour very
quickly once peeled, so
mash them only just before
using.
  Do not add the beaten egg
whites until just before you
intend to use the batter. Once
the egg whites are added the
batter will collapse if it is not
used immediately.

●530 calories/2200 kj each

Triple meat sandwiches

SERVES 4

8 large slices white bread
8 large slices brown bread
100 g/4 oz margarine or butter
100 g/4 oz liver sausage
4 small pickled gherkins, chopped
1 teaspoon bottled brown sauce
salt and freshly ground black pepper
4 lettuce heart leaves
100 g/4 oz luncheon meat slices
½ teaspoon made English mustard
50 g/2 oz raw beansprouts (see
   Buying guide)
50 g/2 oz thinly sliced peaches
100 g/4 oz salami slices
2 tomatoes, sliced
1½ tablespoons mild pickle
mustard and cress

TO GARNISH
12 cocktail onions (see Buying
   guide)
parsley sprigs

1 Spread the 8 white and 4 of the brown bread slices with 75 g/3 oz of the margarine.

2 Put the liver sausage in a bowl, add the remaining 25 g/1 oz margarine and mix with a fork to make a smooth spread. Mix in the chopped gherkins and brown sauce

Cook's Notes

TIME
Preparation takes about 30 minutes.

COOK'S TIP
The uncut meat sandwiches can be wrapped in cling film and refrigerated for up to 6 hours, then cut into squares and left at room temperature for 20 minutes before serving.

VARIATIONS
Mashed corned beef can be used instead of liver sausage, and sliced cooked ham instead of luncheon meat. Coleslaw and pineapple chunks can be substituted for the beansprouts and peaches.

BUYING GUIDE
Fresh beansprouts are now readily available from supermarkets, packed in boxes. Do not use canned beansprouts, as they are not crunchy.
   You can buy jars of different coloured cocktail onions, which would make a specially attractive garnish.

SERVING IDEAS
For a lunch or supper snack, serve the sandwiches with a knife and fork. The sandwiches are satisfying by themselves, or may be served with a selection of salads for a more filling meal.

●800 calories/3350 kj per portion

and season to taste with salt and pepper. Spread the mixture over the remaining 4 slices of brown bread. Lay a lettuce leaf on each slice and season with salt and pepper. Cover each with a slice of white bread, buttered side up.

3 Arrange the luncheon meat slices on top and spread with the mustard. Top each sandwich with beansprouts and peach slices. Cover with the remaining brown bread slices, buttered side up.

4 Lay the salami and tomato slices on top and season lightly with salt and pepper. Top each sandwich with pickle and mustard and cress.

5 Cover the sandwiches with the remaining white bread slices, buttered side down, and press down firmly (see Cook's tip).

6 Thread the cocktail onions and parsley sprigs alternately on to 4 cocktail sticks and spear a stick securely into each Triple meat decker sandwich.

Crusty steak sandwiches

SERVES 4

4 slices thin-cut sirloin steak, each
    weighing 75-100 g/3-4 oz (see
    Buying guide)
1 tablespoon vegetable oil
salt and freshly ground black pepper
4 large slices brown bread
1 tablespoon made English mustard
1 egg, beaten
25 g/1 oz Cheddar cheese, finely
    grated
50 g/2 oz margarine or butter

1 Brush the steaks with a little oil
and sprinkle with salt and pepper.
2 Spread the bread on 1 side only
with the mustard. Dip the other side
of the bread into the beaten egg,
then into the grated cheese.
3 Heat the grill to high.

4 Melt the margarine in a large
frying-pan, add the slices of bread,
mustard side down, and fry over
gentle heat for about 5 minutes until
golden brown and crisp (see Cook's
tip). Remove from the pan with a
fish slice and drain well on
absorbent paper. Cut each slice
of bread diagonally in half and keep
them hot.

5 Grill the steaks for 1 minute on
each side for a rare steak, 2-3 minutes
for medium to well-done steak.
6 When the steaks are grilled to
your liking, place each between 2
triangles of fried bread with the
cheese on the inside.
7 Serve the steaks on a warmed
serving dish with the meat juices
from the grill pan poured over.

Cook's Notes

 TIME
Preparation and cooking
take 20 minutes.

 COOK'S TIP
The cheese on the non-
fried side melts and
holds the sandwiches together.

 SERVING IDEAS
Grill halved tomatoes
and place one on top of

each sandwich or garnish with
lettuce leaves.

 BUYING GUIDE
Thin-cut sirloin steaks
are available in packs
from most supermarkets and
also from freezer centres. If
using frozen steaks cook them
for an extra few minutes.

●475 calories/2000 kj per portion

VEGETABLE DISHES

Vegetables are so versatile, they can add goodness and colour as accompaniments to a normal meal with meat, or they can be made into tasty and nutritious main courses in their own right. This section has a varied mixture of appetizers, soups, salads, main dishes and accompanying dishes, plus some more spicy vegetable dishes like *Cauliflower creole* or *Vegetable biriani* to add more interest to a special meal.

This section is ideal for vegetarians who want to try more exciting recipes or for people who just love the taste and texture of vegetables and salads.

Spring rolls

MAKES 6

300 g/10 oz beansprouts
8 spring onions, cut into
  matchstick strips
1 red pepper, deseeded, quartered
  and thinly sliced
100 g/4 oz mushrooms,
  thinly sliced
3 tablespoons vegetable oil
1 slice fresh ginger root, finely
  chopped
1 tablespoon soy sauce
1 tablespoon dry sherry
freshly ground black pepper
vegetable oil, for deep frying
spring onion tassels, to garnish

PASTRY

200 g/7 oz plain flour
½ teaspoon salt
125 ml/4 fl oz warm water

1 Make the pastry: sift the flour and salt into a bowl, then make a well in the centre and pour in the water. Mix with a wooden spoon until well blended, then knead well until the dough is soft and pliable. Wrap in cling film and put in the refrigerator for 30 minutes to chill.
2 Heat the oil in a large frying-pan or wok and add the beansprouts, the spring onions, red pepper, mushrooms and ginger. Fry briskly, stirring, for 2 minutes, then add the soy sauce, sherry, and pepper to taste. Cook for 1 further minute and remove from the heat.
3 Roll out the pastry on a lightly floured surface as thinly as possible to a neat rectangle, 45 × 30 cm/ 18 × 12 inches. Cut the pastry into six 15 cm/6 inch squares.
4 Place 2 tablespoons of the vegetable mixture in the centre of each pastry square. Fold in the sides, brush with a little water then carefully roll up. Dampen underside of pastry ends and press to seal.

5 Heat the oven to 110C/225F/Gas ¼.
6 Heat the oil in a deep-fat frier to 190C/375F or until a stale bread cube browns in 50 seconds.
7 Using a slotted spoon lower 3 rolls into the oil and fry for about 5 minutes until crisp and golden. Remove with a slotted spoon and drain. Keep warm while frying the remainder (see Cook's tip).

Cook's Notes

TIME
1 hour to prepare, including chilling time, then 10 minutes cooking.

COOK'S TIP
The rolls may be made a few hours in advance, allowed to cool, then reheated in a 170C/325F/Gas 3 oven just before serving.

●230 calories/975 kj per roll

Egg and lettuce rolls

MAKES ABOUT 20

5 large crisp lettuce leaves (see
    Buying guide)
3 hard-boiled eggs, roughly
    chopped
about 25 g/1 oz margarine or butter,
    softened
25 g/1 oz Danish Blue cheese,
    crumbled

1 Cut off a thin slice from the stalk
end of each lettuce leaf to remove
the thickest part of the stalk. Wash
and gently pat dry on absorbent
paper. Set aside.

2 Make the filling: put the eggs into
a bowl with 25 g/1 oz margarine and
the cheese. Mash with a fork to
form a smooth paste, adding a little
more margarine if the mixture is too
stiff to blend.

3 Place 1 lettuce leaf on a work
surface and spoon 1 tablespoon of
the egg mixture into the centre.
Gently spread the mixture over the
lettuce leaf right up to the edges.
Starting at the trimmed end, tightly
roll up the leaf to enclose the egg
mixture. Wrap firmly in cling film
immediately after rolling.

4 Spread, roll and wrap the remaining lettuce leaves in the same way
and refrigerate overnight.

5 To serve: unwrap the rolls and
cut with a sharp knife into 2.5 cm/
1 inch lengths. Serve at once.

Cook's Notes

TIME
About 20 minutes pre-
paration, plus over-
night chilling.

BUYING GUIDE
Choose a cos, Webb's
Wonder or iceberg let-
tuce for this recipe.

VARIATIONS
For a milder flavour,
use full-fat soft cheese
instead of blue cheese and season with salt and pepper and a
little sweet paprika.

Alternatively, replace the
blue cheese with anchovy
paste, available in tubes and
jars from delicatessens and
large supermarkets.

SERVING IDEAS
Serve as a summery
starter, garnished with
tomato wedges and cucumber
slices. These type of rolls also
make delicate accompaniments
for cocktails – arrange attractively on a serving platter and
garnish with tomato or sprigs of
watercress and parsley for a
pretty effect.

●25 calories/100 kj per roll

Spinach surprise

SERVES 4

**500 g/1 lb fresh spinach or 250 g/9 oz
    frozen chopped spinach
salt
50 g/2 oz margarine or butter
1 onion, finely chopped
25 g/1 oz plain flour
150 ml/¼ pint milk
good pinch of freshly grated
    nutmeg
freshly ground black pepper
4 eggs, separated
1 tablespoon grated Parmesan
    cheese
margarine, for greasing**

1 If using fresh spinach, wash very thoroughly and remove the stalks and central midribs. Place the spinach in a saucepan with only the water that clings to the leaves, and sprinkle with salt. Cover and cook over moderate heat for about 10 minutes until the spinach is cooked, stirring occasionally. If using frozen spinach, cook according to packet instructions.

2 Drain the spinach well in a sieve, pressing out all the excess water. Chop the spinach, if using fresh. Grease a 1.5 L/2½ pint soufflé dish.

Heat the oven to 190C/375F/Gas 5.
3 Melt the margarine in a large saucepan, add the onion and cook over low heat for about 5 minutes until soft and lightly coloured. Sprinkle in the flour and stir over low heat for 1-2 minutes until straw-coloured. Remove from the heat and gradually stir in the milk. Return to moderate heat and simmer, stirring, until thick.

4 Stir in the chopped spinach and grated nutmeg and season well with salt and pepper. Simmer over gentle heat for 2 minutes.

5 Remove from the heat. Beat the egg yolks and beat them into the spinach mixture.

6 Whisk the egg whites until they are just standing in soft peaks then fold gently into the spinach mixture with a metal spoon.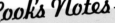

7 Pour the mixture into the greased soufflé dish and sprinkle the top evenly with the grated Parmesan cheese. Bake in the oven for 30-40 minutes until risen and lightly browned on the top. It should be firm to the touch on the outside, and not wobbly if gently shaken, but still moist in the centre. Serve at once straight from the dish.

Cook's Notes

TIME
Preparation takes about 30 minutes, cooking 30-40 minutes.

SERVING IDEAS
This spinach dish is very versatile: serve as a light lunch or supper or as a starter. Or try it as a vegetable accompaniment: it goes very well with veal or lamb dishes.

For individual soufflés, bake in four 300 ml/½ pint greased dishes for 20-30 minutes, or eight 150 ml/¼ pint greased dishes for 15-20 minutes.

WATCHPOINT
Do not overwhisk the egg whites. It is easier to fold in the whites if you first beat 1-2 tablespoons of whisked whites into the spinach mixture to slacken it. Carefully fold in the whites so as not to lose the trapped air.

VARIATION
For a more substantial main-course dish, add 100 g/4 oz finely chopped cooked ham or chicken.

● 250 calories/1050 kj per portion

Mushroom puffs and cheese sauce

SERVES 4

12 cup mushrooms (see Buying guide)
250 g/9 oz frozen puff pastry sheets, defrosted (see Buying guide)
15 g/½ oz butter
½ teaspoon dried marjoram
freshly ground black pepper
1 egg, lightly beaten

CHEESE SAUCE
25 g/1 oz Stilton cheese
150 g/5 oz natural yoghurt
2 spring onions, finely sliced
salt and freshly ground black pepper

1 Trim the mushroom stalks level with the caps, then chop the stalks finely and reserve.

2 Roll out the pastry thinly on a lightly floured surface. Then, using a 7.5 cm/3 inch fluted round cutter, cut out 24 pastry rounds.

3 Place one mushroom, stalk side up, on each of 12 pastry circles. Put a small knob of butter, a pinch of marjoram and a sprinkling of pepper on each mushroom.

4 Brush the edges of each mushroom-topped pastry circle with beaten egg, then place a second circle of pastry on top. Bring together the pastry edges, pressing well to seal. Flute the edges.

5 Dampen 2 baking sheets and transfer the puffs to them. Cover the puffs with cling film and refrigerate for 15 minutes.

6 Heat the oven to 220C/425F/Gas 7.

7 Meanwhile, make the Stilton sauce: crumble the cheese into a serving bowl, add a little yoghurt and mix together with a fork until fairly smooth. Stir in the remaining yoghurt, reserved mushroom stalks and half the spring onions. Sprinkle the remaining spring onions on top of the sauce, cover with cling film and refrigerate.

8 Brush the tops of the puffs with the remaining beaten egg, then bake in the oven for 10-15 minutes until well-risen and golden brown.

9 Pile the hot puffs on to a warm serving plate and serve with the chilled sauce handed separately (see Serving ideas).

Cook's Notes

TIME
Preparing the puffs takes 15-20 minutes. Allow 15 minutes chilling and 10-15 minutes for baking. Making the sauce takes 5 minutes.

SERVING IDEAS
These mushroom puffs make an ideal starter to a meal. Allow 3 puffs per person and serve on plates garnished with celery or spring onion tassels and, if liked, sliced raw mushrooms, and small lettuce leaves.

BUYING GUIDE
Cultivated cup mushrooms are larger than button mushrooms: their caps have begun to open. Choose mushrooms about 3 cm/1¼ inches wide, so the caps will hold the butter and be the right size for the pastry rounds.

Buy a 350 g/12 oz packet ready-made frozen puff pastry sheets and use 3 sheets for this recipe. Keep the remaining sheet frozen for another use.

●340 calories/1425 kj per portion

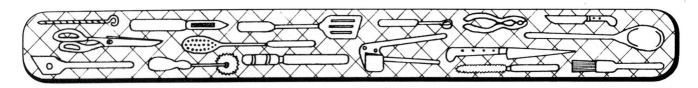

Grapefruit and celery salad

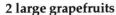

SERVES 4
2 large grapefruits
2 heads celery
4 teaspoons chopped fresh mint
2 tablespoons seedless raisins
4 sprigs mint, to garnish

DRESSING
150 ml/¼ pint natural yoghurt, chilled
1 tablespoon olive oil
1 tablespoon orange juice
salt and freshly ground black pepper

1 Cut each grapefruit in half, into a waterlily shape (see Preparation). Scoop out the flesh, using a curved grapefruit knife. (Alternatively run a small sharp knife between the flesh and the rind, taking care not to pierce the rind, then remove the flesh). Reserve the shells in the refrigerator.
2 Discard the pith, membranes and

pips and put the grapefruit flesh into a bowl.
3 Remove and discard the outer stalks of the celery, leaving the tender, yellowy 'hearts' (see Economy). Cut the celery hearts into 5 mm/¼ inch slices.
4 Add the sliced celery to the bowl, together with the chopped mint and raisins. Toss well.

5 Make the dressing: stir together the yoghurt, olive oil and orange juice and season to taste with salt and pepper.
6 Add the dressing to the salad, toss well and pile the salad into the grapefruit shells. Refrigerate the filled shells for 30 minutes. Garnish with mint sprigs and serve (see Cook's tip).

Cook's Notes

TIME
Preparation takes about 40 minutes.

COOK'S TIP
The shells may be stored and re-used in another dish: wash, pat dry and store for a few days covered in the refrigerator or wrap them and freeze.

ECONOMY
Reserve the outer stalks and leaves of the celery for stock or soup.

PREPARATION
To cut the grapefruits into waterlilies:

Insert knife at an angle through side into centre. Make second cut to form v-shape. Continue all round the grapefruit and pull apart.

● 100 calories/425 kj per portion

Vegetable samosas

MAKES 12

350 g/12 oz potatoes, diced
250 g/9 oz packet frozen mixed
   vegetables
1 tablespoon vegetable oil
1 onion, finely chopped
1 tablespoon curry powder
6 tablespoons water
salt and freshly ground black pepper
vegetable oil, for deep frying

PASTRY
175 g/6 oz plain flour
salt
25 g/1 oz margarine or butter,
   diced
about 4 tablespoons water

1 Make the pastry: sift the flour and salt into a bowl. Add the margarine and rub it into the flour with your fingertips until the mixture resembles fine breadcrumbs. Mix in just enough water to make a soft elastic dough. Wrap dough in cling film and refrigerate for 30 minutes.

2 Meanwhile, make the filling: heat the oil in a saucepan, add the onion and fry gently for 5 minutes until soft and lightly coloured.

3 Stir in the curry powder, then add the potatoes and cook for a further 1-2 minutes.

4 Add the mixed vegetables, water and salt and pepper to taste. Bring to the boil, stirring all the time. Lower the heat slightly, cover and simmer for 15-20 minutes, stirring occasionally, until all the vegetables are tender. Allow to cool slightly.

5 Divide the dough into 12 pieces and roll out each piece on a floured surface to a 10 cm/4 inch square.

6 Place 1 tablespoon filling in the centre of each square. Brush the edges of the pastry with water and bring over one corner to form a triangle. Press the sides together and flute. ✳

7 Heat the oil in a deep-fat frier with a basket to 180C/350F or until a day-old bread cube browns in 60 seconds. Put 3 samosas into the basket, then lower into the oil and cook for 2 minutes or until the pastry bubbles and turns golden. Drain on absorbent paper and keep warm while frying the remaining samosas in the same way. Serve at once.

Cook's Notes

TIME
Samosas take about 35 minutes preparation and cooking, plus 30 minutes chilling time.

 FREEZING
Freeze the samosas before frying: open freeze until solid, then pack into a rigid container or polythene bag. Seal, label and return to the freezer for up to 3 months. To serve: deep-fry from frozen for about 3-4 minutes.

SERVING IDEAS
Samosas are a favourite Indian snack. Serve them as a starter to an Indian meal with mango chutney, or with a tasty sauce made by blending natural yoghurt with mint, finely chopped cucumber, salt and freshly ground black pepper to taste.

● 155 calories/650 kj per samosa

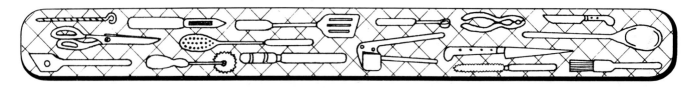

Stuffed green peppers

SERVES 4

4 green peppers (see Buying guide)
150 g/5 oz long-grain rice
1 small onion, chopped
3 tablespoons vegetable oil
2 tablespoons tomato purée
5 tablespoons water
50 g/2 oz flaked almonds
50 g/2 oz sultanas
2 teaspoons dried oregano
grated zest of 1 orange
salt and freshly ground black pepper

1 Heat the oven to 180C/350F/Gas 4.
2 Bring a large saucepan of water to the boil, add the rice, bring back to the boil and cook for about 15 minutes until the rice is tender.
3 Meanwhile, slice the tops off the peppers and reserve them. Carefully remove the seeds from the peppers.
4 Drain the rice thoroughly, rinse under cold running water and then drain again.
5 In a bowl, thoroughly mix the rice together with all the remaining ingredients, reserving 2 table-spoons of the oil and 2 tablespoons of the water.
6 Fill the peppers with the stuffing mixture, packing it in well but taking care not to break the peppers.
7 Put the peppers into a casserole in which they will stand together closely but comfortably (see Cook's tip). Replace the tops.

8 Mix together the reserved oil and water and drizzle it over the peppers.

9 Cover the dish and bake for 25 minutes. Uncover for a further 25 minutes. Serve hot, warm or cold.

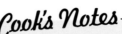
Cook's Notes

TIME
Preparation takes about 30 minutes, including cooking the rice. Cooking in the oven takes 50 minutes.

BUYING GUIDE
Buy firm, squat peppers as they stand up better in the dish and the stuffing will not fall out.

COOK'S TIP
If necessary, put a little crumpled foil between the peppers to keep them upright and remove it before serving.

VARIATION
Red peppers could be used instead of green or use 2 of each.

SERVING IDEAS
These make a filling first course on their own or with a tomato sauce, served with hot garlic or pitta bread. They are especially good served warm. They could also be served as a tasty supper dish.

● 325 calories/1350 kj per portion

Vegetable kebabs

SERVES 4

3 small courgettes, cut into
   4 cm/1½ inch slices
12 whole button onions
salt
12 whole button mushrooms
8 tomatoes, halved
8 small bay leaves
50 g/2 oz margarine or butter,
   melted
vegetable oil, for greasing

MARINADE

6 tablespoons vegetable oil
1 tablespoon lemon juice
1 small onion, finely chopped
2 tablespoons chopped fresh
   parsley
1 clove garlic, crushed (optional)
salt and freshly ground black pepper

1 Bring a saucepan of salted water to the boil, add the courgette slices and button onions and boil gently for 1 minute. Drain and immediately plunge the vegetables into cold water to prevent them cooking further. Drain vegetables well again and pat dry with absorbent paper.
2 Divide the courgette slices, onions, mushrooms, tomatoes and bay leaves into 4 equal portions and

thread them on to 4 greased metal kebab skewers, alternating the shapes and colours as much as possible. Lay the skewers in a shallow dish.
3 To make the marinade: put all the ingredients in a screw-top jar with salt and pepper to taste. Shake well to mix. Pour the marinade over the vegetable kebabs and leave them in a cool place for about 2 hours, turning them occasionally to coat the vegetables evenly.
4 Heat the grill to moderate. Lift the kebabs from the marinade and allow any excess dressing to drain off.

Brush the vegetables with the melted margarine. Grill the kebabs for about 8 minutes, turning them frequently to brown the vegetables evenly. Serve at once, while hot.

Cook's Notes

TIME
Preparation takes about 25 minutes, marinating 2 hours, cooking 8 minutes.

SERVING IDEAS
Serve on a bed of herb-flavoured rice.

●230 calories/975 kj per portion

Mixed vegetable croquettes

MAKES 16

2 onions, very finely chopped
6 celery stalks, very finely chopped
2 carrots, grated
175 g/6 oz mushrooms, very finely chopped
1 tablespoon vegetable oil
1 tablespoon smooth peanut butter
75 g/3 oz unsalted peanuts, ground or very finely chopped
75 g/3 oz fresh wholemeal breadcrumbs
pinch of dried mixed herbs
salt and freshly ground black pepper
2 eggs, beaten
75 g/3 oz dried breadcrumbs (see Economy)
vegetable oil, for deep-frying

1 Heat the oil in a large saucepan, add the onions and celery and fry gently for 5 minutes. Do not allow the vegetables to brown.

2 Add the carrots and mushrooms to the pan and continue cooking for a further 5 minutes, stirring from time to time.

3 Remove from the heat, then stir in the peanut butter until well combined. Add the peanuts, wholemeal breadcrumbs, herbs and salt and pepper to taste. Mix well and bind with half the beaten eggs. Leave until cool enough to handle.

4 Meanwhile, pour the remaining beaten eggs into a shallow bowl or on to a plate. Place the dried breadcrumbs on a separate plate, ready to coat the croquettes.

5 When the mixture is cool, divide it into 16 portions and shape them into croquettes. Dip each croquette in the beaten eggs, then roll in the breadcrumbs until thoroughly coated.

6 Pour enough vegetable oil into a deep-fat frier to come to a depth of 4 cm/1½ inches. Heat to 180C/350F or until a 2.5 cm/1 inch bread cube browns in 60 seconds. Lower in the croquettes and deep-fry for 3 minutes, until golden brown (see Cook's tip). Drain the croquettes very thoroughly on absorbent paper and serve hot.

Herby dip with cheese biscuits

SERVES 4

100 g/4 oz Wensleydale, Caerphilly or white Cheshire cheese, grated
100 g/4 oz unsalted butter, softened
1 tablespoon snipped chives
1 tablespoon finely chopped fresh fennel leaves or mint
1 tablespoon finely chopped fresh parsley
¼ teaspoon sweet paprika
¼ teaspoon caraway seeds
4 tablespoons milk
salt and freshly ground black pepper

CHEESE BISCUITS

100 g/4 oz butter, softened
100 g/4 oz mature Cheddar cheese, grated
100 g/4 oz wholewheat flour
2 tablespoons sesame seeds
margarine, for greasing

1 Make the biscuits: heat oven to 200C/400F/Gas 6 and lightly grease a baking sheet. Sift the flour.
2 In a large bowl, beat the butter until pale and creamy, then beat in the cheese. Add the flour a little at a time, beating thoroughly after each addition, to form a stiff dough.
3 Sprinkle the sesame seeds on a lightly floured work surface and roll out the dough, until about 2 mm/⅛ inch thick. Cut the dough into about 12 rounds using a lightly floured 7.5 cm/3 inch pastry cutter.
4 Using a palette knife, transfer the rounds to the prepared baking sheet, spacing them apart, then bake for 5-8 minutes until golden.
5 Remove from the oven, allow to settle for 1-2 minutes, then transfer to a wire rack and allow to cool.
6 Meanwhile, make the dip: put the Wensleydale cheese into a bowl with the butter, herbs, paprika, caraway seeds and milk. Beat until blended and creamy, then season to taste with salt and pepper.
7 Spoon the mixture into a small serving dish, smooth over the surface and serve with the biscuits.

Spicy bean pâté

SERVES 4

425 g/15 oz can red kidney beans
1 clove garlic, crushed (optional)
1 tablespoon tomato purée
1 teaspoon Worcestershire sauce
1 teaspoon lemon juice
few drops of Tabasco
salt and freshly ground black pepper
parsley sprigs, to garnish

1 Drain the beans, reserving the liquid from the can.
2 Put all the ingredients into a blender and blend to a smooth paste; it will be flecked with pieces of bean skin. Alternatively, place all the ingredients in a bowl, pound them with the end of a rolling pin, then mash thoroughly with a fork. If the mixture becomes too thick, add 2-3 tablespoons of the reserved liquid from the can.
3 Taste and adjust seasoning.
4 Pack the pâté into 4 small ramekins or other individual dishes and carefully smooth the surface of each with a small knife. Serve the pâté cold or chilled, garnished with parsley sprigs.

Cook's Notes

 TIME
Preparation of this pâté takes 15 minutes.

 COOK'S TIP
The pâté may be prepared up to 2 days before then stored in the refrigerator.

 BUYING GUIDE
Different canned pulses can be a very handy store-cupboard standby. They can be used for many quick-to-make dips and sauces.

 SERVING IDEAS
Serve as a quick, easy and different starter with brown bread or toast. For a party, serve the pâté as a dip with sticks of carrot, celery stalks and sliced cucumber, or spread it on cocktail biscuits.

●65 calories/275 kj per portion

Avocado dip

SERVES 4-6

2 ripe avocados (see Buying guide)
juice of 1 lemon
1 clove garlic, crushed (optional)
4 tomatoes, skinned, deseeded and finely chopped
1 small onion, finely chopped
4 tablespoons finely chopped celery
2-3 tablespoons olive oil
1 tablespoon chopped fresh parsley
salt and freshly ground black pepper

1 Cut the avocados in half lengthways (see Cook's tip), remove the stones then scoop out the flesh with a teaspoon. Put the flesh in a bowl and mash it with a wooden spoon.

2 Add the lemon juice, garlic, if using, tomatoes, onion and celery.

3 Stir in enough olive oil to make a soft, smooth mixture, then add the chopped parsley and season with salt and pepper to taste.

4 Transfer the dip to a serving bowl, cover with cling film and chill in the refrigerator for about 30 minutes. Serve chilled.

Cook's Notes

TIME
This dip takes 20 minutes preparation, then 30 minutes chilling.

BUYING GUIDE
Avocados are ripe when the flesh at the rounded end yields slightly when gently pressed. Reject any avocados that are hard or very soft or have blotched, dry skins.

COOK'S TIP
When cutting the avocado, use a stainless steel knife to prevent the avocado flesh from discolouring at the beginning.

SERVING IDEAS
Serve with a selection of small crackers, potato crisps or crisp raw vegetables.

●325 calories/1350 kj per portion

Butter bean dip with crudités

SERVES 4

100 g/4 oz dried butter beans, soaked in cold water overnight (see Cook's tips)
4-6 tablespoons good-quality olive oil
1 tablespoon red wine vinegar
1 clove garlic, crushed (optional)
salt and freshly ground black pepper

CRUDITES
1 small cauliflower, broken into florets
1 cucumber, cut into sticks
2 celery stalks, cut into sticks
2 carrots, cut into sticks
1 small green pepper, deseeded and cut into strips
1 small red pepper, deseeded and cut into strips
bunch of radishes

1 Drain the beans and rinse thoroughly under cold running water. Put them in a large saucepan, cover with fresh cold water and bring to the boil. Lower the heat, half cover with a lid and simmer for about 1¼ hours or until the beans are tender. Add more water to the pan during the cooking time if necessary.

2 Drain the beans, reserving the cooking liquid. Put the beans in a blender with 4 tablespoons oil, the vinegar, garlic, if using, a little salt and pepper and 4 tablespoons of the reserved cooking liquid. Blend until thick and smooth, adding a little more liquid if the mixture is too thick.

3 Taste and adjust seasoning, then spoon the mixture into a small bowl and fork over the top; or heap the mixture up in the centre of a large flat serving plate.

4 Serve the crudités in a shallow basket or salad bowl, or stand the bowl of dip in the centre of a large plate and arrange the crudités around the edge of the plate. If you like, drizzle 2 tablespoons oil over the top of the dip just before serving (see Did you know). Serve at room temperature or refrigerate for about 1 hour before serving and serve the dip chilled.

Cook's Notes

TIME
Cooking the dried beans takes 1¼ hours and preparing the dip then takes 30 minutes.

COOK'S TIPS
If you do not have time to soak the beans in cold water overnight, you can cut down the soaking time considerably by using hot water. Put the beans in a large saucepan, cover with cold water and bring to the boil. Drain and repeat, then remove from the heat and leave to soak in the hot water for 2 hours.

To save even more time, you could use a 425 g/15 oz can butter beans, which are pre-cooked. The whole dip can then be made within 30 minutes.

PRESSURE COOKING
Dried butter beans can be cooked in a pressure cooker. Soak and rinse as in recipe, then cook at high (H) pressure for 20 minutes.

SERVING IDEAS
The butter bean dip makes a filling salad meal for 4, or a starter for 8.

FREEZING
The dip freezes well, either in the dish from which it will be served or in a rigid container. Store for up to 3 months and allow 2 hours for defrosting at room temperature before serving.

DID YOU KNOW
Finishing off the dip with extra oil drizzled on top is usual in Middle Eastern countries, where dips and pâtés made from pulses are very popular. If you do not like too oily a taste, this can be easily omitted.

● 225 calories/950 kj per portion

SOUPS

Brussels soup

SERVES 4

500 g/1 lb Brussels sprouts
1 tablespoon vegetable oil
1 small onion, chopped
2 tablespoons medium sherry
  (optional)
700 ml/1¼ pints chicken stock
freshly grated nutmeg
salt and freshly ground black pepper

1 Heat the oil in a saucepan, add the onion and fry gently for 5 minutes until soft and lightly coloured.
2 Stir in the sherry, if using, then add the stock. Bring to the boil, add the sprouts, a pinch of nutmeg and salt and pepper to taste. Lower the heat slightly, cover and simmer for about 30 minutes.
3 Pass the soup through a sieve, or leave to cool slightly, then purée in a blender. ✳ Return the soup to the rinsed-out pan and heat through.
4 Taste and adjust seasoning, then pour immediately into warmed individual soup bowls. Sprinkle each serving with a pinch of nutmeg and serve (see Special occasion).

Cook's Notes

TIME
Preparation and cooking only take about 40 minutes.

SPECIAL OCCASION
Swirl a little single cream into the soup immediately before serving. Alternatively, serve with fried bread croûtons or crumbled crisply fried streaky bacon.

FREEZING
Cool the soup and pour into a rigid container. Seal, label and freeze for up to 4 months. To serve: reheat from frozen in a heavy-based pan, stirring frequently to prevent sticking. Taste and adjust seasoning before pouring into warmed soup bowls.

●75 calories/300 kj per portion

Cream of chestnut soup

SERVES 4-6

750 g/1½ lb fresh chestnuts
1.25 L/2 pints chicken stock

1 bay leaf
2 onions, sliced
about 150 ml/¼ pint milk
1 egg yolk
150 ml/¼ pint whipping cream
pinch of freshly grated nutmeg
salt and freshly ground black pepper
1-2 teaspoons sugar

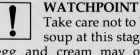

1 Nick the chestnuts with a sharp knife, then place in a saucepan and cover with cold water. Gradually bring to the boil and simmer for 10 minutes.

2 Remove the pan from the heat, then take out the chestnuts, a few at a time (see Cook's tip). Remove both the outside and inside skins.

3 Put the peeled chestnuts into a large pan together with the chicken stock, bay leaf and onions. Bring to the boil, then lower the heat, cover and simmer gently for 1½ hours.

4 Remove the bay leaf, then press the soup through a sieve or work in a blender.

5 Return the soup to the rinsed-out pan and gradually stir in enough milk to make it a smooth con-sistency. Heat through gently. Blend the egg yolk and cream in a bowl. Remove the pan from the heat and stir in the egg and cream. Reheat if necessary, but do not boil.

6 Add the nutmeg, and season to taste with salt and pepper. Add the sugar, a little at a time, to taste. Pour into warmed individual soup bowls and serve at once.

Lentil and lemon soup

SERVES 4

100 g/4 oz split red lentils
15 g/½ oz margarine or butter

2 celery stalks, chopped
1 medium onion, finely chopped
1 L/1¾ pints boiling water
2 chicken stock cubes
grated zest and juice of 1 lemon
¼ teaspoon ground cumin
   (optional)
salt and freshly ground black pepper
1 red pepper, deseeded and thinly
   sliced into rings

TO GARNISH
1 lemon, thinly sliced
snipped chives (optional)

1 Melt the margarine in a saucepan, add the celery and onion, then cover and cook gently for 4 minutes.
2 Remove the pan from the heat, then stir in the lentils and water, with the stock cubes. Add the lemon zest and juice, and the cumin, if using. Season to taste with salt and pepper. Cover and simmer over very gentle heat for 30 minutes.
3 Add the sliced pepper to the pan,
cover and cook for a further 30 minutes. Taste and adjust seasoning. ✳
4 Pour the soup into warmed serving bowls, float the lemon slices on top, then sprinkle over the chives, if using. Serve at once.

Cook's Notes

TIME
Preparation 20 minutes; cooking takes 65 minutes.

FREEZING
Cool quickly, then freeze without the lemon and chives in a rigid polythene container or freezer bag (do not use foil containers, or the acid in the soup may react against the foil). Seal, label and freeze for up to 6 months. Defrost at room temperature, then reheat until bubbling, adding a little more water if necessary.

SERVING IDEAS
Warm crusty rolls are ideal to serve with this soup. For a luxurious touch, top each serving with 1 tablespoon soured cream.

VARIATIONS
For a lentil and orange soup, use 2 small oranges instead of lemons.
If chives are unavailable, use chopped spring onion tops or parsley, if using another garnish as well as the lemon.

● 135 calories/550 kj per portion

Cream of potato soup

SERVES 4

500 g/1 lb old potatoes, diced
50 g/2 oz butter
2 large onions, finely chopped
425 ml/¾ pint milk
425 ml/¾ pint vegetable or chicken
   stock
salt and freshly ground black pepper
4 tablespoons single cream
chopped chives or parsley, to
   garnish

1 Melt the butter in a large pan and, when the foam has subsided, add the potatoes and onions and cook gently for about 5 minutes until the vegetables are soft. Stir frequently to prevent any of the potato dice or chopped onion from sticking to the bottom of the pan.
2 Add the milk and stock (see

Cook's tip), season to taste with salt and pepper and bring to the boil. Lower heat and simmer for 30 minutes, stirring occasionally, until the potatoes are tender.
3 Allow the mixture to cool a little, then work through a sieve or purée in an electric blender.

4 Return the soup to the rinsed-out pan and reheat. Taste and adjust the seasoning, if necessary, and stir in cream just before serving. ⚠ Pour into a large tureen, or ladle into individual soup bowls, garnish with the chopped chives or parsley and serve at once (see Serving ideas).

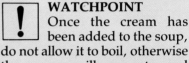

Cook's Notes

TIME
Preparing and cooking take about 1 hour.

COOK'S TIP
The flavour of this soup is vastly improved by the use of homemade stock, rather than a stock cube.

SERVING IDEAS
This filling soup makes a delicious lunch or supper dish served with slices of hot French bread.

VARIATIONS
Instead of using herbs as a garnish, sprinkle the cream of potato soup with sweet paprika or a chopped hard-boiled egg.

WATCHPOINT
Once the cream has been added to the soup, do not allow it to boil, otherwise the cream will separate and spoil the appearance of the soup.

● 305 calories/1275 kj per portion

Green bean soup

SERVES 4

**500 g/1 lb frozen cut green beans
(see Buying guide)**
700 ml/1¼ pints chicken stock
1 small onion, chopped
bay leaf
parsley sprig
**about ½ teaspoon Worcestershire
sauce**
salt and freshly ground black pepper

BEURRE MANIE (kneaded butter)
1 tablespoon plain flour
15 g/½ oz butter

TO GARNISH
**6 black olives, stoned and finely
chopped**
1 hard-boiled egg, finely chopped

1 Pour the stock into a pan, bring to boil and add the beans, onion, bay leaf and parsley. Bring back to the boil, then lower the heat, cover and simmer for about 15 minutes until the beans are soft.

2 Discard the bay leaf and parsley. Allow the soup to cool slightly, then work in a blender until smooth. Return to the rinsed-out pan and set over low heat.

3 Make the beurre manié: blend the flour and butter together with a palette knife to make a paste, then cut the paste into pea-sized pieces. Whisk the pieces into the soup and bring to the boil. Add Worcestershire sauce and salt and pepper to taste. Simmer for a further minute, then remove from heat.

4 Pour the soup into a warmed tureen or 4 individual soup bowls. Mix together the olives and egg, sprinkle over the soup and serve at once (see Serving ideas).

Cook's Notes

 TIME
This soup takes about 30 minutes to prepare.

 SERVING IDEAS
Serve hot with Melba toast or chill and garnish just before serving.

 BUYING GUIDE
Fresh green beans can be used, but you will need 600 g/1¼ lb to allow for trimming ends and side strings. Cut into pieces and cook as described. If the fresh beans are not particularly young and small, blanch them in boiling water for 2 minutes to remove any bitterness before starting.

●90 calories/375 kj per portion

Chunky soya vegetable soup

SERVES 4

100 g/4 oz soya beans, soaked in cold water overnight (see Watchpoint)
1 tablespoon vegetable oil
1 large onion, sliced
2 leeks, thickly sliced
50 g/2 oz carrots, thickly sliced
2 celery stalks, thickly sliced
50 g/2 oz turnips, cut into cubes
850 ml/1½ pints chicken stock
1 tablespoon lemon juice
2 tablespoons tomato puree
1-2 teaspoons dried mixed herbs
100 g/4 oz courgettes, thickly sliced
a few tender cabbage or spinach leaves, finely shredded or chopped
salt and freshly ground black pepper
2 teaspoons toasted sesame seeds, to garnish (optional)

1 Drain the soaked beans, then put into a saucepan and cover with fresh cold water. Bring to the boil and boil for 10 minutes, then lower the heat, cover and carefully simmer for about 1½ hours.
2 After the beans have been cooking 1 hour 20 minutes, heat the oil in a separate large saucepan. Add the sliced onion and fry very gently for 2-3 minutes until brown. Add the leeks, carrots, celery and turnips and cook, stirring, for a further 2 minutes.
3 Stir in the chicken stock, lemon juice, tomato puree and the mixed herbs.
4 Drain the beans and add to the pan. Bring to the boil, then lower the heat slightly, cover the pan and then keep gently simmering for about 1 hour.
5 Add the courgettes and cabbage and continue to cook for a further 15 minutes or until the vegetables and beans are tender. Season to taste with salt and pepper.
6 Pour into warmed individual soup bowls and garnish with a sprinkling of sesame seeds, if liked. Serve the soup at once.

Cook's Notes

TIME
Soaking the beans overnight, then 15 minutes preparation and 2¾ hours cooking time including pre-cooking the beans.

VARIATIONS
Add a 225 g/8 oz can peeled tomatoes instead of the tomato puree.

DID YOU KNOW
Soya beans look quite round in their dried form, but revert to an oval shape after soaking. They are very high in protein, making them an economical meat substitute.

ECONOMY
If possible, buy turnips with their green tops and use the tops in the soup instead of the cabbage leaves.

WATCHPOINT
Do not soak the soya beans for longer than 12 hours and always stand the bowl in a cool place.

SERVING IDEAS
Serve with small bowls of grated cheese and fried bread croutons to sprinkle over the soup.

● 220 calories/925 kj per portion

Jerusalem artichoke soup

SERVES 4-6

1 kg/2 lb Jerusalem artichokes (see Preparation)

15 g/½ oz margarine or butter
2 onions, chopped
600 ml/1 pint milk
425 ml/¾ pint chicken stock
salt and freshly ground black pepper
chopped fresh parsley

1 Melt the margarine in a large saucepan, add the onions and fry gently for 5 minutes until soft and lightly coloured.
2 Add the artichokes to the pan, together with the milk, stock and salt and pepper to taste.
3 Bring to the boil, [!] reduce the heat slightly, cover and simmer for

about 30 minutes, until the artichokes are soft.
4 Leave to cool slightly, then work in a blender or food processor until smooth. Or work through a vegetable mill.

5 Return the soup to the rinsed-out pan and reheat gently. Taste and adjust seasoning, then pour into warmed individual soup bowls. Serve at once, garnished with chopped parsley.

Sunshine soup

SERVES 6

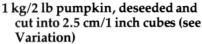
1 kg/2 lb pumpkin, deseeded and
    cut into 2.5 cm/1 inch cubes (see
    Variation)
salt
40 g/1½ oz butter
1 large onion, finely chopped
2 tomatoes, skinned and chopped
1 teaspoon snipped chives
¼ teaspoon freshly grated nutmeg
1 tablespoon desiccated coconut
600 ml/1 pint chicken stock
freshly ground black pepper
300 ml/½ pint single cream
sweet paprika, to garnish

1 Put the pumpkin into a saucepan,
add enough water just to cover and a
good pinch of salt. Bring to the boil,
then lower the heat slightly and
simmer for 15 minutes. Drain well.

2 Melt the butter in a saucepan, add
the onion and fry gently for 5
minutes until soft and lightly
coloured.
3 Add the pumpkin, tomatoes,
chives, nutmeg and coconut and fry
gently for a further 5 minutes.
4 Pour in the stock, season with salt
and pepper to taste and bring to the
boil. Lower the heat slightly, cover
and simmer for about 30 minutes.
5 Remove the pan from the heat,
allow to cool slightly, then purée in a
blender. Stir in half the cream.
6 Pour the soup into warmed soup
bowls, then swirl in the remaining
cream and sprinkle with paprika.
Serve at once.

Cook's Notes

TIME
10 minutes preparation,
55 minutes cooking,
including simmering pumpkin.

 FREEZING
Pour the purée into a
rigid container, leaving
headspace. Cool quickly, then
seal, label and freeze for up to 3
months. To serve: defrost at
room temperature for about 4
hours, then heat through and
add the cream and paprika.

VARIATION
If you are unable to buy
pumpkin, carrots are a
very good substitute and they
do not need precooking.

 SERVING IDEAS
This soup is good either
hot or cold. Serve with
crusty wholemeal bread and
chunks of Cheddar cheese for a
light supper.

●185 calories/775 kj per portion

Carrot soup with egg and rice

SERVES 4-8

750 g/1½ lb new carrots, thinly sliced
25 g/1 oz margarine or butter
600 ml/1 pint chicken stock
1 teaspoon sugar
salt and freshly ground black pepper
150 ml/¼ pint milk
75 g/3 oz cooked rice (see Cook's tips)
4 eggs at room temperature (see Cook's tips)
2 spring onions, finely chopped
150 ml/¼ pint single cream

1 Melt the margarine in a saucepan, add the carrots and fry gently for 2-3 minutes to soften slightly.
2 Add the chicken stock and sugar and season to taste with salt and pepper. Bring to the boil, then lower the heat and simmer, uncovered, for 30 minutes or until the carrots are very tender.
3 Remove the pan from the heat and allow mixture to cool slightly, then pour it into the goblet of a blender and work for a few seconds until smooth. Return the purée to the rinsed-out pan and stir in the milk and the cooked rice. Taste and adjust the seasoning, if necessary.
4 Heat the soup gently until hot but not boiling, then break in the eggs and poach them for about 8 minutes or until they are firm enough to be lifted out with a slotted spoon.
5 Spoon an egg into each of 4 warmed soup bowls and pour over the soup. Sprinkle over the spring onions, swirl in the cream and serve the soup at once.

TIME
Preparation takes 15 minutes, cooking takes about 50 minutes.

SERVING IDEAS
This is a fairly substantial soup, so serve with a light accompaniment such as Melba toast or a selection of crispbreads.

COOK'S TIPS
If cooking raw rice for this dish, you will need 25 g/1 oz to provide 75 g/3 oz of cooked rice.
Remove the eggs from the refrigerator 1 hour before using: cold eggs will require a longer time to set.

●155 calories/650 kj per portion

Creamy mushroom soup

SERVES 4

 250 g/9 oz button mushrooms (see
    Buying guide)
 50 g/2 oz butter
2 tablespoons plain flour
600 ml/1 pint milk
75 g/3 oz full-fat soft
    cheese with chives
2 teaspoons lemon juice
salt and freshly ground black pepper
1 tablespoon snipped chives, to
    garnish

1 Finely chop the mushrooms, reserving 2-3 whole ones for the garnish. Melt half the butter in a frying-pan. Add the chopped mushrooms and fry gently for about 5 minutes until soft. Set aside.
2 Melt the remaining butter in a large saucepan, sprinkle in flour and stir over low heat for 1-2 minutes until it is straw-coloured. Remove from the heat and gradually stir in milk. Return to the heat and simmer, stirring, until the mixture is thick and smooth.
3 Remove from the heat, add the cheese a little at a time and stir until melted. Stir in the mushrooms, their juices and the lemon juice. Season to taste. Return to heat and simmer for 2-3 minutes.
4 Pour into 4 warmed soup bowls. Float a few slices of mushrooms on top of each serving. Sprinkle lightly with chives and serve at once.

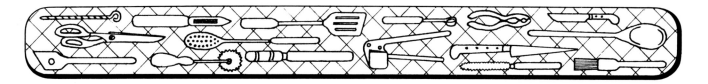

Chilled pea and bean soup

SERVES 4

750 g/1½ lb peas, shelled, and 6 of
    the best pods reserved (see
    Cook's tip)
500 g/l lb broad beans, shelled
25 g/1 oz margarine or butter
1 large onion, finely chopped
850 ml/1½ pints chicken stock
1 sprig fresh mint
salt and freshly ground black pepper
150 ml/¼ pint natural yoghurt
¼ teaspoon curry paste
1 clove garlic, crushed (optional)
4 small mint sprigs, to garnish

1 Melt the margarine in a frying-
pan. Add the onion and fry gently
for 5 minutes until soft and lightly
coloured.
2 Pour in the stock and bring to the
boil, then add the peas, reserved
pods, beans, mint sprig and salt and
pepper to taste. Lower the heat,
cover and simmer for 20 minutes.
3 Remove the pods and mint sprig,
leave the soup to cool slightly, then
work in a blender or food processor
until smooth. Or work through the
medium blade of a vegetable mill.
Leave until completely cold.
4 Mix the yoghurt in a bowl with
the curry paste and garlic, if using,
then beat in about 6 tablespoons of
the soup until smooth. Stir the

yoghurt mixture into the soup,
making sure that it is well mixed in.
Refrigerate for at least 30 minutes.

5 To serve: pour the soup into 4
chilled individual soup bowls and
float a mint sprig on top of each.

Cook's Notes

TIME
Preparation and cook-
ing take 70 minutes, but
allow extra time for cooling and
chilling.

VARIATIONS
Frozen peas and beans
may be used. In this
case, you will need 350 g/12 oz
peas and 225 g/8 oz beans. Do
not defrost them before
cooking.

To serve the soup hot, make
up to the end of stage 3, but do
not cool. Pour into a saucepan,
heat gently without boiling,
then stir in the yoghurt mixture.
Garnish with chopped mint.

FREEZING
Pour the cooled soup in
to a rigid container,
seal, label and freeze for 6-8
weeks. To serve: defrost for 6-8
hours in the refrigerator,

stirring occasionally. If too
thick, stir in a little cold milk.

COOK'S TIP
Pea pods have a
deliciously strong pea
taste. They are too fibrous and
stringy to be included in a soup,
but if added during the first part
of cooking and then removed,
they will add extra flavour.

● 150 calories/625 kj per portion

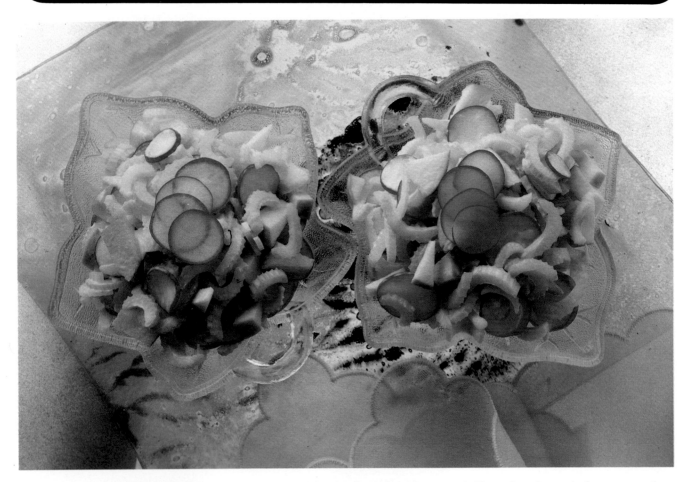

Celery and radish salad

SERVES 4

1 crisp dessert apple
1 small head celery, finely chopped
250 g/9 oz radishes, thinly sliced
   (see Buying guide)
salt and freshly ground black pepper

DRESSING
50 g/2 oz curd cheese
4 tablespoons soured cream
2 tablespoons cider vinegar
1 teaspoon light soft brown sugar
1 clove garlic, crushed (optional)

1 Make the dressing: put the curd cheese into a large bowl and beat until softened. Gradually beat in the soured cream and vinegar, then the sugar and garlic, if using.

2 Core and finely chop (but do not peel) the apple. Add to the dressing with the celery and half the radishes and mix well, adding salt and pepper to taste.

3 Transfer the salad to a serving bowl and arrange the remaining radishes on top in an attractive pattern. Serve as soon as possible, at room temperature.

Cook's Notes

TIME
Preparation takes 25 minutes.

VARIATIONS
Cream cheese may be used instead of curd cheese, and natural yoghurt instead of soured cream.

BUYING GUIDE
The average bunch of radishes available from greengrocers weighs about 100 g/4 oz, so you will need 2 bunches for this recipe.

SERVING IDEAS
This salad goes perfectly with a quiche for lunch, or with cold chicken or turkey. It also makes an attractive starter salad as shown in the photograph, served with Melba toast and butter.

DID YOU KNOW
Celery is rich in mineral salts, vitamins and iron, and is one of the best vegetables for slimmers.

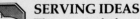
●70 calories/300 kj per portion

Cauliflower salad with sultanas

SERVES 6

1 cauliflower, broken into florets
500 g/1 lb small button onions (see Preparation)
salt
225 ml/8 fl oz white wine
125 ml/4 fl oz water
5 tablespoons olive oil
2 tablespoons wine vinegar
3 tomatoes, skinned, deseeded and chopped
3 tablespoons sultanas
1 teaspoon Demerara sugar
½ teaspoon dried thyme
½ teaspoon ground coriander
freshly ground black pepper

1 Bring 2 pans of salted water to the boil and blanch the cauliflower florets and onions separately for 5 minutes. Drain both together in a colander, then rinse under cold running water to refresh. Drain the vegetables again.

2 Put the remaining ingredients in a large pan with salt to taste and a generous sprinkling of black pepper. Stir well to mix, bring to the boil and boil for 5 minutes.

3 Lower the heat, add the cauliflower and onions and simmer for a further 8 minutes, turning the vegetables occasionally. ⚠

4 Using a slotted spoon, transfer the vegetables to a serving dish. Bring the sauce left in the pan to the boil and boil for 5 minutes to reduce slightly. Pour the sauce over the vegetables and leave until cold. Serve at room temperature.

Cook's Notes

TIME
Preparation 10 minutes, cooking about 20 minutes, but allow time for cooling the salad before serving.

WATCHPOINT
Be careful not to overcook the cauliflower florets. Test them with the point of a knife during cooking to check that they are still crisp.

PREPARATION
Cut off the ends of the onions and remove the skins: keep the onions whole.

SERVING IDEAS
This is an ideal dish for a starter as it can be prepared in advance. Serve with warm French bread.

● 175 calories/725 kj per portion

Crunchy mixed salad

SERVES 4

¼ large cucumber
275 g/10 oz beansprouts (see Buying guide)
175 g/6 oz green grapes
1 small onion, thinly sliced

DRESSING

50 g/2 oz Lancashire cheese
2 tablespoons vegetable oil
1 tablespoon white wine vinegar
½ teaspoon French mustard
¼ teaspoon sugar
salt and freshly ground black pepper

1 Peel the cucumber, cut it in half lengthways, then scoop out the seeds (see Preparation and Cook's tip). Cut into matchstick strips about 5 cm/2 inches long and pat dry on absorbent paper.
2 Wash the beansprouts under cold running water, trim off any roots and drain well on absorbent paper.

3 Cut the grapes in half, or quarter them if large, and remove the pips with the point of a sharp knife.
4 Make the dressing: crumble the cheese finely into a large bowl. Whisk in the oil, vinegar, mustard, sugar and salt and pepper to taste.

5 Add the cucumber, beansprouts, onion and grapes to the dressing and toss well to combine. Cover and leave to stand for 10 minutes to allow the flavours to blend.
6 Just before serving, toss the salad to gather up the juices.

Cook's Notes

 TIME
Preparation takes about 40 minutes, including standing time.

 PREPARATION
To remove the seeds from the cucumber:

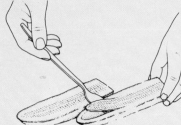

Scoop out the seeds from each half with a teaspoon.

 SERVING IDEAS
The salad goes well with canned fish such as pilchards, tuna or mackerel.

BUYING GUIDE
Beansprouts are often sold in supermarkets in 275 g/10 oz packets. Eat beansprouts within 2 days of buying.

 COOK'S TIP
Removing the cucumber seeds helps to reduce the moisture which can dilute salad dressing.

● 155 calories/650 kj per portion

Waldorf salad

SERVES 4

500 g/1 lb crisp dessert apples (see
    Buying guide)
2 tablespoons lemon juice
1 teaspoon sugar
150 ml/¼ pint thick bottled
    mayonnaise
½ head of celery, chopped
50 g/2 oz shelled walnuts, chopped
    (see Economy)
1 round lettuce, leaves separated
    (optional)

1 Quarter and core the apples but
do not peel them, then cut into neat
dice and put into a bowl. Add the
lemon juice and toss well to prevent
discoloration.

2 Stir in the sugar and 1 tablespoon
of the mayonnaise. Mix until the
apple is well coated, then leave in a
cool place until ready to serve.

3 Just before serving, add the
remaining mayonnaise, celery and
walnuts and toss well together.

4 Place the prepared apple mixture
in a bowl lined, if liked, with
lettuce leaves. Serve at once.

Cook's Notes

TIME
15 minutes advance
preparation, then 5
minutes preparation before
serving.

BUYING GUIDE
To add colour to the
salad, select red-
skinned apples or buy half red
and half green.

SERVING IDEAS
Serve as an accompani-
ment to cold meats or as
part of a buffet selection. For a
more decorative finish, add a
border of thinly-sliced apples
sprinkled with lemon juice, and
garnish with a few whole
walnuts.

DID YOU KNOW
This salad is so-called
because it was first
created by the chef of the
Waldorf-Astoria Hotel in New
York City.

ECONOMY
Buy packets of broken
walnuts or walnut
pieces; they are always less
expensive than whole nuts.

SPECIAL OCCASION
Replace half the mayon-
naise with lightly
whipped cream and gently fold
together until blended. If liked,
add a little tomato purée.

●355 calories/1475 kj per portion

Piquant courgette salad

SERVES 4

4 large courgettes, trimmed
1 small red pepper, deseeded and
    finely chopped
1-2 tablespoons drained capers
1 tablespoon finely chopped fresh
    parsley
1 lettuce, leaves separated, to serve

DRESSING
2 tablespoons vegetable oil
1 tablespoon lemon juice
pinch of caster sugar
pinch of mustard powder
salt and freshly ground black pepper

1 Quarter the courgettes lengthways, then cut them into 1 cm/½

inch slices. Put them in a bowl with
the red pepper, capers and parsley
and mix together with a metal spoon
(see Cook's tips).
2 Put the dressing ingredients in a
small bowl with salt and pepper to
taste, and beat together with a fork.
Pour the dressing over the courgette

Cook's Notes

TIME
Preparation of this
simple salad takes 15-20
minutes.

COOK'S TIPS
Use a metal rather than
a wooden spoon to help
prevent the courgette slices
from breaking up.
    The courgette mixture and
dressing can be stirred together

as much as 1 hour before
serving. Stir the mixture again
and spoon it into the lettuce-
lined bowls at the last minute.

SERVING IDEAS
Serve as a light starter,
or as an accompaniment
to plainly cooked hot meat or
fish dishes.

●90 calories/375 kj per portion

mixture and stir with a metal spoon
until evenly coated.
3 To serve: line 4 individual salad
bowls with the lettuce leaves, then
pile the courgette mixture in the
centre of each lettuce-lined bowl
just before the salads are to be
served (see Cook's tips).

Tomato and Mozzarella salad

SERVES 6

 500 g/1 lb firm ripe tomatoes, cut
    into 5 mm/¼ inch slices
2 tablespoons chopped fresh
    parsley
2 tablespoons chopped fresh basil
    or ½ teaspoon dried basil
pinch of sugar
salt and freshly ground black pepper
175 g/6 oz Mozzarella cheese, cut
    into 5 mm/¼ inch slices (see Did
    you know)
3 tablespoons black olives
4 tablespoons olive oil

1 Arrange the tomato slices in an
overlapping circular pattern around
a flat serving dish. Sprinkle over the
herbs and sugar and season with
salt and pepper to taste. Cover the
dish loosely with foil and chill in the
refrigerator for 30 minutes.
2 Remove the foil and arrange the
cheese slices in the centre of the
tomatoes. Scatter the olives over.
3 Just before serving, pour over the
olive oil and, using a fork, gently lift
up the tomato slices so that the oil
drains through to them. Serve at
once.

Cook's Notes

TIME
Total preparation and
chilling time is 45
minutes.

DID YOU KNOW
 Mozzarella cheese
comes from southern
Italy. Originally made from
buffalo milk, but nowadays
usually made with cow's milk, it
is mild and moist, with a very
definite flavour. It is available
from most delicatessens.

SERVING IDEAS
This classic Italian
tomato salad, which is
dressed with oil alone, and not
the more usual oil and vinegar
dressing, makes a good accompaniment to roast and grilled
meats. Serve it with pork chops
or steak or, for a change, with
roast or grilled chicken. Well
chilled, it also makes a refreshing,
easy-to-prepare first course.

● 205 calories/850 kj per portion

Chinese beansprout salad

SERVES 4

 ½ **large cucumber, peeled**
250 g/9 oz beansprouts
 50 g/2 oz spring greens, stalks
removed and finely shredded
50 g/2 oz roasted peanuts
salt and freshly ground black pepper

DRESSING
50 g/2 oz Danish Blue cheese
6 tablespoons vegetable oil
2 tablespoons wine vinegar
a little milk (optional)

1 Cut the cucumber into 4 cm/1½ inch lengths, then cut these lengthways into thin sticks. Place in a salad bowl with the beansprouts.
2 Add the spring greens and mix all the vegetables together.
3 Make the dressing: crumble the blue cheese into a bowl and mash with a fork. Add the oil a little at a time, mixing it into the cheese with the fork to form a paste. Mix in the vinegar and add a little milk if the mixture seems too thick for a

dressing (see Cook's tips).
4 Just before serving, add the peanuts to the salad and pour over the dressing. Toss until all the ingredients are thoroughly coated in the dressing, then add salt and pepper to taste. Serve at once while the beansprouts and nuts are crunchy.

Cook's Notes

TIME
Preparation takes about 20 minutes.

VARIATIONS
Instead of Danish Blue, try one of the other blue cheeses such as Dolcelatte, Gorgonzola or Stilton.

SERVING IDEAS
Serve as a side dish with beef casseroles, hot roast lamb or grilled white fish.
Alternatively, serve as a first course in individual bowls, topped with garlic-flavoured croûtons (small cubes of bread fried in oil to which 2 crushed garlic cloves have been added).

COOK'S TIPS
If you have a blender or food processor, put all the ingredients in the machine together and work until smooth.
You can prepare the salad ingredients and dressing separately, several hours in advance of serving. Store in covered plastic containers in the refrigerator and combine together with the peanuts just before serving.

SPECIAL OCCASION
If you are feeling extravagant, for a dinner party or special occasion, use the French blue cheese, Roquefort, available from delicatessens and good supermarkets.

 WATCHPOINT
Add the peanuts at the last minute, just before you dress the salad, so that they do not lose their crunchiness.

●345 calories/1425 kj per portion

Crisp and crunchy salad

SERVES 4

175 g/6 oz white cabbage, coarsely
   shredded
175 g/6 oz red cabbage, finely
   shredded
1 large carrot, finely grated
2 celery stalks, chopped
1 small green pepper, deseeded and
   finely chopped
100 g/4 oz fresh beansprouts
   (optional, see Buying guide)
100 g/4 oz salted peanuts

DRESSING

100 g/4 oz Stilton cheese
150 ml/¼ pint olive or sunflower oil
3 tablespoons wine vinegar
½ teaspoon made English mustard
2 tablespoons snipped chives
salt and freshly ground black pepper

1 Put the cabbage in a large salad
bowl (use a glass one, if possible)
with the carrot, celery, green pepper
and beansprouts, if using.

2 Make the dressing: using a fork,
mash the Stilton in a small bowl.
When it is smooth, add the olive oil
a little at a time, and continue
mixing until creamy.
3 Add the vinegar and mix in until
combined, then stir in the mustard

and chives, and salt and pepper to
taste.
4 Just before serving, add the
peanuts to the salad in the bowl,
then pour over the dressing and stir
well to mix. ⚠ Serve as soon as
possible.

Cook's Notes

TIME
This salad takes 30
minutes to prepare.

COOK'S TIP
Try to shred the 2 cab-
bages to different thick-
nesses. The different textures
add interest to the salad.

WATCHPOINT
Do not add the peanuts
until just before you
mix in the dressing otherwise
they will become soft.

VARIATIONS
Add or subtract the in-
gredients according to
what you have available. Keep a
balance of colours and crisp
ingredients. Use another blue
cheese such as Danish Blue or
Dolcelatte instead of the Stilton.

SERVING IDEAS
Serve as a main course
for a healthy lunch—
there is plenty of protein in the
nuts and cheese to balance all
the vegetables.

BUYING GUIDE
Buy fresh beansprouts,
if they are available,
and use the same day. Canned
beansprouts are unsuitable as
they are not crisp.

● 600 calories/2500 kj per portion

Pea and bean salad

SERVES 4

350 g/12 oz peas (weighed in the
 pod), shelled, or 100 g/4 oz frozen
 peas
75 g/3 oz dried red kidney beans,
 soaked overnight, or 215 g/7½ oz
 can red kidney beans
500 g/1 lb broad beans (weighed in
 the pod), shelled, or 100 g/4 oz
 frozen broad beans
salt
1 small red pepper, deseeded and
 finely chopped
1 small green pepper, deseeded and
 finely chopped
1 bunch spring onions, finely
 chopped
2 tablespoons chopped parsley

FRENCH DRESSING
3 tablespoons olive oil
1 tablespoon lemon juice
1 tablespoon white wine or wine
 vinegar
1 teaspoon mild French mustard
1 teaspoon caster sugar
freshly ground black pepper

1 Drain the soaked kidney beans,
cook in boiling water for about 1
hour until tender (see Cook's tips),
then drain and cool slightly. If using
canned beans, drain off the liquid
from the can, then rinse the beans
thoroughly under cold running
water.
2 Cook the fresh broad beans and
peas in separate pans of boiling
salted water until just tender (5-7
minutes). If using frozen beans and
peas, cook according to packet
directions. Drain and cool slightly.
3 Mix together the beans, peas, red
and green peppers, spring onions
and chopped parsley in a bowl.
4 To make the French dressing:
place all the ingredients in a screw-
top jar with salt and pepper to taste.
Replace the lid firmly and shake well
to mix.
5 Pour the French dressing over the
bean mixture and toss well until all
the vegetables are thoroughly
coated. Taste and adjust seasoning.
Cover the bowl with cling film, then
refrigerate for about 2 hours. Transfer to a salad bowl before serving.

Cook's Notes

TIME
Soak red kidney beans
overnight, then cook for
1 hour. Preparation of the other
vegetables 20-30 minutes, and
cooking about 5-7 minutes.
Chill salad for at least 2 hours.

COOK'S TIPS
The kidney beans *must*
boil vigorously for a
good 10 minutes, and then
simmer for the rest of the
cooking time. Do not add salt to
the cooking water; it toughens
the skins.

SERVING IDEAS
This makes a delicious
snack lunch on its own
with wholemeal rolls. It goes
well with all cold meat,
particularly beef, and makes a
colourful addition to a buffet
spread. Serve it, too, as part of a
vegetarian meal.

PRESSURE COOKING
The kidney beans will
cook in 10 minutes in a
pressure cooker at high pressure.

●195 calories/800 kj per portion

Avocado and grapefruit salad

SERVES 4

2 small avocados
1 small grapefruit

2 dessert apples
1 small lettuce, separated into leaves

DRESSING
1 tablespoon clear honey
2 tablespoons cider vinegar
6 tablespoons olive oil
salt and freshly ground black pepper

1 To make the dressing: mix together the honey, vinegar and olive oil in a bowl. Whisk with a fork until the dressing is thick and all the ingredients are thoroughly combined. Season to taste.
2 Peel the grapefruit. Hold it over a bowl to catch the juice and, using a

small, sharp knife, trim away any white pith. Divide the grapefruit into segments and remove the pips. Stir the segments into the dressing.
3 Halve the avocados lengthways, then remove the stones and peel. Slice the flesh and add immediately

to the dressing. Toss thoroughly.
4 Quarter and core the apples. Slice them thinly and toss them in the dressing. Taste and adjust seasoning. Arrange the lettuce leaves in a salad bowl, pile the salad in the centre and serve at once.

Brussels sprouts and date salad

SERVES 6
500 g/1 lb Brussels sprouts
250 g/9 oz carrots, grated
100 g/4 oz stoned dates, chopped

DRESSING
150 g/5 oz natural yoghurt, chilled
2 tablespoons mayonnaise
2 tablespoons fresh orange juice
salt and freshly ground black pepper
2 tablespoons snipped chives

TO SERVE
2 heads chicory or 1 lettuce heart, trimmed and separated into leaves
25 g/1 oz walnut halves (optional)

1 Trim the sprouts, discarding any tough or discoloured outer leaves. Wash and drain them thoroughly, tossing them in a clean tea-towel or on absorbent paper.
2 Shred the sprouts with a sharp knife, then place in a large mixing bowl with the grated carrots and dates. Mix well to combine.
3 To make the dressing: beat together the yoghurt, mayonnaise and orange juice. Add salt and pepper to taste, then stir in the chives.
4 Pour the dressing over the vegetables and mix well. Taste and adjust seasoning. Cover and refrigerate for about 1 hour, or longer.
5 To serve: line a deep serving bowl with the chicory or lettuce leaves, then spoon the chilled salad into the centre, piling it up in a mound. Garnish with the walnuts, if using.

Cook's Notes

TIME
45 minutes preparation, plus at least 1 hour chilling.

SERVING IDEAS
This unusual salad has a slightly 'tangy' flavour, and makes a refreshing first course. It is also a good accompaniment to mixed cold meats, continental sausages, or cold meat pies.

VARIATIONS
Use 2 tablespoons each seedless raisins and sultanas instead of the dates.

● 145 calories/600 kj per portion

Gazpacho salad

SERVES 4

350 g/12 oz tomatoes, skinned and thinly sliced
½ large cucumber, peeled and thinly sliced
1 medium onion, thinly sliced
1 medium red pepper, deseeded and thinly sliced
1 medium green pepper, deseeded and thinly sliced
salt, freshly ground black pepper and sugar
10 tablespoons white or brown breadcrumbs
8 tablespoons French dressing (see Cook's tips)

TO SERVE
10 black olives
1 tablespoon chopped parsley

1 Prepare the tomatoes, cucumber, onion and peppers as indicated above. Plunge the peppers in boiling water for 30 seconds (to blanch), and then immerse them immediately in cold water (to refresh them).

2 In a glass bowl, put a layer of cucumber, followed by a layer of tomatoes and a sprinkling of sugar, a layer of onion and a layer of mixed red and green peppers. Season with salt and pepper and sprinkle over 2 tablespoons breadcrumbs and 2 tablespoons French dressing.

3 Continue these layers, finishing with a layer of 4 tablespoons breadcrumbs. Cover these with French dressing so that they are well soaked, then cover the bowl with cling film and refrigerate for 2-3 hours before serving.

---Cook's Notes---

TIME
The preparation of the salad should take no longer than 20 minutes, but remember you should allow 2-3 hours chilling time in the refrigerator before the gazpacho salad is ready to serve.

COOK'S TIPS
This is a salad version of the better known gazpacho soup. A French dressing well-flavoured with garlic is really essential. Mix together 6 tablespoons olive oil and 2 tablespoons wine vinegar (or lemon juice) and season with freshly ground black pepper. Crush a garlic clove with salt using the blade of a small knife, and blend it into the dressing. (Use only half a clove if your family prefers a mild garlic flavour.) Vegetables are blanched for a variety of reasons – to soften them before further cooking, to retain colour, to get rid of a bitter flavour. Refreshing immediately in cold water stops any further cooking.

SERVING IDEAS
The salad goes particularly well with plain grilled or barbecued meat. It is also a good accompaniment to simple, fried hamburgers.

● 185 calories/775 kj per portion

Leek and potato pie

SERVES 4
500 g/1 lb leeks
salt
750 g/1½ lb potatoes
40 g/1½ oz margarine or butter
25 g/1 oz plain flour
300 ml/½ pint warm milk
pinch of freshly grated nutmeg
freshly ground black pepper
50 g/2 oz Cheddar cheese, grated
margarine or butter, for greasing

1 Trim the leeks, discarding most of the dark green part (see Economy). Slice thickly and wash under cold running water until completely clean. Cook in boiling salted water for 8-10 minutes or until almost tender. Drain thoroughly, reserving the stock.
2 At the same time, cook the potatoes in boiling salted water for about 20-25 minutes or until tender. Drain.
3 While the vegetables are cooking, make the sauce: melt 25 g/1 oz margarine gently in a small saucepan, sprinkle in the flour and stir over low heat for 2 minutes until straw-coloured. Remove from the heat and gradually stir in all but 2 tablespoons of the milk, then return to the heat and simmer, stirring, until thick and smooth. Measure out 150 ml/¼ pint of the leek stock (see Economy); stir gradually into white sauce. Bring back to the boil, stirring constantly, then add the nutmeg and salt and pepper to taste. Remove the pan from the heat.
4 Heat the oven to 190C/375F/Gas 5.
5 Slice one-third of the potatoes, stir them gently into the leeks and turn into the base of a greased 1 L/2 pint ovenproof dish. Pour on the sauce; carefully turn vegetables with a fork, to coat thoroughly.
6 Add remaining margarine and milk to the rest of the potatoes, season with pepper, then mash them until smooth. Beat in half the

cheese with a wooden spoon. Taste and adjust seasoning.
7 Spread the mashed potato over the vegetables, then sprinkle on the

rest of the cheese. Stand the dish on a baking sheet and bake in the oven for 20-25 minutes, or until the topping is golden brown. Serve hot.

Cook's Notes

TIME
Preparation 35-45 minutes, cooking in the oven 20-25 minutes.

SERVING IDEAS
Serve with fried or boiled bacon or any cold cooked meat.

ECONOMY
Reserve the green parts of the leeks and remaining leek stock and use for soup.
Leeks give excellent flavour to a vegetable soup. Remember to wash trimmings thoroughly.

●390 calories/1625 kj per portion

Vegetable pie

SERVES 4-6

100 g/4 oz plain flour
salt
50 g/2 oz margarine or butter, diced
50 g/2 oz Cheddar cheese, grated
about 4 teaspoons chilled water
beaten egg or milk, for glazing

FILLING
500 g/1 lb potatoes, diced
3 carrots, sliced
3 leeks, cut into 1 cm/½ inch slices
1 tablespoon chopped fresh parsley
freshly ground black pepper
25 g/1 oz margarine or butter
25 g/1 oz plain flour
300 ml/½ pint vegetable or chicken
   stock

1 Make the pastry: sift the flour and a pinch of salt into a bowl. Add the margarine and rub it into the flour with your fingertips until the mixture resembles fine crumbs.
2 Mix in the grated cheese and just enough cold water to draw the mixture together to a firm dough. Wrap in cling film and refrigerate for 30 minutes.
3 Heat the oven to 180C/350F/Gas 4. Meanwhile, make the filling: cook the potatoes and carrots in boiling salted water for 10 minutes. Drain thoroughly, then place in an 850 ml/ 1½ pint pie dish with the leeks, mixing them well together. Sprinkle with the parsley and salt and pepper to taste. Set aside.
4 Melt the margarine in a clean saucepan, sprinkle in the flour and stir over low heat for 1-2 minutes until straw-coloured. Gradually stir in the stock, then bring to the boil and simmer, stirring, until thick and smooth. Pour over the vegetables.
5 Roll out the pastry on a floured surface to a shape slightly larger than the top of the pie dish. Cut off a long strip of pastry all around the edge. Reserve this and other trimmings. Brush the rim of the pie dish with water, then press the narrow strip of pastry all around the rim. Brush the strip with a little more water, then place the large piece of pastry on top. Press to seal, then trim, knock up and flute the edge of the pie.
6 Make decorations from the trimmings, brush the undersides with water and place on top of the pie. Brush the pastry lid with a little beaten egg, and make a hole in the centre. Bake in the oven for 40-45 minutes until the pastry is golden brown and the vegetables are tender. Serve at once.

Cook's Notes

TIME
1½ hours preparation and cooking time, including chilling the cheese shortcrust pastry.

VARIATIONS
The vegetables may be replaced by whatever is in season.
   Instead of the cheese pastry crust, use a 215 g/7½ oz packet of frozen puff pastry.

●425 calories/1775 kj per portion

Courgette bake

SERVES 4-6

500 g/1 lb small courgettes, cut into
   2.5 cm/1 inch lengths (see Buying
   guide)
25 g/1 oz margarine or butter
1 onion, chopped
salt
3 eggs, beaten
75 g/3 oz Cheddar cheese, grated
150 ml/¼ pint milk
2 tablespoons chopped fresh
   parsley
good pinch of freshly grated
   nutmeg
freshly ground black pepper
margarine, for greasing

1 Heat the oven to 180C/350F/Gas 4
and grease a 22 cm/8½ inch flan
dish, about 3 cm/1½ inch deep,
with the margarine.

2 Melt the margarine in a frying-
pan, add the onion and fry gently for
10 minutes until browned. Remove
the pan from the heat and cool.
3 Meanwhile, bring a saucepan of
lightly salted water to the boil. Add
the courgettes and simmer for 5
minutes. Drain thoroughly and set
aside.
4 Mix the eggs, cheese, milk,
parsley and nutmeg together in a

bowl. Season to taste with salt and
pepper then stir in the onion.
5 Stand the pieces of courgette
upright in the flan dish, then carefully spoon in the egg mixture,
making sure it is evenly distributed.
6 Bake the dish in the oven for
about 40 minutes until it is set and
the top is golden brown. Leave to
stand for about 10 minutes before
serving, cut into wedges.

Cook's Notes

TIME
The bake takes 20 min-
utes to prepare and 40
minutes to cook.

VARIATION
Chervil may be used
instead of parsley.

SERVING IDEAS
This custard makes
an unusual vegetable

accompaniment to plainly
grilled meat. You may find that
because of the large amount of
courgettes used you will not
need an additional vegetable.

BUYING GUIDE
Buy the smallest cour-
gettes you can find—
there should be 6-9 to 500 g/1 lb.

● 230 calories/975 kj per portion

Vegetable crumble

SERVES 4

2 leeks, cut into 1 cm/½ inch slices (see Preparation)
2 tablespoons olive oil or sunflower oil
2 large carrots, thickly sliced
1 small red pepper, deseeded and diced
500 g/1 lb courgettes, cut into 1 cm/½ inch slices
400 g/14 oz can tomatoes
½ teaspoon dried basil
salt and freshly ground black pepper
25-50 g/1-2 oz pine nuts (see Buying guide)
2 teaspoons wine vinegar

CRUMBLE TOPPING
100 g/4 oz plain or wholewheat flour
¼ teaspoon salt
40 g/1½ oz butter, diced
65 g/2½ oz fresh Parmesan cheese, grated (see Buying guide)

1 Heat the oil in a large saucepan, add the leeks and carrots and fry over moderate heat for 5 minutes, stirring. Add the red pepper and fry for 5 minutes, then add courgettes and fry for a further 5 minutes, stirring constantly.

2 Add the tomatoes and their juices to the pan with the basil and salt and pepper to taste. Bring to the boil, then lower the heat, cover and simmer for 10 minutes.

3 Meanwhile, heat the oven to 200C/400F/Gas 6 and make the crumble: sift the flour and salt into a bowl. Add the butter and rub into the flour with the fingertips until the mixture resembles fine breadcrumbs. Stir in 50 g/2 oz of the Parmesan, and add pepper to taste.

4 Add the pine nuts and vinegar to vegetables, then transfer to a 1.5 L/ 2½ pint casserole. Sprinkle the crumble evenly over vegetables, then top with remaining Parmesan.

5 Bake in the oven for about 40 minutes, until golden.

Cook's Notes

TIME
Preparation time 30-40 minutes, then about 40 minutes baking.

PREPARATION
Wash the leeks, then slice them and put into a colander. Rinse again under cold running water, to remove any remaining grit and dirt.

BUYING GUIDE
Pine nuts are available from health food stores and Italian food shops, but nibbed almonds may be used.
For the best flavour, buy a whole piece of Parmesan and grate it yourself at home when needed. Tightly wrapped in cling film or foil it will keep its flavour for several weeks in the refrigerator. Special graters for this hard cheese can be bought from some kitchen and hardware shops.
If you do not want to go to the trouble of grating the cheese yourself, buy freshly grated Parmesan from an Italian delicatessen; do not buy packets or tubs of grated Parmesan from a supermarket for this dish.

●390 calories/1625 kj per portion

Vegetable fried rice

SERVES 4

250 g/9 oz long-grain rice
salt
250 g/9 oz carrots, diced
1 parsnip, diced
1 small turnip, diced
2 tablespoons vegetable oil
1 large onion, chopped
1 clove garlic, crushed (optional)
50 g/2 oz button mushrooms, sliced
2 large tomatoes, skinned and sliced
50 g/2 oz frozen peas, defrosted
freshly ground black pepper
2 eggs, lightly beaten
1 tablespoon chopped fresh parsley
grated Parmesan cheese, to serve

1 Bring a large saucepan of salted water to the boil, add the rice and cover. Lower the heat and simmer for 10 minutes, or until the rice is just tender.

2 Meanwhile, bring another pan of salted water to the boil. Add the carrots, parsnip and turnip and cover. Lower the heat and cook for about 8-10 minutes, or until all the

vegetables are barely tender.

3 Drain the cooked root vegetables and reserve. Drain the rice in a colander and rinse well under hot running water to separate the grains. Drain again.

4 Heat the oil in a large non-stick saucepan, add the onion and garlic, if using, and fry gently for 5 minutes, until the onion is soft and lightly coloured.

5 Add the drained root vegetables

to the pan, together with the mushrooms, tomatoes, peas and rice. Stir well and season to taste with salt and plenty of pepper. Cover the pan and cook over very low heat for 10 minutes. ✳

6 Stir in the eggs and gently turn the mixture so that the egg cooks. Remove from the heat and turn into a warmed serving dish. Garnish with the parsley and serve at once with the Parmesan cheese.

Potato pizza

SERVES 4

125 g/4 oz self-raising flour
salt
50 g/2 oz margarine or butter
250 g/9 oz cold mashed potatoes
vegetable oil, for greasing

TOPPING
1 tablespoon vegetable oil
1 large onion, sliced
1 red pepper, deseeded and sliced
1 clove garlic, crushed (optional)
125 g/4 oz button mushrooms,
  sliced
pinch of oregano
2 teaspoons malt vinegar
freshly ground black pepper
1 tablespoon tomato purée
175 g/6 oz Cheddar cheese, sliced

1 Heat the oven to 230C/450F/Gas 8.

Oil a large baking sheet.
2 Make the base: sift the flour and salt into a large bowl. Add the margarine and rub it in with your fingertips until the mixture resembles breadcrumbs, then add the mashed potatoes and knead the mixture lightly until smooth.
3 Press the dough into a 25 cm/10 inch round and refrigerate.
4 Meanwhile, make the topping: heat the oil in a frying-pan, add the onion, red pepper and garlic, if using, and fry gently for 5 minutes or until the onion is soft and lightly coloured. Remove the pan from the heat and stir in the mushrooms, oregano, vinegar and salt and pepper to taste.
5 Place the potato base on the baking sheet and spread the tomato purée over it, then top with the onion mixture. Arrange the cheese slices over the top.
6 Bake in the oven for 25-30 minutes or until the base is firm and the cheese is golden brown.

Cook's Notes

TIME
Preparation takes about 40 minutes, including preparing the potatoes; allow time for chilling. Cooking takes 25-30 minutes.

SERVING IDEAS
This delicious pizza makes an excellent supper dish served with a green salad and French bread.

VARIATIONS
For a more Italian flavour, top the cheese with anchovy fillets, slices of salami and black olives, then drizzle with a little olive oil to prevent drying out. Mozzarella cheese can be used instead of Cheddar.

● 500 calories/2090 kj per portion

Red summer flan

250 g/9 oz red peppers, deseeded
  and cut into thin slices
350 g/12 oz tomatoes, thinly sliced
2 tablespoons vegetable oil
4 cloves garlic, crushed
25 g/1 oz fresh white breadcrumbs
½ teaspoon dried basil
salt and freshly ground black pepper
1 teaspoon sugar

PASTRY
175 g/6 oz plain flour
pinch of salt
50 g/2 oz margarine, diced
25 g/1 oz lard, diced
50 g/2 oz Cheddar cheese, finely
  grated
½ teaspoon dried mixed herbs
2 tablespoons cold water
lightly beaten egg white, to seal

1 Heat the oven to 200C/400F/Gas 6.
2 Make the pastry: sift the flour and
salt into a bowl. Add the margarine
and lard and rub in until the mixture resembles fine breadcrumbs.
Stir in the grated cheese and herbs,
then add the cold water and mix to
a fairly firm dough.
3 Turn the dough out on to a lightly
floured surface and roll out thinly.
Use to line a 20 cm/8 inch flan ring,
set on a baking sheet, prick the base
with a fork. Place a large circle of
greaseproof paper or foil in the
pastry case and weight it down with
baking beans. Bake for 10 minutes.
4 Remove the paper or foil lining
and beans, brush the inside of the
pastry case with beaten egg white,
then return the pastry to the oven
for a further 5 minutes. Remove
from the oven and set aside.
5 Make the filling: heat the oil in a
frying-pan, add the peppers and fry
gently for 5 minutes until beginning
to soften. Add the garlic and continue to cook until soft and lightly
coloured. Set aside.
6 Put the breadcrumbs in a bowl
with the basil and salt and pepper
to taste. Mix well.
7 Spread the peppers over the base
of the flan case, then cover with the
tomato slices. Sprinkle with sugar,
then finish with a layer of the
breadcrumb mixture.
8 Bake in the oven for 30-35 minutes until the tomatoes are tender
and the pastry is golden.
9 Serve the flan hot or cold.

Cook's Notes

TIME
35 minutes to prepare
and bake the pastry
case; about 50 minutes to finish.

SERVING IDEAS
This colourful flan
makes a satisfying
lunch or supper dish. Serve hot
with a fresh green vegetable
and new potatoes, or serve cold
with a mixed green salad.

VARIATION
To cut down on prepa-
ration time, use 215 g/
7½ oz frozen shortcrust pastry,
defrosted.
  Canned peppers may be used
instead of fresh peppers – there
is no need to cook them, simply
drain, slice and stir into the
cooked garlic.

●395 calories/1650 kj per slice

Spinach fried with mushrooms

SERVES 4

50 g/2 oz butter
500 g/1 lb spinach, stalks and large
   midribs removed, shredded (see
   Watchpoint)
250 g/9 oz mushrooms, sliced
½ teaspoon freshly grated nutmeg
salt and freshly ground black pepper
4 tablespoons soured cream

1 Melt the butter in a heavy saucepan or flameproof casserole. Add the spinach, sliced mushrooms and nutmeg and season to taste with salt and pepper. Cover the pan and cook over very low heat for 8-10 minutes until the vegetables are just cooked. Stir frequently during this time to ensure even cooking.

2 Transfer the vegetables to a warmed serving dish and drizzle the soured cream over the top in an attractive pattern. Serve at once while still hot.

Cook's Notes

TIME
Preparation and cooking take 20-25 minutes.

VARIATIONS
Single cream may be used as a substitute for the soured cream. Alternatively, to make the dish less expensive, omit the cream altogether and sprinkle with lemon juice before serving.

SERVING IDEAS
Serve this quickly made dish as a vegetable accompaniment for 4, or as a light lunch dish for 2-3 people.

WATCHPOINT
It is important to drain the spinach thoroughly and then to pat it dry.

●145 calories/600 kj per portion

Leek and tomato casserole

SERVES 4-6

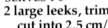

2 large leeks, trimmed, washed and cut into 2.5 cm/1 inch pieces (see Preparation)
2 large onions, cut into eighths
400 g/14 oz can tomatoes
1 tablespoon chopped parsley
1 bay leaf
2 cloves garlic, crushed (optional)
1 teaspoon salt
freshly ground black pepper
150 ml/¼ pint chicken or vegetable stock
4 tablespoons vegetable oil
1 tablespoon lemon juice
pinch of dried thyme

Cook's Notes

 TIME
Preparation of vegetables 15 minutes, cooking time in the oven 1½-2 hours.

 ECONOMY
Save fuel by cooking this dish with something else on the shelf below.

 SERVING IDEAS
Serve this easy-to-make vegetable dish on its own or with roast beef or pork.

 VARIATION
When tomatoes are cheap and plentiful, use fresh instead of canned, in which case you may need a little extra stock. Skin them before mixing with other ingredients.

 PREPARATION
Top and tail leeks; slit them down almost to base. Fan out under cold running water to rinse off all dirt.

● 175 calories/725 kj per portion

Soya burgers

SERVES 4

175 g/6 oz soya beans
2 tablespoons vegetable oil
1 onion, finely chopped
1 small carrot, grated
1 small green pepper, deseeded and
    chopped
1 tablespoon tomato purée
1 teaspoon dried mixed herbs
salt
freshly ground black pepper
1 egg
1 tablespoon water
dried breadcrumbs, for coating
vegetable oil, for frying

1 Put the beans into a bowl, cover with plenty of cold water and leave to soak overnight. Drain the soaked beans and put them into a saucepan; cover with cold water.

2 Bring the beans to the boil, then lower the heat and simmer over very gentle heat for 3 hours until tender, topping up with more water if necessary. Transfer to a colander and drain thoroughly. ✳

3 Heat the oil in a frying-pan and gently fry the onion and carrot for 5 minutes, until the onion is soft and lightly coloured. Add the green pepper and fry for a further 5 minutes, until the vegetables are just tender.

4 Add the beans, tomato purée and herbs to the pan, mashing the beans with a spoon to make the mixture hold together. Season with salt and pepper to taste.

5 Divide the mixture into 8 and shape each piece into a neat, flat circle. Beat egg and water together in a shallow bowl and spread the breadcrumbs out on a plate. Dip the burgers first into the beaten egg mixture, then into the dried breadcrumbs, making sure they are well coated.

6 Heat the vegetable oil in a large frying-pan, add 4 burgers and fry over moderately high heat for 3 minutes on each side until crisp and browned. Remove with a slotted spoon, place on a serving platter, and keep warm. Fry the remaining burgers in the same way and serve at once.

Cook's Notes

TIME
Allow for the overnight soaking of the beans, followed by 3 hours cooking. Preparation and cooking then take about 30 minutes.

PRESSURE COOKING
Soya beans can be cooked in a pressure-cooker. Soak and rinse as in the recipe, then cook at high (H) pressure for 1 hour.

FREEZING
Drained, cooked soya beans can be frozen in polythene bags or rigid containers ready for use. Soya bean burgers can be frozen before frying: open-freeze until solid, then pack in a rigid container, separating the layers with foil. Seal, label and return to the freezer for up to 2 months. To serve: fry from frozen.

SERVING IDEAS
Serve the burgers with mashed potatoes or French fries and parsley sauce; or with chutney and soft rolls.

 DID YOU KNOW
Soya beans are one of the richest sources of protein, described in China as 'meat without bones'.

●360 calories/1525 kj per portion

Creamy spring vegetables

SERVES 4

1 small onion, sliced
2 large spring onions, cut into
   1 cm/½ inch slices
2 carrots, cut into 1 cm/½ inch
   slices
50 g/2 oz butter
300 ml/½ pint hot chicken stock
pinch of caster sugar
salt and freshly ground black pepper
250 g/9 oz broad beans (shelled
   weight)
250 g/9 oz peas (shelled weight)
1 teaspoon cornflour
6 tablespoons double cream
1 tablespoon chopped fresh parsley,
   to garnish (optional)

1 Melt the butter in a saucepan, add the sliced onion and spring onions and cook over moderate heat for 2 minutes. Add the sliced carrots and cook for a further 2 minutes, stirring to coat thoroughly.

Cook's Notes

TIME
Preparation, if using fresh vegetables, takes 20-25 minutes. Cooking the Creamy spring vegetables takes about 35 minutes.

SERVING IDEAS
This dish is delicious with. roast or grilled chicken, pork, lamb or veal. It is also very good as a light lunch or supper dish, simply served with boiled rice, tiny new potatoes or wholewheat rolls.

VARIATIONS
When fresh broad beans and peas are not in season, use frozen ones. Add them to the pan after the carrots have been cooking for 10 minutes, then cook for 8-10 minutes or according to packet instructions.

Add ½-1 teaspoon curry powder to the cornflour when making the sauce to give a mild spiciness to the dish.

●295 calories/1225 kj per portion

2 Pour the hot stock into the pan, add the sugar and salt and pepper to taste, then bring to the boil. Lower the heat, cover and simmer gently for 10 minutes. Add the broad beans and simmer for a further 5 minutes. Add the peas and continue simmering for another 10 minutes, until all the vegetables are tender.

3 Put the cornflour into a small bowl and stir in 1 tablespoon of the hot vegetable stock from the pan. Stir to make a smooth paste, then pour back into the pan. Stir the contents of the pan over low heat for about 4-5 minutes, until the sauce thickens and clears. Stir in the cream and allow just to heat through.

4 Turn the vegetables with the sauce into a warmed serving dish. Sprinkle with parsley, if liked, and serve at once.

Cheesy bubble and squeak

SERVES 4

1 kg/2 lb potatoes, quartered
salt
500 g/1 lb green cabbage, cored and
    shredded
175 g/6 oz mature Cheddar cheese,
    grated (see Buying guide)
1 large egg, beaten
freshly ground black pepper
6-8 spring onions, chopped
25 g/1 oz dripping or lard

1 Cook the potatoes in boiling salted water for 20 minutes or until tender.
2 Meanwhile, cook the cabbage in boiling salted water for 5 minutes. Drain thoroughly.
3 Drain the potatoes well, then return them to the saucepan. Dry out over gentle heat, then mash with 100 g/4 oz cheese, the beaten egg and plenty of salt and pepper. Stir in the cabbage and spring onions.
4 Melt the dripping in a large frying-pan over high heat and swirl

it around to cover the base and sides. Add the bubble and squeak mixture and spread it out evenly. Cook for 3 minutes or until underside is golden (see Cook's tip).

5 Sprinkle with the remaining cheese, then put under a moderate grill for about 5 minutes, until the top is golden brown. Serve at once straight from pan cut in wedges.

Cook's Notes

TIME
Total preparation and cooking time is about 30 minutes.

COOK'S TIP
To see if the underside of the bubble and squeak is golden brown, gently lift up the edge with a palette knife. The centre will become brown before the outside, so take care not to let the centre burn.

VARIATIONS
Traditional bubble and squeak is made with left-over mashed potato and cooked Brussels sprouts. If you prefer the stronger flavour of sprouts, then use these instead of the cabbage. A dash of

Worcestershire sauce is a good complement to the cheese. Add it when mashing the potatoes and, if liked, mix a few drops in with the grated cheese for the topping.

SERVING IDEAS
Serve on its own as a vegetable or with sausages, bacon, chops, etc., or add chopped left-over cooked meat such as ham or bacon to the bubble and squeak to make a more substantial dish.

BUYING GUIDE
Canadian Cheddar cheese has just the right amount of flavour to give a 'kick' to the potatoes and cabbage.

●510 calories/2125 kj per portion

Potato and radish crunch

SERVES 4

500 g/1 lb new potatoes (see Buying guide)

salt

50 g/2 oz butter

3 thick slices white bread, crusts removed and cut into 1 cm/½ inch dice

5 cm/2 inch piece of cucumber, diced

6 radishes, thinly sliced

25 g/1 oz dry roasted peanuts

1 teaspoon snipped chives

freshly ground black pepper

4 tablespoons soured cream

1 Boil a saucepan of salted water and cook the potatoes for 15-20 minutes until just tender. ⚠ Drain well and, when cool enough to handle, cut into 1 cm/½ inch dice. Leave to cool completely.

2 To make the croûtons: melt the butter in a frying-pan. When it is sizzling, add the diced bread and fry gently, turning as necessary, until golden. Drain well on absorbent paper. Leave to cool completely.

3 Place the diced potato, fried croûtons, cucumber, radishes, peanuts and chives into a bowl. Season to taste with salt and pepper. Add the soured cream and mix gently. ⚠ Serve at once.

Cook's Notes

TIME
Preparation, including cooking the potatoes and frying the croûtons, takes about 30 minutes. Allow 30 minutes for cooling. Preparing the salad takes 5 minutes.

BUYING GUIDE
Choose a waxy type of potato such as Pentland Javelin or Ulster Sceptre which will not break up during cooking.

WATCHPOINTS
Watch the potatoes carefully: they should be cooked through but still firm. If overcooked, they will break up instead of cutting into neat dice.

Mix gently so that the ingredients are thoroughly coated in the soured cream but remain separate.

VARIATIONS
Add a small chopped green pepper instead of cucumber.

Omit the peanuts and sprinkle the top of the salad with toasted, flaked almonds.

● 310 calories/1300 kj per portion

Potato 'n' tomato gratin

SERVES 4
750 g/1½ lb waxy potatoes, sliced
  (see Watchpoint)
300 ml/½ pint milk
100 g/4 oz Cheddar cheese, grated

TOMATO SAUCE
40 g/1½ oz margarine or butter
1 medium onion, sliced
1 tablespoon plain flour
400 g/14 oz can tomatoes
½ teaspoon sugar
1 teaspoon dried oregano
salt and freshly ground black pepper

1 Make the tomato sauce: melt 25 g/ 1 oz margarine in a small saucepan, add the onion and fry gently for 3 minutes, stirring occasionally. Do not allow the onion to brown. Sprinkle in the flour and cook for 2 minutes, stirring constantly.
2 Add the tomatoes with their juice to the pan, stir in the sugar and oregano and season with salt and pepper to taste. Simmer for 20 minutes until the tomato sauce has thickened, stirring occasionally.
3 Meanwhile, put the potatoes in a saucepan with the milk and ½ teaspoon salt. Bring slowly to the boil, then lower the heat and simmer uncovered for 10-12 minutes. The potatoes should be tender when pierced with a fine skewer, but not beginning to break up. Drain thoroughly.
4 Grease the inside of a shallow 850 ml/1½ pint flameproof dish with remaining margarine, then arrange the potatoes in overlapping circles over the base.
5 Heat the grill to moderate. Taste and adjust seasoning of the tomato sauce. Pour over the potatoes  and sprinkle the cheese over the top. Place the dish under the grill until the cheese topping is golden brown and bubbling. Serve the gratin very hot, straight from the dish.

Cook's Notes

TIME
Preparation 10 minutes. Boiling the potatoes, preparing sauce and browning under the grill takes 25 minutes.

FREEZING
You can freeze the dish completely assembled, or without the cheese topping. Defrost at room temperature before grilling. Alternatively, cook it in the oven straight from the freezer: heat the oven to 190C/375F/Gas 5 and cook for 35-40 minutes or until the topping is golden brown.

WATCHPOINT
Make sure that you cut the potatoes into even, thick slices and be careful not to overcook them as well. The dish would be very unattractive if made with squashy, moist potatoes. They must be in whole slices and still slightly firm.

VARIATION
Leeks, cooked till just tender and thoroughly drained, could be successfully used instead of the potatoes.

●400 calories/1675 kj per portion

Bulgur wheat casserole

SERVES 4

225 g/8 oz bulgur wheat (see Did you know)
50 g/2 oz margarine or butter
1 tablespoon vegetable oil
1 large onion, finely chopped
2 large leeks, thinly sliced
2 large carrots, diced
1 small red pepper, deseeded and diced
300 ml/½ pint boiling water
2 tomatoes, skinned and chopped
50 g/2 oz seedless raisins
100 g/4 oz Cheddar cheese, diced
salt and freshly ground black pepper

1 Melt half the margarine with the oil in a large saucepan. Add the onion, leeks, carrots and red pepper, cover and cook gently for about 20 minutes.

2 Meanwhile, melt the remaining margarine in a large saucepan. Add the bulgur wheat and stir until the grains are thoroughly coated with margarine. Stir in the boiling water, cover and place over gentle heat. Cook for 10 minutes until the water has been absorbed.

3 Using a fork, gently mix the cooked vegetables into the bulgur wheat. Lightly stir in the tomatoes, raisins and cheese and fork through until the cheese is melted. Season to taste with salt and pepper. Transfer to a warmed serving dish and serve at once.

TIME
This is a quick dish to make: the preparation and cooking only take about 30 minutes.

DID YOU KNOW
Bulgur wheat is wheat which has been cracked by a steaming process. It is widely used in Middle Eastern cooking and can be bought from health food shops and Asian food stores. It is sometimes also known simply as 'cracked wheat'.

● 500 calories/2075 kj per portion

Cabbage gratin

SERVES 4

1 green cabbage, weighing
   approximately 500 g/1 lb,
   coarsely shredded
1 teaspoon salt
6 juniper berries, crushed (optional)
25 g/1 oz butter
25 g/1 oz plain flour
150 ml/¼ pint milk
150 ml/¼ pint single cream
pinch of white pepper
pinch of cayenne pepper
½ teaspoon freshly grated nutmeg
3 tablespoons fresh breadcrumbs
25 g/1 oz good melting cheese (e.g.
   Leicester, Cheddar), grated
extra 15 g/½ oz butter

1 Heat the oven to 190C/375F/Gas 5.
2 Cook the cabbage until just tender, but still crisp, in boiling salted water. Drain thoroughly and mix in the juniper berries, if used.
3 Make a thick creamy sauce with the butter, flour, milk and cream mixed (see Preparation). Add salt, peppers and nutmeg, then taste and adjust seasoning; the sauce should be very highly flavoured.
4 Stir the cabbage into the sauce and pour into a buttered ovenproof dish.
5 Mix together the breadcrumbs and grated cheese. Sprinkle over the cabbage and sauce and top with flecks of butter.
6 Cook for about 15 minutes and then raise the heat to 220C/425F/Gas 7 for 10 minutes, until the cheese has melted and the top is crisp and bubbling.

Cook's Notes

TIME
Preparation 20 minutes, cooking 20-25 minutes.

SERVING IDEAS
Add peeled, chopped tomatoes to the sauce and scatter some crispy, fried bacon bits on top to make a complete supper dish.
   Serve on own or as an accompaniment to grilled or roast meat.

PREPARATION
To make the sauce: melt the butter in a small saucepan, sprinkle in the flour and stir over low heat for 1-2 minutes until straw-coloured. Remove from the heat and gradually stir in the milk and cream. Return to the heat and simmer, stirring, until thick and smooth.

VARIATIONS
Substitute cauliflower for cabbage to make the classic dish, cauliflower cheese. If you like your vegetable gratin really cheesy, add 25 g/1 oz more cheese to the sauce. Mixing a little mustard into the white sauce in Stage 3 makes it a bit more tangy (you will need about ¼-½ teaspoon).

• 255 calories/1050 kj per portion

Creamy swede bake

SERVES 4

 1 kg/2 lb swede, cut into 4 cm/1½ inch pieces
40 g/1½ oz margarine or butter
salt and freshly ground black pepper
freshly grated nutmeg
1 bunch spring onions, chopped
2 tablespoons single cream
3-4 tablespoons fresh white breadcrumbs
vegetable oil, for greasing

1 Heat the oven to 190C/375F/Gas 5. Lightly grease an ovenproof dish or casserole.
2 Put the swede in a large saucepan with just enough cold water to cover. Bring to the boil, then lower the heat. Cover, simmer for 20 minutes or until tender, then drain.
3 Mash the cooked swede with 25 g/1 oz margarine and season. Stir in nutmeg, spring onions and cream.
4 Put the swede mixture into the greased dish, smooth the top and sprinkle evenly with the breadcrumbs. Dot with the remaining margarine. Bake for 40 minutes, until golden on top. Serve hot.

Cook's Notes

TIME
Preparation takes about 30 minutes, cooking 40 minutes.

ECONOMY
Save fuel by serving the bake with a main course such as cottage pie, toad-in-the-hole or a savoury quiche which can be baked in the oven at the same time.

●120 calories/500 kj per portion

Stir-fried celery

SERVES 4

1 head celery, stalks cut into 1 cm/
   ½ inch diagonal slices
1-2 tablespoons vegetable oil
3 spring onions, thinly sliced
salt and freshly ground black pepper
2 tablespoons flaked almonds
2 tablespoons dry sherry
1 teaspoon soy sauce
1 teaspoon tomato purée
½ teaspoon caster sugar
¼ teaspoon ground ginger

1 Heat the oil in a large frying-pan. Add the sliced celery and spring onions and season with salt and pepper. Stir-fry over moderate heat for 5-7 minutes, until the celery has lost its raw taste but is still crunchy (see Cook's tip). Add the flaked almonds and stir-fry for 1 minute.
2 Mix together the remaining ingredients, pour into the pan and stir-fry for 2 minutes. Serve at once.

Cook's Notes

TIME
Preparation takes 15 minutes, cooking 10 minutes.

SERVING IDEAS
Serve stir-fried celery as part of a Chinese meal that you have prepared yourself or bought from a takeaway. It goes well with almost any meat or fish dish, or with a savoury flan or a vegetarian dish such as macaroni cheese.

VARIATIONS
If you do not have any dry sherry, you can use vermouth or white wine instead.

COOK'S TIP
Use a wooden spoon or spatula to stir-fry, keeping the ingredients on the move all the time, so that they cook evenly.

●85 calories/350 kj per portion

Cheesy aubergine bake

SERVES 4

2 aubergines
salt
125 ml/4 fl oz vegetable oil
175 g/6 oz Gruyère or Mozzarella
  cheese, very thinly sliced
  (see Economy)
1 egg
225 g/8 oz can tomatoes
½ onion, finely chopped
1 tablespoon tomato purée
1 tablespoon water
salt and freshly ground black pepper
margarine, for greasing
1 large tomato, sliced

1 Cut the aubergines into 5 mm/
¼ inch slices and put them in a
colander in layers, sprinkling salt
between each layer. Cover with a
plate and place a heavy weight on
top. Leave for about 1 hour to draw
out the bitter juices, then rinse the
slices under cold running water and
pat dry on absorbent paper.
2 Heat the oven to 180C/350F/Gas 4.
Grease a shallow baking dish.
3 Pour enough of the oil into a large
frying-pan to cover the base. Heat
the oil, put a layer of aubergine
slices in the pan and fry for 3-4
minutes on each side, turning once,
until golden brown on both sides.
Remove from the pan and drain on
absorbent paper. Continue in the
same way until all the aubergine
slices are browned.

4 Place layers of aubergines and
cheese alternately in prepared dish,
finishing with a layer of cheese
on top.
5 Put the egg, canned tomatoes,
onion, tomato purée and water in a
blender and blend until smooth.
Season with a little salt and pepper,
then pour over the aubergines and
the cheese. Arrange the tomato
slices on top.
6 Bake, uncovered, for 25 minutes,
until heated through and bubbling.
Serve straight from the dish.

Cook's Notes

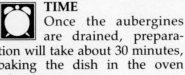

TIME
Once the aubergines
are drained, prepara-
tion will take about 30 minutes,
baking the dish in the oven
takes 25 minutes.

ECONOMY
While the Gruyère or
Mozzarella cheese gives
the best flavour to this dish, a
less expensive mature Cheddar
cheese can be used as a substitute quite successfully.

SERVING IDEAS
Serve this dish with
plenty of warm, fresh
bread and a green salad as a
vegetarian meal.

●405 calories/1770 kj per portion

Creamed lemon spinach

SERVES 4

750 g/1½ lb fresh spinach leaves
1 teaspoon salt
25 g/1 oz butter
15 g/½ oz plain flour
150 ml/¼ pint double cream
grated zest and juice of ½ lemon
freshly ground black pepper
pinch of freshly grated nutmeg
2 hard-boiled eggs, yolks and
    whites separated and finely
    chopped, to garnish

1 If using fresh spinach, thoroughly wash it in several changes of cold water to remove all the grit. Remove the stalks and midribs and discard. Put the spinach in a large saucepan with just the water that adheres to the leaves after washing. ! Sprinkle over the salt.

2 Cook the spinach over moderate heat for about 15 minutes, stirring occasionally with a wooden spoon. Turn the cooked spinach into a colander and drain thoroughly, pressing the spinach with a large spoon or a saucer to extract as much moisture as possible.

3 Melt the butter in the rinsed-out pan, sprinkle in the flour and stir over moderate heat for 3 minutes. Remove from heat, pour in the cream, and when it is completely blended, add the lemon zest and juice. ! Season to taste with salt, pepper and nutmeg. Stir the spinach into the cream sauce and return to very low heat, just to heat through. !

4 Turn the spinach into a heated serving dish and arrange the chopped hard-boiled eggs in rows over the top. Serve at once

Cook's Notes

TIME
Preparation, if using fresh spinach, takes about 15 minutes. Cooking takes about 20 minutes.

WATCHPOINTS
It is best to cook spinach in its own juices—added water only makes it soggy.

Do not add lemon juice until butter, flour and cream are well blended. Otherwise, the acid will curdle the cream.

On no account allow the cream sauce to boil when heating through, or it will curdle.

BUYING GUIDE
If fresh spinach is not available, use 2 × 275g/10 oz packs frozen cut leaf spinach, defrosted and all moisture pressed out. Stir into the sauce and cook 5 minutes.

● 295 calories/1225 kj per portion

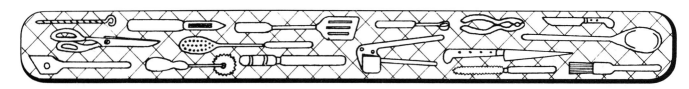

Carrots in orange juice

SERVES 4

750 g/1½ lb small carrots, thinly sliced
finely grated zest of ½ orange
juice of 1 orange
25 g/1 oz margarine or butter
1 teaspoon light soft brown sugar
½ teaspoon salt
freshly ground black pepper

TO GARNISH
twist of orange (see Preparation)
sprig of parsley

1 Put the sliced carrots in a saucepan with the orange zest and juice, margarine, sugar, salt and pepper to taste. Add enough cold water just to cover the carrots.
2 Bring to the boil over high heat, then simmer very gently, uncovered, over the lowest possible heat for 40-45 minutes, until the carrots are just tender.

3 Increase the heat and boil the carrots for 4-5 minutes until the amount of cooking liquid has reduced to a few tablespoonfuls. ⚠
4 Transfer the carrots to a warmed serving dish and pour over the remaining cooking liquid. Garnish in one corner with the twist of orange and the sprig of parsley. Serve at once.

Cook's Notes

TIME
20 minutes preparation, then 45-50 minutes cooking.

VARIATION
Use the finely grated zest of 1 lemon and 2 tablespoons lemon juice in place of the orange zest and juice.

SERVING IDEAS
This dish makes a refreshing accompaniment to any chicken, beef or lamb dish.

WATCHPOINT
The carrots are boiled for the last 4-5 minutes of cooking to evaporate the water and give the remaining cooking liquid a more concentrated flavour. This is known in cookery terms as 'reduction'. Be careful that you do not reduce the liquid too far, or the little that remains will burn on the bottom of the pan.

PREPARATION
To make a twist of orange to garnish the carrots, cut a thin slice from the halved orange before you grate it. Cut through the orange slice to the centre, then twist each half in opposite directions. Keep covered with cling film until required.

●100 calories/425 kj per portion

Peperonata

4 red or green peppers, deseeded
   and cut into thin strips
25 g/1 oz butter
2 tablespoons vegetable oil
1 onion, chopped
8 large tomatoes, skinned and
   chopped (see Preparation)
1 clove garlic, crushed
pinch of caster sugar
salt and freshly ground black pepper

1 Heat the butter in a saucepan with the oil. Add the peppers and onion and fry gently for 5 minutes until the onion is soft and lightly coloured. Cover the pan with a lid and continue frying gently until the peppers are soft.

2 Add the tomatoes, garlic, sugar and salt and pepper to taste. Stir gently.

3 Cover and simmer over a very low heat, stirring from time to time, for 25-30 minutes, or until the mixture is soft and the tomato juices have evaporated.

4 Spoon the mixture into a warmed serving dish and either serve hot or allow to cool and serve cold, but not chilled.

Cook's Notes

 TIME
Easy to make, this dish takes 20 minutes to prepare and 25-30 minutes to cook.

 PREPARATION
It is important to skin the tomatoes: put them in a bowl, cover with boiling water and leave for 1 minute. Remove with a slotted spoon, plunge into a bowl of cold water, then peel off the skins with a sharp knife.

 SERVING IDEAS
This versatile casserole of peppers and tomatoes can be served hot with grilled meat or fish, or cold as a side salad or starter.

 DID YOU KNOW
This dish originates from Italy, where peppers and tomatoes grow in abundance. An Italian cook would use olive oil for frying.

●150 calories/625 kj per portion

Peas portugaise

SERVES 4

500 g/1 lb frozen peas
2 tablespoons vegetable oil
1 medium onion, finely chopped
1 clove garlic, crushed (optional)
2 teaspoons sweet paprika
400 g/14 oz can tomatoes (see Variation)
1 teaspoon caster sugar
celery salt and freshly ground black pepper

1 Heat the oil in a saucepan, add the onion and garlic, if using, and fry over moderate heat for 3-4 minutes, stirring occasionally, until the onion is soft but not coloured. Stir in the paprika and cook for a further 2 minutes, then stir in the tomatoes with their juice, the sugar, celery salt and pepper to taste. Bring to the boil, lower the heat and simmer, uncovered, for about 10 minutes until the tomato sauce is reduced to a thick purée.

2 Meanwhile, cook the peas in a small quantity of boiling salted water, according to packet directions. Drain well.

3 Turn the peas into a warmed serving dish. Taste and adjust the seasoning of the tomato sauce, then spoon it over the peas and fork through lightly so that the sauce can run through the peas to flavour them. Serve the peas at once, while very hot.

Baked potatoes with apple

SERVES 4

4 large potatoes, about 250 g/9 oz
   each (see Buying guide)
½ medium cooking apple
25 g/1 oz margarine or butter
1 large onion, finely chopped
4 sage leaves, chopped, or 1
   teaspoon dried sage
½ teaspoon mustard powder
salt
margarine or butter, for greasing

1 Heat the oven to 200C/400F/Gas 6.
2 Scrub the potatoes and with a fork prick each one in 2 places on both sides. Bake the potatoes in the oven for 1½ hours.
3 Remove the potatoes from the oven (leaving the oven on), allow to cool slightly, then cut each one in half lengthways. Scoop the cooked potato into a bowl, leaving the shells intact. Mash the potato well. Peel, core and finely chop the apple.
4 Melt the margarine in a small frying-pan, add the onion and fry gently until it begins to soften, stirring occasionally. Stir in the apple and cook for a further 2-3 minutes, until soft.
5 Stir the apple and onion mixture into the mashed potato. Add the sage, mustard and a little salt. Mix thoroughly.
6 Spoon the mixture back into the potato shells and make criss-cross patterns on the top with a fork for a decorative finish.
7 Put the potato shells in a greased shallow ovenproof dish and return to the oven. Bake for 15 minutes until the tops are browned. Serve piping hot. Alternatively, top the potatoes with grated cheese (see Serving ideas).

Cabbage and lemon sauce

SERVES 4-6
1 large green cabbage, finely sliced
salt

SAUCE
20 g/¾ oz margarine or butter
1½ tablespoons plain flour
300 ml/½ pint warm milk
grated zest and juice of 1 large lemon
freshly grated nutmeg
freshly ground black pepper
lemon slices and 2 teaspoons snipped chives, to garnish (see Variations)

1 Bring a saucepan of salted water to the boil.
2 Meanwhile, make the sauce: melt the margarine in a separate saucepan, sprinkle in the flour and stir over low heat for 1-2 minutes until straw-coloured. Remove from the heat and gradually stir in the milk. Return to heat; or simmer, stirring, until thickened and smooth.
3 Plunge the cabbage into the boiling water and boil gently for 5 minutes, stirring frequently.
4 Stir the lemon zest and juice into the sauce, then season to taste with nutmeg, and plenty of salt and pepper (see Cook's tip).
5 Drain the cabbage well, then return to the rinsed-out pan. Pour in the sauce, then toss over gentle heat until the cabbage is lightly coated in the sauce.
6 Turn into a warmed serving dish. Garnish with the lemon slices and chives and serve at once.

Cook's Notes

TIME
Preparation 10 minutes, cooking 10 minutes.

COOK'S TIP
The sauce needs plenty of salt to bring out the lemon flavour.

WATCHPOINT
It is essential that the cabbage is tossed quickly in the sauce, so that it still has a 'bite' to it. Do not overcook it at this stage, or the finished dish will be soggy.

VARIATIONS
If chives are not available, use finely chopped spring onion tops instead. Or use fresh tarragon if available.

SERVING IDEAS
The lemon sauce makes this a delicious accompaniment to poached, grilled or fried white fish.
It is also good with a joint of roast lamb or grilled lamb chops or cutlets.

●125 calories/525 kj per portion

Mange-tout with water chestnuts

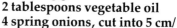

SERVES 4

250 g/9 oz mange-tout (see Buying guide)
2 tablespoons vegetable oil
4 spring onions, cut into 5 cm/ 2 inch lengths
225 g/8 oz can water chestnuts, drained and sliced
2 tablespoons soy sauce
½ teaspoon sugar
4 tablespoons chicken stock
salt and freshly ground black pepper

1 Top and tail the mange-tout and, if necessary, remove any strings from the pod sides.
2 Heat the oil in a wok or a large frying-pan, add the spring onions, mange-tout and water chestnuts and stir until the vegetables are coated with oil.
3 Add the soy sauce, sugar and chicken stock and stir-fry over moderate heat for about 5 minutes, stirring constantly, until the vegetables are hot but still crisp.
4 Season to taste with salt and pepper, turn into a warmed serving dish and serve at once.

Cook's Notes

TIME
15 minutes preparation and cooking.

SERVING IDEAS
Serve as part of a Chinese meal with a beef dish or crispy roast duck.

BUYING GUIDE
Mange-tout tend to be quite expensive, but are well worth buying occasionally for their delicate flavour.
    If fresh mange-tout are not available, buy them frozen from freezer centres.

VARIATION
Use 100 g/4 oz sliced mushrooms instead of the water chestnuts.

●100 calories/425 kj per portion

Brussels sprouts country style

SERVES 4

 750 g/1½ lb Brussels sprouts
salt
 1 tablespoon vegetable oil
1 large onion, sliced
1 green pepper, deseeded and
chopped
500 g/1 lb tomatoes
½ teaspoon dried basil
freshly ground black pepper

1 Trim the sprouts. Wash them thoroughly and cut a cross in the base of each one.
2 Cook the sprouts in boiling salted water until just tender (about 10-12 minutes). ! Drain well.
3 Meanwhile, heat the oil in a frying-pan over moderate heat. Fry the onion and green pepper until the pepper is soft and the onion brown.
4 Peel the tomatoes and chop them roughly (see Preparation).
5 Add the sprouts, tomatoes and basil to the pan and heat through. Season well with black pepper and serve immediately.

388

Creamed onions

SERVES 4-6
750 g/1½ lb onions
salt
150 ml/¼ pint soured cream
freshly ground black pepper
sweet paprika
25 g/1 oz margarine or butter
4 tablespoons day-old white
    breadcrumbs (see Cook's tip)
1 tablespoon chopped fresh parsley
2 hard-boiled eggs
parsley, to garnish

1 Cook the onions in boiling salted water for 15-20 minutes. Drain them thoroughly, reserving 1 tablespoon of the cooking liquid. Leave the onions to cool slightly, then pat them dry with absorbent paper.
2 Heat the oven to 180C/350F/Gas 4.
3 Put the onions on a board and slice them (see Preparation). Arrange the sliced onions in an ovenproof dish.

4 Beat the soured cream with the reserved onion liquid and season with salt, pepper and sweet paprika to taste. Pour the cream over the onions in the dish.
5 Melt the margarine in a small frying-pan, add the breadcrumbs and fry for about 5 minutes over moderate heat, stirring frequently, until they are golden and crisp. ⚠
6 Remove the pan from the heat and

stir in the parsley. Chop 1 hard-boiled egg and stir it into the fried crumb mixture. Spoon the mixture evenly over the onions.
7 Bake in the oven for 15 minutes. Meanwhile, slice the remaining hard-boiled egg.
8 Arrange the egg slices in a row along the top of the dish. Sprinkle with paprika, garnish with parsley and serve at once.

Farmhouse lentils

SERVES 4

250 g/9 oz split red lentils
1 tablespoon vegetable oil
1 large onion, thinly sliced
850 ml/1½ pints chicken stock
500 g/1 lb potatoes, cut into even-
    sized chunks
4 tomatoes, skinned, quartered and
    deseeded
½ teaspoon dried marjoram or
    thyme
½ teaspoon sweet paprika
salt and freshly ground black pepper
100 g/4 oz frozen peas
100 g/4 oz button mushrooms,
    thinly sliced

1 Heat the oil in a large saucepan,
add the onion and fry over moderate
heat for 3-4 minutes, stirring
occasionally.
2 Add the stock to the pan and
bring to the boil. Add the lentils,
potatoes, tomatoes, herbs, paprika
and salt and pepper to taste. Stir
well, then cover and simmer for 20
minutes, stirring occasionally. [!]
3 Add the frozen peas and mushrooms to the pan, cover and simmer
for a further 5-10 minutes, stirring
occasionally, until the lentils are soft
and the potatoes are cooked.
4 To serve: taste and adjust
seasoning, then transfer to a
warmed shallow dish. Serve hot.

Cook's Notes

TIME
Preparation 10 minutes,
cooking 30-45 minutes.

 WATCHPOINT
It is important to stir the
simmering mixture from
time to time, to prevent it
sticking to the bottom of the pan
as it cooks.

SERVING IDEAS
This dish would go very
well with bacon or ham,
or plump sausages—especially
herb-flavoured ones.

●355 calories/1500 kj per portion

Green beans provençal

SERVES 4

350 g/12 oz frozen green or French beans
1 tablespoon vegetable oil
1 medium onion, chopped
1 large clove garlic, crushed
250 g/9 oz tomatoes, skinned and chopped
1 teaspoon dried basil
salt and freshly ground black pepper

1 Heat the oil in a heavy-based saucepan. Add the onion and garlic and fry gently for 10-15 minutes, or until the onion is soft.

2 Add the tomatoes, plus the basil and salt and pepper to taste, then simmer over moderate heat, uncovered, for 10 minutes, stirring occasionally.

3 Meanwhile, cook the beans according to packet directions in boiling salted water until they are tender but still crisp to the bite. Drain thoroughly.

4 Stir the beans into the tomato mixture, then taste and adjust seasoning. Serve hot.

Cook's Notes

TIME
Total preparation and cooking, 30 minutes.

VARIATIONS
Use fresh French or runner beans in season, or fresh courgettes.

SERVING IDEAS
To make this a more substantial dish, place the cooked mixture in a buttered ovenproof dish, top with a mixture of 75 g/3 oz grated Cheddar cheese and 50 g/2 oz breadcrumbs, then place on a high shelf in a hot oven (220C/425F/Gas 7) for 15-20 minutes until the top has browned. Serve hot for a light lunch or supper.

●65 calories/275 kj per portion

New potatoes with wine

SERVES 4

750 g/1½ lb new potatoes, scrubbed
25 g/1 oz butter
½ small can anchovies, drained,
   soaked in milk for 20 minutes,
   then drained and chopped
1 tablespoon finely chopped fresh
   mint, chives or parsley
salt and freshly ground black pepper
150 ml/¼ pint dry white wine
1 tablespoon finely grated
   Parmesan cheese

1 Heat the oven to 190C/375F/Gas 5
and grease a shallow ovenproof
dish with half of the butter.
2 Bring the potatoes to the boil in
salted water, lower the heat and
cook for 12-15 minutes or until
barely tender. Drain and leave until
cool enough to handle.

3 Slice the potatoes into the prepared dish, sprinkling each layer
with anchovies, mint, chives or parsley and salt and pepper to taste. ⚠
4 Pour the wine over the top, then
sprinkle evenly with Parmesan
cheese and then finally dot the

potatoes with the remaining butter.
5 Bake above centre of the oven for
about 30 minutes or until the potatoes are cooked through and the top
is crisp and golden brown. Serve at
once, straight from the dish (see
Serving ideas).

Cook's Notes

TIME
This dish only takes
about 1 hour to make.

ECONOMY
Cook the potatoes in
this style when the
oven is already in use for other
dishes, for example, when
roasting meat or poultry (see
Serving ideas) or baking.

WATCHPOINT
Anchovies are salty, so
only a very light sea-
soning of salt is necessary.

SERVING IDEAS
A deliciously different
way of cooking new
potatoes, this dish can be
served as a light meal with
crisply grilled bacon or topped
with poached eggs, or as an
unusual and tasty vegetable
accompaniment to roast meat
and poultry.
   Because this dish includes
anchovies, it is also particularly
suitable for serving with a main
course of fish.

●220 calories/925 kj per portion

SPICY VEGETABLES

Curried cauliflower salad

SERVES 4

1 medium cauliflower, broken into
  bite-sized florets
2 medium dessert apples
2 medium carrots, coarsely grated
75 g/3 oz sultanas

DRESSING
1 tablespoon vegetable oil
10 spring onions, trimmed and
  finely chopped
2 teaspoons hot curry powder
6 tablespoons mayonnaise
1 tablespoon lemon juice
salt and freshly ground black pepper

1 To make the dressing: heat the oil in a frying-pan, add the spring onions and fry over gentle heat until they begin to brown. Stir in the curry powder and cook for 1-2 minutes, then remove from the heat and leave to cool slightly. Stir in the mayonnaise and lemon juice, then

season to taste with salt and pepper.
2 Plunge the cauliflower into a saucepan of boiling salted water, then blanch by boiling for 2 minutes (see Cook's tip). Drain and immediately refresh under cold running water. Drain the cauliflower florets thoroughly again, then put them into a large bowl.
3 Core and dice the apples, but do not peel them. Add to the cauliflower with the carrots and sultanas,

then fold gently to mix, being careful not to break up the cauliflower. Add the dressing and gently toss the vegetables in it, turning them over lightly with a fork, to coat them evenly.
4 Pile the salad into a serving bowl. Cover tightly with cling film and chill the salad in the refrigerator for at least 2 hours. Remove the salad from the refrigerator 10 minutes before serving.

Cook's Notes

 TIME
Preparation, including making the dressing, takes 30 minutes. Allow at least 2 hours for chilling the salad.

 SERVING IDEAS
This is a versatile salad which can be served with any cold meal, or as part of a buffet. It would make a tasty part of an hors d'oeuvre selection, or it could be served on its own as a starter.

VARIATION
Use 1 medium onion, finely chopped, if spring onions are not available.

COOK'S TIP
Blanching the cauliflower slightly lessens its strong flavour, and the florets remain quite crisp. However, if you want a very crunchy salad, use the cauliflower raw.

●280 calories/1175 kj per portion

Spicy potato sticks

SERVES 4

500 g/1 lb even-sized potatoes
salt
2 cloves garlic, crushed
1 small onion, finely chopped
1 teaspoon ground cumin
1 teaspoon ground turmeric
½ teaspoon chilli powder
2 tablespoons water
vegetable oil, for frying

1 Boil the potatoes in salted water for 5 minutes. Drain in a colander, then rinse under cold running water until cool enough to handle. Pat dry on absorbent paper.
2 Cut the potatoes into 5 mm/¼ inch thick slices, then cut each slice lengthways into 2 mm/⅛ inch wide sticks. Set aside.
3 Put the garlic with the onion, spices, 1 teaspoon salt and the water into a blender and blend until the mixture is very smooth.
4 Heat 1 tablespoon oil in a large frying-pan, add the spice mixture and cook gently for 5 minutes, stirring often. Remove from heat.
5 Fill a large heavy-based frying-pan to a depth of 1 cm/½ inch with oil and heat until a stale bread cube browns in 50 seconds.
6 Fry a batch of the potato sticks in the oil until golden. [!] Remove with a slotted spoon and drain on absorbent paper. Fry the rest.
7 While frying the last batch, return the pan of spice mixture to low heat and heat through.
8 Add the potato sticks to the spice mixture and toss to coat well.
9 Turn the sticks into a warmed serving dish and serve at once.

Cook's Notes

TIME
Preparation and cooking take about 20 minutes in total.

COOK'S TIP
This is a mildly spicy dish – for a hotter taste, increase the amount of chilli powder slightly.

SERVING IDEAS
These tasty potato sticks are excellent for brightening up plain dishes such as roast or grilled chicken or lamb. Alternatively, they make a delicious addition to an Indian meal.
For a dash of colour, garnish with fresh coriander sprigs.

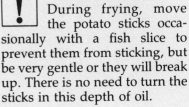
WATCHPOINT
During frying, move the potato sticks occasionally with a fish slice to prevent them from sticking, but be very gentle or they will break up. There is no need to turn the sticks in this depth of oil.

●195 calories/825 kj per portion

Indonesian salads

SERVES 4

100 g/4 oz beansprouts
225 g/8 oz can pineapple rings (see Buying guide)
7.5 cm/3 inch length of cucumber, diced
1 dessert apple
juice of ½ lemon

SAUCE
2 tablespoons smooth peanut butter
2 teaspoons soy sauce
juice of ½ lemon

1 Divide the beansprouts between 4 serving plates.
2 Drain the pineapple, reserving the juice, and chop finely. Put in a bowl and set aside.
3 Make the sauce: put the peanut butter in a bowl and beat in the soy sauce and lemon juice to form a thick cream. Add about 2 tablespoons of the reserved pineapple juice. Set aside.
4 Mix the cucumber into the chopped pineapple. Core and dice the apple, toss in the lemon juice and add to the pineapple mixture. Immediately divide this mixture between the 4 plates, piling it on to the beansprouts.
5 Pour the sauce over each salad and serve at once.

Cook's Notes

TIME
This quickly prepared dish only takes about 15 minutes to make.

BUYING GUIDE
If you are watching your weight, look out for pineapple rings in natural fruit juice. These do not have any added sugar and so the calorie count will be lower.

SERVING IDEAS
Serve this tasty and refreshing salad as a starter, or as an accompaniment.

●85 calories/350 kj per portion

Okra Mediterranean-style

SERVES 4

500 g/1 lb okra (see Buying guide
  and Preparation)
4 tablespoons vegetable oil
1 large onion, chopped
500 g/1 lb tomatoes, skinned and
  quartered
1 clove garlic, crushed
1 teaspoon ground coriander
salt and freshly ground black pepper
coriander leaves, to garnish

1 Heat the oil in a large saucepan,
add onion and fry for 5 minutes.
2 Add the okra to the pan, stir to
coat well with the oil, then add the
tomatoes, garlic and coriander. Stir
well to mix, then season to taste.
3 Bring to the boil, then lower the
heat slightly, cover and simmer for
30 minutes until okra is tender.
Serve garnished with coriander.

Cook's Notes

 TIME
Preparation and cook-
ing take about 40 min-
utes in total.

 SERVING IDEAS
This dish is a natural
accompaniment to gril-
led lamb chops or kebabs. It is
also delicious served with either
plain boiled or fried rice as a
main course.

 BUYING GUIDE
Okra can be bought at
Asian, Greek and West
Indian food shops, as well as
street markets and some large
supermarkets.
  Canned okra is also available
and may be used in this recipe,
but the flavour and texture will
not be as good.

● 165 calories/700 kj per portion

PREPARATION
To prepare the okra for
this dish:

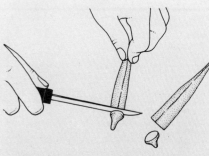

*Cut ends off the okra and remove
any blemishes with a sharp knife. It
is not necessary to peel the okra
before they are cooked.*

 VARIATION
Replace the fresh toma-
toes with 400 g/14 oz
can tomatoes, but use only half
the canned juice, otherwise the
dish will be too watery.

Noodles Chinese-style

SERVES 4

100 g/4 oz Chinese egg noodles (see Buying guide)
salt
2 tablespoons vegetable oil
6 spring onions, sliced
1 tablespoon grated fresh root ginger
500 g/1 lb Chinese leaves, cut into 1 cm/½ inch thick slices
100 g/4 oz lean cooked ham, chopped (see Economy)
100 g/4 oz beansprouts
1 tablespoon soy sauce (see Buying guide)
4 tablespoons chicken stock, dry sherry or water
freshly ground black pepper

1 Bring a large saucepan of salted water to the boil. Add the noodles, bring back to the boil and cook for about 3 minutes or according to packet instructions, until just tender. Drain and set aside.

Cook's Notes

TIME
10 minutes preparation, 10 minutes cooking.

ECONOMY
Any left-over lean cooked meat can be substituted for the ham.

SERVING IDEAS
This Chinese-style dish is particularly good served as a vegetable accompaniment to grilled or fried fish, chops or chicken.

To serve as a quick, economical light lunch or supper dish, double the quantities. If liked, add extra ingredients such as sliced mushrooms or cooked shelled prawns.

BUYING GUIDE
Thin Chinese egg noodles are available at supermarkets and delicatessens, but if difficult to obtain, Italian spaghetti or egg noodles can be used instead. These will need longer initial cooking in water—follow packet instructions.

Some supermarkets may have a choice of soy sauces—choose the lighter type for this dish.

● 230 calories/975 kj per portion

2 Heat the oil in a wok or large frying-pan, add the onions and ginger and fry gently for 2 minutes, stirring constantly.
3 Add the Chinese leaves to the pan with the chopped ham. Fry for a further 2 minutes, stirring the mixture constantly.
4 Add the drained noodles, together with the beansprouts, soy sauce, stock and salt and pepper to taste. Increase the heat to moderate and stir-fry for about 5 minutes until the vegetables are tender but still crisp and most of the liquid in the pan has evaporated.
5 Taste and adjust seasoning. Turn into a warmed serving dish.

Stir-fried beans and beansprouts

SERVES 4

250 g/9 oz small French beans,
   left whole (see Buying guide)
2 tablespoons vegetable oil
1 onion, sliced
4 tablespoons water
1 tablespoon light soy sauce
1 tablespoon lemon juice
salt and freshly ground black pepper
50 g/2 oz mushrooms, sliced (see
   Buying guide)
250 g/9 oz beansprouts

1 Heat the oil in a wok or large heavy-based pan. Fry the onion for 2 minutes, then add the beans and stir-fry for 1 minute.
2 Add the water, soy sauce, lemon juice and season to taste with salt and pepper. Cook for 5 minutes, tossing the beans in the liquid until it has evaporated
3 Add the mushrooms and stir constantly until they are tender. Add beansprouts and stir-fry for a further 2 minutes until the beansprouts are heated through and just tender, but still crisp. Transfer to a warmed serving dish and serve at once (see Serving ideas).

Cook's Notes

TIME
Preparation time is 5 minutes and cooking time about 10 minutes.

SERVING IDEAS
This crunchy dish makes an excellent accompaniment to roast or grilled meats, particularly steaks and chops.

BUYING GUIDE
Small, thin French beans are best for stir-frying and they will give the crunchiest result.
Choose button mushrooms for this recipe – they make an attractive addition and will give the dish a lighter colour.

●85 calories/350 kj per portion

Chinese lettuce parcels

SERVES 6

6 large crisp lettuce leaves (see Preparation)
2 tablespoons vegetable oil
4 spring onions, finely chopped
1 teaspoon ground ginger
1 celery stalk, finely chopped
75 g/3 oz mushrooms, finely chopped
50 g/2 oz canned water chestnuts, drained and finely sliced
100 g/4 oz long-grain rice, cooked
100 g/4 oz frozen peas, cooked and drained
1½ tablespoons soy sauce
1 egg, beaten
extra soy sauce, to serve

1 Heat the oil in a wok or large frying-pan. Add the spring onions and ginger and fry gently for 2-3 minutes until soft.
2 Add the celery, mushrooms and water chestnuts and fry for a further 5 minutes.
3 Stir in the rice, peas and soy sauce. Remove the pan from the heat and stir in the egg.
4 Lay the lettuce leaves out flat on a work surface. Put about 2 generous tablespoons of the mixture at the base of each lettuce leaf. Fold the leaf around the mixture and roll up to form neat parcels. Secure with cocktail sticks, if necessary.
5 Place the parcels in a steamer. If you do not have a steamer, use a metal colander which fits neatly inside a saucepan (the base must not touch the water). Fill the pan with boiling water, place the parcels in the colander and place the colander in the pan. Cover with foil or lid of steamer and steam for 5 minutes.
6 Remove the cocktail sticks from the parcels, if using, then place the parcels on a warmed serving dish. Serve at once, with extra soy sauce handed separately.

Cauliflower creole

SERVES 4

1 cauliflower
1 tablespoon vegetable oil
1 large onion, chopped
1 clove garlic, crushed (optional)
400 g/14 oz can tomatoes
salt
25 g/1 oz margarine or butter
1 large green pepper, deseeded and
     chopped
½-1 teaspoon Tabasco sauce
freshly ground black pepper

1 Heat the oil in a large saucepan, add the onion and garlic, if using, and fry for 2-3 minutes until just tender.

2 Stir in the tomatoes, breaking them up against the sides of the pan with a wooden spoon. Cover and simmer gently for 20-30 minutes.

3 Meanwhile, bring a pan of salted water to the boil, plunge the cauliflower head down in it and cook for about 20 minutes ! until just tender. Heat the oven to 130C/250F/ Gas ½. Drain the cauliflower well, place on a warmed serving dish and keep hot in the oven.

4 Add the margarine and green pepper to the tomato sauce, stir well and simmer for 5 minutes. Season to taste with Tabasco sauce, salt and pepper.

5 Pour a little of the sauce over the cauliflower, leaving some of the white flower showing. Pour the remaining sauce round the sides.

Cook's Notes

TIME
Preparation takes 10 minutes, cooking about 35 minutes.

VARIATION
Add a little Worcestershire sauce instead of Tabasco, for a different, less hot flavour.

SERVING IDEAS
Serve. the cauliflower with plainly cooked but not too bland meat: it would go well with fried liver and bacon.

WATCHPOINT
It is important not to overcook the cauliflower: it should be just tender. Cooking time will vary according to size.

DID YOU KNOW
Tabasco sauce is a hot pepper sauce made of spirit vinegar, red pepper and salt. Use sparingly to give a piquant flavour—too much would prove very fiery.

●115 calories/475 kj per portion

400

Sweet and sour Brussels sprouts

SERVES 4

700 g/1¼ lb fresh Brussels sprouts (see Buying guide), or 500 g/1 lb frozen
50 g/2 oz margarine or butter
1 medium onion, finely chopped
2 Cox's Orange Pippin apples
2 tablespoons seedless raisins
3 tablespoons lemon juice (see Cook's tip)
3 tablespoons clear honey
salt and freshly ground black pepper

1 Cook the sprouts in boiling salted water for about 10-15 minutes until just tender. If using frozen sprouts, cook according to packet instructions.
2 Meanwhile, melt the margarine in a saucepan, add the onion and fry gently until soft but not coloured. Peel, core and chop the apples fairly coarsely, then add to the onion with the raisins and stir well. Season well with salt and pepper.
3 Mix together the lemon juice and honey and pour into a serving jug.
4 When the sprouts are cooked, drain well, add to onion mixture and stir well to mix. Transfer to a serving bowl pour over the sauce and serve.

Cook's Notes

 TIME
Total preparation and cooking time, if using fresh sprouts, is 25 minutes.

 VARIATIONS
Broccoli may be substituted for Brussels sprouts and any other crisp dessert apple such as a Worcester Pearmain or Starking may be used instead of Cox's.

 COOK'S TIP
The average lemon yields 2 tablespoons of juice, so for this recipe you will need 1½ lemons.

 BUYING GUIDE
When buying Brussels sprouts, choose ones which are small, compact and a good green colour with no signs of yellowing. If buying sprouts packed in a polythene bag from a supermarket, make sure there are no signs of mould on them.

 SERVING IDEAS
You can serve this unusual dish of Brussels sprouts in place of ordinary boiled sprouts with roast or grilled meats.

●190 calories/800 kj per portion

Oriental vegetable fritters

SERVES 4

 1 large cauliflower, broken into bite-sized florets

 2 bunches large spring onions, trimmed and halved lengthways

500 g/1 lb carrots, halved lengthways and cut into 6 cm/2½ inch lengths

vegetable oil, for deep-frying

BATTER
100 g/4 oz plain flour
¼ teaspoon bicarbonate of soda
¼ teaspoon salt
¼ teaspoon ground ginger
1 egg yolk
200 ml/7 fl oz cold water

DIPPING SAUCE
3 tablespoons tomato purée
1½ tablespoons soy sauce
1½ tablespoons clear honey
4 tablespoons chicken stock

1 Make the dipping sauce: stir together the ingredients for the sauce, then divide the mixture between 4 tiny dishes or ramekins. Set aside.

2 Make the batter: sift the flour, bicarbonate of soda, salt and ginger into a bowl. Beat the egg yolk with the cold water and add gradually to the flour, stirring with a wooden spoon, to make a smooth thin batter.

3 Heat the oven to 130C/250F/Gas ½. Heat the oil in a deep-fat frier to 190C/375F, or until a cube of bread browns in 50 seconds.

4 Dip the vegetable pieces a few at a time into the batter. Transfer them to the hot oil with a slotted spoon and deep-fry for about 3 minutes or until golden brown, turning once with the spoon. Remove from the pan with the slotted spoon and drain well on absorbent paper. ! Arrange on a warmed large serving platter and keep warm in the oven while frying the remaining vegetable pieces in the same way.

5 Serve the fritters as soon as they are all cooked: provide each person with a bowl of sauce so that they can dip their vegetables into it.

Cook's Notes

TIME
10-15 minutes preparation, then 30-40 minutes frying.

WATCHPOINT
Use plenty of absorbent paper to drain the fritters, so that they are not excessively oily.

VARIATIONS
Delicious alternatives are thickly sliced courgettes, wide strips of green and red pepper, aubergine slices, whole button mushrooms and whole or halved French beans.

DID YOU KNOW
These fritters are a version of the Japanese tempura—vegetables deep fried in a batter. Tempura batter is different from other fritter batters because it contains no oil or butter and must be used immediately.

●400 calories/1675 kj per portion

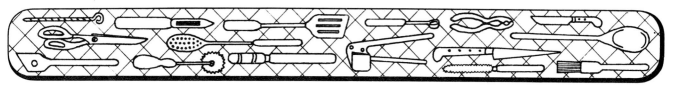

Vegetable biriani

SERVES 4-6

2 tablespoons vegetable oil
1 large onion, chopped
2 cloves garlic, crushed (optional)
2 teaspoons hot curry powder
½ teaspoon ground cinnamon
½ teaspoon ground ginger
425 ml/¾ pint water
1 tablespoon tomato purée
1 large carrot, diced
2 teaspoons salt
225 g/8 oz long-grain rice
75 g/3 oz seedless raisins
250 g/9 oz sliced runner or French
   beans, fresh or frozen
175 g/6 oz frozen peas

1 Heat the oil in a large saucepan. Add the onion and garlic, if using, and fry gently for about 10 minutes until the onion is soft but not browned, stirring frequently.

Cook's Notes

TIME
Preparation and cooking take about 45 minutes.

WATCHPOINT
Try not to lift the lid of the pan during the cooking and do not stir unless absolutely necessary: this way the rice will be tender and fluffy. Heat must be low at this stage.

COOK'S TIP
If using frozen beans, cook them straight from the freezer, without defrosting.

DID YOU KNOW
Biriani is an Indian rice dish usually served as an accompaniment to a main-course curry, although sometimes it has meat, fish or poultry added to it and is served with a curry sauce, in which case it becomes a main course in its own right. If you like the flavour of curry, you can serve this biriani as a vegetable accompaniment to any main-course meat or fish dish.

●365 calories/1525 kj per portion

2 Add the spices to the pan, stir well and cook for a further 2 minutes.
3 Add the water, tomato purée, carrot and salt. Bring to the boil.
4 Add the rice, raisins and fresh or frozen beans, and stir well (see Cook's tip).
5 Lower the heat, cover the pan tightly and simmer very gently for 20 minutes, without stirring.
6 Gently fork in the frozen peas, cover the pan and simmer very gently for a further 5 minutes. Taste and adjust seasoning. Pile the biriani into a warmed serving dish and serve hot.

Sambols

SERVES 5-6

200 g/8 oz tomatoes, skinned and chopped
2 tablespoons coconut milk (water and desiccated coconut)
1 green chilli, deseeded and sliced
1 large onion, sliced
juice of ½ lemon (see Cook's tip)
salt
½ cucumber, thinly sliced
50 g/2 oz desiccated coconut
2 tablespoons hot water
pinch of chilli powder

1 Make the tomato sambol: put the tomatoes into a bowl and stir in half the coconut milk, half the chilli and one-third of the onion. Mix well, then add ½ teaspoon lemon juice and season to taste with salt.

2 Make the cucumber sambol: arrange the cucumber slices in a shallow dish and sprinkle with salt. Leave for 30 minutes.
3 Meanwhile, make the coconut sambol: put coconut in bowl, pour over hot water and leave 15 minutes. Stir in chilli powder, one third of onion and ½ teaspoon lemon juice. Season with salt.
4 Rinse and pat the cucumber dry and transfer to a bowl. Mix in the remaining coconut milk, lemon juice and almost all remaining green chilli and onion. Season with salt.
5 Transfer sambols to individual dishes; garnish with onion and chilli rings and more chilli powder.

PARTY COOKING

Entertaining family and friends can be fun; but it can also involve a great deal of time and expense. This need not be so, 'Party Cooking' shows you how entertaining can be economic and fun for the busy cook. There is a full three-course menu for each meal with detailed planners on when to prepare each course. Each meal is attractively illustrated in full colour so that you can see the finished effect. Menus have been planned with an international flair – treat your friends to a Mexican evening, for example. Those special occasions like a romantic Valentine's dinner for two or entertaining friends at a New Year's party are also catered for. A more formal cocktail party menu is also included, as are special birthday and party meals just for the kids.

If you really need to cook to a strict budget or are in a hurry, several menus on this theme have been included – try the *Cheap and cheerful supper* or the *Meal in under an hour*.

MEXICAN EVENING

Throw an unusual buffet party centred around two savoury dishes that are made with tortillas, the famous Mexican pancakes: Chicken enchiladas and Beef tacos. Start with a tequila cocktail, and finish with a pineapple pudding to complete the exotic flavour.

Flour tortillas

MAKES 12
- 225 g/8 oz plain flour
- 1 teaspoon salt
- 1 teaspoon baking powder
- 15 g/½ oz lard, diced
- 175 ml/6 fl oz water

1 Sift the flour, salt and baking powder into a bowl. Add the lard and rub it into the flour with your fingertips until the mixture resembles fine breadcrumbs. Mix in the water to form a stiff dough.
2 Divide the dough into 12 pieces and shape into balls. Roll each ball out thinly on a lightly floured surface to form 10 cm/4 inch rounds.
3 Put an ungreased heavy-based frying-pan over moderate heat until hot, then add a dough round and cook for 2 minutes on each side until lightly flecked with brown. Wrap tortilla in a tea-towel. ⚠
4 Fry remaining rounds adding them to the tea-towel as they are cooked (see Cook's tip).

Chicken enchiladas

SERVES 6
- 12 warm tortillas
- 500 g/1 lb boneless cooked chicken, shredded (see Buying guide)
- vegetable oil, for frying
- 50 g/2 oz Parmesan cheese, grated

SAUCE
- 100 g/4 oz canned jalapeño peppers, (see Buying guide)
- 1 small onion, roughly chopped
- 400 g/14 oz can tomatoes
- 2 tablespoons vegetable oil
- 1 large egg
- 225 ml/8 fl oz double cream
- salt
- about 2 tablespoons chicken stock

1 Make the sauce: rinse the peppers under cold running water, pat dry, then chop roughly. Purée the peppers, onion and tomatoes in their juice in a blender until smooth.
2 Heat the oil in a frying-pan, add the purée and cook over moderate heat, stirring constantly for 3 minutes. Remove pan from the heat.
3 Beat the egg with cream, and salt to taste.
4 Gradually stir the cream mixture into the cooked purée. Return the pan to low heat and cook, stirring, for 1 minute. If sauce is too thick, thin slightly with chicken stock. Remove from heat; set aside.
5 Put the shredded chicken into a bowl and stir in 2-3 tablespoons of the sauce to moisten it. Set aside.
6 Heat the oven to 180C/350F/Gas 4.
7 Fill a heavy-based frying-pan with oil to a depth of 1 cm/½ inch and heat over moderate heat. When the oil is sizzling, add a tortilla and fry for a few seconds on each side. Lift out with tongs and dip into the sauce, which should still be warm.
8 Place the sauce-coated tortilla in a shallow ovenproof dish, 30 × 20 cm/12 × 8 inches. Put a spoonful of the chicken mixture on to the tortilla, then fold in half.
9 Fry, dip and fill the remaining tortillas in same way, arranging them neatly in the dish. Pour over the remaining sauce, then sprinkle with cheese.
10 Bake for 20 minutes.

Beef tacos

SERVES 6

12 warm tortillas

BEEF FILLING
500 g/1 lb lean minced beef
2 tablespoons vegetable oil
1 onion, finely chopped
1 clove garlic, crushed
225 g/8 oz can tomatoes
2 teaspoons chilli powder
½ teaspoon ground cumin
½ teaspoon dried oregano
salt

1 Make the beef filling: heat the oil in a frying-pan, add the onion and fry gently for 5 minutes until soft and lightly coloured. Add the garlic and continue to fry for a further 2 minutes.

2 Add the beef and fry briskly, stirring with a wooden spoon to remove lumps, for about 5 minutes until the meat is evenly browned.

3 Stir in the tomatoes with their juice, the chilli powder, cumin, oregano and salt to taste. Bring to the boil, then lower the heat and simmer, stirring, for about 20 minutes until the meat is cooked.

4 To serve: spoon a little beef filling into the tortilla, then fold over and eat with your fingers (see Serving ideas).

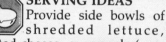

Cook's Notes

Flour tortillas

TIME
The tortillas take 1 hour to make in total.

WATCHPOINT
Keep the tortillas warm in the tea-towel, so that they remain soft and pliable and do not crack when folded.

COOK'S TIP
These tortillas can be made up to 45 minutes in advance: wrap them, still in their tea-towel, in foil and keep warm in an oven heated to 110C/225F/Gas ¼.

DID YOU KNOW
Tortillas of this type are very popular in northern Mexico where they are known as *Tortillas de harina del norte*. The other kind of tortillas famous to Mexico use a special flour, *masa harina*, which is made from boiled maize. Traditionally they are cooked on an ungreased girdle called a *comal*.

●80 calories/325 kj per tortilla

Chicken enchiladas

TIME
About 1 hour to prepare and cook.

BUYING GUIDE
1 kg/2 lb cooked chicken yields 500 g/1 lb meat. Jalapeño peppers are sold in larger supermarkets.

●580 calories/2425 kj per portion

Beef tacos

TIME
The beef filling takes 35 minutes to make.

SERVING IDEAS
Provide side bowls of shredded lettuce, grated cheese, guacamole (avocado dip), finely chopped onion and bottled taco sauce or any other hot chilli sauce. Each person can then add a little of each to the beef filling before folding.
  As an appetizer, serve tortilla chips, if wished, to dip into the taco sauce.

●340 calories/1425 kj per portion

Acapulco pineapple pudding

SERVES 6

6 trifle sponges
3 tablespoons apricot jam
300 ml/½ pint soured cream
50 g/2 oz flaked almonds,
   toasted

PINEAPPLE SAUCE
375 g/13 oz can crushed pineapple
175 g/6 oz sugar
50 g/2 oz ground almonds
4 egg yolks, lightly beaten
generous pinch of ground
   cinnamon
125 ml/4 fl oz dry sherry

1 Make the sauce: put the pineapple with its juice in a saucepan with the sugar, almonds, egg yolks, cinnamon and half the sherry. Stir with a wooden spoon until the ingredients are well mixed.

2 Place the pan over very low heat and cook, stirring constantly, for about 5 minutes or until the sauce has thickened. Set aside to cool for 15 minutes.

3 Meanwhile, split the trifle sponges in half horizontally, then spread the cut sides evenly with the apricot jam.

4 Arrange half the trifle sponges, jam side up, in a glass serving dish large enough to hold the sponges in a single layer.

5 Sprinkle with half the remaining sherry, then spread half the pineapple sauce over the top. Repeat these layers once more, using the remaining sponges, sherry and sauce. Refrigerate for 2-3 hours.

6 Remove the pudding from the refrigerator and spread the soured cream over the top. Sprinkle the surface with the toasted almonds and serve at once.

CHINESE MEAL

For an exotic and delicious change, try making a Chinese meal—it will provide a complete break from Western foods and eating traditions. The ginger-flavoured fried prawn starter has to be eaten with the fingers to be enjoyed, while the glazed pork is fun to eat with chopsticks. The meal ends on a light and refreshing note with a delicately flavoured fruit salad.

Gingered deep-fried prawns

SERVES 6
500 g/1 lb large prawns (see Buying guide)
vegetable oil, for frying

BATTER
50 g/2 oz plain flour
1/4 teaspoon salt
1 egg
150 ml/1/4 pint water
1 teaspoon chopped root ginger
1/4 teaspoon freshly ground black pepper

1 Peel the prawns, then make a shallow cut down the centre back of each prawn and gently scrape away the black vein with the point of a knife. Rinse well, then pat dry.
2 Make the batter: sift the flour with the salt into a bowl and make a well in the centre. Beat the egg with the water, pour into the well and, using a wire whisk, gradually draw the flour into the liquid. When all the flour is incorporated, beat well, then whisk in the ginger and pepper.
3 Fill a frying-pan with oil to a depth of 2 cm/3/4 inch and put over moderate heat. When the oil is on the point of smoking, dip a few prawns in the batter: coat well with batter, then drop into the hot oil.
4 Fry the prawns for 1 minute on each side, until the batter turns golden brown. Transfer with a slotted spoon to a serving platter; keep hot while frying the rest.
5 Serve hot, accompanied by dips (see Serving ideas).

Marinated roast pork

SERVES 6
1.4 kg/3 lb pork fillet, cut into 15 cm/6 inch lengths
3 tablespoons sunflower or groundnut oil
3 tablespoons clear honey
shredded lettuce, to garnish

MARINADE
5 tablespoons soy sauce
3 tablespoons medium-dry sherry
1 1/2 tablespoons brown sugar
2 cloves garlic, crushed
1/2 teaspoon freshly ground black pepper
1/2 teaspoon salt
1/2 teaspoon mixed dried sage and thyme
1/4 teaspoon ground cinnamon

1 Place the pork fillet lengths in a single layer in a deep dish.
2 Make the marinade: beat the marinade ingredients together until thoroughly combined.
3 Pour the marinade over the pork and leave to marinate for at least 2 1/2 hours, turning occasionally.
4 Heat the oven to 220C/425F/Gas 7. Remove the pork from the marinade with a slotted spoon, reserving the marinade. Place the pork on a rack in a roasting tin.
5 Roast the pork in the oven for 15 minutes, then remove from the oven and reduce the oven temperature to 180C/350F/Gas 4. Brush the pork with the reserved marinade and the oil to coat thoroughly, then return to the oven for a further 10 minutes.

6 Just before the end of the cooking time, warm the honey in a small pan over low heat. Remove the pork from the oven, brush with the warmed honey, then return to the oven to roast for a further 5 minutes.
7 Cut the fillets crossways into 5 mm/1/4 inch thick slices. Serve hot, garnished with shredded lettuce.

Fried rice

SERVES 6
350 g/12 oz long-grain rice, boiled
5 tablespoons vegetable oil
1 large onion, chopped
50 g/2 oz frozen peas
1/2 green pepper, deseeded and diced
50 g/2 oz lettuce, shredded
1 tablespoon soy sauce
salt and freshly ground black pepper

1 Heat 3 tablespoons of the oil in a large frying-pan, add the onion and fry gently for 5 minutes until soft and lightly coloured.
2 Add the peas, green pepper and lettuce, stir for 1 minute, then push to the side of the pan.
3 Pour the remaining oil into the centre of the pan, heat gently, then add the rice and fry for 1 minute, stirring. Draw the vegetables from the sides of the pan into the rice and stir together.
4 Stir in the soy sauce, then add salt and pepper to taste. Remove the pan from the heat and continue to stir for a further minute off the heat. Transfer to a warmed dish.

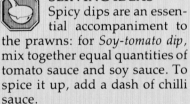

Cook's Notes

Gingered deep-fried prawns

TIME
Preparation and cooking take 30 minutes.

BUYING GUIDE
The jumbo-sized prawns suitable for this dish may be fresh or frozen (defrost before peeling), and can be of various species. Pacific prawns and Dublin Bay prawns (also called scampi) are equally good.

SERVING IDEAS
Spicy dips are an essential accompaniment to the prawns: for *Soy-tomato dip*, mix together equal quantities of tomato sauce and soy sauce. To spice it up, add a dash of chilli sauce.

For *Soy-mustard dip*, mix 1 part English mustard with 2 parts soy sauce.

●105 calories/450 kj per portion

Marinated roast pork

TIME
2 1/2 hours marinating, 30 minutes cooking.

●420 calories/1750 kj per portion

Fried rice

TIME
20 minutes for boiling rice, then 15 minutes.

●330 calories/1375 kj per portion

Oriental fruit salad

SERVES 6

1 small honeydew or ogen
   melon
300 g/11 oz can mandarins,
   drained
50 ml/2 fl oz medium-dry
   sherry
600 g/1¼ lb can lychees

1 Cut the melon in half and scoop
out the seeds. Cut the flesh into balls
using a melon baller, then put in a
glass bowl.
2 Add the drained mandarins and
sherry to the melon, then pour the
lychees, together with their juice,
into the bowl.
3 Stir the fruit gently, cover and
refrigerate for 2 hours before serving
the salad.

Cook's Notes

TIME
This delicately-flavoured
fruit salad only takes 15
minutes preparation, plus
chilling time.

VARIATION
Use fresh mandarins
and lychees when in
season and substitute the
canned lychee juice with a sugar
syrup: dissolve 50 g/2 oz sugar
in 150 ml/¼ pint water, add the
sherry, then boil for 2-3
minutes. Leave the syrup to cool
completely before mixing with
the fruit.

The sherry in the salad may be
replaced by dry white wine, or,
for added zing, by an orange
liqueur, such as Cointreau.

● 110 calories/475 kj per portion

COUNTDOWN
In the afternoon
● Marinate the pork for the
Marinated roast pork.
● Boil the rice for the Fried rice.
● Make the Oriental fruit salad and
refrigerate.
1½ hours before
● Prepare the vegetables for the
Fried rice.
● Peel the prawns and refrigerate.
● Make the accompanying dips for
the Gingered deep-fried prawns.
45 minutes before
● Heat the oven.
● Make the batter for the prawns.
30 minutes before
● Start roasting the pork.
● Fry the prawns; keep hot.
15 minutes before
● Reduce the oven temperature,
baste the pork and continue to roast.
● Make the Fried rice.
5 minutes before
● Baste the pork with honey; con-
tinue to roast. Slice before serving.

CARIBBEAN-STYLE DINNER

The colourful atmosphere of the Caribbean is captured in this exciting menu for six. The flavours that are the very essence of West Indian cookery feature strongly in every dish, and the choice of three knockout cocktails gives the meal a sensational lift!

Piña colada

MAKES 6 LONG DRINKS
700 ml/1¼ pints unsweetened
   pineapple juice
300 ml/½ pint canned coconut
   cream (see Buying guide)
350 ml/12 fl oz white or golden rum
plenty of crushed ice

1 Quarter fill a glass jug with ice, add one-third of the ingredients and mix briskly. Or blend for 2-4 seconds in a blender.

2 Pour into 2 chilled glasses and serve at once. Mix up 2 more batches with the remaining ingredients.

Caribbean blues

MAKES 6 SHORT DRINKS
350 ml/12 fl oz vodka
75 ml/3 fl oz blue Curaçao
75 ml/3 fl oz dry vermouth
plenty of crushed ice, to serve

1 Put all the ingredients, except the ice, in a large glass jug mix well.
2 Fill 6 chilled cocktail glasses with crushed ice, pour the cocktail over the ice and serve at once.

Planter's punch

MAKES 6 LONG DRINKS
350 ml/12 fl oz dark rum
175 ml/6 fl oz lemon juice
4 teaspoons grenadine
300 ml/½ pint orange juice
300 ml/½ pint pineapple juice
few dashes of Angostura bitters
plenty of crushed ice, to serve

TO GARNISH
6 orange slices
6 lemon slices
6 cocktail cherries

1 Put all the ingredients, except the ice, in a large glass jug and stir well.
2 Fill 6 large tumblers with crushed ice and pour the punch over the ice. Garnish each glass with an orange and lemon slice and a cherry.

Cook's Notes

Piña colada

TIME
20 minutes preparation in total.

BUYING GUIDE
Canned coconut cream is available in some large supermarkets, but if you find it difficult to obtain, use 175 g/6 oz block creamed coconut and dissolve it in 300 ml/½ pint hot water. Creamed coconut is available from most supermarkets, and shops specializing in Indian food.

DID YOU KNOW
The name piña colada means soaked pineapple in Spanish.

●365 calories/1530 kj per glass

Caribbean blues

TIME
5-10 minutes preparation in total.

COOK'S TIP
To make crushed ice: crush ice cubes in a strong blender or in a food processor. If you do not have either, place the ice in a strong polythene bag, squeeze out the air and tie firmly. Place the bag on a folded tea-towel and beat with a rolling pin until the ice is reduced to fragments.

●160 calories/680 kj per glass

Planter's punch

TIME
5 minutes preparation in total.

●170 calories/720 kj per glass

West Indian fish patties

SERVES 6

250 g/9 oz cod or haddock fillets
1 tablespoon wine vinegar
300 ml/½ pint cold water
1 tablespoon vegetable oil
½ small onion, chopped
¼ red pepper, deseeded and
   chopped
2 tablespoons chopped parsley
2 tablespoons canned chopped
   tomatoes
juice of ½ lemon
3 dashes Tabasco
salt and freshly ground black pepper
400 g/13 oz frozen puff pastry,
   defrosted
1 egg white, lightly beaten

1 Put the fish in a heavy pan with the vinegar and water, bring just to the boil, then lower the heat slightly and simmer gently for 10 minutes.
2 Drain the fish and, when cool enough to handle, skin, bone and flake the flesh.
3 Heat the oil in a pan, add the onion and fry gently for 5 minutes until soft and lightly coloured. Add the red pepper and parsley and cook for a further 5 minutes.
4 Add the flaked fish, together with tomatoes, lemon juice, Tabasco, 1 teaspoon salt and a generous sprinkling of pepper. Simmer, uncovered, stirring occasionally, for a further 10-12 minutes until most of the liquid has evaporated. Transfer to a bowl, taste, adjust seasoning and leave to cool.
5 Roll out the pastry on a lightly floured surface to a 40 × 30 cm/16 × 12 inch rectangle.
6 Heat the oven to 220C/425F/Gas 7.
7 Cut the pastry into twelve 10 cm/4 inch squares. Place a portion of the fish mixture in the centre of each square, then lightly dampen the pastry edges with cold water and fold each square into a triangle. Press the edges together, then crimp with a fork to seal well.
8 Arrange the patties well apart on 2 baking sheets and brush the surfaces with egg white, then prick each patty with a fork 2-3 times. Bake in the oven for about 20 minutes until golden brown.

Pork roast with rum

SERVES 6

2 kg/4½ lb loin of pork on the bone
   (see Buying guide)
1 teaspoon salt
1 teaspoon ground ginger
½ teaspoon freshly ground black
   pepper
½ teaspoon ground cloves
3 cloves garlic, crushed
3 bay leaves
600 ml/1 pint chicken stock
175 ml/6 fl oz dark rum
100 g/4 oz soft brown sugar
4 tablespoons lime juice
1 tablespoon plain flour

1 Using a very sharp knife, score the skin of the pork fairly deeply, almost through to the fat, in a diamond pattern.
2 Heat the oven to 170C/325F/Gas 3.
3 Pound the salt, ginger, pepper, cloves and garlic to a paste in a mortar and pestle. Rub the paste well into the scored surface of the pork; place bay leaves on top.
4 Pour 150 ml/¼ pint of the stock into a roasting pan, together with one-third of the rum. Put the meat, skin-side up, on a rack in the pan and roast in the oven for 1 hour.
5 Meanwhile, mix the brown sugar, lime juice and remaining rum in a bowl.
6 Remove the meat from the oven and baste with the sugar and lime mixture. Return the meat to the

oven and continue to roast for a further 1¼ hours. Add more stock to the pan during this time, if the liquid appears to be drying out.

7 Transfer the meat to a warmed serving platter and discard the bay leaves. Keep the meat hot.

8 Pour off the liquid from the roasting pan into a jug, skim off the excess fat and return 1 tablespoon to the roasting pan. Place the pan on top of the cooker and sprinkle in the flour. Stir over low heat for 1 minute, then stir in the remaining stock and the reserved cooking liquid. Simmer, stirring constantly, until the sauce has thickened. Season to taste with salt and pepper, transfer to a warmed sauceboat and hand separately.

Coconut soufflé

SERVES 6

350 ml/12 fl oz canned coconut
   cream (see Buying guide)
6 eggs, separated
75 g/3 oz caster sugar
1½ rounded tablespoons (1½
   sachets) gelatine
4 tablespoons cold water
2 limes (see Preparation)
90 g/3½ oz unsweetened desiccated
   coconut

1 Put the coconut cream into a pan
and gently bring almost to
simmering point. Remove from the
heat and set aside.
2 Put the egg yolks and sugar in a
heatproof bowl that will fit over a
pan of water. Whisk together until
thick and pale, then stir in the
warmed coconut cream until
thoroughly mixed in.
3 Set the bowl over a pan of barely
simmering water and cook, stirring
constantly, for about 10 minutes
until the mixture is smooth and

slightly thickened. Remove the
bowl from the heat.
4 Sprinkle the gelatine over the
water in a heatproof bowl. Leave to
soak for 5 minutes until spongy,
then stand the bowl in the pan of
gently simmering water for 1-2
minutes, stirring occasionally, until
the gelatine has dissolved.
5 Whisk the gelatine into the
coconut cream mixture, together
with the lime zest and 75 g/3 oz of
the desiccated coconut. Allow the
mixture to cool for about 30
minutes.
6 Meanwhile, secure a paper collar
carefully around an 850 ml/1½ pint
soufflé dish.

7 In a spotlessly clean, dry bowl,
whisk the egg whites until they
stand in stiff peaks, then fold into
the cooled coconut cream mixture.
Transfer to the prepared soufflé
dish and refrigerate for at least 3
hours until set.
8 Meanwhile, brown the remaining
desiccated coconut: put the coconut
on a foil-covered grill rack and toast
under a fairly hot grill for 2 minutes,
turning constantly, until evenly
browned.
9 Carefully remove the paper collar
from the soufflé, then, using a
palette knife, press the toasted
coconut on to the sides. Decorate the
top with lime slices.

Cook's Notes

TIME
Preparation takes 1
hour, plus 30 minutes
cooling and at least 3 hours
chilling.

BUYING GUIDE
If canned coconut cream
is difficult to obtain, use
115 g/4½ oz block creamed

coconut dissolved in 225 ml/8 fl
oz hot water.

PREPARATION
Finely grate the zest
from 1½ limes, then
cut the remaining half into very
thin slices for decorating.

●680 calories/2860 kj per portion

FRENCH DINNER PARTY

Style and elegance are the hallmarks of French cookery, and here is a superb menu that captures these qualities. The three distinguished dishes include mouthwatering Garlic mushrooms, Dijon lamb noisettes in a gloriously creamy sauce and a fruity Blackcurrant sorbet – a selection of dishes that any French chef would be proud to serve. Bon appétit!

COUNTDOWN

The day before
● Make the Blackcurrant sorbet.
In the morning
● Prepare the Garlic mushrooms.
1 hour before
● Start the Dijon lamb nóisettes.
40 minutes before
● Put the lamb dish in the oven.
20 minutes before
● Fry the Garlic mushrooms.
Just before the main course
● Remove the Blackcurrant sorbet from the refrigerator to soften.
● Make the mustard sauce, pour over the lamb and shallots.

Garlic mushrooms

SERVES 4

24 cup-shaped mushrooms (see Buying guide)
100 g/4 oz unsalted butter, softened
2 cloves garlic, crushed
1 tablespoon finely chopped fresh tarragon, or 1½ teaspoons dried tarragon
finely grated zest of ½ lemon
freshly ground black pepper
2 eggs
75 g/3 oz dried white breadcrumbs
vegetable oil, for deep-frying
lemon wedges, to garnish

1 Heat the oven to 110C/225F/Gas ¼.
2 Carefully remove the mushroom stalks and chop the stalks finely.
3 Beat the butter with the mushroom stalks, garlic, tarragon, lemon zest and pepper to taste, then spoon into the cavities of the mushroom caps. Sandwich the mushrooms together in pairs and secure with cocktail sticks.
4 Lightly beat the eggs in a bowl and spread the breadcrumbs out on a plate. Dip each mushroom pair, first in the egg, then roll in the breadcrumbs. Repeat once more, then refrigerate for at least 1 hour.
5 Heat the oil in a deep-fat frier to 190C/375F or until a stale bread cube browns in 50 seconds. Fry a few of the mushrooms for about 5 minutes until golden brown. Drain on absorbent paper and keep hot in the oven while frying the rest.
6 To serve: remove the cocktail sticks and serve at once.

Dijon lamb noisettes

SERVES 4

4 noisettes of lamb, each about 4 cm/1½ inches thick
2 tablespoons vegetable oil
15 g/½ oz butter
12 shallots or button onions
100 ml/4 fl oz white wine
salt and freshly ground black pepper
bouquet garni
2 egg yolks
150 ml/¼ pint double cream
about 2 tablespoons Dijon mustard (see Buying guide)
1 bunch fresh herbs, to garnish (optional)

1 Heat the oven to 190C/375F/Gas 5.
2 Heat the oil and butter in a large frying-pan, add the lamb and fry briskly for about 2 minutes on each side until browned. Transfer the lamb to a small roasting tin or shallow casserole into which they will fit neatly in a single layer.
3 Add the shallots to the fat remaining in the pan and fry gently for 10 minutes until browned. Transfer to a plate with a slotted spoon.
4 Pour the wine into the pan and bring to the boil, scraping up all the sediment from the bottom of the pan. Season to taste with salt and pepper, then pour over the lamb. Add the bouquet garni, cover with foil or a lid and bake in the oven for about 1 hour.
5 In a bowl, mix together the egg yolks, cream and 2 tablespoons of the mustard. Set aside.
6 Using a slotted spoon, transfer the cooked lamb and the shallots to a serving dish and keep warm.
7 Discard the bouquet garni and strain the cooking liquid into a small, heavy-based saucepan. Boil briskly until the liquid is reduced by about half.
8 Pour a little of the hot cooking liquid into the egg yolk mixture, stirring vigorously all the time, then pour this mixture back into the pan. Heat through, stirring constantly, until thick and on the point of boiling. ⚠ Taste and adjust the seasoning, if necessary.
9 To serve: pour sauce over lamb and garnish with herbs, if liked.

Cook's Notes

Garlic mushrooms
 TIME
About 45 minutes preparation, plus at least 1 hour chilling, then about 20 minutes frying.

 BUYING GUIDE
Buy the medium-sized cultivated mushrooms for this recipe, rather than the small button or large, flat open varieties. The mushrooms must have cups deep enough to hold the filling.

● 380 calories/1600 kj per portion

Dijon lamb noisettes
TIME
Preparation takes about 20 minutes. Total cooking time is about 1 hour 10 minutes.

⚠ **WATCHPOINT**
Do not let the sauce boil or it may curdle and the mustard will turn bitter.

BUYING GUIDE
Dijon mustard, from the area of Burgundy south east of Paris, is available at most good supermarkets and delicatessens. Made from brown mustard seeds, it is a smooth mustard with a distinctive flavour. Dijon is also available with green peppercorns added—*moutarde au poivre vert*. Or, use a herb mustard based on Dijon mustard.

SERVING IDEAS
Serve with plainly boiled potatoes tossed in chopped parsley, if liked, plus broccoli or mange-tout. For a really authentic flavour, serve a light, red French wine to complement the food – a Bordeaux wine (claret) would be the perfect choice.
    If wished, follow the French custom of serving a tossed green salad or selection of cheese after the main course.

● 660 calories/2775 kj per portion

418

Blackcurrant sorbet

SERVES 4

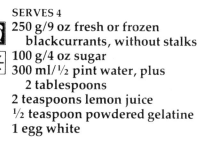
250 g/9 oz fresh or frozen
  blackcurrants, without stalks
100 g/4 oz sugar
300 ml/½ pint water, plus
  2 tablespoons
2 teaspoons lemon juice
½ teaspoon powdered gelatine
1 egg white

1 Put the sugar and 300 ml/½ pint water in a heavy-based pan and heat gently until the sugar has dissolved. Boil for 10 minutes until syrupy, then remove from the heat and set aside to cool.

2 Put the blackcurrants in a pan with the lemon juice and heat gently for about 10 minutes until softened. Allow to cool slightly, then purée in a blender. Press the puréed blackcurrants through a sieve into a bowl to remove seeds and skin.

3 Sprinkle the gelatine over the 2 tablespoons water in a heatproof bowl and leave to soak for 5 minutes until spongy. Stand the bowl in a pan of gently simmering water and heat gently for 1-2 minutes stirring occasionally until the gelatine has dissolved. Stir the gelatine into the cooled sugar syrup.

4 Stir the sugar syrup into the blackcurrant purée and mix well. Turn into a rigid container and freeze, uncovered, (see Cook's tip) for about 3 hours until the mixture is firm around the edges.

5 Remove the blackcurrant mixture from the freezer and break up with a fork. Whisk the egg white until it stands in stiff peaks, then fold into the blackcurrant mixture. ✳ Cover and freeze overnight, until solid.

6 To serve: stand at room temperature for about 30 minutes until the sorbet is soft enough to scoop into individual glasses.

SANGRIA EVENING

Conjure up an exotic, festive atmosphere at any time of year with a Sangria party. The delicious wine cup Sangria is a perfect accompaniment to food with a Spanish flavour – crunchy raw vegetables with a creamy dip, the Mediterranean Chicken catalan, and Spanish caramel custards with the sunny taste of orange.

To help create the informal atmosphere typical of a meal eaten in Spain, hand round the crudités before you and your guests sit down at the dinner table.

Sangria

SERVES 6

2 x 70 cl/1¼ pint bottles sweet red Spanish wine
5 fresh peaches, thinly sliced, or 400 g/14 oz can sliced peaches, drained
juice of 1 lemon
4 tablespoons brandy (optional)
1 eating apple
1 lemon
600 ml/1 pint soda water
ice cubes

1 Put the peaches in a large jug or glass bowl. Add the wine, lemon juice and brandy and allow to soak for about 2 hours.
2 Just before serving, slice the apple and lemon thinly and add to the jug with the soda water and ice cubes.

Cook's Notes

TIME
10 minutes to prepare, but allow 2 hours for the full flavour to develop.

● 240 calories/1000 kj per portion

Crudités and dip

CRUDITÉS

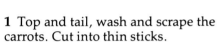

SERVES 6
6 carrots
6 celery stalks
6 small or 3 large tomatoes
½ cucumber
8 radishes (optional)
1 small cauliflower

1 Top and tail, wash and scrape the carrots. Cut into thin sticks.
2 Wash celery and cut into sticks.
3 Cut large tomatoes into quarters, leave small ones whole.
4 Cut the tails off the cucumber and peel it if you prefer. Divide into 2 both lengthways and widthways. Cut each piece into 4 long strips.
5 Wash, top and tail the radishes.
6 Wash the cauliflower. Cut off the base then separate the head into florets. !
7 Arrange the crudités in groups around the edge of a tray, shallow basket or dish, leaving room for the dip in the centre.

COTTAGE CHEESE AND YOGHURT DIP

SERVES 6
225 g/8 oz cottage cheese
2 tablespoons natural yoghurt
2 spring onions or ½ onion
4 gherkins, finely chopped
salt and freshly ground black pepper
dash of Tabasco sauce (optional)

1 Sieve or blend the cottage cheese until smooth.
2 Add the yoghurt and mix well.
3 Wash and trim the spring onions. Chop finely and add to mixture.
4 Add finely chopped gherkins.
5 Season to taste and add Tabasco, if using.
6 Give a final mixing. Transfer to a serving bowl and place in centre of crudités.

Cook's Notes

TIME
Allow 45 minutes to prepare the vegetables and make the dip.

COOK'S TIP
Save time by preparing the dip in a blender. Blend all the ingredients except the onions and gherkins. Add these at the end and switch on for about 2 seconds so that they are only partially chopped.

● 40 calories/150 kj per portion

WATCHPOINT
If vegetables are prepared in advance store them in a plastic box or in the salad drawer of the refrigerator to avoid browning.

VARIATIONS
Use different varieties of vegetables such as red or green peppers, raw button mushrooms or small French beans.

● 45 calories/175 kj per portion

Chicken catalan

SERVES 6

6 small chicken breasts, skinned
6 tablespoons olive oil
3 medium onions, thinly sliced
2 cloves garlic, crushed
450 g/1 lb long-grain rice
1-2 tablespoons tomato purée
pinch of saffron strands (see
    Steps) or few drops of
    yellow food colouring
1 L/2 pints boiling chicken stock
1 teaspoon sweet paprika
salt and freshly ground black pepper
100 g/4 oz Spanish chorizo sausage
    or other firm garlic sausage
    (optional), cut into large chunks
1 green pepper, deseeded and sliced
    into rings
1 red pepper, deseeded and sliced
    into rings
100 g/4 oz stuffed olives
chopped parsley, to garnish

1 Heat half the oil in a large flame-proof casserole. Fry the chicken breasts over moderate heat until golden brown in colour and half cooked through (about 7 minutes each side).

2 Reserve chicken pieces and keep them warm.

3 Add 1 tablespoon more oil to the casserole. Cook the onions over low heat for 2 minutes until transparent but not brown.

4 Add the garlic, the remaining oil and the rice. Stir for a few minutes with a wooden spoon until the rice starts to colour.

5 Meanwhile, stir the tomato purée and colouring, if used, into the boiling stock.

6 Stir stock, with saffron liquid, if used, into the rice mixture, add paprika and salt and pepper to taste, then bring to the boil, stirring constantly.

7 Add the chicken to the casserole with the sausage and peppers, pressing them well down into all the rice.

8 Lower the heat, cover and simmer for about 30 minutes or until the rice is just tender, stirring occasionally with a wooden spoon. Be careful not to overcook the rice so that it becomes mushy.

9 Add the olives to the rice and heat through for a few minutes. Taste and adjust seasoning.

10 Transfer to a large warmed serving dish. Sprinkle the chopped parsley over the top to garnish and serve at once.

Cook's Notes

TIME
10-15 minutes for preparation plus 1 hour cooking.

ECONOMY
Chicken breasts are meaty and convenient to use, because they are sold boned or partially boned, but they do tend to be rather expensive. Ordinary chicken pieces are not so expensive as breasts, and they can be used just as well but will need to be cooked for about 10 minutes on each side in stage 1. (You could even buy a whole chicken and joint it yourself.) If you prefer not to have awkward-looking bones in the finished dish, it is quite simple to remove the bones before the chicken is cooked.

DID YOU KNOW
Saffron is an immensely popular spice in Spain, where it is used for colouring rice (it has hardly any taste). It was introduced to the Spaniards by the Arabs, and has for centuries been used as a colouring agent, especially in Arab and Eastern cooking. It is used in this recipe to give the rice a bright, golden-yellow colour, but as it is so expensive, we have suggested yellow food colouring as a cheaper alternative. If you have ground turmeric this can also be used, but it has a more distinctive flavour than saffron. Saffron strands and turmeric are available from delicatessens, good supermarkets and Indian specialist shops.

BUYING GUIDE
Spanish chorizo sausages can be obtained at most good delicatessens, and are easily recognizable by their bright red appearance. They are made from pure pork flavoured with pimiento (hot red pepper), and so are hot and spicy. If you find them difficult to obtain, use any continental-type cured sausage with a spicy flavour.

● 605 calories/2525kj per portion

HOW TO USE SAFFRON

 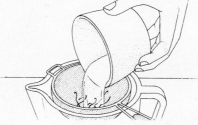 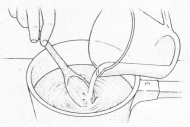

1 *Crush a few strands of saffron in your fingers and drop them into a small bowl of boiling water.*

2 *Leave to infuse for at least 2 hours, then strain the water, discarding the saffron strands.*

3 *Stir the saffron-coloured liquid into the stock used in recipe.*

Spanish caramel custards

SERVES 6

CUSTARD
1 orange
600 ml/1 pint milk
4 eggs
75 g/3 oz caster sugar

CARAMEL
6 tablespoons granulated sugar
6 tablespoons water

1 Heat the oven to 150C/300F/Gas 2.
2 Wash and dry the orange, then pare off the rind with a potato peeler.
3 Place the orange rind and milk in a saucepan and allow to infuse over low heat. This means bringing the milk to the boil slowly and allowing it to stand for 10 minutes.
4 Beat the eggs and sugar together in a bowl and strain over the milk. Beat lightly to mix.
5 Half fill a roasting tin with warm water and place in the oven.
6 To make the caramel: put the sugar and water in a saucepan. Heat slowly until the sugar has dissolved, then boil steadily without stirring until the sugar turns a pale golden brown. !
7 Pour caramel into individual soufflé dishes or a 15 cm/6 inch diameter soufflé dish. Leave for about 2 minutes to set.
8 Remove roasting tin from the oven.
9 Strain the egg and milk mixture on to the caramel in the moulds and place in the roasting tin. Replace in the oven and cook until the custard is set – about 40 minutes to an hour.
10 Cool for at least 3 hours, then chill in the refrigerator.
11 Remove the pith from the orange with a sharp knife and divide the flesh into segments.
12 Turn the custards on to a plate and arrange the orange segments on top or around the plate.

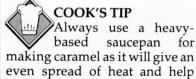

Cook's Notes

TIME
The custards take about 30 minutes to prepare and 1 hour to cook. Remember to allow at least 4 hours afterwards for the custards to cool and for chilling.

COOK'S TIP
Always use a heavy-based saucepan for making caramel as it will give an even spread of heat and help prevent burning.

WATCHPOINT
Do not take your eyes off the caramel once it begins to turn brown as it burns very easily.

• 215 calories/900 kj per portion

MEDITERRANEAN MEAL

Transport your guests to the sunny shores of the Mediterranean with this continental-style menu. Small onion tarts provide a tempting appetizer, before the magnificent Provençal fish stew. And, to finish, sophisticated fruit salad captures all the sunshine flavour of the meal.

Genoese onion tarts

SERVES 6

215 g/7½ oz frozen puff pastry, defrosted
50 g/2 oz can anchovy fillets (see Preparation)
12 black olives, halved and stoned

FILLING
500 g/1 lb onions, finely chopped
25 g/1 oz margarine or butter
1 tablespoon olive oil or corn oil
4 streaky bacon rashers, chopped
1 teaspoon dried mixed herbs
½ teaspoon French mustard
1 egg, beaten
2 tablespoons milk
salt and freshly ground black pepper

1 Make the filling: heat the margarine and oil in a frying-pan, add the bacon and fry over moderate heat for 7-8 minutes. Remove the bacon from the pan with a slotted spoon and set aside. Remove the pan from heat and cool for 10 minutes.
2 Add the onions to the fat remaining in the pan and fry very gently for 15 minutes until they are soft and lightly coloured.
3 Heat the oven to 220C/425F/Gas 7.
4 Meanwhile, dampen 6 individual 7.5 cm/3 inch tart tins. Roll out the pastry very thinly on a lightly floured surface and cut out 6 rounds with a 9 cm/3½ inch plain cutter. Use to line tart tins and then prick base of each pastry case with a fork.
5 Add the herbs to the onions in the pan, together with the mustard, egg and milk. Mix well together, then season with salt and pepper.
6 Divide the filling between the pastry cases, spread evenly and garnish with a cross made of anchovy strips and 4 olive halves.
7 Bake above centre of the oven for 25-30 minutes until the pastry is crisp and the filling is browned on top. Remove the tarts from the oven then carefully transfer them to a platter and serve while still warm.

Provençal fish stew

SERVES 6
1-1.25 kg/2-2½ lb mixed fish fillets, skinned and cut into 5 cm/2 inch pieces (see Buying guide)
6 tablespoons olive oil
2 large cloves garlic, crushed
1 sprig fresh fennel
bouquet garni
1-2 strips orange zest
300 ml/½ pint dry white wine
salt and freshly ground black pepper
2 onions, thinly sliced
2 celery stalks, sliced
4 tomatoes, skinned, deseeded and chopped
2 tablespoons tomato purée
1 L/2 pints fish stock or water
pinch of powdered saffron (optional)
100 g/4 oz peeled prawns, defrosted if frozen
few cooked mussels, shelled
6 slices French bread, to serve
chopped parsley, to garnish

ROUILLE SAUCE
1 slice bread, crusts removed, soaked in water
1 chilli, deseeded and chopped
3 cloves garlic, crushed
1 egg yolk
150 ml/¼ pint olive oil

1 Place the fish in a large dish. Add 2 tablespoons olive oil, the garlic, fennel, bouquet garni and orange zest, then pour in the wine. Season well with salt and pepper, cover and leave to marinate at room temperature for about 1 hour, stirring occasionally.
2 Heat 2 tablespoons of the olive oil in a large, heavy-based frying-pan or flameproof casserole, then add the onions and celery and fry gently for 5 minutes until onions are soft and lightly coloured then stir in the chopped tomatoes and the tomato purée and fry for a further 2 minutes, stirring constantly with a wooden spoon.
3 Drain the fish and add the marinade to the pan. Stir in the fish stock and sprinkle in the powdered saffron, if using. Bring to boil, then simmer for 20 minutes.
4 Meanwhile make the sauce: squeeze the bread dry and put it into a bowl with the chilli, garlic, egg yolk and a pinch of salt. Beat together with a little of the oil until well blended. Gradually whisk in the remaining oil and season to taste with salt and pepper. Transfer the sauce to a serving bowl, cover with cling film and set aside until it is required.
5 Discard the fennel, bouquet garni and orange zest from the drained fish, then add the marinated fish pieces and any remaining juices to the pan. Bring to the boil and then simmer, uncovered, for about 15 minutes.
6 Add the prawns and mussels. Simmer for a further 5 minutes or until the fish is still in pieces but flakes easily when it is tested with a fork.
7 Meanwhile, fry the French bread in the remaining 2 tablespoons of oil until crisp.
8 To serve: taste the stew and adjust seasoning, if necessary. Transfer to large, individual soup plates, sprinkle with parsley and serve at once. Serve the fried French bread and rouille sauce separately (see Serving ideas).

Cook's Notes

Genoese onion tarts

 TIME
35 minutes preparation;
25-30 minutes cooking.

 PREPARATION
Drain the anchovies,
then soak in milk for 20
minutes. Drain again and cut
into 12 even-sized strips.

● 280 calories/1175 kj per portion

Provençal fish stew

 TIME
Preparation 30 minutes
plus marinating; cook-
ing about 50 minutes.

 SERVING IDEAS
Guests spread French
bread with sauce and
dip it in their dish of stew.

● 570 calories/2400 kj per portion

? DID YOU KNOW
This is a simplified ver-
sion of the classic
Provençal fish stew known as
bouillabaisse. Rouille sauce is a
traditional accompaniment.

 BUYING GUIDE
Buy as wide a variety of
fish as possible. Choose
from cod, halibut, monkfish,
whiting, mackerel or mullet.

Riviera fruit salad

SERVES 6
425 ml/¾ pint double cream
4 teaspoons Strega liqueur (see Did you know and Variations)
175 g/6 oz strawberries, hulled
2 bananas
2 dessert apples
100 g/4 oz green grapes, halved and deseeded

CARAMEL SAUCE
200 g/7 oz caster sugar
8 tablespoons water

1 Make the caramel sauce: put the caster sugar in a small, heavy-based saucepan together with 2 table-spoons water. Heat very gently, until the sugar has dissolved. Bring to the boil and boil rapidly without stirring, until the syrup turns a rich caramel colour. ⚠
2 Remove from the heat and add the remaining water, 1 tablespoon at a time, taking care as it will splutter when the water is added to the very hot caramel. Stir well together, returning to the heat if necessary, until well blended. Set aside to cool for about 2½ hours.
3 Whip the cream until standing in soft peaks, then fold in the liqueur (see Cook's tip). Divide between 6 individual shallow glass dishes, about 12.5 cm/5 inches in diameter, and smooth over top with a knife. Cover and refrigerate for at least 1-2 hours.
4 Just before serving, slice the strawberries, slice the bananas, then core and slice the apples. Arrange, with the grapes, in neat rows on top of the chilled cream and carefully coat with the caramel sauce. Serve the fruit salad at once.

Cook's Notes

TIME
45 minutes preparation, plus cooling the syrup and chilling the cream, then 10 minutes finishing the salad.

DID YOU KNOW
Strega is a sweet, citrus liqueur from Italy.

VARIATIONS
Use different varieties of fruit or liqueur to taste — apricot- or cherry-flavoured liqueurs are both suitable.

COOK'S TIP
Sugar is not added to the cream – the caramel sauce sweetens the dish.

WATCHPOINT
It is important not to stir the syrup while it is boiling as this may crystallize the caster sugar. Watch the caramel carefully — if it is too dark, it will taste strong and rather bitter.

●525 calories/2200 kj per portion

NEW YEAR'S PARTY

Celebrate New Year's Eve with a flourish. Start the evening with drinks accompanied by Smoked haddock tarts, then launch into a full-flavoured Scotch beef casserole. End the meal in spirited style with Drambuie creams.

Smoked haddock tarts

MAKES 24 TARTS
400 g/13 oz frozen shortcrust pastry, defrosted
600 g/1¼ lb smoked haddock
1 teaspoon ground mace
2 bay leaves, crumbled
freshly grated nutmeg
freshly ground black pepper
milk
25 g/1 oz butter
1 tablespoon plain flour
1 egg yolk, beaten
salt and freshly ground black pepper
pinch of cayenne pepper
grated Parmesan cheese

1 Heat the oven to 190C/375F/Gas 5.
2 Roll out the pastry on a lightly floured surface and cut out 24 circles with a 7.5 cm/3 inch fluted pastry cutter. Use to line 24 tart tins and prick the base of each with a fork.
3 Line each case with foil and weight down with baking beans. Bake blind in the oven for 10-15 minutes. Remove the foil and beans and set aside to cool.
4 Meanwhile, put the smoked haddock in a large saucepan with the mace, bay leaves, and a generous sprinkling of nutmeg and black pepper. Add enough milk to cover the fish, then poach gently for about 15 minutes or until it flakes easily with a fork.
5 Using a slotted spoon, transfer the fish to a plate, then strain the cooking liquid. Make up the cooking liquid to 300 ml/½ pint with milk and reserve.
6 Remove the skin and bones from the fish, then transfer to a bowl and mash thoroughly with a fork.
7 Melt the butter in a small saucepan, sprinkle in the flour and stir over low heat for 1-2 minutes until

straw-coloured. Remove from the heat and gradually stir in the reserved milky cooking liquid. Return to the heat and, stirring constantly, simmer until thick and smooth.
8 Add 1 beaten egg yolk and the mashed haddock, stirring well to mix thoroughly. Taste and adjust seasoning, adding more salt, pepper and nutmeg if necessary.
9 Heat the grill to high. Carefully remove the pastry cases from the tins, put on a large flameproof serving dish and divide the fish mixture between the cases. Sprinkle each one with a pinch of cayenne and a little Parmesan cheese.
10 Put under the grill for 3-4 minutes until the cheese is melted and the tops of the tarts bubbly and golden. Serve at once.

Scotch beef casserole

SERVES 12
2.3 kg/5 lb chuck steak, cut into 2.5 cm/1 inch cubes (see Buying guide)
3 tablespoons olive oil
50 g/2 oz butter
3 Spanish onions, thinly sliced
2 tablespoons plain flour
750 g/1½ lb tomatoes, skinned
600 ml/1 pint beef stock
salt and freshly ground black pepper
500 g/1 lb button mushrooms
1 tablespoon redcurrant jelly
2 teaspoons French mustard

MARINADE
600 ml/1 pint medium red wine
3 tablespoons olive oil
3 cloves garlic, crushed
1 teaspoon juniper berries, crushed
3 bay leaves
2 sprigs fresh thyme, or ¾ teaspoon dried thyme
1 teaspoon ground caraway seeds

1 Mix the marinade ingredients together. Put the beef cubes in a large bowl and pour the marinade over them. Stir well to mix, then cover and marinate overnight.
2 Drain the meat, reserving the marinade. Remove the bay leaves and sprigs of thyme from the drained meat, then pat dry.
3 Heat the oil and butter in a large deep flameproof casserole. Add enough meat to cover the base of the pan and fry briskly for 3-4 minutes until brown on all sides. Remove the meat with a slotted spoon, set aside. Fry remaining meat in batches.
4 Add the onions to the pan and fry gently for 5 minutes until soft and lightly coloured. Return the meat to the pan, sprinkle over the flour and fry, stirring, for a further 5 minutes.
5 Add the tomatoes, stock and reserved marinade to the casserole with salt and pepper to taste. Bring to the boil, then lower the heat, cover and simmer for 2-2½ hours.
6 Add the mushrooms to the casserole and simmer for 5 minutes.
7 Add the redcurrant jelly and mustard to the pan and simmer for a further 10 minutes, stirring occasionally. Taste and adjust seasoning, if necessary. Serve hot.

COUNTDOWN
The day before
● Marinate meat for casserole.
In the morning
● Make and bake blind the pastry cases for the Smoked haddock tarts.
● Toast the oatmeal for the creams.
3½ hours before
● Start cooking the casserole.
1 hour before
● Make the filling for the tarts.
30 minutes before
● Make the Drambuie creams.
15 minutes before
● Add mushrooms to casserole.
10 minutes before
● Complete the casserole.
● Fill the tarts and grill them.

Cook's Notes

Smoked haddock tarts

 TIME
30 minutes preparation,
50 minutes cooking.

● 100 calories/425 kj per tart

Scotch beef casserole

TIME
30 minutes preparation,
plus 12 hours marinat-
ing, then 3-3½ hours cooking.

 BUYING GUIDE
Scotch beef will give the
best flavour to this dish,
but any other type of beef will
be quite adequate.

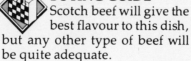 **VARIATION**
For a different, more
'gamey', flavour, try
using stewing venison. It is very
rich so decrease the amount to 2
kg/4½ lb.

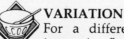 **SERVING IDEAS**
Serve with generous
helpings of mashed
swedes mixed with mashed
potatoes and butter and
seasoned generously with
freshly ground black pepper
and salt – it is a delicious way
to mop up the rich sauce of
the casserole.

● 480 calories/2025 kj per portion

Drambuie creams

SERVES 12

850 ml/1½ pints double cream
75 g/3 oz fine oatmeal
50 g/2 oz icing sugar
4 tablespoons Drambuie

1 Heat the grill to moderate.
2 Spread the oatmeal out in a thin layer on a baking sheet, and grill for 3-4 minutes, turning once, until lightly toasted. Remove and leave to stand until completely cold.
3 Pour the cream into a large bowl and whip until it stands in soft peaks. ⚠
4 Add the cold oatmeal, icing sugar and Drambuie and stir until thoroughly mixed.
5 Spoon into individual glasses or small ramekins and chill in the refrigerator for 30 minutes before serving.

Cook's Notes

TIME
8-10 minutes preparation, plus cooling time and 30 minutes chilling.

WATCHPOINT
Be careful not to whip the cream too stiffly otherwise the dessert may become too thick when the other ingredients are added.

DID YOU KNOW
This is an unusual adaptation of the famous Scottish drink Atholl Brose, which is made from Scotch whisky, cream and oatmeal.
   Drambuie is a famous Scottish liqueur, based on the finest Scotch whisky. The name Drambuie is derived from the Gaelic *an dram buideach:* 'the drink that satisfies'. The secret recipe is alleged to have been given to the Mackinnon family by Bonnie Prince Charlie in return for saving his life.

●365 calories/1525 kj per portion

VALENTINE'S DINNER

Valentine's day is traditionally a day for romance, so this year why not whet the appetite with a delicious dinner just for two. The dishes chosen – avocados, stuffed trout and a creamy heart-shaped dessert — have a seductive delicacy about them that sets the tone for a romantic and very intimate evening.

Avocado special

SERVES 2
1 large ripe avocado
juice of ½ lemon
50 ml/2 fl oz thick bottled
    mayonnaise
1 slice cooked ham, finely chopped
1 tablespoon snipped chives
¼ teaspoon French mustard
salt and freshly ground black pepper

TO GARNISH
lettuce leaves
tomato flesh, cut into heart shapes
    (see Preparation)

1 Cut the avocado in half lengthways and remove the stone. Scoop out the flesh with a teaspoon, leaving a thin lining of flesh on the inside of the shells.
2 Put the flesh in a bowl, sprinkle over the lemon juice, then beat until smooth. Add the mayonnaise, ham, chives and mustard, mix well and season to taste with salt and pepper.
3 Pile the mixture back into the avocado shells.
4 Line 2 individual plates with lettuce leaves, and arrange the filled avocados on the lined plates. Garnish the avocados with the tomato shapes and serve at once.

Trout with mushroom stuffing

SERVES 2
2 fresh or frozen trout, each
    weighing about 500 g/1 lb (see
    Preparation)
75 g/3 oz butter
1 small onion, finely chopped
250 g/9 oz mushrooms, finely
    chopped
juice of ½ lemon
1 tablespoon chopped fresh parsley
25 g/1 oz fresh white breadcrumbs
salt and freshly ground black pepper

TO GARNISH
sliced stuffed olives
parsley sprigs
4 lemon wedges

1 Heat the oven to 190C/375F/Gas 5.
2 Melt 25 g/1 oz of the butter in a frying-pan, add the onion and fry gently for about 5 minutes until soft and lightly coloured.
3 Add the mushrooms to the onion with the lemon juice and cook gently for 5 minutes until the mushrooms are soft and all the liquid has evaporated.
4 Remove the pan from the heat and stir in the parsley and breadcrumbs. Season to taste with salt and pepper and allow to cool.

5 Fill each trout with mushroom stuffing, then close openings with 2-3 wooden cocktail sticks.
6 Put the remaining butter into a shallow ovenproof dish large enough to hold the trout side-by-side. Place the dish in the oven for a few minutes until the butter melts. Remove from the oven.
7 Place the stuffed trout in the dish and turn them in the melted butter until they are well coated. Sprinkle with salt and pepper to taste.
8 Bake the trout, uncovered, for 25-30 minutes until the flesh flakes easily when tested with a fork. Baste frequently during cooking.
9 Transfer trout to a hot serving plate, remove the cocktail sticks and garnish attractively with sliced olives and parsley sprigs. Serve at once, with lemon wedges.

COUNTDOWN
The day before
● Make the *Coeurs à la crème* and refrigerate overnight.
1¾ hours before
● Fill the Trout with mushroom stuffing and make the garnishes.
1 hour before
● Sprinkle the soft fruit with sugar for *Coeurs*.
30 minutes before
● Heat oven and put in trout.
● Prepare the Avocado special.
Just before the dessert
● Unmould *Coeurs* and decorate.

Cook's Notes

Avocado special
 TIME
This starter takes 20 minutes to make.

 PREPARATION
Use a petits fours cutter to cut out hearts.

●420 calories/1750 kj per portion

Trout with mushroom stuffing
TIME
About 30 minutes preparation, and 25-30 minutes cooking.

PREPARATION
Fresh trout should be gutted, rinsed under cold running water and patted inside and out with absorbent paper. Your fishmonger will gut them for you, if asked.

 SERVING IDEAS
Serve with sauté potatoes and tender, young peas (*petits pois*).

●605 calories/2525 kj per portion

Coeurs à la crème

SERVES 2

100 g/4 oz curd cheese
1 tablespoon caster sugar
finely grated zest of ½ lemon
150 ml/¼ pint double cream
1 egg white
250 g/9 oz fresh or frozen small
  strawberries or raspberries
extra caster sugar, for sweetening

1 Line 2 *coeurs à la crème* moulds (see Buying guide) with large squares of wet muslin. ⚠ Allow the muslin to hang over the sides.

2 Pass the curd cheese through a nylon sieve into a bowl, add the caster sugar and lemon zest and beat well until very soft.

3 Whisk 4 tablespoons of the cream until it forms soft peaks, then mix into the cheese mixture.

4 Whisk the egg white in a clean, dry bowl until it stands in stiff peaks. Fold 1 tablespoon of the egg white into the cheese mixture to lighten it, then fold in the rest.

5 Spoon the cheese mixture into the prepared moulds and smooth the

tops. Fold the overhanging pieces of muslin over the cheese mixture to enclose it completely. Put the moulds on a flat plate and refrigerate them overnight.

6 About 1 hour before serving, sprinkle the strawberries with caster sugar to sweeten.

7 To serve: remove the moulds from the refrigerator and unwrap the

tops. Place a small serving plate on top of each mould, then carefully invert the plate and mould together. Shake gently, unmould, then carefully remove the muslin.

8 Decorate with some of the fruit then pour over the remaining unwhipped cream. Put the remaining fruit in the empty moulds and serve separately.

EASTER WEEKEND

Pretty, colourful eggs, whether to eat or to exchange, and the family gathering for a leisurely weekend meal, are what make Easter such an enjoyable occasion. Attractively marbled boiled eggs will make breakfast a special treat and the festively decorated eggs, which can be made in advance, may be passed round later on. For the main meal, a fruity starter, stuffed lamb and a triumphant meringue-topped pudding will appeal to both young and old.

Marbled eggs

SERVES 6

6 large eggs
2 teaspoons each of green, red and blue food colourings (see Watchpoints)
12 slices white or brown bread, crusts removed
butter, for spreading
2-3 tablespoons sesame seeds

1 Heat the grill to high.
2 Put 2 eggs in each of 3 small saucepans and cover the eggs with water. Add 2 teaspoons of one of the food colourings to each pan and stir well. Bring the water to the boil and boil the eggs for 2 minutes.
3 Meanwhile, toast the bread slices on one side only. Remove from the grill and butter the untoasted sides, then sprinkle generously with sesame seeds. Set aside.
4 Remove the eggs from the water with a slotted spoon and, holding them in an oven glove, gently tap the shells all over with the back of a teaspoon, until they are cracked and crazed. [!]
5 Return the eggs to their pans, [!] bring back to the boil and boil for a further 1-2 minutes for soft eggs or 6-8 minutes for hard-boiled eggs.
6 Meanwhile, toast the sesame-coated sides of the bread until golden brown. Cut the toast into fingers or small triangles.
7 Drain the eggs and rinse under cold running water, then carefully remove the shells. Serve at once, with the sesame seed toast.

Chocolate eggs

MAKES 6
6 large eggs
750 g/1½ lb plain or milk dessert chocolate

DECORATIONS
a little lightly beaten egg white
about 150 g/5 oz icing sugar, sifted
few drops of food colouring (optional)
sugar flowers or other cake decorations

1 Using a small skewer or a large darning needle, very carefully pierce a small hole in both ends of the eggshells. Enlarge one hole in each egg to about 5 mm/¼ inch wide. Hold eggs over a bowl and blow out contents through the larger of the holes.
2 Wash the eggs well in cold water, shaking out any remaining contents and put back in the egg box to drain and dry for about 30 minutes.
3 Meanwhile, make a large and a small piping bag from greaseproof paper, without cutting off the ends.
4 When the eggshells are dry, place a small piece of sticky tape over each of the smaller holes.
5 Put the chocolate in a heatproof bowl over a pan of barely simmering water. Heat gently until melted, stirring occasionally, then pour into the large piping bag.
6 Cut a small hole in the end of the bag and pipe the chocolate into the eggshells. Stand the eggs, sticky tape end downwards, back in the egg box. Allow the chocolate to settle for a few minutes, then top up with a little more chocolate, if necessary. Refrigerate the eggs in the box overnight until set.
7 When the eggs are set, crack them gently, then carefully peel off shells.
8 To decorate: stand each egg in an egg cup. Add a little of the beaten egg white to the sugar and beat until the icing forms stiff peaks, beating in more egg or sugar, if needed. Dot a little icing on to the undersides of the decorations and fix in attractive designs to each egg (see Variations). Add a few drops of food colouring to the remaining icing, if liked, then use to fill the small piping bag. Cut a small hole in the end and pipe leaves or other designs on to eggs.
9 Leave for about 1 hour until set completely. Tie a small ribbon around each egg, fixing with a little icing if necessary.

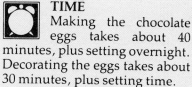

Cook's Notes

Marbled eggs

TIME
Preparing and cooking the eggs and toast take about 20 minutes.

WATCHPOINTS
It is very important to use only edible food colourings to tint the eggs.
Tap the shells very gently to avoid damaging the eggs.
Remember to put the eggs back in the same colour water.

VARIATIONS
Try creating your own designs on the shells of hard-boiled eggs. Use eggs with pale shells and draw or paint on patterns or faces with felt-tip pens, water or oil paints.
The eggs can also be boiled in food colouring to give colour to the shell itself. To create patterns, cut out shapes from masking tape, stick them on to the eggs before boiling in coloured water, then peel the tape away after boiling.

●400 calories/1675 kj per serving

Chocolate eggs

TIME
Making the chocolate eggs takes about 40 minutes, plus setting overnight. Decorating the eggs takes about 30 minutes, plus setting time.

STORAGE
The decorated eggs can be made up to 1 week in advance, if stored in an airtight container in a cool dry place.

VARIATIONS
Here is a chance for the equipped cake decorator to be really creative. Use 250 g/9 oz icing sugar and 1 large egg white to make the icing. Divide into bowls and add a few drops of food colouring to each. Using a petal nozzle, pipe your own flowers such as pretty daffodils on to non-stick paper, then peel off and fix on to the eggs.

●755 calories/3175 kj per serving

Melon and orange appetizers

SERVES 6

1 small honeydew melon
3 oranges
1 teaspoon chopped fresh mint, or
    ¼ teaspoon dried mint
2-3 teaspoons caster sugar
6 mint sprigs or matchstick
    strips of blanched orange zest,
    to garnish

1 Cut the melon in half and scoop
out the seeds. Cut the flesh into balls
with a melon baller and put into a
bowl, together with the melon juice
(see Variations).
2 Squeeze the juice from half an
orange and add to the melon balls.
Peel the remaining half orange and
the 2 whole oranges over a bowl to
catch the juices. Use a fine serrated
knife and a sawing action so that the
rind is removed together with the
pith. Segment the oranges and
discard the pips and membranes
from between the segments.
3 Add the orange segments and
juice to the melon with the mint.
Sweeten to taste with caster sugar
and mix lightly together.
4 Divide the melon and orange mixture between 6 individual glass
dishes and garnish each portion
with a sprig of mint.
5 Cover and refrigerate for up to 1
hour before serving.

Lamb with walnut stuffing

SERVES 6
1.5 kg/3-3½ lb leg of lamb,
    boned (see Buying guide)
250 g/9 oz sausagemeat
100 g/4 oz shelled walnuts, finely
    chopped
2 tablespoons chopped fresh
    parsley
¼ teaspoon freshly grated nutmeg
1 teaspoon dried rosemary
salt and freshly ground black pepper
fresh parsley, to garnish

1 Heat the oven to 200C/400F/Gas 6.
2 Put the sausagemeat in a bowl
together with the walnuts, parsley,
nutmeg and half the rosemary.
Season to taste and mix well.
3 Pack the stuffing into the boned
cavity of the lamb, then secure with
a trussing needle and fine string or
meat skewers.
4 Place the lamb, fat side up, on a
rack in a roasting tin and sprinkle
with the remaining rosemary and
salt and pepper to taste. Cover with
foil. Roast in the oven for 30
minutes, then lower the heat to
170C/325F/Gas 3 and roast for a
further 1½ hours. Remove the foil
for the final 30 minutes.
5 Transfer to a serving platter,
remove the string or skewers and
serve, carved into slices and
garnished with parsley.

Cook's Notes

Melon and orange appetizers

TIME
Preparation time is
about 15 minutes, chill-
ing time 1 hour.

VARIATIONS
Instead of cutting the
melon flesh into balls,
thickly peel off the skin and cut
the melon into cubes.
    Use mandarins or satsumas in
place of oranges—use 4 if they
are small.
    Add 1 tablespoon toasted
almonds for extra crunch.

● 55 calories/225 kj per portion

Lamb with walnut stuffing

TIME
30 minutes preparation,
cooking 2 hours.

BUYING GUIDE
Ask your butcher to
bone the leg of lamb:
it is essential to order in advance, especially at Easter time.

SERVING IDEAS
Serve with a selection of
buttered carrots, turnips
and new potatoes, and hand
round mint jelly.

● 520 calories/2175 kj per portion

Princess pudding

SERVES 6

25 g/1 oz butter
100 g/4 oz wholemeal breadcrumbs
finely grated zest of ½ lemon
425 ml/¾ pint milk
3 eggs, separated
3 tablespoons black cherry jam
150 g/5 oz light soft brown sugar

1 Heat the oven to 170C/325F/Gas 3. Generously grease a 1 L/1¾ pint ovenproof dish with some of the butter.

2 Mix the breadcrumbs with the lemon zest, milk and egg yolks. Pour into the greased dish and dot with the remaining butter.

3 Bake in the oven for about 40 minutes or until the mixture is set. Remove from oven (see Cook's tip).

4 Put the jam in a small saucepan, heat gently until melted, then drizzle over breadcrumb mixture.

5 In a clean, dry bowl, whisk the egg whites until they stand in stiff peaks. Whisk in the sugar, 1 tablespoon at a time, whisking thoroughly after each addition. Pile on top of the jam and return to the oven for about 20 minutes or until the surface of the meringue is crisp and lightly browned. Serve the pudding at once.

Cook's Notes

 TIME
Preparation 20 minutes, cooking 1 hour.

SERVING IDEAS
Serve the pudding with single cream.

 COOK'S TIP
For convenience, bake the breadcrumb base before cooking the lamb. When the lamb is cooked, return the pudding to the oven with the jam and meringue topping and cook for just 10 minutes. Turn off oven and finish cooking as the oven cools for 30-40 minutes.

●280 calories/1175 kj per portion

MIDSUMMER NIGHTS DINNER

Conjure up your own midsummer night's dream with an elegant dinner-party menu that takes full advantage of all that's fresh and good in summer. Glowing with soft summer colours, our heady meal starts with a delicate asparagus soup and is followed by a sumptuous vision of cucumbered salmon. Frosted fruit and rose petals provide a fantasy finish.

Chilled asparagus soup

SERVES 8
500 g/1 lb fresh asparagus, cut into 5 cm/2 inch lengths (see Buying guide)
1 chicken stock cube
salt and freshly ground white pepper
125 ml/4 fl oz single cream
juice of 2 limes

TO GARNISH
8 whole unpeeled prawns
8 thin fresh slices of lime, cut through to the centre
about 3 tablespoons single cream

1 Bring a large pan of cold water to the boil, add the asparagus pieces and cook for about 15 minutes until soft. Remove the asparagus with a slotted spoon and put in the goblet of a blender.
2 Rapidly boil the liquid left in the pan for 5 minutes, then measure out 1.25 L/2 pints. Add the stock cube to the measured liquid and stir until dissolved. Leave the liquid to cool slightly.
3 Add a little of the stock to the asparagus in the blender and blend until smooth.
4 Pour the asparagus purée into a large bowl, gradually stir in the remaining stock and season to taste with salt and pepper.
5 Stir in cream, blend thoroughly, then gradually add the lime juice. Cover the bowl of soup with cling film and refrigerate for 2 hours until well chilled.
6 To serve: pour the soup into 8 chilled individual soup bowls and hook 1 prawn and a lime slice over the side of each bowl. Swirl 1 teaspoon of cream into each bowl of soup, and serve at once.

Salmon with fennel mayonnaise

SERVES 8
1.8 kg/4 lb fresh salmon, cleaned and trimmed with head and tail left on (see Buying guide)
1.5 L/2½ pints water
175 ml/6 fl oz dry white wine
1 small onion, finely sliced
1 lemon slice
2 sprigs fresh fennel
1 parsley sprig
1 bay leaf
6 whole black peppercorns
generous pinch of salt

FENNEL MAYONNAISE
150 ml/¼ pint thick bottled mayonnaise
4 tablespoons chopped fresh fennel
1 teaspoon Pernod (see Did you know)

TO GARNISH
1 slice stuffed olive (optional)
1 large unpeeled cucumber, thinly sliced
8 small lettuce leaves
finely chopped fresh fennel
sprigs fresh fennel

1 Pour the water and wine into a large saucepan, then add the onion, lemon slice, fennel, parsley, bay leaf, peppercorns and salt. Bring to boil, then lower heat and simmer for 30 minutes. Cool then strain.
2 Put the salmon into a fish kettle or a large roasting tin and pour over the strained stock. Bring to boil, then turn to the lowest possible heat, cover and simmer gently for 20 minutes until the fish flakes with a fork. Remove the pan from heat and leave fish, still covered, to cool in the liquid overnight.

3 Make the fennel mayonnaise: put the mayonnaise in a bowl with the fennel and Pernod and mix well together. Cover and refrigerate.
4 When the fish is completely cold, dampen a sheet of greaseproof paper with water. Remove the fish carefully from the cooking liquid with 2 fish slices, then transfer to the dampened greaseproof paper.
5 Using the tip of a round-bladed knife, carefully peel off and discard the skin.
6 Roll the fish gently over and remove the skin from the other side, then gently scrape away any bones along sides of fish. Transfer fish to a long serving platter.
7 Garnish the salmon: place the olive slice over the eye, if liked, then completely cover the side of the fish with cucumber slices (see Preparation). Arrange remaining thin cucumber slices around the edge. Arrange the lettuce along one edge of the salmon, and spoon the fennel mayonnaise into the centre of each leaf. Sprinkle the mayonnaise with chopped fennel, then garnish the edge of the dish with fresh fennel sprigs.

COUNTDOWN
The day before
● Cook the salmon and leave to cool overnight.
● Prepare frosted grapes and rose petals and leave to set overnight.
2¾ hours before
● Make the chilled asparagus soup and refrigerate.
2 hours before
● Make the fennel mayonnaise. Skin the salmon and garnish.
● Frost the strawberries.
Just before the meal
● Pour the soup into individual soup bowls and garnish.
Just before the dessert
● Assemble the frosted fruit and rose petals on a dish.

Cook's Notes

Chilled asparagus soup

 TIME
35 minutes to make, plus 2 hours chilling.

 WATCHPOINT
The stock cube will add a certain amount of salt to the liquid so be careful when seasoning.

BUYING GUIDE
Buy the thin green asparagus for this soup or, if available, the kind sold as *sprue* — very thin stalks not regarded good enough for eating whole. They are just as delicious for soup — and much less expensive than the graded varieties of asparagus spears.

●55 calories/250 kj per portion

Salmon with fennel mayonnaise

 TIME
1½ hours preparation, including cooking the salmon; then overnight cooling, plus 20 minutes finishing.

PREPARATION
Start arranging the cucumber slices at the tail end and overlap them so that they resemble fish scales.

BUYING GUIDE
If a small salmon is difficult to obtain or if you are wanting to economize, substitute salmon trout instead — the colour of the fish is the same and the flavour, though less distinct, is also delicious.

DID YOU KNOW
Pernod is a French aniseed-tasting drink and is available in miniature-sized bottles. When water is added to Pernod, it turns quite white and cloudy.

●450 calories/1875 kj per portion

Frosted fruit and rose petals
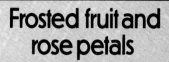

SERVES 8

large pink rose petals (see Watchpoint)

2 egg whites

100 g/4 oz caster sugar

32 green seedless grapes, separated into small bunches

16 whole fresh strawberries, stalks still attached

1 Lightly beat the egg whites in a bowl and spread the caster sugar on to a flat plate.

2 Frost the rose petals: holding each by tweezers, dip first into the egg white, then sprinkle with the sugar, to coat both sides thoroughly. Spread out in a single layer on a plate, and leave to dry overnight.

3 Frost the green grapes: holding each fruit by its stalk, dip first into lightly beaten egg white, then roll in the sugar. Place on a large flat plate, making sure they do not touch each other, and leave to dry overnight.

4 Two hours before serving, repeat process with the strawberries.

5 To serve: pile the strawberries and grapes carefully into a pyramid on a flat dish, then arrange the rose petals on top.

Cook's Notes

TIME
30 minutes for frosting the rose petals and fruit, plus drying time.

WATCHPOINT
Do not pick rose petals that have been sprayed with chemicals. Use unblemished petals and wash them carefully but gently before frosting. Hold each at base with a pair of tweezers and quickly dip in very cold water, gently pat dry with absorbent paper.

SERVING IDEAS
These sophisticated frosted fruits and petals are delicious served with lemon sorbet or with Tea sorbet (see page 227).

●65 calories/275 kj per portion

HALLOWE'EN PARTY

The pumpkins, apples and jacket potatoes in this menu are all traditional Hallowe'en fare, which are sure to be popular with children and adults alike. To add to the fun there is for the adults a vivid witches' brew.

Witches' brew

MAKES 30 GLASSES
600 ml/1 pint dry vermouth
150 ml/¼ pint lime cordial
150 ml/¼ pint crème de menthe
1.5 L/2½ pints soda water
Angostura bitters, to taste (optional)
about 24 ice cubes
3 limes, thinly sliced

1 Crush the ice cubes (see Cook's tips) and place in a large jug or punch bowl.
2 Stir in the vermouth, lime cordial and crème de menthe, then the soda water. Mix well and add Angostura bitters to taste, if liked.
3 Float slices of lime on top; serve.

Lamb and pumpkin casserole

SERVES 12
1.5 kg/3 lb boned lamb, trimmed of fat and cut into 2.5 cm/1 inch cubes (see Buying guide)
1 kg/2 lb pumpkin, peeled and cut into 1 cm/½ inch cubes
4 tablespoons vegetable oil
2 large onions, chopped
4 cloves garlic, crushed
400 g/14 oz can tomatoes
600 ml/1 pint beef stock
1 teaspoon dried oregano
salt
freshly ground black pepper
350 g/12 oz chorizo sausages, sliced (see Buying guide)
2 × 400 g/14 oz cans chick-peas
sprigs of parsley, to garnish

1 Heat the oil in a large flameproof casserole, add the lamb (in batches if necessary) and fry over brisk heat until evenly browned on all sides. Remove the casserole from the heat and transfer the browned meat with a slotted spoon to a large plate. Set aside.
2 Return casserole to the heat. Lower the heat, add the onions and garlic and fry gently for 5 minutes until the onions are soft and lightly coloured.
3 Add the tomatoes with their juice, the stock, oregano and salt and pepper to taste. Bring to the boil, return the meat with its juices to the casserole, then add the chorizos. Stir well, lower the heat slightly, then cover and simmer gently for 30 minutes.
4 Add the pumpkin cubes to the casserole together with the chick-peas and their canned liquid. Cover, bring back to the boil, then reduce the heat slightly and simmer gently for a further 30 minutes.
5 Skim off any excess fat from the surface and taste and adjust seasoning if necessary.
6 Garnish with sprigs of fresh parsley and serve at once, straight from the casserole.

West country potatoes

SERVES 12
12 even-sized potatoes, scrubbed
vegetable oil, for brushing
salt
225 g/8 oz Double Gloucester cheese with chives and onion (see Buying guide)

1 Heat the oven to 220C/425F/Gas 7.
2 Prick the potatoes well with a fork, then brush each one with a very little oil.
3 Sprinkle the potatoes with salt and place in the oven, directly on the shelves. Bake for about 1 hour or until they feel soft in the centre when pierced with a skewer.
4 Just before serving, cut the cheese into 24 thin slices. Make 2 slits in each potato and put a slice of cheese in each slit. Serve at once while the potatoes are still hot.

Cook's Notes

Witches' brew

TIME
Preparation takes about 5 minutes.

COOK'S TIPS
Crush the ice in a strong blender, or in a food processor. If you do not have either, place the ice in a strong polythene bag, squeeze out the air and tie firmly. Beat with a wooden mallet or rolling pin.

VARIATION
Add a little green food colouring if you prefer a darker green drink.

● 35 calories/155 kj per glass

Lamb and pumpkin casserole
TIME
30 minutes preparation, 1 hour cooking.

FREEZING
After adding the pumpkin and chick-peas, cook for 15 minutes only. Cool quickly, lift off and discard any excess solidified fat, then pack into a rigid container. Seal, label and freeze for up to 3 months. To serve: defrost over-night in the refrigerator, then turn into a casserole and simmer for about 20 minutes or until heated through.

BUYING GUIDE
Frozen joints of boneless lamb, such as shoulder, can be found in most super-markets.
Spanish chorizos are sold cooked and uncooked: either type can be used for this casserole, but the cooked type is the most commonly available. If you have difficulty buying chorizos, use kabanos or a similar type of strong-flavoured sausage.

● 520 calories/2190 kj per portion

West Country potatoes
TIME
5 minutes preparation, 1 hour cooking.

BUYING GUIDE
If you have difficulty in buying the cheese, use plain Cheddar and sprinkle with finely snipped chives or chopped onions.

● 245 calories/1025 kj per portion

Caramel-topped apples

SERVES 12
6 crisp dessert apples
4 × 150 ml/¼ pint cartons soured cream
75 g/3 oz caster sugar
finely grated zest and juice of 3 oranges
matchstick strips of orange zest, to decorate

CARAMEL CHIPS
100 g/4 oz granulated sugar
150 ml/¼ pint water
vegetable oil, for greasing

1 Make the caramel chips: grease a baking tray and put the sugar and water into a small, heavy-based saucepan. Heat gently, without stirring, until the sugar has dissolved, then bring to the boil and boil for 5 minutes, until the syrup turns a deep golden colour. !

2 Immediately remove from the heat and plunge the base of the pan into a bowl of iced water. ! Leave for a few seconds until the sizzling stops, then remove pan from water.
3 Pour the syrup immediately into the greased baking tray to make a thin layer. Allow it to become completely cold.
4 Meanwhile, pour the soured cream into a large bowl and stir in sugar. Add orange zest and juice.
5 Core and slice the apples, mix into the soured cream, then turn into a large, shallow serving dish. Cover and refrigerate until ready to serve.
6 Crack the set caramel with a rolling pin to form fine chips and sprinkle over the apple mixture (see Cook's tip). Top with orange zest.

Cook's Notes

 TIME
20 minutes preparation, plus setting time for the caramel.

 WATCHPOINTS
Watch the syrup constantly and be sure to remove it from the heat immediately it turns a deep golden colour.
Plunging the pan into cold water stops the cooking: take care that no water splashes into the syrup, otherwise it will spit.

COOK'S TIP
Do not sprinkle the chips over the dessert until just before serving, otherwise the caramel will become soft and melt into the mixture.

 STORAGE
The caramel chips will keep in a dry, airtight container for a day or two, but after that they will become sticky.

●205 calories/865 kj per portion

TEENAGE PARTY

The key to keeping a crowd of young teenagers happy is to provide heaps of hearty, unfussy food that they can tuck into with gusto. An authentic Italian lasagne, accompanied by garlic bread, is the perfect 'come-and-grab-it' style food. Served with an exciting-looking punch and rounded off with ice cream topped with hot sauces, this party is sure to be a winner!

Italian wine cup

MAKES ABOUT 60 GLASSES
4 × 70 cl/1¼ pints Italian red wine
  (see Variations)
1 L/1¾ pints ginger ale
2 L/3½ pints lemonade or soda
  water
3 lemons, thinly sliced
2 oranges, thinly sliced
2 red-skinned apples
fresh mint sprigs
crushed ice

1 Put the wine, ginger ale and
lemonade into a large bowl.
2 Add the sliced lemons and
oranges. Leave the punch to stand
for 1 hour.
3 Just before serving, core and thinly slice the apples. Add to the
punch with the mint sprigs and the
crushed ice.
4 To serve: ladle into large jugs
together with some of the fruit,
then pour into glasses.

Garlic bread

SERVES 10-12
3 long French loaves
350 g/12 oz butter, softened
6 cloves garlic, crushed
4 tablespoons chopped parsley
  (optional)

1 Heat the oven to 190C/375F/Gas 5.
2 Beat the butter until creamy, then
beat in the garlic and parsley, if
using, until well mixed.
3 Cut each loaf diagonally into
slices, about 5 cm/2 inches thick,
slicing to the bottom of the loaf but
not cutting through it.
4 Spread the cut surfaces of the
bread with the butter, then reform
into a loaf shape. ✳ Wrap each loaf
firmly in foil and place on a baking
tray join side up.
5 Bake in the oven for 15 minutes.
Open the foil and bake for a further
5 minutes to crisp the bread.
6 Remove the garlic bread from
oven and serve it at once, straight
from the foil.

Lasagne al forno

SERVES 10-12
750 g/1½ lb green lasagne
  (see Buying guide)
3 tablespoons olive oil
3 large onions, chopped
4 cloves garlic, chopped
1.5 kg/3-3½ lb lean minced beef
2 × 400 g/14 oz cans tomatoes
4 tablespoons tomato purée
300 ml/½ pint Italian red wine
350 g/12 oz mushrooms, sliced
  (optional)
2 teaspoons dried basil
salt and freshly ground black pepper
75 g/3 oz Parmesan cheese, grated
margarine, for greasing

SAUCE
75 g/3 oz butter
75 g/3 oz plain flour
850 ml/1½ pints milk
freshly grated nutmeg

1 Heat the oil in large heavy-based
frying-pan, add onions and garlic
and fry gently for 5 minutes.
2 Add the meat, turn the heat to
high and fry until the meat is evenly
browned, stirring with a wooden
spoon to remove any lumps. Add
the tomatoes with their juice, the
tomato purée, wine, mushrooms, if
using, basil and salt and pepper to
taste. Bring to the boil, stirring well,
cover and cook for 30 minutes.
3 Heat the oven to 190C/375F/Gas 5
and grease an ovenproof dish about
38 × 25 cm/15 × 10 inches.
4 Make sauce: melt butter in a pan,
sprinkle in the flour and stir over
low heat for 1-2 minutes until straw-
coloured. Remove from the heat
and gradually stir in all the milk.
Return pan to the heat and simmer,
stirring, until thick and smooth. Remove from the heat and season to
taste with nutmeg, salt and pepper.
5 Spread one-third of the meat mixture in the bottom of the prepared
dish. Place one-third of the lasagne
on top in an overlapping layer, then
spread over one-third of the white
sauce. Repeat these layers twice
more, ending with a layer of sauce.
6 Sprinkle with grated Parmesan
cheese and bake in the oven for
about 45 minutes.

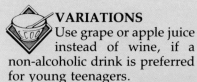
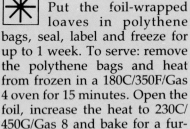
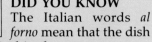

Hot-topped ice cream

SERVES 20
4 L/7 pints vanilla ice cream

CHOCOLATE SAUCE
250 g/9 oz plain dessert chocolate,
broken into pieces
50 g/2 oz butter, softened
4 tablespoons milk
4 tablespoons clear honey or
golden syrup
1 teaspoon vanilla flavouring

BUTTERSCOTCH SAUCE
175 g/6 oz butter
175 g/6 oz light soft brown sugar
2 tablespoons golden syrup

RASPBERRY SAUCE
6 tablespoons raspberry jam
juice of 1 lemon
2 teaspoons cornflour
150 ml/¼ pint water

1 Make the chocolate sauce: put the chocolate pieces in a small heavy-based saucepan. Beat in the butter, milk and honey and heat gently until the chocolate has melted. Add the vanilla (see Cook's tips).

2 Make the butterscotch sauce: put all the ingredients in a heavy-based saucepan and heat gently until the sugar has dissolved. Bring to the boil and cook over high heat for 3-4 minutes until the mixture is golden brown and thick (see Cook's tips).

3 Make the raspberry sauce: put the jam with the lemon juice in a heavy-based saucepan. Blend the cornflour with 1 tablespoon of the water, then gradually stir in the remaining water. Stir into the jam.

4 Heat gently until the jam has melted, then bring to the boil and cook for 2-3 minutes until the mixture is thick. Strain, return to the pan and heat through gently for 2 minutes (see Cook's tips).

5 To serve: pour the hot sauces into individual warmed jugs and serve at once with the ice cream.

FAMILY PICNIC

A picnic by the sea is a great way to entertain the family, as long as the food is well planned. We have devised a picnic for six that can be made in advance and is easy to serve: we suggest a savoury selection of pasties, ham rolls and chicken drumsticks, all of which are easy to eat with your fingers and can be neatly packed. The Banana creams for pudding are ready-made in sandproof containers, and are accompanied by crunchy shortbread fingers.

Tuna puff pasties

SERVES 6

2 × 200 g/7 oz cans tuna fish, drained and flaked
1 tablespoon vegetable oil
1 onion, finely chopped
3 hard-boiled eggs, chopped
2 potatoes, boiled and diced
3 tablespoons tomato ketchup
1 teaspoon dried mixed herbs
grated zest of 1 lemon
2 eggs, beaten
1 clove garlic (optional)
dash of Worcestershire sauce (optional)
salt and freshly ground black pepper
400 g/13 oz frozen puff pastry, defrosted

1 Heat the oil in a frying-pan, add the onion and fry gently for 5 minutes until soft and lightly coloured. Transfer with a slotted spoon to a bowl.
2 Add the tuna to the bowl [!] together with the hard-boiled eggs, potatoes, tomato ketchup, herbs, lemon zest, half the beaten egg, garlic and Worcestershire sauce, if using. Season with salt and pepper to taste and mix well.
3 Heat the oven to 220C/425F/Gas 7.
4 Roll out the pastry on a lightly floured surface to a 35 cm/14 inch square. Trim the edges straight, then cut the pastry in half. Cut each half in 3 crossways.
5 Spoon a portion of the tuna and egg mixture on to the centre of each piece of pastry. Brush the edges of each piece of pastry with water, then draw up the 2 long sides to meet over the filling. Firmly seal the edges together and crimp. Press the short sides together to seal them,

making a neat parcel. Repeat this process with the remaining pastry pieces.
6 Place the 6 parcels on a dampened baking sheet and brush them with the remaining beaten egg. Bake in the oven for 15-20 minutes until the pastry is golden brown and the underside is dry. Carefully transfer to a wire rack and leave to cool.

Herby chicken drumsticks

SERVES 6

6 chicken drumsticks
75 g/3 oz dried white breadcrumbs (see Preparation)
1 teaspoon dried rosemary
1 teaspoon dried thyme
1 teaspoon dried marjoram
salt and freshly ground black pepper
2 tablespoons plain flour
2 eggs, beaten
2 tablespoons milk
2 tablespoons vegetable oil
50 g/2 oz butter

1 Mix together the breadcrumbs and herbs in a bowl and season well with salt and pepper. Place the flour in a polythene bag.
2 Put the beaten eggs in a shallow bowl and stir in the milk and a drop of oil. Put the breadcrumb mixture on a plate. Shake each drumstick in the bag of flour to coat, then dip first into the egg mixture and then into the breadcrumbs.
3 Heat the oil and butter in a large frying-pan over moderate heat. When the butter foams, add the drumsticks and fry gently for about 20 minutes until cooked through and golden brown on all sides.
4 Remove the drumsticks, drain on absorbent paper and cool.

Ham rolls

SERVES 6

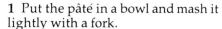

12 thin slices cooked ham
225 g/8 oz smooth liver pâté
3 tablespoons medium-dry sherry
2 tablespoons single cream
salt and freshly ground black pepper

1 Put the pâté in a bowl and mash it lightly with a fork.
2 Add the sherry and cream and mash well into the pâté until the mixture is smooth. Season with salt and pepper to taste.
3 Divide the mixture between the 12 slices of ham, spreading it evenly over each slice with a knife.
4 Carefully roll up each slice of ham as tightly as possible and secure with a cocktail stick.

Orange shortbread fingers

SERVES 6

100 g/4 oz plain flour
50 g/2 oz ground rice
pinch of salt
100 g/4 oz butter, softened
50 g/2 oz caster sugar
grated zest of 1 small orange
butter, for greasing
caster sugar, to decorate

1 Heat the oven to 170C/325F/Gas 3 and lightly grease a baking sheet.
2 Sift the flour, ground rice and salt on to a piece of greaseproof paper. Using a wooden spoon, beat the butter in a bowl until creamy, then beat in the sugar and orange zest until thoroughly combined.
3 Gradually work the sifted flour mixture into the butter mixture, using a wooden spoon at first and finishing by gathering the dough into a ball with your hands.
4 Roll the dough out on a floured surface to a rectangle about 1 cm/½ inch thick, patting the shortbread into shape with your fingers to give a neat edge.
5 With a fish slice, carefully lift the shortbread on to the greased baking sheet and prick all over with a fork.

Bake in the oven for 45 minutes until lightly coloured. Immediately cut in half lengthways, then cut into fingers.
6 Cool for 10 minutes on the baking sheet until firm, then transfer to a wire rack to cool completely. Sprinkle with caster sugar if wished.

Banana creams

SERVES 6

4 bananas
400 g/14 oz can evaporated milk
2 teaspoons sugar
juice of 1 lemon

1 Slice 3 bananas and put in a blender with the evaporated milk, sugar and lemon juice. Blend until thick and smooth. Alternatively, mash the sliced bananas with a fork until they form a smooth pulp, then whisk in the remaining ingredients.
2 Divide the banana cream among 6 plastic containers (see Serving ideas) and refrigerate.
3 Just before serving, cut the remaining banana into diagonal slices and arrange on top of each portion. Serve the creams in the plastic containers

CHILDREN'S BIRTHDAY PARTY

Give a children's fancy-dress birthday party with an 'animal' theme. Animal-shaped cheese biscuits are good fun, and for those who like savouries there are also sausages and bacon rolls stuck into a 'caterpillar' made from a cucumber. For an impressive centrepiece make our colourful butterfly cake, decorated with feather icing.

The day before
● Make the animal biscuits.
● Make the cake.
On the day
In the morning:
● Assemble and feather ice cake.
2 hours before
● Decorate the cake with sugar-coated chocolate buttons and add the liquorice 'antennae'.
1 hour before
● Prepare the cucumber and begin to cook the sausages and bacon and pineapple rolls.

Cucumber caterpillar

SERVES 12
1 large cucumber, preferably slightly curved
2 glace cherries
500 g/1 lb cocktail sausages (see Cook's tips)
6 rashers streaky bacon, rinds removed and cut in half crossways
225 g/8 oz can pineapple pieces, drained

1 Cutting at a slant, slice off the thicker end of the cucumber. To make the eyes: spear each cherry on to the end of half a cocktail stick; press sticks in cut end of cucumber.
2 At the other end, with a sharp knife, make a few small cuts across the cucumber, about 2 mm/⅛ inch apart, for the 'tail'.
3 Heat the grill to high.
4 Prick the sausages with a fork and fry over gentle heat until they are golden brown on all sides.
5 Meanwhile, wrap each half bacon rasher around a piece of pineapple and secure with a wooden cocktail stick. Grill the bacon and pineapple rolls for 3-4 minutes until the bacon is crisp. Drain on absorbent paper.

6 Drain the sausages and spear a cocktail stick into each one. Stick the sausages in a ridge down the centre of the cucumber and the bacon rolls on either side and serve at once (see Cook's tips).

Animal cheese biscuits

MAKES 50
225 g/8 oz plain flour
pinch of salt
¼ teaspoon mustard powder
100 g/4 oz margarine or butter
75 g/3 oz strong Cheddar cheese, finely grated (see Watchpoint)
1 egg yolk
2 tablespoons water
little milk, for glazing
sesame seeds and/or poppy seeds
margarine, for greasing

1 Sift the flour, salt and mustard powder into a large bowl. Rub in the margarine until mixture resembles fine breadcrumbs, then add the cheese. Mix in the egg yolk and water with a knife, then gather up the pastry in your hands to make a firm dough.
2 Turn the dough on to a lightly floured surface and knead briefly until smooth. Place in a polythene bag and leave to rest in the refrigerator for 30 minutes.
3 Heat the oven to 200C/400F/Gas 6 and grease 2 baking sheets.
4 Roll out the pastry on a floured surface until it is about 2 mm/⅛ inch thick. Using different-shaped animal biscuit cutters, cut out shapes and place on the greased baking sheets spacing them apart to allow for them spreading during baking. Brush all over with milk. Using a skewer or the point of a knife, make holes for the eyes, mouths, noses, etc.
5 Decorate the biscuits with sesame seeds and/or poppy seeds.
6 Bake in the oven in 2 batches for 15-20 minutes each until golden brown. Remove from the oven, allow to settle for 1-2 minutes, then place on a wire rack and leave to cool before serving.

Cook's Notes

Cucumber caterpillar

TIME
Preparation time is about 30 minutes, cooking time about 10 minutes.

COOK'S TIPS
If you have difficulty buying cocktail sausages, buy chipolatas and cut each in half by twisting skin in the middle then cutting it.
If you wish, keep the cucumber warm for 30 minutes in a 110C/225F/Gas ¼ oven.

●180 calories/750 kj per portion

Animal cheese biscuits

TIME
30 minutes preparation, 30-40 minutes cooking, plus resting and cooling time.

WATCHPOINT
Use a strong Cheddar cheese or the biscuits will lack flavour.

STORAGE
These biscuits will keep for 1 week in an airtight container in a cool, dry place.

●35 calories/150 kj per biscuit

Butterfly birthday cake

MAKES 24 SLICES

225 g/8 oz self-raising flour
2 teaspoons baking powder
225 g/8 oz soft tub margarine
225 g/8 oz caster sugar
grated zest of 2 oranges
4 large eggs
margarine, for greasing

FILLING AND DECORATION
225 g/8 oz apricot jam
25-50 g/1-2 oz desiccated coconut
225 g/8 oz icing sugar
2-3 tablespoons water
gravy browning

TO FINISH
30 cm/12 inch silver cake-board
3 chocolate flake bars
candles and candle-holders
3 small packets of sugar-coated chocolate buttons
2 liquorice 'pipes'

1 Heat the oven to 170C/325F/Gas 3. Grease a deep 23 cm/9 inch square cake tin. Line the sides and base of the tin with greaseproof paper, then grease the paper.
2 Sift the flour and baking powder into a large bowl. Add the margarine, caster sugar, orange zest and eggs. Mix well, then beat with a wooden spoon for 2-3 minutes, or with a hand-held electric whisk for 1 minute, until blended and glossy.
3 Turn the mixture into the prepared tin and level the surface, then make a slight hollow in the centre. Bake in the oven for about 65 minutes, until the top of the cake is golden and springy to the touch.

4 Cool the cake in the tin for 5 minutes, then turn out on to a wire rack and peel off the lining paper. Leave the cake upside down to cool completely.
5 Trim the cake to level it off, if necessary. Slice the cold cake in half horizontally and sandwich together with 5 tablespoons of the apricot jam. Cut the cake in half diagonally to make 2 triangles, then trim off the triangle tips opposite the cut edge.

6 Sieve all but 1 tablespoon of the remaining jam into a small, heavy-based saucepan and stir over low heat until melted. Brush the sides of the cakes, except the trimmed corners, with some melted jam.
7 Spread a thick layer of coconut on a large plate. Press the jam-coated sides of cake into the coconut one at a time until evenly coated. (Add more coconut to plate if needed.)
8 Brush the trimmed corner of each cake with melted jam. Place the 2 pieces of cake on the cake-board, with the trimmed corners almost touching to make a butterfly shape. Place the chocolate flakes in the gap, one on top of another, then push the 2 'wings' together.
9 Make the glacé icing (see Cook's tips): sift the icing sugar into a bowl, then beat in enough water to give a thick coating consistency.

10 Put 2 tablespoons of the icing into a small bowl. Add several drops of gravy browning, stirring well, to make a fairly dark brown icing. Spoon this icing into a small piping bag fitted with a writing nozzle.
11 Brush the top of the cakes with the remaining melted jam. Spread the white glacé icing smoothly and evenly over the top with a knife. Immediately ! pipe parallel lines of brown icing down the 'wings'.

12 Draw a skewer through the brown lines to give a 'feather' effect.

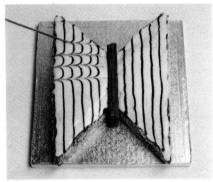

13 Neaten edges, removing surplus icing, then arrange the candles in their holders on top. Leave to set.
14 Two hours before the party, melt the remaining tablespoon of jam. Brush a little jam on each chocolate button and stick them round the edges of the cake. Stick in 2 pieces of liquorice for the 'antennae' and curl them round slightly.

Cook's Notes

TIME
20 minutes preparation, 65 minutes baking, plus cooling time. Shaping and decorating take about 1 hour.

COOK'S TIPS
Very fresh cake is difficult to cut and ice neatly, so bake the cake a day before decorating.

You can assemble and ice the cake on the evening before the party, but not before, otherwise the icing will dry out and crack.

WATCHPOINT
Speed is essential: the icing must not start to set before 'feathering'.

●265 calories/1125 kj per slice

BURGER AND PIZZA PARTY

Create a relaxed atmosphere for family and friends, and cater for all ages from 4 to 50 plus, with a burger and pizza party. Featuring food that is both popular and easy to make, the menu also includes an unusual American-style chocolate fondue which will add to the fun and informality. For outsize appetites you can double up on the quantities given here.

THE DAY BEFORE
● Make the tomato sauce for the pizzas, cover and refrigerate.
● Make the pizza dough and put into refrigerator to rise slowly overnight.
● Prepare and shape the burgers. Cover and refrigerate.
● Make the syrup for the fruit cup.
● Wash salad ingredients, wrap and refrigerate; make salad dressings and store in the refrigerator.

ON THE DAY
● Prepare ingredients for the pizza toppings and cake for the fondue.

JUST BEFORE THE PARTY
Remove pizza dough from the refrigerator, allow it to return to room temperature then knead again.
● Assemble the salads, but do not dress them.
● Prepare the fruit dips and the chocolate for the fondue.

PARTY TIME
● Finish making the fruit cup.
● Cook and serve the burgers.
● Complete and bake the pizzas.
● Dress the salads.

1 To make the burgers: mince the meat finely by passing it through the mincer twice. Mince the onion.
2 Put the minced meat, onion and breadcrumbs into a bowl and season with salt and pepper. Add the egg and stock and mix together with your hands until combined.
3 Divide the mixture into 12. On a floured board, shape each piece into a neat, flat 10 cm/4 inch circle.
4 Line a baking sheet or tray with cling film, place the shaped burgers on top, then cover with cling film. Refrigerate until required.
5 To serve: heat 2 tablespoons oil in a large frying-pan, add the onion slices and fry gently until soft and lightly browned. Remove with a slotted spoon and drain on absorbent paper.
6 Heat the oven to 130C/250F/Gas ½, then put the burger buns in the oven to warm while cooking the burgers. Keep the fried onions warm in the oven at the same time.
7 Heat 2 tablespoons oil in each of 2 large frying-pans. Put 6 burgers in each pan and fry gently for about 5 minutes on each side, or until lightly browned and cooked.
8 Cut open the warm burger buns and fill each with a lettuce leaf, a burger, a slice of tomato and some fried onions. Serve at once.

Beefburgers

MAKES 12 BURGERS
750 g/1½ lb chuck steak
   (see Buying guide)
1 large onion
100 g/4 oz fresh breadcrumbs
salt and freshly
   ground black pepper
1 egg, beaten
2 tablespoons beef
   stock or water

TO SERVE
6 tablespoons vegetable oil
6 onions, sliced
12 burger buns
   (see Buying guide)
lettuce leaves
tomato slices

Cook's Notes

 TIME
Preparation 45 minutes, cooking 10-15 minutes.

 BUYING GUIDE
Alternatively, buy best-quality minced beef for the burgers. If burger buns are not available, buy ordinary round baps or soft rolls instead.

 FREEZING
Open freeze, pack in a polythene bag, seal, label and freeze. Store for up to 2 months. To serve: cook from frozen as in recipe.

SERVING IDEAS
Wrap each cooked burger in a paper napkin. Serve with a selection of pickles, relishes, and mustards.

● 305 calories/1275 kj per portion

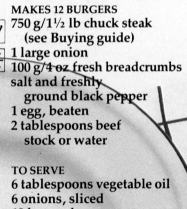

Lemon and apple cup

MAKES ABOUT 2 L/3½ PINTS

thinly peeled rind and strained
    juice of 2 lemons
275 g/10 oz sugar
600 ml/1 pint cold water
1 red-skinned dessert apple
1 orange
1 lemon
1 L/1¾ pints apple juice or dry
    cider, chilled (see Cook's tip)
600 ml/1 pint fizzy lemonade,
    chilled
mint leaves, to serve (optional)

1 Put the lemon rind and sugar into
a saucepan with the water. Heat
gently until sugar has dissolved,
then bring to the boil and boil for 3
minutes. Remove from the heat,
cover and leave to stand for at least 3
hours, preferably overnight.
2 Just before serving, strain the
lemon syrup into a chilled serving
bowl. Stir in the lemon juice.

3 Quarter and core the apple, but do
not peel, then slice it thinly and add
to the lemon syrup. Thinly slice the
orange and lemon (including the
peel) and add to the syrup. Pour the
apple juice and lemonade into the
bowl and stir well. Decorate with
mint leaves if liked; serve at once.

Cook's Notes

TIME
Preparation time 15
minutes, cooking time
5 minutes, but allow at least 3
hours standing time for the
flavour of the lemon syrup to
develop.

VARIATION
If fresh mint is out of
season, soak 1 teaspoon
dried mint in boiling water,
drain and add to the cup before
serving.

COOK'S TIP
Choose apple juice or
cider for the cup accord-
ing to the age and preferences of
your guests.

●145 calories/600 kj per serving

Party pizzas

SERVES 12

PIZZA DOUGH
450 g/1 lb strong white flour
1 teaspoon salt
50 g/2 oz margarine or butter
7 g/¼ oz sachet easy-blend dried
   yeast
300 ml/½ pint tepid water
vegetable oil, for brushing and
   drizzling

TOMATO SAUCE
2 tablespoons olive or vegetable oil
3 medium onions, finely chopped
800 g/1 lb 12 oz can tomatoes
2 tablespoons tomato purée
1 tablespoon dried mixed herbs
2 beef stock cubes
salt and freshly ground black pepper

TOPPINGS
350 g/12 oz Mozzarella cheese,
   thinly sliced
100 g/4 oz thinly sliced salami, rinds
   removed, cut into strips
100 g/4 oz cooked ham, cut into
   strips
100 g/4 oz button mushrooms,
   thinly sliced
1 red pepper, deseeded and thinly
   sliced
1 green pepper, deseeded and
   thinly sliced
4 teaspoons capers
1 large onion, chopped (optional)
2 × 50 g/2 oz cans anchovy fillets,
   well drained
24 black olives

1 First make the tomato sauce: heat the oil in a large saucepan. Add the onions and fry gently for 5 minutes or until soft but not coloured. Stir in the tomatoes with their juice, the tomato purée and the herbs. Crumble in the stock cubes. Break up the tomatoes with a wooden spoon, then add salt and pepper to taste. Bring to the boil, stirring all the time. Reduce the heat to low, partially cover the pan and simmer for about 1 hour, stirring occasionally, until the sauce is thick and reduced in volume by about half. Taste and adjust seasoning, then set aside to cool.

2 Next make the pizza dough (see Cook's tips): sift the flour and salt into a large bowl. Rub in the margarine then stir in the easy-blend yeast. Make a well in the centre of the flour and stir in the tepid water. Mix together with your hands to form a stiff dough.

3 Turn the dough on to a very lightly floured surface, then knead for 10 minutes until smooth and elastic. Alternatively, knead it in an electric mixer, using a dough hook, for 3 minutes. Put the dough back into the bowl, cover with cling film or a clean tea-towel and leave in a warm place for about 1 hour or until more than doubled in size.

4 Heat the oven to 200C/400F/Gas 6. Lightly brush two 30 cm/12 inch round ovenproof plates or two 35 × 25 cm/14 × 12 inch oblong baking sheets with vegetable oil (see Cook's tips).

5 Turn the risen dough on to a lightly floured surface and knead again for 3 minutes. Roll the dough out into an oblong shape and brush with a little oil. Roll up the dough like a Swiss roll.

6 Roll the dough out again, cut it in half, then roll out each piece to fit the prepared plates or baking sheets. Place the dough in position and press firmly with your fingertips until it fits neatly.

7 Brush the dough with a little more oil, then spread with tomato sauce. Cover with the cheese to within 5 mm/¼ inch from the edge. Arrange the salami, ham, mushrooms, peppers, capers, onion, if using, on top, in separate sections or mixed together (see Serving ideas). Divide off the sections with anchovy fillets and place black olives in each section. ✳

8 Drizzle a little oil over the surface, then bake in the oven for about 25 minutes, or until the cheese is bubbling and golden. Cut the pizza into sections and serve at once accompanied by a varied selection of salads.

Cook's Notes

TIME
Preparation time is 1½ hours, including rising time. Cooking time is about 25 minutes

COOK'S TIPS
To save time you can use three 140 g/5 oz packets pizza dough mix to make the pizza base. Cook according to packet instructions.

Choose baking sheets with sides to contain the pizza dough neatly and stop it spreading.

SERVING IDEAS
Invite party guests into the kitchen to select their own toppings which can be arranged in separate sections.

FREEZING
Open freeze after stage 7, seal in polythene bags, label and freeze. Store for up to 3 months. To serve: cook from frozen at 220C/425F/Gas 7 for about 30 minutes.

● 375 calories/1575 kj per portion

Chocolate fondue

SERVES 12
400 g/14 oz plain dessert chocolate,
 broken into small pieces
300 ml/½ pint double cream
6 tablespoons sweet sherry
50 g/2 oz unsalted butter

DIPPERS
20 cm/8 inch Victoria sandwich or
 sponge cake
apricot jam, for spreading
4 large bananas
2 tablespoons lemon juice
2 large dessert apples
450 g/16 oz can sliced peaches
 in syrup, well drained

1 First prepare the dippers: slice the cake in half horizontally and sandwich with apricot jam. Cut into neat 2.5 cm/1 inch cubes. Peel the bananas, cut into slices 1 cm/½ inch thick and toss in 1 tablespoon lemon juice. Quarter, core and slice the apples and toss in the remaining lemon juice. Leave peach slices whole, or cut into chunks if large. ⚠
2 Arrange in separate bowls.
3 Put the chocolate into a heavy-based fondue pan or small saucepan and add the cream and sherry.
4 Just before serving, gently heat the chocolate, cream and sherry together until the chocolate melts, stirring all the time. Continue until almost, but not quite boiling. ⚠ Stir in the butter until melted.
5 Place the pan over a small spirit burner on the table. Arrange the bowls of cake and fruit around the fondue, along with fondue or ordinary forks for spearing the cake and fruit before they are dipped in.

Cook's Notes

TIME
Preparation 30 minutes, cooking time 10 minutes.

VARIATIONS
Use 500 g/1 lb Madeira cake in place of the Victoria sandwich or sponge. Use other well-drained canned fruit, such as pears, pineapple, cherries or apricots in place of, or in addition to, peaches.

WATCHPOINTS
Prepare the fruit as soon as possible before serving to prevent discolouring.
 Do not let the chocolate mixture boil or it will separate.

FOR CHILDREN
Replace the sherry with orange juice.

●540 calories/2250 kj per portion

SUNDAY LUNCH FOR SIX

Sunday lunch is traditionally a time when the whole family sits down for a meal together. Even if you have little time for cooking during the week, it is worth treating Sunday lunch as a special occasion and making an extra effort, particularly if you have guests as well as the family.

If you have any spare time, you can begin the preparations the day before, to ease your workload next morning. Use the countdown below to help you time both cooking operations and the serving of the meal to perfection.

The day before
Defrost the puff pastry overnight so that you can make the dumplings in the morning.

Defrost the prawns overnight if using frozen.

On Sunday morning
Make the grapefruit cocktails and then refrigerate.

Peel the potatoes and keep them in water to prevent browning. Peel the apples and onion. Keep the apples in salted water to prevent browning and wrap onion in cling film. Prepare the other vegetables you have chosen for the meal.

11.00 Prepare the pork for cooking in its roasting pan and put in the oven for the time required.

11.45 Prepare the fruit filling and roll out and cut the pastry. Make the dumplings and put them on a baking sheet.

12.10 Drain the potatoes, dry them with a clean cloth and coat in oil. Slice the onion and apples, place them around the pork and put the potatoes on top. Pour over the cider and return the roasting pan to the oven (see Recipe).

12.30 Cook the other vegetables. Make gravy in your usual way (you can also use the thin cooking juices under the pork). Drain vegetables when they are ready and put them in warm serving dishes. Cover and keep hot.

1.00 Serve the first course.

1.15 or 1.30 Bake the dumplings.

Grapefruit and prawn cocktail

SERVES 6
3 small grapefruit
175 g/6 oz peeled prawns
1 tablespoon chopped parsley
5 tablespoons mayonnaise
salt
pinch of cayenne pepper (optional)
3 lettuce leaves, finely shredded
1 teaspoon ground ginger (optional)
parsley to garnish

1 Halve the grapefruit, vandyking the edges: to do this use a sharp knife to cut V-shapes all round, cutting right through to the centre of the grapefruit. Separate the halves and remove the flesh, discarding all the white pith. Reserve the shells.

2 Separate the grapefruit flesh from the pith and the membranes.

3 Drain the grapefruit flesh and prawns well, then mix them with the parsley and mayonnaise. Add salt and cayenne pepper to taste.

4 Line each reserved grapefruit shell with lettuce, then divide the prawn mixture equally between them and place each on a small plate.

5 Cover and chill for at least 30 minutes before serving.

6 Sprinkle on ground ginger, if using, and garnish with parsley.

Cook's Notes

TIME
Preparation time 20 minutes. Allow at least 30 minutes chilling time.

COOK'S TIP
Use a good commercial mayonnaise—a home-made one may separate.

●120 calories/500 kj per portion

Cider apple roast pork

SERVES 6

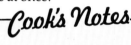

1.5 kg/3 lb boneless pork joint
salt
3 tablespoons vegetable oil
2 sprigs fresh rosemary, or 2
  teaspoons dried rosemary
1.5 kg/3 lb potatoes, thickly cut
2 dessert apples
1 medium onion, thinly sliced
175 ml/6 fl oz dry cider
freshly ground black pepper

1 Heat the oven to 180C/350F/Gas 4. Weigh the joint of pork and calculate the exact cooking time, allowing 25 minutes per 500 g/1 lb plus an extra 25 minutes.
2 Check that the butcher has scored the skin of the pork to make crackling. If he has not, do this yourself with a sharp knife (see Preparation).
3 Wipe the pork dry. Sprinkle the skin with salt and rub it lightly with ½ tablespoon oil.
4 Put the rosemary sprigs in a roasting pan or sprinkle in the dried herb. Place the pork on top.
5 Roast the joint in the oven for about 1¾ hours, or according to the calculated cooking time per weight.
6 About 1¼ hours before the end of the cooking time, put the potatoes in a bowl with the remaining oil and shake well to coat. Peel, core and slice the apples.
7 Remove the pork from the oven, scatter the apple and onion around the joint, then place the potato pieces on top of them. Pour in the cider. Sprinkle with salt and pepper.
8 Return the pan to the oven and continue roasting a further 30 minutes.
9 Turn up the oven to 250C/500F/Gas 9 and cook for a further 30 minutes. The pork crackling should be crisp and the potatoes golden.
10 Place the pork on a warmed carving dish and arrange the apple, onion and potato around the pork or, for easier carving, in a separate dish. Serve at once.

Cook's Notes

TIME
Preparation time is 5 minutes. Exact cooking time will depend on the size of the joint, but will be approximately 1¾ hours for the weight recommended here.

If the meat is cooked before you are ready, turn down the oven and keep the roast warm.

SERVING IDEAS
Shredded red cabbage baked in the oven with sliced cooking apple, onion, chicken stock and a dash of vinegar is a good sharp accompaniment to the richness of the roast pork and crackling.

Serve dry cider as a drink with the meal to complement the flavours of the food.

PREPARATION
Scoring pork: using a very sharp knife, make parallel cuts in the pork skin about 1.5 cm/½ inch apart. Make sure that you cut right through the skin to the thin layer of fat beneath.

Crush dried rosemary well, to avoid any sharp spikes.

● 1110 calories/4650 kj per portion

Appleberry dumplings

SERVES 6

6 dessert apples
375 g/13 oz can blackberries, drained
juice of lemon
500 g/1 lb frozen puff pastry,
   defrosted
1 large egg, beaten
caster sugar
cream or custard, to serve

1 Heat the oven to 220C/425F/Gas 7.
2 Peel the apples and core carefully with an apple corer or potato peeler. Brush with the lemon juice.
3 Roll out the pastry on a lightly floured surface — and trim to a 30 × 45 cm/12 × 18 inch rectangle, then cut into 6 squares.
4 Pat the apples dry with absorbent paper. Place an apple on each square of pastry, then divide the drained blackberries equally between the apples, pressing them into the apple cavities.
5 Brush the pastry edges with some of the beaten egg, then wrap each apple loosely but completely, sealing the joins firmly.
6 Place the dumplings, seam-side down on a dampened baking sheet. Roll out the pastry trimmings and use to make leaves. Brush with cold water and place on top of the dumplings. Brush each one with the remaining egg and sprinkle with caster sugar. Make a small hole in the top of each dumpling to allow steam to escape during baking.
7 Bake in the oven for 15 minutes then reduce heat to 180C/350F/Gas 4 and cook for a further 10 minutes until the apples are tender when pierced with a skewer.
8 Serve with cream or custard.

Cook's Notes

TIME
Preparation and cooking can be completed in 50 minutes.

VARIATIONS
When in season, use fresh blackberries. Also try using blackberry jam or jelly.

! WATCHPOINT
While cooking, the apples expand. It is therefore essential to wrap them *loosely* in the pastry or it will break open.
   To help prevent the pastry bursting open, make sure the joins are well sealed with egg.

COOK'S TIP
Serve the dumplings straight from the oven. If they are allowed to cool, the apple shrinks back and looks rather sad when you cut through the pastry.

●490 calories/2050 kj per portion

CHEAP AND CHEERFUL SUPPER

Here is a menu that conjures up a colourful and tasty meal for six without breaking the bank! The starter uses inexpensive seasonal vegetables served with an unusual hot dip, while the main course, an economical version of a traditional paella, is filling and substantial. A frothy citrus dessert is the perfect foil for the richer taste of the main course.

Cook's Notes

Smoky dip with vegetables

TIME
20 minutes to prepare the vegetables and 10-15 minutes to cook the dip.

ECONOMY
The tomato juice may be used in the Mock paella, if wished—add at stage 1 with the tomatoes.

COOK'S TIP
To ensure that the sauce is really smooth, put it back into the blender for a few seconds at this stage.

VARIATION
For a slightly more spicy dip, add a few drops of Tabasco sauce.

● 135 calories/550 kj per portion

Mock paella

TIME
15 minutes preparation, 35-40 minutes cooking.

SERVING IDEAS
The dish is a meal in itself, but serve with a green salad, if liked.

VARIATIONS
The ingredients can be varied according to taste and what stores you have to hand. For instance, try using left-over chicken or pork instead of the luncheon meat. Add a jar of drained mussels if your purse can stretch to it. A small can of sweetcorn makes an interesting addition, too.

● 705 calories/2950 kj per portion

Smoky dip with vegetables

SERVES 6
100 g/4 oz button mushrooms
1 large green pepper, deseeded and cut into thin strips
4 carrots, cut into thin strips
1 cauliflower, broken into florets
1 bunch spring onions

DIP
225 g/8 oz can tomatoes
150 ml/¼ pint milk
25 g/1 oz margarine or butter
2 tablespoons plain flour
1 teaspoon French mustard
½-1 teaspoon chilli powder
100 g/4 oz smoked cheese, grated
black pepper

1 Make the dip: drain the tomatoes (see Economy) and blend with the milk in a blender until smooth.
2 Melt the margarine in a pan, sprinkle in the flour. Add the French mustard and chilli powder to taste, and stir over low heat for 1-2 minutes. Remove from the heat and gradually stir in the tomato and milk mixture. Return to the heat and simmer, stirring, until thick.
3 Add the grated cheese and stir over low heat until the cheese has melted (see Cook's tip).
4 Season to taste with pepper, transfer to a small serving bowl and place in the centre of a large plate. Arrange the vegetables around the dip and serve while dip is warm.

Mock paella

SERVES 6

3 kabanos sausages, chopped into 1 cm/½ inch lengths
340 g/11 oz can luncheon meat, cut into 1 cm/½ inch dice
2 tablespoons vegetable oil
1 large onion, chopped
1 large red pepper, deseeded and chopped
2 cloves garlic, crushed (optional)
175 g/6 oz smoked streaky bacon rashers, rinds removed and chopped
3 tomatoes, skinned and chopped
1 teaspoon ground turmeric
350 g/12 oz long-grain rice, rinsed
225 g/8 oz frozen peas
600-700 ml/1-1¼ pints chicken stock
2 bay leaves
salt and freshly ground black pepper
198 g/7 oz can shrimps, drained
lemon wedges, to garnish

1 Heat the oil in a large frying-pan, add the onion, red pepper and garlic, if using, and fry gently for 5 minutes until the onion is soft and lightly coloured. Add the bacon and continue to cook for 3 minutes, then add the tomatoes and cook for a further 5 minutes.

2 Add the chopped kabanos and luncheon meat and continue to cook, stirring, for 2 minutes.

3 Stir in the turmeric, rice and frozen peas. Add about 600 ml/1 pint of chicken stock, stir well and add the bay leaves. Season with salt and pepper to taste and simmer gently for 20-25 minutes, stirring occasionally until the rice is tender and the liquid has been absorbed. Stir in the remaining stock, a little at a time, during cooking if the paella begins to look dry and the rice is not quite cooked.

4 Add the shrimps and stir until they are heated through. Discard the bay leaves, transfer the paella to a warmed serving dish and serve at once, garnished with lemon wedges.

Citrus snow

SERVES 6

1 small orange
1 lemon
1 lime
300 ml/½ pint cold water
1 rounded tablespoon (1 sachet)
   powdered gelatine
100 g/4 oz sugar
3 egg whites (see Economy)
candied orange and lemon slices, to
   decorate

1 Pour the cold water into a small saucepan and sprinkle in the gelatine. Leave to soak for 5 minutes.
2 Meanwhile, using a potato peeler, thinly pare the rind from the orange, lemon and lime. Add to the spongy gelatine with the sugar.
3 Over low heat stir the mixture with a metal spoon until the sugar and gelatine have both dissolved. Remove from the heat and leave to stand for about 10 minutes.
4 Meanwhile, squeeze the juice from the orange, lemon and lime.
5 Strain the gelatine mixture through a nylon sieve into a large bowl and add the squeezed fruit juices. Stir well, then refrigerate for about 45 minutes, stirring occasionally, until the mixture begins to thicken and turn syrupy.
6 Add the egg whites and whisk until very thick (see Cook's tip). Turn into individual glasses and refrigerate for 3 hours.
7 Decorate the tops with candied orange and lemon slices just before serving up.

COUNTDOWN
In the morning
● Prepare the vegetables for the Smoky dip and refrigerate: put the green pepper, cauliflower and spring onions in a polythene bag, the carrots in a bowl of iced water and mushrooms in a covered bowl.
4 hours before
● Make Citrus snow; refrigerate.
1 hour before
● Make the Mock paella up to the end of stage 2.

15 minutes before
● Make the Smoky dip.
● Add the turmeric, rice, peas, stock and seasoning to the paella and simmer.
Just before the meal
● Transfer the dip to a serving dish and surround with the vegetables.
Just before the main course
● Stir the shrimps into the paella, garnish and serve.
Just before the dessert
● Decorate the Citrus snow.

Cook's Notes

TIME
25 minutes preparation, plus thickening and chilling time.

COOK'S TIP
Whisking with an electric beater will take about 10 minutes. Do not be tempted to skimp this operation; the mixture should be really fluffy and thick.

ECONOMY
If you do not want to use the left-over egg yolks straightaway, you can freeze them. Decide whether you want them for a sweet or savoury dish and beat ¼ teaspoon sugar or salt into them. Pour into a small rigid container, seal, label and freeze for up to 6 months with salt and 8 months with sugar. Use as soon as defrosted.

VARIATION
Use 3 lemons instead of the mixed fruits.

WATCHPOINTS
Do not allow the mixture to boil.
The mixture must be stirred occasionally to prevent it from setting at the bottom.

●90 calories/375 kj per portion

464

FREEZER DINNER

Make the most of your freezer with this delicious three-course meal! Scallops in tomato sauce, Orange chicken casserole and Frozen raspberry favourite, can be cooked in advance and stored in the freezer until required, leaving you free on the day to enjoy your own dinner party.

Scallops in tomato sauce

SERVES 6
12 cleaned scallops, fresh or frozen (see Cook's tips)
150 ml/¼ pint dry cider or white wine
150 ml/¼ pint water
1 bay leaf
10 peppercorns

SAUCE
1 small onion, finely chopped
1 small clove garlic, finely chopped (optional)
1 tablespoon olive oil or vegetable oil
500 g/1 lb tomatoes, skinned and chopped
pinch of sugar
2 teaspoons chopped fresh basil (optional)
1 teaspoon dried oregano
pinch of dry thyme
salt and freshly ground black pepper

TO GARNISH
50 g/2 oz margarine or butter
500 g/1 lb potatoes, boiled and mashed
2-3 tablespoons warm milk

TO SERVE
25 g/1 oz butter
2-3 tablespoons fine breadcrumbs
1-2 tablespoons chopped fresh parsley

1 Bring the cider and water to the boil in a shallow pan with the bay leaf and peppercorns. Put in the scallops, cover the pan, and remove from the heat immediately, leaving the scallops in the liquid. !
2 Heat the oven to 200C/400F/Gas 6.
3 To make the sauce: heat the oil in a pan, add onion and garlic, if using, and fry gently until soft and lightly coloured. Add the tomatoes, sugar, herbs and salt and pepper to taste, then strain in the liquid from the scallops. Bring to the boil, then lower the heat and simmer about 15 minutes until sauce is thick and almost all liquid has evaporated.

4 Slice the scallops, stir them into the sauce, then taste and adjust seasoning. Spoon into individual ovenproof dishes or scallop shells.
5 To prepare the garnish: beat the margarine into the mashed potato and add enough warm milk to give a smooth creamy mixture, stiff enough to pipe. Spoon into a piping bag fitted with a plain or star nozzle, then pipe a decorative border around each dish.
6 Allow the scallops to cool completely. Open-freeze until solid, then wrap and seal in cling film and label and return to the freezer.
7 To serve: unwrap and reheat from frozen in a 190C/3735F/Gas 5 oven for 15 minutes. Remove from the oven, dot with the butter and sprinkle with the breadcrumbs. Return to the oven for a further 15 minutes or until the topping is golden brown. Serve at once, sprinkled with parsley.

COUNTDOWN
3 months before
● Make the chicken casserole and freeze. Make the ice cream mixture and the raspberry sauce and freeze.

1 month before
● Prepare the scallops and freeze.

The day before
● Take the chicken casserole out of the freezer and allow to defrost overnight at room temperature.

4 hours before
● Take the raspberry sauce out of the freezer.

30 minutes before
● Take the scallops out of the freezer and defrost in the oven.

Immediately before serving
● Take the ice cream mixture out of the freezer. Decorate and pour sauce into a jug.

Cook's Notes

TIME
Total preparation time before freezing is about 40 minutes. (Can be stored in the freezer for up to 1 month.) The scallops then take about 30 minutes to defrost and finish before serving.

COOK'S TIPS
If using fresh scallops, reserve 6 of the deepest shells for serving. Frozen scallops are available off the shell in large supermarkets, freezer centres and high-class fishmongers. Shells can be bought separately at fish-mongers and specialist kitchen shops. They can be kept and used again.

If using frozen scallops, there is no need to defrost them. Add them to the hot cider liquid while still frozen, but bring the liquid back to the boil before removing from heat.

WATCHPOINT
Like all shellfish, scallops need very little cooking or they will become tough. The standing time in the hot liquid plus the browning in the oven is sufficient to cook them through.

● 300 calories/1250 kj per portion

Orange chicken casserole

SERVES 6

6 chicken joints
2 tablespoons plain flour
salt and freshly ground black pepper
50 g/2 oz margarine or butter
1 tablespoon vegetable oil
300 ml/½ pint dry cider or white
  wine
150 ml/¼ pint orange juice
½ teaspoon ground coriander
½ teaspoon dried tarragon or
  chervil

TO SERVE

150 ml/¼ pint double cream
2 large oranges, peeled and
  sliced
50 g/2 oz black olives, halved and
  stoned

1 Put the flour in a polythene bag and season with salt and pepper. Wipe the chicken joints dry with absorbent paper, place in the bag and shake until they are well coated.

2 Melt the margarine with the oil in a large flameproof casserole and fry the chicken joints until golden.

3 Pour the cider and orange juice into the casserole and add the coriander, tarragon and salt and pepper to taste. Cover and simmer over low heat for about 45 minutes, or until the chicken juices run clear when pierced with a skewer.

4 Transfer chicken and sauce to a rigid container, leaving headspace. Cool quickly, seal, label and freeze.

5 To serve: defrost in container overnight in the refrigerator, or for 4-5 hours at room temperature. Turn into a flameproof casserole and reheat gently until bubbling, stirring occasionally. Remove the chicken from the sauce with a slotted spoon, place in a warmed serving dish and keep hot. Boil the sauce until reduced, stir in the cream and adjust seasoning.

6 Pour the sauce over the chicken. Cut the orange slices in half, then arrange a few on the chicken and remainder around the dish. Scatter over olives and serve at once.

Cook's Notes

TIME
Allow about 75 minutes for preparation and cooking before freezing. (Can be stored in the freezer for up to 3 months.) The chicken and sauce will take 4-5 hours or overnight to defrost, then about 30 minutes to finish before serving.

● 490 calories/2050 kj per portion

Frozen raspberry favourite

SERVES 6

300 ml/½ pint double cream
3 tablespoons kirsch or medium
   sweet sherry
8 ready-made meringue shells
   (see Buying guide), roughly
   broken
50 g/2 oz icing sugar, sifted
500 g/1 lb fresh or frozen
   raspberries, defrosted (see
   Variation)
vegetable oil, for greasing

TO SERVE

50 g/2 oz fresh or frozen
   raspberries, defrosted

1 Brush the inside of a 500 g/1 lb
loaf tin with oil and place in the
bottom of the refrigerator to chill
for 1 hour.
2 Whip the cream until it forms soft

peaks, then add the kirsch and whip
again until thickened.
3 Fold in the meringue pieces with
a metal spoon and 1 tablespoon of
the icing sugar.
4 Turn the mixture into the chilled
tin, cover with foil, seal, label and
freeze.
5 Prepare the raspberry sauce:
press the raspberries through a
sieve into a bowl, or work in a
blender. Stir in the icing sugar and
mix well. Pour into a rigid
container, seal, label and freeze.
6 To serve: defrost the raspberry
sauce for 2-4 hours at room
temperature. Just before serving,
remove the ice cream from the
freezer and remove wrappings. Dip
the base of the tin into hot water for
1-2 seconds, then invert a serving
platter on top. Quickly invert the tin
on to the platter, giving a sharp
shake halfway round. Pour a little of
the sauce over the mould, decorate
with raspberries and serve at once.
Pour the remaining sauce into a jug
and hand separately.

467

MEAL IN UNDER AN HOUR

Friends are coming round for dinner at short notice! Don't panic, just follow this super-quick, super-delicious menu: the ingredients are uncomplicated and the meal can be on the table in under an hour. Open with a light egg starter, follow with steaks in a luscious vermouth sauce, and end with Peach flambé – your guests will think you've spent hours in the kitchen!

Egg mayonnaise appetizer

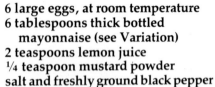

SERVES 4

6 large eggs, at room temperature
6 tablespoons thick bottled
   mayonnaise (see Variation)
2 teaspoons lemon juice
¼ teaspoon mustard powder
salt and freshly ground black pepper

GARNISH
4 lettuce leaves
sweet paprika

1 Put the eggs in a saucepan and cover with water. Bring to the boil, then lower the heat and simmer gently for 8-10 minutes. Drain off water and hold the pan under cold running water to cool the eggs quickly. As soon as the eggs are cool enough to handle, tap each one once against a hard surface to crack the shell, then cool (see Cook's tip).

2 Put the mayonnaise in a bowl and stir in the lemon juice, mustard and salt and pepper to taste.

3 Remove the shells from the cold eggs, then slice the eggs. Reserve 8 slices and chop the rest. Mix the chopped egg into the mayonnaise.

4 Arrange the lettuce leaves on individual serving plates and spoon the egg mixture on to them. Garnish each portion with 2 egg slices and sprinkle with paprika.

Steak with vermouth sauce

SERVES 4

4 beef steaks (see Buying guide)
freshly ground black pepper
25 g/1 oz margarine or butter
1 tablespoon vegetable oil
sprigs of watercress, to garnish

SAUCE

25 g/1 oz butter
150 ml/¼ pint red vermouth
½ teaspoon French grainy mustard
salt

1 Sprinkle the steaks with pepper on both sides.

2 Heat the margarine and oil in a large frying-pan, add the steaks and fry over brisk heat until browned on both sides, turning once. Remove the steaks from the pan with a slotted spoon, arrange on a warmed serving platter and keep hot.

3 Make the sauce: melt the butter in the pan over moderate heat. When it begins to froth, stir in the vermouth, mustard and salt and pepper to taste. Boil quickly until the liquid has become slightly syrupy.

4 Pour the sauce immediately over the steaks, garnish with watercress and serve at once.

Cook's Notes

Egg mayonnaise appetizer

TIME
35 minutes to boil and cool the eggs, then 10 minutes preparation.

COOK'S TIP
Cracking the shell will prevent a dark rim forming around the yolk.

VARIATION
Homemade mayonnaise made with olive oil will give a richer flavour to the dish.

SERVING IDEAS
The egg mayonnaise can also be served on triangles of buttered brown bread. Garnish with chopped walnuts and cress. Or, serve it in stemmed glasses on shredded lettuce, layered with well-drained chopped tomato and cucumber.

● 280 calories/1180 kj per portion

Steak with vermouth sauce

TIME
10 minutes preparation and cooking time in total.

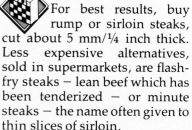

BUYING GUIDE
For best results, buy rump or sirloin steaks, cut about 5 mm/¼ inch thick. Less expensive alternatives, sold in supermarkets, are flash-fry steaks – lean beef which has been tenderized – or minute steaks – the name often given to thin slices of sirloin.

SERVING IDEAS
Serve the steaks with small potatoes baked in their jackets, a frozen vegetable and baked tomatoes. Alternatively, serve with garlic bread and a fresh green salad, tossed in a dressing.

DID YOU KNOW
Vermouth is a wine-based drink to which alcohol and herbs have been added. The herb flavour makes it ideal for cooking. Available in both dry and sweet forms, it is sold under various well-known trade names. For cooking, the sweeter red vermouth goes well with steak, while the drier white marries well with chicken and fish.

● 455 calories/1910 kj per portion

COUNTDOWN

50 minutes before

● Put the potatoes in the oven (see Serving ideas) or prepare the garlic bread and green salad.
● Put the eggs on to boil for the Egg mayonnaise appetizer, and prepare the mayonnaise mixture; cover and refrigerate.

35 minutes before

● Drain the eggs, crack the shells, then leave to cool.
● Start making the Peach flambé: dissolve the sugar in the butter, stir in the wine, add the peaches and remove the pan from the heat. Set aside until needed.

15 minutes before

● Bake the tomatoes, if using, or put the garlic bread in the oven.

10 minutes before

● Complete the Egg mayonnaise appetizer and refrigerate until needed.
● Put the frozen vegetables on to cook, if using.

Just before the main course

● Cook the steak, make the sauce, pour over the steak, garnish and serve.

Just before the dessert

● Warm the brandy, reheat the peaches, flambé and serve sprinkled with the walnuts.

Peach flambé

SERVES 4

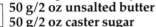

825 g/1 lb 13 oz can peach halves
4 tablespoons brandy

50 g/2 oz unsalted butter
50 g/2 oz caster sugar
75 ml/3 fl oz medium-dry white
   wine
15 g/½ oz shelled walnuts, finely
   chopped

1 Drain the peaches well (see
Cook's tip).
2 Pour the brandy into a cup and
stand in a pan or bowl of hot water
to warm through gently.
3 Melt the butter in a large, heavy-
based pan. Add the sugar and cook
over low heat, stirring occasionally,
until the sugar has dissolved.
4 Stir in the wine, bring the mixture
to a gentle simmer and add the
peaches. Turn the peaches several
times in the liquid to heat through
and absorb the flavour. ☐
5 Remove the pan from the heat,
pour the warmed brandy over the
peaches and set alight. ☐
6 Allow the flames to die down,
spoon into individual bowls and
sprinkle with the walnuts. Serve.

Cook's Notes

TIME
This special party dish
takes just 15 minutes to
prepare and serve.

WATCHPOINT

Turn the peaches gently
with a fish slice and a
palette knife so that they do not
break up.
  When lighting the brandy,
stand well back and hold the
match just above the side of
the pan.

SERVING IDEAS

Serve with whipped
cream or ice cream and
wafers or thin sweet biscuits.

COOK'S TIP

The canned syrup is too
sweet to be used in the
flambé sauce. If stored, covered,
in the refrigerator it will keep
2-3 days. Use it as the liquid for
poaching fresh fruit.

● 400 calories/1675 kj per portion

470

BUDGET DINNER

A budget dinner need not mean a dull dinner. With a little forethought and imagination, some of the most delicious dishes can be made from the most economical of ingredients—and without spending hours in the kitchen. This menu of home-made soup, kebabs with rice and a barbecue sauce, and traditional Manchester pudding is both economical and impressive.

Nearly all home-made soups are less expensive than bought ones, and also have an infinitely better flavour. So impress your guests by making a soup such as creamy watercress, which is not only economical, but unobtainable from a packet or can.

For the main course of the meal, show just what can be done with everyday mince by making it into mouthwatering kebabs topped with a spicy sauce. Cut main course costs even further by choosing the best of the vegetables in season to accompany the kebabs. Budget desserts are often uninspiring, but not this Manchester pudding, an English dish which is a perfect all-year standby, most useful in the dark days of winter when there are few interesting and inexpensive fresh fruits in season.

When entertaining, it is always important, and polite, to know your guests' likes and dislikes. This is particularly so with budget food—many bargain buys are cheap simply because they are not popular! If you know what to buy, and how to prepare it—then your family and friends will be in for a pleasant surprise and a tasty treat.

Creamy watercress soup

SERVES 4

2 bunches watercress
1 medium onion, quartered
600 ml/1 pint well-flavoured
   chicken stock (preferably home-
   made, see Economy)
1 teaspoon lemon juice
salt and freshly ground black pepper
25 g/1 oz cornflour
300 ml/½ pint milk
pinch of freshly grated nutmeg

Cook's Notes

TIME
This soup takes 45 minutes to make.

VARIATION
Substitute 250 g/9 oz frozen leaf or chopped spinach for the watercress.

ECONOMY
To be even more economical, and improve the flavour, make your own stock from a left-over chicken carcass.

COOK'S TIP
A quick way to blend the cornflour and milk without first making a paste is to whizz it for a few seconds in the blender, after puréeing the soup.

● 95 calories/400 kj per portion

---

1 Put watercress into a saucepan, reserving a few sprigs for the garnish. Add the onion, chicken stock, lemon juice and salt and pepper to taste.
2 Bring to the boil, then lower the heat, cover the pan and simmer for 30 minutes. Remove from the heat and leave to cool slightly.
3 Work the soup to a smooth purée in a blender or rub through a sieve.
4 Return the soup to the rinsed-out pan. Mix the cornflour to a paste with a little of the milk, then stir in the remaining milk. Stir this mixture slowly into the soup, then bring to the boil, stirring all the time. Simmer for 2 minutes.
5 Add the nutmeg, taste and adjust seasoning, then pour into warmed individual soup bowls. Serve piping hot, garnished with watercress sprigs.

Beefball and apricot kebabs

SERVES 4
500 g/1 lb lean minced beef
1 small onion, grated
25 g/1 oz fresh white breadcrumbs
½ teaspoon ground ginger
¼ teaspoon dried thyme
½ teaspoon salt
¼ teaspoon freshly ground black
   pepper
1 egg, lightly beaten
6 rashers streaky bacon, rinds
   removed
6 large dried apricots, halved

BARBECUE SAUCE
3 tablespoons wine vinegar
2 tablespoons dark soft brown sugar
2 tablespoons tomato ketchup
2 tablespoons fruit chutney
2 teaspoons cornflour
2 teaspoons soy sauce
300 ml/½ pint water
salt and freshly ground black pepper

1 Heat the grill to high.
2 Mix together the beef, onion, breadcrumbs, ginger, thyme and salt and pepper. Add the egg, then mix with your hands until combined (see Cook's tip). Shape into 16 balls.
3 Cut each bacon rasher in half, then wrap around each apricot half.
4 Thread the meatballs and apricots in bacon alternately on to 4 skewers, allowing 4 meatballs and 3 apricots in bacon for each. ✳
5 Grill the kebabs for 7-10 minutes, turning them over frequently until browned and cooked through. !
6 Meanwhile, make the sauce: put all the ingredients into a saucepan and bring to the boil, stirring constantly. Boil for 2 minutes.
7 Serve at once on a bed of rice, with the sauce poured over.

TIME
The kebabs take 35 minutes.

COOK'S TIP
Mixing the meat with your hands is quick, and makes it easier to shape.

BUYING GUIDE
Make sure you buy really lean minced beef for this dish. Fatty minced beef will make the meatballs shrink and lose their shape when cooked, so it is a false economy.

WATCHPOINT
If the kebabs look as if they are going to burn, reduce the heat and continue to grill until they are cooked through. Remember to keep turning them frequently.

FREEZING
The uncooked kebabs can be frozen on their skewers for up to 1 month, wrapped individually in foil or cling film. To use, unwrap and grill from frozen for about 15 minutes. Uncooked meatballs can be frozen individually, then packed together in a polythene bag or rigid container. They can then be used for quick family snacks and suppers since you can take out only as many as you need.

●525 calories/2200 kj per portion

Manchester pudding

SERVES 4

175 g/6 oz shortcrust pastry,
  defrosted if frozen

FILLING

300 ml/½ pint milk
grated zest of 1 lemon
50 g/2 oz fresh white breadcrumbs
2 medium eggs, separated
50 g/2 oz margarine or butter
100 g/4 oz caster sugar
1 teaspoon vanilla essence
3 tablespoons raspberry jam

Cook's Notes

TIME
Preparation time about 30 minutes, including time for making fresh pastry. Allow an extra 30 minutes for the pastry to chill before using. Baking time is 1 hour.

WATCHPOINTS
Take care when putting the pie in the oven with the uncooked filling; it is fairly runny and can easily spill over on to the baking sheet.

Whisk the egg whites for the meringue topping immediately before they are put on the pudding. If whisked in advance they will deflate, and become watery.

Make sure the meringue touches the pastry all round or it will shrink back during cooking and look unsightly.

COOK'S TIP
The quantities given here will produce at least 4 ample portions. Any left-over pudding is delicious eaten cold.

●535 calories/2250 kj per portion

1 Heat the oven to 180C/350F/Gas 4.
2 Roll out the dough on a floured board and use to line a 20 cm/8 inch flan ring standing on a baking sheet. Set aside to rest while you prepare the filling.
3 Bring the milk to the boil in a saucepan, remove from the heat, then add the lemon zest, breadcrumbs, egg yolks, margarine, 25 g/ 1 oz sugar and the vanilla essence. Stir well with a wooden spoon until the breadcrumbs have absorbed most of the milk. Leave to cool.
4 Spread the jam over the base of the uncooked flan case, then pour the breadcrumb mixture on top.
5 Bake in the oven for 45 minutes until the filling is set, then carefully remove the flan ring.
6 Whisk the egg whites until they stand in soft peaks. Fold in the remaining sugar with a metal spoon, then pile the meringue on top of the cooked pudding.
7 Return to the oven and bake for a further 15 minutes, or until the meringue is browned. Transfer to a serving plate and serve either warm or cold.

COCKTAIL PARTY

Inviting a few friends round for drinks? Why not be adventurous — and serve cocktails? Choose one or two from the chart on page 1256, offer them with our two sophisticated nibbles, and your evening is sure to be a wild success!

Mixing cocktails

The ingredients for cocktails are either stirred or shaken together. Traditionally, a cocktail shaker is used for shaking the ingredients, and many of these have built-in strainers, but rather than going to the expense of buying one specially for this occasion, you can easily improvise with a tight-lidded jar and a clean tea-strainer.

To shake a cocktail, put enough crushed ice into the shaker to cover the base to a depth of about 2.5 cm/1 inch. Then add the ingredients, shake and strain into the glass.

Crushed ice is often a vital ingredient of the drink — to prepare the ice, either crush ice cubes in a strong blender or food processor, or put ice in a strong polythene bag and crush with a wooden mallet or rolling pin.

A proper cocktail measure is very helpful, but a standard measuring jug and spoon can be used if ingredients are kept in the proportions given in the recipes. As a useful guide remember that 30 ml/ 1¼ fl oz equals 2 tablespoons.

The proportions given on page 476 are for one serving only.

Hot cheese and crab dip

SERVES 12

175 g/6 oz mature Cheddar cheese, grated
50 g/2 oz margarine or butter
50 g/2 oz plain flour
425 ml/¾ pint milk
1 tablespoon lemon juice
1 teaspoon Worcestershire sauce
1 teaspoon French mustard
salt and freshly ground white pepper
2-3 tablespoons finely chopped canned pimientos
2-3 tablespoons finely chopped green pepper
6 black olives, stoned and finely chopped
4 tablespoons dry white wine
175 g/6 oz canned crabmeat, drained and all cartilage removed

TO SERVE

small Melba toast squares
small cubes of French bread
small savoury biscuits

1 Melt the margarine in a saucepan, sprinkle in the flour and stir over low heat for 1-2 minutes until straw-coloured. Remove from the heat and gradually stir in the milk. Return to the heat and simmer, stirring, until thick and smooth.

2 Remove from the heat and stir in the cheese until melted and smooth. Add the lemon juice, Worcestershire sauce, mustard and salt and pepper to taste and mix well.

3 Stir in the pimientos, green pepper, olives, wine and crabmeat, then heat through gently, stirring.

4 Pour into a warmed serving dish. Serve at once with small Melba toast squares, cubes of French bread and savoury biscuits (see Cook's tip).

Cook's Notes

TIME
10 minutes preparation; 10 minutes cooking.

COOK'S TIP
This dip is best if served piping hot. If possible, stand it on a warmed serving tray or hostess trolley.

● 160 calories/675 kj per portion

Chilli meat balls

MAKES 36-40

500 g/1 lb lean minced beef
2 tablespoons tomato ketchup
2 tablespoons mild chilli sauce
1 tablespoon Worcestershire sauce
25 g/1 oz cornflakes, finely crushed
125 ml/4 fl oz canned evaporated milk
salt and freshly ground black pepper
vegetable oil, for greasing

DIPPING SAUCE
5 tablespoons tomato ketchup
3 tablespoons mild chilli sauce
1 tablespoon lemon juice
¾ teaspoon creamed horseradish
¾ teaspoon Worcestershire sauce
few drops of Tabasco

1 Heat the oven to 200C/400F/Gas 6. Grease 2 baking trays with oil.
2 Place the beef in a large bowl together with the tomato ketchup, chilli sauce, Worcestershire sauce, cornflakes and evaporated milk. Season with salt and pepper to taste, then mix well together with your fingers.
3 Shape the beef mixture into about 40 bite-sized meat balls (see Cook's tip) and arrange on the greased baking trays. Cook in the oven for 15-20 minutes or until browned.
4 Meanwhile, make the sauce: put the tomato ketchup in a small serving bowl and stir in the rest of the 'sauce ingredients. Place the bowl of sauce in the centre of a large platter.
5 Serve the meat balls on a warmed serving dish accompanied by the dipping sauce (see Serving ideas).

Cook's Notes

TIME
The meat balls take about 10 minutes preparation, then 15-20 minutes cooking.

COOK'S TIP
The meat balls should be about the same size as walnuts, so that they are easy to eat in one mouthful.

SERVING IDEAS
Provide wooden or coloured plastic cocktail sticks so that the meat balls can be dipped into the sauce and eaten without difficulty.

● 130 calories/550 kj per portion

COCKTAILS

COCKTAIL	INGREDIENTS	METHOD	TO SERVE
Gin-based:			
Boxcar	**30 ml/1¼ fl oz gin** **30 ml/1¼ fl oz Cointreau** **1 teaspoon lime juice** **1 egg white** **1-2 dashes grenadine**	Put all ingredients in shaker with crushed ice and shake well	First frost rim of champagne glass: dip glass into forked egg white and then caster sugar. Strain cocktail into glass
Gimlet	**50 ml/2 fl oz gin** **2 teaspoons lime juice cordial**	Put ingredients in shaker with crushed ice and shake well	Strain into squat whisky glass and add ice cubes
Martini	**50 ml/2 fl oz gin** **1-2 teaspoons dry vermouth**	Stir ingredients together	Serve in chilled cocktail glass garnished with an olive or twist of lemon rind
Bourbon or whisky-based:			
Horse's Neck	**65 ml/2½ fl oz whisky** **few drops of lemon juice** **ginger ale**	Stir whisky and lemon juice together, then add ice cubes and fill glass with ginger ale	Serve in tall glass garnished with a long spiral of lemon rind
Manhattan	**65 ml/2½ fl oz whisky** **25 ml/1 fl oz sweet vermouth**	Stir ingredients together	Serve in cocktail glass garnished with maraschino cherry
Vodka-based:			
Black Russian	**40 ml/1½ fl oz vodka** **20 ml/¾ fl oz coffee liqueur**	Put ingredients in shaker with crushed ice and shake well	Strain into squat whisky glass and add crushed ice
Bloody Mary	**40 ml/1½ fl oz vodka** **75 ml/3 fl oz tomato juice** **1 tablespoon lemon juice** **dash of Worcestershire sauce** **few drops of Tabasco** **salt and black pepper**	Put all ingredients in shaker with crushed ice and shake well. Strain and season to taste with salt and pepper	Serve in tall glass garnished with stick of cucumber and mint sprigs or lemon wedge
Harvey Wallbanger	**25 ml/1 fl oz vodka** **orange juice** **2 teaspoons galliano**	Put vodka in glass, add ice cubes and fill with orange juice. Stir, then float galliano on top	Serve in tall glass
Rum-based:			
Between the sheets	**25 ml/1 fl oz white rum** **25 ml/1 fl oz brandy** **25 ml/1 fl oz Cointreau** **1 teaspoon lemon juice**	Put all ingredients in shaker with crushed ice and shake well	Strain into squat whisky glass and add crushed ice
Daiquiri	**50 ml/2 fl oz white rum** **25 ml/1 fl oz lime juice** **1 teaspoon sugar syrup**	Put all ingredients in shaker with crushed ice and shake well	Strain into cocktail glass and add crushed ice
Tequila-based:			
Marguerita	**50 ml/2 fl oz tequila** **2 teaspoons Cointreau** **1 tablespoon lime juice**	Place all ingredients in shaker with crushed ice and shake well	Frost rim of cocktail glass: dip glass into lime juice and then salt. Strain cocktail into glass
Tequila Sunrise	**50 ml/2 fl oz tequila** **125 ml/4 fl oz orange juice** **2 teaspoons grenadine**	Put tequila in glass, add ice cubes and fill glass with orange juice. Stir. Slowly pour in grenadine so it settles on bottom of glass	Serve in tall glass garnished with lemon slice. Stir cocktail before drinking

FESTIVE MEAL

This menu has been created to serve on that special festive occasion when traditional charm and flavour are appropriate. The meal begins with a melon and prawn cocktail that is suitably light and refreshing before the main course of stuffed turkey which is half boned to make carving easier. The pudding is impressively flambéed with the added surprise of a fruity, creamy centre. So, gather your friends and celebrate with our festive meal.

Melon and prawn cocktail

SERVES 8

1 small honeydew melon, deseeded
  and peeled
2 tablespoons red wine vinegar
4 tablespoons vegetable oil
1 teaspoon French mustard
1 tablespoon chopped fresh parsley
salt and freshly ground black pepper
1 large red dessert apple
3 celery stalks, thinly sliced
250 g/9 oz peeled prawns
8 unpeeled prawns, to garnish

1 Put the vinegar, oil, mustard and parsley into a bowl. Season with salt and pepper. Beat well.
2 Cut the melon into small neat cubes. Quarter and core the apple but do not peel it, then cut the flesh into neat cubes.
3 Put the melon, celery, apple and prawns into the dressing and mix lightly together. Spoon the melon and prawn mixture into 6 serving glasses. Garnish and serve at once.

Festive turkey

SERVES 8

4 kg/9 lb turkey, boned (see Buying
  guide and Preparation)
75 g/3 oz butter, softened
2 tablespoons plain flour
600 ml/1 pint turkey stock, made
  from the giblets and bones
sliced red and green pepper, to
  garnish

STUFFING

1 tablespoon corn oil
1 large onion, finely chopped
1 small red pepper, deseeded and
  chopped
1 small green pepper, deseeded and
  chopped
250 g/9 oz lean ham, chopped
175 g/6 oz fresh white breadcrumbs
2 teaspoons dried mixed herbs
3 tablespoons chopped fresh
  parsley
500 g/1 lb pork sausagemeat
1 egg
salt and freshly ground black pepper

1 Make the stuffing: heat the oil in a large frying-pan, add the onion and peppers and fry gently for 5 minutes until the onion is soft and lightly coloured. Cool completely.
2 Put the ham, breadcrumbs, herbs, sausagemeat and egg into a large bowl. Add the onion and peppers and season well with salt and pepper. Mix thoroughly together.
3 Heat the oven to 190C/375F/Gas 5.
4 Lay the boned turkey out flat on a board, skin-side down, and tuck in the small pieces of wing. Then trim off the excess skin at the neck and season the turkey well with salt and pepper. Stuff the body cavity and upper part of the legs where the bone has gone (to stop legs collapsing during roasting). Bring the sides of the turkey neatly up and over the stuffing to enclose it completely.
5 Using a large trussing needle and fine string, neatly sew up the turkey along the backbone where it was cut, to seal in the stuffing.
6 Turn the turkey over so that it is breast side up again. Press into a neat shape and tie the legs tightly together. Spread the skin with the softened butter and season with salt and pepper.
7 Wrap tightly in foil, put in roasting tin and roast for 2½ hours.
8 Remove the foil from the turkey and continue to roast for 60 minutes until the turkey is tender and the juices run clear when the thickest part of the thigh is pierced with a skewer.
9 Transfer the turkey to a warmed serving platter and allow to stand for at least 30 minutes to firm up before carving.
10 Meanwhile, make the gravy: drain off all the fat from the roasting tin, leaving behind the turkey juices. Sprinkle in the flour and cook over low heat until lightly coloured. Stir in the stock and bring to the boil, scraping up all the sediment from the base of the tin. Reduce the heat slightly and simmer gently for 10-15 minutes. Strain into a warmed sauceboat.
11 Just before serving, remove the string from the turkey and garnish with red and green pepper slices. To serve, carve into slices, cutting right across the bird. Remove the legs in the normal way.

Cook's Notes

Melon and prawn cocktail

TIME
This light starter takes 20 minutes to prepare.

● 120 calories/500 kj per portion

Festive turkey

TIME
2 hours preparation, then 3½ hours roasting.

PREPARATION
To bone the turkey, first cut off the parson's nose.

1 *Place the turkey breast-side down and cut through skin all along backbone. Carefully scrape flesh away from carcass, close to ribs, cutting thighs and wings free.*

2 *To remove top leg bone and top wing bone, scrape flesh from all round bones, then break ball and socket joints and pull out top bones. Repeat on other side. Ease knife between skin and breastbone and lift out the carcass. Do not cut through breast skin.*

BUYING GUIDE
Boning is fairly difficult but becomes easier with practice. Use a fresh turkey, as the skin of a frozen bird is more likely to break. You can ask your butcher to bone it, but give him plenty of advance warning.

● 820 calories/3450 kj per portion

Flambéed iced cream pudding

SERVES 8

50 g/2 oz glacé cherries
50 g/2 oz dried apricots
50 g/2 oz stoned dates
25 g/1 oz sultanas
25 g/1 oz seedless raisins
25 g/1 oz cut mixed peel
6 tablespoons brandy
425 ml/¾ pint double cream
100 g/4 oz icing sugar, sifted
1 teaspoon vanilla flavouring

CHOCOLATE COATING
175 g/6 oz plain dessert chocolate,
   broken into small pieces
2 tablespoons water
25 g/1 oz butter

1 Cut the cherries, apricots and dates into small pieces, then put them in a bowl with the sultanas, raisins and peel.
2 Add half the brandy to fruits and mix well. Cover and leave to stand for at least 2 hours, stirring occasionally, until the fruits have softened and absorbed all the alcohol.
3 Pour the cream into a bowl, add the icing sugar and vanilla and whisk until the cream forms soft peaks. Fold in the soaked fruits.
4 Spoon the cream mixture into a 1 L/1¾ pint pudding basin and smooth the top. Cover with cling film and freeze for 4-5 hours until frozen solid.
5 Remove from the freezer, then dip a palette knife in hot water and run around the edge of the pudding. Place a round of foil on top of the pudding, turn out on to a small wire rack and return to the freezer while you are preparing the chocolate coating.
6 Put the chocolate, water and butter in a heatproof bowl. Set the bowl over a pan half full of simmering water and leave, stirring occasionally, until the chocolate is melted.
7 Remove the pudding from the freezer and place the rack over a plate. Pour the chocolate coating over the frozen pudding, smoothing it round the sides with a palette knife to coat completely—the

chocolate does not have to be completely smooth. Return to the freezer until chocolate hardens.
8 Pour remaining brandy into a pan and heat through gently.
9 To serve: remove the pudding from the freezer, peel off the foil round the base and place the pudding on a serving plate. Set light to the warmed brandy and pour, flaming, over the pudding. Allow to flame until the chocolate starts to bubble round the base, then blow out the flames and serve.

Cook's Notes

TIME
30 minutes to prepare, plus 2 hours soaking the fruit and 4½-5½ hours freezing.

FREEZING
Wrap in cling film and foil then seal, label and freeze for up to 3 months. To serve: unwrap and flame as described in recipe.

COOK'S TIP
This spectacular pudding gives the impression that a great deal of skill is needed to produce it—but it is, in fact, very simple, although time-consuming, to make.

●515 calories/2150 kj per portion

COUNTDOWN
2 days before
●Make and freeze the Flambéed iced cream pudding.
The day before
●Bone the turkey and make the turkey stock.
In the morning
●Defrost the prawns for the Melon and prawn cocktail.
●Make the stuffing for the Festive turkey, stuff the turkey and sew up.
3½ hours before
●Roast the turkey.
20 minutes before
●Prepare the Melon and prawn cocktail.
Just before the meal
●Transfer the turkey to a platter.
Just before the main course
●Make the gravy and carve turkey.
Just before the dessert
●Remove the pudding from the freezer, heat the brandy, ignite and pour over the pudding.

BARBECUE PARTY

A barbecue party is the perfect way to relax with friends on a warm summer's evening. Cooking in the open is a lot of fun, and so easy to organize—less washing up for you, and guests can join in with the cooking! Try our exotic selection of three spicy dishes using marinated pork, chicken and lamb from which guests can pick and choose. Accompany them with an unusual Coconut rice salad and finish with a refreshing Orange and lemon water-ice.

BARBECUE KNOW-HOW

Equipment: there are many portable barbecues which can be bought or hired, but you can improvise by building your own with bricks or using a container such as a garden refuse burner. All you really need is a hole for the draught to keep the fire burning and a grid (oven shelves are ideal).

Fuel: always use charcoal for burning. This can be bought in bags from hardware shops, garden centres and some large supermarkets. Briquettes are more expensive than ordinary charcoal pieces, but they usually burn for longer and are, therefore, more economical in the long run—they are also less messy to use. You will also need a stock of firelighters.

Tools: long-handled barbecue tool sets, which usually comprise tongs, a spatula and a two-pronged fork, are a must for easy handling of food—and for safety; they are widely available and inexpensive.

Other general utensils: you will need a brush for brushing oil or marinade on to the food to keep it moist during barbecuing, and prevent it sticking to the grid; long metal skewers for kebabs; a slotted spoon for removing meat from marinades and oven gloves for protecting your hands and paper napkins for mopping up.

Lighting the barbecue: light the charcoal 45-60 minutes before you intend to cook. The simplest way to light the coals is to mound them up in a pyramid in the centre of the barbecue and insert some fire-lighters in between the coals. Barbecue lighting fluid can also be used—it is very efficient; so too are special barbecue pokers, but these are expensive and only worth buying if you intend to do a lot of barbecuing. When the flames have subsided and the coals look grey or

glow red in the dark, you can start cooking. Always oil the grid before starting to cook.

Cooking: a constant eye must be kept on the food to make sure that it does not burn. For a party to serve 12

people such as this one, it is unlikely that all the meats will fit on the grid at the same time so the food will have to be cooked in batches—the idea of our menu is that guests can pick and choose from the selection of meats and cook their own at their leisure.

Since appetites will be stimulated in the open air, it is a good idea to serve lots of accompaniments with the barbecued meat. The rice dish we suggest is a good filler and the Indian flavour combines well with the spiciness of the meat. A selection of different salads would make a refreshing addition. Potatoes wrapped in foil and baked over the grill are delicious served with soured cream, or try barbecuing foil parcels of vegetables, such as drained canned sweetcorn or sliced mushrooms, mixed with a little butter.

A clever tip for creating an extra herby flavour, is to sprinkle the hot coals with mixed dried herbs.

COUNTDOWN
2-3 days before
● Make the Orange and lemon water-ice.

The day before
● Prepare the coconut and cook the rice for the Coconut rice salad.
4 hours before
● Prepare the 3 marinades.
● Put the chicken, pork and lamb in their marinades.
1 hour before
● Light the barbecue.
● Mix the dressing for rice salad.
15 minutes before
● Begin cooking on the barbecue.
● Mix together all the ingredients for the Coconut rice salad.
Just before serving
● Take water-ice out of the freezer.

Curried pork

SERVES 12
3 pork fillets (tenderloins), total
    weight about 1.25 kg/2½ lb,
    trimmed and halved lengthways
    (see Buying guide)

MARINADE
8 tablespoons vegetable oil
2 tablespoons curry powder
2 tablespoons tomato purée
1 large onion, finely chopped
salt and freshly ground black pepper

1 First make the marinade: put the
oil into a large bowl with the curry
powder, tomato purée, onion and
salt and pepper to taste. Mix well.
2 Cut each tenderloin half into bite-
sized pieces.
3 Put the meat into the marinade
and stir well to make sure each piece
is well coated. Cover and leave to
marinate in a cool place for at least 3
hours.
4 Thread the pork pieces on to 12
oiled skewers, reserving any
marinade left in the bowl.
5 To cook: place the skewers on the
oiled grid and barbecue for about 10
minutes until cooked through,
turning several times and brushing
occasionally with any reserved
marinade during cooking.

Chicken in yoghurt and ginger

SERVES 12
12 boned and skinned chicken
    breasts, each weighing about
    150 g/5 oz
vegetable oil, for brushing

MARINADE
300 g/10 oz natural yoghurt
2 tablespoons finely chopped fresh
    root ginger (see Buying guide), or
    2 teaspoons ground ginger
½ teaspoon ground cardamom
½ teaspoon cayenne pepper
2 tablespoons finely chopped fresh
    coriander or parsley
1 teaspoon salt
2 cloves garlic, crushed (optional)

1 Put all the marinade ingredients,
including the garlic, if using, into a
large bowl and stir well to mix.
2 Pat the chicken breasts dry with
absorbent paper, then place in the
marinade, making sure they are well
coated. Cover and leave to marinate
in a cool place for at least 3 hours.
3 To cook: remove the chicken
breasts from the marinade with a
slotted spoon, place on the oiled
grid and barbecue for about 10
minutes until cooked through,
turning several times. Brush occasionally with oil during cooking.

Spiced lamb

SERVES 12
12 lean lamb chops, each weighing
    about 100 g/4 oz
vegetable oil, for brushing

DRY MARINADE
1 tablespoon finely chopped fresh
    root ginger, or 1 teaspoon ground
    ginger
2 cloves garlic, crushed (optional)
1 teaspoon ground cardamom
½ teaspoon ground cinnamon
1 teaspoon ground cumin
¼ teaspoon cayenne pepper
2 teaspoons ground turmeric
salt and freshly ground black pepper

1 First make the dry marinade: mix
the ginger and garlic, if using, in a
shallow dish with all the spices and
plenty of salt and pepper.
2 Place the lamb chops in the dish
and turn them in the spice mixture
to make sure each chop is well
coated. Cover the dish and leave to
marinate in a cool place for at least 3
hours.
3 To cook: place the chops on the
oiled grid and barbecue for 10-15
minutes until cooked through,
turning several times with tongs
and a fork. Brush occasionally with
oil during cooking.

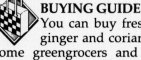

Cook's Notes

Curried pork

TIME
15 minutes to prepare,
then at least 3 hours to
marinate, 10 minutes cooking.

BUYING GUIDE
Pork fillet or tenderloin
is an expensive cut, but
there is so little fat on it that it is
not so uneconomical as it may
seem at first. Each tenderloin
weighs about 350 g/12 oz.

●235 calories/975 kj per portion

Chicken in yoghurt and ginger
TIME
20 minutes to prepare,
then at least 3 hours to

marinate, 10 minutes cooking.

BUYING GUIDE
You can buy fresh root
ginger and coriander at
some greengrocers and larger
supermarkets. Peel fresh ginger
with a potato peeler before
chopping.

●190 calories/800 kj per portion

Spiced lamb
TIME
10 minutes to prepare,
then at least 3 hours to
marinate and 10-15 minutes
cooking.

●175 calories/725 kj per portion

Coconut rice salad

SERVES 12
500 g/1 lb long-grain rice
salt
3 chicken stock cubes, crumbled
2 teaspoons cumin seeds
1 small coconut, broken open and
    flesh removed (see Preparation),
    or 225 g/8 oz packet shredded
    coconut
4 tablespoons corn or vegetable oil
2 tablespoons red wine vinegar
3 tablespoons finely chopped fresh
    parsley
¼ teaspoon mustard powder
freshly ground black pepper
3 bananas
175 g/6 oz salted peanuts

1 Fill a large saucepan with salted water and add the crumbled stock cubes. Bring to the boil, then add the rice and cumin seeds. Stir once to mix the ingredients together, then cover and simmer gently for 20-25 minutes until the rice is tender.

2 Pour the cooked rice into a colander and rinse well under cold running water. Leave to cool and drain well.

3 Meanwhile, grate the coconut flesh finely.

4 Put the oil in a large serving bowl with vinegar, parsley, mustard and pepper to taste. Mix well.

5 Just before serving: peel the bananas and slice them directly into the dressing. Mix lightly. Add the rice, grated coconut and peanuts and fork lightly together.

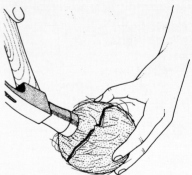

until it has frozen to a width of 2.5 cm/1 inch around the edge, then remove from the freezer and stir well with a large metal spoon until evenly blended. Return to the freezer and freeze for a further 3 hours or until the water-ice is frozen to a firm mushy consistency, not completely hard. Stir with a metal spoon once every hour during this freezing process.

8 Fill the orange cases with the water-ice, mounding it up well on top. Replace the 'lids', pressing them in at an angle. Return the oranges to the freezer for 1-2 hours or until the water-ice is frozen.

9 When ready to serve, remove the oranges from the freezer and place on small decorative plates or saucers. Serve at once.

Cook's Notes

TIME
About 2 hours to make and 8-9 hours to freeze.

WATCHPOINT
Be careful not to split the skins of the oranges when squeezing out the juice.

BUYING GUIDE
Choose oranges with good unmarked skins and try to find 12 more or less the same size.

COOK'S TIP
If the orange cases do not stand level, take a very thin slice off the bases.

PREPARATION
To remove all flesh from inside the oranges:

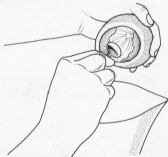

Use a teaspoon to scrape out all the flesh from the orange shells.

● 190 calories/800 kj per portion

Orange and lemon water-ice

SERVES 12

12 oranges (see Buying guide)
8-9 lemons
225 ml/8 fl oz water
450 g/1 lb sugar

1 Set the refrigerator or freezer at its coldest setting.

2 Wash the oranges and 3 of the lemons. With a potato peeler, peel the rinds from the 3 lemons thinly, then put them into a saucepan with the water and sugar. Stir over a low heat until the sugar has dissolved, then bring to the boil. Boil for 2 minutes, without stirring, then remove from the heat, cover and leave the syrup to stand for 1 hour.

3 Squeeze all the lemons and measure 450 ml/16 fl oz juice, making up the quantity with water if necessary. Cut the top third off each orange and carefully squeeze out the juice from the bottom two-thirds. Strain both lemon and orange juices together—you should have about 1.3 L/2¼ pints.

4 Remove all the remaining flesh from the orange cases (see Preparation). Put the orange cases and 'lids' on a tray (see Cook's tip) and put into the freezer.

5 Choose a very large bowl that will fit into the freezer compartment of a refrigerator or fast-freeze compartment of a freezer.

6 Pour the orange and lemon juice into the bowl then strain in the sugar syrup and stir well.

7 Freeze the juice for about 4 hours,

INDEX